Law, Governance and Technology Series

Volume 43

The *Law-Governance and Technology Series* is intended to attract manuscripts arising from an interdisciplinary approach in law, artificial intelligence and information technologies. The idea is to bridge the gap between research in IT law and IT-applications for lawyers developing a unifying techno-legal perspective. The series will welcome proposals that have a fairly specific focus on problems or projects that will lead to innovative research charting the course for new interdisciplinary developments in law, legal theory, and law and society research as well as in computer technologies, artificial intelligence and cognitive sciences. In broad strokes, manuscripts for this series may be mainly located in the fields of the Internet law (data protection, intellectual property, Internet rights, etc.), Computational models of the legal contents and legal reasoning, Legal Information Retrieval, Electronic Data Discovery, Collaborative Tools (e.g. Online Dispute Resolution platforms), Metadata and XML Technologies (for Semantic Web Services), Technologies in Courtrooms and Judicial Offices (E-Court), Technologies for Governments and Administrations (E-Government), Legal Multimedia, and Legal Electronic Institutions (Multi-Agent Systems and Artificial Societies).

More information about this series at http://www.springer.com/series/8808

Santa Slokenberga • Olga Tzortzatou
Jane Reichel
Editors

GDPR and Biobanking

Individual Rights, Public Interest and Research Regulation across Europe

Springer

Editors
Santa Slokenberga
Faculty of Law
Uppsala University
Uppsala, Sweden

Olga Tzortzatou
Academy of Athens
Biomedical Research Foundation
Athens, Greece

Jane Reichel
Faculty of Law
Stockholm University
Stockholm, Sweden

ISSN 2352-1902 ISSN 2352-1910 (electronic)
Law, Governance and Technology Series
ISBN 978-3-030-49387-5 ISBN 978-3-030-49388-2 (eBook)
https://doi.org/10.1007/978-3-030-49388-2

This book is an open access publication.

This Springer imprint is published by the registered company Springer Nature Switzerland AG.
The registered company address is: Gewerbestrasse 11, 6330 Cham, Switzerland

Contents

Introduction

Santa Slokenberga, Olga Tzortzatou, and Jane Reichel

Discrepancies in biobank research regulations have commonly been regarded as one of the most significant hurdles for effective research collaboration. One of the more central aspects of biobank research regulation concerns the use of personal data—health and genetic data and other information related to individuals, either as individual research subjects or participants in a particular scientific study or as one of many in a registry. Accordingly, the adoption of the EU General Data Protection Regulation (GDPR) in 2016 and its applicability from May 2018 had been long awaited by the biobank community. Although the GDPR is not a research regulatory instrument, in the attempt to regulate personal data processing activities it creates a rather complex 'research regime', also known as 'scientific research regime' or 'research exemption', through which it shapes how scientific research in so far as personal data are concerned is regulated by the EU and could further be shaped either by the EU itself or the Member States. The GDPR sets forth stringent requirements for the processing of health and genetic data and a set of data subject rights and imposes considerable obligations on biobanks and researchers, while simultaneously allowing for considerable derogations, directly applicable or enabled through the Member State or the EU law, for the purposes of scientific research. Occasionally, further derogations from individual rights could be possible and other requirements apply if research can be regarded as in the public interest.

S. Slokenberga (✉)
Faculty of Law, Uppsala University, Uppsala, Sweden
e-mail: santa.slokenberga@jur.uu.se

O. Tzortzatou
Academy of Athens, Biomedical Research Foundation, Athens, Greece
e-mail: otzortzatou@bioacademy.gr

J. Reichel
Stockholm University, Faculty of Law, Stockholm, Sweden
e-mail: Jane.Reichel@juridicum.su.se

S. Slokenberga et al. (eds.), *GDPR and Biobanking*, Law, Governance and Technology Series 43, https://doi.org/10.1007/978-3-030-49388-2_1

Article 89 is the central provision that regulates scientific research under the GDPR. It is also a key provision in enabling derogations from individual rights for the purposes of scientific research. Following operationalisation of Article 89, these derogations can be made by directly invoking the provisions of the GDPR on a case-by-case basis, as well as through the national laws of the Member States of the EU, as well as laws of the EU. Consequently, although the GDPR harmonises data protection requirements for resarch, and in that way contributes to the governance of biobanking, considerable divergences between requirements in different EU Member States could occur. Additionally, the Member States of the EU as well as the EU may address questions of public interest that could open up for further fragmentation. This room for divergence, while it offers flexibility for accommodating various standards and values, also creates uncertainty and poses questions about scientific collaboration and data sharing when different standards apply. One can therefore question whether the EU has built a platform upon which biobanking can accelerate or it has created a platform that allows for fragmentation of the regulatory landscape, and thereby creates risks of slowing down research collaborations and scientific advances.

In this book, a comprehensive approach is taken to determine how the GDPR affects the regulatory regimes on the use of personal data in biobank research in the EU Member States. The aim is to examine the GDPR research regime in biobanking starting with the research exception enabled through Article 89 GDPR. In order to achieve this aim, the book takes on two tasks: first, to scrutinize the GDPR research regime, its objective and constituting elements, impact on biobanking, as well as role in a changing EU landscape, especially post-Brexit arrangements; second, to review how various derogations have been operationalised nationally, and what challenges and opportunities this diversification can bring. It thereby captures the complexity GDPR creates for biobanking and sheds light on various approaches to tackling the challenges that have emerged.

More specifically, Part I sets the foundations for this book. The approach in this part rests on three main pillars, namely, the notion of individual rights, public interest and scientific research. In Chapter, 'Individual rights, public interest and biobank research', Santa Slokenberga maps out how biobanking has found its place in the GDPR and traces the main avenues of co-existence of these three pillars.

Biobanking is a field with well-established research ethics traditions in which the research ethics committees have a considerable role to play. In Chapter, 'Striking a balance between personalized genetics and privacy protection from the perspective of GDPR', Mats G. Hansson takes an ethicist's perspective examines how Research Ethics Committees could balance the need for scientific research for scientific advances, on the one hand, and privacy protection, on the other hand, in the absence of clear guidance from law and policy makers. In his contribution, Hansson proposes three premises that could help balancing the aspiration to further research with the aim to ensure the study participants privacy protection.

Part II is devoted to the analysis of GDPR requirements for biobanking. In research, data access and data sharing are of paramount importance. One of the critical concerns is how to comply with the GDPR while still allowing for these two to occur. In Chapter, 'Biobank governance and the impact of the GDPR on the regulation of biobank research', Mahsa Shabani, Gauthier Chassang, Luca Marelli examine the governance models for accessing genomic and health data, and key tools and mechanisms to further compliance with the GDPR. It is clear the GDPR leaves considerable room for further governance interventions by policy makers to uphold good research practices, to ensure research is not hindered and to safeguard the privacy of research participants as sample donors and data subjects. These governance mechanisms need to be up to date in order to be able to mitigate risks and take advantage of the opportunities brought by new and emerging technologies.

In Chapter, 'Biobank and Biomedical Research: Responsibilities of Controllers and Processors under the EU General Data Protection Regulation', Ana Nordberg scrutinises key obligations biobanks and researchers face as controllers and processors. She also identifies key compliance challenges faced by biobanks as data controllers and processors, and discusses different compliance avenues. Furthermore, she highlights challenges that emerge in the area of biobanking as we move towards a data-driven society in which artificial intelligence and big data have a prominent role to play.

In Chapter, 'Individual rights in biobank research under GDPR', Ciara Staunton examines what rights the GDPR provides to the data subjects and their operationalisation in the area of biobanking. She takes a close look at each of the individual rights protected by the GDPR and considers their impact in biobanking. She argues that even though the individual rights in the GDPR are intended to give greater autonomy and control over the use of a data subject's personal data, this may not necessarily be so in the area of biobanking. Not only might data subjects lack awareness about their data being processed, and hence be unable to protect their rights, but they might also be left with few, if any, enforceable rights as a result of different derogations. As a compensatory measure to ensure a high level of data protection, adequate safeguards are offered instead.

Anne-Marie Duguet and Jean Herveg in Chapter, 'Safeguards and derogations relating to processing for scientific research: Article 89 analysis for biobank research', scrutinize the requirement of adequate safeguards and argue that failing to comply with them could render the intended processing for scientific research purposes non-compliant with the GDPR. The GDPR might not appear overly generous in specifying what these safeguards could be but, together with the established research standardsand practice in the field, the authors have found it possible to highlight three elements: respect for the essence of data protection, proportionality and appropriate and specific measures to safeguard the fundamental rights of the data subjects. The authors put forward eight measures that could serve as appropriate safeguards and accordingly as tools to operationalise the generous research exemptions offered by the GDPR.

In Chapter, 'Biobank Oversight and Sanctions under the General Data Protection Regulation', Dara Hallinan examines the function and problems with the oversight and sanctions mechanisms outlined in the GDPR as they relate to the biobanking context. Hallinan has identified four types of oversight (*ex ante* assessment, prior notification and approval, ongoing oversight and general oversight) and two key types of sanction (liability and compensation sanctions, and administrative sanctions). Although these mechanisms are prima facie comprehensive, as Hallinan argues, they are not immune from critique. His chapter shows that problems appear in relation to the standard of protection provided for data subject rights, the disproportionate impact on legitimate interests tied up with the biobanking process—particularly genomic research interests—and their practical implementability in biobanking.

The requirements the GDPR sets forth apply to the EU Member States and the European Economic Area (EEA) states, and through extraterritoriality clauses to others targeting EU data subjects. It also sets forth stringent rules when personal data are being transferred to third countries. Brexit presents an interesting situation as on the one hand the UK is expected to leave the EU, becoming a third country for the purposes of data protection, but on the other hand the UK is a current Member State of the EU as of June 2020 and has adopted a national data protection framework in line with the GDPR. It could transpire that the EU Member States are required to comply with the GDPR through Chapter V rules, namely rules that address data transfers to the third countries or international organisations. In Chapter, 'Brexit and biobanking: GDPR perspectives', Andelka M. Phillips and Tamara K. Hervey provide insights into possible post-Brexit legal futures. In addition to illuminating possible scenarios Brexit poses for biobanking and highlighting the possible post January 31, 2021 scenario, this chapter also provides an insight into the situation for biobanking that any EU Member State could face if an analogue to Brexit occurs.

Part III, Chapters are focuses on how GDPR has been implemented in the selected EU Member States. Teodora Lalova, Anastassia Negrouk, Laurent Dollé, Sofie Bekaert, Annelies Debucquoy, Jean-Jacques Derèze, Peggy Valcke, Els Kindt and Isabelle Huys provide 'An Overview of Belgian Legislation Applicable to Biobank Research and its Interplay with Data Protection Rules'. Mette Hartlev examines the 'Balancing of Individual Rights and Research Interests in Danish Biobank Regulation'. Kärt Pormeister provides insights into the 'Regulatory Environment for Biobanking in Estonia'. Tom Southerington scrutinizes 'Access to Biomedical Research Material and the Right to Data Protection in Finland'. Gauthier Chassang, Michael Hisbergues and Emmanuelle RialSebbag examine 'Research biobanking, personal data protection and implementation of the GDPR in France'. Nils Hoppe scrutinizes 'The Regulation of Biobanking in Germany'. Olga Tzortzatou and Anastasia Siapka have provided 'Mapping the Biobank Landscape in Greece'. Simone Penasa and Marta Tomas have examined 'The Italian Way for Research Biobanks after GDPR: Hybrid Normative Solutions to Balance the Protection of Individuals and Freedom of Research'. Anne Kjersti Befring has provided insights into 'Norwegian Biobanks: Increased Complexity with GDPR and National Law'. Carla Barbosa and Andreia da Costa Andrade have offered 'Biobanks and GDPR: a look at the Portuguese panorama'. Carlos M. Romeo Casabona has offered insights into 'The new European Legal Framework on Personal Data Protection and the Legal Status of Biological Samples and Biobanks for Biomedical Research Purposes in Spanish Law'. Finally, Magnus Stenbeck, Sonja Eaker Fält and Jane Reichel have provided insights into 'Swedish law on Personal Data in Biobank Research: Permissible but Complex'.

These country studies have several common central pillars. They begin by providing an overview of the biobank infrastructure and regulatory environment in the respective country. In particular, they cover issues such as what types of biobanks are there in their respective countries, how biobank research is regulated, how individuals are involved in the sample collection and what procedures are being followed, what are the oversight bodies in the field etc. Thereafter they examine the approach to individual rights and safeguards in the respective national legal order and assess how the rules work in practice and how the balance between individual rights and development of science is struck in the country. Finally, they reflect on the GDPR impact and future possibilities for biobanking, and cover other issues that have been of relevance, such as reflections on the biobank and research governance, the capacity building and sustainability and the collaboration challenges, in the respective country's settings.

In the final Part IV, some conclusions are drawn to the central question this book set out to examine; the impact of the GDPR in the area of biobanking.

In Chapter, 'Biobanking Across Europe post-GDPR: A Deliberately Fragmented Landscape', Olga Tzortzatou and scholars representing 19 countries, namely Teodora Lalova, Anastassia Negrouk, Laurent Dollé, Sofie Bekaert, Annelies Debucquoy, JeanJacques Derèze, Peggy Valcke, Els Kindt and Isabelle Huys (Belgium); Radek Halouzka (Czech Republic); Maja Šutalo (Croatia); Mette Hartlev (Denmark); Kärt Pormeister (Estonia); Tom Southerington (Finland); Gauthier Chassang, Michael Hisbergues and Emmanuelle Ria l-Sebbag (France); Nils Hoppe (Germany); Olga Tzortzatou, Anastasia Siapka (Greece); Katharina Ó Cathaoir (Ireland); Simone Penasa and Marta Tomas (Italy); Ruth Vella Falzon (Malta); Evert-Ben van Veen (the Netherlands); Anne Kjersti Befring (Norway and Liechtenstein); Jakub Pawlikowski, Dorota Krekora-Zajac and Lukasz Kozera (Poland); Carla Barbosa and Andreia da Costa Andrade (Portugal); Carlos M. Romeo-Casabona (Spain); Magnus Stenbeck, Sonja Eaker Fält and Jane Reichel (Sweden); and Santa Slokenberga (Latvia) take a comprehensive insight into the fragmented landscape that GDPR has created. It reviews the biobank regulatory environment; whether and how derogations under Article 89(2) GDPR are enabled; the legal basis for scientific research and the role of consent in biobanking post-GDPR; the balance between individual rights and public interest in national law; and finally, GDPR impact and future possibilities for biobanking. In the conclusion, this chapter underlines the importance of research ethics committees and the coalition regarding data flow or exchange issues, among the several ongoing sector-specific initiatives for Code of Conducts.

In Chapter, 'Allocation of Regulatory Responsibilities: Who Will Balance Individual Rights, the Public Interest and Biobank Research Under the GDPR?', Jane Reichel takes a bird's eye view of the situation and reflects on the allocation of regulatory responsibilities for research under the GDPR. The question is what legislator will in the end perform the balancing of the competing interests of individual rights, the public interest and biobank research? An analysis is given of the division of powers within the regulatory space created by the GDPR in relation to the processing of personal data for research; the legislative competences of the EU and the space left to the Member States. Further, international obligations within bioethics are taken into account. Building on the analysis presented throughout the book, it is concluded that the GDPR has not fulfilled its aim to diminish regulatory fragmentation in regard to processing of data within biobank research. Two mechanisms of overcoming fragmentation in practice are discussed; via forum shopping and via administrative cooperation and soft law tools provided by the GDPR. The conclusion of the chapter it is while forum shopping in ethical issues might be problematic, it is more likely that unity could be brought by the later, administrative cooperation and soft law tools. Even though these tools lack the democratic legitimacy of statutory law, as the law stands today it may be the best we can hope for.

The editors would like to acknowledge the contributions of BBMRI-ERIC in meeting the research goal of the comparative analysis in chapter 'Biobanking Across Europe post-GDPR: A Deliberately Fragmented Landscape'. In the context of the H2020 project ADOPT BBMRI-ERIC (GA No 676550), BBMRI-ERIC, the research infrastructure for biobanking, set up a first screening table based on which national laws were screened for further details relating to operationalization of the GDPR in the national context. For the purpose of this book project, the table was further adapted and enlarged beyond the member states of BBMRI-ERIC. To date, it consists of 20 member states and one international organization. Among other things, its ELSI Services and Research unit provides guidance on ethical, legal and societal aspects relevant for facilitating access to Pan-European biobanks. Several authors of this book are affiliated to BBMRI-ERIC or its National Nodes in various capacities.[1]

Finally, on behalf of the editors team, we would like to thank Nick Cleary for his help with the editing the text and BBMRI-ERIC for covering the open access fee.

Acknowledgements Santa Slokenberga's work has been funded by her postdoctoral fellowship at Lund University, Faculty of Law (Sweden).

[1] http://www.bbmri-eric.eu.

Part I
Setting the Foundations

Setting the Foundations: Individual Rights, Public Interest, Scientific Research and Biobanking

Santa Slokenberga

Abstract The principle of conferral tames the EU competence to regulate research in a comprehensive manner, yet furthering research is one of its aspirations. Data protection, however, is an area within which the EU has legislated extensively. During the development of the General Data Protection Regulation (GDPR), an important issue to tackle was how to balance the ambitious EU aspirations and differing stakeholder interests, on the one hand, with limited competences in research regulation, on the other, and how to determine the extent to which data protection could be used as a means to further scientific research in the EU legal order. The outcome is the GDPR multifaceted research regime that sets forth EU policy and opens up for further regulations from the Member States as well as the EU.

The research regime that the GDPR has created poses numerous questions. Key among these is, what are the implications of the operationalisation of Article 89 GDPR in biobanking? This chapter sets out some of the underlying tensions in the area and pins down key conceptual foundations for the book. It provides insights into the EU's interests in the area of biobanking and maps out central elements of the research regime that has been built within the GDPR. Thereafter, it analyses the key concepts used in the book, including biobank and biobanking, scientific research as undertaken under the GDPR, individual rights and public interest. Lastly, it shares some preliminary reflections as starting points for the analysis to come.

1 Introduction

The availability, accessibility, acceptability and quality of medical goods and services are of paramount importance to create conditions under which the highest attainable standard of health can be realised.[1] In achieving these objectives,

---

[1] See ICESCR Article 12 and General Comment No. 14.E/C.12/2000/4 (2000).

S. Slokenberga (✉)
Faculty of Law, Uppsala University, Uppsala, Sweden
e-mail: santa.slokenberga@jur.uu.se

S. Slokenberga et al. (eds.), *GDPR and Biobanking*, Law, Governance and Technology Series 43, https://doi.org/10.1007/978-3-030-49388-2_2

scientific research, the development of new medicinal products and devices is crucial. In the long term, personalised medicine bears the potential to deliver important changes in medicine as it offers hope for improving health care while also lowering costs. These advances are difficult to achieve unless solid foundations for biobanks are in place and research is furthered.[2]

When scientific research is conceptualised in terms of human rights, the link between biobanking and the right to enjoy the benefits of scientific progress and its applications emerges.[3] Even though the content of this right is still to be fully appraised,[4] it is clear that to enjoy the benefits of scientific progress and its applications, there has to be a benefit in the first place.[5] Therefore, it is crucial that adequate circumstances are created to enable scientific progress to occur.

A coherent regulatory framework has long been seen as key to furthering scientific research and collaboration, within the EU, between the EU and third countries and among the third countries. As has been pointed out on many occasions,[6] the regulatory landscape is fragmented and this has been a challenge that needs to be tackled.[7] The first EU legislation in the area of data protection, the Data Protection Directive, made a considerable contribution to shaping the data protection framework for scientific research. However, through foreseeing considerable room for national regulatory autonomy it created a divergent and fragmented lanscape. As will become apparent in this book, the General Data Protection Regulation (GDPR) does not seem to have a strong potential to rectify these divergences. It also has a predisposition to the fragmentation that stems from its DNA, which has already shown some far-reaching implications.

The aim of this chapter is to set out the conceptual foundations for this book. The hope is that it will provide insights into the EU's interest in the area of biobanking and map out the research regime that has been built around the GDPR. To do this, it analyses the key concepts used in this book: biobank and biobanking, scientific research as undertaken under the GDPR, individual rights and public interest.

---

[2] Hewitt (2011), pp. 112–119.

[3] As a human right, it is set forth in Article 27.1 of the Universal Declaration of Human Rights and Article 15 of the International Covenant of Economic, Social and Cultural Rights. Article 27.1 of UDHR states that '[e]veryone has the right freely... to share in scientific advancement and its benefits'. In a similar vein, Article 15.1.b ICESCR states that '[t]he States Parties to the present Covenant recognize the right of everyone:... [t]o enjoy the benefits of scientific progress and its applications'.

[4] Among most recent contributions see Committee on Economic, Social and Cultural Rights, General comment No. 25 (2020) on science and economic, social and cultural rights (article 15 (1) (b), (2), (3) and (4) of the International Covenant on Economic, Social and Cultural Rights),E/C.12/GC/25.

[5] Slokenberga and Howard (2019).

[6] See, for example, Directorate-General for Research and Innovation (European Commission) (2012), pp. 46–48.

[7] See, for example, Chen and Pang (2014), pp. 113–117. Furthermore, biobank governance remains also a regional challenge Kaye (2006), pp. 245–248. In that regard, solutions have also been sought, among which there is the Code of Conduct for international genomic research. See Knoppers et al. (2011).

Lastly, it shares some preliminary reflections as starting points for the analysis carried out in this book, namely on whether the research regime created within the GDPR, which entails the trade-off between the data subjects' rights and adequate safeguards, is a means to further scientific research and ensure a high level of personal data protection in the EU legal order, and on the implications of such an approach for researchers, law and policymakers, research funders and other stakeholders.

2 EU and Biobanking: Building a Research Regime in the Data Protection Framework?

In Europe, historically, the competence to regulate biomedical research has to a considerable degree been placed at the national level, although often it has been exercised with due regard to the hard and soft law instruments in the international fora.[8] Except for such areas as clinical trials, in the area of biomedical research the EU has traditionally taken a back seat.[9] However, in biobanking, research is not merely about research regulation, which embraces such questions as the ethical recruitment of research participants and collection of human biospecimens, but also about data protection, which in the EU legal order is classified as a human right under Article 8 of the Charter of Fundamental Rights of the European Union (CFREU) and an area in which the EU has legislative competence under Article 16 of the Treaty on the Functioning of the European Union (TFEU). Against this backdrop, the GDPR, similarly to some degree to its predecessor the Data Protection Directive, faced a considerable challenge in how to effectively operationalise a fundamental right to data protection and further free movement of personal data whilst also accounting for the limits surrounding its competence in research set forth in Article 4(3) of the TFEU, and simultaneously furthering the EU's objective of competitiveness in the global arena. Arguably, this tension and the legislator's approach to tackling it is best captured in Recital 4 of the GDPR where it is explained that '[t]he processing of personal data should be designed to serve mankind', and thereafter elaborated that the non-absolute nature of this right entails necessity to balance it against other rights in a proportional manner. Although some of the rights have been mentioned by way of illustration, neither freedom of sciences as protected under Article 13 CFREU nor health care as safeguarded under Article 35 CFREU is

[8] For example, Council of Europe treaties, such as Convention for the protection of Human Rights and Dignity of the Human Being with regard to the Application of Biology and Medicine: Convention on Human Rights and Biomedicine and its Additional Protocol to the Convention, concerning Biomedical Research, various recommendations in the field, as well as WMA Helsinki declaration, and CIOMS International Ethical Guidelines for Health-related Research Involving Humans.

[9] This, however, is undergoing changes. The *In Vitro Diagnostic Medical Devices Regulation* (applicable from 2022) contains provisions relevant to biobanking.

indicated. Nonetheless, as the GDPR scientific research regime structure suggests, these two aspirations are inherent elements of the GDPR.

Generally, for the EU, limitations to its competence have not been an issue. In fact, data protection, similar to other areas such as the framework for in vitro diagnostic medical devices, originated as a policy within the Internal Market.[10] The factual circumstances were that at the time of the Treaty establishing the European Community the European Community's general competence to regulate the Internal Market was deployed as a tool to develop policies within the Internal Market.[11] With the Treaty of Lisbon, the circumstances changed and the data protection policy acquired its own legal basis in the Treaty.

This brief historical insight leads to an obvious question, namely, whether the EU's competence in the area of data protection is now used to push for policies in the areas where the EU currently lacks the competence to adopt harmonisation measures. It is clear the GDPR establishes a research regime, which to some degree can be seen as research harmonisation through the back door: firstly, intra-EU; but secondly, through the extraterritorial clauses and data transfer rules, so also globally.[12] Yet, this acknowledgement does not come without a 'however'. The GDPR is a sector-neutral legislation, but each research field comes with its own history and traditions. For example, the area of medical research has been influenced by the horrors of WWII, and the area of biobanking has faced some initial struggles to depart from the stringent rules surrounding research involving human beings.[13] More recently, biobanking specific research governance measures have been adopted, such as the (revised) World Medical Association Declaration of Taipei on Ethical Considerations Regarding Health Databases and Biobanks (Taipei Declaration).[14] In terms of competences, the national legal orders have retained varying degrees, and often these competences have been exercised differently, with due regard to the traditions, historical experiences, societal values and objects of public interest. Respect for this diversity was already afforded under the Data Protection Directive. With this background in mind, even if the EU might have possibly desired a different approach and was to assume the test for the limits of its interventions in the area where it lacks direct legislative competence, as the legislative history of the GDPR shows,[15] this is neither easy to achieve nor realistic. In fact, awareness of the EU's weakness in the field and the initially-perceived strength of the Council of Europe was demonstrated by an expert group on the ethical and regulatory challenges of international biobank research set up by the European Commission, where in the report 'Biobanks for Europe. A Challenge for Governance'

[10] Slokenberga (2016), ch. 6.2.3.3.

[11] De Witte (2006).

[12] Slokenberga et al. (2019), pp. 30–48.

[13] Stjernschantz Forsberg (2012).

[14] World Medical Association (2016).

[15] See Reichel J, Lind A-S (2015) The new general data protection regulation—where are we are and where might we be heading? In: Mascalzoni D (ed) Ethics, law and governance of biobanking: national, European and international approaches. Springer, Dordrecht, pp 95–100.

it pointed out that the Council of Europe 'is in a strong position to develop an additional protocol to the Oviedo [Biomedicine] Convention, specifically on biobanking'.[16] For reasons that are not widely discussed, but arguably relate to the low ratification levels of the previous Biomedicine Convention protocols, instead of an additional protocol the Council of Europe opted for revising its recommendation in the field.[17]

3 Building Blocks of the GDPR and the Research Regime

The GDPR can be said to consist of several interrelated fundamental building blocks: principles, individual rights, responsibilities, and oversight and enforcement which give expression to Article 8 CFREU. The principles seek to ensure that personal data are handled properly. The GDPR delineates obligations of the controllers and processors when processing personal data, empowers the data subjects with rights, not only for them to manage their data but also to ensure bottom-up enforcement, and sets forth rules on oversight and enforcement. In practice, however, the lines between these building blocks are rather blurred and the content of these building blocks allows to pose questions about the exact requirements that are stemming from the GDPR. For example, the obligations of controllers and processors are anchored in the data protection principles, but their exact meaning for scientific research is in some respects is unclear, and the oversight and enforcement closely relate to the responsibilities of controllers and processors set forth in the GDPR as well as the data subject rights.

The research regime, which is in-built in the GDPR and rooted in Article 89 GDPR, rests on these building blocks. In terms of principles, the GDPR enables purpose limitation compatibility, permitting secondary use of previously collected data and the processing of these data for scientific research purposes, and storage limitation compatibility, allowing the data to be stored for longer periods if so necessary for scientific research. Yet, reliance on these principles is surrounded by some ambiguity. For example, generally, the GDPR treats the principles of lawfulness and purpose limitation as two distinct principles. Consequently, one could question, whether or not any reuse of data for scientific research purposes needs to have a separate legal ground. In that regard, recital 50 guides that 'no legal basis separate from which allowed the collection of the personal data is required' and it adds that '[f]urther processing for ... scientific ... research purposes ... should be considered to be compatible lawful processing operations.' Despite this guidance from the EU legislator, recently it has been argued that '[a]s the recital is not accompanied by a specific provision in the main body of the GDPR, this appears not so much a blanket exemption ... but rather advisory'. Therefore, a suggestion

[16] Directorate General for Research and Innovation (2012), p.47.

[17] See Recommendation CM/Rec(2016)6 of the Committee of Ministers to member States on research on biological materials of human origin (Adopted by the Committee of Ministers on 11 May 2016 at the 1256th meeting of the Ministers' Deputies).

to consider purpose compatibility test set forth in Article 6(4) GDPR before proceeding with scientific research has been put forward.[18] While this precaution can be understandable in the absence of guidance from the Court of Justice of the European Union (CJEU), which holds the ultimate authority under Article 19(1) Treaty on European Union on 'ensur[ing] that in the interpretation and application of the Treaties [and by extension, secondary law] the law is observed', one could also take a different stand. It could be argued that scientific research is 'inbuilt' in the lawfulness requirements, but in the cases when the EU or the Member States determine and specify the tasks and purposes for the further processing as guided under recital 50 and set forth in Article 6(2) specific consideration to further processing for scientific research could be given. One could also question how the storage limitation should be operationalized, for example, whether it is enough that a controller has the ambition to process the data for scientific research at some point in the future, or this ambition needs to be more concrete. While it is clear that scientific research should not be a guise for storing personal data for other purposes,[19] it could be argued that the lawmaker has not put constraints for scientific research, disregarding when the research is carried out. However, to avoid unlimited and uncontrolled storage, the research intention should be genuine and demonstrable.

The GDPR provides the data subjects with several rights, known as individual rights, but at the same time through Article 89 it enables two co-existing avenues of depriving the subjects of these rights if necessary for research: first, one that permits the researchers to invoke the GDPR norms directly for the purposes of a particular project; second, one that requires the Member State national law or EU law to be adopted so that derogations can take place.[20] Both require an individual assessment to take place on whether in a particular case it can be justified to invoke the derogations. Moreover, both make the derogations possible, subject to the conditions and safeguards referred to in Article 89(1) GDPR. Additionally, although it formally does not belong to the research regime that has been set up around Article 89, extensive derogations from individual rights could also be possible through the application of Article 23. The GDPR does not clearly spell out the interplay between Article 23 and 89, nonetheless one could argue that the nature of Article 23 requires that it is applied in exceptional cases only when other avenues are insufficient. Although it cannot be precluded that it could be relied upon in the context of scientific research, those could be expected to be rather rare occasions.

---

[18] See European Data Protection Supervisor, A Preliminary Opinion on data protection and scientific research, 6 January 2020, pp. 20–21. Such a cautions approach has also been flagged by scholars, for example Bell et al. (2019), pp. 43–53, at 48.

[19] European Data Protection Supervisor, A Preliminary Opinion on data protection and scientific research, 6 January 2020, pp. 23–24.

[20] While this assessment is intended to be case-by-case-based in accordance with the wording of the GDPR, as the analysis carried out by Tzortzatou et al. show some Member States opt for generic derogations, potentially leaving room for further specification in their national, biobank-specific laws.

Additionally, within the research regime as well as outside it, the GDPR puts forward a public interest concept, adding to it different qualifiers in different contexts (see below Sect. 4.3.3). This concept enables the application of different data protection requirements to activities that are carried out in the public interest in comparison with those that are not. Likewise, it enables different treatment of those activities that relate to 'reasons of important public interest' in comparison with those activities that relate to public interest only.

Generally, the research support afforded under the principles of lawfulness and the possibility to derogate from data subjects' rights comes with a number of responsibilities for biobanks and researchers. Apart from such practicalities as case-by-case assessments on the necessity and possibility to invoke these derogations, they have to ensure that 'appropriate safeguards, in accordance with this Regulation, for the rights and freedoms of the data subject' are in place.[21] Article 89(1) GDPR further elaborates that '[t]hose safeguards shall ensure that technical and organisational measures are in place in particular in order to ensure respect for the principle of data minimisation'. However, the text of the GDPR is not forthcoming on what these safeguards are apart from pinpointing in Article 89(1) that '[t]hose measures may include pseudonymisation provided that those purposes can be fulfilled in that manner', and unpacking what pseudonymisation is under Article 4(5) GDPR. One could argue that reference to the provisions of the Regulation tames the interpretation of 'appropriate safeguards' to those GDPR requirements that the controller or processor shall fulfil for a particular scientific research activity (processing), disregarding whether these requirements are set forth in the GDPR or adopted by the Member States when operationalizing provisions of the GDPR, and those that are compatible with the GDPR, for example, because of different scopes of application. However, one can question to what extent they could accommodate safeguards that create obstacles to achieving the GDPR objectives.[22]

Even though the EU is not a research regulator *stricto sensu*, the research regime that is set forth within the GDPR shapes research regulations and thereby practices nationally. To some countries, it may even act as an incentive to revise their frameworks drafted in the early 2000s with great caution vis-à-vis the developments in science and technology. As for countries where biobank legal frameworks have been absent, it can act as an incentive to develop them. However, at the same time it should be kept in mind that although biobanking is an important area, it is only one of the many that a general data protection framework such as the GDPR captures, and that the GDPR in itself cannot be expected to function as the sole base of a research regime for the EU.

---

[21] Article 89(1) GDPR. See Anne-Marie Duguet Jean Herveg 'Safeguards and derogations relating to processing for scientific purposes: Article 89 analysis for biobank research' in this book.

[22] See further analysis on appropriate safeguards by Anne-Marie Duguet Jean Herveg 'Safeguards and derogations relating to processing for scientific purposes: Article 89 analysis for biobank research' in this book.

4 Clarifying Key Concepts and Definitions

4.1 Concepts of Interest

To create a deeper understanding of how Article 89 GDPR has been operationalised in biobank research, it is necessary to pin down two essentials: first, the concept of a biobank and biobanking; second, the approach to individual rights and public interest under the GDPR and within this book.

4.2 Biobank and Biobanking

Biobanks are extensively discussed by scholars as well as law and policy makers, and they are surrounded by a thick layer of governance and regulatory frameworks—hard and soft law measures—but they lack a universally agreed definition. Moreover, sometimes more than one term is used to refer to biobanks, for example, biorepositories and biological resource centres,[23] and sometimes a distinction between the two is drawn.[24]

Arguably, the term was first used in 1996 and at that time it was mainly used to refer to human population-based biobanks,[25] despite the fact that collections were being stored at various hospitals and academic institutions even before that time. Moreover, it was a considerable time after the first paraffin embedded tissue sample collections had emerged, which are regarded as 'the predecessors of today's biobanks'.[26]

Among law and policy makers, as well as in the literature, a range of definitions can be found.[27] For example, the 2006 OECD report 'Creation and Governance of Human Genetic Research Databases' referred to a biobank as follows: 'a collection of biological material and the associated data and information stored in an organised system, for a population or a large subset of a population'. However, already in 2009 in the OECD Recommendation on Human Biobanks and Genetic Research Databases, human biobanks and genetic research databases were described as 'structured resources that can be used for the purpose of genetic research, and which include: (a) human biological materials and/or information generated from their analysis; and (b) extensive associated information'.[28] This clearly shows the shift from the early focus on a population scale biobank to a more inclusive approach.

[23] Parodi (2015).

[24] See, for example, Siwek (2015).

[25] Hewitt and Watson (2013), p. 309.

[26] Biobanking and Biomolecular Resources Research Infrastructure (2013).

[27] Shaw et al. (2014), pp. 223, 226.

[28] OECD (2009), p. 22.

Nationally, diverse uses of biobank terminology have appeared. For example, the Swedish Biobanks in Medical Care Act defines a biobank as '[b]iological material from one or more human beings that is collected and preserved for an indefinite period, and whose origin is traceable to an individual or individuals'.[29] The Latvian Human Genome Research Law does not define a biobank but uses the term genome database to refer to what in other countries could be understood as a biobank. In particular, it describes it as 'a set of data containing coded descriptions of the DNA, coded descriptions of the state of health, coded genealogical and genetic data, as well as coded DNA samples and coded tissue samples to be used for genetic research'.[30]

In practice, however, there is a considerable variation in the types of biobank and their purpose. The term biobank has now commonly been applied not only to refer to human specimen collections but also to plant, animal or microbial samples.[31] In regard to human biospecimen biobanks, several types can be identified and they can be classified differently.[32] For example, Harris et al. classify four types, namely: (1) biobanks established as part of the health care process; (2) biobanks established in the context of clinical trials; (3) biobanks comprising specific research project sample collections that can be re-used for other research; and (4) population-based biobanks, which may have a more general research purpose.[33]

Apart from shifts in the content of the biobank concept and the emergence of research data banks (collections of data for further research), changes have occurred in regard to infrastructures and operational management governance. In the early days of biobanking, it was common for record keeping to be confined to a laboratory notebook and specimen storage was in a small number of ultra-low freezers. This is what De Souza and Greenspan describe as a 'modest style of banking'. Biobanking and its associated science has become a far more complex enterprise.[34] Driven by technological advances such as automation and computerisation, the management of biobanks has been modernised. Today, specimen annotation and storage location are maintained through electronic records in databases, with the tracking of samples done via a laboratory information management system (LIMS).[35] Moreover, various software solutions, including with robotic elements, are available and these support biobanks in administrative as well as research practices.[36] There is also software associated with processes that integrate with LIMS and catalogues of available specimens for an external audience. In the last decade, virtual biobanks have become common,[37] allowing for easier and faster biospecimen and data

[29] Sveriges Riksdag (2002), Chapter 1 Section 2.

[30] LR Saeima (2002), Section 1 Subparagraph 8.

[31] Hewitt and Peter (2013), pp. 309, 313.

[32] EU Commission (2012), pp. 14–17.

[33] Harris et al. (2012).

[34] De Souza and Greenspan (2013).

[35] See Bendou et al. (2017).

[36] De Souza and Greenspan (2013). For a more detailed insight, see Müller et al. (2017).

[37] Reijs et al. (2015).

transfer and exchange in comparison with centralized model biobanks.[38] In terms of infrastructure network, BBMRI-ERIC became an important initiative as it created a pan-European directory of biobanks and collection sites that has brought together stakeholders in the field.[39]

For the purposes of this book, given the differences in approaches and lack of universally agreed definition, a broad and inclusive approach to a biobank has been chosen, viewing it as a collection of biospecimens and associated data, including clinical and sample data. The primary focus has been on research biobanks. This approach is in line with what, according to Shaw et al., are seen among the stakeholders as 'the basic requirements for a biobank'.[40] By approaching biobanks in such a broad way, the size of a biobank has been rejected as an area of concern. A biobank can be a valuable resource, even without containing a large number of specimens or particularly detailed associated data.[41]

In addition to 'biobank', the term 'biobanking' is also regularly used in this book. Biobanking involves multiple steps. According to De Souza, with some simplification, they can be expressed in three steps: the collection of a specimen and data, biospecimen processing and storage, and biospecimen dissemination.[42] This approach was also confirmed in later studies, for example, by Hewitt and Watson.[43] Therefore, for the purposes of this book, the term has been applied to refer to 'the collection, processing and storage' of a specimen and associated data.

4.3 Scientific Research, Individual Rights and Public Interest Under the GDPR and Implications

4.3.1 Scientific Research

Although the GDPR establishes a scientific research regime, it does not exhaustively define what scientific research is. In line with guidance provided by the EU legislature in Recital 159,[44] research can encompass a wide array of activities. It

[38] Somiari and Somiari (2015), pp. 12–27, at 19

[39] BBMRI-ERIC http://www.bbmri-eric.eu/.

[40] Shaw et al. (2014), p. 226. These seem to be shared in a study by Hewitt and Watson, Defining Biobank. Additionally, they point at the importance of managing biobanks according to professional standards. Hewitt and Watson (2013), pp. 309, 313. As this is a governance question rather than directly related to individual rights, we have ommitted this criterion from the approach.

[41] Shaw et al. (2014), p. 227.

[42] De Souza and Greenspan (2013).

[43] Hewitt and Watson (2013), p. 311.

[44] It states '[w]here personal data are processed for scientific research purposes, this Regulation should also apply to that processing. For the purposes of this Regulation, the processing of personal data for scientific research purposes should be interpreted in a broad manner including for example technological development and demonstration, fundamental research, applied research and privately funded research. In addition, it should take into account the Union's objective under

emphasises that 'the processing of personal data for scientific research purposes should be interpreted in a broad manner including, for example, technological development and demonstration, fundamental research, applied research and privately funded research'. The Article 29 Working Party has indicated that it 'considers the notion may not be stretched beyond its common meaning and understands that "scientific research" in this context means a research project set up in accordance with relevant sector-related methodological and ethical standards, in conformity with good practice'.[45] This view is now accepted by the European Data Protection Board.[46] From this it follows that research within the meaning of the GDPR, albeit on the surface appearing open to interpretation, in fact could be a type of research that follows the requirements of a particular research field.

Recently, the European Data Protection Supervisor, an actor that has been established under another regulation and is tasked to act in regard to personal data protection matters by EU institutions and bodies,[47] has gone even further and in addition to indicating the importance that 'relevant sectorial standards of methodology and ethics apply' for the processing of 'personal data' has added that in order scientific research can benefit from the GDPR research regime, 'the research ... [needs to be] carried out with the aim of growing society's collective knowledge and wellbeing, as opposed to serving primarily one or several private interests.'[48] Putting aside the question of the (vague) authority of this actor on the GDPR matters and the fact that the released document is a preliminary opinion only, it suffices to note that although for many reasons it might be appealing to draw a distinction between 'collective knowledge and well-being' and 'primarily one or several private interests', there are several problems with such an approach. They include uncertainty and ambiguity of the content of these elements and interplay, lack of adequate consideration for the complex reality in which scientific research takes place and commercialization as means to drive the scientific advances forward (e.g. in the area of medicinal products for paediatric use). As derives from the explanations relating to CFREU, Article

---

Article 179(1) TFEU of achieving a European Research Area. Scientific research purposes should also include studies conducted in the public interest in the area of public health. To meet the specificities of processing personal data for scientific research purposes, specific conditions should apply in particular as regards the publication or otherwise disclosure of personal data in the context of scientific research purposes. If the result of scientific research in particular in the health context gives reason for further measures in the interest of the data subject, the general rules of this Regulation should apply in view of those measures.'

[45] EU Article 29 Working Party Guidelines on consent under Regulation 2016/679 (2017), pp. 27–28.

[46] See the European Data Protection Board, Endorsement 1/2018.

[47] Regulation (EU) 2018/1725 of the European Parliament and of the Council of 23 October 2018 on the protection of natural persons with regard to the processing of personal data by the Union institutions, bodies, offices and agencies and on the free movement of such data, and repealing Regulation (EC) No 45/2001 and Decision No 1247/2002/EC, OJ L 295, 21.11.2018, pp. 39–98, Article 52.2.

[48] European Data Protection Supervisor, A Preliminary Opinion on data protection and scientific research, 6 January 2020, p. 12.

13 that protects scientific research relates to Article 10 of European Convention on Human Rights (ECHR), which is not an absolute right. It can be restricted to protect other rights, including privacy (and thereby data protection) of the data subjects under Article 8 ECHR. At the same time, also Article 8 does not contain an absolute right and could be restricted for a number of grounds, including, the economic well-being of the country, the protection of health or morals, or for the protection of the rights and freedoms of others. From such a perspective, a complex balancing act between privacy protection and freedom of expression needs to be exercised, which has strong parallels to that, which is set forth in Article 52(1) CFREU. While carrying out this exercise is beyond the scope of this contribution, it is clear that it should not lead to depriving the data subject of her rights with no (public good) in return and in that way become carte blanche approach to defining scientific research. From such a perspective, one could agree with the Supervisor on the benefits that the research should deliver,[49] adding that this notion should be generously interpreted. However, it could be argued that the contrast element ('primarily one or several private interests') could be difficult to uphold due to the reasons for and the reality in which scientific research is carried out. One can understand that the Supervisor has drawn inspiration from different sources and areas, including the field of copyright, and reasons for doing that, however, one should not be ignorant to the fact that each area comes with its principles that might not necessarily be easily transferable to another field, such as data protection. Finally, although the proposal to defining scientific research that has been put forward by the Supervisor on the surface resonates with the CJEU long-established approach in defining exceptions to rules narrowly, it does not sit well with the legislator's intention for the field expressed in recital 159 that 'the processing of personal data for scientific research purposes should be interpreted in a broad manner'. One can only question what reasons should emerge for the CJEU to disregard the signals provided by the legislator for interpreting the text of the GDPR. Acknowledging the complex reality that this uncertainty could create and need for further inquiries, this book proceeds on the assumption that biobanking has a great potential to benefit from the GDPR research regime, disregarding whether or not the Supervisor's approach is upheld and followed.

4.3.2 Individual Rights

A key requirement in biobanking is safeguarding trust. Usually this is achieved through various protections, and is often also expressed in terms of rights of the research participants.[50] The GDPR does not ignore the rights of individuals and in Chapter III GDPR sets forth a range of data subject rights, in particular the right to information, and it gives further modalities depending on whether or not data are collected directly from the data subject in Articles 13 and 14 respectively. It also

---

[49] European Data Protection Supervisor, A Preliminary Opinion on data protection and scientific research, 6 January 2020, p. 12.

[50] For an overview, see Staunton et al. (2019).

provides a right of access under Article 15, a right to rectification under Article 16, a right to erasure under Article 17, a right to restrict processing under Article 18, a right to data portability under Article 20, as well as a right to object and a right not to be subjected to automated decision-making under Article 21. Moreover, Article 19 contains the so-called notification entitlement, whereby a data subject can request to be informed about recipients to whom Article 19 applies.[51] However, unlike in the human rights discourse and research regulations, under the GDPR self-determination exercised through informed consent is not a right per se but a means to fulfil the lawfulness requirement and could also be seen as a type of adequate safeguards under Article 89(1). The importance of these rights is significant as a means of empowering research participants as data subjects and enabling obstacles related to participants that hold back the work of biobanking to be overcome. On the other hand, in some cases these very same rights can also hinder research if they are exercised. To overcome this, the GDPR sets forth the already-noted derogation mechanism, which has previously been characterised as a mechanism that strips individuals of their rights.[52]

4.3.3 Public Interest

There are different approaches how to approach the notion of public interest. A theory of public interest has been conceptualized as 'the process of defining the scope of rights and the justification for securing public goods as the objects of collective rights'.[53] However, the GDPR seems to depart from this complex public good and public interest tangle and takes a more practical approach. It approaches public interest as an end in itself, allowing for additional regulatory privileges. As highlighted below, this usually comes at the expense of individual rights, but is not necessarily limited to that. Hence, more broadly under the GDPR public interest can be described as an object worth safeguarding for the needs or interests of the Member States or the EU for the purposes of which a number of specific measures could be taken, including the rights of a data subject could be constrained.

In relation to biobanking and public interest a number of questions emerge. One can discuss, under what circumstances, if at all, is biobanking a public interest. One

[51] Notification obligation regarding rectification or erasure of personal data or restriction of processing.

> The controller shall communicate any rectification or erasure of personal data or restriction of processing carried out in accordance with Article 16, Article 17(1) and Article 18 to each recipient to whom the personal data have been disclosed, unless this proves impossible or involves disproportionate effort. The controller shall inform the data subject about those recipients if the data subject requests it.

[52] Staunton et al. (2019).

[53] Capps (2012), p. 240.

can also question, whether there is a difference for what purpose research is conducted and who the researcher or research institution. For example, whether it is a non-profit actor carrying out research in the area of non-communicable diseases, which is a large cause of death across the world,[54] or commercially-driven research relating to the identification of genes attributed to traits or a child's potential talent. If so, who is the one to decide?

In the GDPR, public interest is mentioned 70 times, yet on none of these occasions is the concept fully explained. Moreover, qualifiers can be found, for example, Recital 50 refers to the 'general public interest', Recital 70 to 'important objectives of general public interest', Recital 112 to 'important reasons of public interest' and Article 18(2) GDPR to 'reasons of important public interest'. In spite of this, a number of clues can be found that indicate that these qualifiers have different meanings. Therefore, while as guided by Recital 159 research in the area of public health could be located in the area of public interest in some situations, this very same research might not necessarily benefit from laxed measures applicable to activities falling under 'important reasons of public interest'.

Perhaps the most central operationalisation of public interest relates to the lawful processing of personal data. It can be derived from Articles 6(2) and 6(3) GDPR that research can be considered by a Member State to be in the Member State's public interest.[55] Moreover, for the purposes of tasks carried out in the public interest, the implicit prohibition on the processing of personal data can be lifted.[56] This possibility has to be further regulated by EU law or Member State national law.[57] One could say that by using the open-ended concept of public interest, the GDPR allows Member States to choose their own policies. As mapped out by Reichel and Lind, in the earlier drafts of the GDPR it was suggested that the Commission should define the concept of public interest (at that time, 'high public interest'). This was heavily criticised since it would de facto mean that the Commission could control the Member States in areas that were politically sensitive.[58] Hence, this approach was not retained in the GDPR. Therefore, Member States could decide that, for example, tackling Covid-19 or the development of personalised medicine are matters of public interest. However, that in itself would not be sufficient to proceed with the

[54] World Health Organization (2018).

[55] Recital 45 guides that '[i]t should also be for Union or Member State law to determine whether the controller performing a task carried out in the public interest or in the exercise of official authority should be a public authority or another natural or legal person governed by public law, or, where it is in the public interest to do so, including for health purposes such as public health and social protection and the management of health care services, by private law, such as a professional association.'

[56] Recital 10, Article 6(1)(f) and 6(2) GDPR.

[57] As clarified in Recital 45, '[t]his Regulation does not require a specific law for each individual processing. A law as a basis for several processing operations based on a legal obligation to which the controller is subject or where processing is necessary for the performance of a task carried out in the public interest or in the exercise of an official authority may be sufficient.'

[58] Reichel and Lind (2015), pp. 95–100.

processing of personal data as other requirements, including those set forth in Article 9 also shall be met.

4.3.4 Interaction Between Scientific Research, Individual Rights and Public Interest

On a number of occasions in the GDPR public interest coexists with the research regulatory framework for individual rights. However, for example, under Article 17(3) the two are addressed differently. Article 18(2) GDPR *expressis verbis* relates to 'reasons of important public interest of the Union or of a Member State', which may well be research. Similarly, also Article 20(3) refers to 'the performance of a task carried out in the public interest', but does not in itself contain provisions relating to research. This differentiation is also present in Article 21(6) GDPR, which merges these two regimes, the research and the public interest. Under Article 21(1) GDPR, '[t]he data subject shall have the right to object, on grounds relating to his or her particular situation, at any time to processing of personal data concerning him or her which is based on point (e) or (f) of Article 6(1), including profiling based on those provisions'. In accordance with Article 21(6) GDPR, '[w]here personal data are processed for scientific (...) research purposes (...) pursuant to Article 89(1), the data subject, on grounds relating to his or her particular situation, shall have the right to object to processing of personal data concerning him or her, unless the processing is necessary for the performance of a task carried out for reasons of public interest'. In that way, the operational scope of the right to object is restricted when research is carried out in the public interest.

However, this public interest interplay with research regulation has to be characterised even more specifically. Article 89(2) GDPR permits derogations from individual rights for Articles 15, 16, 18 and 21 GDPR. In that way, research in the public interest in comparison with research not falling in the public interest benefits from an Article 20 and Article 21 derogation.

Furthermore, apart from these avenues, Article 23 GDPR is of interest. Article 23(1) GDPR states that 'Union or Member State law to which the data controller or processor is subject may restrict by way of a legislative measure the scope of the obligations and rights provided for in Articles 12 to 22 and Article 34, as well as Article 5 in so far as its provisions correspond to the rights and obligations provided for in Articles 12 to 22, when such a restriction respects the essence of the fundamental rights and freedoms and is a necessary and proportionate measure in a democratic society to safeguard '(e) other important objectives of general public interest of the Union or of a Member State, in particular (..) public health (..)'. It cannot be excluded that there could be a possibility for the Member States to rely on this provision for particular research purposes.

There is a rather subtle difference in terms of individual rights for how a Member State approaches research, and whether and to what extent it locates it in the area of public interest. However, for obligations stemming from the GDPR,[59] as well as data transfer to third countries and international organisations, public interest conceptualization has a considerable role to play.[60] Nevertheless, as this book will show, there are Member States that have not afforded any particular consideration to research being or not being in the public interest within the GDPR. Moreover, this term is occasionally used interchangeably with 'public goods'—in this way explaining to what extent, if at all, biobanking is seen as an interest worth safeguarding and what means are used to further this interest.

4.3.5 Implications

It is rather clear that theoretically permissible differences between the level of protection in different EU Member States should not become an obstacle to free movement of personal data. It could, however, be different in practice. One could also question, to what extent, if at all, could forum shopping take place? Arguably, the most relevant guidance on the question of choice of jurisdiction may be inferred from the *Weltimmo* case in which the place of establishment of a controller was emphasized.[61] However, that establishment is subject 'to any real and effective activity—even a minimal one—exercised through stable arrangements'.[62] This very same approach is now specified in Recital 22 of the GDPR, though without the requirement of 'even a minimal one'.[63] It is unclear yet whether absence of the indication of this minimum threshold will have any practical significance under the GDPR.

In practice, for collaborative research projects, as long as the real and effective activity requirement exercised through the stable arrangements requirement can be met, then forum shopping could take place. For this, private international law could, to some degree, become handy. Yet, what is the practical significance of this forum shopping is another question to ask as the research ethics committees are not necessarily required to approve lawful research that appears unethical.[64] On the other hand, ethics is not necessarily ethics only (not binding, but highly recommended). Often it is a legal requirement to receive an ethics review and the research ethics committees operate under a legal framework. It may well happen that the research ethics committee's decision becomes an obstacle to free movement of personal data in scientific research, and then it could ultimately be for the CJEU to address it and

---

[59] For example, regarding processors under Article 28(3)(a), regarding data protection impact assessment under Article 35(9), in regard to a prior consultation under Article 36(5) GDPR.

[60] Recital 115, Article 49 GDPR. See further, the European Data Protection Board (2018), pp. 10–11.

[61] Weltimmo s. r. o. V Nemzeti Adatvédelmi és Információszabadság Hatóság, ECLI:EU:C:2015:639, para 24. For a discussion on territoriality under the Data Protection Directive see Maja Brkan (2016). For insights under the GDPR see Pormeister (2018).

[62] Court of Justice of the European Union, Weltimmo s. r. o. V Nemzeti Adatvédelmi és Információszabadság Hatóság, ECLI:EU:C:2015:639, para 31.

[63] Recital 22, GDPR.

[64] See also Article WP 29 (2017).

contextualize in relation to the GDPR. If ethical approval is treated as safeguards, then indeed, such an obstacle could be justified. However, if the wording in Article 89(1) 'in accordance with this regulation' applies only to measures under the GDPR stricto sensu, one could question whether the approach taken by Article 29 Working Party can be upheld. As the CJEU has demonstrated in a different context, it is willing to accommodate genuine ethics concerns even when the legislator has not done that in a clear manner,[65] and therefore it could be argued that a similar approach could also be taken under the GDPR.

5 Concluding Remarks

Concerns over the restrictive approach to data protection were expressed when the Commission's initial text was negotiated in the legislative procedure.[66] In particular, there were concerns that the draft GDPR, if adopted, may 'challenge the survival of retrospective clinical research, biobanking, and population-based cancer registries in the EU'[67] and over whether the trilogue—key players in the EU ordinary legislative procedure (the Commission, the European Parliament and the Council)—would accept the importance of health research and would not hinder it.[68]

The text of the GDPR as adopted and applicable continues to raise concerns. For the law and policy makers, it opens up room for considerable variation in how data protection is further regulated nationally. For researchers and biobankers, it raises questions on compliance with the rules of the GDPR as invoked directly and further specified nationally when carrying out research. For the data subjects, it raises questions of the level of protection the GDPR provides them and on the meaning of the fundamental right to the protection of personal data as safeguarded under Article 8 CFREU. As Pormeister questions, does the GDPR go too far?[69] Staunton et al. also implicitly point in that direction as they agree that the GDPR is stripping data subjects of their rights,[70] but this does not necessarily mean that no protection has been afforded to the data subjects. The limitations to individual rights are prescribed at the expense of appropriate safeguards, to ensure that a high level of protection of personal data is not undermined. Therefore, it is important that these safeguards are fully operationalized and a fair balance between valid objectives, in particular data privacy protection and scientific research, is struck.

However, in the case of biobanking and from the perspective of the GDPR, it is the Member States who have the ultimate say whether the flexibility that the GDPR

[65] See Case C-165/08, Commission of the European Communities v Republic of Poland, ECLI:EU:C:2009:473.

[66] Gottweis et al. (2012).

[67] Kerr (2014), p. 563.

[68] Coppen et al. (2015), p. 757.

[69] Pormeister (2017), pp. 137–146.

[70] Staunton et al. (2019).

offers could and should be used with due regard to their particular circumstances, such as history, traditions, cultural values and prevailing views in society. Whether the stakeholders will manage to reconcile these divergences with a view to further research through the elaboration and adoption of a code of conduct in the field pursued by BBMRI-ERIC remains to be seen.[71] One could call such a task ambitious as the stakeholders through the code of conduct are attempting to resolve this when the trilogue together with the Member States could not do so during the legislative procedure.

Acknowledgement This work has been funded by Santa Slokenberga's postdoctoral fellowship at Lund University, Faculty of Law (Sweden). The author wishes to thank Dr.h.c., former judge of the CJEU Egils Levits for a research visit at his cabinet that allowed setting foundations for this work. The author would also like to thank Dr. Carmen Swanepoel for comments on an earlier draft of this chapter.

References

A Code of Conduct for Health Research. http://code-of-conduct-for-health-research.eu/. Accessed 30 June 2019

A Report from the BBMRI Project (2013) Biobanks and the public. Governing biomedical research resources in Europe

Article 29 Working Party Guidelines on consent under Regulation 2016/679, Adopted on 28 November 2017 As last Revised and Adopted on 10 April 2018, 17/EN WP259 rev.01

Barzilai N et al (2012) The place of genetics in ageing research. Nat Rev Genet 13:589–594

BBMRI-ERIC, http://www.bbmri-eric.eu/. Accessed 30 June 2019

Bell J, Aidinlis S, Smith H, Mourby M, Gowans H, Wallace SE, Kaye K (2019) Balancing data subjects' rights and public interest in research: examining the interplay between UK Law, EU Human Rights Law and the GDPR. Eur Data Prot L Rev 5(43):43–53

Bendou H et al (2017) Baobab laboratory information management system: Development of an open-source laboratory information management system for biobanking. Biopreservation Biobanking 15:116–120

Berr C et al (2016) How to optimize the use of biobanks from population-based cohorts in aging research. Biogerontology 17:221–227

Capps B (2012) The public interest, public goods, and third-party access to UK biobank. Public Health Ethics 5:240–251

Chen H, Pang T (2014) A call for global governance of biobanks. Bull World Health Organ 93(2):113–117. https://doi.org/10.2471/BLT.14.138420:113–117

Coppen R et al (2015) Will the trilogue on the EU data protection regulation recognise the importance of health research? Eur J Public Health 25:757–758

De Souza YG, Greenspan JS (2013) Biobanking past, present and future: responsibilities and benefits. AIDS 27:303–312

De Witte B (2006) Non-market values in internal market legislation in Shuibhne (ed). Edward Elgar Publishing, Cheltenham, pp 61–86

Directorate-General for Research and Innovation (European Commission) (2012) Biobanks for Europe. A Challenge for Governance. EUR 25302 EN: 46–48

[71] See http://code-of-conduct-for-health-research.eu/.

European Commission (2018) The 2018 ageing report economic & budgetary projections for the 28 EU Member States (2016–2070). Institutional paper 079
European Data Protection Board, Endorsement 1/2018
Fulop T (2016) Biological research into aging: from cells to clinic. Biogerontology 17:1–6
Gottweis H et al (2012) Biobanks for Europe. A challenge for governance, report of the expert group with ethical and regulatory challenges of international biobank research. directorate-general for research and innovation. European Commission, Brussels
Harris J et al (2012) Toward a roadmap in global biobanking for health. Eur J Hum Genet 20:1105–1011
Hewitt R (2011) Biobanking: the foundation of personalized medicine. Curr Opinion Oncol 23:112–119
Hewitt R, Watson P (2013) Defining Biobank. Biopreservation Biobanking 11(5):309–315
Joanna Stjernschantz Forsberg (2012) Biobank research: individual rights and public benefit. Uppsala University, Uppsala
Kaye J (2006) Do we need a uniform regulatory system for Biobanks across Europe? Eur J Hum Genet 14(2):245–248
Kerr D (2014) Policy: EU data protection regulation—harming cancer research. Nat Rev Clin Oncol 11:563–564
Knoppers BM et al (2011) Towards a data sharing code of conduct for international genomic research. Genome Med 3:46
LR Saeima (2002) Human genome research law. Latvijas Vēstnesis, 99 (2674), 03.07.2002
Müller H et al (2017) From the evaluation of existing solutions to an all-inclusive package for Biobanks. Health Technol 7:89–95
Maja Brkan (2016) Data Protection and Conflict-of-Laws: A Challenging Relationship. 2 Eur Data Prot L Rev 324–341
OECD (2009) Guidelines on human biobanks and genetic research databases. p 22
Parodi B (2015) Biobanks: a definition. In: Mascalzoni D (ed) Ethics, law and governance of biobanking: national, European and international approaches. Springer, Dordrecht
Partridge L, Deelen J, Slagboom P (2018) Facing up to the global challenges of ageing. Nature 561:45–56
Pormeister K (2017) Genetic data and the research exemption: is the GDPR going too far? Int Data Privacy Law 7(2):137–146
Pormeister K (2018) Genetic research and applicable law: the intra-EU conflict of laws as a regulatory challenge to cross-border genetic research. J Law Biosci 5(3):706–723. https://doi.org/10.1093/jlb/lsy023
Reichel J, Lind AS (2015) The new general data protection regulation—where are we are and where might we be heading? In: Mascalzoni D (ed) Ethics, law and governance of biobanking: national, European and international approaches. Springer, Dordrecht, pp 95–100
Reijs B et al (2015) The Central Biobank and virtual biobank of BIOMARKAPD: a resource for studies on neurodegenerative diseases. Front Neurol 6:1–7
Shaw DM, Elger BS, Colledge F (2014) What is a Biobank? Differing definitions among Biobank stakeholders. Clin Genet 85:223–226
Siwek M (2015) An overview of biorepositories—past, present, and future. Mil Med 180:57–66
Slokenberga S (2016) European legal perspectives on health-related direct-to-consumer genetic testing. Jure
Slokenberga S, Howard HC (2019) The right to science and human germline editing: Sweden, its external commitments and the ambiguous national responses under the Genetic Integrity Act. Förvaltningsrättslig Tidskrift 2:199–222
Slokenberga S, Reichel J, Niringiye R, Croxton T, Swanepoel C, Okal J (2019) EU data transfer rules and African legal realities: is data exchange for biobank research realistic? Int Data Privacy Law 9(1):30–48
Somiari SB, Somiari RI (2015) The future of biobanking: a conceptual look at how biobanks can respond to the growing human biospecimen needs of researchers. In: Karimi-Busheri F (ed) Biobanking in the 21st century. Advances in experimental medicine and biology, vol 864. Springer, Cham, pp 12–27

Staunton C, Slokenberga S, Mascalzoni D (2019) The GDPR and the research exemption: considerations on the necessary safeguards for research Biobanks. Eur J Hum Genet 27(8):1159–1167

Sveriges Riksdag (2002) Lag (2002:297) om biobanker i hälso- och sjukvården m.m. SFS nr: 2002:297

The European Commission (2012) Proposal for a regulation of the European Parliament and of the Council on the protection of individuals with regard to the processing of personal data and on the free movement of such data (General Data Protection Regulation). https://eur-lex.europa.eu/LexUriServ/LexUriServ.do?uri=COM:2012:0011:FIN:EN:PDF. Accessed 30 June 2019

The European Data Protection Board (2018) Guidelines 2/2018 on derogations of Article 49 under Regulation 2016/679

UN Committee on Economic, Social and Cultural Rights, General Comment No. 14: The Right to the Highest Attainable Standard of Health (Art. 12 of the Covenant), 11 August 2000

WMA Declaration of Taipei On Ethical Considerations Regarding Health Databases and Biobanks. Adopted by the 53rd WMA General Assembly, Washington, DC, USA, October 2002 and revised by the 67th WMA General Assembly, Taipei, Taiwan, October 2016

World Health Organization (2018) Noncommunicable diseases. https://www.who.int/news-room/fact-sheets/detail/noncommunicable-diseases. Accessed 30 June 2019

World Medical Association (2016) WMA declaration of Taipei on ethical considerations regarding health databases and Biobanks. https://www.wma.net/policies-post/wma-declaration-of-taipei-on-ethical-considerations-regarding-health-databases-and-biobanks/. Accessed 30 June 2019

Striking a Balance Between Personalised Genetics and Privacy Protection from the Perspective of GDPR

Mats G. Hansson

Abstract GDPR is currently being implemented across Europe and researchers, ethical review boards and national authorities are waiting for guidance on how to do the ethical balancing of the interests of privacy and the interest of conducting effective scientific, e.g. biomedical research, in practice. In order to reach this one must both understand the specific challenges that are related to new developments within the field of personalised medicine where massive uses of personal data are foreseen and what it really means to protect someone's privacy. In this chapter I will suggest how a balance may be reached between personalised medicine and privacy protection based on the premises of genetic science, ethics and the GDPR.

1 Introduction

The dominant current trend in genetics is trying to become more precise in targeting individual characteristics related to genotype and environmental factors that are decisive for diagnosis, treatment and prevention of disease. This development has been called *personalised* or precision medicine. Individuals are exposed to different risks of illness and risk profiling is part of the goal to stratify medical intervention and prevention in accordance with individual characteristics. This development stands in apparent conflict with the parallel aim to strengthen privacy protection as laid down and explicated in detail through the GDPR. One may rightfully ask how much of the private sphere that will be left as a secluded protected sphere as medicine gets more and more personal.

M. G. Hansson (✉)
Uppsala University, Center for Research Ethics and Bioethics, Uppsala, Sweden
e-mail: mats.hansson@crb.uu.se

S. Slokenberga et al. (eds.), *GDPR and Biobanking*, Law, Governance and Technology Series 43, https://doi.org/10.1007/978-3-030-49388-2_3

2 Personalised Genetics

There is a massive production of genetic information by academic- and industry-associated scientists. A common feature of this research is its focus on future medical and clinical application. Large prospective biobanks and—omic-databases are created as research infrastructures with links made to medical and personal data. They are intended to revolutionize the whole understanding of clinical and medical application by 'personalizing medicine'. Advances in genomics and Next Generation Sequencing are leading to the discovery of new genes that cause disease or at least correlate with a higher risk. From the perspective of current and future patients, the development of the field of genetic and life-style related risk information is of immense interest. The vision that is now being established and applied in the clinics is that we may move from trial-and-error therapies to evidence-based personalised medicine in clinical practice. It should be observed that the term 'personalised' does not imply medicine tailored to the needs of each individual but rather an approach whereby populations of patients are stratified into groups of good and bad responders before treatment is started, or to groups with special sensitivity to toxicity of drugs.[1] However, within a relatively short time frame one can foresee the usage of pre-emptive screening of an individual's genome, perpetually available as part of an individual's genetic examination, i.e. genetic examination performed in anticipation of future medical needs, and the associated development of medical record systems that can accommodate large-scale patient-specific genotypic information to be used in future medical consultations by general practitioners, specialist doctors and by their patients.[2]

Traditionally, genetic testing was confined to specialist medical genetic services, focused on relatively rare, high penetrance inherited diseases. In contrast, the common, complex disorders such as dementia, heart diseases, diabetes, and cancer are usually the result of variation in many genes, each contributing a small amount of genetic susceptibility, acting in concert with environmental or epigenetic factors. Some of the environmental factors might be changeable (as nutrition, exercise, avoiding toxic substances) while other rather less (such as pollution of air or water, psycho-social stress). Being genetically higher at risk might give individuals a reason to avoid those manageable factors to counterbalance their risk. But the interpretation of such information is generally very complicated already in a traditional clinical setting. The challenge for the health care system is illustrated by the following Fig. 1:[3]

The numeral I at the left of the figure represents diseases in which an individual can do very little to control his or her risk. At the other extreme, IV on the right, we find diseases where almost the entire risk may be managed if the individual changes health-related behaviour. One example here is Cardiovascular Diseases where for

[1] Nuffield Council of Bioethics (2010).

[2] O'Donnel and Ratain (2012).

[3] Figure from Hansson (2010).

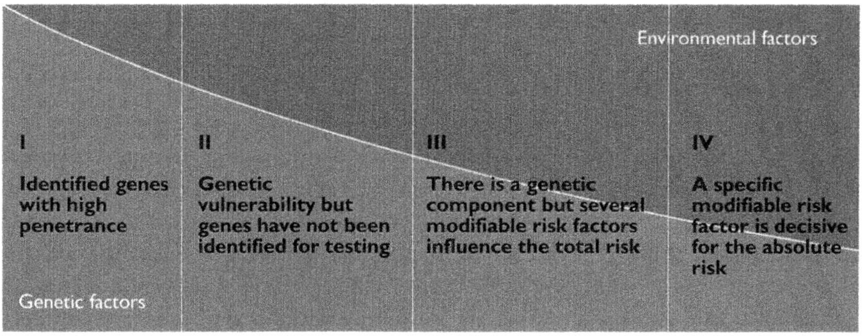

Fig. 1 Relative importance of genetic and environmental factors affecting an individual's prospect of modifying his or her health risk

Heart Infarction 90% of the total risk is related to modifiable factors.[4] Another challenge in bringing new pre-emptive information to the clinic is related to risk perception. Interpretation of risk language as well as risk perception is variable and in order for clinicians, counsellors and their patients to engage in meaningful shared decision-making more knowledge is needed about individuals' perceptions as well as of how to apply different models of risk communication and informed consent that respects autonomy. Risk communication in the clinic has been criticized for leaving the patient alone with difficult assessments and decisions to make.[5] At the same time, one should acknowledge that genetic profiling with identification of biomarkers is estimated to enable prediction and facilitate early treatment as well as preventive interventions of great benefit for individuals carrying an increased risk.

Genetic, medical and environmental data are the key tools for this development in personalised medicine and sharing of data between different research groups across national borders an intrinsic feature. Sharing and access to data is vital for most health-related research but it is of highest importance for research in Rare Diseases because of the scarcity of research participants and their associated data.[6] GDPR recognizes the special sensitivity and need for protection of genetic data. Genetic data is defined as 'personal data relating to the inherited or acquired genetic characteristics of a natural person which result from the analysis of a biological sample from the natural person in question, in particular chromosomal, deoxyribonucleic acid (DNA) or ribonucleic acid (RNA) analysis, or from the analysis of another element enabling equivalent information to be obtained'.[7] With this definition also proteins and other biomarkers, that are playing an increasing role in personalised medicine, are covered.

---

[4] Yusuf (2004).

[5] Politi et al. (2007).

[6] Mascalzoni (2014).

[7] Recital 34, GDPR.

3 The Central Value of Privacy

The central value of privacy and the recognition of each individual's claim of a protected private sphere can be thought to be justified by the circumstance that every human being has the right to determine who is allowed to have an insight into personal matters or to have access to information relating to that person as a private individual. This is how the notion of privacy protection is laid out in the EU Charter of Fundamental Rights.[8] This Charter emphasizes the right of each individual to protection of privacy within the fields of medicine and biology, implying a free and informed consent regarding access to their data according to procedures laid down by law (Article 3). Article 8 of the Charter also grants the individual the right to the protection of personal data implying that the processing of such data requires consent of the person concerned or other legally-recognized means. These articles conform to the European Convention for the Protection of Human Rights and Fundamental Freedoms, and the Social Charters adopted by the Council of Europe.

From a psychological viewpoint, the scope of the private sphere which a person wishes to define in this way, will be found to vary greatly. Whereas one person may be very unwilling to provide private information, another will freely expose themselves, both physically and with regard to their inner tendencies and thoughts. Some people look upon the fact that they can be observed through a window by a stranger as invasive, whereas others accept it without difficulty as part of the price to be paid for living in a town. From a historical and a philosophical point of view there are several accounts of privacy and its central importance in society.[9] James Rachels has suggested the enjoyment of a protected private sphere as a necessary condition for social diversity where we may have different kinds of relationships with our fellow beings.[10] According to Rachels, a private sphere is necessary in order to maintain a variety of social relations and he argues for the value of private life as a necessary requirement for being at all able to participate in several *different* types of relations. In Rachels' view, there is a close connection between human beings' control over who has access to personal information and their capacity to maintain different types of relationships with different people. If all had the same right to intimacy and access to the same information about an individual, it becomes difficult for the individual to live a socially fully adequate life together with family members, friends, colleagues, neighbours, cosignatories to an agreement or the man in the street or subway.

Historically and culturally the importance and practical implementation of a protected private sphere has varied but two central features seem to be common.[11] It is important (1) that an individual has access to a secluded private sphere and (2) that

[8] CFREU (2010/C 83/02).

[9] For an overview, see Hansson (2008).

[10] James (1984).

[11] Philippe and Georges (1989).

each individual is free to decide who will have access to this sphere, for example, to private information or to a private space. Invasion of privacy can lead to injustice through unfairly discriminatory use of personal information though an individual may be harmed merely by having exposed to the public gaze what they would prefer to be private. Respect for privacy is a means of respecting an individual but it can also be instrumental to establish trust, for example, in medical research contexts. Privacy is a central social value but it is not an absolute value. It has sometimes to be balanced against other important interests, both for society at large and for the individual citizens themselves. The individual has an interest in being allowed to be left in peace but at the same time participating in a community together with other people. Individuals seek an opportunity for a private sphere, which is part of a larger social space in which they participate in various types of social relationships together with other individuals. Within the family, individuals wish people to respect that certain matters are deeply personal, but at the same time they wish to participate in the inner life of the family. So too, in the case of friendship. There is a desire both for privacy and for participation. Genetic research has provided insight into the individual's genetic material in a way which was previously impossible, but thereby allowing new possibilities for the diagnosis and treatment of hereditary illnesses. Individuals have an interest in non-interference but also an interest in profiting from the results, which such interference can give. It is only through participation in research projects and the establishment of large infrastructures for biobanking, genetic and -omic research an individual may reap the fruits in terms of improved diagnosis, treatment and prevention. This central feature of having to balance privacy against other vital interests is well reflected both in accounts of human rights and, as we will see, in the legal premises as laid down in *Recital 4* of GDPR.

4 Balancing Privacy with Research Interests from a Human Rights Perspective and the Principle of Proportionality

As described, the Charter of Fundamental Rights of the European Union emphasizes the right of each individual to protection of privacy. In addition, the Charter also lays down human fundamental rights of each individual to social security benefits and social services in cases of illness (Article 34) as well as the rights to preventive health care and to benefit from medical treatment under the conditions established by national laws and practices (Article 35). Accordingly, the founding document of the European Union recognizes both the privacy right leading to requirements of respecting autonomy, providing information, obtaining consent etc., and the right to health care and social services in cases of illness as fundamental individual rights, notwithstanding that there may also be societal and public health related interests concerned. Normally we consider a right to be empty and rather meaningless if there is no corresponding duty. This is usually the case with rights to health, they require someone to take on the corresponding duty, to provide the necessary means for fulfilling the right and to monitor how the rights to health are recognized. Within the European context these duties will fall on the national governments who will have to provide the resources needed for implementing rights to health, medicine and social services. This will not be part of the EU competencies and the European Commission powers. However, they have both the competence and the powers to lay down the principles that should guide how the balancing of the different rights and interests should be made. This is the role of the GDPR regarding the protection of privacy.

The basic principle in this regard is the principle of proportionality as stated in Recital 4: 'The processing of personal data should be designed to serve mankind. The right to the protection of personal data is not an absolute right; it must be considered in relation to its function in society and be balanced against other fundamental rights, in accordance with the principle of proportionality'. This guiding principle reflects indeed very well the need of ethical balancing privacy interests against other interests such as those related to carrying out scientific research and using genetic data for the benefit of current and future patients, in accord with the account provided regarding privacy above. With this principle of proportionality, with its emphasis of taking into account both privacy concerns and the use of personal data for vital ends such as to be accomplished through research, in mind I will now turn to some of the detailed regulations in the GDPR and what they may imply for scientific research using genetic as well as other kinds of personal data.

From a doctrinal legal perspective it remains to be seen how exactly the different interests of privacy and scientific research should be balanced, something that should be based on case law from the European Court of Human Rights and the Court of Justice of the European Union. Meanwhile and pending such cases, there is a need for national legislators, national authorities, ethical review boards and researchers to steer in a way that takes account of the basic ethical values as discussed and exemplified in GDPR. It should in this context be observed that, generally speaking, researchers are loyal to the law and that they rarely, if ever, appeal a decision made by a public authority, or go to court in order to get their way through regarding, e.g. issues related to the use of personal data or informed consent procedures. The intention in this analysis is that the premises provided will be helpful as a guide for the national implementation of GDPR in the context of scientific research.

4.1 Premise 1: Promote the Free and Secure Flow of Data Across Borders

The sharing of genomic and health-related data for biomedical research is of key importance in ensuring continued progress in our understanding of human health and wellbeing. In particular for rare diseases but to an increasing extent also in other disease areas sharing of data is necessary in order to validate biological and clinical findings made in smaller local and national cohorts. As exemplified by a case in the area of rare diseases, a clinical trial in the rare disease juvenile dermatomyositis had to engage with 103 clinical centers in 30 different countries worldwide in order to collect the needed number of 130 patients.[12] On this background Recital 53 of GDPR is pertinent: 'Member States should be allowed to maintain or introduce further conditions, including limitations, with regard to the processing of genetic data, biometric data or data concerning health. However, this should not hamper the free flow of personal data within the Union when those conditions apply to cross-border processing of such data'. Further support for this may be found in Article 27 of the 1948 Universal Declaration of Human Rights which lays down the rights of every individual in the world 'to share in scientific advancement and its benefits' *(including to freely engage in responsible scientific inquiry), and at the same time* 'to the protection of the moral and material interests resulting from any scientific... production of which [a person] is the author.'

It should be observed that open access and free flow of data does not imply unconditional flow. GDPR sets up several precautionary measures in order to protect data from unauthorised use, as will be presented shortly. There are also interests of researchers, institutions and research subjects that needs to be considered. The following five principles for the stewardship of bio-specimens and data repositories may constitute a common premise for sharing and access to data, as well as human biological samples.[13]

I. Respect for privacy and autonomy: stewardship implies protection of participants' privacy. Privacy protection measures should be in place and informed consent must provide provisions for future research purposes described in general terms using data and biospecimens.
II. Reciprocity: stewardship also implies giving back. Feedback of general results should be channeled to institutions and patients.
III. Freedom of scientific enquiry: stewardship should encourage openness of scientific enquiry, and maximize data and bio-specimen use and sharing so as to exploit their full potential to promote health.
IV. Attribution: the intellectual investment of investigators involved in the creation of data registries and bio-repositories is often substantial, and should be acknowledged by mutual agreement.
V. Respect for intellectual property: the sharing of data and biospecimens needs to protect proprietary information and address the requirements of institutions and third-party funders.

It is made clear in the GDPR that use and sharing of data should always be made in a secure manner. As stated in Recital 39, 'Personal data should be processed in a manner that ensures appropriate security and confidentiality of the personal data,

[12] Hansson et al. (2012).

[13] Mascalzoni (2014) and Ness (2007).

including for preventing unauthorised access to or use of personal data and the equipment used for the processing'.

The chief instrument for achieving this is to protect individuals from identification by using a mechanism for pseudonymization. The definition of this is described in Article 4.5, pseudonymization 'means the processing of personal data in such a manner that the personal data can no longer be attributed to a specific data subject without the use of additional information, provided that such additional information is kept separately and is subject to technical and organisational measures to ensure that the personal data are not attributed to an identified or identifiable natural person'. In practice there are several technical solutions available. When designing such a system of protection one must always keep in mind that while there should be strong measures for protection of privacy one must not make it too cumbersome for researchers to use and share data in an efficient way.

4.2 Premise 2: Make Sure Informed Consent and/or Ethical Approval Covers All Use of Data

Following Article 6.1.a end e, for research purposes there are in essence two applicable legal grounds for the use of personal data: an informed consent followed by an approval by an ethical review board or such an approval based on the recognition of a research project as being of public interest. It should be observed here that also private research institutes and companies may refer to handling of personal data for a research purpose as being a public interest, provided that national law lays down that research performed by them can be regarded as a public interest. The latter ground is of particular interest for retrospective studies where it may be impractical to contact research subjects and ask for a renewed consent. This is evident from the wordings of Recital 62: 'However, it is not necessary to impose the obligation to provide information where the data subject already possesses the information, where the recording or disclosure of the personal data is expressly laid down by law or where the provision of information to the data subject proves to be impossible or would involve a disproportionate effort. The latter could in particular be the case where processing is carried out for archiving purposes in the public interest, scientific or historical research purposes or statistical purposes'. In any case a research project processing personal data needs approval by a legitimate ethical review board, also when claiming public interest as the legal ground.

Regarding informed consent it should be observed that GDPR recognizes the need and option for a broad consent covering future yet unspecified research projects, to an extent that was not the case with the preceding directive of data protection. Recital 33 states that 'It is often not possible to fully identify the purpose of personal data processing for scientific research purposes at the time of data collection. Therefore, data subjects should be allowed to give their consent to certain areas of scientific research when in keeping with recognised ethical standards for scientific research. Data subjects should have the opportunity to give their consent only to certain areas of research or parts of research projects to the extent allowed by the intended purpose'.

As is stated in the guidelines on informed consent from the Article 29 Working Party this does not disapply the obligations with regard to the requirements of specific informed consent whenever that is feasible: 'This means that, in principle, scientific research projects can only include personal data on the basis of consent if they have a well-described purpose. For the cases where purposes for data processing within a scientific research project cannot be specified at the outset, Recital 33 allows as an exception that the purpose may be described at a more general level'.[14] For a further clarification on how to deal with this possibility of a broad consent while adhering to standards for privacy protection there is a long tradition of ethics research.[15] The basic approach suggested is to make a distinction between the purpose of research—that may be described in general terms (e.g. lung cancer research or research in rare diseases)—and the elements of the process and design of a research project where different designs may imply different levels of risk for privacy intrusion with subsequent harm for the research subject—where the description should be more specific. One should then try to be specific about issues like, the identity of the data controller, the nature of research (e.g. will it include whole genome sequencing), if data is going to be shared with other research partners and across national borders, if collaboration is planned with commercial partners, if there will be linkage to registry data, if there will be feed-back of research results or incidental findings and how data will be protected from unauthorized use. There should always be an option provided for withdrawal from a project and the way to do this needs to be clearly described in the consent form.

4.3 *Premise 3: Establish Codes of Conduct for Facilitating Joint Research Projects*

As research is to a growing extent carried out in large international networks there is a need to have agreement on basic elements. The GDPR will provide the basic requirements regarding personal data protection but that is often provided on a rather general level. The need for further specification is also recognized in this legislation. Recitals 77 and 98 states that guidance on the implementation of GDPR, e.g. regarding identification of risks and best practices to mitigate these risk, may be provided by means of approved codes of conduct or guidelines by the Data Protection Board.

---

[14] Working Party (2018).

[15] e.g. Hansson (1998, 2009, 2010), Hansson et al. (2006, 2013), Wendler (2006), Steinsbekk (2013), Stjernschantz-Forsberg (2011) and Grady (2015).

It is essential that these codes of conduct reflect the needs and conditions related to different research contexts since the way personal data is used may vary in different contexts. However, there are examples of such codes of conduct that may serve as inspiration and provide guidance on what to include and how to design them. One such example is the RD-Connect Code of Conduct.[16] The research project RD-Connect was established in November 2012 through a grant from the European Commission under the seventh framework programme (FP7). It provided infrastructure, tools and resources to facilitate and accelerate rare disease research by maximizing the availability, analysis and (re)use of rare disease data and biological samples. It is sustained on an ongoing basis by European and national funding mechanisms and close connection with pan-European biomedical research infrastructures, in particular ELIXIR and BBMRI-ERIC. The RD-Connect Genome-Phenome Analysis Platform (GPAP) is an online, controlled-access suite of software tools and underlying secure database that enables the standardized collection, integration, storage, real-time analysis and reuse of linked genomic and phenotypic data and metadata on individuals with rare diseases. The GPAP interface enables clinicians and researchers to analyze and interpret the full genomic datasets they submit for both diagnosis and gene discovery on an individual patient basis and to link these with phenotypic data and biosample availability for the same individual. A Code of Conduct was developed to regulate the terms on which users gain access to the RD-Connect Genome-Phenome Analysis Platform. Other RD-Connect tools and resources share the same goal of enabling rare disease research and data and sample sharing for the benefit of patients. The Code of Conduct specified definitions of crucial terms based on the GDPR, gave a motivation as well as principles and specific rules for sharing and access to data. An adherence agreement was signed with each user.

A Code of Conduct, with associated Adherence Agreement, may provide a helpful tool for balancing privacy interests with research interests in line with what is argued in this chapter, in addition to implementations of GDPR in national law. An advantage with such codes of conduct is that they can have attention to contextual conditions related to specific research contexts and areas, as well as have regard to challenges and concerns related to the advancement of scientific research and the development of new tools, e.g. for combining massive amounts of data from different sources (Big Data).

[16]Connect Code of Conduct. https://rd-connect.eu/wp-content/uploads/2018/05/RD-Connect_Code-of-Conduct_GPAP_20180525.pdf. Accessed 9 May 2019.

5 Conclusions

GDPR has laid down the legal premises for processing of personal data. National laws and specific regulations by national authorities will provide further guidance to researchers. It is essential that all this rule making is having regard to and is taking into account the basic need and prerogative to balance privacy interests against research interests, since privacy protection cannot be an absolute condition when engaging in scientific research. This has then implications also for when researchers propose e.g. protection measures regarding access to personal data. Protection measures should not be so strict so that they hinder important research from being carried out. In a similar vein, ethical review boards should take into account the need to balance privacy interests, not only against risks of intrusions but also against the estimated utility of research.

References

Grady C, Eckstein L, Berkman B, Brock D, Cook-Deegan R, Fullerton SM, Greely H, Hansson MG, Hull S, Kim S, Lo B, Pentz R, Rodriguez L, Weil C, Wilfond BS, Wendler D (2015) Broad consent for research with biological samples: workshop conclusions. Am J Bioethics 15(9):34–42

Hansson MG (1998) Balancing the quality of consent. J Med Ethics 24(3):182–187

Hansson MG (2008) The private sphere. An emotional territory and its agent. Springer, Dordrecht

Hansson MG (2009) Ethics and biobanks. Br J Cancer 100:8–12

Hansson MG (2010) Taking the patient's side: the ethics of pharmacogenetics. Pers Med 7(1):75–85

Hansson MG, Dillner J, Bartram CR, Carlsson J, Helgesson G (2006) Should donors be allowed to give broad consent to future biobank research? Lancet Oncol 7:266–269

Hansson MG, Gattorno M, Stjernschantz Forsberg J, Feltelius N, Martini A, Ruperto N (2012) Ethics bureaucracy – a significant hurdle for collaborative follow-up of drug effectiveness in rare childhood diseases. Archiv Dis Childhood 97:561–563

Hansson MG, Van Ommen GJ, Chadwick R, Dillner J (2013) Patients would benefit from simplified ethical review and consent. Lancet Oncol 14(6):451–453

James R (1984) Why privacy is important. In: Schoeman FD (ed) Philosophical dimensions of privacy: an anthology. Cambridge University Press, New York, pp 290–299

Mascalzoni D, Dove E, Rubinstein Y, Dawkins H, Kole A, Mc McCormack P, Woods S, Riess O, Schaefer F, Lochmüller H, Bartha Knoppers B, Hansson MG (2014) International charter of principles for sharing bio-specimens and data. Eur J Hum Genet 23:721–728

Ness RB (2007) On behalf of the American College of Epidemiology Policy Committee: Biospecimen "ownership": point. Cancer Epidemiol Prev Biomarkers 16:188–189

Nuffield Council of Bioethics (2010) Annual Report 2010. http://nuffieldbioethics.org/wp-content/uploads/2014/06/Nuffield_Council_on_Bioethics_Annual_Report_2010.pdf. Accessed

O'Donnel PH, Ratain MJ (2012) Germline pharmacogenomics in oncology: decoding the patient for targeting therapy. Mol Oncol 6(2):251–259

Philippe A, Georges D (eds) (1989) A history of private life, vol I–V. The Belknap Press of Harvard University Press, Cambridge

Politi MC, Han PK, Col NF (2007) Communicating the uncertainty of harms and benefits of medical interventions. Med Decision Making 27(5):681–695

Steinsbekk KS, Kåre Myskja B, Solberg B (2013) Broad consent versus dynamic consent in biobank research: is passive participation an ethical problem? Eur J Hum Genet 21(9):897–902

Stjernschantz-Forsberg J, Hansson MG, Eriksson S (2011) Biobank research: who benefits from individual consent? Br Med J 343:d5647

Wendler D (2006) One-time general consent for research on biological samples. BMJ 332(7540):544–547

Yusuf S, Hawken S, Ôunpuu S et al (2004) Effect of potentially modifiable risk factors associated with myocardial infarction in 52 countries (the INTERHEART study): case–control study. Lancet 364:937–952

Part II
GDPR Insights

The Impact of the GDPR on the Governance of Biobank Research

Mahsa Shabani, Gauthier Chassang, and Luca Marelli

Abstract Governance of health and genomic data access in the context of biobanking is of salient importance in implementing the EU General Data Protection Regulation (GDPR). Various components of data access governance could be considered as 'organizational measures' which are stressed in the Article 89(1) GDPR together with technical measures that should be used in order to safeguard rights of the data subjects when processing data under research exemption rules. In this chapter, we address the core elements regarding governance of biobanks in the view of GDPR, including conditions for processing personal data, data access models, oversight bodies and data access agreements. We conclude by highlighting the importance of guidelines and policy documents in helping the biobanks in improving the data access governance. In addition, we stress that it is important to ensure the existing and emerging oversight bodies are equipped with adequate expertise regarding using and sharing health and genomic data and are aware of the associated informational risks.

M. Shabani (✉)
Metamedica, Faculty of Law and Criminology, Ghent University, Ghent, Belgium
e-mail: mahsa.shabani@ugent.be

G. Chassang
Inserm, Faculté de Médecine, Toulouse, France
e-mail: gauthier.chassang@bbmri-eric.eu

L. Marelli
Life Sciences and Society Lab, Centre for Sociological Research (CeSO), University of Leuven, Leuven, Belgium

Department of Experimental Oncology, IEO, European Institute of Oncology IRCCS, Milan, Italy
e-mail: luca.marelli@kuleuven.be

S. Slokenberga et al. (eds.), *GDPR and Biobanking*, Law, Governance and Technology Series 43, https://doi.org/10.1007/978-3-030-49388-2_4

1 Introduction

Governance of health and genomic data access in the context of biobanking is of salient importance in implementing the EU General Data Protection Regulation (GDPR). Various components of data access governance could be considered as 'organizational measures' which are stressed in the Article 89(1) GDPR together with technical measures that should be used in order to safeguard rights of the data subjects when processing data under research exemption rules. By establishing adequate governance mechanisms from the outset in the process of personal data processing, the ultimate goal of the regulation in terms of 'privacy by design' will be facilitated, in which data protection safeguards will be built into the products and services from the earliest stage of development.

According to the GDPR Article 9(2)(j), personal data, including sensitive data, could be processed for scientific research purposes under the conditions set out in the Article 89. As Article 9(2)(j) states: 'processing is necessary for archiving purposes in the public interest, scientific or historical research purposes or statistical purposes in accordance with Article 89(1) based on Union or Member State law which shall be proportionate to the aim pursued, respect the essence of the right to data protection and provide for suitable and specific measures to safeguard the fundamental rights and the interests of the data subject.'

In principle, adopting adequate governance models that are foreseen by the GDPR will establish additional controls, to protect the rights of the data subjects when processing personal data for research purposes. A similar approach has been supported by a report on the *Collection, linking and use of data in biomedical research and health care* by Nuffield Council on Bioethics, which noted, 'Because of the risk of misuse and consequential privacy infringement, de-identification and consent measures may be supplemented by further governance arrangements.'[1]

One key element in biobank governance is developing transparent and fair data access rules, which should address the core elements regarding data access review and oversight procedures. Generally speaking, rules for data access should delineate criteria for data user's qualification, the review procedure, and terms and conditions of access. The ultimate goal is to decrease the risks of harms to the research participants that may arise from unauthorized access to the datasets for unintended purposes. In principle, the development of the data sharing and access rules must be in compliance with the applicable national laws. The relevant international and national data sharing policies and guidelines that are issued by various professional communities may guide the development of data access rules.

Moreover, data access rules should be developed in the view of suitable data access models, which could range from fully open-access to controlled-access. The nature of the data in terms of identifiability and the associated privacy risks for the data subjects significantly influences the model of data access. It should be noted that biobanks and data-intensive genomics and health studies might use external

[1] Nuffield Council on Bioethics (2014), p. 7.

data repositories for data sharing such as the NIH database of Genotypes and Phenotypes (dbGaP) or the European Genome-phenome Archive (EGA).[2] This could be requested by funding organizations or journals in order to facilitate broad access to the data. In case of using external databases, it is essential for the researchers to ensure that the data governance models of the databases conform with the applicable national laws and institutional policies.[3]

In this chapter, we address a number of issues essential in discussion regarding governance of biobanks in the view of GDPR. First, we will investigate the GDPR's relevant provisions regarding processing personal data under research exemption. This is particularly pertinent for the governance of biobanks, as personal data harvested from biological samples may include a wide range of health and genomic data. Second, we will provide an overview of the major data access models, namely open access, registered access and controlled access. This overview will enable us to show the level of control that biobanks could maintain on data based on the selected model of data access. Finally, we will review the functions of the relevant oversight committees in the framework of governance of data access. Some of these oversight committees, such as Data Access Committees are not defined by the GDPR, yet they are essential in the governance of data access in biobanks. We will also refer to data transfer agreements as an important tool used in the governance of data access.

2 Processing Personal Data for Scientific Research Purposes

The GDPR provides a certain degree of flexibility for the processing of personal data for scientific research purposes. Notably, the GDPR upholds a 'research exemption' to the general prohibition otherwise imposed on the processing of 'special categories of data'[4] (a label under which are grouped sensitive data like genetic, biometric and health-related data that are recognized as warranting the implementation of higher forms of protection from the part of data controllers.[5]) In addition, Article 6 recognizes processing personal data for public interest or legitimate interest in the list of lawful grounds for processing data. When read in conjunction with Art. 9(2)(j), this can, in turn, provide a legal basis for processing data for scientific research purposes. The so-called research exemption allows the processing of data for scientific research purposes, where the processing is proportionate to the aim pursued, that is, only personal data which is adequate and relevant for the purposes of the processing is collected and processed.

---

[2] Paltoo et al. (2014), pp. 692–695.

[3] Mascalzoni et al. (2019).

[4] Article 9(2)(j), GDPR.

[5] Recital 53, GDPR.

Additionally, the Regulation[6] relaxes the stringent requirements for specific consent and data storage—two key aspects directly impinging on biobanking—, allowing use of broad consent whenever required by the intended research purposes,[7] and to extend the period in which personal data can be legally stored.[8,9]

Crucially, subject to the provision of technical and organizational safeguards, the GDPR further allows Member States to introduce derogations from the core data subject rights of data access, rectification, restriction of processing, and object to the processing,[10] whenever upholding such rights is 'likely to render impossible or seriously impair' the achievement of the desired scientific research purposes, and such derogations are deemed essential for the fulfilment of these purposes.[11] More in general, in line with the principle of subsidiarity and the (historically) national competence in the field of health, Article 9(4) of the Regulation allows Member States to maintain or introduce further conditions, including limitations, with regard to the processing of genetic, biometric and health-related data. On a par with the derogations foreseen under Article 89(2) that are further elaborated in this volume by Anne-Marie Duguet and Jean Heveg, this could potentially lead to the fragmentation of the regulatory landscape underpinning the operations of European biobanks.[12]

3 Pseudonymized and Anonymized Data

3.1 Introductory Remarks

In order to identify the adequate organizational and technical measures in accessing and sharing genomic and health data in the context of biobanks, it is crucial to investigate the status of data, and whether the data is being considered as personal data under the GDPR. A relevant distinction enshrined in the GDPR, with significant implications for the processing and governance of access to sensitive data in the field of biobanking, is the one between pseudonymized and anonymized data.

[6] Recital 33, GDPR.

[7] Article 29 Working Group Party (2018).

[8] Article 5(1)(e), GDPR.

[9] Marelli and Testa (2018), pp. 496–498.

[10] Article 15, 16, 18 and 21, GDPR.

[11] Article 89(2), GDPR. LERU (2016).

[12] For insights in how Article 89(2) has been implemented in different EU Member States and EEA states, see Tzortzatou et al. 'Biobanking across Europe post-GDPR: A deliberately created fragmented landscape' in this volume.

3.2 *Pseudonymized Data*

Pseudonymized data are defined, in Article 4(5), as data that 'can no longer be attributed to a specific data subject without the use of additional information, provided that such additional information is kept separately and is subject to technical and organizational measures to ensure that the personal data are not attributed to an identified or identifiable natural person'. This is typically the case of key-coded data, which allows (among other things) the traceability and correlation of genotypic and phenotypic data, as well as the possibility to recontact research participants, while still preserving the de-identification of personal data in the day-to-day operations of the organization. Accordingly, *insofar* as they are not irreversibly de-identified, pseudonymized data are considered as personal data, falling under the scope of the GDPR.

On the contrary, according to Recital 26, *irreversible* de-identification is defined as 'information which does not relate to an identified or identifiable natural person' or as 'personal data rendered anonymous in such a manner that the data subject is not or no longer identifiable'. As further specified in Recital 26, anonymized data fall outside the remit of the GDPR. However, it should be noted that the act of anonymization itself should be considered as an act of processing personal data, which should occur, accordingly, in compliance with the GDPR.

3.3 *Anonymization of Data*

When we focus on anonymization, the main question to be addressed is: Under what circumstances, if any, can genomic and health data be anonymous in light of the GDPR?[13] Interestingly, the GDPR differs conspicuously, in this respect, from other major data protection legislations, such as the Health Insurance Portability and Accountability Act (HIPAA) Privacy Rule in the US.[14] Within the Privacy Rule, the Safe Harbor standard for achieving the de-identification of personal data singles out 18 distinct identifiers, the removal of which is said to make the resulting information 'not individually identifiable', and thus anonymous.[15]

Differently from this approach, recital 26 of the GDPR states instead that personal data should be considered anonymous insofar as the data subject cannot be identified 'by any means reasonably likely to be used [...] either by the controller or by any other person'.[16] To ascertain whether means are reasonably likely to be used to identify the natural person, the GDPR further states that 'account should be taken

---

[13] For a broader overview of this issue in relation to genomic data, cf. Shabani and Marelli (2019).

[14] Shabani et al. (2018).

[15] U.S. Department of Health & Human Services (2012), p. 6.

[16] Recital 26, GDPR; see also: Court of Justice of the European Union (CJEU), Case C-582/14: Patrick Breyer v Bundesrepublik Deutschland, ECLI:EU:C:2016:779.

of all objective factors, such as the costs of and the amount of time required for identification, taking into consideration the available technology at the time of the processing and technological developments' (Recital 26). In addition, opinion 05/2014 of the Article 29 Working Party has outlined other factors that should be taken into consideration, such as the existence of publicly available data which can be cross-referenced with the original dataset, thus heightening the risk of de-anonymization. As such, and in line with the overall decentralized thrust of the Regulation, the GDPR can be said to adopt a context-base criterion to determine whether personal data should be considered as irreversibly de-identified (and thus anonymous), bestowing upon controllers the responsibility to address such a question (is there a 'reasonable likelihood' that re-identification techniques can be effectively used to de-anonymize my given dataset?) in the context of their concrete processing activities.

4 Governance Models for Accessing Genomic and Health Data

4.1 Governance Models: An Overview

Samples and data collected by biobanks can be accessed for various research purposes. Such access may not be limited only to the researchers/clinicians who collected the data, but also a broader range of researchers. Adopting adequate governance models would assist to protect data subjects against potential privacy breaches. The current governance model can be grouped under three major models of open access, controlled-access and registered access, which are explained below.

4.2 Open-Access

Open-access models generally refer to making data available for the users through various online platforms without any constraint. Sharing data through open-access models has been initially pursued by the Human Genome Project, which sequenced the whole human genome for a first time in the course of 13 years.[17] However, the concerns related to identifiability of genomic data that has been demonstrated by a number of re-identification studies, questioned the adequacy of adopting such model when sharing health and genomic data.[18] Consequently, genomic data have

[17] Cook-Deegan and McGuire (2017), pp. 897–901.

[18] Homer et al. (2008), pp. 321–324.

been moved to the controlled-access databases.[19] This has been mainly the case when sharing personal level information rather than aggregate data.

A key question here is when genomic data could be considered as non-identifiable under GDPR, therefore suitable for sharing through open-access models? The regulation states that the principles of data protection 'should not apply to anonymous information, namely information which does not relate to an identified or identifiable natural person or to personal data rendered anonymous in such a manner that the data subject is not or no longer identifiable' (Recital 26).

As it has been shown in the previous part, GDPR adopts a context-based criterion to determine whether personal data should be considered as irreversibly de-identified (and thus anonymous) and do not define the standards for de-identification itself. Hence, it is important, to decide when data can be considered as anonymous and do not fall under GDPR protection. Thereby, this is the responsibility of the data controllers to confirm whether the data is not identifiable by reasonable likelihood. For example, in the context of genomics, only sharing variant-level aggregate data may not be considered as identifying personal data, therefore adopting open-access model for sharing such data would seem acceptable under the GDPR. In a same vein, recently National Institutes of Health (NIH) updated its Genomic Data Sharing Policy and allowed unrestricted access to genomic summary results that do not raise privacy concerns.

4.3 Controlled-Access

In the view of privacy concerns when sharing health and genomic data, adopting a controlled-access model for data sharing is favored. Thereby, the data controllers can set rules for data access and limit access to the datasets to the approved users and under the determined terms and conditions. Such access control mechanisms can be considered as technical and organizational measures, which are mentioned in Article 89(1). Although there is no single model for controlled-access, a common approach is to establish oversight committees, or so-called Data Access Committees (DACs) to review the data access requests for the purpose of approval or disapproval. One of the important aspects of controlled-access data sharing is to use tools such as data access agreements (see Sect. 5), which are legally binding documents, in order to hold users accountable against potential misuses of data. This is in contrast with the open-access model where the users do not enter to any agreement with the data holders.

Oversight by DACs could be considered as an example of organizational measures that have been stressed in Article 89. Thereby, further safeguards could be offered to protect the privacy of the data subjects and ensure the downstream data

[19] Rodriguez et al. (2013), pp. 275–276.

uses conform to the original consent forms.[20] However, the recent studies have showed that the current oversight by DACs are not always efficient or effective.[21] One major reason for the identified shortcomings is DACs are not always equipped with sufficient tools and oversight mechanisms to effectively review the data access requests or detect the potential violations of data access agreements.

In response, novel approaches to data access oversight are being developed. In particular, it has been suggested to replace or supplement review by DACs by automated tools.[22] In addition, not all steps of data access review are deemed to be necessary for all types of health and genomic data sharing. In the next section, we will provide an overview of one of these recently suggested methods for data governance, namely the Registered Access model.

4.4 Registered Access

Registered access is likely to be suitable as a mechanism for access to data types that are less sensitive and low risk, such as non-stigmatizing health-related data from non-vulnerable individuals who would expect, or have consented to, data sharing for the purposes envisaged.[23] This model would focus primarily on ensuring that the data users are *bona fide* researchers. The rationale behind the registered model is that if processing data is not creating high risks of identifiability and the users are trusted, then further access review (for instance reviewing the ethical or scientific aspects of the proposals) would be redundant or disproportionate.

The 'registered access' model hinges on a number of core elements, namely authentication, authorization and attestation. First, the data use applicants should provide personal and professional information within a registration process, including their name, title, position, affiliation, email address, institutional website and mailing address for the purpose of authentication. In contrast to a controlled-access model, a registered-access model would not entail verification on a case-by-case basis by a DAC of the users' qualifications. In addition, the applicants should declare that they are 'bona fide' researchers in order to be authorized access. At last, the applicants should agree with the terms and conditions of the data access. Within the registered access model, data users would not need to sign a data access agreement in a paper-based format but could instead agree via clickwrap-type online agreements. Indeed, the procedure for signing data access agreements by DACs,

---

[20] Shabani and Borry (2017), pp. 149–156.

[21] Shabani and Borry (2016), pp. 892–897.

[22] Woolley et al. (2018), p. 17.

[23] Dyke et al. (2016), pp. 1676–1680.

and users and their home institution, is administratively heavy and this proposed alternative approach could reduce pressure on DACs and create rapid, open and efficient access to data.

A Registered-access model is only one proposed solution in response to the limitations of the controlled-access model. It is expected that novel governance models will emerge in the coming years in order to address the identified shortcomings of the controlled-access models, and in line with the principles of responsible data sharing. In addition to emerging governance mechanisms, novel technical solutions are also proposed,[24] including the introduction of federated networks in which multiple distributed databases are connected.[25] By using federated networks, users would be able to have (a level of) access to data in a protected virtual environment, and each database would be able to monitor data uses in real time. To date, few models of federated data computation have been suggested.[26] Considering the limitations of controlled-access models, there is a pressing need for the introduction of such innovative solutions. Concurrently, it is important to ensure the core elements of secure data computational environments are in line with data protection principles.

5 Relevant Data Sharing and Access Oversight Bodies and Tools

5.1 Data Access Committees

The need to establish an extra layer of oversight through DACs is grounded in the nature of data sharing, which allows downstream data uses that are not known at the time of the initial sample and data collection. Therefore, research ethics committees cannot foresee all downstream data uses when they approve the research protocol in the beginning. In that sense DACs are considered as an extra layer of oversight next to research ethics committees, which review the proposals in the beginning of the studies. In particular, DACs are established to receive data access requests from actual users and assess them for the purpose of approving or disapproving their access to data.[27] DACs are not mentioned in the GDPR, but their role in governance of data access is important. This can indeed be considered as part of research self-regulation in order to ensure data sharing and use is in line with the overarching principles and the relevant regulations.

---

[24] Joly et al. (2016), pp. 1150–1154.

[25] Philippakis et al. (2015), pp. 915–921.

[26] Wallace et al. (2014), pp. 149–157. See also: Ardeshirdavani et al. (2014).

[27] Lowrance (2012), p. 23.

DACs, function in different ways. As Lowrance illustrates, 'some of these groups are formally constituted, have terms of reference and hold regular meetings. Others, are casual, rarely meeting but existing to be consulted from time to time by the custodian and in a position to address serious problems should any arise'.[28]

The composition of DACs varies across the institutions. Ideally, such committees should be consisting of internal and independent members with expertise in technical, ethical and legal aspects of processing health and genomic data. Some have suggested establishing two-layer committee is beneficial, namely an advisory committees together with operational access committees. The advisory committees will be tasked with auditing the performance of the operational access committees, while the operational committee will be responsible for reviewing the access requests.

Moreover, the oversight committees, such as DACs and Research Ethics Committees, should be given the opportunity to assess the data access rules on a regular basis, and propose revision of the provisions when needed. This could ultimately strengthening effective operation of the organizational measures under Article 89(1). In addition, transparency of the data access governance could be considerably enhanced if adequate information dissemination policies are adopted. It is expected that the oversight bodies within the institutions provide information about the access review procedure, incoming data access requests and approved and disapproved requests to enhance transparency and facilitate external scrutiny. Furthermore, data access governance models should adopt mechanisms that hold users accountable.

5.2 Data Protection Impact Assessment and Appointment of Data Protection Officers (DPOs)

The GDPR sets further requirements in terms of governance of data processing when higher risks for the freedoms and the rights of the data subjects are perceived. One of the relevant organizational measures foreseen by the GDPR is to appoint a data protection officer (DPO) and conduct data protection impact assessment when specific conditions are met. The biobanks as entities that process health and genomic data should adhere to these provisions.

The Regulation in Article 37 provides a set of rules for designating the DPO when the processing of personal data within institutions meets certain criteria. According to the explanation provided by the European Data Protection Supervisor: 'the main task of the data protection officer is to ensure, in an independent manner, the internal application of the provisions of the Regulation in his/her institution. The data protection officer is also required to keep a register of all of the processing operations involving personal data carried out by the institution. The Register,

[28] Lowrance (2012), p. 23.

which must contain information explaining the purpose and conditions of the processing operations, should be accessible to any interested person.'[29] The appointment of a DPO must of course be based on her personal and professional qualities, but particular attention must be paid to her expert knowledge of data protection.

In addition, according to Article 35, a privacy impact assessment is necessary: 'where a type of processing in particular using new technologies, and taking into account the nature, scope, context and purpose of the processing is likely to result in a high risk to the rights and freedoms of natural persons, the controller shall, prior to the processing, carry out an assessment of the impact of the envisaged processing operations on the protection of personal data.' Therefore, a broad scope for these data protection impact assessments is expected, which goes beyond compliance with the Regulation and privacy rights and includes consideration of a plethora of individual's fundamental rights. This will therefore provide an opportunity to take into account a broader range of concerns relating to the rights of individuals in processing personal data and not only those that are related to storage and safety. Article 35(b) adds that the data protection impact assessment shall in particular be required in cases where there is 'processing on a large scale of special categories of data referred to in Article 9(1)'.

The controller shall receive a data protection officer's advice (if he/she has been appointed) when carrying out a data protection impact assessment. Consequently, the data controller shall consult the supervisory authority prior to processing 'where a data protection impact assessment under Article 35 indicates that the processing would result in high risk.'[30] Article 35(9) also requires the data controller, where appropriate, to 'seek views of data subjects or their representatives on the intended processing'.

The impact assessment will therefore replace the previous obligation to notify the data protection authority, which was outlined by the Directive 95/46/EC on the protection of individuals with regard to the processing of personal data. This change was welcomed by commentators, who argued against the effectiveness of the previous notification requirement. As Townend argues: 'Although data controllers are required to register their activity with the relevant supervisory authorities and that authority has power to investigate and prosecute breaches of the data subject's rights, the sheer amount of processing that goes on within any jurisdiction at any given time makes it impossible for a supervisory authority to be seen as the primary protector in the system'.[31] In turn, the new requirements will see a shift towards the accountability of the controllers and reinforce their role in establishing adequate safeguards in the course of the processing, not only limiting it to the outset of the project.[32] This could also draw the attention of the data controllers towards the

[29] European Data Protection Supervisor. https://edps.europa.eu/data-protection/eu-institutions-dpo_en.

[30] Article 36, GDPR.

[31] Townend (2016), pp. 128–142.

[32] de Hert and Papakonstantinou (2016), pp. 179–194.

ethical concerns associated with data processing and take the concerns into account in the design of the processing.

5.3 Data Access Agreements and Data/Material Transfer Agreements

Contractual agreements are essential operational instruments intended to legally bind the parties to specific rules ensuring adequate individuals' privacy protection throughout personal data processing. Such contracts can take many forms and be labelled differently such as 'Data Access Agreements' (DAAs), 'Data Transfer Agreements' (DTAs) or 'Confidential Data Agreements' (CDAs). Personal data protection measures are also included within other special research agreements, in particular within the so-called 'material transfer agreements' (MTAs) when biological samples are also transferred. In particular, it is widely recommended to include in MTAs provisions regarding samples' quality, transportation, conditions and restrictions of use (e.g. derivations of original material) and storage (biosafety/biosecurity).

The nature and scope of the contract can vary depending on the internal practices of operators or applicable national legal framework, the requester's processing operation and purposes, the database governance model (cf. supra) and on the cross-border features of the access (intra-EU or including outside-EU elements). For example, where data is managed within a closed controlled system (e.g. digital data analysis platform), an access agreement could take the form of terms and conditions in the view of the applicable regulations. In addition, a decentralized infrastructure could rely on a general Access policy having a contractual value. For example, BBMRI-ERIC[33] provides such template while allowing its members to adopt specific and compliant contractual activities to frame collaborations.[34]

The legal qualification of the parties to such agreements is context-dependent and needs a case-by-case analysis of the role and activities of each stakeholder. Access could be requested in a framework of a research collaboration with the biobank or by an external researcher to conduct an independent research project. Thereby, the contract will define a controller-processor relationship or a joint-controllers relationship. This is in line with the GDPR that requires setting up a contract for organizing joint-controllers[35] and/or controller-processor relationships[36] in terms of duties and rights in processing data.

---

[33] BBMRI-ERIC (2018).

[34] B3Africa, Checklist: For a good governance of transcontinental collaborative biobank research. http://biobanklearning.iarc.fr/course/checklist-elsi/#llms-lesson-locked. Accessed 9 May 2019.

[35] Article 26, GDPR.

[36] Article 28, GDPR.

The data access agreements usually include negotiable and non-negotiable provisions. Contracts shall echo and respect the will of the initial donor and facilitate the exercise of the donors' rights. The parties shall commit to respect confidentiality and plan cooperation procedures, in particular regarding personal data breach notifications. The agreement must also clearly describe any restriction specified by the initial controller during the deposit of the data/sample in the biobank or imposed by the biobank policy based on a legitimate interest (e.g. regarding onward transfers possibilities, the return of the data/samples or destruction, intellectual property issues). For ensuring proper legal security, agreements must include information about the applicable laws and dispute resolution mechanisms, including out-of-court proceedings. Financial provisions could also be included but should not be indexed on the intrinsic personal data or sample value but on the necessary investments performed for ensuring samples or data quality, integrity and FAIRness for example.

In addition, the GDPR is setting specific conditions when transferring data/and samples to non-EU countries. Accordingly, materials can only be transferred to a third entity in a country that ensures an appropriate level of protection of individuals' rights and freedoms compared to the one guaranteed within the EU. Therefore, such a transfer can be permitted where it is based on an adequacy decision adopted by the European Commission after analysis of a country general and sectorial legislation,[37] or where appropriate safeguards are in place.[38] This is including the use of binding corporate rules (applying to cross-border personal data transfers in a group of undertaking or a between entities of a multinational enterprise), or of standard contractual clauses adopted by the European Commission[39] (provided that they are not modified, otherwise the competent supervisory authority should be consulted to validate the adapted clauses), the respect of an approved Code of Conduct or the use of an approved certification mechanism together with binding and enforceable commitments of the controller or processor in the third country to apply the appropriate safeguards, including as regards data subjects' rights.

In exceptional circumstances, in the absence of an adequacy decision and of appropriate safeguards a transfer shall take place only if one of the conditions of Article 49 GDPR are met. This includes situations where the data subject has explicitly consented to the transfer, after having been informed of the possible risks of such transfers for the data subject due to the absence of an adequacy decision and appropriate safeguards, or the transfer is necessary for protecting the vital interests of the data subject, or is necessary for important reasons of public interest recognized in the Union or relevant Member State law (e.g. fight against cross-border public health threats), or is made from a public register intended to provide

---

[37] Article 45, GDPR.

[38] Article 46, GDPR.

[39] European Commission. Model contracts for the transfer of personal data to third countries. https://ec.europa.eu/info/law/law-topic/data-protection/data-transfers-outside-eu/model-contracts-transfer-personal-data-third-countries_en. Accessed 9 May 2019.

information to the public and which is open to consultation either by the public in general or by any person who can demonstrate a legitimate interest.

6 Conclusions

In developing data access rules and governance models biobanks could be assisted by soft law measures, which have traditionally had considerable importance in the field. It seems that GDPR leaves considerable room to operationalize its provisions through these soft law measures. One area that soft law measure can be useful is in elaborating on what organizational measures should be when processing data under research exemptions. In particular, such measures can provide guidance on the adequate models of data governance, oversight bodies, data access rules and implementation of data protection best practices.

Oversight bodies can be considered as a crucial part under organizational measures. In particular, oversight bodies such as ethics committees and data access committees are in the good place to hold control over the access and use of data. It is important to ensure the existing and emerging oversight bodies are equipped with adequate expertise regarding using and sharing genomic data and are aware of the associated informational risks. In order to achieve this, soliciting the attitudes of the involved parties regarding the associated risks would be necessary. Thereby, the overall governance of personal data processing will go beyond legal requirements and will take into account the pertinent individual or social concerns that may not be explicitly outlined in the legal provisions. That said, DACs often lack adequate tools to keep ongoing oversight on actual use of data once data access has been granted. Such limitations on the oversight on data access should be taken into considerations, when assessing the potential risks and the adequacy of the current oversight tools and mechanisms.

Moreover, the oversight of personal data processing by competent authorities should keep pace with recent developments in the field of data science, bioinformatics and genetics, among others. The risks associated with emerging technologies and the safeguards in protecting the privacy of data subjects should be treated as moving targets. Otherwise, the safeguards will become obsolete and unable to safeguard data subjects in an adequate fashion.

Finally, increasing cross-border data sharing underlines the importance of the harmonization of legal frameworks concerning personal data protection. One of the main goals of the Regulation has been to achieve this by harmonizing the personal data protection landscape across EU. However, concerns remain regarding the real impact of the Regulation on unifying the national regulations towards processing health and genetic data for research purposes, across Member States. Arguably, the Regulation still leaves room for varying interpretations, for instance, concerning the safeguards that should be established and also in setting further conditions for processing data on the basis of the research exemption provisions. This may challenge development of European sample repositories and data sharing platforms, as different safeguards may be required to be adopted for samples/data collected in different member states.

Acknowledgements L.M has received funding from the European Union's Horizon 2020 research and innovation programme under the Marie Sklodowska-Curie grant agreement No 753531.

References

Ardeshirdavani A, Souche E, Dehaspe L et al (2014) NGS-logistics: federated analysis of NGS sequence variants across multiple locations. Genome Med 6:71

Article 29 Data Protection Working Party (2014) Opinion 05/2014 on anonymization techniques. https://ec.europa.eu/justice/article-29/documentation/opinion-recommendation/index_en.htm. Accessed 27 May 2019

Article 29 Data Protection Working Party (2018) Guidelines on consent under regulation 2016/679 (wp259rev.01). https://ec.europa.eu/newsroom/article29/item-detail.cfm?item_id=623051. Accessed 29 May 2019

B3Africa, Checklist: For a good governance of transcontinental collaborative biobank research. http://biobanklearning.iarc.fr/course/checklist-elsi/#llms-lesson-locked. Accessed 27 May 2019

BBMRI-ERIC (2018) BBMRI-ERIC policy for access to and sharing of biological samples and data. Available on line at: http://www.bbmri-eric.eu/wp-content/uploads/AoM_10_8_Access-Policy_FINAL.pdf. Accessed 27 May 2019

Cook-Deegan R, McGuire AL (2017) Moving beyond Bermuda: sharing data to build a medical information commons. Genome Res 27:897–901

Court of Justice of the European Union (CJEU), Case C-582/14: Patrick Breyer v Bundesrepublik Deutschland. http://curia.europa.eu/juris/document/document.jsf?docid=184668&doclang=EN. Accessed 27 May 2019

de Hert P, Papakonstantinou V (2016) The new general data protection regulation: still a sound system for the protection of individuals? Comp Law Secur Rev 32(2):179–194

Dyke SO, Kirby E, Shabani M et al (2016) Registered access: a 'Triple-A'approach. Eur J Hum Genet 24:1676–1680

European Commission. Model contracts for the transfer of personal data to third countries. Available online at: https://ec.europa.eu/info/law/law-topic/data-protection/data-transfers-outside-eu/model-contracts-transfer-personal-data-third-countries_en. Accessed 27 May 2019

Homer N, Szelinger S, Redman M et al (2008) Resolving individuals contributing trace amounts of DNA to highly complex mixtures using high-density SNP genotyping microarrays. PLoS Genet 4:e1000167

Joly Y, Dyke SO, Knoppers BM et al (2016) Are data sharing and privacy protection mutually exclusive? Cell 167:1150–1154

LERU (2016) Policy Brief: the new EU general data protection regulation: why it worries universities and researchers. Available at: https://www.leru.org/files/The-New-EU-General-Data-Protection-Regulation-Why-It-Worries-Universities-and-Researchers-Full-paper.pdf. Accessed 27 May 2019

Lowrance WW (2012) Privacy, confidentiality, and health research. Cambridge University Press, Cambridge

Marelli L, Testa G (2018) Scrutinizing the EU general data protection regulation. Science 360(6388):496–498

Mascalzoni D, Bentzen HB, Budin-Ljøsne I et al (2019) Are requirements to deposit data in research repositories compatible with the European Union's general data protection regulation? Ann Intern Med 170(5):332–334
Nuffield Council on Bioethics (2014) Collection, linking and use of data in biomedical research and health care
Paltoo DN, Rodriguez LL, Feolo M et al (2014) Data use under the NIH GWAS data sharing policy and future directions. Nat Genet 46:934
Philippakis AA, Azzariti DR, Beltran S et al (2015) The matchmaker exchange: a platform for rare disease gene discovery. Hum Mutat 36:915–921
Rodriguez LL, Brooks LD, Greenberg JH et al (2013) The complexities of genomic identifiability. Science 339:275–276
Shabani M, Borry P (2016) "You want the right amount of oversight": interviews with data access committee members and experts on genomic data access. Genet Med 18:892–897
Shabani M, Borry P (2017) Rules for processing genetic data for research purposes in view of the new EU General Data Protection Regulation. Eur J Hum Genet 26:149–156
Shabani M, Marelli L (2019) Re-identifiability of genomic data and the GDPR: assessing the re-identifiability of genomic data in light of the EU General Data Protection Regulation. EMBO Rep:e48316
Shabani M, Dyke SO, Marelli L et al (2018) Variant data sharing by clinical laboratories through public databases: consent, privacy and further contact for research policies. Genet Med 21:1031–1037
Townend D (2016) EU laws on privacy in genomic databases and biobanking. J Law Med Ethics 44:128–142
U.S. Department of Health & Human Services (2012) Guidance regarding methods for de-identification of protected health information in accordance with the Health Insurance Portability and Accountability Act (HIPAA) privacy rule. Available at: https://www.hhs.gov/hipaa/for-professionals/privacy/special-topics/de-identification/index.html#standard. Accessed 27 May 2019
Wallace SE, Gaye A, Shoush O et al (2014) Protecting personal data in epidemiological research: DataSHIELD and UK law. Public Health Genomics 17:149–157
Woolley JP, Kirby E, Leslie J et al (2018) Responsible sharing of biomedical data and biospecimens via the "Automatable Discovery and Access Matrix"(ADA-M). NPJ Genomic Med 3:17

Biobank and Biomedical Research: Responsibilities of Controllers and Processors Under the EU General Data Protection Regulation

Ana Nordberg

Abstract Biobanks are essential infrastructures in current health and biomedical research. Advanced scientific research increasingly relies on processing and correlating large amounts of genetic, clinical and behavioural data. These data are particularly sensitive in nature and the risk of privacy invasion and misuse is high. The EU General Data Protection Regulation (GDPR) developed and increased harmonisation, resulting in a framework in which the specific duties and obligations of entities processing personal data—controllers and processors—were defined. Biobanks, in the exercise of their functions, assume the role of controllers and/or processors and as such need to comply with a number of complex rules. This chapter analyses these rules in the light of Article 89 GDPR, which creates safeguards and derogations relating to 'processing for archiving purposes in the public interest, scientific or historical research purposes or statistical purposes'. It identifies key compliance challenges faced by biobanks as data controllers and processors, such as determining whether the GDPR is applicable and its intersection with other regulations; when a biobank should be considered controller and processor; and what are the main duties of biobanks as data controllers and processors and options for compliance.

1 Introduction

Biobanks, broadly understood, play a central role in contemporaneous medical and biomedical research. For its part, scientific biomedical research is essential in modern developed societies and serves the realisation of important fundamental rights, namely the right to life and health care.[1] Cutting-edge health research increasingly

[1] Article 2 'Right to Life'; Article 35 'Right to health care', Charter of Fundamental Rights of the European Union *OJ C 326, 26.10.2012, p. 391–407.*

A. Nordberg (✉)
Lund University, Faculty of Law, Lund, Sweden
e-mail: ana.nordberg@jur.lu.se

S. Slokenberga et al. (eds.), *GDPR and Biobanking*, Law, Governance and Technology Series 43, https://doi.org/10.1007/978-3-030-49388-2_5

relies on large amounts of genetic, clinical and behavioural data. These data are particularly sensitive and enjoy increased legal protection,[2] thus creating complex intersections between fundamental values. Data protection law has a long history in Europe, and unlike other jurisdictions such as the USA it is based on the principle that personal data processing is prohibited unless explicitly allowed under a specific legal basis.[3] The latest data protection development in the EU is the GDPR,[4] which replaced the previous framework set forth by the Data Protection Directive.[5]

The present chapter focuses specifically on the duties of biobanks as data controllers and data processors under the GDPR. The GDPR has created an increasingly harmonised framework as to the duties and obligations of entities which retrieve, store and analyse personal data, i.e. data controllers and data processors. Biobanks, in their typical operating functions, assume the roles of controllers and processors of personal data. From the perspective of biobank compliance with the duties and obligations imposed by EU data protection law, relevant key changes include: (1) higher penalties for contravention; (2) new requirements for appointment of a data protection officer (DPO) when an entity processes significant amounts of sensitive data; (3) recognition of genetic data as sensitive personal data; (4) strong promotion of a privacy by design approach; (5) new direct obligations imposed on data processors; (6) broader territorial scope, now expanding to non-EU entities which process EU citizens' data; (7) time limitation on the storage of data; (8) specific permission for broad consent for scientific research; (9) exemption from some individual data subject rights concerning data 'for archiving purposes in the public interest, scientific or historical research purposes or statistical purposes'.[6]

Whether or not biobanks assume the roles of data controllers and/or data processors for GDPR compliance purposes will largely depend on their actual functions, manner of operating and whether the specific tasks can be considered data processing of personal data. In order to contextualise the debate on the duties of biobanks as data controllers and processors, it should be briefly mentioned that data protection rules intersect with the general regulatory frameworks applicable to biobanking activities in the EU and EU Member States. Among the European biomedical community, biobanking terminology tends to vary.[7] There is therefore

[2] The right to privacy is a fundamental right linked to the notions of human dignity, equality and autonomy. See for example Article 7 'Respect for private and family life; Article 8 'protection of personal Data'; Article 21 'Non-discrimination' EU Charter of Fundamental rights.

[3] Dove (2019).

[4] Regulation (EU) 2016/679 of the European Parliament and of the Council of 27 April 2016 on the protection of natural persons with regard to the processing of personal data and on the free movement of such data, and repealing Directive 95/46/EC, *OJ L 119, 4.5.2016, p. 1–88.*

[5] Directive 95/46/EC of the European Parliament and of the Council of 24 October 1995 on the protection of individuals with regard to the processing of personal data and on the free movement of such data, *OJ L 281, 23.11.1995 P. 31 – 50.*

[6] Article 9(2)(j) GDPR; Morrison et al. (2017), pp. 693–703.

[7] Fransson et al. (2015), pp. 22–28; Watson (2014), pp. 163–164; Hewitt and Watson (2013), pp. 309–315; Shaw et al. (2014), pp. 223–227.

neither a common understanding of what a biobank is nor agreement on a taxonomy of different types of biobanks. Legislation across EU Member States reflects the difficulties in establishing precise legal definitions of biobanks and biobanking activities.[8] At the national level, regulative approaches to biobanks reflect the pluralism of ethical, research and legal traditions and have their roots in significant socio-political, cultural and religious normative diversity.[9] Only a minority of EU Member States have specific legislation on biobanks.[10] The majority either do not have any domestic legislation[11] or rely on non-specific existing laws, often accompanied by soft law instruments, such as ethical guidelines, to regulate biobanks.[12] Lack of EU harmonisation and diversity of solutions, and in some cases vague and dispersed legislation, are all considered problematic for the development of biobanking activities.[13]

Overall, biobanks are quite diverse in terms of features such as the number, type and nature of samples, population covered, type of associated information, purpose and activities developed (e.g. sample hosting, processing and curation). These specific features influence the intersections between legal regulation of biobanking activities (mainly national) and the EU data protection framework and have practical implications for compliance with the obligations imposed by the GDPR on controllers and processors of personal data. There is a lack of specific, harmonised EU legislation on biobanks and biobanking activities. Existing EU regulation applicable to biobanks and biobank research is dispersed through a number of areas of law, including data protection, clinical trials[14] and tissue regulation.[15] An exhaustive analysis is outside the scope of this chapter. However, it can be noted for example the complex interplay between clinical trials regulation and the GDPR.[16]

---

[8] Beier and Lenk (2015), pp. 69–81; Briceño Moraia et al. (2014), pp. 187–212.

[9] Penasa et al. (2018), pp. 241–255.

[10] Belgium, Estonia, Finland, Hungary, Latvia, Lithuania, Portugal, Spain, Sweden and UK.

[11] Bulgaria, Croatia, Czech Republic, Malta, Romania, Slovakia.

[12] Austria, Cyprus, Denmark, France, Germany, Greece, Italy, Luxembourg, the Netherlands, Poland, Republic of Ireland and Slovenia. See Beier and Lenk (2015). See also: Nicola (2015), pp. 800–815; Sandor et al. (2009).

[13] In this sense, see a for example Penasa et al. (2018), with further references to national commentators defending the introduction of specific codified legislation in their respective jurisdictions.

[14] Directive 2001/20/EC of the European Parliament and of the Council of 4 April 2001 on the approximation of the laws, regulations and administrative provisions of the Member States relating to the implementation of good clinical practice in the conduct of clinical trials on medicinal products for human use, OJ L 121, 1.5.2001, p. 34, soon to be replaced by entry into effect of Regulation 536/2014 of the European Parliament and of the Council of 16 April 2014 on clinical trials on medicinal products for human use, and repealing Directive 2001/20/EC, OJ L 158 27.05.2004, p. 1–76 [hereinafter Clinical Trials Regulation].

[15] Directive 2004/23/EC of the European Parliament and of the Council of 31 March 2004 on setting standards of quality and safety for the donation, procurement, testing, processing, preservation, storage and distribution of human tissues and cells, *OJ L 102, 7.4.2004, p. 48–58.*

[16] See European Data Protection Board, Opinion 3/2019 concerning the Questions and Answers on the interplay between the Clinical Trials Regulation (CTR) and the General Data Protection regulation (GDPR) (art. 70.1.b)), Adopted on 23 January 2019.

This chapter examines the obligations imposed by the GDPR on biobanks in their role as controllers or processors of human personal data. After this introduction which sets out the contextual background of the application of data protection norms to biobanking activities, Sect. 2 addresses the material and geographic scope of applicability of the GDPR concerning biobanking activities. Section 3 then examines the concepts of controller and processor, their relationships and how these apply in a biobanking context. Section 4 analyses the duties of biobanks as data controllers and processors by reference to general data processing principles and the related duties imposed on biobanks, including obligations to respect data protection rights of data subjects. Adopting the perspective of biobanks as controllers and processors of data, it addresses possible compliance routes, with particular emphasis on rules concerning data processing of health and genetic data and exemptions provided for data processing 'for archiving purposes in the public interest, scientific or historical research purposes or statistical purposes'.[17] Section 5 will conclude this chapter with a general summary of the main points addressed.

2 GDPR and Biobanking Activities

2.1 Substantive Scope of the GDPR

Data protection obligations of biobanks depend largely on their geographical establishment, location of data subjects, functioning, tasks performed and whether these allow their classification as controllers and/or processors of personal data under the EU jurisdiction. In other words, in order to determine whether in a specific situation a biobank has to comply with the GDPR rules, it is necessary to establish whether it falls both under the substantive and the geographic scope of application of the Regulation.

In substantive terms, the GDPR applies to data processing activities and these are defined broadly and generally, which means that in practice they will include most biobanking activities and related research. Any activity involving personal data, performed either by automated or manual means, is in principle subject to the GDPR. This includes, for example, 'collection, recording, organisation, structuring, storage, adaptation or alteration, retrieval, consultation, use, disclosure by transmission, dissemination or otherwise making available, alignment or combination, restriction, erasure or destruction'.[18]

Data protection rules only apply to personal data, which means information relating to an identified or identifiable living, natural person. The concept of identifiable natural person is broadly defined and identification does not need to be immediate and direct. Data will still be personal if an individual can be identified by

[17] Article 9(2)(j) and Article 89(1) GDPR.

[18] Article 4 (2) GDPR.

reference to an identifier, for example, name, number, IP or physical address, or specific physical, physiological, genetic, mental, economic, cultural or social descriptors.[19] The concept of personal data only applies to living persons, and therefore *prima facie* it will not apply to samples obtained from deceased individuals. However, personal data of living relatives can be inferred from historical samples, thus arguably when inferences are established concerning, for example, the health of a living relative, such might constitute personal data processing under the GDPR.

2.2 Geographical Scope of the GDPR

Biobanks often collect, receive, keep or analyse transnational samples or data, which raises the question of the geographic scope of applicability of data protection rules. Generally, there are two factors that are relevant to determine the territorial scope of application: the establishment criterion, and the targeting criterion.[20] These will be further examined below.

Concerning the establishment criterion, the European Data Protection Board (EDPB) recommends consideration of three aspects: (a) establishment in the EU; (b) processing of personal data carried out 'in the context of the activities of' an establishment; and (c) application of the GDPR to the establishment of a controller or a processor in the EU regardless of whether the processing takes place in the EU or not.[21] The GDPR has a broad scope of applicability as it does so regardless of where the data processing activities are conducted and to any processing of personal data done by a controller or a processor with an establishment in the EU.[22] Recital 22 clarifies that 'establishment implies the effective and real exercise of activity through stable arrangements'.[23] Factual elements and not legal formalities are the determining factor to assess whether a data controller or processor has an establishment in the EU. In some circumstances, the GDPR rules also apply even if the controller or processor is not established in the EU as long as the data subject is located in the EU. In a biobank context, whether the data processing is considered carried out in the context of the activities of an establishment does not depend necessarily on whether the processing in question is carried out 'by' the biobank itself.[24] Assessment will have to be made on a case by case basis. For example, in cases of data and sample sharing, the activities of a biobank in a Member State and the data processing activities of a third party (data controller or processor) outside the EU may be inextricably linked, and thereby may

[19] Article 4 (1) GDPR.

[20] EDPB Guidelines 3/2018 on the territorial scope of the GDPR (Article 3) Adopted on 16 November 2018.

[21] EDPB Guidelines 3/2018, p. 4–7.

[22] Article 3 (1) GDPR.

[23] Recital 22 GDPR.

[24] Article 3(1)

trigger the applicability of EU data protection law even if the biobank by itself does not have an active role in the data processing.[25] Finally, the place of processing is not relevant in determining whether or not the data processing, carried out in the context of the activities of an EU biobank, falls within the scope of the GDPR. For example, when samples and information are collected outside the EU and later the data are processed by a biobank operating in an EU Member State or when a clinical trial is conducted outside the EU by a branch or subsidiary not legally distinct from an EU entity which determines the purpose and means of the data processing carried out on its behalf.[26]

In regards to the targeting criterion, Article 3 contains international private law rules that extend the jurisdiction of the GDPR to data controllers and processors not established in the EU and regardless of where the data processing activities take place. The connecting factor here is the location of the data subject and the purpose of the data processing activities. The GDPR applies to data subjects located in the EU[27] independently of their legal status concerning nationality or residence.[28] The second cumulative jurisdiction connecting factor concerns the type of data processing activities. Article 3(2) GDPR defines these as:

(a) the offering of goods or services, irrespective of whether a payment of the data subject is required, to such data subjects in the Union; or
(b) the monitoring of their behaviour as far as their behaviour takes place within the Union.

Biobanking activities may involve offering goods or services, such as where tissues and living materials are preserved as a service, for example, preservation of stem cells present in the umbilical cord or preservation of gametes and embryos for future use in an IVF context. The EDPB considers that it is necessary to have an actual 'connection between the processing activity and the offering of good or service, but both direct and indirect connections are relevant and to be taken into account'.[29]

The second type of activity that triggers the application of the GDPR to controllers or processors not established in the EU is the monitoring of data subject

---

[25] EDPB Guidelines 3/2018. See: Judgment of the Court (Third Chamber) 1 October 2015, Case C-230/14, Weltimmo s. r. o. *v* Nemzeti Adatvédelmi és Információszabadság Hatóság, Digital Reports: ECLI:EU:C:2015:639 para. 25, and Judgment of the Court (Grand Chamber), 13 May 2014, *Google Spain SL and Google Inc. v Agencia Española de Protección de Datos* (AEPD) *and Mario Costeja González*, Case C-131/12, *Digital reports:* ECLI identifier: ECLI:EU:C:2014:317, para. 5.3.

[26] Adapted from EDPB Guidelines 3/2018, p. 8.

[27] Article 3 (2) GDPR, see also Article 8 EU Charter where the right to data protection is not limited to 'citizens but intended for 'everyone'.

[28] Recitals 2, 14 and 24 GDPR.

[29] EDPB Guidelines 3/2018, p. 21. see also Recital 23 GDPR and CJEU case law based on Regulation 44/2001 on jurisdiction and the recognition and enforcement of judgments in civil and commercial matters, for example, Joined Cases C-585/08 and C-144/09: Judgment of the Court (Grand Chamber) of 7 December 2010 (references for a preliminary ruling from the Oberster Gerichtshof (Austria))—Peter Pammer v Reederei Karl Schlüter GmbH & Co KG (C-585/08) and Hotel Alpenhof GesmbH v Oliver Heller (C-144/09), *OJ C 55, 19.2.2011, p. 4–5.*

behaviour as far as their behaviour takes place within the Union.[30] These are two cumulative criteria. The nature of the processing activity that can be considered as behavioural monitoring is further specified in Recital 24, which focuses exclusively on the monitoring of a behaviour through the tracking of a person on the internet. However, the EDPB considers that tracking through other types of network or technology involving personal data processing should also be taken into account, for example, through wearable and other smart devices. In a biobanking research context, monitoring may occur in longitudinal studies involving multiple samples and health information retrieved over time or where data subject information is regularly updated. However, it is not clear whether this represents behaviour monitoring since the spirit of the GDPR elucidated in Recital 24 GDPR clearly points to commercial monitoring of consumers. Regardless of this, since health and genetic data enjoys additional protection, there is good reason to understand that health monitoring can also be included and will thus trigger the application of the GDPR.

3 Notion of Controller and Processor in Biobanking

3.1 Definition of Controller and Processor

In the GDPR, the duties of data controllers and processors have been framed as positive obligations which emanate from the individual rights of data subjects,[31] for example, the rights to information, access, rectification, erasure and blocking, and to object to the processing of personal data. From a compliance perspective, this means that the first and foremost important task is to ensure a full understanding of the role each intervenient in biobanking research assumes for data protection purposes.

The legal concepts of controller and processor are established in Article 4 (7) and (8) GDPR as follows:

> 'controller' means the natural or legal person, public authority, agency or other body which, alone or jointly with others, determines the purposes and means of the processing of personal data; where the purposes and means of such processing are determined by Union or Member State law, the controller or the specific criteria for its nomination may be provided for by Union or Member State law;
>
> 'processor' means a natural or legal person, public authority, agency or other body which processes personal data on behalf of the controller;

These definitions have been transplanted without modification from the Data Protection Directive[32] and have their origin in a similar text in the Council of

---

[30] Article 3(2)(b) and Recital 24 GDPR.

[31] See Chapter, Staunton C (2019) Individual rights in Biobank research under the GDPR.

[32] *Directive 95/46/EC*. The concept of 'controller' was adopted with a few modifications from the Council of Europe's Convention for the Protection of Individuals with regard to Automatic Processing of Personal Data, Strasbourg, 28/01/1981 (CoE ETS 108).

Europe's Convention for the Protection of Individuals with regard to Automatic Processing of Personal Data[33] concluded in 1981. Although the wording appears relatively straightforward, in practice it may not be so simple to assert who is the entity responsible for determining the purposes and means of data processing and identify the (various) entities processing data on behalf of a controller. This is due to contemporaneous organisational differentiation and complexity in both the public sector and private industrial fabric. The scope of these concepts was clarified by Opinion 1/2010 of the Article 29 Data Protection Working Party (WP29).[34] This soft law instrument analysed each operative concept of the definitions or its three main building blocks: (1) the personal aspect; (2) the possibility of pluralistic control; and (3) the essential elements to distinguish the controller from other actors—'determination' of 'purpose' and 'means'.[35] Controller and processor are independent functional EU concepts to be concretely determined by reference to the factual reality. This means that the type of activities of a biobank will have a bearing on whether and what entities are considered controllers and processors.

A controller is defined by its function and ability to decide on the purposes of processing and the means used. This role is based on a notion of control which can stem from any form of legal entitlement, including both explicit and implicit legal competence or from factual influence. The controller is also defined by its ability to determine the substantive content of the data processing. This ability must not be absolute: there is room for discretion and delegation. Whoever makes a de facto determination of the 'purpose' of processing is a controller while concrete methodologic issues concerning the choice of 'means' of processing can be delegated. In short, in a biobanking context the controller is whichever entity decides on issues pertaining to those substantial questions which are essential to the core of lawfulness of processing, for example, decisions on the legal basis for processing (e.g. consent or an exception), length of time a biological sample and related data are to be stored and who has access to the personal data processed.

The concept of processor is dependent on the organisational decisions and structure of the controller. The GDPR establishes two basic conditions for qualifying as processor: being a separate legal entity and processing data on behalf of a controller. Since, the controller decides either to process data within the organisation or to delegate all or part of the processing activities to an external entity, generally, processing data 'on behalf' means serving someone else's interest and is linked to the general concepts of 'delegation' and 'representation'. A processor implements

[33] CoE ETS No.108. This convention, was the only international legally binding instrument on the protection of private life and personal data open to any country in the world, and has been revised by the Protocol amending the Convention for the Protection of Individuals with regard to Automatic Processing of Personal Data (CoE ETS No. 223), 128th Session of the Committee of Ministers, Elsinore, 17–18 May 2018.

[34] Opinion 1/2010 issued by reference to the data protection directive, remains valid since these definitions transited unchanged to the GDPR.

[35] Opinion 1/2010.

instructions and decisions of the controller at least with regard to the purpose of the processing and the essential elements of the means.

3.2 *Joint-Controllers and Joint-Processors*

Data processing responsibilities may be borne by any natural or legal person and if shared will give rise to the notion of joint-controllers and joint-processors. In biobanking practice, situations involving putative joint-controllers and joint-processors present challenges, in particular when different entities submit samples and data to a biobank and/or when such data are shared, used and re-used by a diverse number of research institutions. The jurisprudence of the CJEU supports a broad concept of controller. In *Wirtschaftsakademie*[36] the Court of Justice of the EU (CJEU) ruled on joint-controllers, reaffirming the broad concept of controller previously established in *Google Spain.*[37] The court based its ruling on the criteria of whether a processor contributes, in the specific context, to determining, jointly with the main controller, the purpose and means of processing the personal data.[38] Applying this reasoning to a biobanking research context, both biobanks, researchers and entities conducting, sponsoring or financially supporting research, may be considered data controllers either by themselves or jointly. Their role differentiation and attribution will depend on the contractual relationships and de facto organisation of the research activities. Any entity which processes data on behalf of the controller will be considered a data processor. These activities comprise 'collection, recording, organisation, structuring, storage, adaptation or alteration, retrieval, consultation, use, disclosure by transmission, dissemination or otherwise making available, alignment or combination, restriction, erasure or destruction'.[39]

3.3 *Relationship Between Controllers and Processors*

Controllers are responsible to ensure that those entities that process the data comply with data protection rules. Contractual relationships established between biobanks and research institutions or commercial companies should set up an allocation of tasks, rights and obligations between the parties, including provisions concerning

[36] Judgment of the Court (Grand Chamber) of 5 June 2018, *Unabhängiges Landeszentrum für Datenschutz Schleswig-Holstein v Wirtschaftsakademie Schleswig-Holstein GmbH*, Case C 210/16, OJ C 260, 18.7.2016, ECLI:EUC:2018:388.

[37] Judgment of the Court (Grand Chamber), 13 May 2014, *Google Spain SL and Google Inc. v Agencia Española de Protección de Datos* (AEPD) and Mario Costeja González, Case C-131/12, *Digital reports:* ECLI identifier: ECLI:EU:C:2014:317.

[38] C-210/16 *Wirtschaftsakademie*.

[39] Article 4(2) GDPR.

the purpose of processing, type of personal data and categories of data subject involved. Among other specific subjects, data processing contracts should address the issue of transfers of data to countries outside the EU or to international organisations.[40] Contracts should also include clauses on subcontracting of data processing activities as processors are precluded from subcontracting without the controller's prior written agreement.[41]

Territorial scope is also relevant here as often biobanking activities are conducted in collaboration with international research institutions and repositories. Firstly, the EDPB takes the view that the existence of a relationship between a controller and a processor does not necessarily trigger the application of the GDPR to both if one is not established in the Union. This means that 'when it comes to the identification of the different obligations triggered by the applicability of the GDPR, the processing by each entity must be considered separately'.[42] Secondly, when an EU biobank acting as a controller uses a processor located outside the EU, it will be necessary for the controller to ensure by contract or other legal act[43] that the processor will conduct its activities in accordance with the GDPR. This will include imposing on the processors by contract clauses all the relevant obligations placed by the GDPR on processors, and thus extending by contractual means the GDPR scope of application to processors outside the EU. Thirdly, the opposite situation—a biobank processing data on behalf of an institution/controller outside of the EU—is also a recurrent one. In such cases, while the provisions of the GDPR do not apply to the data controller, the biobank, as a processor established in the EU, will still continue to be required to comply with the GDPR obligations imposed on data processors provided that such activities are carried out in the context of its activities.[44]

4 Duties of Biobanks as Controllers and Processors

4.1 Accountability

Biobanks are responsible and accountable for compliance with data protection rules in their various activities as data controllers, for example, in receiving, holding or distributing biological samples or materials and associated data.[45] This means that biobanks in their capacity as data controllers are responsible for implementing the appropriate technical and organisational measures both to ensure compliance and to be able to demonstrate compliance with GDPR principles and rules.

---

[40] Article 26(3) GDPR.
[41] Article 26(2) GDPR.
[42] EDPB 3/2018, p. 9.
[43] Article 28(3) GDPR.
[44] EDPB 3/2018, pp. 10–11.
[45] Article 5(2) GDPR.

As seen above, the accountability obligations of biobanks also include exercising a supervisor function and ensuring that researchers and entities in the position of personal data processors follow data protection rules.[46] If several entities are in the position of data controller, they become joint-controllers. For reasons of legal certainty, joint-controllers have the additional responsibility to determine in a transparent manner the allocation of the shared responsibilities for compliance.

Data protection rules establish the rights of data subjects and impose corresponding duties on controllers and processors. These comprise both the general duty to assure compliance with general principles of data protection stemming from the principle of accountability and specific duties pertaining to the factual relationship and conduct towards data subjects in the course of data processing activities. General data protection principles include: (1) lawfulness, fairness and transparency; (2) purpose limitation; (3) data minimisation; (4) accuracy; (5) storage limitation; and (6) integrity and confidentiality.[47]

The principle of 'accountability' inverts the burden of proof, imposing on biobanks acting in the capacity of data controllers the responsibility for demonstrating that all data processing activities are conducted lawfully, fairly and in a transparent manner in relation to the data subject.[48] 'Lawfulness' of data processing activities is the fundamental basis for compliance with all other duties of controllers and processors under EU data protection law. If data are processed unlawfully, compliance with other duties and obligations will not preclude eventual sanctions. This means that, in the absence of legitimate grounds for data processing, all ensuing biobanking activities will be tainted by the unlawfullness of data processing. Because the right to data protection and privacy are fundamental rights protected by the EU Charter, the legal consequences of unlawful data processing may even expand beyond data protection sanctions. For example, it may hinder the ethical acceptance of the research for patentability purposes.[49] Once lawfulness of processing has been established, biobanks and biobank researchers will have to ensure effective compliance with the other principles of data protection mentioned above and the associated duties imposed on data controllers and processors. 'Purpose limitation' means that personal data can only be processed for specified, explicit and legitimate purposes. Further processing outside the initial purpose/conditions is generally not allowed. An exception is made for 'processing for public interest, scientific or historical research or statistical purposes'.[50] 'Data minimisation' means that processing activities are required to be adequate and relevant to the purposes, and the privacy intrusion is limited to the minimum necessary to achieve such purposes.[51] The principle of accuracy imposes the duty to take reasonable steps to ensure that inaccurate or

---

46 Article 28(1) GDPR.

47 Article 5 GDPR.

48 Article 5(2) GDPR.

49 Nordberg and Minssen (2016), pp. 138–177; Hellstadius and Schovsbo (2018).

50 Article 5(1)(b) GDPR.

51 Article 5(1)(c) GDPR.

out of date information is rectified or erased.[52] 'Storage limitation' refers to the duty to anonymise or erase data once it is no longer necessary for achieving the original purposes. This principle is also an object of limitation if the personal data are processed solely 'for archiving purposes in the public interest, scientific or historical research purposes or statistical purposes' provided that the processing is subject to appropriate technical and organisational measures to safeguard the rights and freedoms of data subjects.[53] Finally, 'integrity and confidentiality' of personal data against unauthorised or unlawful processing, as well as accidental loss, destruction or damage, is to be ensured by the use of appropriate technical or organisational measures.[54]

4.2 Lawfulness of Data Processing

4.2.1 Categories of Personal Data and Lawfulness in Biobanking

It is critical to consider data types and their relevance for determining the concrete duties and compliance obligations of data controllers and processors. Unlike data subjects, not all personal data are born equal. Some types of informational content are liable to cause greater intrusion in the data subject's personal private sphere and/or have a higher risk of being misused for discriminatory practices or outcomes. The rapid development and availability of DNA sequencing, big data techniques and artificial intelligence (AI) has in recent years changed biomedical research and biobanks. Biological samples are now accompanied by personal data that can be aggregated and correlated through data mining techniques in a variety of ways. Such personal data may originate from health and medical records but also from research and clinical trials and other sources. It may include genetic and genomic data and other epistemological biomedical information but also environmental, lifestyle or social data.

As mentioned, processing personal data is only allowed under specific grounds and stricter rules apply concerning processing of special categories of personal data, including health data and genetic data.[55] It is therefore important, as a matter of compliance, that biobanks distinguish between non-personal and personal data but also between general personal data and special categories of personal data.

The concept of health data is defined in the GDPR as 'personal data related to the physical or mental health of a natural person, including the provision of health care services, which reveal information about his or her health status'[56] and this includes 'all data pertaining to the health status of a data subject which reveal information

[52] Article 5(1)(d) GDPR.

[53] Article 5(1)(e) GDPR.

[54] Article 5(1)(f) GDPR.

[55] Article 9 GDPR.

[56] Article 4(15) GDPR.

relating to the past, current or future physical or mental health status of the data subject'.[57] Health data include both information derived from health records and 'information derived from the testing or examination of a body part or bodily substance, including from genetic data and biological samples'.[58]

Genetic data means 'personal data relating to the inherited or acquired genetic characteristics of a natural person which give unique information about the physiology or the health of that natural person and which result, in particular from an analysis of a biological sample from the natural person in question',[59] in particular, 'chromosomal, deoxyribonucleic acid (DNA) or ribonucleic acid (RNA) analysis, or from the analysis of another element enabling equivalent information to be obtained'.[60] The GDPR imposes obligations on data controllers and processors with a focus on regulating data processing from the perspective of lawfulness of such processing. However, it does not regulate what types of derivative information can be obtained (correlations and inferences) nor what types of uses of data are permissible. Particularly problematic data uses, such as predictions and correlations based on big data analytics and AI, are still only timidly regulated.[61] The type of research activities developed by each biobank will have a bearing on determining the most suitable legal basis to rely upon for compliance with the principles of lawfulness, fairness and transparency. In any case, this decision must be made beforehand since controllers have the duty to inform individual sample donors/owners of the legal grounds allowing the data processing before collecting or in any way processing data.[62] Because new data processing technologies such as big data analytics allow category jumping inferences, it will often be the case that all data will become personal data, if not immediately then at least in the future. Moreover, the use of biological samples will equate to actual or potential genetic data and health data, and thus a cautionary approach would lead to generally considering that most data processed by biobanks and biobanking research are likely to pertain to one of the special categories of personal data.

4.2.2 Modalities for Lawful Data Processing in Biobanking

General Remarks

Ensuring the lawfulness of data processing is the most essential duty of controllers and processors. In ensuring lawfulness, choosing an appropriate legal basis for processing the data is of utmost importance and has to be performed prior to the

[57] Recital 35 GDPR.

[58] Recital 35 GDPR.

[59] Article 4(13) GDPR.

[60] Recital 35 GDPR.

[61] Article 22 GDPR.

[62] Article 7 GDPR.

collection of data. The GDPR contains several legal basis for data processing. These can be conceptualized as two main models for lawfulness of data processing in biobanks and bio-banking research: (a) consent-based model, and (b) necessity-based model. Depending on the ground for lawfulness, different obligations will be imposed on biobanks in the capacity of either data controllers or data processors. In order to simplify the compliance analysis, in this section it will be assumed that most human data processed by biobanks or in biobanking research are special categories of personal data (e.g. health data and genetic data), and thus attention will focus on the lawfulness grounds established in Article 9 GDPR.

Necessity-Based Model

Generally, the processing of special categories of personal data, such as genetic and health data, is prohibited. However, biobanks can choose to rely on the exceptions and exemptions provided in Article 9(2) GDPR and so implement either a consent or necessity-based model or a mixture. Among the various exceptions conferring lawfulness of processing, of particular interest for biobanks is data processing justified by the necessity 'for archiving purposes in the public interest, scientific or historical research purposes'[63] and processing justified by the necessity 'for reasons of public interest in the area of public health'.[64] This data processing model can be suitable where obtaining consent is not possible or excessively burdensome (for example, when data is re-purposed and contact information is missing or outdated), or when consent is insufficient, redrawn or denied. The definition of 'scientific research purposes' is broadly constructed and includes 'technological development and demonstration, fundamental research, applied research and privately funded research'.[65]

In biobanking research, re-use and repurposing of data has become a necessity where new digital technologies offer increased possibilities to cross-reference large quantities and types of data from multiple sources (big data analytics), including health and medical records. However, data have to be collected 'for specified, explicit and legitimate purposes and not further processed in a manner that is incompatible with those purposes'.[66] This means that the lawfulness of data processing has to be established prior to the data collection and is connected to the purpose for which the data were collected. The result of this is that a necessity-based model may offer advantages to biobanks and in certain circumstances be the preferred option to establish lawfulness since repurposing of data for archiving or research purposes is generally presumed compatible with the original purpose as long as the controller

[63] Article 9(2)(j) GDPR.

[64] Article 9(2)(i).

[65] Recital 159 GDPR. The recital mentions specifically 'studies conducted in the public interest in the area of public health'.

[66] Article 5(1)(b) GDPR.

demonstrates respect for individual rights and freedoms of the data subject and implements appropriate safeguards, such as pseudonymisation (unless this is impossible or impairs the archiving or research purposes).[67]

Under Article 9(2)(j), processing of health and genetic data without consent is possible for scientific research purposes provided that processing is: (a) necessary for scientific research purposes; (b) proportionate to the aims pursued; (c) and respects the essence of the right to data protection.[68] These requirements will be relatively simple to fulfil in the case of biobanking activities directly connected with a specific research project aimed at studying a serious medical condition. However, concerning biobanking activities not directly linked to a specific research project or where such a link is less immediate or evident, data controllers will need to carefully justify that the use of the data is necessary and proportionate. In any case, the essence of the data protection right must be respected. This means that all processing activities must respect the general principles of data protection: lawfulness, fairness and transparency; purpose limitation; data minimisation; accuracy; storage limitation; integrity and confidentiality; and accountability.

Article 9(2)(i) GDPR allows Member States to establish the lawfulness of data processing for public interest reasons in the area of public health. Provided that a legal basis exists and specific measures to safeguard the rights and freedoms of data subjects and the confidentiality of health records are enacted, samples collected in the course of medical treatment might be stored in biobanks and made available for research, alongside patient records. However, a non-consenting data subject is unlikely to collaborate and provide additional samples or necessary specific information, thus affecting the ability to monitor an individual's health over time or study the health impact of specific lifestyle or social and environmental factors. Because patient records, even if standardised and comprehensive, are often of limited interest to researchers, the consent-based model will remain vital in any research project where collaboration of the data subject is imposed by methodological considerations.

Processing of data under a necessity framework also implies special obligations to safeguard the rights and interest of data subjects, in particular, the use of technical measures to ensure respect for the principle of data minimisation, including the default use of either pseudonymisation or complete anonymisation if the research proposed can be achieved in that manner.[69] All rights of data subjects and respective duties imposed on controllers and processors are to be observed, including specific national limitations on the processing of health and genetic data,[70] unless a derogation from data protection rights is established either by EU or national law.[71] Concerning genetic, biometric and health data, Member States are given additional

[67] Data sharing and repurposing data is a very important issue for biobanking. See below Sect. 4.4.

[68] Article 9(2)(j) GDPR.

[69] Article 89(1) GDPR.

[70] Article 9(4) GDPR.

[71] Article 89(2) GDPR.

room for manoeuvre and are allowed to introduce more stringent requirements and impose further obligations on data controllers and processors which may amount to further limitations on the processing of these special categories of data.

Article 89 GDPR gives Member States additional leeway to enact specifications and derogations from the rights of data subjects when lawfulness is based on a necessity framework.[72] Exemptions to the duties of controllers and processors may be provided in national law concerning the information requirements[73] and rights to rectification,[74] to erasure,[75] to restriction of processing,[76] to data portability[77] and to object when processing personal data 'for archiving purposes in the public interest, scientific or historical research purposes or statistical purposes'.[78] These derogations from the rights of data subjects have a subsidiary nature and are only admissible as far as the data subject rights render impossible or seriously impair the achievement of the 'scientific or historical research purposes or statistical purposes'.[79] Derogations also have to be specified and accompanied by appropriate safeguards as to the general principles of data protection. In particular, all exemptions must follow data minimisation, proportionality and necessity principles.[80]

Biobanks may be able to use these exemptions in national law. However, the question of applicable jurisdiction has to be carefully considered, in particular the possibility that a data set might include individual data which are subject to different national exemptions and complementary rules concerning, for example, the use of genetic data.[81] If the legal basis for lawfulness is necessity for research under Article 89(2) GDPR, exemptions to the duties of controllers and processors may be provided in national or EU law concerning: (1) the right of any person to obtain from the controller confirmation as to whether or not their personal data are being processed, and the right to information concerning such processing;[82] (2) the right to rectification;[83] (3) the right to restrict processing;[84] and (4) the right to object to processing.[85] Where biobanks serve as repositories and data processing is justified for archiving purposes in the public interest under Article 89(3) GDPR, exemptions

---

[72] See Chapter Duguet A-M, Herveg J 'Safeguards and derogations relating to processing for scientific research: Article 89 analysis for biobank research'.

[73] Article 15 GDPR.

[74] Article 16 GDPR.

[75] Article 17 GDPR.

[76] Article 18 GDPR.

[77] Article 20 GDPR.

[78] Article 21 GDPR.

[79] Article 89(1) GDPR.

[80] Recital 156 GDPR.

[81] For an overview of existing national legislation see: Penasa et al. (2018); p. 252; Briceño Moraia et al. (2014).

[82] Article 15 GDPR.

[83] Article 16 GDPR.

[84] Article 18 GDPR.

[85] Article 21 GDPR.

established in EU or national law may also extend to the controller's obligation to notify any restriction or erasure of personal data to each third party to whom the data has been disclosed[86] and the data subject's right to data portability.[87]

The right of data subjects to request erasure of their personal data cannot be subject to national derogations under Article 89 GDPR. However, Article 17 GDPR does exempt data processing activities for archiving purposes 'in the public interest, scientific or historical research purposes or statistical purposes' in accordance with Article 89(1) GDPR[88] provided that erasing the data is likely to render impossible or seriously impair the achievement of these objectives.[89] If the data are essential but can be fully anonymised, then such an option should prevail. Controllers are under an obligation to justify the refusal to erase and to disclose information about the specific use of the data in a specific project.

Consent-Based Model

When a necessity-based lawfulness basis cannot be established, biobanks will need to resort to a consent-based model in order to avoid data protection liability. It is also a solid strategy through which to build trust and ensure recruitment of research participants while fostering the willingness of participants to provide accurate data, be monitored over time and provide multiple samples and data entries and allow multi-purpose processing.

The literature shows that prior to the GDPR Member States had different frameworks for consent.[90] Taking into account the GDPR flexibilities, the situation is likely to be maintained, at least insofar as additional specific requirements and regulatory oversight are concerned. Under the GDPR, the type of consent necessary for data processing is defined as necessarily being freely given, purpose specific, informed and unambiguous.[91] In order to be legally binding, consent does not need to be given in the form of a signed written document but should be given by a clear affirmative act. Documented oral statements and electronic means are allowed but controllers should avoid 'silence, pre-ticked boxes or inactivity' since only affirmative consent is legally binding.[92]

Compliance with the principle of fairness and transparency imposes that pre-formulated consent forms must be written in a manner that is intelligible and easily accessible to the data subject using clear and plain language.[93] The use of legal or

[86] Article 19 GDPR.
[87] Article 20 GDPR.
[88] Article 17(3)(d).
[89] Article 17(3)(d).
[90] Kaye et al. (2016), pp. 195–200.
[91] Article 4 11) GDPR.
[92] Recital 32 GDPR.
[93] Recital 42 GDPR.

technical terms should be avoided and, if applicable, translated into the native language of the data subjects. The standard for consent is 'free and informed consent'. Documents or information provided orally should contain clear mention of the identity of the controllers and the purpose of the data processing. Consent will not be valid if the data subject has no genuine or free choice or if refusal or withdrawal of consent is detrimental to the data subject.[94] This would be the case for multipurpose consent without the possibility to separately consent to different processing purposes or if broad consent is demanded for access to treatment or a service and the data processing exceeds what is necessary for fulfilling such goals (e.g. deposit and conservation of biological materials for future use: blood, stem cells, ova, sperm, embryos, etc.).[95]

Often in biobanking activities samples and information originate from outside the EU. In some cases, local cultural and legal traditions may result in different frameworks, rules and procedures for consent.[96] EU data protection rules are based on the EU Charter right to data protection[97] and have an extensive territorial application. Thus, if the controller or processor is established in the EU, reliance on local law or customary social norms is not possible and individual data subject informed specific consent or another legal ground for data processing remains necessary under the GDPR.

Consent should also be specific and cover every purpose and all processing activities carried out for each purpose.[98] The legislators acknowledged that in the case of data used for scientific research it is often difficult to identify beforehand all possible data processing purposes and so this opened the door to broad consent. In this sense, Recital 33 clarifies that broad consent—defined by reference to certain areas of scientific research—can be accepted if procedures comply with 'recognised ethical standards for scientific research', for example, through an ethical board review.[99] WP29 pointed out that Recital 33 does not necessarily mean that specific consent is not necessary but rather that as an exception and if research purposes cannot be specified at the time of data processing (sample collecting), it is possible to obtain valid consent and only describe the purpose in a more general manner. However, it also alerts us to the fact that 'when special categories of data are processed on the basis of explicit consent, applying the flexible approach of Recital 33 will be subject to a stricter interpretation and requires a high degree of scrutiny'.[100]

---

[94] Recital 42 and 43 GDPR.

[95] In such cases, specific national legislation may contain more strict rules.

[96] For an overview see for example: De Vries et al. (2017).

[97] Article 8 EU Charter.

[98] Recital 32 GDPR.

[99] See Marelli and Testa (2019), pp. 496–498.

[100] Article 29 Working Party, Guidelines on Consent under Regulation 2016/679, last Revised and Adopted on 10 April 2018.

The notion of dynamic consent[101] is indirectly accepted. On the one side, data subjects have several rights that can be exercised over a period of time: right to rectification of inaccurate personal data and to add supplementary information to incomplete data;[102] right to erasure;[103] right to restriction of processing;[104] right to data portability;[105] and right to not be subject to a decision based solely on automated processing.[106] On the other side, the re-purposing of data will require informing the data subject and renewed consent. Dynamic consent models offer biobanks the possibility to allow data subjects to exercise their rights to object to specific types of data processing, specific purposes, projects or users while simultaneously maintaining consent to a broad range of processing activities. These also simplify procedures for consent for further processing purposes and improve fairness and transparency of data processing. However, it should be noted that overall repurposing of data in biobanking remains a complex matter subject to specific national regulations[107] and where determining if the new use is compatible with the consent provided may not be easy to ascertain.[108]

Biobanks as data controllers have a duty to implement technical measures to assure that data subjects can, on request, receive the personal data provided in a structured, commonly used and machine-readable format and transmit those data to another controller.[109] It is debatable whether data portability duties apply only to raw data or also to established correlations, probabilities or predictions, for example, a diagnosis. As long as a person is identifiable then the information is considered personal data and thus subject to the GDPR.[110] Inferred data and derived data, such as the outcome of an assessment regarding the health of a user, are, according to WP29, excluded from the right to data portability.[111] Furthermore, this information

---

[101] Kaye et al. (2015), pp. 141–146.

[102] Article 16 GDPR.

[103] Article 17 GDPR.

[104] Article 18 GDPR.

[105] Article 20 GDPR.

[106] Article 22 GDPR.

[107] See: Tassé (2016), pp. 207–216; Kondylakis et al. (2017), pp. 282–292.

[108] See the landmark Italian case concerning the acquisition by United Kingdom–based commercial company Tiziana Life Sciences Plc of Shardna an Italian genomic biobank (Tribunal of Cagliari, Sentenza n. 1569, 6 June 2017) described in Marelli & Testa n.101; see also recent Clinical Research Development Ireland (CRDI) 'Submission to the Data Protection Commission on the topic of the General Data Protection Regulation in relation to Biobanking'(3 May 2018), signed by 28 Representatives of Irish Research Institutions. Available: https://www.crdi.ie/wp-content/uploads/2018/06/CRDI_Submission_GDPR-and-Biobanking.pdf.

[109] Article 20 GDPR.

[110] Article 4 (1) GDPR defines an identifiable person as 'one who can be identified, directly or indirectly, in particular by reference to an identifier such as a name, an identification number, location data, an online identifier or to one or more factors specific to the physical, physiological, genetic, mental, economic, cultural or social identity of that natural person'.

[111] Article 29 data protection working party, Guidelines on the Right to data Portability, adopted on 13 December 2016.

may constitute a trade secret or be copyright protected and proportionality arguments may arise, while specific contractual or patient rights statutory provisions may provide further obligations.

In the context of big data analytics, where data are obtained from a plurality of sources, the controller always has general information duties that may be difficult to comply with, including providing individual information concerning categories of data, origin, legal basis and purpose of processing and use in automated decision-making.[112] These duties are waived if providing information to data subjects proves impossible or involves a disproportionate effort, and where the processing is for scientific research purposes and compliance with such duties would render impossible or seriously impair the research.[113] Either way, repurposing of data must always have a legal basis; either it has to be covered by original consent or an exception.

Consent can be withdrawn and the data subject can request that further processing is restricted or that the data is erased. The right to erasure, known as the right to be forgotten, is often considered a potential challenge. However, research activities are protected if the data are necessary for research and their erasure would 'render impossible or seriously impair the achievement of the objectives of that processing'.[114] This is not a complete exemption; an erasure request must still be complied with if under the specific circumstances that individual's personal information is not essential and can be erased without compromising the entire study. In any case, if the data are not erased due to being essential, it might have to be erased from other research projects and cannot continue to be processed in the future unless another ground for processing exists.

Finally, consent to participation in scientific research activities in clinical trials is subject to specific legislation—the Clinical Trials Regulation (CTR).[115] GDPR principles and other rules remain applicable to data processing in the context of clinical trials.[116] Consent for data processing in the context of biobanking samples and data originated or procured for clinical trials will also follow the GDPR rules and should not be confused with informed consent for participation in clinical trials and/or medical treatment.[117] Informed consent for these activities is regulated by specific frameworks and follows a different legal reasoning.[118] As explained by the EDPB in Opinion 3/2019, the provisions on informed consent in the Clinical Trials

---

[112] Article 14(1) GDPR.

[113] Article 14(5) GDPR.

[114] Article 17(3)(d) GDPR.

[115] Articles 28–35, Regulation (EU) No 536/2014 of the European Parliament and of the Council of 16 April 2014 on clinical trials on medicinal products for human use, and repealing Directive 2001/20/EC, *OJ L 158, 27.5.2014, p. 1–76.*

[116] See the recent, European Data protection board, Opinion 3/2019 concerning the Questions and Answers on the interplay between the Clinical Trials Regulation (CTR) and the General Data Protection regulation (GDPR) (art. 70.1.b)) Adopted on 23 January 2019.

[117] Idem, para 15.

[118] Minssen and Rajam (2019); Chico (2018), p. 116.

Regulation[119] respond primarily to core ethical requirements of research involving humans subjects and derive from the Helsinki Declaration. The obligation to obtain informed consent of participants in a clinical trial is primarily required to ensure respect for the right to human dignity and the right to integrity of individuals under Articles 1 and 3 of the Charter of Fundamental Rights of the EU and is not an instrument for data protection compliance.[120]

This means that informed consent obtained for clinical trials may not be sufficient for data processing purposes. In particular, a 'clear situation of imbalance of powers between the participant and the sponsor/investigator will imply that the consent is not 'freely given' in the meaning of the GDPR'[121] (e.g. when a participant is not in good health, belongs to an economically or socially disadvantaged group or is in any situation of institutional or hierarchical dependence). Therefore, consent will not be the appropriate legal basis in most cases and other legal bases than consent must be relied upon.[122] Biobanks storing samples or data obtained or used in clinical trials have to conduct a separate assessment on the legal basis of data processing to rely upon and eventually obtain consent for initial or further biobanking activities, unless the so-called presumption of compatibility provided under Article 5(1)(b) GDPR can be relied upon under the specific circumstances.[123]

4.3 *Fairness and Transparency of Data Processing*

Although biobanks operating under the framework for lawfulness established under Article 89 'Interest for scientific research-based model' are exempted from a number of specific obligations, the principle of transparency imposes an obligation to inform data subjects at the time data are obtained of the following: (1) identity and the contact details of the controller and, where applicable, of the controller's representative; (2) contact details of the DPO; (3) purposes and legal basis of the processing; (4) recipients or categories of recipients of the personal data; and (5) whether the controller intends to transfer personal data to a third country or international organisation, and the existence or absence of an adequacy decision by the Commission, or reference to the appropriate or suitable safeguards and the means by which to obtain a copy of them or where they have been made available.[124]

In addition to this information, biobanks acting as data controllers also have a duty to provide to the data subject at the time personal data are obtained additional information to ensure fair and transparent processing, namely, (1) length of time

---

[119] CTR Chapter V, Article 28 e sq.

[120] EDPB Opinion 3/2019, para 16.

[121] EDPB Opinion 3/2019, para 20.

[122] Idem.

[123] EDPB Opinion 3/2019, para 29-32.

[124] Article 13(1) GDPR.

data will be stored (either a fixed date or criteria used to determine it); (2) details about the right to lodge a complaint with a supervisory authority; and (3) the existence of automated decision-making, including profiling and meaningful information about the logic involved, as well as the significance and the envisaged consequences of such processing for the data subject.[125]

Although the rule is that data subjects have the right to object to automated decision-making and profiling, automated decisions and profiling (e.g. diagnostic, epidemiologic studies, categorisations of genetic risk, etc.) based on special categories of data, such as health and genetic data, are not prohibited. In fact, these can be acceptable if based on explicit consent for specified purposes or if based on the necessity of the processing for reasons of substantial public interest.[126]

If the ground for data processing is consent, biobanks as data controllers are also required to provide information on the existence of the right to request access to and rectification or erasure of personal data or restriction of processing concerning the data subject or to object to processing as well as the right to data portability. Biobanks will also be obliged to inform data subjects that they have the right to withdraw consent at any time, and that this will not affect retroactively the lawfulness of previous processing. These obligations will not subsist if data is processed based on other grounds.[127]

4.4 Purpose Limitation of Data Processing

Data sharing is increasingly necessary for scientific research, and there is a growing international trend towards open science,[128] with major funding agencies and scientific journals imposing data sharing policies.[129] Such policies may implicitly result in imposing the need to share or make public available research data outside the EU. In their turn, EU initiatives also place considerable emphasis on open research data and open access to scholarly publication and communication and reuse of scientific information.[130]

[125] Article 13(2) GDPR

[126] Article 13(2)(f), Article 22(4) and Article 9(2 (a) and (g) GDPR.

[127] Article 13(2) GDPR.

[128] Groves and Godlee (2012), p. e4383.

[129] Taichman et al. (2017), pp. 63–65; National Institutes of Health (NIH) (2003); Wellcome Trust (2017); European Commission DG for research and Innovation (2017).

[130] Commission Recommendation of 17 July 2012 on access to and preservation of scientific information (2012/417/EU); see also Declaration of the Budapest Open Access Initiative https://www.budapestopenaccessinitiative.org/read; Berlin Declaration on Open Access to Knowledge in the Sciences and Humanities https://openaccess.mpg.de/67605/berlin_declaration_engl.pdf; The ECHO Charter https://echo.mpiwg-berlin.mpg.de/policy/oa_basics/charter, and the Bethesda Statement on Open Access Publishing http://legacy.earlham.edu/~peters/fos/bethesda.htm.

Biobanking research by its nature involves the possibility to re-use and repurpose collected samples and information in several research projects. New digital technologies offer increased possibilities to cross-reference large quantities and types of data from multiple sources. The interpretation of the principle of purpose limitation has become a central issue in biobanking as both data sharing and data repurposing raise considerable data protection and ethical issues;[131] a balance needs to be achieved with the protection of the rights of data subjects.

The principle of purpose limitation ensures that as a rule all data must be 'collected for specified, explicit and legitimate purposes and not further processed in a manner that is incompatible with those purposes',[132] and it can be particularly controversial to apply in the context of biobanking sharing and re-use of research data. Subsequent uses may rely either on consent or another ground for lawfulness; both these grounds have to be established at the time a biological sample, tissue or information is collected and further processing has to be compatible with the purpose for which the personal data are initially collected.[133] If the lawfulness of data processing is based on necessity for archiving purposes in the public interest, scientific or historical research, the re-purpose of data for archiving or research is generally presumed compatible with the original purpose as long as the controller demonstrates respect for the individual rights and freedoms of the data subject and implements appropriate safeguards, such as pseudonymisation (unless this is impossible or impairs the archiving or research purposes).[134] However, the presumption appears to only apply if it is the same type of research or research project, for example, the EDPB does not think that it necessarily applies to clinical trials data reuse.[135] Moreover, if the data processing is based on another lawfulness ground, then compatibility can never be presumed and it is either necessary to establish that the specific research conducted is compatible with the original purpose or predict and establish at the time of data collection several possible specific, explicit and legitimate data purposes.

When biobanks intend to further process the personal data for a purpose other than that for which the personal data were collected, information must be provided to the data subjects prior to that further processing concerning such further processing and its purpose, as well as any other relevant information.[136] Moreover, often biobanks will store and process data that was not obtained directly from data subjects but instead was originally collected from a third party, for example, biological samples obtained in a clinical setting or use of health records. In such cases, and in

[131] For an overview on open questions see: Global Forum on Bioethics in Research (2018).

[132] Article 5(1)(b) GDPR.

[133] Article 6(4) GDPR. See with adaptations Article 29 Data Protection Working Party Opinion 03/2013 on purpose limitation Adopted on 2 April 2013.

[134] Article 5(1)(b) and Article 89(1) GDPR; Recitals 157 to 160.

[135] See EDPB Opinion 3/2019 para 28, recognizing that further guidance in this respect is necessary.

[136] Article 13(3) GDPR.

the absence of more specific national or EU legislation,[137] information duties subsist in accordance with Article 14 GDPR. There are, however, some exceptions: compliance with information duties is not required if the data subject already has the information. Regarding processing based in public interest and research purposes, there is no duty to provide information if this has been proven to be impossible or would involve a disproportionate effort, or if it is likely to render impossible or seriously impair the objectives of the biobanking activity. The biobank neverthelesss must take appropriate measures to protect the data subjects' rights and freedoms and legitimate interests, including making the information publicly available.[138]

4.5 *Data Protection by Design*

As controllers, biobanks are also responsible to implement measures leading to 'data protection by design and default'. Data protection by design implements the principle of data minimisation and is imposed under a standard of reasonability taking into consideration a number of factors, such as the state of the art, the cost of implementation and the nature, scope, context and purposes of processing as well as the risks of varying likelihood and severity for rights and freedoms of natural persons posed by the processing.[139] Appropriate technical measures include pseudonymisation[140] but also measures for ensuring that personal data are only used if necessary for a specific purpose. This means that all data processed must be relevant for a specific research question. The data minimisation obligation also applies to ensure that the amount of personal data collected, the extent of their processing, the period of their storage and who is granted access is linked and necessary for the purpose of data processing.[141] Generally, biobanks acting as data controllers are always responsible for implementing appropriate technical and organisational measures to ensure compliance with data protection rules. Compliance may be demonstrated inter alia by specific data protection policies, adherence to approved codes of conduct[142] or through use of approved certification mechanisms.[143]

---

[137] Article 14(5)(c) and (d) GDPR 'obtaining or disclosure is expressly laid down by Union or Member State law to which the controller is subject and which provides appropriate measures to protect the data subject's legitimate interests; or where the personal data must remain confidential subject to an obligation of professional secrecy regulated by Union or Member State law, including a statutory obligation of secrecy.'

[138] Article 14(5)(a) and (b) GDPR.

[139] Article 25(1) GDPR.

[140] Idem. Cf. notion of pseudo-anonymisation in Article 4(5) GDPR with different understandings in other normative sources see: Phillips et al. (2017), pp. 483–496.

[141] Article 25(2) GDPR. On compliance strategies See: Holub et al. (2018), pp. 97–105.

[142] Article 24 and 40 GDPR.

[143] Articles 24 and 42 GDPR.

4.6 *Data Stewardship*

Biobanks are also entrusted with data stewardship duties. These are formulated as the principles of data accuracy, storage limitation, integrity and confidentiality. Data controllers have the obligation to keep records of all processing activities. This obligation is related to the principle of transparency and has the purpose of guaranteeing compliance with data subjects' rights and preventing controllers from alleging insufficient knowledge based on deficient records as a defence.[144] Biobanks acting as controllers are also responsible for guaranteeing the security of data processing activities,[145] cooperating with data protection authorities (DPA);[146] and notifying the DPA of any data breaches within 72 h[147] and each data subject provided that there is a high risk to their rights and freedoms. Data controllers should conduct data protection impact assessments (DPIAs),[148] implement measures to mitigate the risks discovered and consult with data protection authorities where such DPIAs determine a high risk that cannot be mitigated.[149] Biobanks process special categories of personal data and therefore DPIAs are mandatory.[150] Controllers and processors may also be responsible for jointly designating a DPO.[151] This duty will apply to biobanks and biobank researchers insofar as their core activity entails processing large amounts of special categories of personal data.[152]

5 Conclusion

The recent reform of data protection rules in the EU is in several ways a positive step in the direction of balancing individual rights and ensuring that scientific research and innovation in a data-driven economy are not hindered. A number of exemptions and exceptions are provided for research activities, with Article 89 GDPR making it possible for Member States to adopt further exceptions and exemptions. While this has a positive side, it also favours forum shopping, creates difficulties in pan-European studies and risks reducing harmonisation and transforming the GDPR almost into a de facto *directive* as far as the scientific research context is concerned.

[144] Article 30 GDPR.

[145] Article 32 GDPR.

[146] Article 31 GDPR.

[147] Article 33 GDPR.

[148] Article 35 GDPR.

[149] Article 36 GDPR.

[150] Article 35 (3) (b) GDPR.

[151] Article 37 GDPR.

[152] Article 37(1)(c) GDPR.

Its broad scope of geographic application expands the application of GDPR to many data processing situations that have a connection with the EU even when the data are not processed in the EU, i.e. either through the data controller or data processor being considered established in the EU or when the data pertain to data subjects in the EU. Local data protection rules might no longer be considered sufficient and, given the level of international collaboration in the field of biobanking, the GDPR rules might become a *de facto* international data protection standard.

The main restriction imposed on data controllers and processors is the duty to ensure the lawfulness of such activities. The GDPR contains two main legal bases for data processing of interest to biobanks: consent-based model and necessity-based model. It will remain critical to carefully consider which to apply to each data set because combining data sets based on different lawfulness grounds may generate increased compliance complexity.

Finally, the GDPR maintains a regulatory approach based on types of data (personal and special) and general lawfulness grounds for processing. It does not provide specific rules for particular activities of data processing and types of data uses. Legal persons data are left subject to national laws as the GDPR rules only applies to natural persons data and there is no differentiation between types of more or less intrusive uses. It does not clearly differentiate between raw data and inferred data and derived data. Neither does it consider the privacy impact of cumulative or network effects of data aggregation and cross-reference.

Compliance with the GDPR presents challenges for biobank and biobank researchers using advanced digital technologies. The use of big data analytics has brought tremendous benefits to scientific research, particularly in the field of genetics. Developments in this area include cost-effective sequencing of entire genomes and the possibility to share and combine multiple sources of complementary data. The very nature of research using big data analytics in general and genetic data in particular suggests that compliance may be onerous and difficult to implement in research protocols and institutional procedures. As we move deeper into a digitalised and data-driven society, particularly problematic data uses will require further clarification and improved approaches to data protection. Growing use of AI and big data analytics in biobanking activities means that special attention to compliance procedures will be necessary and that in the long term further legal developments and interpretative guidance should be expected.

References

Article 29 Data Protection Working Party, Guidelines on Consent under Regulation 2016/679, last Revised and Adopted on 10 April 2018

Article 29 Data Protection Working Party, Guidelines on the Right to data Portability, adopted on 13 December 2016

Article 29 Data Protection Working Party, Opinion 03/2013 on purpose limitation Adopted on 2 April 2013

Article 29 Data Protection Working Party, Opinion 1/2010 on the concepts of "controller" and "processor", adopted on 16 February 2010

Beier K, Lenk C (2015) Biobanking strategies and regulative approaches in the EU: recent perspectives. J Biorepository Sci Appl Med 3:69–81

Briceño Moraia L et al (2014) A comparative analysis of the requirements for the use of data in biobanks based in Finland, Germany, the Netherlands, Norway and the United Kingdom. Med Law Int 14(4):187–212

Chico V (2018) The impact of the general data protection regulation on health research. Br Med Bull 128(1):109–118, p.116

Commission Recommendation of 17 July 2012 on access to and preservation of scientific information (2012/417/EU)

Council of Europe Recommendation CM/Rec 2016 (6) of the Committee of Ministers to member states, adopted by the Committee of Ministers on 11 May 2016 at the 1256th meeting of the Ministers' Deputies

Council of Europe Recommendation Rec 2006 (4) of the Committee of Ministers to member states on research on biological materials of human origin, adopted by the Committee of Ministers on 15 March 2006 at the 958th meeting of the Ministers' Deputies

Council of Europe's Convention for the Protection of Individuals with regard to Automatic Processing of Personal Data (Coe ETS No.108), Strasbourg, 28/01/1981

De Vries J et al (2017) Regulation of genomic and biobanking research in Africa: a content analysis of ethics guidelines, policies and procedures from 22 African countries. BMC Med Ethics 18(8):8

Declaration of the Budapest Open Access Initiative. https://www.budapestopenaccessinitiative.org/read; Berlin Declaration on Open Access to Knowledge in the Sciences and Humanities. Available at: https://openaccess.mpg.de/67605/berlin_declaration_engl.pdf

Directive 2001/20/EC of the European Parliament and of the Council of 4 April 2001 on the approximation of the laws, regulations and administrative provisions of the Member States relating to the implementation of good clinical practice in the conduct of clinical trials on medicinal products for human use, OJ L 121, 1.5.2001, p. 34

Directive 2004/23/EC of the European Parliament and of the Council of 31 March 2004 on setting standards of quality and safety for the donation, procurement, testing, processing, preservation, storage and distribution of human tissues and cells, *OJ L 102, 7.4.2004, p. 48–58*

Directive 95/46/EC of the European Parliament and of the Council of 24 October 1995 on the protection of individuals with regard to the processing of personal data and on the free movement of such data, *Official Journal L 281, 23/11/1995 P. 0031 – 0050*

Dove ES (2019) The EU general data protection regulation: implications for international scientific research in the digital era. J Law Med Ethics 46(4):1013–1030. https://doi.org/10.1177/1073110518822003

ECHO Charter. https://echo.mpiwg-berlin.mpg.de/policy/oa_basics/charter, and the Bethesda Statement on Open Access Publishing http://legacy.earlham.edu/~peters/fos/bethesda.htm

European Commission DG for research and Innovation (2017) H2020 programme guidelines to the rules on open access to scientific publications and open access to research data in Horizon 2020. Available at: http://ec.europa.eu/research/participants/data/ref/h2020/grants_manual/hi/oa_pilot/h2020-hi-oa-pilot-guide_en.pdf

European Data protection board, Opinion 3/2019 concerning the Questions and Answers on the interplay between the Clinical Trials Regulation (CTR) and the General Data Protection regulation (GDPR) (art. 70.1.b)) Adopted on 23 January 2019

Fransson MN, Rial-Sebbag E, Brochhausen M et al (2015) Toward a common language for biobanking. Eur J Hum Genet 23(1):22–28

Global Forum on Bioethics in Research (2018) Background paper: the ethics of data sharing and biobanking in health research, Meeting in Cape Town, 13–14 November 2018. Available at: http://www.gfbr.global/wp-content/uploads/2018/04/GFBR-2018-background-paper-FINAL.pdf

Groves T, Godlee F (2012) Open science and reproducible research. BMJ 344:e4383
Hellstadius A, Schovsbo J (2018) You told me, right? - Free and informed consent in European patent law. In: Minssen T, Herrmann JR, Schovsbo J (eds) Global genes, local concerns: legal, ethical and scientific challenges in international biobanking. Edward Elgar, Cheltenham
Hewitt R, Watson P (2013) Defining biobank. Biopreserv Biobank 11(5):309–315
Holub P et al (2018) Enhancing reuse of data and biological material in medical research: from FAIR to FAIR-Health. Biopreserv Biobank 16(2):97–105
Judgment of the Court (Grand Chamber), 13 May 2014, *Google Spain SL and Google Inc. v Agencia Española de Protección de Datos* (AEPD) and Mario Costeja González, Case C-131/12, *Digital reports:* ECLI identifier: ECLI:EU:C:2014:317
Judgment of the Court (Grand Chamber) of 5 June 2018, *Unabhängiges Landeszentrum für Datenschutz Schleswig-Holstein v Wirtschaftsakademie Schleswig-Holstein GmbH*, Case C-210/16, OJ C 260, 18.7.2016, ECLI:EUC:2018:388
Kaye J et al (2015) Dynamic consent: a patient interface for twenty-first century research networks. Eur J Hum Genet 23(2):141–146
Kaye J et al (2016) Consent for biobanking: the legal frameworks of countries in the BioSHaRE-EU Project. Biopreserv Biobank 14(3):195–200
Kondylakis H et al (2017) Donor's support tool: enabling informed secondary use of patient's biomaterial and personal data. Int J Med Inform 97:282–292
Marelli L, Testa G (2019) Scrutinizing the EU general data protection regulation. Science 360(6388):496–498
Minssen T, Rajam BM (2019) Clinical trials data transparency & GDPR compliance: what are the effects on data sharing and open innovation?, Science and public policy scaa014
Morrison M et al (2017) The European general data protection regulation: challenges and considerations for iPSC researchers and biobanks. Regen Med 12(6):693–703
National Institutes of Health (NIH) (2003) Final NIH statement on sharing research data. Available at: https://grants.nih.gov/grants/guide/notice-files/NOT-OD-03-032.html
Nicola P (2015) Spanish regulation on biobanks. J Law Med Ethics 43(4):800–815
Nordberg A, Minssen T (2016) A 'Ray of Hope' for European stem cell patents or 'Out of the Smog into the Fog'?: an analysis of recent European case law and how it compares to the US. IIC 47(2):138–177
OECD, Recommendation on human biobanks and genetic research databases, adopted by the OECD Council on 22 October 2009
Penasa S et al (2018) The EU general data protection regulation: how will it impact the regulation of research biobanks? Setting the legal frame in the Mediterranean and Eastern European area. Med Law Intern 18(4):241–255
Phillips A, Borry P, Shabani M (2017) Research ethics review for the use of anonymized samples and data: a systematic review of normative documents. Account Res 24(8):483–496
Protocol amending the Convention for the Protection of Individuals with regard to Automatic Processing of Personal Data (CoE ETS No. 223), 128th Session of the Committee of Ministers, Elsinore, 17–18 May 2018
Regulation 536/2014 of the European Parliament and of the Council of 16 April 2014 on clinical trials on medicinal products for human use, and repealing Directive 2001/20/EC, OJ L 158 27.05.2004, p. 1–76
Sandor J, Drakopoulou A, Bard P (2009) The legal regulation of biobanks: National Report: Greece. CELAB Paper Series No. 2. Available at https://doi.org/10.2139/ssrn.2295967
Shaw DM, Elger BS, Colledge F (2014) What is a biobank? Differing definitions among biobank stakeholders. Clin Genet 85(3):223–227
Taichman DB et al (2017) Data sharing statements for clinical trials: a requirement of the International Committee of Medical Journal Editors. Ann Intern Med 167(1):63–65
Tassé AM (2016) A comparative analysis of the legal and bioethical frameworks governing the secondary use of data for research purposes. Biopreserv Biobank 14(3):207–216

Watson PH (2014) Biobank classification: communicating biorepository diversity. Biopreserv Biobank 12(3):163–164

Wellcome Trust (2017) Policy on data, software and material management and sharing at https://wellcome.ac.uk/funding/managing-grant/policy-data-software-materials-management-andsharing

Individual Rights in Biobank Research Under the GDPR

Ciara Staunton

Abstract The coming into force of the General Data Protection Regulation (GDPR) on 25 May 2018 has brought about considerable changes in how data may collected, stored and used. Biobanks, which require the collection, use and re-use of large quantities of biological samples and data, will be affected by the proposed changes. In seeking to require 'data protection by design', the GDPR provides data subjects with certain individual rights. They are, the right to be informed, the right of access, the right to rectification, the right to erasure, the right to restrict processing, the right to data portability, the right to object and rights in relation to automated decision making and profiling.

This chapter will consider each of these individual rights in turn and discuss the impact on biobank research. In particular, it will discuss the challenges that are now facing biobanks in upholding the individual rights, the limits of these rights in light of the technical realities of biobanks, and the potential impact that they may have on the collection, sharing, use and re-use of biological data and material.

1 Introduction

The General Data Protection Regulation (GDPR) seeks to strengthen the protection of personal data and it makes explicit provision for certain personal rights for data subjects: the right to information (Article 13 & 14), the right of access (Article 15), the right to rectification (Article 16), the right to erasure (Article 17), the right to restriction of processing (Article 18), the right to data portability (Article 20), the right to object, (Article 21) and the right regarding automated individual decision-making (Article 22). The rights are intended to enhance the autonomy and control that a data subject has over the processing of their personal data, and as such, could control and limit the use of a data subjects' personal data.

The author would like to thank Drs. Edward S Dove and Deborah Mascalzoni for comments on an earlier draft of this paper and Dr. Carmen Swanepoel for discussion on aspects of this paper.

C. Staunton (✉)
Middlesex University, School of Law, London, UK

Institute for Biomedicine, Eurac Research, Bolzano, Italy
e-mail: Staunton@mdx.ac.uk

S. Slokenberga et al. (eds.), *GDPR and Biobanking*, Law, Governance and Technology Series 43, https://doi.org/10.1007/978-3-030-49388-2_6

Biobanks are repositories that store large quantities of biological samples and data. The data may be in the form of information that a data subject may have given the biobank themselves, or it may be data that is derived from a biological sample. In the processing of this data, biobanks will now need to consider and uphold the individual rights under the GDPR. Biobanks are often involved in collaborative research projects requiring the transfer of data across borders, but differing legal rules can slow down and hinder cross-border transfer. In response, there have been calls for a harmonisation of rules at an international level[1] or development of a global governance of biobanks that is based on key principles and norms.[2] As such, the GDPR should be welcomed as it seeks to harmonise data protection legislation across the EU, while also facilitating the free movement of personal data across Member States (Article 1). On the face of it, a regulation that promotes the sharing of data and harmonisation of legislation in this realm should support collaborative transnational research.

These individual rights can however be derogated either directly by the biobank or through Member State derogations under Article 89 if the data is to be used for scientific research, potentially negating the rights of data subjects. Thus, when biobanks are processing data for research purposes they may not have to follow the rights of data subjects where to do so would impair research. The exact scope of these rights will depend on derogations that may be invoked either directly by biobanks, or through Member State derogations. These derogations will be examined in Chapter 'Safeguards and derogations relating to processing for scientific purposes: Article 89 analysis for biobank research' by Anne-Marie Duguet and Jean Herveg. This chapter will consider the individual rights of data subjects provided by the GDPR. Each right will be discussed in turn and the possible impact that they may have on biobanks.

2 Individual Rights and the Impact on Biobank Research

2.1 The Right to Be Informed

The importance of public trust in biobanks has been well documented[3] and inherent in this trust is transparency in the use and re-use of personal data. The right to information contained in Article 13, (information to be provided when personal data is collected from the data subject), and Article 14 (information to be provided when data has not been obtained directly from the research subject), strengthens the principle of transparency.

[1] International Bioethics Committee (2015).

[2] Chen and Pang (2015), p. 113.

[3] Lipworth et al. (2019), pp. 119–132; Johnsson (2013), p. 142.

Article 13(1) and Article 14(1) details certain information that must be provided to the data subject when their data is collected. The data subject must be provided with information about the data controller, a data protection officer if applicable, the purpose of the research and its legal basis, the legitimate interests if processing is based on Article 6(1)(f), the recipients of the data, if it is intended to transfer the data to a third country, and the safeguards in place to protect their data in that country. In addition to this, under Article 13(2) and Article 14(2) a data subject must also be told about the duration of the storage of data, criteria to determine duration if it is not known, the right to withdraw if consent is the lawful basis of processing, and the right to lodge a complaint with a supervisory authority. Similarly, under Article 13(3) and Article 14(4), if a data controller intends to process the personal data for research that was not intended at the time of data collection, the foregoing information must be provided to the data subject prior to the further processing of that data.

Thus, irrespective of whether a biobank itself collects data from a data subject or obtains data through other means (e.g. from residual samples or from another biobank), it must provide the data subject with the foregoing information. The difference is that this information must be provided at the time of collection if the biobank itself collects the data, or within 1 month if it obtains the data through other means (Article 14(3)). If a biobank intends to use personal data for research that was not envisaged at the point of data collection, they must inform the data subject in advance of the research if no exception applies.

It is important to note that the right in Articles 13 & 14 is for information purposes only. For ease of compliance with Articles 13 & 14, consent forms should detail the information outlined in Article 13(1)&(2) and Article 14(1)&(2) (where consent is the lawful basis of processing), but the right to information should not be confused with informed consent. The right to information does require biobanks to envisage at the outset who it may collaborate and share the data with, as well as the possible duration of the research.

Article 13 and 14 do provide for instances when the right to information does not apply. Under Article 13, the right to information does not apply when 'the data subject already has the information' (Article 13(4)). The exceptions under Article 14 are wider and are particularly pertinent for research: where the provision of information would prove impossible for research purposes; where it would constitute a disproportionate effort, in particular for research; where provision of the information would seriously impair or make the objectives of the processing (i.e. the research) impossible (Article 14(5)(b)).

If a biobank seeks to rely on the exemption under the impossibility scenario, they would have to clearly demonstrate that the research would be impossible. This could apply if individual data subjects are uncontactable, but it is unclear whether a lack of contact information is sufficient on its own as a basis to rely on impossibility, or whether reasonable efforts should be made to contact data subjects. In any case, such an exemption would apply on a case-by-case basis and would be burdensome. It is thus more likely that any exemption to the right to information for biobanks would fall under grounds of disproportionate effort under Article 14(5)(b).

In determining what could constitute a 'disproportionate effort', Recital 62 states that the number of data sets, the age of the data, and any appropriate safeguards should be taken into consideration. Biobanks will generally have very large data sets; thus, provided there are appropriate safeguards in place under Article 89(1),[4] biobanks could be granted an exemption to the right to information when they have not collected the data under Article 14(5)(b). To rely on this exemption, biobanks should conduct a data protection impact assessment (DIPA) to balance the effort of informing data subjects with the risks to the research, and this should be documented.[5] This DIPA should be carried out before relying on this exemption and following Article 35(7), the assessment should include a systematic description of the envisaged processing operations and the purposes of the processing, including where applicable, the legitimate interest pursued by the controller; an assessment of the necessity and proportionality of the processing operations in relation to the purposes; an assessment of the risks to the rights and freedoms of data subjects referred to in paragraph 1; and the measures envisaged to address the risks, including safeguards, security measures and mechanisms to ensure the protection of personal data.[6]

The right to information does seem to be potentially limited in the context of research under Article 14(5)(b) when data was not collected from the data subject. As will discussed in the following sections, the exercise of other rights is contingent on data subjects being aware of the processing of their personal data, thus the right to information is important in the exercise of their other rights and any limits on the right to information could impact other rights. However, Article 13(1)(e) requires data subjects to be informed about 'the recipients or categories of recipients of the personal data'. A narrow interpretation of this provision would require biobanks to simply inform data subjects about those to whom the biobank itself shared data. On the other hand, when one considers the importance of transparency in the processing of personal data, it could be suggested that biobanks have an obligation to inform data subjects about all those to whom the data has been shared with, irrespective of whether they shared the data themselves. In reality, this would likely constitute an undue burden on biobanks, particularly when one considers the importance of research in the GDPR. The principle of accountability most likely requires a biobank to be transparent in its own processing of personal information. Thus, under Article 13(1)(e) a biobank will likely only be obliged to inform a data subject about any third party to whom it has shared personal data. Biobanks must thus ensure that they have systems or a register in place that documents all data transfers.

[4] See Chapter 'Safeguards and Derogations Relating to Processing for Scientific Purposes: Article 89 Analysis for Biobank Research'.

[5] Art 29 WP (2018), ICO (2018).

[6] For more on DIPA's see Dara Hallinan's contribution in Chapter, 'Biobank Oversight and Sanctions under the General Data Protection Regulation'.

2.2 The Right of Access

In a further effort to promote transparency, Article 15 provides the data subject with the right to access information about their personal data, including confirmation as to whether a data controller is processing their personal data and the purpose; other recipients of their personal data, including to third countries (and the safeguards in place); where the data controller obtained the data when the data was not collected from the data subject; and the expected storage period or the criteria to determine the storage period. Under this right, data subjects can access information regarding the research projects that their data is used in, and other biobanks or researchers with whom the data may have been shared.

A data subject is unlikely to be able to exercise their right of access without knowledge that the data controller was processing their data. The right of access is thus dependent upon the right to information and it would be unlikely that a data subject would be in a position to exercise their right to access if a biobank invoked an Article 14(5) exception.

Importantly for research, Article 15(3) provides that the data subject has a right to access a copy of their personal data that is being processed. This can include genetic data, results of particular tests, and results of research and may include information about genetic mutations, conditions that may be inherited and passed onto their children, and conditions that the data subject may be predisposed or susceptible to. To fulfil their obligations under the GDPR, a biobank will be required to provide the data subject with the raw data, but not an interpretation of that genetic data. Meeting this requirement may be tricky considering the wider evolving debate on communication of incidental findings.[7] A right to access thus does not equate to a right to feedback of findings, if requested, but biobanks are now legally required to provide data subjects with access to their data which can include raw genetic data. Direct to consumer (DTC) genetic testing companies have faced criticisms for making raw genetic data available to its consumers. DTC companies do generally include a disclaimer that the information has not been validated for accuracy, nor do they provide an interpretation of the data, but the risks of possible inaccuracy and false positives have been highlighted.[8] Biobanks will now be in a similar position whereby may be legally required to return raw genetic data if requested, without any obligation of the interpretation of that data. Thus arguably biobanks can no longer have a 'no returns' policy, but in returning such data, they must make it clear that they have not interpreted the data and any such interpretation should be done by a trained genetic counsellor.

[7] De Clercq et al. (2017), pp. 128–131; Wolf et al. (2012), pp. 361–384.

[8] Tandy-Connor et al. (2018).

2.3 The Right to Rectification

The right to rectification provides the data subject with the right to have inaccurate personal data corrected and incomplete data to be completed. This rectification must then be communicated to any other recipient who has received the data, unless it involves a disproportionate effort (Article 19). This right is linked with the principle of transparency under Article 5(1)(d) that requires that personal data be accurate, kept up to date and every 'reasonable step' be taken to rectify any inaccuracy.

Genetic and genomic research is rapidly evolving, but genome sequencing and genetic testing may lead to results that are of uncertain significance or relevance and this uncertainty is inherent in genomic research. Uncertainty does not equate to inaccuracies, and biobanks will only be required to update any inaccurate information. This rectification must be communicated to any third party that has been provided with the data. Similar to Article 15, a data subject will likely only be in a position to exercise that right if they have been informed that their data is being processed. However, unlike Article 15, this obligation to notify third parties can be limited if it would prove to be impossible or require a 'disproportionate effort'. Assessments of 'disproportionate effort' will need to be carried out and determined on a case-by-case basis, and should be recorded in the interests of transparency. Rectification of data that has formed part of research results that is published will most likely be considered disproportionate, if not impossible.

2.4 The Right to Erasure

Article 17 (a)–(f) describes when the right to erasure (more commonly known as the right to be forgotten) may be invoked, but in the context of biobanks, the right to erasure is most likely to be invoked under Article (a)–(c), namely that the personal data is no longer required for the purposes for which it was obtained (Article 17(a)), the data subject withdraws consent where consent is the lawful basis for processing (Article 17(b)), and the data subject objects to the processing under Article 21(1) (discussed below) when public interest or legitimate interest is the lawful basis of processing (Article 17(c)). Thus, data subjects can invoke a right to erasure when the research has been completed, they withdraw their consent (where consent was the lawful basis of processing), or they object to the public interest or legitimate interests as the basis for the use of their research. Data subjects have the right to request the erasure of their personal data from all data controllers that are processing their data under Article 17(2). Biobanks thus must communicate with those they have shared the data of this request for erasure.

Upon receipt of a request for erasure, a biobank will be required to erase all personal data that they have about that data subject and, as discussed, inform all other subsequent data controllers about this request. The data must then be removed from ongoing research and will not be used in any future research or shared with other data controllers. The erasure of the retrospective use of data is more challenging as the data may have formed part of published results, and it such erasure is likely to be challenging in practice if not impossible. As noted by Melham et al 'past uses of data and samples cannot be undone'.[9]

This right to erasure is, however, limited. First, similar to other rights, invoking the right to erasure pre-supposes that a data subject is aware of the processing of their personal data. As earlier discussed, this is only likely to occur where data was collected from the data subject. Second, Article 19 states that data controllers do not have to communicate to those with whom it has shared personal data a request for erasure if it is impossible or would involve a disproportionate effort. Similar to Article 16, what is considered to be disproportionate will depend on the circumstances of the case and the reasons for any decisions should be recorded. Third, Article 17(3)(c) states that a request for erasure and notification to other controllers processing the data does not have be complied with if processing is in the publics' interest in the area of public health under Article 9(2)(h) and (i), subject to Article 9(3). Thus, a biobank can be exempt from a request to erasure if the research is for the purposes of preventive or occupational medicine, protect against serious cross-border threats to health, or ensure high standards of quality and safety of health care, medicinal products or medicinal devices.

Finally, Article 17(3)(d) states that a request for erasure does not have to be complied with if the processing is for research purposes, subject to the safeguards in Article 89(1), where fulfilment of the right to erasure would 'render impossible or seriously impair the achievement of the objectives of that processing'. Thus, subject to Article 89(1) safeguards, a biobank processing personal data for research purposes would not have to comply with a request for erasure.

The right to erasure is significantly limited in the research context. Biobanks that are seeking to be exempt from any request for erasure should conduct an assessment, make a record of its assessment and communicate its decision to the data subject, in the interests of transparency.

2.5 *The Right to Restrict Processing*

Article 18 gives the data subject the right to restrict the processing of their personal data on a number of grounds: if they are contesting the accuracy of the data; if the processing is unlawful and the data subject opts for restriction of data processing over the erasure of data; if the data is no longer needed for processing but the data subject requires it for a legal purpose; or if the data subject has objected to the processing of data under Article 21(1) (to be discussed below). Although in the biobank context its practical impact may be limited, if the right to restriction is invoked on one of those grounds, the biobank can continue to store the data, but they can no

[9] Melham et al. (2014).

longer process the data. Thus, there will be no obligation on the data controller to remove or erase the data from previously published results. As such, the right to restriction applies to both current and future research.

Similar to Articles 15, 16 and 17, a data subject can only exercise this right if they are aware that their data is being processed for research. Furthermore, it is also limited by Article 19, and therefore the biobank is under no obligation to inform subsequent data controllers about this notice of rectification if it would prove to be impossible or involve a 'disproportionate effort'.

2.6 *The Right to Data Portability*

In keeping with the aim of giving data subjects greater control over their personal data, under Article 20, data subjects have the right to data portability. For biobanks, this will mean that data subjects can now move their data from one biobank to another, in circumstances where they have provided the data to the biobank. The biobank must make this data available in a 'structured, commonly used and machine-readable format' to another biobank that the data subject may have selected. That transfer can either be carried out by the data subject or they can require the biobank to make that transfer. As the transfer must be made 'without hindrance from the controller', there is an obligation to put in place measures to facilitate such a transfer. Interoperable formats are encouraged, but this does not extend to requiring controllers to adopt systems that are technically compatible with other organisations (Recital 68).

This right only applies in circumstances where the following conditions have been met: the data subject has provided the data controller with the data, consent is the lawful basis of processing and the processing is carried out by automated means (Article 20(1)). Thus, if a biobank is processing data for research on any other legal basis, they will not be required to comply with a request under Article 20. Equally, the use of shared data, irrespective of the legal basis of processing, will not be subject to Article 20. This right will have limited applicability in the biobank context as the Art 29 Working Party makes it clear that 'inferred data and derived data are created by the data controller'. Thus any data derived from a biological sample will not come under the definition 'provided by the data subject'.[10]

In circumstances where a data subject seeks to enforce their data portability right, exercise of Article 20 does not amount to erasure and is not a withdrawal of consent. Rather, it is a transfer of data only and the Article 29 Working Party has made it clear that the data controller can continue to process the data after a transfer has been made.[11] This means that under Article 20, biobanks will be required to transfer the data if requested, but can continue to use the data in current and future

[10] Art 29 WP (2017).

[11] Art 29 WP (2017).

research. The biobank to which the data subject originally gave and consented to the use of their personal data in research can continue to use that data after Article 20 has been invoked.

2.7 *The Right to Object*

Article 21 provides data subjects with the right to object to the processing of their data if the lawful basis of processing is either public interest (Article 6(1)(e)) or legitimate interests (Article 6(1)(f)). Thus, if a biobank is relying on either of these claims as the lawful basis of processing, a data subject can object to the use of their data in the research. The impact of the right to object for a biobank is that it can no longer use that data for research purposes, but does not amount to an erasure of data.

In practice, the exercise of this right could be limited for biobank research. Similar to Articles 15–18, exercise of this right will only be possible where the data subject is aware that their data is used for research. In circumstances where the data subject is aware of such use, Article 21(1) states that the data controller can continue to process data if they can demonstrate 'compelling legitimate grounds' that override the rights of the data subject. Article 21(6) also states that while a data subject can object to processing of data for research purposes under Article 89(1), this right can be derogated from where the processing is in the public interest.

Furthermore, although a data subject does have the right to object to the processing of data for research pursuant to Article 89(1), a data controller can continue to use the data for research purposes if it is necessary 'for reasons of public interest'. Recital 45 states that health purposes could come within the meaning of 'public interest' and Pormeister argues that due to the importance of research in the GDPR, research that benefits society such as genetic research could be a legitimate claim on which to continue processing.[12]

2.8 *Rights in Relation to Automated Decision Making and Profiling*

Finally, under Article 22, a data subject has the right not to be subject to a decision solely on automated decision making, which includes profiling, if this produces 'legal effects' on the data subject, or 'significantly affects' them. Profiling is defined in Article 4(4) as 'any form of automated processing of personal data consisting of the use of personal data to evaluate certain personal aspects relating to a natural person, in particular to analyse or predict aspects concerning that natural person's

[12] Pormeister (2017), p. 141.

performance at work, economic situation, health, personal preferences, interests, reliability, behaviour, location or movements'.

Profiling is commonly used in biobank research as samples and data can be classified according to certain characteristics (e.g. age, sex, disease profile). Artificial intelligence can help researchers analyse and sequence DNA much quicker, enabling researchers to interpret and turn it into clinically actionable knowledge.[13] They can predict the odds of an individual developing a disease or how they may respond to a particular drug or therapy. The use of Artifical Intelligence (AI) and machine learning in genomic research is likely to increase as it assists in the analysis of increasingly complex data sets.[14]

A data subject can exercise their right not to be subject to profiling or automated decision-making if it has a legal effect, or if they are similarly affected. Healthcare decisions based on such means would likely come under such a definition. The requirement of the automated decision-making having 'legal effect' likely leaves research biobanks outside of the application of this right. Article 22(2) provides for some derogations from this right, including if the data subject consents, or it is authorised by Member State law and subject to safeguards. Such derogations do not apply to the processing of special categories of data (which includes genetic data and data concerning health), unless processing is based on the data subject's consent (Article 9(2)(a)), or necessary for reasons of substantial public interest that is based on EU or Member State law (Article 9(2)(g)) and subject to suitable safeguards.

The extent to which a biobank may use automated decision making and profiling depends on the activities of the biobank. However, if it intends to use automated decision making and/or profiling for genetic or genomic research, it must have either the express consent of the data subject, or this must be provided for by law and subject to safeguards.

3 Limits on Individual Rights

3.1 Limitations

Despite the promise of greater autonomy for data subjects, the individual rights for data subjects in research are severely limited and potentially unenforceable. The GDPR itself provides for EU and Member State derogations that can limit some rights, but equally important is the limitation not grounded in law whereby a data subject may not be aware of the processing of their data. Thus a Data Protection Officer (DPO) will be unable to enforce the rights on behalf of the data subject.

---

[13] Williams et al. (2018), p. 237.

[14] Libbrecht and Stafford Noble (2015), p. 231.

3.2 *Knowledge of the Processing of Data*

As discussed, the exercise of many individual rights is contingent on the right to be informed and a data subject's awareness that their data is being processed for research. Biobanks that collect data from the data subject must inform them about the research under Article 13. However, in circumstances where a biobank did not collect data from the data subject, they do not have to inform the data subject about the processing if it would constitute a disproportionate effort, impair the research, or make the research impossible. If either of these grounds under Article 14(5) are satisfied, a data subject may be unaware of the processing of their data for research and from the foregoing analysis, it is likely to impact upon the exercise of a data subject's Article 15, 16, 17, 18, and 21 rights. A data subject does have these rights under the GDPR, but the implication of Article 14(5) is that it may not be practically possible to exercise those rights.

3.3 *Lawful Derogations*

Articles 15 (right of access), Article 17 (right to erasure) and Article 21 (right to object) provide that biobanks can be exempted from these rights if processing is for research purposes and exercise of the right would 'render impossible or seriously impair' the research. If a biobank seeks to directly invoke this derogation, it can take into consideration the number of data subjects and the age of the data (Recital 62). A biobank should undertake a DPIA and consider whether it has to contact a large amount of data subjects, whether it has all relevant and up-to-date contact information, cost implications, as well as the impact it may have on the completion of the research. This is subjective test that will depend upon the research, and the outcome of this assessment must be recorded. Importantly, it is subject to safeguards as required by Article 89(1) and further discussed in Chapter 'Safeguards and Derogations Relating to Processing for Scientific Purposes: Article 89 Analysis for Biobank Research'.

Article 89(2) specifically provides that a biobank may derogate from Article 15 (right of access), Article 16 (right to rectification), Article 18 (right to restriction of processing), and Article 21 (right to object) where the processing is for research purposes and these rights are likely 'to render impossible or seriously impair the achievement of the research, and such derogations are provided for by law.

Under Article 89(3), a biobank can derogate from Article 15, Article 16, Article 18, Article 19 (notification obligations), Article 20 (right to data portability) and Article 21, if personal data is being processed for archiving purposes in the public interest. This is contingent on the exercise of those rights likely 'to render impossible or seriously impair' the research, and the derogations are provided for law and subject to safeguards. This would apply to biobanks or permanent archives such as the European Genome-Phenome Archive (EGA) that is archiving data that may in the future be re-analysed, provided it can be demonstrated that the retention is in the public interest. The scope of the research exemption and the appropriate safeguards are considered in Chapter 'Safeguards and Derogations Relating to Processing for Scientific Purposes: Article 89 Analysis for Biobank Research', but some points on the impact of the research exemption on individual rights are worth noting here. First, the research exemption severely limits the operation of the specified rights and, depending on the wording of the derogations in Member State law, may leave them completely unenforceable. Second, as it is for individual Member States to determine the derogations and decide on the scope of the appropriate safeguards, the scope of data subject's rights will differ across the EU. Data that is initially processed in one jurisdiction may be shared with a data controller in other jurisdictions with weaker protections in place for data subjects. Thus, the rights of data subjects cannot be guaranteed during the consent process (where consent is the lawful basis of consent) and for all secondary use of data the rights of the data subject will vary according to its location. The same data will be subject to different rights and protections, likely resulting in confusion for the data subject (assuming, of course, that they are aware of the use of their data in research) and lacking in transparency. Third, the potential wide scope of the research exemptions means that the data subject loses almost all rights once their data is in a biobank. If all possible exemptions and derogations were to be invoked, only Article 13 would remain. The individual rights that are intended to give the data subject greater autonomy over the use of their personal data are circumvented by the potentially far reaching research exemption and it is therefore essential that robust safeguards and protections are in place, as required by Article 89.

Article 19 requires the biobank to notify any biobank or researcher to whom it may have shared data about a communication regarding rectification (Article 16), erasure (Article 17(1)), or restriction (Article 18) of processing. Such a requirement can help ensure that a data subject can fully exercise their rights. Article 19 does, however, provide that a biobank is not obliged to follow this if it would be impossible or involve a disproportionate effort. Again, such a decision will be on a case-by-case basis and any decision must be recorded and communicated to the data subject, but it has the effect of limiting the scope of these rights.

4 Conclusion

The individual rights in the GDPR are intended to give greater autonomy and control over the use of a data subject's personal data. However, they may be severely limited in the biobank context owing to the limits that may be placed on these rights. These limits may simply be due to the lack of a data subjects' awareness of the processing of their personal data. If a data subject is unaware that their personal data is used in research, it is unlikely that they can exercise their other rights. The GDPR itself also provides for derogations that biobanks may invoke, leaving the data subject with very limited rights. Considering the intention of the GDPR and the importance of public and participant trust in biobanks, the importance of the undefined safeguards in Article 89 cannot be overstated and must provide protection of the fundamental rights of data subjects. The national derogations (considered further by Tzortzatou et al. in Chapter 'Biobanking across Europe post-GDPR: A deliberately created fragmented landscape') are potentially wide ranging and the ability to introduce local exemptions provides little clarity and transparency to data subjects. The practical implication of the individual rights as written and the research exemption is to render the data subject with little, if any, rights once a biobank has begun to process their data. Rather, they are dependent on safeguards to be put in place to uphold and protect their rights. Finally, despite the intention of the GDPR to harmonise data protection across the EU, as the research exemption begins to be invoked, the standard of protection of individual rights will begin to vary across jurisdictions as well as biobanks,. Once again researchers will be left to navigate the differing levels of data protection afforded to data in biobanks across the EU.

References

Article 29 Data Protection Working Party (2017) Guidelines on the right to data portability. WP 242 rev.01

Article 29 Data Protection Working Party (2018) Guidelines on transparency under Regulation 2016/679. WP260

Chen H, Pang T (2015) A call for global governance of biobanks. Bull World Health Organ 93:113–117

De Clercq E, Kaye J, Wolf SM, Koenig BA, Elger BS (2017) Returning results in biobank research: global trends and solutions. Genet Test Mol Biomarkers 21(3):128–131

Information Commissioner's Office (2018) The right to be informed. Available at https://ico.org.uk/media/for-organisations/guide-to-the-general-data-protection-regulation-gdpr/the-right-to-be-informed-1-0.pdf. Accessed 25 March 2019

International Bioethics Committee (2015) Report of the IBC on updating its reflection on the human genome and human rights SHS/YES/IBC-22/15/2 REV.2 Paris, 2 October 2015

Johnsson L (2013) Trust in biobank research: meaning and moral significance. Acta Universitatis Upsaliensis. Digital comprehensive summaries of Uppsala Dissertations from the Faculty of Medicine 861. 142 pp. Uppsala. ISBN 978-91-554-8585-6

Libbrecht MW, Noble WS (2015) Machine learning applications in genetics and genomics. Nat Rev Genet 16:321–332

Lipworth W, Morrell B, Irvine R, Kerridge I (2019) An empirical reappraisal of public trust in biobanking research: rethinking restrictive consent requirements. J Law Med 17(1):119–132

Melham K, Briceno Moraia L, Mitchell C, Morrison M, Teare H, Kaye J (2014) The evolution of withdrawal: negotiating research relationships in biobanking. Life Sci Soc Policy 10:16

Pormeister K (2017) Genetic data and the research exemption: is the GDPR going too far? Pormeister Int Data Privacy Law 7(2):137–146

Tandy-Connor S, Guiltinan J, Krempely K, LaDuca H, Reineke P, Gutierrez S, Gray P, Tippin Davis B (2018) False-positive results released by direct-to-consumer genetic tests highlight the importance of clinical confirmation testing for appropriate patient care. Genet Med advance online publication 22 March 2018. https://doi.org/10.1038/gim.2018.38

Williams AM, Liu Y, Regner KR, Jotterand F, Liu P, Liang M (2018) Artificial intelligence, physiological genomics, and precision medicine. Physiol Genom 50(4):237–243

Wolf SM, Crock BN, Brian Van Ness B, Lawrenz F, Kahn JP, Beskow LM, Cho MK, Christman MF, Green RC, Hall R, Illes J, Keane M, Knoppers BM, Koenig BA, Kohane IS, LeRoy B, Maschke KJ, McGeveran W, Ossorio P, Parker LS, Petersen GM, Richardson HS, Scott JA, Terry SF, Wilfond BS, Wolf WA (2012) Managing incidental findings and research results in genomic research involving biobanks and archived data sets. Genet Med 14(4):361–384

Safeguards and Derogations Relating to Processing for Scientific Purposes: Article 89 Analysis for Biobank Research

Anne-Marie Duguet and Jean Herveg

Abstract When complying with appropriate safeguards, the processing of personal data for scientific research under the GDPR benefits from a special regime which is of interest for biobank research. On the one hand, under this condition, the further processing of personal data will not be incompatible with the initial purposes for which the data were originally collected and processed and it allows for retaining data for longer periods of time for scientific research. Complying with this condition is a condition to lift the prohibition to process special categories of personal data in the context of scientific research. On the other hand, complying with this condition makes it possible to derogate to some extent to several data subjects' rights such as the right of access, the right to rectification, the right to the restriction of processing and the right to object to the processing.

Possible safeguards range from specific procedures to support the exercise of data subjects' rights to the use of anonymous data or (where necessary) of pseudonymised data, the appointment of a data protection officer, enforcing a procedure to ensure a feedback to data subjects on the results of the research, requiring specific professional accreditations, creating a specific supervisory body for the biobank research, or the creation of a specific Code of conduct for biobank research activities.

This double regime under the GDPR is finally compared with the 2009 OECD Guidelines in biobanks and genetic research databases.

1 Introduction

The GDPR regulates the processing of personal data and recognizes subjective rights to data subjects. In particular, it provides special rules for processing personal data for scientific research. Thereby, as a rule, the processing of personal data for scientific research must be subject to appropriate safeguards for the rights and

A.-M. Duguet (✉)
UMR/INSERM 1027 Université Paul Sabatier, Toulouse, France

J. Herveg
Centre de recherches information, droit et société, University of Namur, Namur, Belgium
e-mail: jean.herveg@unamur.be; http://www.crids.eu

S. Slokenberga et al. (eds.), *GDPR and Biobanking*, Law, Governance and Technology Series 43, https://doi.org/10.1007/978-3-030-49388-2_7

freedoms of the data subject, in accordance with Article 89.1,[1] without prejudice to respecting the other rules imposed by the GDPR.[2]

The obligation to comply with appropriate safeguards applies to all data processing for scientific research, whether it is a primary or secondary data processing or an initial or further data processing.

Complying with these appropriate safeguards opens the door to a specific regime for processing personal data for scientific research: relaxing of some rules applicable to all data processing and possibility for Member States to provide for derogations to data subject's rights.

This chapter aims at grasping the specificities of this regime in the matter of data processing for scientific research and studying the ways to conceive these appropriate safeguards, in the field of biobanks.

2 The Special Regime for Processing of Personal Data for Scientific Research Applied to Biobanks

Biobanks for research consist of a collection of biological materials and associated medical data. The biological material collected is variable: blood, urine, tissue samples, surgical pieces, organ fragments, tumors, etc. Data of different nature are associated with the samples: data relating to the subject's identity (first name, name, age, date of birth, etc.), data relating to the pathology and the state of health (diagnosis, results of biological tests, treatments, risk factors, etc.), data relating to the results of the research which has been carried out (identification of biological markers, responses to certain treatments, genetic analysis, etc.). Sometimes, the data subject is not even aware about the mere existence of these data. Studies carried out in the domain of Public Health are epidemiological (and/or statistical) studies and population studies, in which cohorts of subjects are monitored over the long term and information about each individual should be nominative or coded to avoid duplication.

In principle, it is prohibited to process special categories of personal data such as those revealing racial or ethnic origin, political opinions, religious or philosophical

[1] Compare with Articles 4.1.b & 15.1 of Council of Europe Recommendation CM/Rec(2019)2 of the Committee of Ministers to member States on the protection of health-related data (Adopted by the Committee of Ministers on 27 March 2019 at the 1342nd meeting of the Ministers' Deputies).

[2] See e.g. Article 5 (b) for the purpose limitation principle, Article 9 (i) & (j) for the regime applicable to personal data concerning health and without prejudice to the power of Member State to maintain or introduce further conditions, including limitations, with regard to the processing of genetic data, biometric data or data concerning health. On the GDPR, please consult: de Terwangne et al. (2018); Herveg (2018b), pp. 333–392; Herveg and Van Gyseghem (2018), pp. 703–762. On the specific topic of biobank, please refer to : Herveg J (2018a).

beliefs, or trade union membership, genetic data, biometric data for the purpose of uniquely identifying a natural person, data concerning health or data concerning a natural person's sex life or sexual orientation.[3]

However, the GDPR provides derogations to the prohibition to process special categories of personal data such as e.g. having the explicit consent of the data subject or pursuing a substantial public interest or for reasons of public interest in the area of public health or for scientific research.[4] Directive 95/46/EC already provided exemptions to this prohibition which were useful for biobank activities such as e.g. the explicit consent of the data subject or appropriate national provisions applicable to biobank activities.

In comparison with the Data Protection Directive, the GDPR may be seen as having extended the notion of personal data concerning health. Indeed, it is defined as 'personal data related to the physical or mental health of a natural person, including the provision of health care services, which reveal information about his or her health status' (Article 4.15). Recital 35 precises that:

> Personal data concerning health should include all data pertaining to the health status of a data subject which reveal information relating to the past, current or future physical or mental health status of the data subject. This includes information about the natural person collected in the course of the registration for, or the provision of, health care services as referred to in Directive 2011/24/EU of the European Parliament and of the Council (1) to that natural person; a number, symbol or particular assigned to a natural person to uniquely identify the natural person for health purposes; information derived from the testing or examination of a body part or bodily substance, including from genetic data and biological samples; and any information on, for example, a disease, disability, disease risk, medical history, clinical treatment or the physiological or biomedical state of the data subject independent of its source, for example from a physician or other health professional, a hospital, a medical device or an in vitro diagnostic test.

Moreover, the strict application of data protection rules (such as the purpose limitation, the data minimization or the storage limitation principles) may be seen as being in conflict with certain research activities, particularly in the secondary use of data which requires extending the shelf life. By instance, it is not always possible to determine, at the time of data collection, the exact purposes for which data are going to be processed for scientific research purposes.

However, recital 33 recognizes that data subjects should be allowed to consent to the processing of data relating to them, in accordance with recognized ethical standards and recital 157 confirms that the prohibition to process personal data should be lifted in order to facilitate scientific research, subject to appropriate conditions and safeguards provided for in Union law or the law of Member States.

> By coupling information from registries, researchers can obtain new knowledge of great value with regard to widespread medical conditions such as cardiovascular disease, cancer and depression. On the basis of registries, research results can be enhanced, as they draw on

---

[3] Article 9(1), GDPR.

[4] Article 9.2 (a), (g), (i) & (j), GDPR.

> a larger population. Within social science, research on the basis of registries enables researchers to obtain essential knowledge about the long-term correlation of a number of social conditions such as unemployment and education with other life conditions. Research results obtained through registries provide solid, high-quality knowledge which can provide the basis for the formulation and implementation of knowledge-based policy, improve the quality of life for a number of people and improve the efficiency of social services. In order to facilitate scientific research, personal data can be processed for scientific research purposes, subject to appropriate conditions and safeguards set out in Union or Member State law.

Thus, as long as it complies with the requirement of appropriate safeguards imposed by Article 89(1) of the GDPR, the further processing of personal data for scientific research purposes will not be incompatible with the original purposes for which the data were collected and processed.[5] The further processing then constitutes a compatible and therefore lawful processing operation.[6] This means, a contrario, that the further processing of personal data for scientific research, which does not offer adequate guarantees and therefore does not comply with the requirement laid down in Article 89(1) of the GDPR, is incompatible with the original purposes for which the data were collected and processed. Being incompatible, the processing is prohibited [unlawful] and the person who nevertheless ventures in this direction would be exposed to the risk of being prosecuted, if necessary, taking into account all the circumstances and regarding the penalties provided for by the applicable national legislation.

Similarly, compliance with Article 89(1) of the GDPR allows data to be retained for longer periods of time for scientific research purposes. More precisely, the data controller may retain the data for a longer period than is necessary for the purposes for which the data were initially processed, but only insofar as, on the one hand, the data are processed exclusively for the purposes of scientific research in accordance with Article 89(1) and, on the other hand, provided that the appropriate technical and organizational measures required by the GDPR are implemented in order to guarantee the rights and freedoms of the data subject.[7]

As seen before, compliance with Article 89(1) of the GDPR also makes it possible to lift the prohibition on processing special categories of data insofar as their processing is necessary for scientific research purposes. However, the processing must, in addition, be authorized either under Union law or under the law of a Member State, and this legal basis must (1) be proportionate to the objective pursued, (2) respect the essence of the right to data protection and (3) provide for appropriate and specific measures to safeguard the fundamental rights and interests of the data subject.[8] In any event, it should be recalled that Member States may maintain or introduce additional conditions, including limitations, for the processing of genetic, biometric or health-related data.[9] It means that there is no need to collect data subjects' consent in this case.

---

[5] Article 5(1)(b), GDPR.

[6] Recital 50, GDPR.

[7] Article 5(1)(e), GDPR.

[8] Article 9(2)(j) and recitals 52 and 53, GDPR.

[9] Article 9(4), GDPR.

It remains to find an agreement on the notion of 'scientific research', the latter being open to debate. In any case, the GDPR defines research as studies or evaluations in the health field. Recital 159 states in this respect that:

> (...) For the purposes of this Regulation, the processing of personal data for scientific research purposes should be interpreted in a broad manner including for example technological development and demonstration, fundamental research, applied research and privately funded research. In addition, it should take into account the Union's objective under Article 179(1) TFEU of achieving a European Research Area. Scientific research purposes should also include studies conducted in the public interest in the area of public health. To meet the specificities of processing personal data for scientific research purposes, specific conditions should apply in particular as regards the publication or otherwise disclosure of personal data in the context of scientific research purposes. If the result of scientific research in particular in the health context gives reason for further measures in the interest of the data subject, the general rules of this Regulation should apply in view of those measures. (...)

3 Derogations to Data Subjects' Rights When Processing Personal Data for Scientific Research in the Context of Biobanks

3.1 On Derogations

Compliance with the requirement of appropriate safeguards imposed by Article 89(1) of the GDPR also makes it possible to derogate from certain rights of the data subject insofar as (1) their exercise would risk making impossible or seriously impair the achievement of a specific scientific research purpose and (2) the derogation from these rights is necessary to achieve that purpose (Article 89(2) of the GDPR).

It means that Member States may elaborate specific options in their national law in order to offer derogations to data subjects' rights vis-à-vis data controllers in the field of scientific research. This concerns the following rights: right of access (Article 15), right to rectification (Article 16), right to restriction of processing (Article 18) and right to object (Article 21). The same applies to studies for statistical purposes.

3.2 Derogation to the Information Requirements

Articles 13& 14 of the GDPR impose to data controllers to provide information to data subjects whether the data are obtained from the data subject or not.

When data are collected from data subjects, data controllers must provide them with the following minimal information (Article 13(1) of the GDPR):

(a) the identity and the contact details of the controller and, where applicable, of the controller's representative;
(b) the contact details of the data protection officer, where applicable;

(c) the purposes of the processing for which the personal data are intended as well as the legal basis for the processing;
(d) where the processing is based on point (f) of Article 6(1), the legitimate interests pursued by the controller or by a third party;
(e) the recipients or categories of recipients of the personal data, if any;
(f) where applicable, the fact that the controller intends to transfer personal data to a third country or international organisation and the existence or absence of an adequacy decision by the Commission, or in the case of transfers referred to in Article 46 or 47, or the second subparagraph of Article 49.1, reference to the appropriate or suitable safeguards and the means by which to obtain a copy of them or where they have been made available.

Article 13.2 imposes to the data controller to provide additional information when necessary to ensure fair and transparent processing. Data controllers must also provide information to data subjects when they plan to further process the personal data for a purpose other than that for which the personal data were collected.[10] Of course, providing information is not required when data subjects already have the information.[11]

But researchers may collect personal data from a third party. Indeed, as seen previously, as long as it complies with the requirement of appropriate safeguards imposed by Article 89(1) of the GDPR, the further processing of personal data for scientific research purposes will not be incompatible with the original purposes for which the data were collected and processed.[12] The further processing then constitutes a compatible and therefore lawful processing operation.[13] In this situation, data controllers are exempted from informing data subjects if the processing is subject to appropriate safeguards imposed pursuant to Article 89(1) of the GDPR and that, in two cases:[14]

(1) the provision of such information would prove impossible or would involve a disproportionate effort, in particular for processing for scientific research purposes;
(2) the obligation is likely to render impossible or seriously impair the achievement of the objectives of that processing.

In such cases, data controllers will take appropriate measures to protect the data subject's rights and freedoms and legitimate interests, including making the information publicly available.

This means that in the event of data recovery from third parties to conduct a research, it is possible not to inform individuals, if this act of information proves impossible to perform or would require disproportionate effort.

In practice, the question is to ascertain when it really is not possible to inform the data subject. GDPR recitals indicate that account must be taken of the number of

[10] Article 13.3, GDPR.

[11] Article 13.4, GDPR.

[12] Article 5.1(b), GDPR.

[13] Recital 50, GDPR.

[14] Article 14.5 (b), GDPR.

persons concerned, the age of the data and the appropriate safeguards that would be implemented.[15] For example, one can imagine that this will be the case if too many people were to be contacted without having the necessary information to do so. However, while it is conceivable that individual information may give rise to operational or financial problems, collective information, for example through the press, is easily accessible, at least in local press and through public media.

It must also be borne in mind that the impossibility or disproportionate difficulty of informing cannot be the result of erroneous or avoidable choices made by the data controller. In other words, the latter cannot rely on his poor organization or errors or negligence in the organization of the data processing. The data controller cannot deliberately organize data processing in such a way as to make it impossible or too difficult to inform the data subject. Thus, if the data controller failed to collect contact details or any other information that would have made it possible to contact data subjects, he cannot use it to justify the impossibility or disproportionate difficulty of complying with the obligation to inform data subjects. The data controller must respect the spirit of data protection and must not attempt to identify situations in which he could be exempted from informing data subjects. On the contrary, he must do everything possible to ensure that data subjects are duly informed. This is also a requirement from the principles of privacy by design and by default.

In addition, situations in which the information could make impossible or seriously impair the achievement of the objectives pursued by the data processing must also be exceptional. Such justifications must be detailed and documented and their assessment must be particularly severe because they are in total contradiction with the basic principles of data protection, including transparency and fairness principles. Again, it should be stressed that the controller must do everything possible to avoid having to evade his obligation to inform data subjects. Data controllers acting in the opposite direction would seriously breach their obligations under the GDPR.

Where the data controller intends to further process personal data for a purpose other than that for which the personal data were obtained, he shall first provide the data subject with information about that other purpose and any other relevant information to ensure fair and transparent processing.[16]

3.3 Derogation to the Duration Requirements

As seen previously, compliance with Article 89(1) of the GDPR allows data to be retained for longer periods of time for scientific research purposes. More precisely, the data controller may retain the data for a longer period than is necessary for the purposes for which the data were initially processed, but only insofar as, on the one hand, the data are processed exclusively for the purposes of scientific research in

[15] Recital 62, GDPR.

[16] Article 14.2, GDPR.

accordance with Article 89(1) and, on the other hand, provided that the appropriate technical and organizational measures required by the GDPR are implemented in order to guarantee the rights and freedoms of the data subject.[17]

This implies that data may be stored beyond the time that was necessary to achieve the research (for example, beyond the duration of a specific research project) as long as they are then stored only for use for research purposes.

Compliance with the requirement of appropriate safeguards imposed by Article 89(1) of the GDPR also makes it possible to oppose the claim of a right to oblivion or erasure on the part of the data subject when the processing of data is necessary for the purposes of scientific research insofar as this right is likely to make impossible or seriously jeopardize the achievement of the objectives pursued by the processing of personal data.[18] Similarly, data controller may not seek to oppose this right; they must, as far as possible, make its exercise possible. It is only as a last resort that they may oppose it.

The right to forget or erase is a new feature of the GDPR which allows individuals to require data controllers to delete data relating to them without having to provide justification. Exceptions are provided for, one of which is applicable to scientific research:

> for (…) scientific (…) research purposes (…) purposes in accordance with Article 89(1) in so far as the right referred to in paragraph 1 is likely to render impossible or seriously impair the achievement of the objectives of that processing.[19]

Data controllers may therefore refuse to grant a request for deletion when processing personal data for scientific research, but this is not a discretionary power: they must be able to prove that such deletion prevents the planned research or seriously compromises it. It is quite unlikely that anonymizing or deleting the data of a single person on a panel would in itself compromise a research project. On the other hand, the repetition of deletion requests from different individuals may eventually weaken the relevance of a dataset. However, it is difficult to know whether researchers could refuse to grant requests for deletion based on a certain amount of data deleted on the basis of the right to delete.

It should be recalled that even where the data controller complies with Article 89(1) of the GDPR, the data subject still has the right to object, for reasons relating to his or her particular situation, to the processing of data relating to him or her for the purposes of scientific research, unless their processing is necessary for the performance of a task in the public interest.[20] There is no derogation to this right to object in the context of research activities, but the person who requests it must give reasons for it, citing reasons relating to his or her particular situation. It is then theoretically possible for researchers to refuse to grant this type of opposition request, but only if the processing they carry out is 'necessary for the performance

[17] Article 5.1(e), GDPR.

[18] Article 17.3 and recital 65, GDPR.

[19] Article 17.3(d), GDPR.

[20] Article 21.6, GDPR.

of a mission in the public interest', which will probably be uncommon in the case of research activities.

4 Possible Appropriate Safeguards When Processing Personal Data for Scientific Research in the Field of Biobanks

The purpose limitation set forth in Article 5.1(b) of the GDPR requires that collected data should be processed for specified, explicit and legitimate purposes. Purposes for data collection in research and biobanks are predetermined, explicit and legitimate[21] and in accordance with ethical standards.

The principle of proportionality and necessity provides that only what is necessary should be collected upstream and only if it is really necessary to achieve the stated purpose.

Recital 156 explains that:

> The processing of personal data for (...) scientific (...) research purposes (...) should be subject to appropriate safeguards for the rights and freedoms of the data subject pursuant to this Regulation. Those safeguards should ensure that technical and organisational measures are in place in order to ensure, in particular, the principle of data minimisation. The further processing of personal data for (...) scientific (...) research purposes (...) is to be carried out when the controller has assessed the feasibility to fulfil those purposes by processing data which do not permit or no longer permit the identification of data subjects, provided that appropriate safeguards exist (such as, for instance, pseudonymisation of the data). Member States should provide for appropriate safeguards for the processing of personal data for (...) scientific (...) research purposes (...). Member States should be authorised to provide, under specific conditions and subject to appropriate safeguards for data subjects, specifications and derogations with regard to the information requirements and rights to rectification, to erasure, to be forgotten, to restriction of processing, to data portability, and to object when processing personal data for archiving purposes in the public interest, scientific or historical research purposes or statistical purposes. The conditions and safeguards in question may entail specific procedures for data subjects to exercise those rights if this is appropriate in the light of the purposes sought by the specific processing along with technical and organisational measures aimed at minimising the processing of personal data in pursuance of the proportionality and necessity principles. The processing of personal data for scientific purposes should also comply with other relevant legislation such as on clinical trials.

Insofar as the GDPR relaxes the regime applicable to the processing of personal data for scientific research purposes and also allows Member States to derogate under certain conditions to the data subjects' rights, the appropriate safeguards referred to in Article 89.1 of the GDPR should be understood as measures to compensate for reducing data subjects' protection as a result of relaxing the rules

[21] See recital 33, GDPR.

applicable to the processing of data for scientific research purposes as well as to compensate for the infringement of data subjects' rights.

It should be kept in mind that, in accordance with the principles of data protection by design and by default, the data controller should not seek to evade the general regime, but rather to comply with it as far as possible. Only when this is no longer possible should the implementation of the relaxation of rules and derogations from the rights of the data subject be understood.

It now remains to agree on the notion of appropriate guarantees under Article 89(1) of the GDPR. This one specifies that:

> Processing for archiving purposes in the public interest, scientific or historical research purposes or statistical purposes, shall be subject to appropriate safeguards, in accordance with this Regulation, for the rights and freedoms of the data subject. Those safeguards shall ensure that technical and organisational measures are in place in particular in order to ensure respect for the principle of data minimisation. Those measures may include pseudonymisation provided that those purposes can be fulfilled in that manner. Where those purposes can be fulfilled by further processing which does not permit or no longer permits the identification of data subjects, those purposes shall be fulfilled in that manner.

Therefore, as an example of appropriate safeguards, we can mention the implementation of specific procedures allowing data subjects to exercise their rights with regard to data relating to them which are processed within the scope of the GDPR (such as collective information campaigns instead of individual information), the adoption and implementation of technical and organisational measures to reduce data processing to a minimum (in accordance with the principles of proportionality and necessity) and compliance with the rules on clinical trials, if relevant.

However, it seems impossible to determine the kind of measures that could help securing appropriate safeguards for data subjects' rights and freedoms without first considering performing a data protection impact assessment, whether Article 35 is applicable (when the data processing is likely to result in a high risk to the rights and freedoms of data subjects) or not, knowing that, in the first case, the data controller will have to consult the data protection officer and sometimes the supervisory authority. This data protection impact assessment must provide,[22] a minima:

(a) a systematic description of the envisaged processing operations and the purposes of the processing, including, where applicable, the legitimate interest pursued by the controller;
(b) an assessment of the necessity and proportionality of the processing operations in relation to the purposes;
(c) an assessment of the risks to the rights and freedoms of data subjects; and
(d) the measures envisaged to address the risks, including safeguards, security measures and mechanisms to ensure the protection of personal data and to demonstrate compliance with the GDPR rules taking into account the rights and legitimate interests of data subjects and other persons concerned.

[22] For detailed insights in data protection imact assessment see Dara Hallinan 'Biobank Oversight and Sanctions under the General Data Protection Regulation' in this book.

The results of this impact assessment must guide the determination of the measures aiming at securing the protection of data subjects' rights and freedoms, who are concerned by the data processing carried out in biobanks' activities.

A first measure to consider is the way to implement the data minimization principle.

The principle of minimization consists in processing only the data strictly necessary for the purpose. There can be no question of collecting data that would not be directly justified by the purpose of the research. This could be the case for collecting genetic data.

The GDPR acknowledges that research activities may derogate to some extent from the rights of individuals, but the text insists that even in this case, the principle of necessity and minimization must be strictly respected:

> The conditions and guarantees in question may include specific procedures allowing the data subjects to exercise these rights if appropriate having regard to the purposes of the specific processing operation concerned, as well as technical and organisational measures aimed at reducing the processing of personal data to a minimum in accordance with the principles of proportionality and necessity.

This implies that the GDPR allows for derogations from the rights of individuals for scientific research but only on the condition that researchers strictly apply the principle of minimization upstream (collect only what is necessary and only if it is really necessary).

As a rule, the data controller should favor the use of anonymous data. If it is not possible to realize the scientific research with anonymous data, the data controller must use coded or pseudonymized data. 'Pseudonymisation' means the processing of personal data in such a manner that the personal data can no longer be attributed to a specific data subject without the use of additional information, provided that such additional information is kept separately and is subject to technical and organisational measures to ensure that the personal data are not attributed to an identified or identifiable natural person (Article 4.5 of the GDPR).

In a way, pseudonymised data are those that can be attributed to a natural person by using additional information (in this sense, see recital 26), such as a conversion table.

Clearly, the GDPR encourages researchers to process at least pseudonymised data (see supra Article 89.1 of the GDPR).

Pseudonymisation is favoured by the GDPR as it is likely to reduce the risks for data subjects and to help data controllers and processors to fulfil their data protection obligations. However, the use of pseudonymisation should not be understood as being exclusive of other data protection measures.[23] In other words, pseudonymization does not exempt from compliance with the other obligations imposed by the GDPR, and its implementation does not imply that no further action should be taken.

Recital 29 adds that:

[23] See recital 28, GDPR.

> In order to create incentives to apply pseudonymisation when processing personal data, measures of pseudonymisation should, whilst allowing general analysis, be possible within the same controller when that controller has taken technical and organisational measures necessary to ensure, for the processing concerned, that this Regulation is implemented, and that additional information for attributing the personal data to a specific data subject is kept separately. The controller processing the personal data should indicate the authorised persons within the same controller.

Pseudonymisation is a security measure promoted by the GDPR, but it should not be confused with anonymisation (the process of making it impossible to identify individuals from the data). Pseudonymized data remain subject to the application of the GDPR, unlike anonymized data, which are excluded.

Anonymization could be a good way to use data secondarily without having to collect new consent. However, in the context of scientific research, it is necessary to be able to identify the person in order to enrich the data with the results of the new research.

Pseudonymization raises several issues: when should it happen (after data collection or before the further processing), who may have access to the pseudonymization keys, what about de-pseudonymization, who should realize the pseudonymization (a trusted third party especially when they are several sources from which the data are collected?), etc.

If it is not possible to use coded or pseudonymized data, the data controller may, to some extent, use non-coded or non-pseudonymized data.

Another measure consists in considering the appointment of a data protection officer knowing that the latter is mandatory where data controller's core activities consist of processing on a large scale of special categories of personal data such as genetic data or data concerning health, by instance.

A third measure to consider consists of adequately fill in the record of processing activities on basis of the data protection impact assessment. By instance, the record should contain the justification to process pseudonymized data or not, the reasons to restrict data subjects' rights when they are likely to render impossible or seriously impair the achievement of the specific purposes, and the impact assessment itself. The information to be provided to data subjects should also be attached to the record.

A fourth measure that could help securing the protection of the data subjects' rights and freedoms regarding the data processing carried out in the framework of biobanks activities consists in studying the way to implement mechanisms that could offer data subjects with a general or individual feedback on the results of the scientific research (by way of information campaigns notably through the medias), taking into account all the circumstances and the result of the data protection impact assessment.

A fifth measure could consist of requiring specific professional accreditation to the persons involved in the processing of personal data for scientific research activities and to the persons in charge of supervising their activities.

A sixth measure could consist in improving procedures for answering data subjects' requests and, considering the scale of the biobank and its impact on data subjects' rights and freedoms, creating a supervisory body in charge of deliberating on the fundamental options of the biobank functioning.

A seventh measure could consist in confirming the data subject's right to refuse to participate to the research and the right to withdraw at any time without justification.[24]

Finally, certification or even the creation of a specific Code of conduct could help biobanks in uniformizing their practices in the field of data protection, without forgetting to be prepared to be audited by the data protection supervisory authority.

5 Concluding Reflections

The GDPR defines a very broad scope for scientific research. Kart Pormeister[25] considers that the exemptions for the processing of sensitive data for research purposes allow the processing of data without sufficient guarantees since the exemptions refer to national legislation or European Union regulations. This is the case for the important public interest,[26] large population biobanks commonly fall within this framework, and scientific research.[27]

In fact, it seems that the GDPR has confirmed certain practices that previously existed in the field and removed the vagueness that could exist in the eyes of researchers who usually processed health data according to national regulations (very variable between states).

Guidelines were proposed in 2009 by the OECD[28] that set out a number of principles to guide biobanks for genetic research. They collect particularly sensitive samples and data since genetic data are subject to a special regime in some European countries, particularly in France. These recommendations are not binding but serve as a reference in OECD countries (Europe, North America and Asia), which have very different national regulations.

It is interesting to reconcile what these guidelines say about consent and purpose change with the provisions of the GDPR. In that regard, review of addressing the purpose, specification, consent, rules for the secondary use of personal data and the changing of purpose, and data protection are of importance.

First, regarding the purpose it is clear that for the OECD, the purpose of biobanks in human genetics is to stimulate research for the advancement of scientific knowledge, while respecting the fundamental rights and privacy of participants. Operators must comply with documented and transparent procedures. Collective and general

---

[24] See Article 15.4 of recommendation CM/Rec(2019)2 of the Committee of Ministers on protection of data related to health, adopted on 27 March 2019.

[25] Pormeister (2017), pp. 137–146.

[26] Article 9(2)(g), GDPR.

[27] Art 9(2)(j), GDPR.

[28] OECD 2009 Guidelines for Human Biobanks and Genetic Research Databases.

research results should be published. The purpose of the biobank, both now and in the foreseeable future, must be clearly formulated and communicated.

These goals do not differ from those defined for research in the GDPR.

Second, consent. Free and informed consent is provided for in paragraph 4b. However, if consent cannot be obtained, it is the authorization of the decision-maker, an appropriate substitute, or the exemption granted by an ethics committee or a competent authority in accordance with the legal framework applicable to the research that allows the bank to be implemented.

Consent does not appear to be an essential prerequisite for the establishment of biobanks for the OECD, which gives priority to facilitating research with biobanks, while the rights of the subjects involved are secondary and in accordance with national legislation.

For its part, the GDPR, while laying down the principle of consent as means to process health and genetic data, organizes limited conditions under which the subject's consent is not sought.

Thirdly, the secondary use of personal data and the changing of purpose. Some collections and associated data can be used for large-scale epidemiological or genetic studies of samples and data from different collection modes and locations are consolidated in a new database. Article 3.1 sets out procedures for monitoring the terms of consent. If broad general consent has been given at the time of initial collection, appropriate information mechanisms are proposed. But if the research topics were impossible to predict, the purpose is not specified at the time of collection, and in this case Article 4.6 requires additional safeguards to ensure the protection of participants.

When additional data are associated from personal medical records, Article 5.1 defines access procedures and use. In principle, specific consent is obtained to access the medical file compiled outside the collection, unless an exemption is given by an ethics committee or a competent authority.

It is clear that the OECD greatly facilitates secondary use and exchanges through its guidelines, just as the GDPR goes very far in recognizing secondary use, in all circumstances, as a compatible lawful processing.

Finally, data protection. Article 6.1 designates a data protection and privacy officer. Specific provisions are provided for the possibility of withholding certain data that would make secondary identification possible (Article 6.3) or the separation of data allowing direct identification of a subject from other data, in particular genotypic data.

Appropriate measures for the protection of privacy and confidentiality are proposed in Article 6.5: secure storage, data encryption or encryption, sample and data access logs, infrastructure to prevent unauthorized access.

Access to the bank must be in accordance with the consent given, requests must be accompanied by a scientifically and ethically appropriate research plan (Article 7B) Third party access for purposes other than research is prohibited (Article 7F). An agreement organizes access, users sign confidentiality (Article 7.5) or transfer (Article 7.6) agreements.

Article 14 of the GDPR provides for the information to be given where the data have not been obtained from the data subject: it concerns the possibility of secondary use and the possible transfer of data. This information is likely to enable the person, at the time of obtaining initial consent, to object to subsequent use or transfer. Clear and fair advance information should be provided.

The transfer of data is authorised by Article 46 of the GDPR with appropriate safeguards, including binding corporate rules,[29] an approved code of conduct[30] or a certification mechanism.[31]

References

2009 Guidelines for Human Biobanks and Genetic Research Databases

Article 29 Data Protection Working Party. Guidelines on consent under Regulation 2016/679. WP 259 rev.01

Article 29 Data Protection Working Party. Guidelines on Data Protection Officers ('DPOs'). WP 243 rev.01

Article 29 Data Protection Working Party. Guidelines on Data Protection Impact Assessment (DPIA) and determining whether processing is "likely to result in a high risk" for the purposes of Regulation 2016/679. WP 248 rev.01

Article 29 Data Protection Working Party. Guidelines on the right to data portability. 13 December 2016 & revised on 5 April 2017. WP 242 rev.01

Article 29 Data Protection Working Party. Guidelines on transparency under Regulation 2016/679. 29 November 2017 & revised on 11 April 2018. WP 260 rev.01

Article 29 Data Protection Working Party. Opinion 03/2013 on purpose limitation. WP 203

Article 29 Data Protection Working Party. Opinion 05/2014 on Anonymisation Techniques. WP 216

Article 29 Data Protection Working Party. Opinion 10/2004 on More Harmonised Information Provisions. WP 100

Article 29 Data Protection Working Party. Opinion 15/2011 on the definition of consent. WP 187

Article 29 Data Protection Working Party. Opinion 4/2007 on the concept of personal data. WP 136

Council of Europe Recommendation CM/Rec (2019) 2 of the Committee of Ministers on protection of data related to health, adopted on 27 March 2019

de Terwangne C, Degrave E, Dusollier S, Queck R (dir.) (2018) Law, norms and freedoms in cyberspace. Droit, normes et libertés dans le cybermonde. Liber Amicorum Yves Poullet. Larcier, Bruxelles. Collection du CRIDS

Herveg J (2018a) Data protection and Biobanks in 2018. Eur J Health Law:515–536

Herveg J (2018b) Réflexions autour de la protection des données et des vulnérabilités. In: Jacquemin H, Nihoul M (coord.) Vulnérabilités et droits dans l'environnement numérique. Larcier, Buxelles. Collection de la Faculté de droit de l'UNamur, pp 333–392

Herveg J, Van Gyseghem JM (2018) L'impact du Règlement général sur la protection des données dans le secteur de la santé. In: Rosier K, de Terwangne C (coord.) Le Règlement général sur la protection des données (RGPD/GDPR). Analyse approfondie. Larcier, Bruxelles. Collection du CRIDS, pp 703–762

Modernised Convention for the protection of individuals with regard to automatic processing of personal data (Treaty n° 108+)

Pormeister K (2017) Genetic data and the research exemption: is the GDPR going too far? Int Data Priv Law 7(2):pp. 137–146

[29] Article 47, GDPR.

[30] Article 40, GDPR.

[31] Article 42, GDPR.

Biobank Oversight and Sanctions Under the General Data Protection Regulation

Dara Hallinan

Abstract This contribution offers an insight into the function and problems of the oversight and sanctions mechanisms outlined in the General Data Protection Regulation as they relate to the biobanking context. These mechanisms might be considered as meta-mechanisms—mechanisms relating to, but not consisting of, substantive legal principles—functioning in tandem to ensure biobank compliance with data protection principles. Each of the mechanisms outlines, on paper at least, comprehensive and impressive compliance architecture—both expanding on their capacity in relation to Directive 95/46. Accordingly, each mechanism looks likely to have a significant and lasting impact on biobanks and biobanking. Despite this comprehensiveness, however, the mechanisms are not immune from critique. Problems appear regarding the standard of protection provided for research subject rights, regarding the disproportionate impact on legitimate interests tied up with the biobanking process—particularly genomic research interests—and regarding their practical implementability in biobanking.

1 Introduction

The oversight and sanction mechanisms are two of the most significant mechanisms in the General Data Protection Regulation (GDPR).[1] Evidence for this might be argued to be found in the extreme build up in data protection compliance activities

[1] European Parliament and Council Regulation (EU) 2016/679 *on the protection of natural persons with regard to the processing of personal data and on the free movement of such data, and repealing Directive 95/46/EC (General Data Protection Regulation).* O.J. L119/1 (2016). This contribution asserts the applicability of the GDPR to biobanking encompasses all processing of biological samples, all associated genomic, health and lifestyle data as well as any individual level research results. See, for further clarification: Hallinan (2018), pp. 263–295; Hallinan and De Hert (2016), pp. 119–139.

D. Hallinan (✉)
FIZ Karlsruhe – Leibniz-Institut für Informationsinfrastruktur, Karlsruhe, Germany
e-mail: dara.hallinan@fiz-karlsruhe.de

S. Slokenberga et al. (eds.), *GDPR and Biobanking*, Law, Governance and Technology Series 43, https://doi.org/10.1007/978-3-030-49388-2_8

prior, and subsequent, to the GDPR coming into force in early 2016 and applying from early 2018—including in the biobanking context. Some might argue this build-up of activity is due to the substantive novelty of the GDPR.[2] Such arguments, however, are swiftly dismissed with reference to the substantive similarity of the GDPR to its forerunner—Directive 95/46. A much more likely explanation is the increase in data controller compliance activities as a consequence of the fear of oversight potentially leading to novel, and crippling, sanctions.[3]

The astute reader might wonder why these two separate mechanisms fall within one contribution. The answer is relatively straightforward: they go together like salt and pepper. The oversight mechanism functions as the mechanism permitting the generation of information about compliance with the GDPR as well as information about violations of the GDPR. The sanctions mechanism then functions as the dissuasive threat pushing data processing actors towards compliance, which becomes reality—usually—on the back of the oversight mechanism's violation-information generation capacity. The two systems function in tandem in the service of compliance.

The oversight and sanctions mechanisms do not directly define the boundaries of the public interest in biobanking under the GDPR, how the concept relates to other rights and interests or to the conditions under which processing in its service is permissible. Nevertheless, they are indirectly determinative of the concept in two ways. First: as meta-systems ensuring compliance with substantive principles of the GDPR, they are key to maintaining the boundaries, and conditions associated with action in, the public interest in biobanking under the GDPR. Second: the emphasis placed on oversight and sanctions is indicative of the importance the legislator attaches to the need to police and control the boundaries and conditions of the public interest under the GDPR generally.

With the above in mind, this contribution is structured as follows. To start, the chapter provides a descriptive analysis of the function of the oversight and sanctions mechanisms in relation to biobanking under the GDPR (Sects. 2 and 3, respectively). Subsequently, and building on the descriptive analysis, the chapter engages in a critical analysis of the problems raised by the mechanisms. This critical analysis identifies, and considers the severity of, problems from three perspectives: mechanisms' negative impacts on research subject rights; mechanisms' disproportionate impacts on research interests; and mechanisms' practical implementability in the biobanking context (Sect. 4).

[2] See, for example: Kuner (2012), pp. 1–2.

[3] There remains little empirical study of GDPR compliance activity. However, early work very much suggests sanctions are a driving factor in compliance efforts. See: Martin et al. (2019).

2 Biobank Oversight Under the GDPR

2.1 *Introduction*

The GDPR foresees an extensive, and complex, oversight mechanism relevant to biobanking. This oversight mechanism might reasonably be considered as consisting of four forms—or stages—of oversight: *ex ante* assessment; prior notification and approval; ongoing oversight; and finally, general oversight. The oversight system under the GDPR consists of several oversight bodies. These include those specifically elaborated by the GDPR as well as national bodies such as research ethics committees (REC) and other *sui generis* bodies—for example data access committees. Accordingly, this section will proceed by considering how each of the four forms of oversight foreseen in the GDPR function, before finally considering how the key oversight actors relate to each other.

2.2 *Ex Ante Assessment Under the GDPR*

Ex ante assessment requires a biobank, prior to engaging in processing, to conduct a Data Protection Impact Assessment (DPIA).[4]

A DPIA is not a general obligation in the GDPR. It will usually, however, be an obligation for biobanks. Article 35(3)(b) clarifies a DPIA will always be required whenever processing includes: 'processing on a large scale of special categories of data'. All personal data processed in biobanking will, as clarified by the Article 29 Working Party, qualify as sensitive personal data by virtue of its planned integration into data driven genomic research.[5] In turn, it seems reasonable that the scale of most biobank projects—even relatively small biobank projects—will already qualify as large scale processing of such personal data.

The base rationale behind a DPIA is the surfacing of information concerning the risks to data subjects' rights and thus to provide an information-base from which to mitigate these risks before processing begins.[6] Where the DPIA obligation is applicable, each aspect of biobank processing falling under the scope of the GDPR must be subject to a DPIA. It is nevertheless possible, however, for one DPIA, to cover 'a

[4] The obligation is outlined in Article 35 of the GDPR. It is true that a DPIA is not oversight in the traditional sense—i.e. an external party checking and confirming behaviour corresponding to some standard. It is, however, so key to the information production process supporting subsequent forms of oversight it might, practically, be regarded as an aspect of oversight.

[5] The Article 29 Working Party observe that all data involved in 'medical research using big data'—such as genomic research—will qualify as data concerning health and therefore as sensitive personal data under Article 9(1) of the GDPR. Article 29 Working Party (2015), p. 3.

[6] See, for example: Van Dijk et al. (2016), p. 289. For more on concrete data subject rights outlined in the GDPR relevant in the biobanking context, please see Ciara Staunton's contribution 'Individual rights in biobank research under the GDPR'.

set of similar processing operations that present similar high risks'.[7] It is logical to conclude that the GDPR permits multiple biobanking operations—even potentially by multiple different biobanks or external researchers—to be subsumed under one single DPIA.

Whilst the GDPR is scant on the procedural and substantive specifics of a DPIA, certain framework conditions are outlined.[8] In particular, the biobank conducting the DPIA must describe processing operations, describe the interests on which the processing is based—where relevant—provide an assessment of the necessity and proportionality of planned processing, offer an assessment of the scale of risks to data subjects and offer an elaboration of steps taken to minimise identified risks. In certain cases—although when exactly remains unclear—a biobank must also seek 'the views of data subjects'.[9] Finally, if any significant change to the proposed processing occurs, the biobanking must go back and review the continued relevance of the original DPIA.[10]

2.3 Prior Notification and Approval Under the GDPR

Prior notification and approval follows, chronologically and legally, from *ex ante* assessment.[11] The prior notification and approval process will tend to involve two types of body under the GDPR. One type of body is specifically elaborated by the GDPR: the Data Protection Authority (DPA).[12] The other type of body will be elaborated by EU Member States following from their obligations to ensure effective safeguards in scientific research under the GDPR.[13] These national bodies will often—although not always, or necessarily—be Research Ethics Committees (RECs).

[7] See Article 35(1) GDPR.

[8] See Articles 35(7)(a)-(d) for these conditions.

[9] See Article 35(9) GDPR.

[10] See Article 35(11) GDPR.

[11] See Article 36 of the GDPR.

[12] DPAs are the national authorities tasked with ensuring compliance with data protection law under the GDPR. They are given life and legal base in Article 51(1) of the GDPR. This clarifies that each State must 'provide for one or more independent public authorities'. Whilst being national authorities, DPAs retain independence from national governments. Article 52(1) of the GDPR states: 'Each supervisory authority shall act with complete independence in performing its tasks and exercising its powers in accordance with this Regulation.'

When biobanking takes place in more than one EU Member State, multiple DPAs may be relevant. In this case, DPAs will collaborate under a specific set of rules. Article 56(1) requires one authority to be designated: 'lead supervisory authority'. This authority will be: 'the supervisory authority of the main establishment or of the single establishment of the controller'. See also: Article 29 Working Party (2016).

[13] See the obligation, in Article 89(1) GDPR, for scientific research to be 'subject to appropriate safeguards, in accordance with this Regulation, for the rights and freedoms of the data subject.' See

DPA prior notification and approval is not always obligatory. In fact, it only becomes relevant in two situations. First: Article 36(1) clarifies that advance approval must only be sought whenever a DPIA process: 'indicates that the processing would result in a high risk in the absence of measures taken by the controller to mitigate the risk'. Significantly, the eventual decision as to whether the prerequisites for notification and approval are fulfilled thus lies, as De Hert and Papakonstantinou observe, with the biobank—although, as will be seen later, in Sect. 2.4, the rationale of this decision is subject to *ex post* checking and verification for compliance with the GDPR.[14] Second: where EU Member States have explicitly clarified that biobanks must consult with the DPA prior to engaging in processing.[15]

When the DPIA has shown a high residual risk or when prior consultation with the DPA is explicitly foreseen in EU Member State law, the biobank must engage in the DPA prior approval process. This process involves the provision to the DPA of all relevant information concerning the planned processing activities. This information will include, in particular, information as to how data protection responsibilities—for example the protection of data subject rights—are distributed between relevant actors, information concerning the 'purposes and means' of processing, information concerning safeguards, DPIA documentation as well as any information specifically requested by the DPA.[16]

Subsequent to DPA checks of information provided, the DPA will then issue the biobank with a decision on the proposed processing. This decision should be available within eight weeks from the start of the process.[17] The decision may take three forms: first, if processing is unproblematic, the DPA will allow it, subject to the conditions of the DPIA, to go ahead; second, if there are specific problematic aspects of processing identified, the DPA will allow it to go ahead only subject to certain conditions;[18] and finally, if processing is irretrievably problematic, the DPA will forbid it in its entirety.[19]

National bodies' prior notification and approval will also not always be necessary. This will depend on whether advance oversight by national bodies constitutes a prerequisite under Member State law. It is not necessarily the case that all Member States require such notification or approval for all, or indeed any, biobanking activity under the GDPR—there is no such comprehensive obligation in the German system, for example.[20] It will subsequently depend on whether national bodies' oversight is required for a specific type of processing. In the UK, for example,

also the subsequent chapters in part III of this book on the implementation of Article 89 by EU Member States.

[14] De Hert and Papkonstantinou (2016), p. 192.

[15] See Article 36(5) GDPR.

[16] See Article 36(3)(a)–(e) for lists of types of information to be provided. Article 36(1)(f) includes an open requirement to provide the DPA with 'any other information requested'.

[17] See Article 36(2) GDPR.

[18] See Article 58(2)(d) GDPR.

[19] See Article 58(2)(f) GDPR.

[20] Hallinan (2018), p. 191.

certain biobank activity may be exempted from specific REC oversight under a principle of generic oversight: 'NHS RECs can give generic ethical approval for a research tissue bank's arrangements for collection, storage and release of tissue'.[21]

Where national bodies' prior notification and oversight is necessary, the process and consequences of oversight will depend on the conditions of the relevant body's constitution and the powers bestowed on that body by national law. For example, whilst some REC prior notification and approval mechanisms will require REC approval before biobanking activity can go ahead, this is not universally the case. This is not the case, for example, in relation to the advance oversight procedures of the REC of the Estonian Biobank. According to Article 29(1) of the Estonian Human Genes Research Act: '[the advance] assessment of the Ethics Committee is not binding [in terms of whether processing proceeds]'.[22]

2.4 *Ongoing Oversight Under the GDPR*

Ongoing oversight—oversight which takes place during processing activity—in the GDPR is carried out by three different types of bodies. Two of these types of bodies are specifically elaborated by the GDPR: the DPA; and the Data Protection Officer (DPO).[23] The final type of body will be—as above—elaborated by EU Member States following from their obligations to ensure effective safeguards in scientific research under the GDPR.[24] As above, these bodies will often—although not always, or necessarily—be Research Ethics Committees.

[21] https://www.hta.gov.uk/policies/information-research-tissue-banks. Accessed 4 Mar 2019.

[22] Riigikogu RT I 2000 104 685 *Human Genes Research Act* (2000), Article 29(1). Unofficial English translation available at: https://www.riigiteataja.ee/en/eli/531102013003/consolide. Accessed 4 Mar 2019.

[23] Ongoing oversight is outlined in Articles 39, 57 and 58 of the GDPR. A DPO is an employee of a data controller—or data processor—discussed in chapter IV, section 4, of the GDPR. Despite being an employee, the DPO is required by the GDPR to be allowed to act independently of the interests of their employer. Article 38(3) clarifies: 'The controller and processor shall ensure that the data protection officer does not receive any instructions regarding the exercise of those tasks. He or she shall not be dismissed or penalised by the controller or the processor for performing his tasks. The data protection officer shall directly report to the highest management level of the controller or the processor.' It is true that DPOs are not a mandatory requirement for all data controllers and processors in the GDPR. However, Article 37(1)(c) clarifies that they are obligatory whenever: 'the core activities of the controller…consist of processing on a large scale of special categories of data'. As discussed above, in Sect. 2.2, in relation to the DPIA obligation, this description will cover much biobanking activity. The obligation to employ a DPO may sound like an arduous and expensive one for many biobanking actors. In this regard, it should be noted, perhaps with a sigh of relief, that Article 37(2) allows one DPO to be appointed to represent multiple biobanking actors. The Article specifically allows: '[a] group of undertakings [to] appoint a single data protection officer'.

[24] See Article 89(1) GDPR.

DPAs, in principle, are under no strict requirement to engage in oversight of all, or any particular, biobanking activity. Nevertheless, the GDPR empowers them to engage in specific and detailed oversight of any biobanking activity they see fit.[25] Provided the processing falls within the material scope of the GDPR, there is no limitation to the type of biobank processing—or indeed any other type of data processing—which falls within the scope of this form of DPA oversight. There is, however, little material guidance on how the process of ongoing DPA oversight under the GDPR should look.

If a DPA decides to engage in oversight of biobank activity, the GDPR provides the DPA with investigative powers.[26] These powers include the ability to order the biobanking actor 'to provide any information [the DPA] requires for the performance of its tasks'.[27] If, in the course of an investigation, problems are identified, the DPA is endowed with corrective powers. These powers are wide ranging.[28] They include, for example, the power to order the biobanking actor to bring processing into line with the GDPR.[29] The DPA also has administrative sanctioning powers—these will be discussed later, in Sect. 3.3.

DPOs have a dual function in ongoing oversight. First, the DPO has an advisory role in relation to the biobanking actor. This role requires the DPO to 'inform and advise the…[biobanking actor] of their obligations pursuant to…[the] Regulation and…other…data protection provisions'.[30] Second, the DPO must engage in activities normally associated with external oversight bodies and monitor a biobanking actor's compliance with the GDPR. In this regard, the DPO must: 'monitor compliance with this Regulation, with other Union or Member State data protection provisions and with the policies of the [biobanking actor]'.[31]

The biobanking actor is obliged to provide the DPO with all relevant support in the conduct of their oversight activities. This obligation encompasses the obligation to provide the DPO with all necessary financial and administrative support and with informational resources and access privileges.[32] The DPO has no explicit power to remedy any problems they identify. Significantly, the extent to which the DPO is obliged to initiate coordination and collaboration with external authorities—in particular DPAs—in the case of regulatory breach remains unclear.[33]

---

[25] This power is outlined in Article 57(1)(a) GDPR, which states a DPA has the power to: 'monitor and enforce the application of this Regulation'.

[26] These are outlined under Article 58(1) GDPR.

[27] See Article 58(1)(a) GDPR.

[28] See, for example, Article 58(2) GDPR.

[29] See Article 58(2)(d) GDPR.

[30] See Article 39(1)(a) GDPR.

[31] See Article 39(1)(b) GDPR.

[32] See Article 38(2) GDPR.

[33] See, for example, Bergt (2018a). Art. 39, paras 17–20. The consequences of the resolution of this issue are likely to be significant for the role of the DPO in biobanking. In the case the DPO is eventually found to have no DPA collaboration obligation, it seems likely the DPO will become more trusted as a point of data protection reference within biobanks but will also become less

National bodies will have varied capacities in relation to ongoing oversight. As above, this variation will result from bodies' differing constitution and powers under their respective Member States' laws. As above, it is not always the case that Member States will have chosen to require national bodies' ongoing oversight of biobank activity. Even in cases in which they have, it will not always be the case that the relevant national bodies will have the power to conduct ongoing oversight. For example, the Estonian Human Genes Research Act does not task the Estonian Biobank's REC with any form of ongoing oversight.[34]

The process and consequences of national body ongoing oversight will also depend on the conditions of constitution and powers of the national body in the Member State law in question. Most significantly, these conditions and powers will define whether the national body has pro-active oversight capacities comparable to DPAs—or whether they may only react to changes in processing—when they must be consulted in the case of changes in a processing operation and the consequences of their decisions. For example, whilst the UK Human Tissue Act—in Part 2 and Schedule 2—endows the Human Tissue Authority with pro-active oversight capacity, Norwegian law only empowers RECs to be consulted subsequent to changes in biobank processing operations.[35]

2.5 General Oversight Under the GDPR

As opposed to the ongoing oversight process, the general oversight process concerns biobanking activity generally rather than specific biobanking activity.[36] The GDPR foresees participation of two types of oversight body: the DPA; and the European Data Protection Board (EDPB).[37]

DPAs are under no obligation to engage in general oversight. They, however, have the option to engage in general oversight and have the power to 'monitor relevant developments, insofar as they have an impact on the protection of personal data, in particular the development of information and communication

trusted by external actors. If the DPO is found to have DPA collaboration obligations, it seems likely the DPO will be less trusted by biobanks as a point of data protection reference but will become more trusted by external entities.

[34] Riigikogu RT I 2000 104 685 *Human Genes Research Act* (2000), Article 29. Unofficial English translation available at: https://www.riigiteataja.ee/en/eli/531102013003/consolide. Accessed 4 Mar 2019.

[35] UK Parliament *Human Tissue Act 2004* (2004), Part 2 and Schedule 2. http://www.legislation.gov.uk/ukpga/2004/30/introduction. Accessed 4 Mar 2019; Storting no. 44 *Act on Medical and Health Research* (2008), Article 11. Unofficial English translation available at: http://www.ub.uio.no/ujur/ulovdata/lov-20080620-044-eng.pdf. Accessed 4 Mar 2019.

[36] The general oversight process is elaborated in Articles 57 and 70 GDPR.

[37] The EDPB is the EU body tasked with providing interpretation and adaptation of the GDPR to ensure the ongoing EU level harmony and suitability of the GDPR. Its composition and function is discussed extensively in Chapter VII, section 3 GDPR.

technologies'.[38] DPAs thus have the power to engage in oversight of biobanking generally, or of specific types of processing activity or technological development which partially overlap with biobanking. As far as DPA interpretations are legal, DPAs may enforce them—see Sect. 3.3, below.

The EDPB also has discretion to engage in general oversight. The key difference between DPA and EDPB oversight is that EDPB oversight operates at EU level. Article 70(1)(e) permits the Board to: '[examine], on its own initiative, on request of [its] members, or...the Commission, any question covering the application of [the] Regulation'. The result will be guidelines or recommendations.[39] These guidelines are technically non-binding. However, they may be difficult for biobanking actors to ignore. As De Hert and Papakonstantinou observe, 'this is a: strong...Board...capable of deciding...and enforcing...opinions'.[40]

2.6 *The Interplay of Actors in the GDPR Biobank Oversight Ecosystem*

As discussed in the previous sections, oversight under the GDPR consists of a mix of both oversight bodies constituted by the GDPR—most importantly DPAs—as well as national oversight bodies served with discharging EU Member States obligations under the GDPR.[41] These national bodies show considerable variation across Europe in terms of form, function and legal constitution. The most important actors are RECs—common across Europe—although these may be joined by *sui generis* legally and non-legally constituted actors—for example data access committees—in relation to specific biobanking activities in specific Member States.[42]

[38] See Article 57(1)(i) GDPR.

[39] See also Article 70(1)(e) GDPR.

[40] De Hert and Papkonstantinou (2016), p. 193. Whilst the EDPB—and its forerunner the Article 29 Working Party—have not yet adopted any guidance specifically targeted to biobanking, they have adopted numerous opinions and guidance documents touching aspects of the applicability of data protection law to biobanking. See, for example, the relevant opinions in the references section of this contribution. Whilst these documents are not always used or followed in Court of Justice of the European Union case law on data protection, they may nevertheless be regarded as significant pieces of guidance on EU data protection law. See their use in, for example: Wachter and Mittelstadt (2019), p. 25. There are three reasons for this significance. First: the EDPB is populated by each of the national DPAs—i.e. the bodies tasked with interpreting and applying the GDPR at national level. Second: the EDPB itself has been given broad powers in interpreting and applying the Regulation to ensure EU level harmony. These powers bolster the normative power of anything the Board says, regardless of its format. Third: EDPB opinions can be issued much faster and with much greater flexibility than CJEU case-law. Accordingly, they cover many phenomena in relation to which CJEU jurisprudence is silent.

[41] See Article 89(1) GDPR.

[42] Expert Group on Dealing with Ethical and Regulatory Challenges of International Biobank Research (2012), p. 43.

Given the lack of homogeneity of national oversight actors across the EU, it is hard to monolithically assert the relationship between actors in the biobank oversight ecosystem under the GDPR.[43] Nevertheless, certain observations might be made.

In the first instance, DPAs will usually enjoy higher legal status than other oversight bodies. This results from their express creation as executive authorities in EU law.[44] As EU law takes precedence over national law, this means DPAs sit above other nationally constituted—by law or otherwise—biobank supervisory authorities in the legal hierarchy.[45] For example, the UK DPA occupies a higher legal status than the UK Human Tissue Authority.[46] The exception to this legal superiority concerns RECs in biobanks linked to clinical trials. Here, the EU Clinical Trials Regulation—for example under Article 4—elevates RECs to the status of EU level oversight bodies.[47]

This hierarchical relationship is normatively significant regarding oversight decisions. Where the hierarchical relationship is in place, if a decision by a DPA concerning problematic aspects of biobank processing contradicts that of another body, the DPA's decision will technically take precedence. Generally, however, it is not the case that a DPA's confirmation that processing is acceptable will overrule another body's decision that processing is problematic. Here, a cumulative logic will apply. For example, if a German DPA finds a biobanking actor's proposed processing acceptable, yet an REC—under Article 15(1) of the Musterberufsordnung für Ärzte—disagrees, processing could not go ahead.[48]

[43] In terms of RECs: it should be noted that the form, precise oversight function and legal status of RECs will also vary between EU Member States. For example, in Estonia, they are legally obliged to play a role in the oversight of the Estonian biobank project—although not technically in oversight of other biobanks. Riigikogu *Human Genes Research Act* (2000), Art. 29. Unofficial English translation: https://www.riigiteataja.ee/en/eli/531102013003/consolide. Accessed 4 Mar 2019. In the UK, their legal status in relation to biobanking is much more indirect—secured through institution requirements and executive agency decisions. In terms of other types of biobank oversight actors: in certain Member States, RECs are joined by other, *sui generis* bodies in biobank oversight. In the UK, for example, the Human Tissue Authority—the executive authority responsible for the oversight of the Human Tissue Act—plays a significant role. UK Parliament *Human Tissue Act 2004* (2004), Arts. 13–15. http://www.legislation.gov.uk/ukpga/2004/30/introduction. Accessed 4 Mar 2019.

[44] Indeed, their legitimacy stems not only under the GDPR but also directly—under Article 8—from the Charter of Fundamental Rights of the European Union. European Union *Charter of Fundamental Rights of the European Union*. O.J. C 326/02 (2012), Article 8.

[45] It does, however, seem inevitable that hard cases will emerge in which national oversight entities, constituted by law as safeguards under Article 89(1) GDPR and are better placed than DPAs—in terms of proximity to the object of biobanking oversight as well as in terms of expertise. In such cases, attempts to define hierarchical relationships will likely be difficult and counter-productive.

[46] UK Parliament *Human Tissue Act 2004* (2004), Arts. 13–15. http://www.legislation.gov.uk/ukpga/2004/30/introduction. Accessed 4 Mar 2019.

[47] European Parliament and Council Regulation (EU) No 536/2014 *on clinical trials on medicinal products for human use, and repealing Directive 2001/20/EC*. O.J. L 158 (2014), Article 4.

[48] Bundesärztekammer *Musterberufsordnung für die in Deutschland tätigen Ärztinnen und Ärzte* (1997 (updated 2018)), Article 15(1). https://www.bundesaerztekammer.de/fileadmin/user_upload/downloads/pdf-Ordner/MBO/MBO-AE.pdf. Accessed 4 Mar 2019.

There will be overlap in the oversight tasks performed by DPAs and those performed by other national bodies. This overlap stems, in the first instance, from the broad functionality already taken on by certain biobank oversight bodies. RECs, for example, have traditionally—and will continue to under the GDPR—considered data privacy issues.[49] In turn, in many Member States, the overlap will be exacerbated by the lack of formal clarification of the distribution of oversight tasks among relevant oversight bodies. This duplication of roles may, from a research perspective, be seen as somewhat frustrating. It is not, however, solely a negative—see Sect. 4.3, below, for a discussion of advantages.

How task duplication and division between DPAs and other oversight bodies will precisely function will be context dependent. Nevertheless, it seems likely DPAs will tend toward restraint in scope and means of oversight. This has been documented—at least in the UK context—by Gibbons under Directive 95/46.[50] There seems little reason to think this should change under the GDPR. A number of reasons for this might be proposed. Two seem highly likely: the inaccessible nature—to the layperson at least—of genomic research and limited DPA staff expertise; and the political nature of DPAs and their aversion from interfering in normatively legitimate and publicly supported research—more in Sect. 4.3, below.

One aspect of the oversight relationship between DPAs and other oversight bodies—particularly RECs—under the GDPR is particularly interesting. Anecdotally, under Directive 95/46, many RECs had taken to dealing with data privacy issues by requiring DPA authorizations from biobanks and researchers. Under the GDPR, there is no longer any requirement to gain prior DPA authorisation. Accordingly, this approach will no longer automatically function, and a new approach will need to be sought. In certain cases where no DPA oversight is required, an informal relationship between DPAs, biobanks and genomic researchers, and RECs may develop. In other cases, RECs will simply need to internalise the advance data privacy oversight process themselves.

3 Biobank Sanctions Under the GDPR

3.1 Introduction

In the case that a biobanking actor infringes the substantive principles outlined in the GDPR, two different types of sanctions are envisaged: liability and compensation sanctions; and administrative sanctions. The sanctions mechanism under the

[49] Even if there are doubts as to their efficacy in this regard. See, for example, Dove and his observation that: 'the misalignment of data privacy laws and ethics review boards and committees is an ongoing challenge… [T]hese entities may impose higher standards of privacy protection than privacy laws require… Moreover, there is an inconsistent level or lack of privacy expertise, training, and oversight of many REC members.' Dove (2016), p. 682.

[50] Gibbons (2012), pp. 74–75.

GDPR also fits into a broader biobanking sanctions ecosystem. Accordingly, this section will proceed by considering each of the two forms of sanction foreseen in the GDPR, before finally considering how these relate to the broader biobank sanctions ecosystem.

3.2 *Liability and Compensation Sanctions*

In order for liability and compensation sanctions[51] to become relevant, a complaint must be lodged. This may happen via the research subject approaching a national court.[52] Significantly, the research subject may choose the location of the court.[53] They may lodge a complaint in their country of residence, or, if the biobanking is located elsewhere, in that country. This may also happen via a research subject mandating a non-profit to approach the national courts on their behalf.[54] However, only non-profits which have been 'properly constituted in accordance with the law of a Member State…[may] lodge the complaint'.[55]

A biobanking actor found liable for causing either material or non-material damage resulting from a violation of the principles of the GDPR will then be liable to pay the research subject compensation.[56] In clarification, the GDPR explicitly includes, in Recital 75, a set of examples of non-material damage. With relevance for the biobanking context, compensation is available for cases in which: 'data subjects might be…prevented from exercising control over…personal data…[or] where [sensitive] personal data are [illegitimately] processed'.

The recognition of the possibility to claim compensation for non-material harm is highly significant in the biobanking context. Laurie et al. had observed that the lack of clarity as to whether this was possible under Directive 95/46 had led, in certain Member States—in the UK, at least—to: 'damage [simply being] equated with financial loss'.[57] Accordingly, before the GDPR, it would have been very difficult for a research subject to obtain compensation for harms concerning, for example, the illegitimate processing of sensitive personal data—precisely the kinds of harms most likely to occur in the biobanking context.

In the case that compensation is found to be payable, the GDPR foresees the possibility for fault to be spread across multiple biobank actors. In this case, the GDPR gives the research subject the power to chase each actor at fault for the complete

---

[51] Liability and compensation sanctions relevant for biobanking actors are elaborated in Articles 79, 80 and 82 GDPR.

[52] See Article 79(1) GDPR.

[53] See Article 79(2) GDPR.

[54] See Article 80(1) GDPR.

[55] See Article 80(1) GDPR.

[56] See Article 82(1) GDPR.

[57] Laurie et al. (2014), p. 37.

damage.[58] Fortunately, the GDPR also permits any actor held completely liable to recoup any disproportionate losses by chasing other responsible actors for 'compensation corresponding to their part of responsibility for the damage'.[59]

3.3 *Administrative Sanctions*

In order for administrative sanctions[60] to become relevant, a DPA investigation must be started in one of three ways. First, the DPA itself may begin an investigation—under its ongoing oversight powers, discussed in more detail above, in Sect. 2.4.[61] Second, a research subject may begin an investigation by lodging a complaint with a DPA.[62] Finally, a research subject may also mandate a non-profit to lodge a complaint with the DPA.[63] In the final two cases, the DPA is obliged to investigate the complaint.[64]

In the case that a DPA's investigation finds a violation of the principles of the GDPR, they are endowed with a wide range of administrative sanctioning powers. Certain of these are described as corrective powers—these have been discussed above, in Sect. 2.4. Perhaps most significantly, these include the ability to 'impose a temporary or definitive limitation including a ban on processing'.[65] Beyond these powers, however, DPAs also have the power to impose administrative fines. The scale of these fines is colossal. The power is, as Wybitul puts it: 'drastic'.[66] This power is, arguably, the primary driver of all reaction to the GDPR.

There are two levels of fine relevant for biobanking actors. First level: Article 83(4) outlines fines of '10,000,000 EUR, or…up to 2% of the total…annual turnover' relevant for violations of certain substantive provisions—for example data controller obligations or certification obligations.[67] Second level: Article 83(5) outlines fines of '20,000,000 EUR, or…up to 4% of the total…annual turnover' relevant for violations of other substantive provisions—for example core data protection principles, sensitive data processing prohibitions and data subject rights.[68]

[58] See Article 82(4) GDPR. '[E]ach controller or processor shall be held liable for the entire damage in order to ensure effective compensation'.

[59] See Article 82(5) GDPR.

[60] Administrative sanctions relevant for biobanking actors are elaborated in Articles 57, 58, 77, 83 and 84 of the GDPR.

[61] See Articles 57(1)(a) and 58(1)(b) GDPR.

[62] See Article 57(1)(f) GDPR.

[63] See Article 80(1) GDPR.

[64] See Article 57(1)(f) GDPR.

[65] See Article 58(2)(f) GDPR.

[66] Translation by the author of 'drastisch'. Wybitul (2016), p. 203.

[67] See Articles 25–39 GDPR and Articles 42 and 43 GDPR respectively.

[68] See Article 5 GDPR, Article 9 GDPR and Articles 13–20 GDPR respectively.

Fines need not, however, always be imposed at maximum levels. The GDPR provides DPAs with certain leeway in light of the specifics of the case. The GDPR provides, what Schwartz describes as 'a multi-factor test for calculation of administrative fines'. This test—subsequently refined and clarified by EDPB guidance—requires DPAs to consider factors such as the gravity and intentionality of the infringement.[69] In light of such considerations the DPA is permitted to—in relation to minor infringements—waive the fine altogether or impose the fine at discretionary level.[70]

3.4 *The GDPR's Sanctions Mechanism in the Biobank Sanctions Ecosystem*

There are many sanctioning regimes available for violations of data privacy principles relevant for biobanking actors identifiable across EU Member States. For example, evident in the German context, but in few others, are civil sanctions under Articles 253 or 823 of the Bürgerliches Gesetzbuch for misappropriation of biological samples.[71] Owing to the variety of sanctions and sanctioning regimes operational across Europe, it is not possible to monolithically assert exactly how the GDPR's sanction mechanisms will fit into the biobank sanctions ecosystem. Nevertheless, general observations might be made.

In the first instance, despite DPA discretion and the variety of sanctioning regimes, sanctions under the GDPR are intended to have a harmonizing effect across the EU. This results from the GDPR's nature as an instrument of EU law directly binding in all EU Member States as well as the limited direct capacity for derogation from its sanctions regime. Accordingly, no extensive deviation between Member States is intended. Such deviation would lead to Member States in which conditions for data processing were favourable compared to other Member States—bringing the risk of 'forum shopping'. Whilst the dangers of forum shopping seem rather small in relation to biobanks, the harmonization rationale remains relevant.

Indeed, the need for harmonization in fines has been recently explicitly enunciated by the Article 29 Working Party. In their opinion on administrative fines, they conclude: '[Infringements] should lead to the imposition of 'equivalent sanctions'.[72] They explicitly base this conclusion on the recognition that: 'equivalent sanctions in all Member States as well as effective cooperation between supervisory authorities

69 Schwartz (2013), p. 1997. See Article 83(2) GDPR.

70 See Recital 148 and Recital 150 GDPR.

71 Bundestag *Bürgerliches Gesetzbuch* 1896 (updated 2002), Arts 253 and 283. http://www.gesetze-im-internet.de/bgb/BJNR001950896.html#BJNR001950896BJNG000102377. Accessed 4 Mar 2019.

72 Article 29 Working Party (2017b), p. 5.

of different Member States is seen as a way 'to prevent divergences hampering the free movement of personal data within the internal market', in line with [one of the core aims of] of the Regulation.'[73]

Regardless of the base harmonization rationale, there will still be instances in which the sanctions for violations of the GDPR's principles in biobanking will differ across EU Member States. Two cases are noteworthy. First, certain public biobanks, in certain Member States may not be subject to administrative fines at all. The GDPR clarifies Member States may limit or exclude fines as they relate to public bodies.[74] Second, supplementary sanctions—beyond those in the GDPR—are still permissible in certain cases. The GDPR clarifies that Member States may define sanctions for violations of the GDPR not already covered by administrative fines.[75] This includes, as Gola observes, the possibility to outline criminal sanctions for biobanking actors.[76]

Despite the above clarifications, it remains unclear just how far Member States can take the possibility to impose supplementary sanctions in outlining sanctions for infringements not covered by administrative fines—in terms of the type of violation which may be addressed as well as the form and degree of sanctions. For example, the relevant Article simply states that Member State sanctions must be: 'effective, proportionate and dissuasive'.[77] There is, however, no common standard regarding this concept. Such vagaries leave considerable room for manoeuvre which will doubtless be exploited by Member States.

Looking across the oversight and sanctions mechanisms, one cannot help but admire their comprehensiveness—at least on paper. Indeed, this comprehensiveness becomes starkly evident when one compares them to many of the alternative oversight and sanctions mechanisms outlined for biobanking—both on international and European level.[78] Despite this comprehensiveness, however, there are problems identifiable with these mechanisms. The most important of these will be discussed in the following section.

---

[73] Ibid.

[74] See Article 83(7) GDPR.

[75] See Article 84 GDPR.

[76] Gola (2017), Article 84, para 1.

[77] See Article 84 GDPR.

[78] Hallinan (2018), p. 370.

4 Problems with Biobank Oversight and Sanction Mechanisms Under the GDPR

4.1 Introduction

A framework for the critical analysis of the oversight and sanctions mechanisms might consider them from three perspectives: whether they provide adequate protection for data subject rights; whether they disproportionately impact other interests—particularly research interests—tied up with the biobanking process; and whether they are practically implementable in the biobanking context. A critical glance at the mechanisms from these perspectives reveals a number of issues. Three seem particularly worthy of discussion.[79]

4.2 The Lack of Clarity in the DPIA Obligation (Problem 1)

There is much text in the GDPR outlining the DPIA obligation. This is, unfortunately insufficient to remove uncertainty in the biobanking context. As Wright observes generally, the provisions in the GDPR remain 'rather sketchy'.[80] This is a problem of practical implementation.

In the first instance, there remains a lack of clarity about the focus of a DPIA. In particular, it remains unclear whether a DPIA represents another exercise in compliance with the GDPR or whether it represents an effort to go beyond the boundaries of the GDPR's concrete substantive principles to identify and mitigate all potential harms to research subjects.[81] The text of the GDPR seems to suggest the latter, requiring that a DPIA consider and mitigate risks to all 'rights and freedoms'.[82] The practical consequences of this broader approach for the conduct and outcome of, as well as the legal obligations flowing from, a DPIA, however, remain unclear.[83]

In turn, there is a lack of clarity around the method and modalities of a DPIA.[84] Here, four significant issues persist. First, the range of biobanking operations one DPIA may address is unclear. The GDPR explains that multiple similar operations can fall under one DPIA but is silent as to how different operations might be.[85]

---

[79] Problems are dealt with according to the order in which the aspect of the oversight or sanction mechanism to which they relate was dealt with in the descriptive part of the contribution—parts 2 and 3.

[80] Wright (2013), p. 307.

[81] Hallinan and Martin (2020).

[82] See Article 35(7)(c) GDPR.

[83] Ibid.

[84] See, for early reference to the significance of the lack of specificity of the scope of DPIAs in relation to medical research: Fears et al. (2014), p. 4.

[85] See Article 35(1) GDPR.

Second, the precise method to be used to conduct a DPIA is unclear. The GDPR provides some instructions, but these are far from an operationalisable methodology.[86] Third, the effect of a change in processing is unclear. The GDPR requires a review of the DPIA but is silent as to what the consequences of incompatibility should be.[87] Finally, the question of the resources to be invested to conduct an efficacious DPIA remain completely unaddressed.[88]

Finally, there is a lack of clarity as to how the DPIA relates to documentation required by other national bodies' approval processes. Compare, for example, the information and process of a DPIA in the GDPR with the information and process of submission of an application for REC approval under Articles 5–7 of the Clinical Trials Regulation.[89] The overlap is significant—both processes require the production of an outline of the foreseen processing activity as well as a consideration of the foreseen benefits and risks to research subjects. The blunt answer that both processes are legally required is technically correct but substantially unsatisfactory—at the very least, this may require an inefficient use of resources.

Despite the apparently myriad problems, there is reason to think that the lack of clarity in the DPIA obligation will not have a significant impact on in biobanking. Two points are significant. First, a DPIA itself is best considered as an information surfacing process.[90] The substantive impact of an improperly conducted DPIA thus seems likely to be minimal—a DPIA itself will neither ensure or prevent compliance with the GDPR. Second, the DPIA obligation is novel for all actors—biobanking actors and enforcement actors. It thus seems likely that the lack of clarity in the process—including as to how it relates to other assessment processes—will crystalize over time. Until then, it seems unlikely that DPAs or other national oversight bodies will not be too zealous in enforcement.

Equally, the GDPR does facilitate solutions to the lack of clarity in the DPIA obligation both from within and from without. In terms of internal solutions, the GDPR clarifies the EDPB can act to clarify the DPIA obligation.[91] Indeed, the power has already been used in the adoption, by the Article 29 Working Party—the EDPB's forerunner—of DPIA guidelines.[92] In terms of external solutions, both

[86] See Article 35(7) GDPR. There are DPIA methodologies which seek to address this lack of clarity. It is, however, not certain that these are compatible with the GDPR or that the can be effectively used by biobanking actors. See, for example: Commission Nationale de l'Informatique et des Libertés (CNIL) (2015); Information Commissioner's Office (2018).

[87] See Article 35(11). Bieker et al. (2016), p. 24.

[88] Wright et al. (2014), p. 10.

[89] European Parliament and Council Regulation (EU) No 536/2014 *on clinical trials on medicinal products for human use, and repealing Directive 2001/20/EC*. O.J. L 158 (2014), Article 4.

[90] Gellert (2017), p. 216.

[91] See Article 64(1)(a) GDPR.

[92] Article 29 Working Party (2017a). The EDPB would do well to look to the DPIA methodology developed in the context of the Datenschutz-Folgenabschätzung (DSFA) für die betriebliche und behördliche Praxis project. The goal of the project is: 'to…refine a process for implementing a DPIA…suitable for different technologies and data processing techniques…equally applicable to institutions of different sizes'. The methodology builds upon that developed by the Forum

Articles 9(4) and Article 89(1) permit EU Member States to enact supplementary conditions clarifying—including in terms of substance, process and relationships to other comparable processes—the DPIA obligation in biobanking.[93]

4.3 The Lack of Obligation to Seek Prior Approval (Problem 2)

As discussed in Sect. 2.3, prior approval by an oversight body is not an obligation in the GDPR. In comparison with international norms this represents an insufficient standard of research subject protection. As will be discussed below, this is a problem for the standard of protection offered to research subject rights.

The obligation to seek prior approval for all genomic research activity may be seen as a minimum standard of research subject protection to be provided by all efficacious biobank law. This is arguable by virtue of the fact the obligation constitutes a norm evident across all biobank relevant international instruments.[94] The World Medical Association Declaration of Taipei states, for example, in Article 19: 'the ethics committee must approve use of data and biological material.'

The GDPR does not explicitly foresee an obligation to gain prior approval from a DPA before engaging in biobank processing. It is true that the GDPR includes provisions on prior approval by DPAs of biobanking processing. These provisions only become relevant, however '[when] a data protection impact assessment … indicates that processing would result in a high risk in the absence of measures taken by the controller'.[95] Recall here the observation of De Hert et al., that the decision as to whether the Article is triggered is eventually with the biobanking actor.[96] It is also true that the GDPR foresees the possibility for Member States to derogate from the GDPR and require prior consultation with a DPA for specific types of

Privatheit project and appears to be the most legally comprehensive and methodologically sound available. https://www.dsfa.eu/index.php/en/home-en/. Accessed 4 Mar 2019.

[93] The wording of the article permits Member States to adopt derogations 'including limitations'. How far this possibility to adopt limitations on the applicability of the Regulations's provisions extends, is not clear. This would be ideally clarified as quickly as possible by the EDPB or by the CJEU.

[94] See Hallinan (2018), pp. 145–146 and the following instruments: Organization for Economic Co-Operation and Development *Guidelines on Human Biobanks and Genetic Research Databases*, 2009. http://www.oecd.org/sti/biotech/44054609.pdf. Accessed 4 Mar 2019; Council of Europe Recommendation CM/Rec(2016)6 of the Committee of Ministers to member States *on research on biological materials of human origin, 2016. Available at* (2016). https://search.coe.int/cm/Pages/result_details.aspx?ObjectId=090000168064e8ff. Accessed 4 Mar 2019; World Medical Association *Declaration of Taipei on Ethical Considerations regarding health databases and biobanks* (2002 (updated 2016)). https://www.wma.net/policies-post/wma-declaration-of-taipei-on-ethical-considerations-regarding-health-databases-and-biobanks/. Accessed 4 Mar 2019.

[95] See Article 36 GDPR.

[96] De Hert and Papkonstantinou (2016), p. 192.

processing.[97] It remains to be seen, however, how many Member States will implement this requirement.

Nor does the GDPR foresee the obligation to gain prior approval from a national body before engaging in biobank processing. The GDPR does foresee the establishment, at national level, of safeguards for scientific research which may translate into the obligation, in certain Member States, for biobanks to obtain prior approval for processing operations.[98] This may prove a panacea for the issue in future. It does not, however, constitute a panacea now. It is not the case that national body advance approval procedures are comprehensively present in all EU Member States. Even where such advance approval procedures are in place, it is not necessarily the case that they have the power to prevent biobank processing from going ahead. Recall the example of the non-binding nature of the Estonian Biobank's REC decisions.[99]

Despite the apparent significance of the issue, the substantial consequences of the lack of the obligation in the GDPR look likely to be, practically, of diminished significance. Two factors are significant. First: the GDPR will, as discussed above, require prior consultation in certain cases—for example, in cases in which it is uncertain whether risks have been adequately addressed in the DPIA. Second: whilst supporting national oversight bodies are, from a legal perspective, not a panacea in providing a perfect advance approval landscape, their prevalence and efficacy should not be underestimated. For example, whilst certain RECs may not have the power to issue binding decisions on whether biobank processing may proceed, it would also, practically, be highly unusual for their decisions to be ignored.

Equally, the GDPR does facilitate solutions to the issue both via internal and external approaches. In terms of internal approaches: there is no doubt the EDPB could issue guidance highlighting the need to seek prior approval before engaging in biobank processing.[100] In terms of external approaches: Articles 9(4), Article 36(5) and Article 89(1) grant power to EU Member States to elaborate supplemental rules concerning the processing of sensitive personal data in research in relation to the obligation for biobanking actors to seek prior approval from DPAs, other national oversight bodies, or both.

4.4 *The Size of Administrative Fines (Problem 3)*

The huge size of potential administrative fines outlined in the GDPR is justified based on the need to give data protection law teeth in the face multinational internet companies. This is an image of perpetrator which does not match the majority of

[97] See Article 36(5) GDPR.

[98] See Article 89(1) GDPR.

[99] According to Article 29(1) of the Estonian Human Genes Research Act: '[the advance] assessment of the Ethics Committee is not binding [in terms of whether processing proceeds]'.

[100] Under the power to issue opinions in Article 70(1)(e) GDPR.

public research biobanks at all.[101] As a consequence, for such biobanks, fines are disproportionate. This is a problem concerning the disproportionate impact on interests tied up with the biobanking process.

The reasoning behind the scale of fines—up to 20,000,000 EUR or up to 4% of turnover—makes sense when placed in context. In the legislative process, the scale of fines was discussed as necessary as a deterrent to multinational internet companies' violating the GDPR.[102] Further proof the legislator had this model of target perpetrator in mind when drafting the fines is found in the recognition by certain legal scholars, for example Faust et al. and Bergt, that fines share scale and form with those in EU monopolies law—law concerned with the regulation of cartels and market dominance.[103]

However, the typical public biobanking actor does not compare to such a perpetrator. How then, should such fines be proportionate? Public biobanking actors do not compare in size, financial clout or purpose with large internet companies—or indeed any organisation the target of monopolies law. In this regard, it is enlightening to consider some of the—although admittedly limited—empirical work on the financial constitution of biobanks in the EU. Here, Zika et al. clarify that only 3% of biobanks which answered their large-scale survey were even privately owned.[104] An absurd position: the tiny biobanks of the EuroBioBank rare disease network face the same sanctions as Google.[105]

Despite the potentially crippling, disproportionate nature of fines, there are factors which look likely to, practically, significantly diminish the impact of the problem on biobanking—although the possibility of huge fines will still hang, like the sword of Damocles, above biobanking actors' heads. As discussed in Sect. 3.3, DPAs have significant discretion in setting the quantities of fines. For a number of reasons, it seems unlikely DPAs will ever set maximum—or even near maximum—fines. Quite apart from the fact these would seldom be proportionate, such an act would unlikely be in a DPA's best interest. DPAs operate in a politicised

[101] This will also be true for many private biobanks. There are, however, certain companies building large scale biobanks with huge financial backing and operating with economic imperatives. For such biobanks, the fines seem less disproportionate. See, for example: https://www.23andme.com/about/biobanking/. Accessed 4 Mar 2019.

[102] See, for example, Jan Philipp Albrecht—EU Parliament Rapporteur for the GDPR: 'Companies which violate the new rules must pay fines of up to four per-cent of their yearly turnover. That could be billions for the global internet companies'. Author translation of: 'Unternehmen, die gegen die neuen Regeln verstoßen, müssen Strafen von bis zu vier Prozent ihres Jahresweltumsatzes zahlen, das können für die großen globalen Internetkonzerne Milliarden sein'. Albrecht, Jan Philipp. 2015. Starke Verbraucherrechte und mehr Wettbewerb: EU-Datenschutzreform. https://www.janalbrecht.eu/2015/12/2015-12-21-starke-verbraucherrechte-und-mehr-wettbewerb/. Accessed 4 Mar 2019.

[103] Faust et al. (2016), p. 120; Bergt (2018b), Art. 83, para 2.

[104] Zika et al. (2010), p. 19. http://ipts.jrc.ec.europa.eu/publications/pub.cfm?id=3259. Accessed 4 Mar 2019.

[105] http://www.eurobiobank.org/. Accessed 4 Mar 2019.

environment. They are likely to have little appetite to interfere with biobanking activity with normative legitimacy and, as observed by Simon et al., public support.[106]

Equally, solutions to the disproportionate scale of fines are also available through the GDPR as well as parallel law. In terms of solutions available through the GDPR: Article 70(k) is clear the EDPB should: '[draw] up guidelines for supervisory authorities concerning the application of…and the setting of administrative fines'. In terms of parallel law: the flexible construction of Article 9(4)—which specifically permits Member States to enact 'limitations' on the principles of the GDPR in relation to sensitive data—could legitimate Member State derogations restricting the scale of fines relating to biobanking.

5 Conclusion

This contribution dealt with two of the key mechanisms concerning biobanking outlined in the GDPR: the oversight mechanism; and the sanctions mechanism. Indeed, it is arguable that the provisions of the sanctions mechanism—in particular the huge potential scale of administrative fines—are one of the key factors driving the rise in concern for, and efforts toward compliance with, data protection law since the GDPR came into force in early 2016 and since its application in early 2018.

The oversight and sanctions mechanisms play no substantive role in the definition of the public interest—or the conditions pertaining to processing in service of the concept—in relation to biobanking under the GDPR. Nevertheless, they are indirectly determinative of the concept in two key ways. In the first instance, as meta-systems ensuring compliance with the substantive principles outlined in the GDPR, these mechanisms ensure respect for the boundaries of, and conditions attached to, the public interest under the GDPR. In turn, the emphasis on each mechanism acts as an indicator of the level of the legislator's general concern with the ability to police and control the boundaries and conditions of the public interest under the GDPR.

The oversight mechanism in the GDPR applicable to biobanking is—at least on paper—extensive.[107] Indeed, it consists of four types of oversight. First: *ex ante* assessment—the need for biobanking actors to conduct a DPIA. Second: prior notification and approval—the need for certain biobanking actors to obtain approval from a DPA and, potentially, national bodies, prior to processing. Third: ongoing oversight—the need for biobanking actors to submit to investigation by a DPA, a DPO and, potentially, national bodies. Fourth: general oversight—the power for DPAs and the EDPB to issue general opinions on the biobanking sector. It remains,

[106] Simon et al. (2013), pp. 821–831.

[107] Time will tell whether the legislator's presumptions as to the efficacy of the oversight mechanism will play out in practise. Moving forward, biobank oversight under the GDPR looks likely to be a fascinating subject for research.

however, somewhat unclear how the various oversight bodies—in particular DPAs and national bodies—will engage with each other.

The sanctions mechanism in the GDPR applicable to biobanking is also—at least on paper—extensive. The mechanism consists of two key types of sanction. First: liability and compensation sanctions. In the case a biobanking actor is brought before court and found guilty of an infringement of the GDPR, this actor will be liable to pay compensation. Second: administrative sanctions. The range of administrative sanctions available is broad, but perhaps most important are the colossal potential administrative fines—up to 20,000,000 EUR or 4% of turnover. It remains to be seen how the sanctions mechanism explicitly elaborated in the GDPR will fit with supplemental Member State sanctions.

Whilst these two mechanisms display an impressive comprehensiveness in approach, several problems concerning their negative impacts on research subject rights, research interests and their practical implementability to biobanking, are also evident. Three might be highlighted as particularly significant. First: the lack of clarity in the DPIA obligation. Second: the lack of obligation to seek prior DPA approval. And third: the huge scale of potential administrative fines. Although each problem initially seems significant, however, a closer consideration reveals each is subject to practically mitigating factors as well as to resolution through the GDPR, or parallel Member State law, or both.

References

Article 29 Working Party (2015) 'health data in apps and devices', Annex to Communication between the Article 29 Working Party and DG Connect

Article 29 Working Party (2016) Guidelines for identifying a controller or processor's lead supervisory authority. http://ec.europa.eu/information_society/newsroom/image/document/2016-51/wp244_en_40857.pdf. Accessed 4 Mar 2019

Article 29 Working Party (2017a) Guidelines on Data Protection Impact Assessment (DPIA) and determining whether processing is "likely to result in a high risk" for the purposes of Regulation 2016/679. https://ec.europa.eu/newsroom/article29/item-detail.cfm?item_id=611236. Accessed 4 Mar 2019

Article 29 Working Party (2017b) Guidelines on the application and setting of administrative fines for the purposes of the Regulation 2016/679. https://ec.europa.eu/newsroom/article29/item-detail.cfm?item_id=611237. Accessed 4 Mar 2019

Bergt M (2018a) Art. 39: Aufgaben des Datenschutzbeauftragten. In: Kühling J, Buchner B (eds) DatenschutzGrundverordnung/BDSG. Beck, Munich, pp 753–762

Bergt M (2018b) Art. 83: Allgemeine Bedingungen für die Verhängung von Geldbußen. In: Kühling J, Buchner B (eds) DatenschutzGrundverordnung/BDSG. Beck, Munich, pp 1122–1147

Bieker F et al (2016) A process for Data Protection Impact Assessment under the European General Data Protection Regulation. In: Schiffner S et al (eds) Privacy technologies and policy. Springer, Dordrecht, pp 21–38

Commission Nationale de l'Informatique et des Libertés (CNIL) (2015) Privacy Impact Assessment: methodology (how to carry out a PIA). https://www.cnil.fr/sites/default/files/typo/document/CNIL-PIA-1-Methodology.pdf. Accessed 4 Mar 2019

De Hert P, Papkonstantinou V (2016) The new General Data Protection Regulation: still a sound system for the protection of individuals? Comput Law Secur Rev 32(2):179–194

Dove E (2016) Biobanks, data sharing, and the drive for a global privacy governance framework. J Law Med Ethics 44(4, part. 1):675–689

Expert Group on Dealing with Ethical and Regulatory Challenges of International Biobank Research (2012) Biobanks for Europe: a challenge for governance. https://www.coe.int/t/dg3/healthbioethic/activities/10_biobanks/biobanks_for_Europe.pdf. Accessed 4 Mar 2019

Faust S et al (2016) Milliardenbußgelder nach der DS-GVO: Ein überblick über die neuen Sanktionen bei Verstößen gegen den Datenschutz. Zeitschrift für Datenschutz 3:120–125

Fears R et al (2014) Data protection regulation and the promotion of health research: getting the balance right. Q J Med 107:3–5

Gellert R (2017) The Article 29 Working Party's Provisional Guidelines on Data Protection Impact Assessment. Eur Data Protect Law Rev 3(2):212–217

Gibbons S (2012) Mapping the regulatory space. In: Kaye J et al (eds) Governing biobanks: understanding the interplay between law and practice. Hart Publishing, Oxford, pp 51–93

Gola P (2017) Artikel 84: Sanktionen. In: Gola P (ed) DS-GVO Datenschutz-Grundverordnung VO (EU) 2016/679 Kommentar. Beck, Munich, pp 756–758

Hallinan D (2018) Feeding biobanks with genetic data: what role can the General Data Protection Regulation play in the protection of genetic privacy in research biobanking in the European Union? VUB Doctoral Thesis, Brussels

Hallinan D, De Hert P (2016) Many have it wrong – samples do contain personal data: the data protection regulation as a superior framework to protect donor interests in biobanking and genomic research. In: Mittelstadt B, Floridi L (eds) The ethics of biomedical big data. Springer, Basel, pp 119–139

Hallinan D, Martin N (2020 Forthcoming) Fundamental Rights, the Normative Keystone of DPIA. European Data Protection Law Review.

Information Commissioner's Office (2018) Sample DPIA Template. https://ico.org.uk/media/for-organisations/documents/1595/pia-code-of-practice.pdf. Accessed 4 Mar 2019

Kuner C (2012) The European Commission's Proposed Data Protection Regulation: a Copernican revolution in European data protection law. Priv Secur Law Rep 11:1–15

Laurie et al (2014) A review of evidence relating to harm resulting from the uses of health and biomedical data. http://nuffieldbioethics.org/wp-content/uploads/FINAL-Report-on-Harms-Arising-from-Use-of-Health-and-Biomedical-Data-30-JUNE-2014.pdf. Accessed 4 Mar 2019

Martin N et al (2019) How data protection regulation affects startup innovation. Working Paper

Schwartz P (2013) The EU-U.S. privacy collision: a turn to institutions and procedures. Harv Law Rev 126:1966–2009

Simon C et al (2013) Active choice but not too active: public perspectives on biobank consent models. Genet Med 13(9):821–831. https://doi.org/10.1097/GIM.0b013e31821d2f88

Van Dijk N et al (2016) A risk to a right? Beyond data protection risk assessments. Comput Law Secur Rev 32(2):286–306

Wachter S, Mittelstadt B (2019) A right to reasonable inferences: re-thinking data protection law in the age of inferences and big data'. Columbia Bus Law Rev 2:1-130.

Wright D (2013) Making Privacy Impact Assessment more effective. Inf Soc 29:307–315

Wright D et al (2014) A guide to surveillance impact assessment — how to identify and prioritise risks arising from surveillance systems. SAPIENT Project Deliverable 4.4. https://zenodo.org/record/1182874#.Wpf3RqjOXIU. Accessed 4 Mar 2019

Wybitul T (2016) Was ändert sich mit dem neuen EU-Datenschutzrecht für Arbeitgeber und Betriebsräte? Anpassungsbedarf bei Beschäftigtendatenschutz und Betriebsvereinbarungen. Zeitschrift für Datenschutz 5:203–209

Zika E et al (2010) Biobanks in Europe: prospects for harmonisation and networking. http://ipts.jrc.ec.europa.eu/publications/pub.cfm?id=3259. Accessed 4 Mar 2019

Brexit and Biobanking: GDPR Perspectives

Andelka M. Phillips and Tamara K. Hervey

Abstract At the time we wrote this chapter, we undertook the almost impossible task of providing a legal analysis of an event (Brexit) that had not happened and might never have happened. This chapter nonetheless contributes to the edited collection in that it reports on the then legal position in the UK, and presents an analysis of two possible immediate post-Brexit legal futures, for data protection law as applicable to biobanking in the UK. These post-Brexit futures are the position if the draft Withdrawal Agreement is ratified and comes into force, and the position if it does not (a so-called 'No Deal' Brexit). The chapter concludes with some thoughts on possible longer term futures. The main message is the deep uncertainties surrounding Brexit and what it means in both legal form and in practice.

1 Introduction

At the time we finished writing this chapter (June 2019), the UK remained a Member State of the European Union (EU). This chapter explores the landscape of biobanking in the UK and the legal framework applicable to biobanks operating in the UK, focussing on the applicable data protection legislation. At that time, there was much uncertainty around Brexit, as a Withdrawal Agreement had not yet been ratified and it was possible that the UK would leave the EU without an agreement, a so-called 'No Deal' Brexit. It was also still possible that the UK would not in fact leave the EU. Given this uncertainty, this chapter outlines two possible post-Brexit legal futures. One of these (the UK leaving the EU without a Withdrawal Agreement) has

The support of the ESRC's *Governance after Brexit* grant ES/S00730X/1 is gratefully acknowledged.

A. M. Phillips (✉)
Te Piringa – Faculty of Law, University of Waikato, Hamilton, New Zealand

HeLEX Centre, University of Oxford, Oxford, UK
e-mail: andelka.phillips@waikato.ac.nz

T. K. Hervey
University of Sheffield, Sheffield, UK
e-mail: t.hervey@sheffield.ac.uk

S. Slokenberga et al. (eds.), *GDPR and Biobanking*, Law, Governance and Technology Series 43, https://doi.org/10.1007/978-3-030-49388-2_9

not come to pass. However, many of the uncertainties associated with it remain, including in the context at which this chapter is now revised (June 2020), of the negotiation of the future EU-UK trade relationship. The chapter primarily focuses on applicable data protection law in this context.

The chapter first describes the context of biobanking in the UK, showing the European and global networks within which the UK's biobanks of various types are embedded (Sect. 2). It outlines the key legal and governance instruments applicable to UK-based biobanks. The chapter then turns to the general political and legal context following the EU referendum vote (Sect. 3), before its detailed discussion of implications of Brexit for biobanking (Sect. 4). A brief conclusion notes the effects of continued uncertainty on UK biobanking and medical research.

2 Biobanking in the UK: The Current Position

2.1 The Context: National Biobanks Within European and Global Networks

A biobank is an entity which collects and stores human biological materials, and data about such materials, organises them on the basis of population, disease type or other pertinent typology, and provides bio specimens and data for both exploratory research and clinical trials.[1] There are five main models for biobanks (small scale/university, governmental/institutional, population, commercial and virtual), four of which are present in the UK.[2] A 2017 list, populated by the University of Nottingham, UCL and the Advanced Data Analysis Centre, covers over 180 UK-based biobanks.[3]

The first biobanks began over a century ago, on a small scale, within universities. Many 'Russell Group' UK Universities[4] still hold smaller scale biobanks, but these are increasingly networked globally. For instance, University College London holds several biobanks focussed on specific conditions.[5] Another example is London School of Hygiene and Tropical Medicine's biobank for Myalgic Encephalomyelitis (ME)/Chronic Fatigue Syndrome.[6] A third is CNMD Biobank, London, which collects tissues and primary cell cultures from skin, muscle, stem cells and nerve cells from patients with genetically determined neuromuscular diseases.[7] Like other university biobanks, it works collaboratively, on primary and translational research,

[1] Geneticist (31 May 2018) https://www.geneticistinc.com/blog/the-importance-of-biorepositories.

[2] The UK does not have a population biobank.

[3] Tissue Directory and Coordination Centre https://biobankinguk.org/biobanks-a-z/.

[4] The UK's 24 leading universities, https://russellgroup.ac.uk.

[5] UCL Human Tissue Biobanks (last updated February 2019) https://www.ucl.ac.uk/human-tissue/hta-biobanks.

[6] London School of Hygiene and Tropical Medicine, CureME https://cureme.lshtm.ac.uk/.

[7] Queen Square Centre For Neuromuscular Diseases, Biobank https://www.ucl.ac.uk/cnmd/research/research-core-activities/biobank.

with the European Network Eurobiobank and the EU Network of Excellence TREAT-NMD.

A major institutional/governmental repository, the UK Biobank, was established as a not-for-profit charity in 2006,[8] as a collaboration between the medical charitable sector, the English National Health Service (NHS), and governments within the UK.[9] It provides services to researchers worldwide. Its website description states:[10]

> UK Biobank is a major national and international health resource, and a registered charity in its own right, with the aim of improving the prevention, diagnosis and treatment of a wide range of serious and life-threatening illnesses – including cancer, heart diseases, stroke, diabetes, arthritis, osteoporosis, eye disorders, depression and forms of dementia. UK Biobank recruited 500,000 people aged between 40-69 years in 2006-2010 from across the country to take part in this project. They have undergone measures, provided blood, urine and saliva samples for future analysis, detailed information about themselves and agreed to have their health followed. Over many years this will build into a powerful resource to help scientists discover why some people develop particular diseases and others do not.

Another significant biobank in the UK is Oxford Biobank. Oxford Biobank holds a 'collection of 30-50 year old healthy men and women living in Oxfordshire. All participants have undergone a detailed examination at a screening visit, donated DNA and given informed consent to be re-approached.'[11] Oxford Biobank is an interesting example of protection of research participants' rights, as they utilise a dynamic consent platform, which enables participants to have more control over how their data and samples are used and allows for the withdrawal of consent.[12]

Many UK-based biobanks have been and are involved in international collaborations, often with partners in the EU. For example, EPIC-Oxford is the Oxford based 'component of European Prospective Investigation into Cancer and Nutrition (EPIC)—a prospective cohort of 65,000 men and women living in the UK, many of whom are vegetarian.'[13] This project 'is the largest detailed study of diet and health ever undertaken'[14] and involves 23 centres from 10 European countries, including collaborators from the UK, Denmark, France, Italy, Germany, Greece, Spain, Sweden, Norway, and the Netherlands.[15] Several UK biobanks also participated in BIOSHARE-EU (Biobank Standardisation and Harmonisation for Research Excellence in the European Union), which has now ended. This included UK

---

[8] Naomi et al. (2012), pp. 123–126 https://www.sciencedirect.com/science/article/pii/S2211883712000597.

[9] The Welcome Trust medical charity, Medical Research Council, Department of Health, Scottish Government, the Northwest Regional Development Agency, the Welsh Government, British Heart Foundation, Cancer Research UK and Diabetes UK, see http://www.ukbiobank.ac.uk/about-biobank-uk/.

[10] UK Biobank, About UK Biobank http://www.ukbiobank.ac.uk/about-biobank-uk/.

[11] Oxford Biobank https://www.oxfordbiobank.org.uk.

[12] Teare and Kaye (2018), p. S3.

[13] EPIC-Oxford (2019) Homepage http://www.epic-oxford.org.

[14] EPIC-Oxford (2019) Introduction http://www.epic-oxford.org/introduction/.

[15] EPIC-Oxford (2019) European Collaboration http://www.epic-oxford.org/europe/.

Biobank and EPIC-Oxford.[16] Currently, both UK Biobank and Oxford Biobank continue to make their resources available to researchers based outside the UK.

The UK Clinical Research Collaboration's Tissue Directory and Coordination Centre, administered by the Medical Research Council, is a virtual biobank: an electronic web-based collection of information about existing biospecimens and data. The Centre does not hold any human material and is independent from physical biobanks, allowing it to adopt a position of neutrality. It holds the UK's first pan-disease Tissue Directory,[17] which is available for any research to search according to disease classification, age, sex, sample type, preservation details, quality indicators and datasets available. In April 2017, it covered 100 bioresources.[18] Its aim is to support research by enhancing the ability of researchers and organisations to find suitable samples. The Centre is the UK node of the BBMRI-ERIC network,[19] which is an EU-funded network of biobanks and biomolecular resources.[20] The UK was not a founding member of BBMRI-ERIC, but joined subsequently. 14 EU Member States and Norway are members; four other states are observers. Member States, third countries as well as intergovernmental organisations may become members of BBMRI-ERIC at any time, subject to approval by the Assembly of Members according to Article 11(8)(b) of its Statutes.[21] Members of BBMRI-ERIC take collective decisions through the Assembly of Members.[22] Both members and observers contribute to the budget.

Due to increasing funding pressures, there may also be collaboration and investment in public biobanks by private entities.[23] There are also commercial biobanks in the UK including, for instance, bioDock, a trading name of Future Health Technologies Ltd (Company number: 04431145), which is a Nottingham-based cryo-genetic facility, with storage facilities in Switzerland and the UK.[24] This biobank currently holds more than '500,000 samples from over 80 different countries'.[25] In the commercial context, businesses that offer direct-to-consumer genetic tests (sometimes called 'personal genomics') also can be viewed as operating biobanks, in that they develop databases from consumers' samples and personal data. Such businesses also operate across borders.

---

[16] BioSHaRE (2015) Biobank Standardisation and Harmonisation for Research Excellence in the European Union (Summary Report) http://www.bioshare.eu/assets/Final%20publishable%20summary%20-%20update%20Jan.pdf.

[17] Tissue Directory and Coordination Centre https://directory.biobankinguk.org.

[18] Quinlan et al. (2017), p. 6.

[19] Mayrhofer et al. (2016), pp. 379–384.

[20] See Council Regulation (EC) No 723/2009 of 25 June 2009 on the Community legal framework for a European Research Infrastructure Consortium (ERIC) amended by Council Regulation (EU) No 1261/2013 of 2 December 2013 OJ 2009 L 206/1.

[21] The Statutes of BBMRI-ERIC were decided for implementation by the European Commission on 22 November 2013, published in the Official Journal of the EU on the 30 November and came into force on 3 December 2013 (2013/701/EU). OJ 2013 L 326/56.

[22] Statutes, Article 9 (3).

[23] Caulfield et al. (2014), pp. 94–110.

[24] BioDock (2019) Homepage http://www.bio-dock.com.

[25] BioDock (2019) Homepage http://www.bio-dock.com.

2.2 *Overview of the Current Law and Governance Arrangements for Biobanks in the UK*

Several pieces of UK legislation have relevance to the governance of biobanks in the UK. The focus in this chapter is primarily on data protection. The key current legal instrument here is the EU's General Data Protection Regulation (GDPR),[26] which replaced the earlier Data Protection Directive.[27] Some UK-based biobanks apparently take the view that legal changes brought in by the GDPR do not affect the lawfulness of their existing practices. For instance, UK Biobank's guidance for researchers states that compliance with the previous data protection regime is sufficient to secure GDPR compliance.[28] This statement has not, to our knowledge, been legally tested.

As a Regulation, from the point of view of EU law, the GDPR is 'directly applicable' in the Member States,[29] which means it has legal effect irrespective of any act of transposition. From the point of view of UK law, under the European Communities Act 1972, section 2, the GDPR takes effect in UK law in accordance with the requirements of EU law. Those requirements include the supremacy of EU law, in that the GDPR must be applied in preference to any contradictory domestic law, which should be 'disapplied' irrespective of its date of enactment (in other words, the normal *lex posteriori* rule is inverted).[30] In practice, however, domestic courts in the UK seek to avoid any 'clash' of norms, but rather to interpret and apply UK Acts of Parliament consistently with EU obligations.[31]

In principle, the GDPR protects the fundamental rights of natural persons whose data are 'processed' within the material scope of EU law,[32] where the entity processing the data is within the EU, or the data subjects are within the EU, if the entity processing the data is not, and the processing activities are 'related to the offering of goods or services, irrespective of whether a payment of the data subject is required'.[33] Thus the GDPR applies in principle to all UK-based biobanks, which must comply with the GDPR's terms on lawful data processing.[34] The GDPR also provides for the

---

[26] Regulation (EU) 2016/679 of the European Parliament and of the Council of 27 April 2016 on the protection of natural persons with regard to the processing of personal data and on the free movement of such data, and repealing Directive 95/46/EC (General Data Protection Regulation) OJ 2016 L 119/1.

[27] Directive 95/46/EC of the European Parliament and of the Council of 24 October 1995 on the protection of individuals with regard to the processing of personal data and on the free movement of such data OJ 1995 L 281/31.

[28] UK Biobank, Researchers https://www.ukbiobank.ac.uk/scientists-3/.

[29] Article 288 TFEU.

[30] *Factortame Ltd v Secretary of State for Transport* [1991] 1 AC 603.

[31] Hervey and Sheldon (2011), pp. 327–375.

[32] GDPR, Article 2 (2) (a).

[33] GDPR, Article 3.

[34] GDPR, Articles 6 ff.

free movement of data both within and into the EU. It does so by providing harmonised minimum level standards of data protection, by requiring Member States to have a 'supervisory authority' to oversee their application,[35] and by setting up institutional fora within which EU Member States cooperate. The UK is currently obliged to participate in those institutional arrangements. Its supervisory authority is the Information Commissioner's Office (ICO).

The GDPR permits Member States to derogate from its terms in various respects. The UK's Data Protection Act 2018 (DPA) both implements the GDPR in domestic law and specifies how the UK takes advantage of this permission. The DPA also outlines how various aspects of the GDPR apply in practice in the UK.[36]

The Human Tissue Act 2004 (HTA), enforced by the Human Tissue Authority, is also significant for UK biobanks. The HTA's purpose is to regulate activities involving the removal, storage, use and disposal of human tissue. The Human Tissue Authority also secures compliance with the EU's human tissue and cells Directives.[37] Under the HTA, like under the GDPR, the fundamental principle of consent underpins the lawful removal, storage and use of body parts, organs and tissue.[38] The HTA provides that analysis of DNA without qualifying consent is a criminal offence.[39] Although the HTA does not specifically define the term biobank, biobanks in the UK come within its remit, as they typically involve the collection of a broad range of human biological materials.[40] The Human Tissue Authority provides licences to organisations that collect and remove human tissue used in research and is thus responsible for licensing biobanks.[41]

Under the guidance issued by the Human Tissue Authority, UK-based biobanks which provide direct-to-consumer services are also obliged to comply with the provisions of the HTA, which means that all such businesses should obtain consent for the initial performance of a genetic test.[42] The law—in particular relevant

---

[35] GDPR, Article 51.

[36] See section 22 of the Data Protection Act 2018: Section 22 (1) The GDPR applies to the processing of personal data to which this Chapter applies but as if its Articles were part of an Act extending to England and Wales, Scotland and Northern Ireland. (2) Chapter 2 of this Part applies for the purposes of the applied GDPR as it applies for the purposes of the GDPR.

[37] Directive (2004/23/EC) which provides the framework legislation and two technical directives (2006/17/EC and 2006/86/EC), which provide the detailed requirements.

[38] Human Tissue Authority, 'Human Tissue Act 2004' https://www.hta.gov.uk/policies/human-tissue-act-2004.

[39] Human Tissue Act 2004, section 45.

[40] This is similar to the position in Estonia, please see K Pormeister's chapter in this volume. K Pormeister, Article 89 GDPR implementation and biobanks in Estonia in Santa Slokenberga, Olga Tzortzatou and Jane Reichel (eds), *Individual rights, public interest and biobank research. Article 89 GDPR and European legal responses* (forthcoming Springer Law, Governance and Technology Series).

[41] Human Tissue Authority, *Guide for the general public to Code of Practice E* (HTA (07e/17)) https://www.hta.gov.uk/sites/default/files/HTA%20%2807e-17%29%206%20Research.pdf.

[42] Human Tissue Authority (2019) Analysis of DNA under the HT Act FAQs, https://www.hta.gov.uk/faqs/analysis-dna-under-ht-act-faqs, note: that the Human Tissue Authority has not altered its

exemptions—will apply differently to such enterprises from its application to public research projects, as the nature of their business differs significantly, involving the direct sale of genetic tests as consumer services, followed often by secondary research on the genetic data generated from such tests. Furthermore, the commercial nature of these businesses means that, as well as data protection law, consumer protection legislation, including the medical devices legislative framework also applies to governance of the industry and their research activities.

In addition to the legislative framework, biobanks in the UK are subject to a range of governance provision. Much of this concerns ethical practice. For example, UK Biobank's funders developed an Ethics and Governance Framework, as well as an Ethics and Governance Council, which is an independent body that oversees the biobank's compliance with the Framework. UK Biobank has been licensed by the Human Tissue Authority, which means that researchers using data or samples from the biobank do not need additional licences.

Finally, in addition to those under the GDPR, DPA and HTA, the common law may afford other protections to data subjects, concerning special categories of personal data. Such special categories include: 'data concerning health'; genetic and genomic data; and 'biometric data that is processed to uniquely identify a natural person'.[43] These are all relevant categories for UK-based biobanks. For instance, claims in contract, the tort of negligence, or in equity could all be applicable in English law where biomedical research activities involve processing special categories of data collected from patients.[44] We do not discuss these further in this chapter.

2.3 Lawfulness of Processing, Transfer of Data Within the EU, and Transfer to 'Third Countries' in the Context of Biobanking in the UK

2.3.1 Lawfulness of Processing and the UK Biobank

To understand how the GDPR impacts in practice on biobanking in the UK, UK Biobank provides a useful illustrative example. According to its website, there are two main grounds for lawfully processing data in this context. These are either consent or legitimate public interest.[45] The HRA guidance does note though that, if it is possible to undertake the relevant research without processing personal data, then

position on this.

[43] See Taylor et al. (2018), p. 639 https://doi.org/10.1007/s00439-018-1921-0; Health Research Authority Legal basis for processing data https://www.hra.nhs.uk/planning-and-improving-research/policies-standards-legislation/data-protection-and-information-governance/gdpr-detailed-guidance/legal-basis-processing-data/.

[44] Health Research Authority Legal basis for processing data (n 43).

[45] UK Biobank (2019) GDPR https://www.ukbiobank.ac.uk/gdpr/; also see their guidance document, UK Biobank (30 May 2018a) Information notice for UK Biobank participants: the General

neither consent nor legitimate interest will be valid as a basis for data processing.[46] UK Biobank believes that their work meets both the consent and legitimate interests bases for processing. Its GDPR Information Notice asserts that:

> Each person who joined UK Biobank provided their explicit consent for us to collect, store and make available information about them (including data from genetic and other assays of the samples that were collected) for health-related research, and for their health to be followed 25 over many years through medical and other health-related records, as well as by being re-contacted by UK Biobank.[47]

UK Biobank also states that they believe that they meet the three step tests necessary for legitimate interest processing, set out in the GDPR, that is the purpose test, the necessity tests, and the balancing tests. Its Information Notice adds an additional note, stating that:

> there is a further requirement under the GDPR for processing "special categories of data" and this includes data concerning an individual's health. This requirement can be satisfied if the processing is necessary "for reasons of public interest in the area of public health of for archiving purposes in the public interest, scientific or historical research purposes ….". The GDPR specifies that "research purposes" include "studies conducted in the public interest in the area of public health". We consider that UK Biobank's activities fall squarely within this requirement.[48]

Where data is lawfully processed within the EU, it may be lawfully transferred anywhere within the EU. This is one of the key aims of the GDPR, to allow the flow of data within the EU's 'single market'. UK-based biobanks, like UK Biobank, that transfer data *out* to other EU countries, and other EU countries that transfer data *in* to the UK, currently rely on these provisions. Further, under the GDPR, standard contractual clauses provide a lawful basis for transfer of data to 'third countries' (i.e. non-EU countries), or international organisations.

2.3.2 Consent as a Basis for Lawful Processing

In general, the GDPR sets a high standard for consent to process personal data and especially specific kinds of data, including health data. This raised concerns during its drafting that this standard could cause difficulties for researchers, as it was common practice for consent to participate in research to be framed on a broad basis.[49] This is a matter which Member States may treat differently in their derogations, but

---

Data Protection Regulation (GDPR) http://www.ukbiobank.ac.uk/wp-content/uploads/2018/10/GDPR.pdf.

[46] Health Research Authority (last updated 19 April 2019) Consent in research. (NHS) https://www.hra.nhs.uk/planning-and-improving-research/policies-standards-legislation/data-protection-and-information-governance/gdpr-guidance/what-law-says/consent-research/.

[47] UK Biobank (27 February 2018b) GDPR Information Notice. https://www.ukbiobank.ac.uk/2018/02/gdpr/.

[48] Ibid.

[49] Taylor et al. (2018), pp. 638–639.

in the UK there is some uncertainty about whether consent can be relied upon as a basis for lawful processing in the context of health and social care research, which obviously includes activities of biobanks. Although consent is central to the HTA, both the Health Research Authority and the ICO have released guidance on consent. Specifically, according to the HRA's website:[50]

> For the purposes of the GDPR, the legal basis for processing data for health and social care research should NOT be consent. This means that requirements in the GDPR relating to consent do NOT apply to health and care research

The logical consequence of this guidance is that the basis of lawful processing of data by UK-based biobanks is legitimate interest, rather than consent. However, the ICO also indicates in its guidance that organisations 'are likely to need to consider consent when no other lawful basis obviously applies'.[51] Furthermore, when dealing with human tissue, as consent is the central principle upon which the Human Tissue Act is based, biobanks that handle tissue samples are likely to be required to obtain consent from research participants in order to collect samples and conduct research.

2.3.3 Legitimate Public Interest as a Basis for Lawful Processing

According to the UK's Data Protection Act, processing of personal data that is 'necessary for scientific … research purposes' is lawful.[52] This includes personal data in one of the GDPR's 'special categories', which include genetic data and data concerning health. The data held by biobanks includes 'special category' data under the GDPR and Data Protection Act. Biobanks may collect and process several different types of 'special category' data. Processing of such data by a biobank that is necessary when carrying out research is lawful, so long as it is consistent with the Data Protection Act's section 19 requirements and so long as it is in the public interest.[53] Section 19 provides that the processing may not, however, be 'likely to cause substantial damage or substantive distress to a data subject'.[54] It is possible that biobanking activities could do so, for instance, if they brought to light information about someone's genetic predispositions to medical conditions. However, where the data processing is necessary for 'the purposes of approved medical research', then

[50] Ibid, citing Health Research Authority (last updated 19 April 2019) Consent in research. (NHS) https://www.hra.nhs.uk/planning-and-improving-research/policies-standards-legislation/data-protection-and-information-governance/gdpr-guidance/what-law-says/consent-research/.

[51] Taylor et al. (2018), p. 639 citing ICO When is consent appropriate? https://ico.org.uk/for-organisations/guide-to-data-protection/guide-to-the-general-data-protection-regulation-gdpr/consent/when-is-consent-appropriate/; Mahsa and Borry (2018), p. 149; Ford et al. (2019), p. e10191; Townend (2018), pp. 657–664; Budin-Ljøsne et al. (2017), p. 4; Mc Cullagh K (2019) UK: GDPR adaptions and preparations for withdrawal from the EU: 108–119. https://ueaeprints.uea.ac.uk/70040/1/national_adaptations_of_the_gdpr_final_version_27_february_1.pdf.

[52] DPA, section 19 (1)(b).

[53] DPA, schedule 1, part 1, section 4.

[54] DPA, section 19 (2).

it is compliant with the Data Protection Act.[55] 'Approved medical research' requires ethical clearance, either under the Health Research Authority, or a body appointed by the NHS or a research institution, such as a University.[56]

Under the Health Research Authority guidance, data subjects who are research participants in public sector research projects must be informed that processing of personal data for research purposes is in the public interest.[57]

2.3.4 Adequacy Decisions, 'Appropriate Safeguards' (Standard Contractual Clauses and Binding Corporate Rules), and Special Circumstances as a Basis for Transfer of Data to 'Third Countries'

Under the GDPR, and Data Protection Act, it is unlawful to transfer personal data to a 'third country' unless there is a lawful basis for such transfer.[58] While the UK remained a Member State of the EU, and during the 'transition' period until end December 2020, organisations (including biobanks) processing data in the UK were able to rely on the grounds set out in chapter V of the GDPR, and chapter 5 of the DPA, as a basis for the lawful transfer of data out of the UK to 'third countries' (i.e. non-EU countries).

Biobanks in the UK may lawfully transfer personal data to a third country where the transfer is based on an 'adequacy decision'.[59] Such adequacy decisions are taken by the European Commission.

In the absence of an adequacy decision, transfer may take place where 'appropriate safeguards' are provided. One such appropriate safeguard is the use of standard contractual clauses. Article 57 of the GDPR provides for each supervisory authority to create standard contractual clauses, which businesses can use in their agreements for data processing and transfer. The UK's ICO has created templates for both controller to processor contracts[60] and controller to controller contracts,[61] which biobanks can use. The ICO has also produced guidance on what organisations need to

[55] DPA, section 19 (3).

[56] DPA, section 19 (4).

[57] Taylor et al. (2018), p. 639 citing Health Research Authority NHS (last updated 8 May 2018) Legal basis for processing data. https://www.hra.nhs.uk/planning-and-improving-research/policies-standards-legislation/data-protection-and-information-governance/gdpr-detailed-guidance/legal-basis-processing-data/.

[58] DPA, section 73.

[59] DPA, section 74.

[60] ICO Build a controller to processor contract. https://ico.org.uk/for-organisations/data-protection-and-brexit/how-to-transfer-data-from-europe-from-the-eea-to-the-uk-using-standard-contractual-clauses-sccs/build-a-controller-to-processor-contract/.

[61] ICO Build a controller to controller contract https://ico.org.uk/for-organisations/data-protection-and-brexit/how-to-transfer-data-from-europe-from-the-eea-to-the-uk-using-standard-contractual-clauses-sccs/build-a-controller-to-controller-contract/.

include in contracts for data transfer.[62] The Health Research Authority's guidance confirms the lawfulness of such data transfers.[63]

However, as Lawlor et al. write, standard contractual clauses may not be the best suited mechanism for biobanking research.[64] Their work is concerned with research conducted by biobanks more generally, rather than specifically those based in the UK. They suggest that making more use of material transfer agreements, and development of a code of conduct, would assist international biobank research collaborations.

BBMRI-ERIC have also called for the development of a Code of Conduct for Health Research.[65] The aim is to 'reach a sector-specific code that explains how the GDPR applies in practice.'[66] 130 individuals representing 80 organisations in the field of health research support the idea of such a Code.[67] This initiative is international in nature. The most recent Code drafting meeting took place in Rome in November 2018.[68] If it is eventually approved under Article 40 of the GDPR, the Code would apply broadly to a wide range of health research and would be of assistance to biobanks engaging in international data transfer into EU Member States and also potentially for those sending data outside the EU.

Another type of appropriate safeguard is 'binding corporate rules'.[69]

It is also permissible for a UK-based biobank to transfer data to a third country on the basis of special circumstances.[70] The most relevant circumstances that could be relied upon are those set out in DPA, section 76(1) (a) and (b), which allow for transfer in order to 'protect the vital interests of the data subject or another person' or 'to safeguard the legitimate interests of the data subject'. Explicit consent of the data subject to the transfer is another possible 'special circumstance' but this would not be practical for biobanks to secure.

[62] ICO What needs to be included in the contract? https://ico.org.uk/for-organisations/guide-to-data-protection/guide-to-the-general-data-protection-regulation-gdpr/contracts-and-liabilities-between-controllers-and-processors-multi/what-needs-to-be-included-in-the-contract/.

[63] Taylor et al. (2018), p. 639 citing Health Research Authority NHS (last updated 8 May 2018) Legal basis for processing data. https://www.hra.nhs.uk/planning-and-improving-research/policies-standards-legislation/data-protection-and-information-governance/gdpr-detailed-guidance/legal-basis-processing-data/.

[64] Lawlor RT, Kozlakidis Z, Bledsoe M (14 November 2018) GDPR in biobanking for precision medicine research: The challenges. Open Access Government https://www.openaccessgovernment.org/gdpr-in-biobanking-for-precision-medicine/54468/.

[65] Code of Conduct for Health Research http://code-of-conduct-for-health-research.eu/faq.

[66] Ibid.

[67] Ibid.

[68] Code of Conduct for Health Research (05/11/2018 – 06/112018) CoC Drafting Group Meeting https://code-of-conduct-for-health-research.eu/events/coc-drafting-group-meeting-6.

[69] GDPR, Article 47.

[70] GDPR, Article 49; DPA, section 75.

3 The Political and Legal Processes of Brexit to Date

This section of the chapter explains the political processes following the EU referendum in June 2016, and sets out the current legal position in general terms. Its specific application to biobanking, especially GDPR aspects, is discussed in Sect. 4 below.

Following an (advisory) referendum, and an Act of Parliament,[71] the latter as required 'in accordance with [the UK's] constitutional requirements',[72] the UK formally notified its intention to leave the EU on 29 March 2017, as specified under Article 50 of the Treaty on European Union. Under Article 50 (3) TEU, the default position was that the UK would leave the EU on 29 March 2019.

Article 50 TEU obliged the EU-27 to negotiate a Withdrawal Agreement with the UK. By 25 November 2018, the UK had agreed a draft Withdrawal Agreement with the EU's negotiating team, which was duly approved by the Council of the EU-27, along with a non-binding political declaration on the future EU-UK relationship.[73] However, the UK government was unable to secure support in Parliament for ratification of the Withdrawal Agreement.[74] Nonetheless, in a non-binding vote, the House of Commons *also* indicated its opposition to leaving the EU without a Withdrawal Agreement in place.[75]

In March 2019,[76] and again in April 2019,[77] the EU and UK agreed, in accordance with Article 50 (3) TEU, to extend the withdrawal negotiation period. As at May 2019, it was agreed that the UK would leave the EU on 31 October 2019, unless the Withdrawal Agreement was ratified before that date, in which case the UK would have left when the Withdrawal Agreement entered into force. As things stood when we originally wrote this chapter, thus, on the date of entry into force of the Withdrawal Agreement, or on 31 October 2019, the UK would have ceased to be

---

[71] European Union (Notification of Withdrawal) Act 2017.

[72] Article 50 TEU; *R on the application of Miller and another v Secretary of State for Exiting the European Union* [2017] UKSC 5.

[73] See Agreement on the withdrawal of the United Kingdom of Great Britain and Northern Ireland from the European Union and the European Atomic Energy Community, OJ 2019 C 66 I/01; Draft Political declaration setting out the framework for the future relationship between the European Union and the United Kingdom, OJ 2019 C 66 I/185; Council Decision (EU) 2019/274 on the signing, on behalf of the European Union and of the European Atomic Energy Community, of the Agreement on the withdrawal of the United Kingdom of Great Britain and Northern Ireland from the European Union and the European Atomic Energy Community OJ 2019 LI 47/1.

[74] As we write, there have been three attempts to secure approval for the Withdrawal Agreement from the UK's House of Commons on 15 January 2019 (defeated by 230 votes); 12 March 2019 (defeated by 149 votes) and 29 March (defeated by 58 votes).

[75] The House of Commons voted, on 13 March 2019, to reject leaving the EU without a Withdrawal Agreement (321 to 278, a margin of 43 votes).

[76] European Council Decision (EU) 2019/476 taken in agreement with the United Kingdom of 22 March 2019 extending the period under Article 50(3)TEU OJ 2019 L 801/1.

[77] European Council Decision (EU) 2019/584 taken in agreement with the United Kingdom of 11 April 2019 extending the period under Article 50(3) TEU OJ 2019 L 101/1.

a Member State of the EU. What actually happened was that the UK did not leave the EU until 31 January 2020, at which point a revised Withdrawal Agreement entered into force.

The Withdrawal Agreement provides for a 'transition' or 'implementation' period, which ends on 31 December 2020.[78] In principle, during the transition period, EU law applies to and in the UK, producing the same legal effects, and being interpreted and applied in accordance with the same methods and principles, as before withdrawal.[79] This means that EU law as it stands at 'Exit Day' *and as it evolves through the transition period* will produce legal effects in the UK during the transition period.[80]

During transition, EU institutions, bodies and agencies, including the Court of Justice of the EU, have powers in relation to the UK, and to natural and legal persons established in the UK.[81] But this is 'unless otherwise provided' in the Withdrawal Agreement.[82] So, for instance, the UK will no longer be included in EU institutions, bodies or agencies, and the UK's institutions will not be considered institutions of a Member State.[83] Access to networks, information systems and EU databases ceases at the end of transition.[84]

The transition period may be extended once, 'to a period up to [31 December XXXX]', by a decision of a 'Joint Committee'[85] made before 1 July 2020.[86] The current political intention of the UK government is not to seek extension.

The UK has made initial domestic provision for withdrawal from the EU through the EU (Withdrawal) Act 2018. The EU (Withdrawal) Act originally provided for an 'Exit Day' of 29 March 2019. This was amended by statutory instrument on 11 April 2019, so that Exit Day is currently defined in UK domestic law as on 30 October 2019, so that Exit Day is defined in UK domestic law as 31 January 2020 [87]

The Act repeals the European Communities Act 1972, which is the domestic provision through which EU law applies in the UK and is a source of UK law. The EU (Withdrawal) Act 2018 creates, on Exit Day, a new source of UK law: 'retained EU law'. In essence, all EU law applicable in the UK on that date will be part of UK law by virtue of the Act.

---

[78] WA, Article 126.

[79] WA, Article 127.

[80] WA, Article 6.

[81] WA, Article 131.

[82] WA, Article 127.

[83] WA, Article 128.

[84] WA, Article 8.

[85] An institution comprising representatives of the EU and UK, established by the WA, Article 164. Its obligations include to supervise and facilitate the implementation of the WA.

[86] WA, Article 132.

[87] European Union (Withdrawal) Act 2018 (Exit Day) (No 3) Regulations 2019 SI 2019/1423 30 October 2019. This statutory instrument makes no provision for an earlier Exit Day in the event that the Withdrawal Agreement is ratified. If it is, a further statutory instrument will be necessary to define Exit Day accordingly.

4 The Legal Position for GDPR Aspects of Biobanking Post-Brexit

All of the different types of biobank structures in the UK have been and will continue to be affected by Brexit, but in different ways. Smaller biobanks that collect, process or share data solely within the UK are affected less, although the applicable law will change. Larger, networked, UK-based biobanks that share data *outward* to the EU and other countries, and those which receive *inward* coming data from the EU and other countries are affected more, because pre-Brexit and pre-transition the basis on which the lawfulness of data protection in those transactions is secured is the UK's membership of the EU and the Withdrawal Agreement. Some biobanks, for instance, commercial operators, may be able to circumvent the inconvenience of Brexit, and continue to operate as before within the EU, by incorporating in an EU Member State. This approach is not open to university-based or governmental/institutional UK biobanks. Those biobanks that rely on EU networks and funding may find that they are totally excluded from such access, depending on the form that the future EU-UK trade relationship takes.

We now focus on the legal position for UK data protection law, as it applies in biobanking contexts, post-Brexit. In the run up to 29 March 2019, the UK government issued several guidance notes and other policy documents giving advice about the post-Brexit legal position. Some of this guidance is relevant to the GDPR and biobanking. Of course, however, the views of the government, even expressed in formal guidance notes, do not have the force of 'hard' law. The section therefore outlines the position under the only relevant primary UK legislation currently enacted at the time of writing: the EU (Withdrawal) Act 2018, and under relevant secondary (delegated) legislation in the form of statutory instruments. These latter are executive acts with the full force of law in the UK.[88] These provisions apply whatever the form of Brexit, and do not distinguish between the position under the Withdrawal Agreement and that in a 'No Deal' situation (which did not, in the end, occur).

We then consider the legal position under each of the possible forms of Brexit discussed in this chapter: under the EU-UK Withdrawal Agreement, and what the position would have been in the event of a No Deal Brexit. We have retained the latter analysis to illustrate both the complexities of Brexit and the position should the EU and UK be unable to agree a trade agreement by the end of December 2020. When we originally wrote this chapter, we did not know how the UK would implement its obligations under the Withdrawal Agreement, so that analysis is by definition more conjectural.

[88] For further information, see UK Parliament Statutory Instruments (Sis) https://www.parliament.uk/site-information/glossary/statutory-instruments-sis/.

4.1 Domestic Legislation, Statutory Instruments, 'Soft Law', Guidance

4.1.1 Soft Law and Guidance on Data Protection Post-Brexit

In December 2018, the UK government issued a technical note giving guidance on data protection post-Brexit. That guidance was withdrawn on 1 March 2019,[89] and replaced with revised guidance adopted on 6 February 2019.[90] It complements guidance from the ICO[91] on the future data protection regime in case of a No Deal Brexit, which remains in place. The guidance applies to all organisations to which the GDPR applies, so it applies to UK biobanks.

4.1.2 Data Protection Under the EU (Withdrawal) Act 2018

As 'retained EU law', the GDPR is in principle part of UK law on Exit Day, under the terms of the EU (Withdrawal) Act 2018.

However, the GDPR (as a source of 'retained EU law') will be subject to future amendments made by the UK legislator. Any such amendments are legally authorised on the basis of powers set out in the EU (Withdrawal) Act 2018, the Data Protection Act 2018, and the European Communities Act 1972. These powers allow the UK government to act unilaterally to remedy any 'deficiencies' in 'retained EU law'. These amendments will take effect through secondary legislation: the Data Protection, Privacy and Electronic Communications (Amendments etc) (EU Exit) Regulations 2019,[92] and any subsequent secondary legislation. The EU (Withdrawal) Act 2018 makes no provision for UK compliance with the Withdrawal Agreement (see further below in Sect. 4.2.3).

---

[89] Department for Digital, Culture, Media & Sports (13 September 2018, this guidance was withdrawn on the 1st of March 2019) Data protection if there's no Brexit deal. https://www.gov.uk/government/publications/data-protection-if-theres-no-brexit-deal/data-protection-if-theres-no-brexit-deal.

[90] Department for Digital, Culture, Media & Sports (6 February 2019) Using personal data after Brexit. https://www.gov.uk/guidance/using-personal-data-after-brexit. We make no further comment on the obvious unsatisfactory nature of guidance from 6 February 2019 not replacing guidance from December 2018 until 1 March 2019.

[91] ICO, Data protection and Brexit https://ico.org.uk/for-organisations/data-protection-and-brexit/.

[92] SI No 419 28 February 2019 http://www.legislation.gov.uk/uksi/2019/419/pdfs/uksi_20190419_en.pdf.

4.1.3 The Data Protection, Privacy and Electronic Communications (Amendments Etc) (EU Exit) Regulations 2019

The Data Protection, Privacy and Electronic Communications (Amendments etc) (EU Exit) Regulations 2019[93] (hereafter, 'the EU Exit Regulations') amend various parts of legislation to take account of the UK leaving the EU. They came into force on Exit Day. In summary, the Regulations amend the Data Protection Act 2018, the GDPR as 'retained EU law' (known in the Regulations as 'the UK GDPR'), and merge provisions of the two.[94] Schedule 1 lists the amendments to the UK GDPR, while schedule 2 deals with the amendments to the Data Protection Act 2018. Schedule 3 deals with consequential amendments to other legislation, and schedule 4 addresses amendments consequential on provisions of the 2018 Act.

The UK government claims[95] that the majority of the changes to the existing law involve removing references to EU institutions and procedures that will not be directly relevant when the UK is outside the EU. This is accurate. Many changes, for instance, simply change 'the Union' or 'a Member State' for 'the UK'; or 'the competent authority' for 'the Commissioner', that is, the Information Commissioner as referred to in the Data Protection Act, section 114 and schedule 12.

However, the EU Exit Regulations do make some changes to the legal position beyond removing references to the EU and its institutions and procedures. The key changes of relevance or potential relevance to biobanking are as follows:

(a) Adequacy decisions
(b) Standard data protection contractual clauses
(c) Information exchange and cooperation
(d) Removal of procedural and remedial safeguards
(e) General principles of EU law.

(a) Adequacy Decisions

The EU Exit Regulations add new sections 17A and 17B, and 74A to the Data Protection Act 2018. These give the Secretary of State power to adopt adequacy decisions by regulations, and oblige the Secretary of State to keep such decisions under periodic review. An adequacy decision may be taken in respect of a third

---

[93] Ibid.

[94] The Explanatory Note to the SI reads 'Among other things, changes made by Schedules 1 and 2 have the effect of merging two pre-existing regimes for the regulation of the processing of personal data – namely that established by the GDPR as supplemented by Chapter 2 of Part 2 of the DPA 2018 as originally enacted, and that established in Chapter 3 of Part 2 of the DPA 2018 as originally enacted (the applied GDPR). The applied GDPR extended GDPR standards to certain processing out of scope of EU law and the GDPR. Regulation 5 makes provision concerning interpretation in relation to processing that prior to exit day was subject to the applied GDPR.'

[95] Department for Digital, Culture, Media & Sports, Data protection if there's no Brexit deal (n 89).

country (which in this context, contrary to its meaning in EU and international law, means a country outside of the UK[96]); a territory or one or more sectors within a third country; an international organisation (such as the EU); or a description of such a country, territory, sector or organisation. Transfer of personal data *from* the UK to such a country, territory, sector or organisation would not be lawful in the absence of an adequacy decision, or other basis for lawful transfer, such as 'special circumstances', or 'standard data protection clauses' (see below in Sect. 4.3.2).

When assessing the adequacy of protection in a third state or international organisation, the Secretary of State must take into account a list of factors outlined in new section 74A of the Data Protection Act. These repeat verbatim the matters that the European Commission should take into account when assessing adequacy, as provided in Article 45 (2) GDPR. Briefly, these include:

> (a) the rule of law, respect for human rights and fundamental freedoms, relevant legislation, both general and sectoral, including concerning public security, defence, national security and criminal law and the access of public authorities to personal data, as well as the implementation of such legislation, data protection rules, professional rules and security measures, including rules for the onward transfer of personal data to another third country or international organisation which are complied with in that country or international organisation, case-law, as well as effective and enforceable data subject rights and effective administrative and judicial redress for the data subjects whose personal data are being transferred;
>
> (b) the existence and effective functioning of one or more independent supervisory authorities in the third country … including adequate enforcement powers, for assisting and advising the data subjects in exercising their rights and for cooperation with the supervisory authorities of the Member States;
>
> and (c) the international commitments the third country … has entered into, or other obligations arising from legally binding conventions or instruments as well as from its participation in multilateral or regional systems…

The Secretary of State must monitor developments in such third countries, sectors etc, and amend or revoke adequacy decisions accordingly, having given the country etc the opportunity to remedy any lack of protection. In addition, each adequacy decision must be reviewed at least once every 4 years.[97]

The UK government's guidance explains that the UK 'will transitionally recognise all EEA countries (including EU Member States) and Gibraltar as 'adequate' to allow data flows from the UK to Europe to continue,' and 'preserve the effect of existing EU adequacy decisions', including the EU-US Privacy Shield, on a transitional basis.[98] The Data Protection, Privacy and Electronic Communications (Amendments etc) (EU Exit) (No. 2), Regulations 2019, schedule 2, article 102,

---

[96] New provision in Article 4 GDPR, after para 26.

[97] Data Protection Act 2018, new Sections 17B and 74B.

[98] Department for Digital, Culture, Media & Sport (updated 11 April 2019) Amendments to UK data protection law in the event the UK leaves the EU without a deal. (UK Government, Guidance Note) https://www.gov.uk/government/publications/data-protection-law-eu-exit/amendments-to-uk-data-protection-law-in-the-event-the-uk-leaves-the-eu-without-a-deal-on-29-march-2019.

inserting a new Schedule 21 into the UK GDPR provides that all EEA states (which of course include all EU27 Member States), Gibraltar, EU and EEA institutions, and all the third countries, territories, sectors or international organisations which the EU recognises with adequacy clauses (Switzerland, Canada, Argentina, Guernsey, Isle of Man, Jersey, Faroe Isles, Andorra, Israel, Uruguay, New Zealand, and the USA) are regarded as countries etc which the UK recognises as having an adequate level of protection for personal data transferred *from* the UK into that country. In the context of biobanking this means that it will be lawful for biobanks in the UK to continue to conduct data transfers of UK citizens' data, and other data they hold, to organisations based in all of these places.

Obviously the UK's EU Exit Regulations can make no provision for the transfer of personal data *into* the UK from another country. Non-EU countries will each need to decide how to treat the UK as a non-EU Member State, when, up to the end of the transition period they have been recognising the UK's treatment of personal data as adequate because the UK is an EU Member State. It was reported in April 2019 that some countries have indicated that they will continue to allow free data flow into the UK, even in the event of a No Deal Brexit.[99] This might be the case also in the event of a failure to agree an EU-UK trade agreement. These countries include Switzerland, Israel, and the USA. The legal nature of these permissions is domestic law within each third country.

Transfer of personal data from EU Member States into the UK post Brexit remains subject to EU law. In the absence of any other provision being in place (but see further below Sects. 4.2.1 and 4.3.1), the UK is treated as a 'third country' in the terms of the GDPR. This will mean that transfer of data to biobanks in the UK is unlawful, unless there is a lawful basis for that transfer as provided for under the GDPR. At present, there is no agreement on how the UK and EU are to treat each other's assessments of adequacy. The biobanking sector, like many (or possibly all) other sectors which rely on sharing of data across borders, have noted that it would be beneficial if some agreement was reached that would allow for mutual recognition. This will be easier to achieve because Brexit took place under the Withdrawal Agreement, as opposed to on a 'No Deal' basis (see further below section 4.2).

(b) Standard Data Protection Contractual Clauses and Binding Corporate Rules

Approach to Standard Data Protection Contractual Clauses and Binding Corporate Rules

The EU Exit Regulations 2019 purport to offer some level of legal continuity, as they amend the Data Protection Act to provide that standard contractual clauses and binding corporate rules that are authorised before Exit Day will remain valid.[100]

---

[99] Linkomies (April 2019), pp. 8–9.

[100] Data Protection Act 2018, new Schedule 21, sections 7, 8 and 9, added by Data Protection, Privacy and Electronic Communications (Amendments etc) (EU Exit) Regulations 2019 http://

UK-based biobanks which currently transfer UK citizens' data, and other data they hold, to organisations based in other countries, on the basis of standard data protection contractual clauses or binding corporate rules, will be able to continue to do so after Exit Day. Post-Brexit, standard contractual clauses become known as 'standard data protection clauses' in UK law.[101] The EU Exit Regulations also empower the Information Commissioner to withdraw authorisation for binding corporate rules.[102]

Schedule 2 of the EU Exit Regulations adds new sections 17C and 119A to the Data Protection Act. These provisions address standard data protection clauses. Such clauses are those which the Secretary of State considers provide appropriate safeguards for transfers of data to a third country or international organisation, in accordance with new sections 17A and 17B. Schedule 3 of the Regulations revokes existing EU law (that otherwise would become retained EU law) which provides for standard contractual clauses.[103] To replace this, the Information Commissioner is empowered, in consultation with the Secretary of State, and any other stakeholders the Commissioner considers appropriate,[104] to specify 'standard data protection clauses' which are sufficient to provide adequate safeguards for the purposes of transfer of data to a third country or international organisation,[105] and also to amend or withdraw such standard clauses.[106] In effect, standard contractual clauses become standard data protection clauses in the Regulations. Documents issued by the Commissioner specifying standard data protection clauses are subject to a negative Parliamentary assent procedure.[107] For UK-based biobanks wishing to continue to conduct data transfers of UK citizens' data, and other data they hold, to

www.legislation.gov.uk/uksi/2019/419/pdfs/uksi_20190419_en.pdf.

[101] Data Protection, Privacy and Electronic Communications (Amendments etc) (EU Exit) Regulations 2019 http://www.legislation.gov.uk/uksi/2019/419/pdfs/uksi_20190419_en.pdf, Schedule 1 of Regulation 3, section 39.

[102] Data Protection Act 2018, new Schedule 21, section 9 (5).

[103] Commission Decision 2001/497/EC of 15th June 2001 on standard contractual clauses for the transfer of personal data to third countries, under Directive 95/46/EC OJ 2001 L 181/19;... (g) Commission Decision 2004/915/EC of 27th December 2004 amending Decision 2001/497/EC as regards the introduction of an alternative set of standard contractual clauses for the transfer of personal data to third countries OJ 2004 L 385/74; (i) Commission Decision 2010/87/EU of 5th February 2010 on standard contractual clauses for the transfer of personal data to processors established in third countries under Directive 95/46/EC of the European Parliament and of the Council OJ 2016 L 344/100;... and (q) Commission Implementing Decision (EU) 2016/2297 of 16th December 2016 amending Decisions 2001/497/EC and 2010/87/EU on standard contractual clauses for the transfer of personal data to third countries and to processors established in such countries, under Directive 95/46/EC of the European Parliament and of the Council OJ 2016 L 344/100.

[104] Data Protection Act 2018, new section 119A (4).

[105] Data Protection Act 2018, new section 119A (1).

[106] Data Protection Act 2018, new section 119A (2).

[107] Data Protection Act 2018, new section 119A (6). Under the negative Parliamentary assent procedure, a statutory instrument laid before Parliament becomes law on the day the Minister signs it, and automatically remains law unless a motion to reject it is agreed by either the House of

organisations based in other countries, standard data protection contractual clauses are a potential basis for lawful transfer of data post-transition.

Again, as with adequacy decisions, the UK's EU Exit Regulations can make no provision for the post-transition transfer of data *from* EU-based entities, or those based in other countries, *to* UK-based biobanks. There is (as yet) no agreement on coordination or mutual recognition of such clauses between the UK and the EU, and in any event the nature of these clauses is currently the subject of litigation before the CJEU (see further below, Sect. 4.3.1).[108] Despite this, the ICO has produced an interactive tool for businesses to deal with standard contractual clauses if the UK does leave the EU without a deal.[109] The ICO recommends that organisations that need 'to maintain the free flow of personal data into the UK from Europe, in the event the UK exits the EU without a deal... should consider using standard contract clauses'.[110] But the ICO can only account for movement of data *out* of the UK, not *into* the UK. To write of 'free flow' of data, as the ICO's recommendations do, is to misrepresent the formal legal position. It is not yet clear what the EU's position will be on data transfer into the UK from the EU following a the failure to agree a trade agreement at the end of transition (see further below in Sect. 4.3.1).

(c) Information Exchange and Cooperation

The EU Exit Regulations remove all obligations on the UK, or entities within the UK, to cooperate within the structures of the EU, or to exchange information with the European Commission. Instead, the Regulations envisage that the Council of Europe's Data Protection Convention[111] (which the UK has signed and ratified) will be the basis of interstate data protection cooperation post transition, through the Convention's obligations to designate one or more authorities to furnish information to authorities in other states on law and administrative practice in data protection.[112] This Convention is the first binding international instrument on individual personal

Commons or the House of Lords within 40 sitting days. See https://www.parliament.uk/site-information/glossary/negative-procedure/.

[108] Case C-311/18 *Schrems II*, reference for a preliminary ruling from the Irish High Court 9 May 2018.

[109] ICO (2019a) *Do I need to use standard contractual clauses (SCCs) for transfers from the EEA to the UK (if we leave the EU with no deal)?* https://ico.org.uk/for-organisations/data-protection-and-brexit/standard-contractual-clauses-for-transfers-from-the-eea-to-the-uk-interactive-tool/.

[110] ICO (2019b) How to transfer data from Europe (from the EEA) to the UK using standard contractual clauses (SCCs) https://ico.org.uk/for-organisations/data-protection-and-brexit/how-to-transfer-data-from-europe-from-the-eea-to-the-uk-using-standard-contractual-clauses-sccs/.

[111] Convention for the Protection of Individuals with regard to Automatic Processing of Personal Data (the Data Protection Convention) ETS No.108, Strasbourg, 1981.

[112] Under the Data Protection Convention, Article 13. See The Data Protection, Privacy and Electronic Communications (Amendments etc) (EU Exit) Regulations 2019 SI No 419 28 February 2019 Reg 3 Sch 1 6(10) http://www.legislation.gov.uk/uksi/2019/419/pdfs/uksi_20190419_en.pdf.

data protection. It seeks to prohibit abuses that may arise when personal data is collected or processed, to ensure that sensitive data (such as concerning health) is subject to legal safeguards, to secure a 'right to know' what information is held, and to regulate the flow of personal data across borders. The UK's data protection law secures compliance with these international obligations. The Data Protection Convention will thus have increased significance to the UK's data protection framework post-Brexit, where there continues to be uncertainty about how the EU will treat the UK for data protection purposes post-transition. This will depend on the type of Brexit (see further below), and what the EU and the UK eventually agree in terms of future EU-UK relationships.

(d) Procedural and Remedial Safeguards

The EU Exit Regulations remove the obligation to the effect that the authority that supervises the application of the GDPR (in the UK, the Information Commissioner) must, when imposing administrative fines, comply with national and EU law on procedural safeguards, including effective judicial remedy and process.[113] Instead, section 115 (9) of the Data Protection Act makes provision about the exercise of the Commissioner's functions when imposing administrative fines. The right to an effective remedy and other general principles of EU law concerning due process are an important feature of EU law in various contexts, including data protection. Essentially driven by the CJEU, these principles have formed an important part of the development of EU data protection law, which includes the entitlement of data subjects to secure effective remedies for breach, part of the overall compliance and sanctions regime under the GDPR.

The Data Protection Act, section 115 (9), as amended, provides that the Commissioner may only exercise its powers to issue administrative fines by giving a penalty notice, as provided for in section 155, having determined that a person has failed, in the sense prescribed in section 149, to comply with provisions of the GDPR. The pre-Brexit position was that this form of implementation is—at least in theory—subject to scrutiny for compliance with general principles of EU law. Post-transition, this layer of scrutiny is removed. However, of course, the UK will retain its obligations to due process under the ECHR, such as a right to a fair hearing.

(e) General Principles of EU Law

The EU Exit Regulations exclude from application any case law or general principles of EU law not relevant to the GDPR, or chapter 2 or Parts 5–7 of the Data Protection Act.[114] These are the parts of the existing law concerning interpretation of

[113] Regulation 3, Schedule 3, chapter 8, Regulation 62 (7), removing Article 83 (8) of the GDPR.

[114] Regulation 5 (3).

the applicable legal provisions. The change made by the EU Exit Regulations means, for instance, that future CJEU interpretations of broader principles of EU law, such as under the EU CFR, and in *Mangold*-type cases,[115] will not apply in the UK as retained EU law. This is consistent with the amendment to the Data Protection Act, section 205, which provides that references in that Act to a 'fundamental right or fundamental freedom' are only to such fundamental rights and freedoms which continue to form part of UK domestic law after Exit Day. The European Union (Withdrawal) Act, section 4, provides that EU law rights, obligations, or remedies that come from the CJEU's jurisprudence continue to be part of 'retained EU law', *only* if they are recognised as such in a case decided by the CJEU *before* Exit Day. The intention seems to be to sever the way that relevant law in the UK is interpreted from how those interpretations develop in the EU, following Exit Day, and to do so irrespective of whether the Withdrawal Agreement—which provides in its Article 131 that the CJEU's jurisdiction continues in the UK during transition—is agreed or not. The implications of this are difficult to ascertain. During transition, the European Union (Withdrawal Agreement) Act 2020 'switches back on' the European Communities Act 1972, to the effect that EU law (including judgments of the CJEU) continues to apply to and within the UK until the end of December 2020. However, after that, the European Union (Withdrawal) Act, section 4, provides that EU law rights, obligations, or remedies that come from the CJEU's jurisprudence continue to be part of 'retained EU law', only if they are recognised as such in a case decided by the CJEU before Exit Day (not the end of transition). The intention seems to be to sever the way that relevant law in the UK is interpreted from how those interpretations develop in the EU, following Exit Day, and to do so despite the fact that the Withdrawal Agreement provides in its Article 131 that the CJEU's jurisdiction continues in the UK during transition. Questions about the significance of this legislation go to questions of future regulatory alignment between the UK and the EU, which itself will then affect the extent to which the EU is able to recognise the UK's regulatory environment as embodying an adequate protection for data, including the kinds of health-related data that biobanks process. These matters are discussed further in Sect. 4.2 below.

4.2 The EU-UK Withdrawal Agreement and Biobanking

4.2.1 Data Protection Law Under the Withdrawal Agreement

We note at the start of this section that aspects of the Withdrawal Agreement's text on data protection are difficult to interpret.[116] Of course, as the Withdrawal Agreement has only recently entered into force, there are no binding judicial rulings

[115] Case C-144/04 *Mangold* ECLI:EU:C:2005:709.

[116] See, for instance, https://privacylawblog.fieldfisher.com/2018/what-does-the-draft-withdrawal-agreement-mean-for-data-protection: 'During the transition period the UK loses its seat at the table

on the meaning of its text. The underlying aim of the Withdrawal Agreement is to ensure an orderly withdrawal of the UK from the EU, and to avoid disruption during the transition period by ensuring that EU law applies to and in the UK during that period.[117] The Withdrawal Agreement's provisions should thus be interpreted with that aimed-for continuity in mind.

In general, the Withdrawal Agreement provides that the UK is to be treated as a Member State of the EU during the transition period.[118] So, in general, EU law continues to apply to and in the UK, as if the UK were still a Member State, from Exit Day until the end of transition.[119] Thus, the GDPR continues to apply in and to the UK during that period. Biobanks in the UK will continue to be required to comply with the GDPR. The Withdrawal Agreement also provides that references to competent authorities of Member States in provisions of EU law made applicable by the Withdrawal Agreement are to include UK competent authorities.[120] This means that, until the end December 2020, the UK's ICO continues to be recognised as an institution of a Member State, even though the UK is no longer a Member State of the EU.

However, this continuity rule applies *only* 'unless otherwise provided' in the Withdrawal Agreement.[121] One of the key exclusions concerns the UK's participation in EU institutions, and in decision-making and governance of the bodies, offices and agencies of the Union. The UK will no longer participates in such entities.[122] The European Data Protection Board, established under the GDPR,[123] is (presumably[124]) a 'body' of the Union for these purposes. The Withdrawal Agreement makes no explicit provision for the UK's continued participation in the European Data Protection Board or its information sharing systems. The precise modalities of the situation where the UK Information Commissioner is excluded from the European Data Protection Board, but the ICO is still recognised as a competent national

---

in the European Data Protection Board ("EDPB"). But that doesn't necessarily mean that all the provisions which have a link to the EDPB fall away. So, for example, it's not clear how the one stop shop will work during the transition period. Just because the UK Information Commissioner loses her seat at the table doesn't necessarily mean that the entire one stop shop mechanism simply won't apply to the UK. If that were the case it would undermine the central policy of the transition period, which is to maintain consistency as between the regimes in the UK and the EU. The detail of how all this will work in practice is still very unclear.'

[117] WA, recitals 5 and 8.

[118] WA, Article 127 (6).

[119] WA, Article 127 (1).

[120] WA, Article 7.

[121] WA, Article 127.

[122] WA, Article 7 (1) (b). This is not the hoped-for outcome that the UK's Information Commissioner would continue to be part of the EDPB post-Brexit (the so-called 'adequacy plus' scenario), see https://www.dpnetwork.org.uk/opinion/brexit-data-protection-update/.

[123] GDPR, Article 68.

[124] GDPR, Article 68 provides 'the European Data Protection Board ... is hereby established as a body of the Union ...'. It is assumed that the interpretation of 'body' in this context under the Withdrawal Agreement would be consistent with the use of the term in EU legislation such as the GDPR.

authority under the GDPR, are far from clear. This may have practical implications for UK-based biobanks, for instance seeking to rely on the European Data Protection Board's guidance on the 'one stop shop' principle, in terms of which national supervisory authority should be the lead supervisory authority after Exit day and during transition. Biobanks which operate across the EU and the UK may find themselves subject to parallel proceedings.[125]

The Withdrawal Agreement has a separate title (Title VII) on data processing. It covers 'Union law on the protection of personal data', which includes the GDPR,[126] but excludes the GDPR's Chapter VII, which covers cooperation between supervisory authorities in the EU, consistency, dispute resolution and the European Data Protection Board. Title VII of the Withdrawal Agreement also includes 'any other provisions of Union law governing the protection of personal data'.[127] Other relevant provisions of Union law include the EU CFR, and 'general principles' of EU law, both of which include the right to protection of personal data[128] and the right to privacy.[129] There is an unresolved question here about whether the EU Exit Regulations' exclusion of general principles of EU law 'not relevant to' the GDPR as it applied immediately before Exit Day[130] is compliant with the UK's obligations under the Withdrawal Agreement.

Title VII consists of just four provisions, two of which are not relevant to biobanking.[131] The remaining two provisions have the following implications.

The Withdrawal Agreement, Article 71 provides

> (1) Union law on the protection of personal data shall apply in the United Kingdom in respect of the processing of the personal data of data subjects outside the United Kingdom, provided that the personal data:
>
> (a) were processed under Union law in the United Kingdom before the end of the transition period; or
> (b) are processed in the United Kingdom after the end of the transition period on the basis of this Agreement.

It is very difficult to make sense of this provision. If the UK is to be treated as if it were a Member State of the EU during the transition period,[132] and if EU law

[125] See, e.g., https://www.twobirds.com/en/news/articles/2018/global/data-protection-and-the-draft-brexit-agreement-first-impressions.

[126] It also includes a Directive on data processing in the context of criminal offences, Directive 2016/680/EU OJ 2016 L 119/89; and a Directive on e-communications privacy, Directive 2002/58/EC OJ 2002 L 201/37.

[127] WA, Article 70.

[128] EUCFR, Article 8.

[129] EUCFR, Article 7; ECHR, Article 8; See, e.g., Case C-139/01 *Österreichischer Rundfunk and Others*: ECLI:EU:C:2003:294; Case C-101/01 *Bodil Lindqvist v Åklagarkammaren i Jönköpin* ECLI:EU:C:2003:596.

[130] Regulation 5 (3).

[131] WA, Article 72 applies to entities in the water, energy, transport and postal services sectors; WA, Article 74 applies to classified information concerning national/EU security.

[132] WA, Article 127 (6).

continues to apply to and in the UK during that time,[133] the GDPR continues to apply as pre-Brexit. Processing in the UK during transition (or afterwards, on the basis of the Agreement, for instance, in the case of coordination of social security entitlements of migrants) of personal data of data subjects in a Member State ('data subjects outside the United Kingdom') is protected under the GDPR and its coordination arrangements, as pre-Brexit. One way to make sense of this provision, therefore, is that it is an exception to the general rules in the Withdrawal Agreement. For the purposes of transfer of data of a data subject in an EU Member State from that EU Member State to the UK for processing, during transition, the UK is *not* to be treated as if it were a Member State, and the GDPR does *not* apply. But if this is the intention of the provision, its drafting is far from clear.

Article 71 covers *only* personal data *of data subjects outside the UK* processed or obtained before the end of the transition period, or on the basis of the Withdrawal Agreement. In effect, it operates as if it were an adequacy decision. It does not cover personal data of data subjects within the UK. The majority of data held by UK-based biobanks is personal data of UK-based data subjects. But, especially given the way in which biobanks are networked, some of their data is personal data of data subjects outside the UK. If this interpretation is correct, the law applicable to UK-based biobanks would differ, depending on the source of the personal data. This would potentially create difficult—or even impossible—situations for UK-based biobanks in terms of data processing, depending on the extent to which UK data protection law diverges from EU data protection law. We noted some possible places of divergence in Sect. 4.1.3 above.

Article 71 (2) provides that paragraph 1 does not apply in the event that the European Commission adopts an adequacy decision under GDPR, Article 45. There is even provision in the Withdrawal Agreement for the withdrawal of an adequacy decision during the transitional period. In that event, Article 71 (3) of the Withdrawal Agreement provides that 'to the extent that a decision referred to in paragraph 2 has ceased to be applicable', the UK is obliged to ensure a level of protection of personal data that is 'essentially equivalent' to that in EU law.

Under the Withdrawal Agreement, Article 73, the EU is obliged to continue to treat data obtained from the UK before the end of transition, or after the end of transition on the basis of the Withdrawal Agreement, the same as data obtained from an EU Member State, or rather, not to treat it differently 'on the sole ground of the UK having withdrawn from the Union'.[134] This drafting is unfortunate, given that the text of the GDPR contemplates only two categories of states: EU Member States and 'third countries'. It is possible that the Withdrawal Agreement's effect, combined with the GDPR rules on 'third countries' is that some kind of provision for data transfer into the EU from the UK is necessary during the transition period—be that an adequacy decision, appropriate safeguard, or special circumstances. But the political declaration on the future relationship between the EU and the UK indicates

[133] WA, Article 127 (1).

[134] WA, Article 73.

that the EU intends to begin the process of adopting an adequacy decision as soon as possible after Exit Day, so as to have such a decision in place by the end of transition. Given that, the better interpretation of the Withdrawal Agreement is intention to continue the current legal position between Exit Day and December 2020 (or the end of transition if a different date).[135]

4.2.2 Other Law Relevant to Biobanking Under the Withdrawal Agreement

Other aspects of the Withdrawal Agreement will also be significant for biobanking. We noted above that the UK participates in the EU-funded BBMRI-ERIC network of biobanks and biomolecular resources.[136] Under the Withdrawal Agreement, during transition, the UK is to be treated as if it were a Member State. The Withdrawal Agreement's financial settlement provisions oblige the UK to continue making contributions to the EU budget as if it were a Member State during 2019 and 2020, and pay a share of the EU's budgetary commitments made under the 2014–2020 Multiannual Financial Framework (but which are not yet paid on 31 December 2020 when that framework comes to an end), on which Horizon 2020 funding is premised.

This means that access to EU funding for UK-based biobanks (and other research organisations) will continue during transition. After the end of transition, the UK could become a member, or an observer, of BBMRI-ERIC, if the Assembly of Members of BBMRI-ERIC grants its approval. The Assembly must do so on the basis of agreement of at least 75% of the Members, representing at least 75% of the Members' annual contributions. This means that no single Member of BBMRI-ERIC has a veto. At present, only EEA states are members (Norway included), but there is no legal impediment to a third country becoming a member.[137]

---

[135] See, e.g., https://www.herbertsmithfreehills.com/latest-thinking/brexit-withdrawal-agreement-impact-for-data-protection.

[136] See Council Regulation (EC) No 723/2009 of 25 June 2009 on the Community legal framework for a European Research Infrastructure Consortium (ERIC) amended by Council Regulation (EU) No 1261/2013 of 2 December 2013 OJ 2009 L 206/1; The Statutes of BBMRI-ERIC were decided for implementation by the European Commission on 22 November 2013, published in the Official Journal of the EU on the 30 November and came into force on 3 December 2013 (2013/701/EU). OJ 2013 L 326/56.

[137] See Regulation (EC) No 723/2009, Article 9 (1) which provides that Member States, associated countries, third countries other than associated countries, and intergovernmental organisations that have agreed to the Statutes are Members of BBMRI-ERIC.

4.2.3 Domestic Implementation of the EU-UK Withdrawal Agreement[138]

The Withdrawal Agreement requires the UK to render its obligations under the EU/UK Withdrawal Agreement into domestic law through domestic primary legislation.[139] As the UK is a 'dualist' state, provisions of an international agreement are conceptualised as an executive act, and do not have automatic legal effect in its legal systems.

The European Union (Withdrawal Agreement) Act 2020 provides for the continued application of the European Communities Act 1972 during transition. This means the continued supremacy and direct effect of law agreed between the UK and the EU (that is, the Withdrawal Agreement). In effect it creates a new source of law in the UK's constitution: that of Withdrawal Agreement law, in the same way that the European Communities Act 1972 is, in the words of the UK Supreme Court in *Miller*, the 'conduit pipe' by which EU law becomes 'an independent and overriding source' of UK law.[140]

The benefits of this approach are that it secures compliance with the provisions of the Withdrawal Agreement, Article 4, which provides that:

(1) The provisions of this Agreement and the provisions of Union law made applicable by this Agreement shall produce in respect of and in the United Kingdom the same legal effects as they produce within the Union and its Member States. Accordingly, legal or natural persons shall in particular be able to rely directly on the provisions contained or referred to in this Agreement which meet the conditions for direct effect under Union law.
(2) The United Kingdom shall ensure compliance with paragraph 1, including as regards the required powers of its judicial and administrative authorities to disapply inconsistent or incompatible domestic provisions, through domestic primary legislation.
(3) The provisions of this Agreement referring to Union law, or to concepts or provisions thereof, shall be interpreted and applied in accordance with the methods and general principles of Union law.
(4) The provisions of this Agreement referring to Union law, or to concepts or provisions thereof shall in their interpretation and application be interpreted in accordance with the relevant case law of the Court of Justice of the European Union handed down before the end of the transition period.
(5) In the interpretation and application of this Agreement, the United Kingdom's judicial and administrative authorities shall have due regard to relevant case law of the Court of Justice of the European Union handed down after the end of the transition period.

Further, there is significant jurisprudence, including from the House of Lords (the predecessor to the UK Supreme Court, the highest court in the land), on the meaning and effect of the relevant parts of the European Communities Act 1972. In

[138] This section is based on T Hervey and S Peers, 'What might have happened in an alternative universe: the EU Withdrawal Agreement Implementation Bill ('WAB') http://eulawanalysis.blogspot.com/search?q=Hervey.

[139] WA, Article 4 (2).

[140] Miller case, (n 72), para 65.

particular, the *Factortame* ruling[141] confirms that domestic legislation, irrespective of its date, that cannot be consistently interpreted with directly effective, validly adopted EU law, must be disapplied. This approach thus entails significant legal certainty and clarity. It is a better approach than either considering the Withdrawal Agreement as 'ordinary' international law (which would potentially fail to fulfil the UK's Withdrawal Agreement obligations despite the presumption that Parliament intends to comply with the UK's obligations in international law[142]) or using the words of the Withdrawal Agreement itself (which would introduce uncertainty about the direct effect of the Withdrawal Agreement, as there is no universal rule in EU law as to direct effect of provisions of treaties to which the EU is a party: it is dependent on the context, aims and objectives of the treaty concerned[143]).

In the biobanking context, the consequences are that the decision of the UK to 'switch back on' the existing obligations under the European Communities Act 1972 makes it easier for the EU to take the view that the UK's data protection regulatory environment is sufficiently protective of personal data to permit data flow into the UK. This goes to questions of adequacy decisions, standard contract clauses, codes of conduct and binding corporate rules, which are the basis on which data from EU Member States (and other countries) may be shared with UK-based biobanks after Exit Day.

4.3 *The Law If 'No Deal' Brexit*

4.3.1 The EU's Position

When we originally wrote this chapter, it was not clear whether the EU and UK would agree a Withdrawal Agreement. At that time, the EU had been consistently clear in its position that, in the event of a No Deal Brexit, the UK would have been treated as an ordinary 'third country'. The implications for matters such as access to EU funding, for instance through the UK's participation in BBMRI-ERIC, were that the existing legal arrangements would have been immediately ceased, unless another legal provision was adopted to respond to the exigencies of 'No Deal' (so-called 'managed No Deal'). In January 2019, the European Commission proposed, on an

[141] *Factortame Ltd v Secretary of State for Transport* (n 30).

[142] See, for instance, *Ghaidan v Goden-Mendoza* [2004] UKHL 30.

[143] See, for instance, Case 12/86, *Demirel*, ECLI:EU:C:1987:400; Case C-262/96, *Sürül*, ECLI:EU:C:1999:228; Case C-63/99, *Gloszczuk*, ECLI:EU:C:2001:488; C-257/99, *Barkoci and Malik*, ECLI:EU:C:2001:491; Case C 16/05 R *(on the application of Veli Tum and Mehmet Dari) v. Secretary of State for the Home Department*, ECLI:EU:C:2007:530; Case C-240/09, *Lesoochranárske Zoskupenie (Slovak Brown Bear)*, ECLI:EU:C:2011:125. See further, Gáspár-Szilágyi (2015), pp. 343–370.

extraordinary legal basis, a transitional provision for 2019,[144] which in effect would have allowed the UK, and UK-based entities, to be treated as eligible for funding, provided that the UK had paid into the EU budget, on a monthly basis. This proposal was not adopted, but it could be if 'No Deal' becomes politically more likely again, for instance in the run up to 31 October 2019. The obvious problem with such transitional measures is that they cannot deal with difficult broader decisions about the nature of the EU-UK relationship after Brexit, which will need to be determined before longer-term collaborative funding arrangements can be secured.

The European Data Protection Board's February 2019 information note is consistent with the position that the UK would have been treated as an ordinary 'third country' immediately on a No Deal Brexit:

> In the absence of an agreement between the EEA and the UK (No Deal Brexit), the UK will become a third country from 00.00 am CET on 30 March 2019. This means that the transfer of personal data to the UK has to be based on one of the following instruments as of 30 March 2019:
>
> - Standard or ad hoc Data Protection Clauses
> - Binding Corporate Rules
> - Codes of Conduct and Certification Mechanisms
> - Derogations.[145]

Note that none of the listed bases of lawful transfer of personal data to the UK, in the event of No Deal Brexit, is that of an adequacy decision. It might be thought that this would have been the most convenient solution for all concerned, including EU-based biobanks which are networked with UK-based biobanks and wish to continue to share data. As noted above, in Sect. 4.1.3, the UK has affirmed that it will regard the EU's data protection provision as adequate for the purposes of transfers of data *to* the EU. The GDPR provides that the Commission may decide that a third country, or one or more specified sectors in that third country (such as the biobanking sector), ensures an adequate level of protection of personal data. Transfer of personal data from the EU to a country or sector within a country that is subject to such an adequacy decision is lawful under the GDPR without any further specific authorisation.[146] The UK has become a 'third country', but its law, up until, the end of transition, was (at least presumptively) compliant with EU data protection law. Indeed, post-transition under the EU (Withdrawal) Act 2018, as amended by the EU (Withdrawal Agreement) Act 2020, the GDPR will become 'retained EU law', a part of the law of the UK. An adequacy decision seems the logical and practical approach.

---

[144] Proposal for a Council Regulation on measures concerning the implementation and financing of the general budget of the Union in 2019 in relation to the withdrawal of the United Kingdom from the Union COM/2019/64 final.

[145] European Data Protection Board, *Information note on data transfers under the GDPR in the event of a No Deal Brexit*, 12 February 2019, https://edpb.europa.eu/sites/edpb/files/files/file1/edpb-2019-02-12-infonote-nodeal-brexit_en.pdf.

[146] GDPR, Article 45 (1).

However, adequacy decisions are formal acts, taken by the Commission, assisted by a committee and according to a specified procedure,[147] lasting for a period of up to 4 years, at which point they are reviewed.[148] Although, on duly justified imperative grounds of urgency, there is a power to adopt immediately applicable implementing acts *revoking or withdrawing* adequacy decisions,[149] there is no equivalent power to *take* an urgent adequacy decision. The GDPR sets the procedures through which adequacy decisions must be taken, and the EU institutions are not competent to depart from those procedures. To do so would have been *ultra vires*. Adequacy decisions are not suitable for the immediate legal ruptures implied by No Deal Brexit: to adopt an adequacy decision would be, in effect, to create a (partial) 'Deal', and would thus have undermined the EU's negotiating position.

The CJEU has already found that aspects of UK data protection law are not compliant with EU law obligations, although not in the context of biobanking.[150] A January 2019 report from the UK Parliament's Joint Committee on Human Rights[151] noted that the Data Protection Act 2018 may not provide as comprehensive a protection as Article 8 of the EU Charter of Fundamental Rights. The onward transfer of data from the UK to countries outside the EU is also an area of contention.[152]

Furthermore, although the GDPR becomes 'retained EU law', as explained above, important changes to the GDPR are implemented by ministerial powers granted under the EU (Withdrawal) Act. Enforcement and remedial provisions also change: there will be no scope for dispute resolution within the European Data Protection Board, no obligation on UK courts to comply with rulings of the CJEU after the end of transition, and no jurisdiction of the CJEU to hear preliminary references from the UK courts.

All of the above explains why the EU's contingency planning for a No Deal Brexit did not include adopting an adequacy decision with respect to the UK. This may become salient again if the EU and UK trade agreement negotiations fail. EU Member States may not lawfully adopt unilateral adequacy decisions: the power to do so rests with the European Commission only.

According to Article 44 of the GDPR, in the absence of a formal adequacy decision taken by the European Commission, or other basis for the lawful transfer of personal data, all data flows from the EU to the UK would immediately be unlawful under the GDPR.[153] If the EU does not take an adequacy decision to come into effect

---

[147] GDPR, Article 93 (2), Regulation (EU) No 182/2011, Article 5.

[148] GDPR, Article 45 (3).

[149] GDPR, Article 45 (5); Article 93(3).

[150] Joined Cases C-203/15 and C-698/15 *Tele2 / Watson* ECLI:EU:C:2016:970, which involves investigatory powers.

[151] https://publications.parliament.uk/pa/jt201719/jtselect/jtrights/774/77404.htm.

[152] https://www.instituteforgovernment.org.uk/explainers/data-adequacy.

[153] GDPR, Article 44. See Mc Cullagh, Karen. UK: GDPR adaptions and preparations for withdrawal from the EU. (n 51) at 119.

at the end of the transitional period, biobanks seeking to lawfully transfer personal data to UK-based biobanks must therefore rely on alternative bases for that data transfer.

As noted above, these include binding corporate rules; standard contractual clauses; codes of conduct; and 'special circumstances'. We were unable to locate examples of binding corporate rules in the context of biobanking which are in the public domain, or plans for adopting such rules in the event of No Deal Brexit, or no EU-UK free trade agreement at the end of transition. Several multinationals in the pharmaceutical and biomedical industry have successfully adopted such binding corporate rules.[154] Given that this approach is more likely to be adopted by commercial biobanks, it is not a surprise that such plans are not available for us to scrutinize. In general, they are costly and time-consuming to put in place.

The most likely mechanism for lawful data transfer from an EU Member State to a non-commercial biobank in the UK in the event of No Deal Brexit was on the basis of standard contractual clauses. Standard contractual clauses may be approved by the competent supervisory authority in any Member State, provided they comply with the conditions set out in the GDPR.[155] In February 2010, the European Commission issued a template for standard contractual clauses (controller to processor) under the Data Protection Directive.[156] The GDPR provides that this template remains in place until it is replaced under the GDPR's new arrangements.[157] The Commission Decision provides that the template may not be varied, although further commercial clauses may be added. This inflexibility may present some difficulties for data transfer from the EU to a UK biobank. Further, this template will apply only where the data controller is in an EU Member State and the processor is in the UK. It will not apply in a situation where the UK-based biobank is the data controller and hosts personal data with an EU-based processor.

Most importantly, moreover, the status of standard contractual clauses as a basis for data transfer to third countries is currently the subject of litigation before the CJEU. This litigation process was not completed before Exit Day, adding to the levels of uncertainty. Case C-311/18 *Schrems II* was referred to the CJEU for a preliminary ruling by the Irish High Court on 9 May 2018. The AG Opinion was issued in December 2019, but the CJEU may not make its decision until after the end of transition.

---

[154] See list at https://ec.europa.eu/info/law/law-topic/data-protection/international-dimension-data-protection/binding-corporate-rules-bcr_en.

[155] GDPR, Article 47.

[156] Commission Decision 2010/87/EU of 5 February 2010 on standard contractual clauses for the transfer of personal data to processors established in third countries under Directive 95/46/EC of the European Parliament and of the Council *OJ 2010 L 39/5–18; Amended to comply with* Case C-362/14 *Maximillian Schrems v Data Protection Commissioner* ECLI.EU.C.2015:650; Commission Implementing Decision (EU) 2016/2297 of 16 December 2016 amending Decisions 2001/497/EC and 2010/87/EU on standard contractual clauses for the transfer of personal data to third countries and to processors established in such countries, under Directive 95/46/EC of the European Parliament and of the Council *OJ 2016 L 344/100–101.*

[157] GDPR, Article 94.

One of the key questions of contention is the consistency of standard contractual clauses with the requirements under EU law for data subjects to access effective remedies for violations of their rights. An important element of standard contractual clauses as a basis for lawful data transfer under the GDPR is that the contract gives data subjects specific rights, even though the data subject is not a party to the contract. Providing effective judicial remedies for private parties is a distinctive feature of EU law in general. These questions engage application of both the GDPR's requirements and those of the EU Charter of Fundamental Rights, Articles 7 (privacy); 8 (data protection) and 47 (right to an effective judicial remedy).

Here the UK's amendments to the GDPR, as 'retained EU law', through the relevant EU Exit Regulations, noted above in Sect. 4.1.3, are important. Will the UK arrangements for remedies and enforcement suffice to secure adequate protection from the point of view of the EU? Bear in mind, first, that the EU Exit Regulations remove all obligations on the UK, or entities within the UK, to cooperate within the structures of the EU, or to exchange information with the European Commission, including in matters of enforcement.

Further, and perhaps more seriously, the EU Exit Regulations,[158] the amended Data Protection Act,[159] and the European Union (Withdrawal) Act,[160] all seek to prevent future developments of EU law that arise through interpretations of the CJEU becoming applicable in the UK. If *Schrems II* is decided after the end of transition, Exit Day, any principles of EU law deriving from that decision would not necessarily be applied in the UK, and data subjects in the UK would not necessarily be able to rely on those principles in seeking to remedy any breaches of their data protection rights.

In view of those concerns, it may be preferable for the biobanking sector to move expeditiously to adopt a sector-specific code of conduct for health research, and have this code approved under Article 40 of the GDPR. Such a code of conduct would provide a lawful basis for transfer of data to UK-based biobanks from the EU post-transition.

One final possibility is that EU-based biobanks transfer data to UK-based biobanks on the basis of 'special circumstances'.[161] This may be the most appropriate basis for lawful transfer following transition where data is being shared in the context of an on-going clinical trial. A patient (data subject) already enrolled in that trial, and who perhaps cannot access any other licensed treatment for their condition, would need to secure continued data transfer to protect their 'vital interests'. For pure research, it might be feasible to argue that 'safeguarding legitimate interests of the data subject' justifies continued sharing of data to the UK, at least in the context of an existing research project which may result in some benefit, however remote, for the data subjects concerned. UK Biobank certainly seems to believe that

158 Regulation 5 (3).

159 DPA, section 205.

160 EU (Withdrawal) Act 2018, section 4.

161 GDPR, Article 49.

legitimate interests and the public interest are an appropriate basis for its data *processing*, although whether it is sufficient for data *transfer* is unclear. There are also discussions regarding a possibility to rely on 'public interest' when collaborating with the US for transfers not covered under the EU's adequacy decision for the US (the 'privacy shield').[162]

The position with regard to personal data *that has already been transferred* from the UK to the EU remains uncertain. By analogy with the revocation of an adequacy decision under Article 45 (5) GDPR, the effects of the UK leaving the EU on the lawfulness of the transfer of the data should not have retroactive effect. In practice, unless the European Data Protection Board or European Commission takes a decision applicable to the whole EU, it is likely to depend on the view adopted by the supervisory authority in the relevant EU Member State. Hence, it may be that data is processed by biobanks in the EU in a situation that is technically unlawful, or perhaps better described as a situation of 'a-legality',[163] failure of the EU and UK to reach agreement on the matter.

4.3.2 The UK Position

The UK government's position was to seek to secure as much continuity as possible in the event of No Deal Brexit, and presumably also a failure to reach agreement on a future trade relationship. For Horizon 2020 funding, the UK Chancellor announced in August and October 2016 that the UK government would guarantee funding for UK participants (but not for their EU collaborating partner organisations) in Horizon 2020 projects in place before Exit Day. A further ministerial statement made to Parliament on 26 July 2018,[164] and accompanied by a statement of liabilities in a departmental Minute laid before the UK House of Commons, assures UK organisations (which includes biobanks) that

> The Treasury is also guaranteeing funding in event of a no deal for UK organisations which bid directly to the European Commission so that they can continue competing for, and securing, funding until the end of 2020. This ensures that UK organisations, such as charities, businesses and universities, will continue to receive funding over a project's lifetime if they successfully bid into EU-funded programmes before December 2020.

The details of how this commitment would have been administered in practice in a No Deal Brexit situation, where funding is shared among consortia involving UK organisations and those in EU Member States, were far from clear, and the UK government has recognised that this was the case.[165]

---

[162] See for example the work of Shabani and Borry (2018), pp. 149–156.

[163] Hervey and Speakman (2018), pp. 65–109.

[164] https://www.parliament.uk/business/publications/written-questions-answers-statements/written-statement/Commons/2018-07-24/HCWS926/.

[165] UK Department for Business, Energy and Industrial Strategy, *Guidance Horizon 2020 funding if there's no deal* 23 August 2018 https://www.gov.uk/government/publications/horizon-2020-funding-if-theres-no-brexit-deal/horizon-2020-funding-if-theres-no-brexit-deal%2D%2D2,

If the UK Clinical Research Collaboration's Tissue Directory and Coordination Centre were excluded from BBMRI-ERIC and/or other EU funding and collaboration arrangements, it may look to intensify other collaborations, for instance with projects in the USA, Russia and China. This approach would obviously only be legally viable if the sharing of data under such collaborations complies with the post-Brexit and post-transition UK regulatory provisions, as outlined above.

The UK government's position under a No Deal Brexit was that there would be no immediate change to data protection law,[166] and this presumably remains the case post-transition. The EU (Withdrawal) Act and secondary legislation based on it, such as the Data Protection, Privacy and Electronic Communications (Amendments etc) (EU Exit) Regulations 2019, discussed above, make no distinction between different types of Brexit. At the end of transition, the Data Protection Act 2018 would remains in place, and the GDPR changes from being EU law to being 'retained EU law'. For data transfers from the UK to the EU, EEA and third countries deemed adequate by the EU at the end of transition, the UK has in effect taken an adequacy decision under the Data Protection, Privacy and Electronic Communications (Amendments etc) (EU Exit) (No. 2), Regulations 2019, schedule 2, article 102, inserting a new Schedule 21 into the UK GDPR.

The assertion that there would be no immediate change to data protection law is self-evidently not the case with regard to data transfer from the EU to the UK, as without an adequacy decision, or other basis on which data may lawfully be transferred to a UK-based entity, such as 'appropriate safeguards' (standard contractual clauses, a code of conduct, or binding corporate rules), or 'special circumstances', the EU will treat the UK as non-compliant with its data protection law. This is also the case for data transfer from other countries which currently rely on the UK's membership of the EU to allow data transfer into the UK. As noted above, the consequence for the activities of biobanks which rely on sharing of data with UK-based biobanks is that any continued sharing of data would potentially be unlawful. Given the difficulties with adequacy decisions, and the need for recognition from the EU, or a national competent authority in the EU, of standard contractual clauses, codes of conduct or binding corporate rules, this situation may be one in which the 'special circumstances' provision of the GDPR may be tested.

However, even with regard to data protection law *as applicable solely within the UK*, a better description of the legal position is that there would be no immediate change to the *content* of data protection law (apart from the changes outlined in

'We are aware of some cases where UK participants lead a consortium and are responsible for distributing funding to the other participants; the UK government is seeking to discuss how this could best be addressed in a "no deal" scenario with the European Commission. These discussions would also need to include consideration of projects where the UK's change in status from member state to third country could lead to concerns about ongoing compliance with Horizon 2020 rules (for example, where a consortium no longer meets the threshold for member state and/or associated country participants).' Updated Guidance 3 December 2018 https://www.gov.uk/government/publications/the-governments-guarantee-for-eu-funded-programmes-if-theres-no-brexit-deal/the-governments-guarantee-for-eu-funded-programmes-if-theres-no-brexit-deal.

[166] Department for Digital, Culture, Media & Sports, Data protection if there's no Brexit deal. (n 89).

Sect. 4.1.3 above), but that the *source* of data protection law would change. With this change of source, there may also be implications for the effects of the relevant law. Indeed, the UK government's December 2018 guidance[167] itself described the GDPR as 'sitting alongside' the Data Protection Act, which is a quite different to the pre-Brexit legal position to the effect that the GDPR is a source of supreme EU law.

5 Conclusion

Since the EU referendum vote in June 2016, despite the considerable uncertainties, many of which are outlined above, biobanks in the UK are adopting a 'business as usual' approach. For instance, UK Biobank continues to receive applications for and approve projects involving EU (and indeed international) partners, and as far as we have been able to ascertain, there is no falling away of the numbers of such projects being approved. For instance, in May 2019, UK Biobank approved a 5 year project with the Ecole Polytechnique Federale de Lausanne (EPFL), France, to explore diet/lifestyle/health factors as causes and modifiers of genetic determinants of healthspan, ageing and longevity.[168] In April 2019, UK Biobank approved a year-long project with Sanofi, France, to support the eventual development of precision medicine.[169] These are far from isolated examples.[170] In 2018 and 2019, UK Biobank approved three projects from researchers based in the Netherlands; eight projects from researchers based in Sweden; a project from researchers based in Germany; and in June 2019 has approved a project from researchers based in Denmark.[171]

This 'biobanking business as usual' approach makes good sense. The UK has not left the EU, but the Withdrawal Agreement was agreed, ratified and entered into force, securing significant levels of continuity will be secured until the end of the transition period (currently until the end of December 2020). By contrast, under a No Deal Brexit, legal continuity was far from guaranteed, and this is the case at the end of transition too, although sharing of data with UK-based biobanks may be able to continue on the basis of appropriate safeguards, including possibly a code of conduct for biomedical research, or even perhaps a (temporary) adequacy decision. Given the uncertainty, inflexibility, cost and time investment that surrounds other types of appropriate safeguards, prompt moves towards a code of conduct, within

[167] Department for Digital, Culture, Media & Sports, Data protection if there's no Brexit deal. (n 89).

[168] https://www.ukbiobank.ac.uk/2019/05/exploring-diet-lifestyle-health-factors-as-causes-and-modifiers-of-genetic-determinants-of-healthspan-ageing-and-longevity/.

[169] https://www.ukbiobank.ac.uk/2019/04/exhaustive-bivariate-genome-wide-interaction-studies-applied-to-the-uk-biobank-datasets/

[170] This database is accessible here https://www.ukbiobank.ac.uk/approved-research/.

[171] The metabolic consequences of adverse early life conditions and subsequent risk for adult cardiovascular disease and type 2 diabetes https://www.ukbiobank.ac.uk/2019/06/the-metabolic-consequences-of-adverse-early-life-conditions-and-subsequent-risk-for-adult-cardio-vascular-disease-and-type-2-diabetes/.

the context of BBMRI-ERIC, would offer timely reassurance to the biobanking sector, both within the UK and on a European and international level, given the ways in which UK biobanks are nested within European and global networks.

At this time (June 2020), it is still not possible to predict what the relationship will be between the UK and the EU in the future, for data transfer, in the biobanking sector and beyond. The political declaration setting out a framework for the future relationship between the EU and the UK,[172] issued at the same time as the draft Withdrawal Agreement, gives a prominent place to data protection.[173] The declaration states that the EU will begin the process of adopting an adequacy decision for transfer of data to the UK, as a 'third country', 'as soon as possible after the UK's withdrawal'. The UK will reciprocate. The EU and UK should also 'make arrangements for appropriate cooperation between regulators'. Of course, this is a political commitment only, and not legally binding on the EU or the UK. Yet, at least at the time it was promulgated, the intention to secure continuity was present, even if the precise legal modalities of how to do so were distinctly elusive.

All that said, given that prominent biobanks in the UK are continuing to collaborate internationally, it seems likely that such collaborations and data transfer will also continue both in to the UK and outwardly to the EU, in one way or another. Nevertheless, the chilling effect of the uncertain legal basis on which future collaborations involving data transfer will take place, is undoubtedly having implications for the biobanking sector in the UK.

References

Agreement on the withdrawal of the United Kingdom of Great Britain and Northern Ireland from the European Union and the European Atomic Energy Community, OJ 2019 C 66 I/01

BioDock (2019) Homepage. http://www.bio-dock.com

BioSHaRE (2015) Biobank Standardisation and Harmonisation for Research Excellence in the European Union (Summary Report) http://www.bioshare.eu/assets/Final%20publishable%20summary%20-%20update%20Jan.pdf

Budin-Ljøsne I, Teare HJA, Kaye J et al (2017) Dynamic consent: a potential solution to some of the challenges of modern biomedical research. BMC Med Ethics 18(1):4

Case C-144/04 Mangold ECLI:EU:C:2005:709

Case C-311/18 Schrems II, reference for a preliminary ruling from the Irish High Court 9 May 2018

Caulfield T, Burningham S, Joly Y et al (2014) A review of the key issues associated with the commercialization of biobanks. J Law Biosci 1(1):94–110

Code of Conduct for Health Research. http://code-of-conduct-for-health-research.eu/faq

Commission Decision 2001/497/EC of 15th June 2001 on standard contractual clauses for the transfer of personal data to third countries, under Directive 95/46/EC

---

[172] Draft Political declaration setting out the framework for the future relationship between the European Union and the United Kingdom (n 73).

[173] It is covered in paragraphs 8–10, under the heading 'I Basis for Cooperation', immediately following a sub-heading on 'Core values and rights'.

Commission Decision 2004/915/EC of 27th December 2004 amending Decision 2001/497/EC as regards the introduction of an alternative set of standard contractual clauses for the transfer of personal data to third countries
Commission Decision 2010/87/EU of 5th February 2010 on standard contractual clauses for the transfer of personal data to processors established in third countries under Directive 95/46/EC of the European Parliament and of the Council
Commission Implementing Decision (EU) 2016/2297 of 16 December 2016 amending Decisions 2001/497/EC and 2010/87/EU on standard contractual clauses for the transfer of personal data to third countries and to processors established in such countries, under Directive 95/46/EC of the European Parliament and of the Council (notified under document C(2016) 8471) C/2016/8471 OJ 2016 L 344/100
Convention for the Protection of Individuals with regard to Automatic Processing of Personal Data (the Data Protection Convention) ETS No.108, Strasbourg, 1981
Council Regulation (EC) No 723/2009 of 25 June 2009 on the Community legal framework for a European Research Infrastructure Consortium (ERIC) amended by Council Regulation (EU) No 1261/2013 of 2 December 2013 OJ 2009 L 206/1
Data Protection Act 2018
Data Protection, Privacy and Electronic Communications (Amendments etc) (EU Exit) Regulations 2019 No 419 28 February 2019. http://www.legislation.gov.uk/uksi/2019/419/pdfs/uksi_20190419_en.pdf
Department for Digital, Culture, Media & Sport (updated 11 April 2019) Amendments to UK data protection law in the event the UK leaves the EU without a deal. (UK Government, Guidance Note) https://www.gov.uk/government/publications/data-protection-law-eu-exit/amendments-to-uk-data-protection-law-in-the-event-the-uk-leaves-the-eu-without-a-deal-on-29-march-2019
Department for Digital, Culture, Media & Sports (13 September 2018, this guidance was withdrawn on the 1st of March 2019) Data protection if there's no Brexit deal. https://www.gov.uk/government/publications/data-protection-if-theres-no-brexit-deal/data-protection-if-theres-no-brexit-deal
Department for Digital, Culture, Media & Sports (6 February 2019) Using personal data after Brexit. https://www.gov.uk/guidance/using-personal-data-after-brexit
Directive 95/46/EC of the European Parliament and of the Council of 24 October 1995 on the protection of individuals with regard to the processing of personal data and on the free movement of such data OJ 1995 L 281/31
Draft Political declaration setting out the framework for the future relationship between the European Union and the United Kingdom, OJ 2019 C 66 I/185
EPIC-Oxford (2019) Homepage. http://www.epic-oxford.or
EU Charter of Fundamental Rights and Freedoms
European Council Decision (EU) 2019/476 taken in agreement with the United Kingdom of 22 March 2019 extending the period under Article 50(3)TEU OJ 2019 L 80/1
European Council Decision (EU) 2019/584 taken in agreement with the United Kingdom of 11 April 2019 extending the period under Article 50(3) TEU OJ 2019 L 101/1
European Data Protection Board, Information note on data transfers under the GDPR in the event of a No Deal Brexit, 12 February 2019. https://edpb.europa.eu/sites/edpb/files/files/file1/edpb-2019-02-12-infonote-nodeal-brexit_en.pdf
European Union (Notification of Withdrawal) Act 2017
European Union (Withdrawal) Act 2018 (Exit Day) (No 2) Regulations 2019 SI 2019/859 11 April 2019
Factortame Ltd v Secretary of State for Transport [1991] 1 AC 603
Ford E, Boyd A, Bowles JKF et al (2019) Our data, our society, our health: a vision for inclusive and transparent health data science in the United Kingdom and beyond. Learn Health Syst. e10191. https://doi.org/10.1002/lrh2.10191

Gáspár-Szilágyi S (2015) The "Primacy" and "Direct Effect" of EU international agreements. Eur Public Law 21:343–370
Geneticist (31 May 2018). https://www.geneticistinc.com/blog/the-importance-of-biorepositories
Health Research Authority (last updated 19 April 2019) Consent in research. (NHS) https://www.hra.nhs.uk/planning-and-improving-research/policies-standards-legislation/data-protection-and-information-governance/gdpr-guidance/what-law-says/consent-research/
Hervey T, Sheldon N (2011) Judicial method of English Courts and tribunals in EU law cases: a case study in employment law. In: Neergard U, Nielsen R, Roseberry L (eds) European legal method: paradoxes and revitalisation. DJØK, Copenhagen, pp 327–375
Hervey T, Speakman EM (2018) The immediate futures of EU health law in the UK after Brexit: law, 'alegality' and uncertainty. Med Law Int 18(2–3):65–109
Human Tissue Act 2004
Human Tissue Authority (2019) Analysis of DNA under the HT Act FAQs. https://www.hta.gov.uk/faqs/analysis-dna-under-ht-act-faqs
Human Tissue Authority, 'Human Tissue Act 2004' https://www.hta.gov.uk/policies/human-tissue-act-2004/
Human Tissue Authority, Guide for the general public to Code of Practice E (HTA (07e/17)) https://www.hta.gov.uk/sites/default/files/HTA%20%2807e-17%29%206%20Research.pdf
ICO (2019a) Do I need to use standard contractual clauses (SCCs) for transfers from the EEA to the UK (if we leave the EU with no deal)? https://ico.org.uk/for-organisations/data-protection-and-brexit/standard-contractual-clauses-for-transfers-from-the-eea-to-the-uk-interactive-tool/
ICO (2019b) How to transfer data from Europe (from the EEA) to the UK using standard contractual clauses (SCCs). https://ico.org.uk/for-organisations/data-protection-and-brexit/how-to-transfer-data-from-europe-from-the-eea-to-the-uk-using-standard-contractual-clauses-sccs/
ICO, Data protection and Brexit. https://ico.org.uk/for-organisations/data-protection-and-brexit/
ICO Build a controller to controller contract. https://ico.org.uk/for-organisations/data-protection-and-brexit/how-to-transfer-data-from-europe-from-the-eea-to-the-uk-using-standard-contractual-clauses-sccs/build-a-controller-to-controller-contract/
ICO Build a controller to processor contract. https://ico.org.uk/for-organisations/data-protection-and-brexit/how-to-transfer-data-from-europe-from-the-eea-to-the-uk-using-standard-contractual-clauses-sccs/build-a-controller-to-processor-contract/
ICO What needs to be included in the contract?. https://ico.org.uk/for-organisations/guide-to-data-protection/guide-to-the-general-data-protection-regulation-gdpr/contracts-and-liabilities-between-controllers-and-processors-multi/what-needs-to-be-included-in-the-contract/
Joined Cases C-203/15 and C-698/15 Tele2 / Watson ECLI:EU:C:2016:970
Lawlor RT, Kozlakidis Z, Bledsoe M (14 November 2018) GDPR in biobanking for precision medicine research: The challenges. Open Access Government. https://www.openaccessgovernment.org/gdpr-in-biobanking-for-precision-medicine/54468/
Linkomies L (April 2019) UK Secures post-Brexit data flow deals with nine countries. Privacy Laws & Business International Report 8–9
London School of Hygiene and Tropical Medicine, CureME https://cureme.lshtm.ac.uk/
Mahsa S, Borry P (2018) Rules for processing genetic data for research purposes in view of the new EU general data protection regulation. Eur J Human Genet 26(2):149
Mayrhofer MT, Holub P, Wutte A, Litton JE (2016) BBMRI-ERIC: the novel gateway to biobanks. From humans to humans. Bundesgesundheitsblatt, Gesundheitsforschung, Gesundheitsschutz 59(3):379–84. https://doi.org/10.1007/s00103-015-2301-8
Naomi A et al (2012) UK Biobank: current status and what it means for epidemiology. Health Policy Technol 1(3):123–126
Oxford Biobank. https://www.oxfordbiobank.org.uk
Proposal for a Council Regulation on measures concerning the implementation and financing of the general budget of the Union in 2019 in relation to the withdrawal of the United Kingdom from the Union COM/2019/64 final

Queen Square Centre For Neuromuscular Diseases, Biobank. https://www.ucl.ac.uk/cnmd/research/research-core-activities/biobank
Quinlan PR, Pourabdolla LE, Sims A et al (2017) The UK clinical research collaboration (UKCRC) tissue Directory and coordination Centre: the UK's Centre for facilitating the usage of human samples for medical research. Open J Bioresour 4(1):6. https://doi.org/10.5334/ojb.31
Regulation (EU) 2016/679 of the European Parliament and of the Council of 27 April 2016 on the protection of natural persons with regard to the processing of personal data and on the free movement of such data, and repealing Directive 95/46/EC (General Data Protection Regulation) OJ 2016 L 119/1
Shabani M, Borry P (2018) Rules for processing genetic data for research purposes in view of the new EU general data protection regulation. Eur J Human Genet 26:149–156. https://doi.org/10.1038/s41431-017-0045-7
Taylor MJ, Wallace SE, Prictor M (2018) United Kingdom: transfers of genomic data to third countries. Human Genet 137(8):637–645
Teare H, Kaye J (2018) Dynamic consent–Improving translational research Pathology 50:S3 https://www.pathologyjournal.rcpa.edu.au/article/S0031-3025(17)30794-8/abstract
Tissue Directory and Coordination Centre. https://biobankinguk.org/biobanks-a-z/
Tissue Directory and Coordination Centre. https://directory.biobankinguk.org
Townend D (2018) Conclusion: harmonisation in genomic and health data sharing for research: an impossible dream? Human Genet 137(8):657–664. https://link.springer.com/content/pdf/10.1007%2Fs00439-018-1924-x.pdf
UCL Human Tissue Biobanks. https://www.ucl.ac.uk/human-tissue/hta-biobanks
UK Biobank (30 May 2018a) Information notice for UK Biobank participants: the General Data Protection Regulation (GDPR). http://www.ukbiobank.ac.uk/wp-content/uploads/2018/10/GDPR.pdf
UK Biobank (27 February 2018b) GDPR Information Notice. https://www.ukbiobank.ac.uk/2018/02/gdpr/
UK Biobank (2019) GDPR. https://www.ukbiobank.ac.uk/gdpr/
UK Biobank, About UK Biobank. http://www.ukbiobank.ac.uk/about-biobank-uk
UK Biobank, Researchers. https://www.ukbiobank.ac.uk/scientists-3/
UK Department for Business, Energy and Industrial Strategy, Guidance Horizon 2020 funding if there's no deal 23 August 2018. https://www.gov.uk/government/publications/horizon-2020-funding-if-theres-no-brexit-deal/horizon-2020-funding-if-theres-no-brexit-deal%2D%2D2

Part III
National Implementation

An Overview of Belgian Legislation Applicable to Biobank Research and Its Interplay with Data Protection Rules

Teodora Lalova, Anastassia Negrouk, Laurent Dollé, Sofie Bekaert, Annelies Debucquoy, Jean-Jacques Derèze, Peggy Valcke, Els J. Kindt, and Isabelle Huys

T. Lalova (✉)
Department of Pharmaceutical and Pharmacological Sciences, KU Leuven, Leuven, Belgium

Centre for IT and IP Law (CiTiP), KU Leuven, Leuven, Belgium
e-mail: teodora.lalova@kuleuven.be

A. Negrouk
European Organisation for Research and Treatment of Cancer, Brussels, Belgium
e-mail: anastassia.negrouk@eortc.org

L. Dollé
Biothèque Wallonie Bruxelles (BWB), Department of Pathology, Erasme Hospital, Brussels, Belgium

S. Bekaert
Department of Public Health and Primary Health Care, Faculty of Medicine and Health Sciences, Ghent University, Ghent, Belgium
e-mail: sofie.bekaert@ugent.be

A. Debucquoy
BBMRI.be, Belgian Cancer Registry, Brussels, Belgium
e-mail: annelies.debucquoy@kankerregister.org

J.-J. Derèze
HUZ Leuven, Leuven, Belgium
e-mail: jean-jacques.dereze@uzleuven.be

P. Valcke
Centre for IT and IP Law (CiTiP), KU Leuven, Leuven, Belgium
e-mail: peggy.valcke@kuleuven.be

E. J. Kindt
Centre for IT and IP Law (CiTiP), KU Leuven, Leuven, Belgium

eLaw, Universiteit Leiden, Leiden, The Netherlands
e-mail: els.kindt@kuleuven.be

I. Huys
Department of Pharmaceutical and Pharmacological Sciences, KU Leuven, Leuven, Belgium
e-mail: isabelle.huys@kuleuven.be

S. Slokenberga et al. (eds.), *GDPR and Biobanking*, Law, Governance and Technology Series 43, https://doi.org/10.1007/978-3-030-49388-2_10

Abstract This contribution aims to present in a clear and concise manner the intricate legal framework for biobank research in Belgium. In Part 1, we describe the Belgian biobank infrastructure, with a focus on the concept of biobank. In Part 2, we provide an overview of the applicable legal framework, namely the Act of 19 December 2008 on Human Body Material (HBM), and its amendments. Attention is given to an essential piece of self-regulation, namely the Compendium on biobanks issued by the Federal Agency on Medicine Products and Health (FAMPH). Furthermore, we delineate the interplay with relevant data protection rules. Part 3 is dedicated to the main research oversight bodies in the field of biobanking. In Part 4, we provides several examples of the 'law in context'. In particular, we discuss issues pertaining to presumed consent, processing of personal data associated with HBM, and information provided to the donor of HBM. Finally, Part 5 and 6 addresses the impact of the EU General Data Protection Regulation (GDPR), suggests lines for further research, and outline the future possibilities for biobanking in Belgium.

1 Biobank Infrastructure

1.1 What Is a Biobank

The applicable Belgian legislation defines a biobank as 'the structure which, for the purpose of scientific research, with the exclusion of research with human medical applications, obtains, processes, stores and makes available human body material, and, where appropriate, the associated data relating to the human body material and the donor' (see Figure 1).[1] It is sufficient to carry out one of the activities listed above for scientific purposes in order to be characterized as a biobank.[2] Such structure may be established within an accredited hospital or faculty of medicine and health sciences, or it may also be created outside of a hospital, for instance by a private organization, such as a pharmaceutical company.[3] The law further requires the positive opinion of an ethics committee concerning the objectives and activities of the biobank.[4]

Human body material (HBM) is defined as 'any human biological material, including human tissues and cells, gametes, embryos, foetuses, as well as substances derived therefrom, and regardless of the degree of their transformation, with the exception of substances of non-human origin'.[5]

[1]Article 2 (27) of the Act of 19 December 2008 regarding the procurement and use of human bodily material destined for human medical applications or for scientific research applies, hereafter the Act on HBM.

[2]For the sake of completeness, it must be noted that the Belgian Act on HBM defines three additional structures that collect HBM and associated data. These are the bank for HBM, the intermediate structure of HBM and the production establishment, all for therapeutic purposes, see Article 2 (24) (25) and (26). The rules for biobanks do not apply to these structures, and vice versa.

[3]Sterckx and Van Assche (2011), p. 249.

[4]Article 22(1) (3) of the Act on HBM.

[5]Article 2 (1) of the Act on HBM.

The majority of Belgian biobanks are organized at a central level, within the framework of an institution, e.g. a hospital or a university. In such situation, these hospitals/universities require their researchers to use that central biobank infrastructure. However, it is possible that even a sole researcher can be regarded as a biobank and will have to abide to the strict applicable legislation. This will be the case if his activity formally falls within the scope of the Belgian biobank legislation.[6]

The biobank manager (often referred to in literature as custodian) is the central responsible authority in the Belgian biobank infrastructure.[7] The custodian must be a doctor who fulfils the conditions laid down in Article 25 of the Law on the exercise of health care professions or a national of one of the Member States of the European Union who is authorized to practice medicine in a Member State other than Belgium.[8] The rights and responsibilities of the custodian, as elaborated in the Act on HBM, are critical for the conduct of biobanking activities and translational biomedical research.[9]

1.2 *Types of Biobanks and Biobank Networks in Belgium*

On a broader European level, there are many different types of biobanks, established for various purposes and reasons. A report issued by the European Commission (EC) has provided a classification of biobanks that can be translated to the Belgian

[6] Examples are provided in the Compendium, issued by the Federal Agency for Medicines and Health Products (FAMHP) in order to address the most pertinent questions in regards the biobank legislation. For instance, if HBM is stored by a researcher for future research and he has not concluded an agreement with a biobank for the storage of the samples, the research himself would be under an obligation to notify himself as a biobank. See the FAMHP Compendium (2018), p. 4 and 9.

[7] However, the legislation features another figure that is entrusted with responsibility vis-à-vis specific biobank activities. This is the so called 'operator' ('exploitant' or 'uitbater' in the French, respectively Dutch language versions of the Act on HBM). Firstly, a biobank that deals with gametes, embryos or foetuses shall be exclusively operated by the operator of an approved laboratory on research on in-vitro embryos, see Article 3(4)(9) of the Act on HBM. Secondly, and more generally, it is required from the operator to conclude the agreement with the third persons or institutions to which HBM is made available, as established in Article 22 (2) (3) of the Act on HBM.

[8] Article 2 (28) of the Act on HBM.

[9] Some specific responsibilities are further elaborated in the Royal Decree of 9 January 2018 on biobanks, in implementation of Article 22 of the Act of December 2008 (hereafter the Royal Decree of 9 January 2018), for instance duties to keep a register on the specific subject of the scientific research (using a predefined template) and responsibilities related to the processing of personal data in the biobank. Opinion No 45 of 19 January 2009 of the Belgian Advisory Committee on Bioethics brings attention to some of the most important custodian duties. These include, inter alia, checking whether the conditions required prior to obtaining HBM are satisfied, whether the associated personal data are limited to those required for research, and whether the data is coded or anonymized in the most suitable way. Furthermore, it is the custodian's responsibility to keep a register of the samples available and an overview of the transfer of HBM made. Finally, he or she is the one responsible for the management of the biobank and for ensuring that the biobank abides to all relevant legal rules, professional directives, and international codes of conduct. The custodian responds to supervisory authorities and to the management committee of the biobank in case a breach of the applicable rules occurs.

context.[10] According to the authors of the report, there are certain biobank characteristics that can be used to distinguish between different types of biobanks. These include size, research design, the types of biological samples collected, the method of sample collection, processing and storage, and the disease/research focus.[11] Hence, the following types of biobanks can be enumerated: large-scale biobanks, small collection biobanks, population-based biobanks, disease-oriented biobanks, case-control biobanks, tissue banks, biobanks in the context of clinical trials, and other specific biobanking formats, such as Guthrie cards (newborn screening), cord blood, or stem cells.[12]

It is hard to provide an exhaustive overview of the types of biobanks in Belgium, as the Belgian legislator has not pronounced itself on the matter and because no official record exists.[13] The only exception concerns the distinction between biobanks created in the context of a clinical trial and biobanks in general.

The sampling and operations carried out on HBM in the context of a clinical trial on medicinal products for human use, are excluded from the scope of the Belgian Act on HBM.[14] The provisions for biobanks created in the framework of a clinical trial are containted in the Act of 10 April 2014. Attention must be paid to situations where HBM and associated data which were initially collected in a clinical trial, are used later for purposes other than the ones defined in the clinical trial protocol. In this case, the collected data and material would fall within the scope of the Act on HBM.[15]

In addition to the foregoing, the concept of a biobank network must be discussed. The term is not defined in the legislation, however a working definition is established in literature, together with a classification of such networks. A biobank network could be described as 'a group of institutions who freely assume the commitment to collaborate in the domain of biobanking and who (often) share the same procedures and quality policies, and who are (or might be) helped by a central hub for coordination in terms of service'.[16] In Europe, Biobanking and BioMolecular Research infrastructure—European Research Infrastructure Consortium

[10] Gottweis et al. (2012).

[11] Gottweis et al. (2012), p. 13.

[12] Gottweis et al. (2012), pp. 15–16.

[13] However, the Belgian Federal Agency for Medicines and Health Products (FAMHP) is currently working on publishing a list of all notified biobanks, which will shed clarity on the matter, as required by Article 22 (1) (8) of the Act on HBM. At the time of preparation of this Chapter, said list is not yet publicly available, though all historical biobanks (meaning the ones who have been conducting biobanking activities prior February 2018) had to be notified before 1 May 2019 to the FAMHP in order to legally pursue their activities.

[14] Article 3 (3) (f) of the Act on HBM. Note that this applies only to clinical trials as defined in the Act of 7 May 2004 or Regulation (EU) 536/2004.

[15] Article 3 (3) (f) of the Act on HBM.

[16] Morente et al. (2011), p. 188.

(BBMRI-ERIC)[17] is the largest and most significant example of a biobank network, as it connects biobanks and researchers from 20 countries.[18] Belgian's BBMRI-ERIC node has been in operation since 2013, under the name of BBMRI.be. It unites the historically established Belgian biobank networks,[19] one of which formally no longer exists.[20] In the period 2013–2019, BBMRI.be has matured into a solid partner network on biobanks in Belgium and has proven to reach out to a broader community beyond the founding partners. From 2019 onwards, BBMRI.be invites all Belgian biobanks with translational research potential, as well as biobank users that are seeking structural research collaborations with the BBMRI.be network to join the BBMRI.be network.

[17] See also the definition provided for BBMRI-ERIC as a biobank network, namely 'a distributed research infrastructure of biobanks and biomolecular resources, which provides [for its Member States] expertise and services (...) and facilitates access to collections of paner biobanks and biomolecular resources', as found on http://www.bbmri-eric.eu/faq/.

[18] Most of the countries participating in BBMRI-ERIC have the status of full Member states (e.g., Austria, Belgium, Bulgaria), while several participate as observers (e.g., Turkey, Switzerland, Cyprus). More information about the national nodes and contact points at http://www.bbmri-eric.eu/national-nodes/.

[19] All historical Belgian network initiatives could be perceived to fall within the type of a catalogue network. According to literature, a catalogue network consists of a central database from which researchers can obtain information whether the participating biobanks provide access to specific HBM and associated data, see e.g., Verlinden (2015), p. 11. See also Shickle et al. (2010) for a detailed distinction between different types of biobank networks, namely storage networks, bring-and-share storage networks, catalogue networks, partnership networks, contribution networks, expertise networks, and networks in population cohorts.

[20] These are the Belgian Virtual Tumourbank (BVT), Biothèque de la Fédération Wallonie-Bruxelle (BWB), and the Flemish Biobank Network (which is officially no longer in operation). The BVT is coordinated by the Belgian Cancer Registry and within it 11 hospitals (including all major Belgian university hospitals) cooperate. Within this network, a standardized set of oncological data is collected centrally in an online catalogue that can be consulted by researchers in the field of oncology to identify samples of interest for their research, see more at http://virtualtumourbank.kankerregister.org/tumourbank.aspx?url=BVT_home. The Biothèque de la Fédération Wallonie-Bruxelle (BWB) unifies eight biobanks from the territory of the Walloon and Brussels capital regions. BWB is an inter-university collaboration platform, stated by the Université Catholique de Louvain (UCL), Université Libre de Bruxelles (ULB) and the University of Liège (ULg). At the time of preparation of this Chapter, BWB is funded by Innoviris. The BWB network has an online catalogue providing rapid access to high-quality specimens and associated medical/biomolecular data, compliant with international quality standards and regulations. See more about BWB at http://bwb.creatix.be/. Finally, the partners of the former Flemish Biobank Network are united within BBMRI.be as well. The Flemish Biobank Network was organized between the four Flemish University hospitals and five universities, and established five central biobank facilities, a harmonized quality and ethical-legal framework, and a central catalogue.

2 Regulatory Environment for Biobank Research in Belgium

2.1 *Legal Framework for Biobanks*

2.1.1 The Act of 19 December 2008 on Human Body Material

The Act on HBM applies to the donation, collection, procurement, control, treatment, storage, distribution, and use of HBM and manufactured products derived from HBM, intended for human applications or for *scientific research purposes*.[21]

Regarding the scope *ratione materiae*, the rules of the Act on HBM are applicable to any human biological material.[22] Although exceptions exist,[23] the scope of application remains extremely broad. For instance, within the scope fall all derived substances irrespective of their degree of transformation.[24] It follows from the foregoing that the Act on HBM is in principle also applicable to DNA and proteins.[25] Gametes, embryos, and foetuses, even if to a limited extent, also fall under the scope of the legislation.[26] The broad scope of the law *ratione materiae* has been subject to criticism from stakeholders in the field, as it does not provide for an adequate nuancing of the different types of HBM, and thus imposes too strict regulations in all cases. Such conclusion follows when the most recent proposal for amendment of the Act on HBM[27] is taken into consideration.

---

[21] This act was designed to implement Directives 2004/23/EC, 2006/17/EC and 2006/86/EC, as stipulated in Article 1.1 therein. The directives, in contrast to the Act on HBM, relate to human tissues and cells intended solely for application on humans and treatment purposes (see e.g., Article 1 of the Directive 2004/23/EC), and not for scientific research use.

[22] Article 2(1) of the Act on HBM.

[23] Pursuant to Article 3(3)(a)-(e) of the Act on HBM, separate legal frameworks are in force as regards organ transplantations; blood; sampling and operations with HBM for autologous use in the context of a single intervention; sampling and operations carried out for the exclusive purpose of diagnosis for the benefit of the person from whom the body material was collected, and finally, hair, nails, urine, mothers milk, tears and sweat. It should be noted, however, that the Act provides for exceptions to the exceptions. Namely, the collection, storage and making available of blood would still fall under the scope of the Act on HBM, when these activities are carried by a biobank, see Article 3(3)(b). The same applies for the use of hair, nails and other regenerative material, when the intended purpose is scientific research, see Article 3(3)(e).

[24] ARTICLE 2(1) and 3(2) of the Act on HBM. 'Transformation' is defined in the law as 'any manipulation that substantially modifies the genetic code of the cells that make up the human body material so that the material does not show a link with the donor and can no longer provide meaningful information about the health status of the donor', see Article 2(3)(7) of the Act on HBM, as translated into English in the FAMHP Compendium (2018), p. 16. Transformation can occur only in the case that the donor of the HBM has consented to that. Human body material can be transformed if the donor has agreed to this.

[25] Verlinden (2015), p. 78.

[26] Article 3(4) of the Act on HBM.

[27] Proposal for legislation, deposited to the Belgian House of Representatives on 21 February 2019, publicly available at: http://www.dekamer.be/FLWB/PDF/54/3589/54K3589001.pdf A critical discussion of the proposal is not within the scope of this Chapter, however in order to better eluci-

Regarding its scope *ratione loci*, the Belgian Act on HBM applies, first, to HBM removed on Belgian territory,[28] but also, second, to samples imported from abroad and used in Belgium.[29]

Finally, regarding the scope of the law *ratione personae*, three conditions must be fulfilled cumulatively to regard any entity as a biobank: (1) the entity must be carrying out one or more of the activities enumerated in the law (*obtains, processes, stores and makes available of HBM and/or associated data*); (2) the use of HBM must be done *for the purposes of scientific research;*[30]and (3) the activities that a structure has to perform in order to be established as a biobank, include the obtaining, processing, storage and making available of HBM *for scientific research.*[31]

The initial text of the Act on HBM contained legal rules on the procurement and use of HBM by biobanks for research purposes that did not enter into force for 10 years, and in the meantime were amended several times. Changes were introduced, first, by the Act of 19 March 2013 containing diverse provisions concerning health. Second, the Act of 10 April 2014 containing diverse provisions concerning

---

date the challenges that the current law poses in practice, it is of importance to bring attention to some of the changes sought. In the preamble, it is acknowledged that the current scope of the biobank rules is too strict vis-à-vis the nature of some type of HBM. Hence, it is proposed that the scope of application of the law is limited to certain key provision when it comes to some materials. Key example is the revision of the notion of 'transformed material'. The proposal introduces two new terms, namely 'artificial' and 'extracted' material, which allow for better nuancing of the nature of the HBM, see Article 3 of the Proposal. 'Artificial material' is to be understood as material that is produced outside the human body, with the main focus being on cell lines, where cells from a human donor have been replaced by 'manufactured' cells. 'Extracted' material, on the other hand, is material that has been cell or tissue extract, but no longer consists of cells, e.g. ribosomes, mitochondria, etc. The legal regime envisaged for these two types of material is less strict, as long as the material is not intended for genetic research. In all cases, however, the proposal maintains the obligation for an ethics committee check of the use of the material. Further, the proposal seeks to remedy problems of interpretation of the law. Finally, it creates a legal basis for the digital sharing of data concerning the health of the patient with the patient himself or healthcare providers, see Chapter 6 of the Proposal, that further builds up on the already existing Belgian eHealth platform, and more specifically on the so-called Personal Health Viewer, available to Belgian citizens on https://www.masante.belgique.be/#/.

[28] Verlinden (2015), p. 79.

[29] The FAMHP Compendium (2018), p. 6. When that is the case, all imported samples must be registered by a Belgian biobank with which a framework agreement or a contract must be concluded.

[30] Article 2(32) defines 'scientific purposes' as 'any use of human body material with a view to development of the knowledge specific to the exercise of the health care profession as referred to in the law concerning the exercise of health care professions, coordinated on 10 May 2015'. The definition requires to treat operations with HBM with caution, as, for instance, from the moment that HBM enters into a biobank, it will no longer be available for direct clinical use, as stipulated in Article 8(2)(1) of the Act on HBM.

[31] Article 2(27) of the Act on HBM. In cases where HBM is temporarily stored in the context of ongoing scientific research, such temporary storage would not require a researcher to notify himself as a biobank, on the conditions that the researcher has concluded an agreement with a biobank and that the research is conducted within a defined time frame or for a specific purpose, see the FAMHP Compendium (2018), p. 4.

health established specific rules for biobanks created in the framework of a clinical trial. Finally, The Act of 22 June 2016 introduced further modifications to the legal framework. All three Acts were scheduled to enter into force only after the publication of one or more executive Royal Decrees.[32] With the adoption of the Royal Decree of 9 January 2018, the legal framework described above finally entered into force.[33]

A recent amendment of the Act on HBM that requires attention, is the Act of 30 October 2018. With its entry into force, the scope of Belgian biobank rules *ratione materiae* was extended to the donation, procurement, control and import of HBM intended for use exclusively in manufactured products, in particular medicinal products, advanced therapy medicinal products (ATMPs)[34] or medical devices.[35] Another significant change brought by the new amendment act, is the establishment of a new service within the Federal Agency for Medicines and Health Products (FAMHP), which should provide advice on access to HBM.[36]

2.1.2 The Royal Decree of 9 January 2018

The Royal Decree[37] establishes rules pertaining to, *inter alia,* the biobank notification procedure; the collection of human material; the approval by and reporting to ethics committees; the organization of a biobank register; the content of the agreement between a biobank and the recipient of the human substances.

2.1.3 The Compendium on Biobanks, Issued by the Federal Agency for Medicines and Health Products (FAMHP)

The Compendium is a form of self-regulation[38] which strives to shed clarity as to how to interpret and implement the complex system of legal requirements. During the preparation of the Compendium, the input of relevant stakeholders was sought,

[32] Article 124 of the Act of 19 March 2013, Article 139 of the Act of 10 April 2014, and Article 45 of the Act of 22 June 2016.

[33] Article 15 of the Royal Decree of 9 January 2018.

[34] Belgian legislation refers directly to the definition for advanced therapy medicinal products provided at European level, namely 'any of the following medicinal products for human use: — a gene therapy medicinal product as defined in Part IV of Annex I to Directive 2001/83/EC, — a somatic cell therapy medicinal product as defined in Part IV of Annex I to Directive 2001/83/EC, — a tissue engineered product', see Article 2(1) of Regulation (EC) No 1394/2007 on advanced therapy medicinal products.

[35] Article 3(1) of the Act on HBM as modified by Article 3 of the Act of 30 October 2018.

[36] The service is titled 'Commité d'allocation du matériel corporel humain' (CAMCH) in French and 'Allocatiecomité voor menselijk lichaamsmateriaal' (ACMLM) in Dutch, translated into English as 'Human Body Material Allocation Committee', see Article 21(3)/1 of the Act on HBM, as amended by Article 15 of the Act of 30 October 2018.

[37] The Royal Decree of 9 January 2018 on biobanks in implementation of Article 22 of the Act of 19 on HBM, entered into force on 01.11.2018.

[38] To be taken as meaning that the relevant stakeholders have voluntarily committed to abide by the guidelines as established in the document.

namely representatives of academic and industrial biobanks, ethical committees and juridical experts. By providing answers to 47 consolidated questions, the document covers a broad range of topics such as, *inter alia*, the scope of the biobank legislation, consent, notification procedure, transformation of HBM, traceability and anonymization, ethics committees.

2.1.4 Belgian Data Protection Legislation

Data protection legislation must always be considered when it comes to biobanking activities. The reason for this lies in the fact that access to associated data[39] is of crucial importance for the proper conduct of most biomedical research. Limited access to such data could result in a lack of reproducibility and risk of misinterpretation of the research results.[40]

2.1.5 'Associated Data' as Personal Data

The Belgian Privacy Commission[41] brought attention to the fact that information about a number of characteristics of the donor must be provided every time an operation is conducted on HBM.[42] This is in line with Article 2 (27) of the Act on HBM, which states that within the scope of the law is also 'where appropriate, *associated data* relating to the human body material and the donor'. The Belgian biobank legislation refers to personal data, although it does not provide a definition of the term itself. However, the Belgian Privacy Commission further established that such biological and medical characteristics of the donor (i.e., associated data) have to be regarded as personal data in relation to the health of the donor in the sense of Article 7 of the Act of 8 December 1992 on the protection of privacy.[43]

[39] Associated data includes data related to the donor, such as demographic data, e.g. age and gender, or data on previous diseases or family history, and data about the quality characteristics of the HBM, see Verlinden (2015), p. 4. However, it should be born in mind that personal data is not only collected upon procurement of HBM, but it can also be generated when samples are being processed. Pursuant to Recital 35 of the GDPR, 'personal data concerning health should include (…) information derived from the testing or examination of a body pa or bodily substance, including from genetic data and biological samples'. This brings another layer of complexity to the matter of associated data (as the new generated personal data necessarily will always fall within the special categories of data provided for in the GDPR). Hence, the crucial importance of taking into consideration data protection legislation when conducting biobank activities.

[40] Verlinden (2015), p. 4.

[41] Operating as the Belgian Data Protection Authority since 25 May 2018, as reformed by a law of 16 November 2017 and.

[42] Opinion No 10/2009.

[43] Opinion No 10/2009.

2.1.6 The Act of 30 July 2018

The Act of 8 December 1992 was replaced by the Act of 30 July 2018.[44] It can be argued that the authoritative guidance issued in the past by the Belgian Privacy Commission applies to the new legislation as well.

The Act of 30 July 2018 stipulates that the definitions of GDPR apply directly.[45] Hence, central concepts such as 'personal data', 'controller', 'processor', or, in the context of biobanking, 'data concerning health' and 'genetic data', are to be understood as they are defined in the GDPR.[46]

2.1.7 Interplay Between the Belgian Data Protection and Biobank Rules

In addition to the reference to personal data described above, the Belgian biobank legislation provides for an interplay with data protection rules on several other grounds, listed below.

- **Data controller and data subject in the context of biobank research:** Responsibility for the processing of personal data in the framework of a biobank is allocated to the biobank custodian.[47] Logically, the data subject is the donor of HBM.[48]
- **Record of processing activities:** On the one hand, Article 191 of the Act of 30 July 2018 lists the additional elements that the controller should add to the record of processing activities in case data is processed for scientific purposes. Besides this list, the legislation does not provide any further guidance or template for this record. On the other hand, the Act on HBM establishes that a biobank should keep a 'register' with information about the nature, origin and destination of the stored HBM,[49] and a template for such a register is provided in the Royal Degree of 9 January 2018. The two types of records complement each other, and the lack of a unified format could be perceived as an additional burden for the data controller/biobank custodian.
- **Storage period:** The maximum storage period for personal data is 50 years after procurement of HBM.[50]

---

[44] Act of 30 July 2018 on the protection of natural persons with regard to the processing of personal data, which implements the EU General Data Protection Regulation (GDPR).

[45] Article 5 of the Act of 30 July.

[46] See Articles 4(1), 4(7), 4(8), 4(13), and 4(15) of the GDPR.

[47] Article 11(3) of the Royal Decree of 9 January 2018.

[48] Verlinden (2015), p. 85.

[49] Article 22 (2) of the Act on HBM.

[50] Article 22 (8) of the Act on HBM. This provision of Belgian law is directly related to the principle of storage limitation, as established in Article 5(e) of the GDPR. However, the Act on HBM does not contradict the principle of storage limitation, as it benefits from the exception provided for personal data processed solely for scientific research.

- **Traceability and identification of personal data:**[51] Traceability is a crucial concept in biobanking. It constitutes the ability to locate and identify HBM and associated personal data at any stage of the biobank process, from procurement to distribution for use, or destruction.[52] Concerning HBM obtained by a living donor, traceability depends on the consent of the donor or of the person who is legally authorized to grant permission for the procurement of HBM.[53] In the case of residual HBM obtained from a diseased person, the determination of whether the material should be traceable could be made by several people, which the law enumarates in a limited manner, including the custodian of the biobank.[54] Hence, such HBM is collected based on a presumed (non-explicit) consent procedure. As traceability is necessarily linked to the processing of personal data, the discussed provisions also bear influence on the degree of control that a donor will have regarding his privacy.[55]
- **Further processing of personal data:** Pursuant to Article 194 of the Act of 30 July 2018, where personal data are not collected from the data subject, the controller should conclude an agreement with the original controller. The Article 195 lists the essential elements of the agreement: the contact details of the original controller and of the controller of the further processing; or, in cases where derogations from certain data subject's rights (i.e., right to access, right to rectification, right to restriction of processing, and right to object) have been adopted, the reasons why the exercise of these rights is likely to make the achievement of the purpose of further processing impossible or seriously hinder it.

  These rules are directly related to Article 21(1), Article 22(2)(3) of the Act on HBM, and Article 10 of the Royal Degree of 9 January 2018, pursuant to which each provision of HBM by a biobank, whether the HBM is transferred to another biobank or a third party, should be subject to a written agreement with the person or institution receiving the material. The agreement should govern the possible processing of the donor's personal data by the entity to which the material is made available.[56] The biobank legislation requires that this type of agreements containt more elements, than what is prescribed in the data protection rules, e.g. the subject of the scientific research for which the HBM is made available; the

---

[51] Article 22 (9) of the Act on HBM establishes that the rules on traceability and identification of the donor (outlined in Article 22(37)) are to be further worked out in a Royal Decree, with the aim of guaranteeing data protection in accordance with the applicable Privacy legislation. The relevant Royal Decree was finally adopted in 2018, hence at the current moment they are enforceable.

[52] Article 2(23) of the Act on HBM.

[53] Article 22(4)(1) of the Act on HBM.

[54] Article 22(4)(2) of the Act on HBM.

[55] Moreover, regard shall be held of Article 11 of the GDPR, according to which 'if the purposes for which a controller processes personal data no longer require the identification of a data subject by the controller, the controller shall not be obliged to maintain, acquire or process additional information in order to identify the data subject for the sole purpose of complying' with the GDPR.

[56] Article 22(2)(3) of the Act on HBM.

responsibilities for ensuring traceability; a description of the appropriate technical and organization measures to be taken in the case personal data is also communicated; a coded copy of the consent of the donor.
Finally, Article 11 of the Royal Decree of 9 January 2018, expressly forbids the transfer of personal data to third parties, but permits it if it occurs between biobanks.

Questions remain regarding the practical implementation of the provisions discussed above. For instance, a detailed account of the appropriate technical and organizational measures to be taken in cases of personal data transfers lacks in the current Belgian data protection legislation.

2.2 *Procedure for Samples Collection*

2.2.1 In Theory

The procedure for samples collection is established in the Act on HBM. Removal of HBM for scientific research is permitted on the condition that it is performed for a specific purpose.[57] The aim should be specified, precise and relevant for the scientific research.

Again, attention should be paid again to the fact that associated data, and more specifically personal data, are collected alongside samples. Hence, in the context of HBM procurement, data protection rules apply as well. According to the purpose limitation principle established in Article 5(1)(b) of the GDPR, personal data must be processed for 'specified, explicit and legitimate purpose'. The purpose limitation principle is thus in line with the condition established in the Act on HBM as regards the obtaining of samples. However, in contrast to the Act on HBM, the GDPR allows the possibility for a broad consent for research, as long as ethical oversight is provided. Pursuant to Recital 33, 'it is often not possible to fully identify the purpose of personal data processing for scientific research purposes at the time of data collection. Therefore, data subjects should be allowed to give their consent to certain areas of scientific research when in keeping with recognised ethical standards for scientific research.'

- **Informed consent: A central place in the samples collection procedure holds the requirement for informed consent.**[58] Consent is also one of the possible legal bases for the valid processing of associated personal data.[59] According to the biobank legislation, informed consent for biobank research shall be given

[57] Article 8(1)(1)(1) of the Act on HBM.

[58] Article 10(1) of the Act on HBM stipulates that as a general principle 'the removal of human body material from a living person can only be carried out on an adult donor (…) who has previously consented thereto in accordance with the provisions of Article 10(5)'.

[59] As stipulated in Article 6.1(a), read in conjunction with Article 9(2)(a) of the GDPR.

without prejudice to the applicable data protection rules.[60] Pursuant to the Act on HBM, the donor's consent for biobank research must be given in an informed, conscious and free manner, and it must be written, dated and signed.[61]

An interesting parallel between the GDPR and the biobank rules can be made vis-à-vis the right to withdrawal. The Act on HBM provides for a right to withdraw one's consent that can be exercised at any time before the HBM has been subjected to any action after having been obtained.[62] It is not necessary to motivate the withdrawal. In literature, this right to withdrawal is perceived as rather symbolic, since the donor loses such it as soon as the custodian stores or processes the HBM.[63] The GDPR also establishes a right to withdraw consent,[64] which holds relatively more weight than the same right under the Act of HBM. Hence, consent for the processing of associated data can be withdrawn at any time, and if done, this would mean that the custodian must delete all processed data, unless the data can be processed on another legal ground. However, the right of withdrawal under GDPR does not affect the lawfulness of the processing conducted before withdrawal.

- **Distinction between primary and secondary use of HBM:** Another important consideration related to the Belgian biobank legal framework pertains to the distinction between primary and secondary use of HBM. Primary use is defined as 'any use of human body material to which the donor has explicitly and specifically given consent in the context of the collection',[65] whereas secondary use is 'any use of human body material other than that to which the donor has given his consent in the context of the collection'.[66] In Article 20(1) an informed and explicit consent is required for the secondary use of HBM. However, pursuant to the same provision, in cases where it is impossible to seek consent, or where such a request would be exceptionally inappropriate, the positive opinion of an ethics committee would be sufficient to allow the collection of samples.
- **Use of residual HBM:** A further essential point relates to the use of residual HBM. Residual HBM is defined as the material collected for 'the diagnosis or treatment of the donor which, after a sufficient and relevant part has been stored for the establishing, refining or completing the diagnosis or treatment of the donor on the basis of new scientific data, is redundant in relation to these purpose and could therefore be destroyed'.[67] In the case of residual HBM, consent is presumed, unless, prior to any operation with the material, the donor announced his/

---

[60] See Article 10(7) of the Act on HBM.

[61] Article 10(5) of the Act on HBM.

[62] Article 10(5)(4)of the Act on HBM.

[63] See Verlinden (2015), p. 81 and Panis and Van Gelder (2008).

[64] Article 7(3) of the GDPR.

[65] Article 2(29) of the Act on HBM.

[66] Article 2(30) of the Act on HBM.

[67] Article 2(33) of the Act on HBM.

her refusal.[68] The refusal must be addressed to the medical specialist referred to in Article 4(1)(1) of the Act on HBM, or to the chief medical officer of the hospital where the sample was taken.

- **Who obtains consent:** The person responsible for obtaining the consent must be a medical specialist.[69]
- **Sample collection from minors and incapacitated persons:** The Act on HBM provides for the possibility to obtain HBM from minors and incapacitated persons (as defined in Article 492 of the Belgian Civil Code) only in cases whereby the collection of samples cannot have serious consequences for the donor and the removal involves cells and tissues that regenerate, or in cases where the removal is carried out with an autologous purpose.[70] Informed consent is required, and it should be given by the donor's representative in accordance with the Belgian Act of 22 August 2002 on Patients' Rights.
- **Sample collection from diseased persons:** The Act on HBM provides that a presumption, established in Article 10–14 of the Act of 13 June 1986 regarding the removal and transplantation of organs, applies for research biobanking as well.[71] According to the relevant provisions, anyone who has been domiciled in Belgium for 6 months, is presumed to consent to a sample collection after his death, unless he has expressed his opposition[72] (orally or in writing, with the municipal administration, their general practitioner, or online via MaSante.Belgique.be). This is known as the 'opt-out' system. A new Royal Decree, issued on 9 February 2020, further details the rules on the registration of declarations of will concerning post mortem removal of HBM and organs. The decree enters into force on 1 July, 2020. Of interest is Article 11, which introduces a sensibilization step. Namely, a month before reaching the age of maturity, all persons will receive a letter which would inform them about the opt-out system, and their right to opt-out or explicitly opt-in. The future consequences of this law cannot be predicted. It may be assumed that the new generation will be more aware of the system of opting-out, in comparison to many people today who do not know about it. However, it can also be argued that as long as the general public is not structurally informed about these provisions, this could induce yet another obstacle in accessing HBM for research purposes. They key lies in setting up information campaigns, which are not yet foreseen by the government.
- **The no (commercial) advantage rule:** The Act on HBM prohibits that any financial or material advantage is offered or received in exchange for the dona-

[68] Article 20(2)(1) of the Act on HBM.

[69] Article 10(5)(6) of the Act on HBM.

[70] Article 10(3) of the Act on HBM.

[71] Article 12 of the Act on HBM.

[72] Soon after the adoption of the Act on HBM, the logic of the Belgian legislator in constructing the cited rule was heavily criticized in literature. For example, Sterckx and Van Assche discuss the illegitimacy of extrapolation of presumed consent for uses of HBM for therapeutic purposes to consent for research uses (see Sterckx and Van Assche 2011). However, at the present moment presumed consent has become accepted in practice.

tion of HBM.[73] The donor can only receive a compensation for the cost or loss of income that is direct results of the donation.[74]

- **Who removes the sample:** The categories of health professionals that have the right to physically obtain HBM are listed in Article 2 of the Royal Decree. These are medical doctors, dentists, nurses, midwives, pharmacists and licensees or masters in chemical sciences authorized to perform clinical biology analysis, and finally, holders of the professional title 'medical laboratory technologist'. It is possible that the collection of HBM from a living donor takes place outside of a hospital, as long as this occurs in an environment where health, safety and discretion are guaranteed.[75]

2.2.2 In Practice

In general, the institutions strictly follow the rules described above. The reliance on presumed consent for the use of residual HBM has not yet become widespread. Because of the need for clarification on the applicable stipulations, explicit consent is often asked also for residual material, as such material in most cases is not anonymized.

Moreover, it could be argued that it anonymization itself is only possible with the donor's consent. The reason lies in the provision of Article 11 of the Act on HBM, according to which, if important information concerning the donor's state of health has been generated during operations conducted on traceable HBM, an obligation is triggered for the biobank to inform the donor about the discovery.

When HBM is procured for secondary purposes, practice shows that in most cases it is impossible to obtain the donor's consent, or it is excetionally inappropriate to seek it.

3 Biobank Research Oversight

3.1 General Remarks

In Belgium research oversight in the context of biobanking, other than by the Belgian Supervisory Authority for data protection, is provided by three main bodies. These are ethics committees, the Federal Agency for Medicines and Health Products (FAMHP), and Data Protection Officers, as required by the Act of 30 July 2018, in implementation of the GDPR.

---

[73] Article 6 of the Act on HBM.

[74] As confirmed by the FAMHP Compendium (2018), p. 38.

[75] FAMHP Compendium (2018), p. 29.

3.2 Ethics Committees

The positive opinion of an ethics committee is required for the establishment of a notified biobank.[76] Pursuant to Article 22(1)(3) of the Act on HBM, such opinions can only be given by ethics committees with full competence.[77]

Once a positive ethics opinion has been obtained in view of a biobank's general aims and activities, the biobank can also rely upon it as an approval covering particular projects.[78] Thus the biobank is alleviated from the burden to seek ethical advice for each new procurement of HBM.[79]

In addition, prior to any secondary use of HBM, an ethics committee must provide a favorable opinion.[80] The ethics committee decides on the relevance of the secondary use and its purpose, the adequacy of the information provided to the donor, and the sufficient specificity and the scope of the donor's consent.[81]

Finally, in cases where it is impossible to seek the donor's consent, or where such a request would be exceptionally inappropriate, the positive opinion of an ethics committee is sufficient to allow the collection of HBM. Whereby such a situation arises, it is also the ethics committee's responsibility to evaluate whether it appears impossible or exceptionally inappropriate to request the donor's consent.[82]

3.3 The Federal Agency for Medicines and Health Products (FAMHP)

All biobanks in Belgium have to submit a notification on their activities to the FAMHP (see also Figure 2).[83]

---

[76] Crucial role is in this respect is played by the Belgian Association of Research Ethics Committees (BAREC). Among its objectives is the provision of support to Belgian ethics committees involved in health care. See more at http://barec.be/index.htm.

In addition, note that an exception from the general rule exists for biobanks created in the framework of a clinical trial. In such cases, the ethics approval given as regard the clinical trial as a whole is also considered sufficient for the valid establishment of biobank activities. See Article 22(1)(6) of the Act on HBM.

[77] In accordance with the Act of 7 May 2004 relating to experiments on humans. For a list of all 25 recognized ethics committees in Belgium, see here https://www.famhp.be/sites/default/files/content/lijst_ecs_-_liste_ce_4.pdf.

[78] Article 22(1)(3), (4), and (5) of the Act on HBM.

[79] Note, however, that the usage of HBM by academic or industrial end-users is still subject to approval by a local ethics committee.

[80] Article 21(1) of the Act on HBM.

[81] Article 21(3) of the Act on HBM.

[82] Article 21(3)(3) of the Act on HBM.

[83] Article 22(1) of the Act on HBM and Article 3 of the Royal Decree. An exception to this rule exists for biobanks that are created in the framework of a clinical trial. In such cases, the approval

For a biobank that has been in operation before the entry into force of the Royal Decree (meaning that samples have already been collected before November 2018), the notification procedure had to be finalized before 1 May 2019, following a 6 months grace period.

For all new biobanks, the notification must be done before the start of any samples collection.

3.4 Data Protection Officer

Article 37.1 of the GDPR stipulates that in cases where the core activities of a controller or processor consist of processing special categories of data pursuant to Article 9 (i.e., genetic data, biometric data, and data concerning health) on a large scale, a data protection officer shall be designated. Having in mind the sensitive character of biobank activities and of HBM and its associated data, it is to be concluded that most biobanks would have to appoint such Data Protection Officer (hereafter DPO). The DPO can be perceived to have a critical role in the oversight of biobank research.

The DPO must be designated on the basis of his professional qualities, in particular expert knowledge of data protection law and practices.[84] The DPO's tasks include, *inter alia*, informing and advising the controller or the processor, and the employees who carry out processing, of their obligations pursuant to the GDPR and to other relevant national provisions; monitoring compliance with the relevant EU and national data protection provisions, as well as the internal policies of the biobank; providing advice as regards data protection impact assessment; cooperating with the data protection supervisory authority.

The Belgian Act of 30 July 2018 also provides for the designation of a DPO, specifically in the cases where personal data are processed for scientific research purposes and the processing may result in high risk.[85] When personal data is processed for scientific purposes, the controller must anonymize or pseudonymize it after it is collected. In cases of further processing, it is possible to de-pseudonymize the personal data only when necessary for the research purposes and, where applicable, after consulting the DPO.[86] Furthermore, under Article 204, the DPO must issue opinions on the use of the various pseudonymization and anonymization methods employed. However, the legislator's decision to createthis obligation may be questioned, as at the current moment there are not enough guarantees that DPOs are sufficiently equipped and educated to provide such opinions.

---

of the clinical trial itself by the FAMHP replaces the requirement to notify the establishment of the biobank, see Article 22(1)(2) of the Act on HBM.

[84] Article 37(5) of the GDPR.

[85] Article 190, read in conjunction with Article 32 of the Act of 30 July 2018.

[86] Article 198–200 of the Act of 30 July 2018.

4 Law in Context: Individual Rights and Public Interests

4.1 General Remarks

Several examples could be provided as regards the question how the legal rules outlined above are applied in practice, and more specifically, how the balance between individual rights and the development of science is struck in Belgium.

4.2 Issues Pertaining to (Presumed) Consent for Obtaining HBM

As established above, informed consent constitutes the general principle in biobank research for the valid procurement of HBM and associated data. However, consent is absolutely required only in situations whereby samples are collected for primary use.

For secondary use of HBM for research purposes, the Belgian legislation gives the possibility to procure HBM without consent. This will be the case if it is impossible to seek the donor's consent (for instance, the donor is deceased), or if such a request would be exceptionally inappropriate. In such instances, the positive opinion of an ethics committee would be sufficient to allow the collection of samples.[87]

Even more significantly, the concept of presumed consent for residual use of HBM is part of Belgian law. It is always presumed that consent has been given, unless the donor has explicitly refused before any operation was performed on the samples.[88] This could be seen as a unique 'opt-out' consent system with very practical roots.

The concept of informed and explicit consent has had a central place in biomedical research since it was first embedded in the Nuremberg code.[89] It is inextricably linked to the principles of human dignity and autonomy, and to the protection of the privacy of the individual, and it is seen as the practical implementation of the right to self-determination.[90] Henceforth, at first glance the Belgian presumed consent system may seem to be in contradiction to the protection of fundamental rights. Indeed, according to some authors the opt-out consent system is 'highly problematic'.[91] However, when discussing the procurement of HBM in practice, and the balance between relevant interests, regard should be held of the following considerations.

The nature of current biomedical research as such calls for the establishment of large pools of samples to ensure genetic representation for the correct testing of

[87] Article 21 of the Act of HBM.

[88] Article 20(2)(1) of the Act on HBM.

[89] The Nuremberg Code (1996) 313 BMJ 1448. See also, Kosta (2011) for an overview of the evolution of the concept of consent in the bioethics field, and an elucidation of consent under data protection rules.

[90] Allen and McNamara (2011).

[91] Sterckx and Van Assche (2011), p. 254.

research hypotheses. This is especially prominent as the precision medicine approach is becoming more widespread. If HBM stored by biobanks is unrepresentative of society as a whole, future treatments for those not represented are likely to become increasingly scarce.[92] A practical way to deal with under-representation is presumed consent. When consent has been already obtained for the procurement of HBM for diagnostic/therapeutic uses, going back to the donor for a second consent for research purposes would result in additional costs (as it will require more time and efforts), or it might prove impossible to obtain. Thus, the Belgian presumed consent fosters the development of science. Koslakidis and el. further argue that an opt-out system may be seen as part of an 'altruistic societal obligation' for the common good.[93] This directly refers to the principle of solidarity, part of the broader bioethical discourse surrounding transplantation for years. For instance, in Belgium, presumed consent for organ donation was established in 1986 with the Law regarding the removal and transplantation of organs. Therefore, the opt-out system in the framework of research biobanking could be viewed as a logical continuation of a long-standing tradition.[94]

4.3 *Issues Pertaining to the Processing of Data Associated to HBM*

With respect to the processing of associated personal data, the GDPR and the implementing Belgian Act of 30 July 2018 apply.

A legal basis is required for the valid processing of personal data. The choice of the correct legal basis is responsibility ofthe data controller.[95] In practice, there is a lack of sufficient authoritative guidance pertaining to the choice of the most suitable legal basis, and much uncertainty remains.

Recently, the European Data Protection Board (EDPB) issued Opinion No 3/2019 which concerns the interplay between the EU Clinical Trials Regulation (CTR) and the GDPR. At the moment, it is the first EPDB opinion to discuss biomedical research. Biobanking is neither harmonized at EU level, nor regulated in the EU CTR, however, some important conclusions related to it can still be drawn on the basis of Opinion No 3/2019, by way of analogy.

Firstly, the EPDB expressly stipulated that explicit consent[96] should not always be regarded as the preferred legal basis for the conduct of scientific research. In the

---

[92] Kozlakidis et al. (2012), p. 115.

[93] Kozlakidis et al. (2012), p. 118.

[94] The adoption of a presumed consent possibility for the valid procurement of HBM offers grounds for a broader critical discussion about the drawbacks and positives of such a system. Such discussion, however, although highly significant from a theoretical point of view, falls outside scope of the present Chapter.

[95] As biobank research deals with sensitive data, the applicable provisions of the GDPR are to be found in Article 9(2) read in conjunction with Article 6.

[96] Article 9(2)(a) of the GDPR.

context of a clinical trial, this is especially the case when processing is carried out for reliability and safety purposes, such as e.g., safety reporting or inspection by national competent authorities. The appropriate legal basis, as established by EPDB, is Article 9(2)(i)—'processing is necessary for reasons of public interest in the area of public health' read in conjunction with Article 6(1)(c)—'legal obligations to which the controller is subject'.

Secondly, for pure research activities conducted in the framework of a clinical trial, the EPDB rightly acknowledged that the informed consent for participation in a trial must not be confused with consent as legal basis for the processing of data. Extrapolated to the context of biobanking, it seems reasonable to draw a similar distinction as regards the informed consent required to obtain HBM for primary use.

Further, the EPDB brought attention to the imbalance of power between a trial participant and the investigator/sponsor of a trial, which could affect one of the conditions for valid data processing consent, namely that it has to be 'freely given'. In the context of biobank research conducted outside the context of a clinical trial, it could be argued that the power imbalance is not of the same nature, by virtue of the fact that sample donation does not involve the same risks pertaining to possible institutional or hierarchical dependencies that could inappropriately influence a patient's decision to participate in a clinical trial. However, consent should still be regarded with caution when considered as the suitable legal basis for processing.[97]

4.4 *Issues Pertaining to Information Provided to the Donor of HBM*

As established above, pursuant to the Belgian Act on HBM the consent of the donor for the procurement of HBM must be *informed*. In addition, concerning associated personal data, the GDPR in its Article 13 establishes an information obligation for the data controller. At the time the personal data is obtained, the data subject, i.e. the donor, must receive all of the information specified in Article 13(1) and (2).

The practice in Belgian biobanks is to provide general information about the biobank research via a patient brochure. This general information is not repeated later to the individual donor. It could be argued that, pursuant to Article 13 and 14 of the GDPR, for each research conducted on human body material and for each related processing of personal data, the donor should be individually informed.

[97] In the case of use of residual HBM, for instance, the opt-out consent system for the procurement of samples applies in Belgium. Contacting the data subject for consent under GDPR could be seen as an undue burden posed on the biobank custodian. In such instances, another legal basis could be seen as more suitable, e.g. Article 6 (1) (e) of the GDPR, which allows data processing 'necessary for the performance of a task carried out in the public interest' or Article 6(1)(f)—'for the purposes of the legitimate interests pursued by the controller or by a third pay, except where such interests are overridden by the interests or fundamental rights and freedoms of the data subject'. The logic expressed here follows the one established in the EPDB Opinion No 3/2019. It could be argued that following such reasoning would be beneficial for striking the right balance between individual rights and public interest. However, an in-depth elaboration on this topic is outside the scope of this Chapter, and it provides ground for a separate study.

Furthermore, more specific information is provided by the biobank when the donor's informed consent is obtained. At the current moment a national sensibilization campaign is in development with the aim to inform the general public about the nature and aims of biobank research, similar to organ donation campaigns in the past.

When it comes to information considerations within the Belgian context, one practical challenge might be present in the case of residual use of HBM, as consent for it is presumed, henceforth the donor does not have access to the more specific information that is typically provided during the informed consent procedure. Another unresolved issue is that under the current legal framework, donors cannot indicate that they do not want to receive information. A parallel could be made with the ongoing debate regarding return of research findings in biomedical research and the psychological stress endured by some donors.[98]

5 GDPR Impact and Future Possibilities for Biobanking

5.1 *The Impact of GDPR on Biobanking in Belgium*

In addition to the points already presented throughout this Chapter, several more issues related to the impact of GDPR on biobanking in Belgium can be selected for discussion. This part aims to open room for debate and pose questions for further research on the theoretical and practical challenges that the current legal frameworks present.

5.2 *Allocation of Responsibilities According to Biobanking and Data Protection Rules*

Article 5(2) of the GDPR establishes the principle of accountability, according to which the data controller is responsible and should be able to demonstrate compliance with all other data protection principles. In the Belgian biobank framework, the unique concept of custodian is established. According to the law, the custodian can only be a natural person, more specifically a medical doctor, and should fulfill a specific set of strict eligibility conditions.[99] It is the custodian who is specifically entrusted with the responsibilities of a data controller.[100] However, the custodian carries a set of additional obligations, assigned to him under the legal framework for biobanking.

It is outside the scope of this article to carry out an in-depth comparative study of the figures of the data controller and the biobank custodian, and more specifically, on how the custodian may exercise most suitably the dual responsibilities allocated

[98] De Clercq et al. (2017).

[99] Article 2 (28) of the Act on HBM.

[100] Article 11(3) of the Royal Decree of 9 January 2018.

to him by the two set of applicable rules. However, a meaningful line for further research may concern the influence that the notion of controller has over the performing of custodian duties in practice. Vice versa, insights into how the concept of custodian may bear an impact on the notion of controller in Belgium would be useful. Such research would be of help for the much-needed alignment between data protection and biobank rules.

Further layers of complexity as regards the allocation of responsibilities exists in the field of clinical trials and other interventional studies. As stated in Sect. 1.2 above, the Act on HBM is not applicable to the sampling and operations conducted in the framework of a clinical trial on medicinal products for human use. However, when it comes to studies performed to test medical devices,[101] studies for in vitro medical devices,[102] or other types of studies, e.g. a surgical study, no such exception is provided for and the biobank legislation applies in full. A collision might be envisaged between the figures of the sponsor of such a study, the biobank custodian, and the notion of data controller. Pursuant to biobank rules, the custodian is in all cases a data controller.[103] In the context of an investigational study, it could be argued that the study sponsor would be the data controller, as the natural or legal person that determines the purposes and means of the processing of personal data, associated to the HBM.[104] A more in-depth discussion is necessary as regards the responsibilities of sponsor and custodian in such a context and vis-à-vis the possibilities for joint controllership. Moreover, the foregoing begs further investigation into the national legislator's reasons to exclude only one type of interventional study, namely clinical trials on medicinal products for human use, from the scope of the Act on HBM.

Finally, it is also of interest to discuss the fact that the Act on HBM becomes applicable to data and samples collected in the scope of a clinical trial, if they are later used for other research (i.e., secondary use). To illustrate, we use a hypothetical case, see Fig. 3. First, HBM and associated data are collected and used in the scope of a clinical trial: the Belgian biobank law would not be applicable, and the clinical trial sponsor would be the data controller. The biobank in which, tissues, samples, and associated data are stored, would be sub-contractor of the sponsor, and, moreover, data processor acting on behalf of the sponsor. Second, a number of years after the end of the trial, the sponsor may decide to conduct new research with the previously collected HBM and data. This would be possible, as long as all legal and ethical requirements for secondary use of data are complied with. In this situation, the Belgian biobank law would become available. Regarding

[101] Regulated in Belgium by the Royal Decree of 15 July 1997 governing the active implantable medical devices, implementing Directive 90/385/EEC, and by the Royal Decree of 18 March 1999 governing medical devices, implementing and by Directive 93/42/EEC.

[102] Regulated in Belgium by the Royal Decree dated 14 November 2001 governing medical devices for in-vitro diagnostics, implementing Directive 98/79/EEC.

[103] Article 11(3) of the Royal Decree of 9 January 2018.

[104] Article 4(7) of the GDPR.

roles and responsibilities, whereas the sponsor would remain data controller for the original full data set, the biobank manager would turn into joint-controller for the sub data set stored and processed in the biobank. Potential issues emerge. For instance, the biobank remains subcontractor, but pursuant to the Act on HBM, the biobank manager would now have the power to agree or not to the release of samples and data for research. Uncertainties exists also with respect to the agreements for further processing of data and samples, described in Sect. 2.1.7 above, as it is not clear whether the contract between the sponsor and a new recipient of HBM would be sufficient, or whether the biobank would have to sign their own agreement.

5.3 Allocation of Research Oversight Responsibilities Between Data Protection Officers and Ethics Committees

Another question that has not been investigated yet and that could present practical challenges in the future, is about the allocation of research oversight responsibilities between DPOs and ethics committees. On the one hand, some of the rights and responsibilities with which DPOs are entrusted seem to require expertise in ethics matters, especially when data processing activities are situated in a biobanking context. For instance, confusion may be brought up by the possibility for a DPO to provide opinion prior to the collection of personal data.[105] In such cases, it is generally expected that the DPOs would seek the advice of an ethical committee. However, ethics committees themselves are often lacking specific expertise when it comes to data protection matters. The right balance should be sought between these two important actors. Furthermore, efforts in education and cross-sharing of experience are required.

6 Future Possibilities for Biobanking

In relation to the many remaining uncertainties in the interpretation of the relevant legal rules, Article 40 of the GDPR offers a welcomed solution by encouraging the drawing up of codes of conducts. The codes of conduct are intended to contribute to the proper application of the data protection legislation in a specific processing sector, and their aim is to overcome fragmentation in implementation. Having in mind the particularly sensitive link between biobanking and data protection, such a comprehensive common interpretation of GDPR norms would have positive influence for fostering biobank research. At present, BBMRI-ERIC is in preparation of a code of conduct. As Belgium is among the few Member

[105] Article 22 of the Act of 30 July 2018.

States who have a distinct biobank legal framework, it could be envisaged that the Belgian experience in regulating biobanking would be of high significance during the drafting of the code.

A second point to be considered when discussing the future, is collaboration, both on a national level (between biobanks), and on a broader European level. In this respect, the Belgian node of BBMRI-ERIC (BBMRI.be) is currently working on strengthening the harmonization of relevant Belgian policies within the broader framework of BBMRI-ERIC policies. In addition, the structure and governance of BBMRI.be was recently changed to allow biobank users to become part of the network besides the biobank providers. This change is an attempt to improve the interaction and best practices for sharing and mutual understanding of needs and challenges in the use and custodianship of HBM.

7 Conclusion

This chapter aimed to shed clarity on the intricate legal framework for biobank research in Belgium, and its interplay with data protection rules. We outlined the key legislative acts and soft law guidance in the field, and critically discussed their practical application. Belgium is among the few countries in Europe which have adopted a specific law for research biobanking. However, gaps and uncertainties remain, especially in relation to the joint application of the biobank and data protection laws. Creating a code of conduct applicable in daily research practice may be the way forward for a pragmatic implementation of all relevant legal and regulatory frameworks. Further suggestions for future investigations and discussions on pertinent questions on the topic were systematically made throughout the chapter.

Acknowledgments TL's PhD is supported by a scholarship awarded by the Research Foundation - Flanders (project number: 11H3720N), and is conducted in collaboration with the European Organisation for Research and Treatment of Cancer (EORTC).

Figures

Figures 1 and 2, have been created by Dr. Laurent Dollé (Biothèque Wallonie Bruxelles), and are used as illustrations on the official website of Biothèque Wallonie Bruxelles as well.

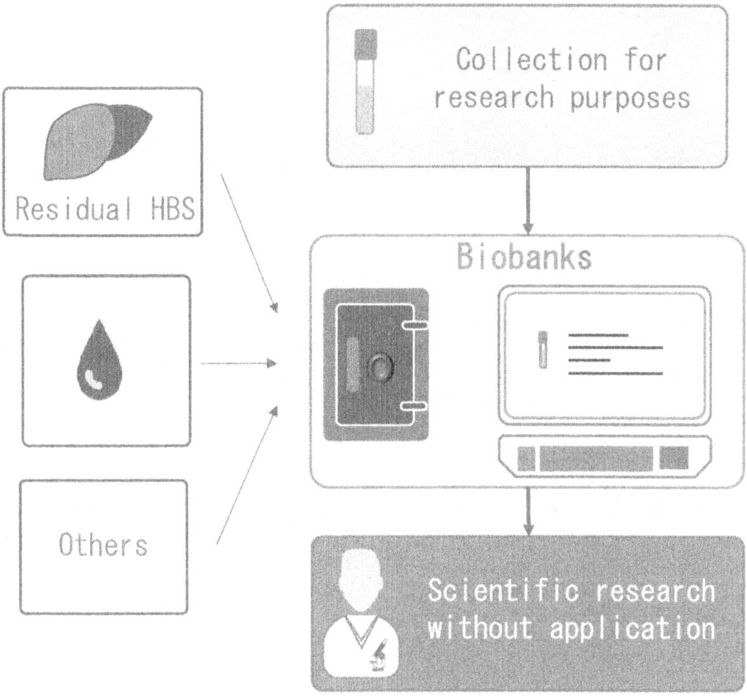

Fig. 1 Concept of biobank: collection of human body material and residual human biological specimen (HBS)

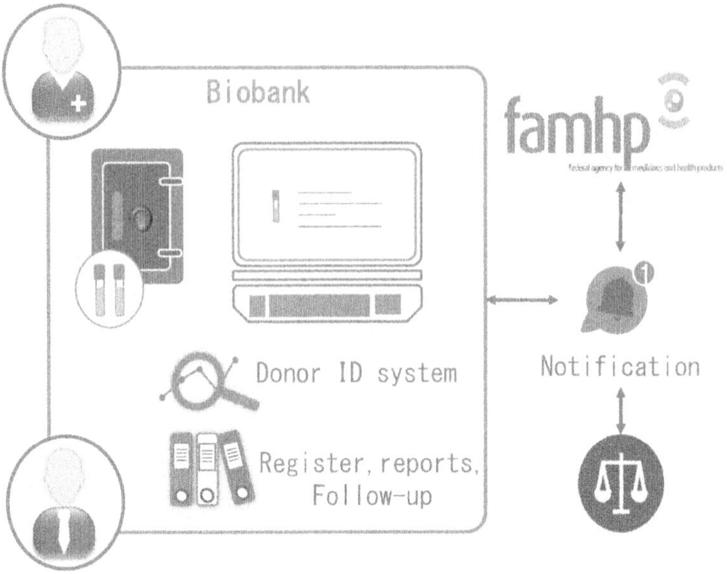

Fig. 2 Notification obligation

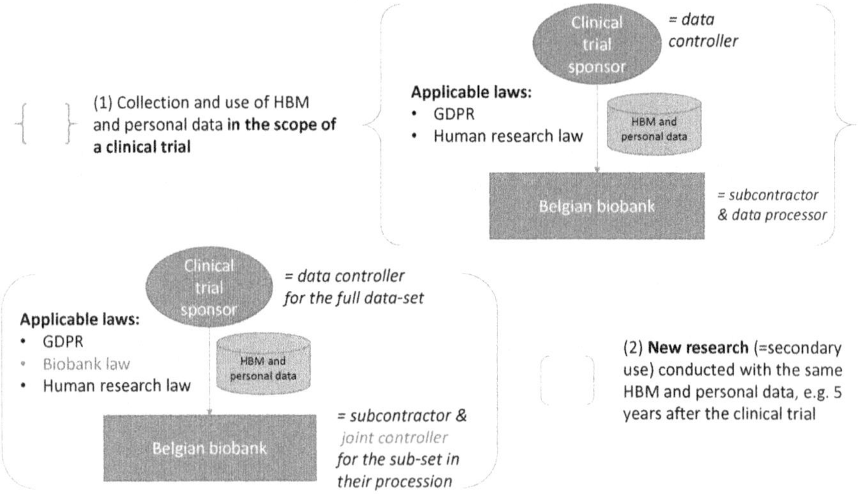

Fig. 3 Secondary use of HBM and personal data outside the scope of a clinical trial

References

Allen J, McNamara B (2011) Reconsidering the value of consent in biobank research. Bioethics 25(3):155–166

Belgian Advisory Committee on Bioethics. Opinion No 45 of 19 January 2009

Belgian Privacy Commission. Opinion No 10/2009

De Clercq E, Kaye J, Wolf SM, Koenig B, Bernice E (2017) Returning results in biobank research: global trends and solutions. Genet Test Mol Biomark 21(3):128–131

European Data Protection Board. Opinion 3/2019 concerning the Questions and Answers on the interplay between the Clinical Trials Regulation (CTR) and the General Data Protection regulation (GDPR)

Federal Agency for Medicines and Health Products (2018) Compendium Biobanken. Available at https://www.bbmri.be/wp-content/uploads/2018/08/compendium_20072018_0.pdf

Gottweis H et al (2012) Biobanks for Europe: a challenge for governance. Report of the Expert Group on Dealing with Ethical and Regulatory Challenges of International Biobank Research. Directorate-General for Research and Innovation, European Commission. Brussels. https://www.coe.int/t/dg3/healthbioethic/Activities/10_Biobanks/biobanks_for_Europe.pdf. Accessed 25 Mar 2019

Kosta E (2011) Untravelling consent in European data protection legislation: a prospective study on consent in electronic communications. PhD Dissertation, KU Leuven

Kozlakidis Z, Cason R, Mant C, Cason J (2012) Human tissue biobanks: the balance between consent and the common good. Res Ethics 8(2):113–123

Morente MM, Cereceda L, Luna-Crespo F et al (2011) Managing a biobank network. Biopreserv Biobank 9(2):187–190

Panis S, Van Gelder N (2008) De Wet Menselijk Lichaamsmateriaal van 19 December 2008: een-grondige analyse. Tijdschr voor Gezondheidsr (4):217–253

Shickle D, Griffin M, El-Arifi K (2010) Inter- and intra-biobank networks: classification of biobanks. Pathobiology. Shickle, D, Academic Unit of Public Health, Institute of Health Sciences, University of Leeds, Leeds, 77(4):181–190

Sterckx S, Van Assche K (2011) The new Belgian law on biobanks: some comments from an ethical perspective. Health Care Anal 19(3):247–258

Verlinden M (2015) Legal framework applicable to access to biobanks. PhD Dissertation, KU Leuven

Balancing of Individual Rights and Research Interests in Danish Biobank Regulation

Mette Hartlev

Abstract Denmark offers very good opportunities for biobank research. There is a vast number of well-structured and comprehensive collections of biological material, which in combination with a 'research generous' legislation provides an excellent environment for biobank research. However, both the Danish biobank landscape and the regulatory environment is rather complex. In contrast to a number of other countries, there is no specific biobank act in Denmark. Instead, various regulatory regimes interact, which makes it challenging to navigate in the legal landscape. It is also rather non-transparent for the individuals, from whom samples have been collected, what samples are used for, and how they can influence the use of samples for research. With the GDPR and the Danish Data Protection Act it seems that research participants' rights have been slightly weakened in Danish law. However, it is argued, that the GDPR has the potential to ensure more awareness of research participants right against the societal and scientific interest in research.

1 Introduction

Denmark possesses excellent opportunities for biobank research and other forms of research relying on collections of human biological material and comprehensive datasets. Biobank and data-based research is facilitated by the use of a unique personal civil registration number, which was introduced in 1968 and is used widely in both the public and private sectors. The Danish legislation is also known to promote biobank research, due to a liberal attitude to the use of tissue samples for research purposes, the presumption being that the population is willing to contribute to research by providing both data and tissue samples.[1] Generally, the data- and biobank resource is also seen as an important competitive asset in attracting and

[1] For a more comprehensive description of the Danish healthcare system and biobank landscape see Hartlev (2015), pp. 743–753.

M. Hartlev (✉)
University of Copenhagen, Faculty of Law, Copenhagen, Denmark
e-mail: mette.hartlev@jur.ku.dk

S. Slokenberga et al. (eds.), *GDPR and Biobanking*, Law, Governance and Technology Series 43, https://doi.org/10.1007/978-3-030-49388-2_11

retaining foreign research and investment in Denmark, in particular in the area of personalized medicine.[2] Given the number of biobanks and the strong interest in promoting biobank research, it is surprising that there is no specific biobank act in Denmark. Instead, the collection, storage and use of tissue samples for various purposes is regulated in a number of different laws, creating a rather complex legal situation.

2 Biobank Infrastructure and Regulatory Environment

2.1 The Danish Biobank Landscape

The Danish biobank landscape is composed of a vast number of public and private biobanks of various sizes and purposes. There are different categories of biobanks: clinical, research, donor, and commercial biobanks. *Clinical* biobanks deposit human tissue samples obtained and stored in a clinical context in which patients have been tested and received treatment in the health care services. *Research* biobanks are established with a research aim and with samples obtained from research participants or from other (clinical) biobanks. *Donor* biobanks have the aim of storing and providing human tissue samples for the treatment of patients. Finally, there are a few *commercial* biobanks that provide storage facilities for individuals, who wishes to deposit biological materials which cannot be stored within the public health care services.[3] In some situations, a biobank could seem to fall within two categories; e.g. when surplus material is collected in a clinical context with the explicit view to store it exclusively for research purposes. In this context, the sample has been obtained in a clinical context and from a patient (and not a research participant), and would therefore still be considered a clinical biobank.

There is no central register of all biobanks. Consequently, the exact number of biobanks and stored biological samples is unknown. There are a number of larger biobanks, most of which are located in the public sector, and with different functions (treatment, quality assurance, research). In the private sector, most biobanks are related to either private research projects or private companies, which uses samples for research (e.g., the pharmaceutical industry) or for commercial purposes (sperm or stem cell biobanks).

The Danish National Biobank was established in 2012, with the aim of strengthening the Danish infrastructure in biobank research to provide an overview easier access to samples for both Danish and international researcher. Organizationally, it is a department under the Statens Serum Institut (SSI), a public body coming under

[2] See Danish Ministry for Business and Growth (2013). https://www.welfaretech.dk/media/3018/2013_06_04_v_kstplan_for_sundheds_og_velf_rdsl_sninger.pdf.

[3] It could be storage of e.g. sperm and stem cells obtained from newborns umbilical cord, where there is no clinical justification of the storage.

the Ministry of Health. The Danish National Biobank has three pillars (1) a register with detailed information about the samples available in the participating biobanks,[4] and which can be linked to disease codes and demographic information from national administrative registers on an individual level, (2) a physical biobank that stores and retrieves samples for researchers, and (3) a coordination center that offers know-how to researchers and external biobanks. The Danish National Biobank does not store the samples from all the participating research biobanks, but the biobanks regularly submit data to the above mentioned register. This should facilitate access for researchers who wish to obtain data from the biobanks and databases involved.

The register holds information about 13 biobanks among which the biggest and most important are:

- The Danish Patobank (more than 17 million tissue samples from pathology departments in Danish hospitals)
- Blood samples from all newborn (in Denmark) since 1982 (more than 2 million samples)
- Cancer biobank (blood and tissue samples from cancer patients).
- Danish birth cohort (more than 600,000 samples from pregnant women and newborns).

2.2 *Collection of Samples*

In contrast to other countries, there is no special biobank legislation in Denmark. The regulation of biobank research in Denmark relies on cluster of acts, of which the Act on Research Ethics Review of Health Research Projects[5] together with the Data Protection Act[6] are the most important. The Health Act[7] is also relevant.

In order better to understand how the different pieces of legislation interact, it is important to know how tissue samples are collected, and how they can end up in biobank research. The focus will here be on clinical and research biobanks, which are the most important tissue collections in regards to biobank research. Most tissue samples are collected when patients seek diagnosis and treatment from the health care services. The right to self-determination is an important patients' right in Denmark, and collecting tissue samples will, according to section 15 and section 16 of the Health Act,[8] normally require the patient's informed consent, as it involves an

[4] It is only a selection of the Danish biobanks, which takes part of the Danish National Biobank.

[5] Consolidated Act no. 1083 of 15 September 2017 on Research Ethics Review of Health Research Projects.

[6] Act no. 502 of 23 May 2018 on supplementary provisions to the regulation on the protection of natural persons with regard to the processing of personal data and on the free movement of such data (the Data Protection Act).

[7] Consolidated Act no. 903 of 26 August 2019 on Health.

[8] Ibid.

intrusion of the body. After having served their clinical purpose, some tissue samples are stored in a biobank, and may subsequently be used for research or other purposes. The storage of tissue samples does not require a separate consent, as it is considered to be authorized by section 7(3) of the Data Protection Act, which refers to Article 9(1) of the GDPR (see more details below).

The general provision regarding informed consent is concerned with consent to *treatment* and medical *interventions* and does not automatically imply a duty to inform the individual patient about the storage and possible future use of tissue samples. However, it is considered to be part of a general administrative service obligation owed to patients to provide general information for example in a general patient information leaflet. The GDPR may also prescribe an obligation to inform the patients (see below).

Patients' right to *self-determination* in relation to stored samples is also recognized in the Health Act (section 29), which entitles patients to opt out with regard to the further use of samples, obtained in a clinical setting, for research purposes. This can be done by signing up in a special 'Use of Tissue Register' (*Vævsanvendelsesregisteret*). There is no obligation to provide individual information to patients about Use of Tissue Register, but it is expected that general information about the register is available, e.g. in a general patient leaflet.[9] Around 3000 individuals have signed up since this register was introduced in 2004.[10] In addition, patients are normally entitled to retrieve the samples or demand their destruction (Health Act, section 33–34). This allows them to have some control over the further use of samples obtained in a clinical setting. Furthermore, it imposes a duty on biobanks to ensure that samples are not handed over for research purposes, when patients have registered in the Use of Tissue Register.

Tissue samples can also be obtained from *deceased* persons, and this will normally also require informed consent from either the deceased person (advance directive) or the relatives (when they consent to an autopsy). Before consenting to an autopsy, the person or relatives must be informed that parts of the deceased's body may be used for research purposes (Health Act, section 187).

Another important setting for collection of tissue samples is *research* projects, where tissue samples are taken from individuals who participate in a research project. The rights of research participants follow from the Act on Research Ethics Review of Health Research Projects.[11] Research participants must provide a written, informed consent to research participation and to the interventions involved in the participation, and they must on beforehand be provided with proper and comprehensive information about the project including the aim of the collection of tissue,

[9] The Ministry of Health has recently (April 2018) committed itself to provide significantly better information being to patients about the options for signing up in the Use of Tissue Register. See answer to question no. 10, 13 April 2018, in connection with the reading of Bill no. 146/2017 on the establishment of a National Genome Center https://www.ft.dk/samling/20171/lovforslag/L146/spm/1/svar/1480847/1880410.pdf.

[10] The specific number was 3070 28 May 2019.

[11] Consolidated Act no. 1083 of 15 September 2017.

the predicted future use and the storage period. Consequently, in this situation, a specific consent is required for both collection, storage and further use of tissue samples.

Tissue samples are also increasingly being collected outside the context of a specific research project, that is, with the aim instead of building up a research biobank, which could be used for unspecified future research projects. Collection for this purpose is taking place in both clinical and research settings, in which patients are asked to donate surplus samples to be stored specifically for future research. The Danish legislation on research ethics review of health research projects does not apply in this situation, as it is restricted to assessing actual research projects. However, collection of samples for those biobanks must comply with the provisions in the Health Act (and in the Data Protection Act) regarding informed consent.

In addition to the Health Act and the Act on Research Ethics Review of Health Research Projects, the *Danish Data Protection Act*[12] and GDPR also have an impact on collection of tissue samples. The Data Protection Act supplements the GDPR in areas where there is room for national discretion. Together with the GDPR, the Data Protection Act substitutes the previous Act on the Processing of Personal Data, which was based on the former EU Directive on Processing of Personal Data. When the Act on the Processing of Personal Data came into force in year 2000, it was debated and decided that tissue samples, which could be related to an identifiable person, should be considered as personal data under the Act.

The new Data Protection Act does not explicitly state in the Act or the preparatory work whether it generally applies to processing of human tissue samples or not. However, the Act has a specific provision concerned with processing of tissues sample (section 10 (3)). Accordingly, it is the general view that the Data Protection Act, like the previous Act on Processing of Personal Data, applies to processing (e.g. collection and storage) of tissue samples, which can be related to an identifiable person.[13] Collection and storage of tissues samples in the health care services is authorized by section 7(3) of the Data Protection Act which stipulates, that processing of data covered by Article 9(1) of the GDPR, can take place, if the processing is '…necessary for the purposes of preventive medicine, medical diagnosis, the provision of care or treatment, or the management of medical and health care services, and where those data are processed by a health professional subject under law to the obligation of professional secrecy, see point h) of Article 9(1) of the General Data Protection Regulation'. This implies, that no explicit consent is needed for the collection and storage of samples. However, there is an obligation to inform the individual about the collection and storage of the data.[14]

To summarize: The collection of tissue samples will always require an informed consent from the patient/research participant. The storage of samples in a biobank

[12] Act no. 503 of 23 May 2018 on supplementary provisions to the regulation on the protection of natural persons with regard to the processing of personal data and on the free movement of such data (the Data Protection Act).

[13] For a possible different opinion, see Blume and Herrmann (2018), pp. 266, 269.

[14] GDPR Articles 13–14.

requires informed consent when samples are collected in a research project, whereas samples collected in a clinical context can be stored without consent. However, the patient has in certain situation a right to retrieve the samples or demand their destruction according to the Health Act. Research participants are entitled to comprehensive information, including information regarding storage of samples and the storage period. Patients' are not entitled to this information according to the Health Act, but the GDPR requires that such information should be provided to all data subjects.

2.3 *Regulation of Biobank Research*

The complexity of the legal framework regarding collection of samples also exists in regards to regulation of biobank research, where the same pieces of legislation interacts.

The *Act on Research Ethics Review of Health Research Projects* governs the establishment of research ethics committees at regional and national level and lay down rules for ethical evaluation and authorization of health research projects. This also includes regulation of informed consent to collection and storage of data and tissue samples for scientific purposes (sections 3–6),[15] and the further use of previously collected tissues samples for scientific purposes (sections 10). The Act applies exclusively to *health research* projects and not to research within other disciplines. Most biobank research will be categorized as health research projects.[16]

All health research projects involving human research subjects or human tissue in biobanks must according to section 14(1) of the Act, obtain prior authorization from a research ethics committee (REC) before it can commence.[17] The overall aim of the Act on Research Ethics Review of Health Research Projects is to ensure a balance between the interests and protection of research subjects and the interests of society and science. Its main focus, therefore, is on scientific quality, risk assessment and respect for research participants' autonomy and right to self-determination. Section 1 of the Act emphasizes, that in balancing the respective interests, the priority should be given to the interests of the research participant. Data protection issues are not explicitly mentioned in the Act, but they are part of the risk assessment, and they are also addressed in an executive order issued with a legal basis in the Act.[18]

[15] The informed consent requirements are further detailed in Executive Order no. 498 of 13 May 2018 on informed consent to participation in a health research project and notification and supervision of health research projects, see especially sections 6–9.

[16] Biobank research could e.g. also be relevant in archeological research.

[17] If the research involves clinical trials of medicines or of medical devices, the special rules in Consolidated Act No. 99 of 16 January 2018 on Medicines also applies.

[18] Sections 6–8 of Executive order No. 498 of 13 May 2018 on right to information and consent to participation in a health research project and on notification and control of health research projects.

In research project involving individuals as *research participants*, the informed consent of the research participant is needed for the collection and storage of tissue samples, and information about the predicted future use and the storage period must also be provided (see also above in Sect. 2.2). However, research projects can also be based exclusively on *tissue samples from a biobank*. Such projects are also subject to the requirement of prior authorization from a REC. The normal rules of the Act on Research Ethics Review of Health Research Projects apply to biobank research projects, which imply that the tissue donor's informed consent is required. However, with regard to biobank research, section 10 of the Act provides for derogation from this legal principle, and the REC may decide to make an exception, provided the project does not possess any risks, or if it would be impossible or disproportionately difficult to obtain consent or proxy consent.[19]

This implies that biobank research based on samples from a *clinical biobank* can take place without the consent and knowledge of the patient, from which the sample was collected. However, as explained above (Sect. 2.2), the patient can prevent the use of samples for research purposes by registering in the Use of Tissue Register. Biobank research can also be based on samples from a *research biobank*, where samples have been collected for another research project (and purpose). Even though the tissue donor has consented to the collection and storage of samples for the original project, this consent does not necessarily cover subsequent use of the samples for another project. The REC will assess the project, but the research participant, from whom the sample was collected, does not have the same option as the patient to prevent further research on the samples by registering in the Use of Tissue Register.[20]

All research projects involving research participants and tissue samples will imply processing of personal data. The Danish *Data Protection Act* takes advantage of the research exemption laid down in Article 89 of the GDPR. According to section 10(1) of the Act, 'Data as mentioned in Article 9(1) and Article 10 of the General Data Protection Regulation may be processed where the processing takes place for the sole purpose of carrying out statistical or scientific studies of significant importance to society and where such processing is necessary in order to carry out these studies'. This means that personal data—including tissue samples which can be related to a person—can be used for research purposes without the data subject's prior, explicit consent. In general, the processing of data and tissue samples must respect the GDPR and the Data Protection Act, but there are some exemptions from the data subjects' rights (see below in Sect. 3). In order to secure the data subjects' rights and interests, section 10(2) stipulates that data used for research purposes may not subsequently be used for other purposes, and according to section 10(3) disclosure of data to third parties requires prior authorization of the

[19] If the data subject has used the right to opt-out in regards to the further use of tissue samples according to Article 29 of the Health Act, the samples cannot be used for research purposes. See more above in Sect. 2.2.

[20] The option to register in the Use of Tissue Register is only available for patients, from whom samples have been taken in a clinical context.

Data Protection Authority, if the disclosure involves human tissues samples, or if data are disclosed to thirds parties outside the jurisdiction of the GDPR.[21] It is generally expected, that data and tissue samples are anonymized or pseudonymized whenever possible, and that the results of the research project are not communicated in a form making the individual, from whom the tissue sample was collected, identifiable.

In general, researchers are themselves responsible for complying with the legislation. However, a number of bodies have *supervisory authority*. The regional research ethics committees together with the National Research Ethics Committee and the Danish Medicine Authority have *supervisory and oversight authority* in regards to health research projects. The Medicines Authority supervises clinical trials, and the regional research ethics committees and the National Research Ethics Committee supervises other health research project, which they have approved.[22] General supervisory functions ensure that results from research projects are reported after being completed, that the researchers apply for an extension of the project, if it cannot be completed within the timeframe set out in the authorization. More targeted supervision and oversight can be initiated based on information received from research participants or third parties, or if a specific research project gives rise to concern in terms of compliance with the rules and regulations. The National Research Ethics Committee also serves as a complaints board for decisions taken by the regional research ethics committees. The Danish Data Protection Agency, which is an independent body, has the responsibility laid down in Chapters VI and VII of the GDPR to monitor the processing of data and tissue covered by the Data Protection Act, the GDPR and other legislation. It can also receive complaints and perform inspections.[23] There are examples of supervision and oversight of research projects which has provoked criticism from the Data Protection Agency.

3 Individual Rights and Safeguards

Individuals have important interests and rights in regards to the use of tissue samples for research purposes, such as the right to self-determination and the right to privacy. The general data protection principles stipulated in the GDPR (Article 5) also emphasises the importance of proportionality and transparency in regards to the processing of data and tissue samples. In addition, the GDPR also outlines more specific right of the data subject (Articles 13–22) and requires that *safeguards* are in place, when national laws accept the use of sensitive personal data for research purposes (Article 89 (1)).

[21] In addition, prior authorization from the Data Protection Authority is also needed, when disclosure is made for the purpose of publication in a recognized scientific journal or similar (section 10(3)(3)).

[22] Sections 28–29 of the Act on Research Ethics Review of Health Research Projects.

[23] Sections 27–36 of the Data Protection Act.

As will be clear from the analyses and description of the regulatory framework for biobank research (Sect. 2), the rights and safeguard for individuals, who contribute with tissue samples to research, depends on how the samples are collected. In general, the protection of *privacy* seems to be observed both when samples are collected in the clinic and as part of a research project. In regards to the *right to self-determination*, it seems that the rights of research participants are better protected than those of patients. In contrast to patients, each individual research participant is entitled to comprehensive written and oral information about the storage and further use of tissue samples, and must give an explicit written consent to research participation. This both support a right to self-determination and serves to ensure *transparency*. In comparison, patients are not entitled to receive individual information about storage and further use of tissue samples. It is sufficient that general information is publicly available; e.g. in a leaflet or on a website.

However, in regards to the further use of tissue samples stored in clinical or research biobanks, patients' right to self-determination may be better protected than the rights of research participants. If patients are aware of their right to retrieve and demand the destruction of tissue samples, they may retain control over the samples. In addition, they have the right to opt out of the further use of the samples for research purposes by registering in the Use of Tissue Register. In comparison, the research participant may experience that tissue samples are handed over to other researchers, or used for other research purposes, without having the same right to opt out as the patient. This is because the Use of Tissue Register only applies to samples stored in clinical biobanks. Consequently, both patients and research participants may end up in situations, where their right to self-determination is poorly protected and with a lack of transparency.

Some of the specific rights of data subjects stipulated in the GDPR could potentially be helpful in this regard, e.g. the duty to inform the data subject, when data are not collected directly from him (Article 14). However, this obligation does not apply, if it is impossible or would involve a disproportionate effort to fulfil it (Article 14(5)(b)). Processing of data for research purposes, subject to the conditions referred to in Article 89(1), is specifically mentioned as an example. Similarly, the right of access (Article 15) could provide some transparency to patients or research participants, who wishes to know for which purposes their data and tissue samples have been used. However, the Danish Data Protection Act (section 22(5)) in accordance with GDPR Article 89(2) explicitly derogates from the rights of the data subjects laid down in GDPR Article 15, and the same derogation apply in regards to GDPR Article 16 (right to rectification), Article 18 (right to restriction of processing) and Article 21 (right to object). Consequently, it seems that the research exemption is a 'carte blanche' for derogation from other rights of the data subjects.

The GDPR Article 89(1) requires that certain *safeguards* must be in place when sensitive data are processed for scientific purposes. These safeguards shall include technical and organizational measures to ensure respect for the data minimization principle, e.g. the use of anonymization or pseudonymization whenever this is possible without hampering the research purpose. According to the preparatory work to the Danish Data Protection Act anonymization or pseudonymization should be used when possible. In addition, the Act also prohibits the use of data obtained for research purposes for other purposes (e.g. administrative purposes). It is, however, possible to derogate from this prohibition by rules laid down by the Minister of Health in situations, where such processing is necessary for safeguarding the vital interests of the data subject (section 10(5)). This could e.g. apply in situations where genetic research reveals incidental findings, which could be of significant importance for individuals' health.

Further safeguards are outlined in section 10(3) which stipulates that an authorization from the Data Protection Authority is needed, when data are transferred to a third party outside the territorial scope of the GDPR, and in all cases where tissues samples are transferred to third parties (both within and outside the territorial scope of the GDPR). In addition, authorization is needed in situations where data will be transferred with a view to be published in a widely recognized scientific journal (or the like).

4 Law in Context: Individual Rights and Public Interest

The Danish Act on Research Ethics Review of Health Research Projects, place the individual at the center of attention when stressing (in section 1) the priority of the research subject against the interests of society and science. However, with regard to biobank research the Act allows for derogations from the consent requirement, and in practice derogation seems to be the main rule and not an exception. This reflects a perception of biobank research being less harmful, than other kinds of research—if just the privacy of the research subject is protected, and data cannot be used for other purposes, what should be the concern? This perception ignores the individual's interest in transparency and self-determination in regards to the use of sensitive data, which are important elements in paying respect to the dignity of the individual. It could also be added, that the possibility of protecting research subjects' privacy may be reduced or disappear in big data and genetic research (as personalized medicine). The Danish National Committee on Health Research Ethics has issued guidelines for genomic research (including biobank research) to ensure better awareness of the interests of research participants.[24]

As explained above (Sect. 2.3), the Act on Research Ethics Review of Health Research Projects only applies to research involving research participants and tissue samples from human beings. Research projects exclusively based on data does not fall under the scope of the Act. This has proven to be problematic in regards to data generated by comprehensive genetic analyses of tissue samples (e.g. using WGS or GWAS techniques). Whereas the analyses of the samples would need REC authorization, subsequent research on the retrieved data (bioinformatic data) was until

[24] National Committee on Health Research Ethics (2018) Guidelines on Genomic Research. June 2018. http://en.nvk.dk/~/media/NVK-EN/General-guidelines/Guidelines-on-Genomics-Research.pdf.

recently exempted from ethics review. As the data reflects the information embedded in the samples, and are just as sensitive and worthy of protection as the actual sample, a recent ammendment to the Act on Research Ethis Review of Health Research Projects (December 2019) requires mandatory ethics review for research projects based on sensitive bioinformatics data, where there is a risk of secundary findings.[25] This reflects how the boundaries between the body and data is being increasingly blurred.

5 GDPR Impact and Future Possibilities for Biobanking

So far, the GDPR has not had any major impact on the Danish legal regulation of biobank research; apart from slightly weakening the former safeguards. Under the previous act, the authorization of the Data Protection Authority was needed for any kind of disclosure of data to third parties, also third parties within Denmark and the EU. However, the GDPR could potentially have an influence on the Danish regulatory environment, especially in regards to stimulating awareness of the rights of data subjects. It will e.g. be interesting to see, whether the Court of Justice of the European Union will require more substantial justification for derogations from the rights of individuals whose data and tissue samples are used for research (e.g. pseudonymization and notification requirements, access rights and right to be forgotten). The Danish Data Protection Act express the perception that any kind of rights assigned to the research subject, will impede the research process. This perception could be challenged to ensure more general awareness of data subjects' rights. In addition, the GDPR could also encourage the development and use of technical solutions which could promote privacy and informational self-determination by design.

6 Conclusion

As will be clear, the Danish regulatory framework for biobank research can be characterized as 'research friendly'. The explicit consent from the research participant is only necessary in projects where individuals are directly recruited as research participants. In other situations, it is presumed that patients and persons, who have previously participated in research, are willing to contribute with samples for research. If this is not the case, the individual must actively opt-out—and in some situations it is even not possible to opt-out. This raises the issue of whether the legal situation is compliant with section 1 of the Act on Research Ethics Review of Health

[25] Act no. 1436 or 17 December 2019 on amendment of the Act on Research Ethics Review of Health Research Projects (Strengthening citizens confidence and trust in health research).

Research Projects which prescribes, that priority should be given to the interests of the research participant, when balancing the interests of respectively society, science and the individual research participant.

However, it also provokes the question what we as individuals owe to society, especially in the context of a welfare society as the Danish. Respect for individual rights are beyond doubt important. However, a solidarity-based approach to research is also needed to ensure that we together with all other individuals can profit from new advances in medical technologies.[26]

References

Blume P, Herrmann JR (2018) Ret, privatliv og teknologi. Jurist- og Økonomforbundets Forlag 4th edn. Copenhagen

Danish Ministry for Business and Growth (2013) Danmark i arbejde. Vækstplan for sundheds- og velfærdsløsninger. Copenhagen

Hartlev M (2015) Genomic databases and biobanks in Denmark. J Law Med Ethics 43(4):743–753

National Committee on Health Research Ethics (2018) Guidelines on Genomic Research

Prainsack B, Buyx A (2017) Solidarity in medicine and beyond. CUP, Cambridge

[26] Prainsack and Buyx (2017).

Regulatory Environment for Biobanking in Estonia

Kärt Pormeister

Abstract The regulatory framework for biobanking in Estonia is fragmented. Whilst a specific law applies to the population-wide biobank, other entities engaged in biobanking are subject to rules stemming from various legal sources. In the case of the population biobank, participants give open consent for their data and tissue to be used in genetic research. Most other entities do not have the possibility to obtain open research consent for the use of personal data. However, national data protection law enables the use of personal data in research without the consent of individuals.

In contrast, since no stricter requirements are set, open consent can be used when tissue is obtained directly from individuals for research purposes. However, if tissue is initially obtained for other (research) purposes, further research use requires written consent in the case of blood, while due notification will suffice for most other types of tissue.

1 Introduction

Estonian law does not define the term or concept of 'biobank'. As observed by Hallinan, '[t]he term has emerged as an umbrella term to describe all collections of biological samples and associated data supporting genomic research'.[1] From this broad perspective a biobank cannot be defined through an institutional prism, and any entity engaged in the collection and preservation of biological samples and associated data for purposes of, *inter alia,* research could be labelled a biobank. For example, hospitals and providers of direct-to-consumer genetic testing (DTCGT) services collect biosamples and relevant genomic data for the purposes of, respectively, clinical care and private testing services. However, the samples and data may be stored for future research purposes. Thus, hospitals and providers of DTCGT

[1] Hallinan (2018), p. 64.

K. Pormeister (✉)
University of Tartu, Law Faculty, Tartu, Estonia

S. Slokenberga et al. (eds.), *GDPR and Biobanking*, Law, Governance and Technology Series 43, https://doi.org/10.1007/978-3-030-49388-2_12

services can be seen as operating biobanks, though that is not their main or sole activity.

Since Estonian law does not define the terms 'biobank' or 'biobanking', and the regulatory environment concerning biobanking activities is, for the most part, not dependent on the institutional nature of the entity engaged in such activities, the general and broad definition proposed above (collection of biosamples and genetic data for research) will be adopted for the purposes of this chapter.

This chapter will first give a brief overview of the legal and regulatory environment of biobanks in Estonia and then introduce the Estonian population biobank. This will be followed by an analysis of the rights and safeguards of biobank participants. The fourth part of this chapter will explore the balance struck under Estonian law between the public interest in biobank research on the one hand and individual rights and interests on the other. Finally, the author will comment on the impact of the GDPR and future possibilities for biobanking in Estonia.

2 Biobank Infrastructure and Regulatory Environment

2.1 The Estonian Biobank and the Human Genes Research Act

The Estonian Biobank (EBB) (*Geenivaramu*) is a population-based biobank that was established in 2002 as a state-run foundation.[2] Since 2007 it has been part of the University of Tartu.[3] As of 2019, the EBB has over 157,000 gene donors[4] out of a population of ca 1.3 million.

The EBB has made recruitment procedures as convenient as possible in order to attract new donors. For example, as of 20 March 2018, informed consent can be given online.[5] After informed consent has been provided, the blood samples can be donated in various locations, such as all major hospitals, certain laboratories collaborating with the EBB located throughout the country,[6] and even some pharmacies.[7]

---

[2] Order no 177 of the Government of the Republic of Estonia, *Sihtasutuse Eesti Geenivaramu Asutamine*, adopted 13 March 2001. – RTL 2001, 37, 512.

[3] Official website of the Estonian Biobank. https://www.geenivaramu.ee/en/access-biobank.

[4] Offical website of the Estonian Biobank. Available only in Estonian. https://www.geenivaramu.ee/et/doonorile/olen-geenidoonor.

[5] See www.geenidoonor.ee. On this website, informed consent can be provided with a digital signature, either via using the national ID card or mobile-ID (both official means for providing a valid digital signature).

[6] Official website of the Estonian Biobank. Available only in Estonian. https://www.geenivaramu.ee/et/geenidoonorile/soovin-saada-geenidoonoriks.

[7] As of September 2019 there were three pharmacies that cooperated with the EBB in obtaining blood samples from new gene donors. *Geenidoonoriks saab nüüd mugavalt hakata juba kolmes apteegis*. 20 Sept 2018 *Postimees: Tervis*. https://tervis.postimees.ee/6409353/geenidoonoriks-saab-nuud-mugavalt-hakata-juba-kolmes-apteegis.

The activities of the EBB are regulated by the Human Genes Research Act[8] (HGRA), which was adopted in 2000 specifically for the operations of the EBB. Aside from a few general clauses, the HGRA does not regulate the biobanking activities of other entities.

In terms of clauses of general applicability, the most notable ones are found in Chapter 5 and establish a general prohibition on genetic discrimination and specific prohibitions in employment and insurance relationships. These prohibitions apply universally.

2.2 *Biobanking Activities Other Than the EBB*

As far as biobanking activities of entities other than the EBB are concerned (e.g. other research institutions, hospitals, DTCGT service providers, etc.), there are no specific regulations. It is noted in the HGRA that genetic testing beyond the activities of the EBB to which Chapters 2 to 4 of the HGRA do not apply 'may be performed pursuant to the procedure and for the purposes provided by law'.[9] However, there is no respective law regulating genetic testing in Estonia—whether for research or other purposes.[10]

As such, biobanking activities of entities other than the EBB are subject to a number of different laws. First, data protection law applies as far as genetic and health (and other associated personal) data are concerned to the extent that they constitute 'personal data' within the meaning of the General Data Protection Regulation[11] (GDPR).[12] Second, in terms of biosamples, international law and a few national legal acts establish a fragmented set of rules for different types of tissue.

---

[8] Human Genes Research Act (HGRA), RT I, 13.03.2019, 64. English translation available at https://www.riigiteataja.ee/en/eli/508042019001/consolide (22 June 2020).

[9] § 6(2) HGRA, ibid.

[10] Regulation (EU) 2017/749 on *in vitro* medical devices, which shall apply from 26 May 2022, will establish a few basic rules in regard to genetic testing in the healthcare setting. However, this will have no impact on genetic testing for research purposes.

See Art. 4 of Regulation (EU) 2017/746 of the European Parliament and of the Council of 5 April 2017 on *in vitro* diagnostic medical devices and repealing Directive 98/79/EC and Commission Decision 2010/227/EU. OJ L117/176.

[11] Regulation (EU) 2016/679 of the European Parliament and of the Council of 27 April 2016 on the protection of natural persons with regard to the processing of personal data and on the free movement of such data, and repealing Directive 95/46/EC (General Data Protection Regulation). OJ L119/1.

[12] Recital 26 and Arts. 1(1), 4(1), 4(13) and 4(15) GDPR, ibid.

2.3 Data Protection and Biobanking

Parallel to possible specific regulations, data protection rules apply to any research involving the use of personal data, including personal data collection for and use by entities engaged in biobanking activities and research. Thus, the GDPR and the Estonian Personal Data Protection Act[13] (the DP Act) serve as regulatory tools relevant for any biobanking facility.

The explanatory note to the DP Act[14] refers to Recital 159 GDPR to define 'research', which indicates that this concept is to be interpreted broadly. This is in contrast with the previous approach under the former Estonian Personal Data Protection Act,[15] according to which generally only certain entities or establishments could rely on the research exemption.[16] The approach of Recital 159 GDPR seems to focus on the research activity itself rather than the nature of the entity or institution carrying out the activity. Thus, in terms of biobanking, any entity engaged in such activities is subject to the general and research clauses of the GDPR and the Estonian DP Act.

In terms of the population biobank EBB, the HGRA does establish that data protection rules do not apply to the EBB as far as the processing of coded tissue samples, coded descriptions of DNA and coded descriptions of state of health is concerned, on the condition that they are processed as a set of data of at least five gene donors at a time.[17] This clause dates back to 2000, and its compliance with the GDPR is questionable as the GDPR clearly defines pseudonymised data as 'personal data'.[18]

[13] Personal Data Protection Act (DP Act), RT I, 04.01.2019, 11. Official English translation. https://www.riigiteataja.ee/en/eli/523012019001/consolide.

The new Estonian DP Act that came into force on 15 January 2019 regulates personal data protection to the extent of specifying and complementing clauses of the GDPR (including but not limited to matters related to research), and implementing Directive (EU) 2016/680.

[14] Explanatory note to the (2019) DP Act. Available in Estonian. https://www.riigikogu.ee/download/b7c9371a-7768-46b5-9d33-9eb4e3b98125, at § 6.

[15] Explanatory note to the (2007) DP Act. Available in Estonian. https://www.aki.ee/et/eraelu-kaitse/oigusaktid, at § 16.

[16] Namely, those that met the conditions set for research and development institutions under § 3 of the Organisation of Research and Development Act. RT I 1997, 30, 471. Official English translation. https://www.riigiteataja.ee/en/eli/513042015012/consolide.

[17] § 7(2) HGRA, supra n 8.

[18] Recital 26 GDPR, supra n 11.

2.4 Research Oversight

Research oversight in Estonia is scarce. The Estonian Data Protection Inspectorate (DPI)[19] conducts oversight of research as far as matters of data protection are concerned.[20] However, oversight of the DPI is in practice highly unlikely to occur unless there is an individual complaint.

Under the former Estonian Personal Data Protection Act that was applicable before 15 January 2019, DPI permission was required for the use of personal data in research without the consent of individuals.[21] This task is now for the most part assigned to ethics committees. Therefore, ethics committees can also be regarded as part of the research oversight system. However, aside from a few exceptions, ethics committees in Estonia are not systematically established under or regulated by law. Legislative revisions lead to the establishing of one central ethics committee at the Ministry of Social Affairs in September 2019, which would oversee ethical matters related to EBB research and the research use of data in the Health Information System (i.e. patient data submitted by health care professional to this state database).[22] All other ethical reviews are left to institutional ethics committees, which are not regulated by law.

Under Estonian law, An ethical review is mandatory for the operations of the EBB,[23] the research use of data in the Health Information System,[24] and for clinical studies under the Medicinal Products Act.

Aside from the explicit ethics review requirements concerning the research use of the data in the Health Information System, the EBB and clinical trials, for any other entity engaged in biobanking activities, an ethics review requirement has been established under the DP Act which is applicable in very limited circumstances in certain cases where personal data are used in research without the consent of individuals.[25] This will be further addressed below.

---

[19] For more information on the Estonian Data Protection Inspectorate (*Andmekaitse Inspektsioon*), see their official website. https://www.aki.ee/en.

[20] This includes oversight of the EBB, see § 29 HGRA, supra n 8.

[21] § 16(3) of the Personal Data Protection Act (2008), RT I 2007, 24, 127. Available in Estonian. https://www.riigiteataja.ee/akt/12802623.

[22] See § 29(5) HGRA and § 59(index 4)(6) Health Services Organisation Act (HSOA). In March 2019, the HGRA and the HSOA were revised in parts. Amongst other things, the revisions included the establishing of a central research ethics committee via a ministerial regulation. This committee consists of expert representatives of a list of different academic and practical fields, and in addition to reviewing ethical matters related to the research of the EBB also oversees the ethics of using data of the Health Information System for research purposes. See Regulation No 60 of the Minister of Social Affairs of 24 September 2019, 'The establishing of a research ethics committee, its rules of procedure, number and appointment of members and the rates for reviewing applications' (as translated by the author of this chapter)—RT I, 26.09.2019, 1.

[23] § 29 HGRA, supra n 8.

[24] § 59(index 4)(6) Health Services Organisation Act (HSOA), RT I, 17.05.2020, 12. English translation available at https://www.riigiteataja.ee/en/eli/518052020003/consolide (23 June 2020).

[25] § 6(4) DP Act, supra n 13; and § 6 of the explanatory note to the (2019) DP Act, supra n 14.

However, the DP Act does not regulate ethics committees but merely presumes their existence. Under the DP Act, in case there is no ethics committee for a given field, the DPI will conduct the review to assess compliance with data protection rules.

3 Individual Rights and Safeguards

3.1 Participation in Biobanks

3.1.1 The Use of Human Tissue in Research

There is little regulation on the use of human tissue under Estonian law. Two general rules can be derived from applicable international law on this and there are also a few national laws that address it.

In 2004, Estonia ratified the Oviedo Convention on human rights in biomedicine.[26] Under Articles 5 and 16(v) of the Convention the physical intervention to obtain tissue, including for research purposes, presumes prior informed consent of the individual. With regard to further uses of already available tissue, which is obtained, for example, for purposes of clinical care like diagnostic tests, the Oviedo Convention establishes in Article 22 a minimum threshold of due notification.[27] These two rules apply in the Estonian context in any scenario which national law does not specifically address.[28]

Estonian law only specifically addresses a few cases regarding the research use of human tissue or body parts. For example, the use of embryos in research requires the consent of both gamete donors.[29] Furthermore, in the case of blood (excluding

[26] Convention for the Protection of Human Rights and Dignity of the Human Being with regard to the Application of Biology and Medicine: Convention on Human Rights and Biomedicine. Oviedo, 4.IV.1997. ETS No. 164.

[27] Explanatory Report to the Convention for the protection of Human Rights and Dignity of the Human Being with regard to the Application of Biology and Medicine: Convention on Human Rights and Biomedicine, at para 137.

[28] § 123(2) of the Estonian Constituion establishes that 'When laws or other legislation of Estonia are in conflict with an international treaty ratified by the *Riigikogu*, provisions of the international treaty apply.' The Constitution of the Republic of Estonia, RT 1992, 26, 349.

Referring to § 123(3) of the Constitution, the Estonian Supreme Court has established in its case law that a legal rule contained in an international treaty can also be directly applied if there is no respective legal rule under national law. The direct applicability of an international treaty presumes that the rule in the treaty is aimed at regulating national relationships, and that the rule is specific enough in order not to need clarification in national law. Judgment no 3-3-1-58-02 of 20 December 2002 of the Estonian Supreme Court. See also Pormeister (2018).

[29] § 32(2) of the Artificial Insemination and Embryo Protection Act. Official English translation. https://www.riigiteataja.ee/en/eli/504012018005/consolide.

other types of tissue), the Blood Act[30] stipulates in § 10 that blood taken from a donor or patient can be used for research purposes upon written consent. The subsequent sequencing of DNA from such blood in the course of research is a matter not directly regulated by law but rather left to ethics.

The HGRA establishes that: 'It is prohibited to take a tissue sample and prepare a description of state of health or genealogy without the specific knowledge and voluntary consent of the person.'[31] However, the referred clause is part of Chapter 2 HGRA which regulates exclusively the rights of the gene donors of the EBB. It is clear from the HGRA that Chapters 2 to 4 do not apply to genetic testing (or research) outside of the EBB.[32] Thus, under the HGRA, it is only the EBB that is prohibited from obtaining tissue samples of individuals without their specific knowledge and voluntary consent.

Therefore, in the case of the further research use of the types of human tissue not clearly addressed in national law a minimum requirement of due notification would apply. Hence, under Estonian law consent is not necessarily required for human tissue to be included in biobank research—the two clear exceptions here remain blood, which requires written consent, and the EBB, which cannot obtain tissue samples without consent.

However, given that the primary research interest in tissue lies in the information that can be derived therefrom, the rules for the use of the data are really the primary question.

3.1.2 Informed Consent for the Use of Personal Data

In the case of the EBB, the consent for the use of an individual's tissue and data for 'genetic research, public health research and statistical purposes' must be in writing and signed by the donor.[33] As such, the consent of the EBB is an open or broad type of research consent allowing donors' tissue and data to be used for essentially any type of ethically acceptable scientific research.

In terms of data protection law and informed consent, general rules under the GDPR apply. Thus, as required by Article 9(2)(a) GDPR, the specific purposes of processing must be laid out in the consent when it comes to the use of special categories of data like genetic or health data. Though Recital 33 GDPR appears to grant Member States the discretion to allow for broader consent in research, the Estonian DP Act does not establish a separate, broader notion of informed consent for research.

[30] Blood Act, RT I 2005, 13, 63. Official English translation. https://www.riigiteataja.ee/en/eli/510042015002/consolide.

[31] § 9(1) HGRA, supra n 8.

[32] § 6(2) HGRA, ibid. This is also evident from the text of the HGRA in Chapters 2 to 4 as it refers clearly to the gene donors and processing activities of the EBB.

[33] § 12(1) HGRA, supra n 8.

The informed consent of the EBB remains the only open or broad informed consent for the research use of data established under Estonian national law. Though the explanatory note to the DP Act makes no mention of the consent of the EBB and how this relates to Article 9(2)(a) GDPR, it can be argued that the consent of the EBB is to be regarded as an exercise of the discretion referred to in Recital 33 GDPR. An alternative interpretation is that the use of personal data by the EBB is based on law and not consent. On 15 March 2019, a number of changes to the HGRA came into force.[34] Amongst these changes is a clause in § 29 concerning ethics committees that obliges the committee to, *inter alia*, review compliance with § 6 of the DP Act. The latter, however, regulates the use of personal data in research without consent. This begs the question whether the use of personal data by the EBB is to be seen as data processing based on national law instead of processing based on the donors' consent. Since no working document relating to these recent changes in the HGRA is publicly available, there are currently no definite answers to this question.

In summary, instead of opting for a broader informed consent to research that would also enable biobanking activities, the Estonian DP Act creates simple options for the use of personal data in research without the consent of individuals. This could arguably serve as an even greater facilitator for biobanking activities than broad or open research consent.

3.1.3 Use of Personal Data Without Consent

The Estonian DP Act creates in § 6 a legal basis for the use of personal data in research without consent.[35] The following two exceptions apply to all types of personal data.

First, personal data can be used for research purposes without consent as long as the data are pseudonymised or any other equally effective method is engaged (i.e. the requirement is technologically neutral).[36] For the use of pseudonymised data in research, no prior approval from an ethics committee or the Estonian Data Protection Inspectorate (DPI)[37] is required. Though pseudonymisation as a safeguard is explicitly mentioned under Article 89(1) GDPR, pseudonymisation of data at the earliest possible point is in any case an underlying principle of the GDPR.[38] Thus, it is arguable whether pseudonymisation of personal data as a stand-alone, though

[34] The latest version of the HGRA (in force as of 15 March 2019) is currently only available in Estonian. Human Genes Research Act, RT I, 13.03.2019, 64.

[35] DP Act, supra n 13.

[36] § 6(1) DP Act, ibid.

[37] For more information on the Estonian Data Protection Inspectorate (Andmekaitse Inspektsioon), see their official website. https://www.aki.ee/en.

[38] See, e.g., Recital 78 GDPR which mentions 'pseudonymising personal data as soon as possible' as one of the measures to demonstrate compliance with the GDPR and in particular with the principles of data protection by design and data protection by default.

'appropriate',[39] safeguard is sufficient to deem the Estonian approach compliant with the GDPR.

Furthermore, according to the explanatory note to the DP Act, neither pseudonymisation nor anonymisation (as processing activities within the meaning of the GDPR) require separate prior approval either.[40] This means that if personal data are available, they can be pseudonymised (or anonymised) for use in research and used in research without the consent of individuals or prior approval of an ethics committee or the DPI. De-pseudonymisation of such data is permitted for the purposes of additional research.[41]

Second, personal data can also be used in research without consent when it is processed with *direct identifiers* if the following three conditions are met:

(1) the purposes of data processing can no longer be achieved after removal of the data enabling identification or it would be unreasonably difficult to achieve these purposes;
(2) there is an overriding public interest for it in the estimation of the persons conducting scientific and historical research or compiling official statistics;
(3) the scope of obligations of the data subject is not changed based on the processed personal data or the rights of the data subject are not excessively damaged in any other manner.[42]

The only additional requirement applicable to specifically special categories of data is an ethics review—or, alternatively, DPI approval—if the second exception is utilized, i.e. if special categories of data are to be used in research with direct identifiers.[43]

However, even in such cases, the explanatory note to the DP Act emphasizes that prior review is only required if the entire research, including the analysis of the data, is to be conducted with direct identifiers,[44] which is rarely the case as most research projects do not require inclusion of direct identifiers in the actual analysis of the data. This comment in the explanatory note is at odds with the text of the law, which requires a review whenever special categories of data are used in research.[45]

---

[39] See Recital 156 GDPR which labels pseudynomisation of data as an 'appropriate safeguard' in the research context.

[40] § 6 of the explanatory note to the (2019) DP Act, supra n 14.

[41] § 6(2) DP Act, supra n 13.

[42] § 6(3) DP Act, ibid.

[43] § 6(4) DP Act, ibid.

[44] § 6 of the explanatory note to the (2019) DP Act, supra n 14.

[45] § 6(4) DP Act reads: 'If scientific and historical research is based on special categories of personal data, the ethics committee of the area concerned shall first verify compliance with the terms and conditions provided for in this section. If there is no ethics committee in the scientific area, the compliance with the requirements shall be verified by the Estonian Data Protection Inspectorate. With regard to any personal data retained at the National Archives, the National Archives shall have the rights of the ethics committee.'

3.2 *Rights of Participants*

3.2.1 Gene Donors of the EBB

The rights of the gene donors of the EBB are established under Chapter 2 of the HGRA. Once individuals become donors to the EBB they have a right to confidentiality, and a donor's identity can only be revealed by the donor or upon his consent.[46] Donors have the right to know and the respective right not to know the information kept about them in the EBB. However, in order to protect the privacy interests of other donors, donors do not have the right to access their genealogies. If a donor wishes to access his or her information, the donor is entitled to counselling.[47]

It must be emphasized that the consent given by donors allows the EBB to collect all donors' health data from all possible state databases. However, donors have the right to prohibit the EBB from further accessing their health data, which can otherwise be done by the EBB for supplementing, renewing and verifying the already obtained data.[48]

If a donor wants to opt out of the EBB, the donor has the right to demand that the de-coding information be destroyed.[49] Although opting out will not have a retrospective effect and the collected tissue and data remain in the EBB and can still be used for research, the donor can no longer be re-identified. A donor has the right to demand that already-obtained tissue and data be destroyed entirely but only if the donor's identity has been unlawfully revealed.[50]

3.2.2 Participants of Other Biobanks

Although the rights of gene donors established under the HGRA are exclusively designed for participants of the EBB, many similar principles arise from data protection law that would cover any biobanking facilities. Under data protection law, all individuals have, for example, the right of access,[51] the right to be forgotten,[52] the right to restrict processing[53] and the right to object to the use of their data.[54]

[46] § 8 HGRA, supra n 8.

[47] § 11(1)-(4), ibid. On 15 March 2019, amongst other changes in the HGRA, § 11(4) was altered so that the donors' right to 'genetic counselling' was reduced to the right to 'counselling', i.e. not specifically genetic counselling. Regrettably, no explanatory notes, impact assessments or other working documents are publicly available regarding this change.

[48] § 11(6), ibid.

[49] § 10(1), ibid.

[50] § 10(2), ibid.

[51] Art. 15 GDPR, supra n 11.

[52] Art. 17 GDPR, ibid.

[53] Art. 18 GDPR, ibid.

[54] Art. 21 GDPR, ibid.

However, taking advantage of Article 89(2) GDPR, the Estonian DP Act creates the possibility to derogate from all of these rights, except the right to be forgotten as this right is not mentioned in the referred article. Nonetheless, an exception to this right in the research context stems directly from the GDPR itself.[55]

Under the DP Act, when it comes to the research use of personal data, the controller or the processor[56] may restrict data subjects' rights referred to in Articles 15, 16, 18 and 21 GDPR as far as such rights are likely to render impossible or seriously impair the achievement of the specific research purposes and such derogations are necessary for the fulfilment of those purposes.[57]

3.3 *Article 89 GDPR and Safeguards Under the DP Act*

The explanatory note to the DP Act refers in the introduction to § 6 to Articles 89 and 6(1)(e) GDPR, which set out that scientific and historical research, and statistics, are tasks carried out in the public interest within the meaning of the latter article.[58] In referring to Article 89 GDPR, the explanatory note sets out that § 6 of the DP Act is designed to establish both the exceptions indicated in that article but also safeguards. However, aside from what is already mentioned directly in Article 89(1) GDPR (i.e. pseudonymisation), no other safeguards are apparent from the national law or its explanatory note.

Article 89(1) GDPR mentions pseudonymisation as one of the possible safeguards to be applied in regard to the research use of personal data. As laid out above, the DP Act allows for all types of personal data to be used in research without consent or any review process provided that the data are 'in a pseudonymised format or a format which provides equivalent level of protection'.[59] Thus, pseudonymisation, or any technological equivalent providing for the same level of protection, is essentially the one safeguard mentioned under Estonian data protection law.

Ethics reviews and the alternative DPI approval might also be regarded as safeguards within the meaning of Article 89(1) GDPR. However, as was explained above, according to the explanatory note under the Estonian DP Act an ethics review requirement would only be triggered if special categories of data were to be used in research without consent and with direct identifiers during the analysis of the data. This means that, at least in light of the explanatory note, an ethics review would

[55] Art. 17(3)(d) GDPR, ibid.

[56] There is no comment in the explanatory note to the DP Act as to why the processor is afforded the right to decide upon derogations from the rights of data subjects.

[57] § 6(6) DP Act, supra n 13.

[58] § 6 of the explanatory note to the (2019) DP Act, supra n 14.

Oddly, there is no reference to Article 9(2)(j) GDPR that grants discretion to Member States to regulate the research use of special categories of data in particular, although § 6 of the DP Act clearly regulates this matter as well.

[59] § 6(1) DP Act, supra n 13.

only be required in very limited circumstances,[60] and the DPI would only ever be involved if there was no ethics committee in a given field, which in practice is not likely ever to be the case in Estonia.

With regard to safeguards under Estonian law and Article 89(1) GDPR, it must be emphasized that the latter requires the implementation of safeguards in the research context regardless of the legal basis for processing (i.e. whether it be consent or national law). However, the Estonian DP Act mentions pseudonymisation only in regard to the use of personal data in research without the consent of individuals, essentially setting all pseudonymised data free as far as research is concerned. Furthermore, as noted above, de-pseudonymisation of the data is permitted for further research purposes.

Therefore, the implementation of Article 89 GDPR in Estonian data protection law is of a limited nature. In terms of safeguards, the national DP Act refers to pseudonymisation or equal measures when it comes to the research use of personal data without consent or any review process. The review process established by the DP Act only applies in limited circumstances, whereas in regard to derogations from the rights of data subjects the DP Act takes full advantage of Article 89(2) GDPR.

4 Law in Context: Individual Rights and Public Interest

It can be concluded from the previous part of this chapter that the Estonian DP Act takes quite a liberal approach to the research use of personal data. The only aspect in which the Estonian approach cannot be labelled liberal is informed consent.

As noted above, the drafters of the 2019 DP Act did not use the discretion granted to them under Recital 33 GDPR.[61] Thus, as a general rule, informed consent in research must comply with Article 9(2)(a) GDPR as far as special categories of data are concerned. This means that the informed consent must set out the specific purposes of processing (i.e. the specific research projects in which the data are to be used[62]). The one clear exception to this general rule under EU law are clinical trials

[60] As noted earlier, however, this extremely narrow approach laid out in the explanatory note to the DP Act is dubious and ethically questionable. Furthermore, it is at odds with the text of the law, See supra n 47.

[61] In the inital version of the draft law for the new DP Act (published in November 2017), the explanatory note of the law referred to Recital 33 GDPR, emphasizing the need for a broader consent in research. However, the draft law itself made no mention of consent in research. In a letter to the Ministry of Justice, the author of this chapter drew attention to this discrepancy, explaining that the consent issue must either be addressed within the law itself or the reference in the explanatory note should be removed. As a result, the reference to Recital 33 GDPR was removed from the explanatory note without any explanation for this choice in the later version.

[62] For arguments supporting this conclusion regarding the approach to (research) consent under the GDPR, see Pormeister (2018).

for pharmaceuticals.[63] The only exception under national law to this general rule of specific consent in research remains the consent established under the HGRA for the EBB.[64]

This approach to consent runs counter to the very essence of biobanks as the collection of tissue and data into biobanks is meant to enable their use for the research community as a whole, not specific single projects or projects in a specific field (though some specialized biobanks might be focused on specific fields).

Entities that do not have the option to obtain an open or broad informed consent can still establish biobanks by taking advantage of § 6 of the DP Act. If the necessary data are already available (i.e. have been obtained from individuals), they can be used for further research purposes regardless of what purposes they were initially obtained for. Even where data are initially obtained based on informed consent for specific purposes, they can still be used later for (different) research. The GDPR sets the data free from the storage and purpose limitations (Arts. 5(1)(b) and (e)), and the national DP Act provides the necessary legal basis for processing without consent.

As laid out above, the use of available human tissue and its inclusion into biobanks is subject to either a general rule of due notification or consent if there is a respective requirement in national law (e.g. written consent for the use of blood of patients and donors in research). In order to physically obtain tissue from an individual, of course, consent is required, but there is no requirement for this consent to set out specific research purposes as is the case with consent for the research use of data.

For example, clinical facilities with competency in clinical genetics accumulate large sets of tissue and genetic data of patients who have been referred to a geneticist and who have undergone genetic testing for the purposes of clinical care. The further research use of the blood sample would require written consent (not limited to specific purposes). The further research use of the genetic data could be either based on an initial limited consent for specific research projects and then later still be used in different research projects based on the DP Act. Alternatively, the step of obtaining initial specific consent could be skipped and the data could be used in research based on the DP Act. An ethics committee would be likely to ask for reasons why the researchers decided not to obtain consent and base their processing activities on the law instead. However, in genetic research the high number of individuals whose data are being handled often constitutes an impractical hardship for obtaining consent, and thus provides an acceptable justification for not obtaining consent for the use of already available data and instead opting for the law as the legal basis for processing.

[63] Article 28(2), Regulation (EU) No 536/2014 of the European Parliament and of the Council of 16 April 2014 on clinical trials on medicinal products for human use, and repealing Directive 2001/20/EC. OJ L158/1. See Pormeister (2020), pp. 47–54.

[64] However, the reference to § 6 of the DP Act introduced into the HGRA on 15 March 2019 leaves room for doubt as to whether in terms of data protection law the data processing of the EBB should be regarded as processing based on national law instead of consent.

It is debatable which approach—broad/open or specific consent—is more considerate of individual rights and interests. On the one hand, broad or open consent arguably does not facilitate an adequate understanding in laymen of how their tissue and data might be used in research in the future. On the other hand, the current approach in Estonia leads to an outcome where an individual might give specific consent for certain research projects but the same data could then be further used in future research projects without renewed consent. Thus, in the Estonian context, specific consent under data protection law does not leave the individual in a stronger position than broad or open consent. On the contrary, by giving broad or open consent the individual must at least be aware that the consent is not limited to specific projects or fields of research, whereas specific consent with the possibility for the same data to be later used in different research projects can be regarded as somewhat deceitful towards the individual as the initial specific consent might create a false sense of certainty.

Adding to this the fact that the Estonian DP Act allows controllers and processors to derogate from the rights of data subjects established in Articles 15, 16, 18 and 21 GDPR (in addition to the derogations within the GDPR itself, like Art. 17(3)(d)), the Estonian approach seems to be shifting the balance between individual rights and public interest strongly towards the latter. This attitude is also reflected in the explanatory note to the DP Act which emphasizes that research in general is seen as a task carried out in the public interest within the meaning of Article 6(1)(e) GDPR.

5 GDPR Impact and Future Possibilities for Biobanking

The GDPR itself cannot be deemed to have had a significant impact on biobanking activities in Estonia. Like its predecessor,[65] the GDPR sets available data free from the purpose and storage limitations as far as research uses are concerned, while the national DP Act facilitates the (further) research use of such data by creating a legal basis for processing that is independent of consent.

Even though the new Estonian DP Act does not establish a broader informed consent for research—as could have been done according to Recital 33 GDPR—it does enable biobanking activities by providing alternative legal bases for already available data to be included in (biobank) research without the consent of individuals. This makes it possible for entities engaged in research to accumulate large sets of data which can be used in various research projects without the need to obtain specific consent for each project, or any type of consent at all. Though not explicitly mentioned in the explanatory note to the DP Act, enabling the accumulation of large

[65] See Recital 29 and Art. 6(1)(b) and (e) of Directive 95/46/EC of the European Parliament and of the Council of 24 October 1995 on the protection of individuals with regard to the processing of personal data and on the free movement of such data. OJ L281.

sets of data is likely to have been the aim of the legislator given that Estonian health care is geared towards personalized medicine.[66]

The possibilities for the use of personal data in research without consent are even more significant in the Estonian context considering that all medical data (both genetic and other health data) are stored electronically. In addition to insitutional e-health records, Health data are stored in the state Health Information System, also referred to as the state-wide e-Health Records system. DNA sequencing data are not yet available through this central system but are electronically stored in institutional databases. However, part of the strategic vision of the e-Health system is to eventually include genetic data in electronic health records and create a database to accumulate pseudonymised health and genetic data that could be used for scientific research and also to further business developments.[67] This means that even today, aside from DNA sequencing data, essentially all the other health data of the whole population are readily available for research and can be used for research purposes without the consent (or knowledge)[68] of individuals.

As such, the creation of biobanks is no longer subject to the will of potential donors but is more a matter of available tissue and data. Although no entities other than the EBB (under national law) and sponsors of clinical trials (under Regulation (EU) 536/2014)[69] have the possibility to obtain open or broad consent for the research use of data, obtaining specific consent does not limit future research uses of already available data. This further enables research collaborations and exchange of available data. Whether this approach is proportional and balanced in regard to individual rights and interests is debatable.

6 Conclusions

For the purpose of transferring tissue and data directly from individuals into biobanks, consent is required for the physical intervention needed to obtain the tissue. Further use of already available tissue is subject to due notification, aside from a few exceptions. Written consent is needed to include the blood (but not other types of tissue) of blood donors and patients in research. As Estonian law does not establish

[66] See, e.g., the official website of the Ministry of Social Affairs regarding personalized medicine. https://www.sm.ee/en/personalised-medicine.

[67] E-Health vision 2025. E-Health strategic development plan 2020. (*E-tervise visioon 2025. E-tervise strateegiline arengukava 2020*). Estonian Health Strategy 2020. Government Office, 29-31. Available in Estonian. https://www.sm.ee/sites/default/files/content-editors/eesmargid_ja_tegevused/Eesti_e_tervise_strateegia/e-tervise_strateegia_2020.pdf.

[68] Art. 14(5)(b) GDPR creates an exception to the controller's obligation to inform data subjects of the processing of their data where the provision of information would 'involve a disproportionate effort', in particular for processing for, *inter alia*, research purposes. In the context of biobanking, the high number of data subjects involved is likely to enable controllers to invoke the exception (See Recital 62 GDPR). See also Pormeister (2020).

[69] Pormeister (2020), pp. 47–54.

any further requirements for this consent, it is not limited to specific projects or even fields of research. However, the population biobank EBB is prohibited from taking tissue samples without the specific knowledge and voluntary consent of individuals. This means that, for example, clinical facilities like hospitals that obtain large quantities of tissue samples during the clinical care of patients, are able to include these in biobank research by providing due notification (or obtaining written consent in the specific case of blood).

As for the data, which is where the core research interest lies, it may be included in research based on either consent or the national DP Act. Consent is an impractical option for biobanks since, in regard to special categories of personal data like genetic and health data, the GDPR requires consent to lay out specific processing purposes—whereas Estonian law does not establish a separate, broader research consent as could have been done. However, the national DP Act creates a legal basis for the use of any type of personal data in research without consent. Hence, available data can be included into biobanks without the consent of individuals. For example, hospitals and DTCGT service providers that obtain tissue and sequence DNA from it for purposes not related to research may store and later use the data for research purposes without consent by relying on the national DP Act as a legal basis. In the same manner, researchers who obtain tissue and sequence DNA from it based on specific consent for certain projects may later be able to still use the data for different research.

References

Hallinan D (2018) Feeding biobanks with genetic data: what role can the general data protection regulation play in the protection of genetic privacy in research biobanking in the European Union? Vrije Universiteit, Brussel

Pormeister K (2018) Genetic research and consent: on the crossroads of human and data research. Bioethics 33(3):347–356. https://doi.org/10.1111/bioe.12475

Pormeister K (2020) Transparency in relation to the data subject in genetic research – an analysis on the example of Estonia. Doctoral thesis defended 13 january 2020, University of Tartu. Available online at https://dspace.ut.ee/bitstream/handle/10062/66697/pormeister_kart.pdf?sequence=1&isAllowed=y. Accessed 22 June 2020

Access to Biomedical Research Material and the Right to Data Protection in Finland

Tom Southerington

Abstract This chapter describes the Finnish regulatory landscape concerning primarily non-interventional biomedical research and in particular the rights of study subjects from the data protection point of view. The GDPR is just one of many pieces of legislation affecting the rights of individuals, and it allows for significant variation between the EU Member States. Finnish law relating to biomedical research has materially changed in recent years and some changes are still pending. Overall, the legislator has aimed at enhancing opportunities for responsible research and enabling research-related innovation ecosystems, but also implemented quite strict limitations for data processing in balance. It is yet too early to evaluate the effects of the legislatory changes. The chapter is therefore mainly descriptive.

1 Introduction

Finland has several advantages over others in relation to biomedical research, such as nationwide tissue sample collections, primarily public health care with electronic health records and other national registers accessible for research, and the national identification number by which it is possible to link information from different sources. The Finnish genome is particularly interesting for research because of the population bottleneck.[1] The Finnish people are generally positive towards research,[2] and the legislation provides the required structure to enable it. In recent years, Finland has materially renewed its legislation concerning biomedical research and this work is still ongoing. A central piece of new legislation is the Biobank Act, which became effective in September 2013 but is now subject to

[1] See, for example, Kääriäinen et al. (2017).

[2] For a critical review, see Snell and Tarkkala (2019).

T. Southerington (✉)
University of Turku, Hospital District of Southwest Finland,
Finnish Biobank Cooperative – FINBB, Turku, Finland
e-mail: tomsou@utu.fi

S. Slokenberga et al. (eds.), *GDPR and Biobanking*, Law, Governance and Technology Series 43, https://doi.org/10.1007/978-3-030-49388-2_13

change, partly due to the GDPR. The new Data Protection Act, which complements the GDPR, entered into force in January 2019. The most recent addition is the Act on the Secondary Use of Social and Health Care Data, gradually becoming effective from May 2019.[3] Data protection and data security have been central themes in the legislative process and as a result the law has in some parts become quite restrictive, while at the same time creating new opportunities. The balance of the legislative measures and different rights and freedoms and the actual effects of legislation warrant keen monitoring.

2 Biobank Infrastructure and Regulatory Environment

2.1 Biobank Infrastructure

In June 2020, Finland has eleven registered biobanks. The term biobank in this context refers only to sample and data collections regulated under the Finnish Biobank Act.[4] Seven biobanks are hospital based, six of these are operated by public hospital districts and one by a private health care provider. The Finnish National Institute of Health and Welfare (THL) and the University of Oulu operate biobanks for collections accumulated in cohort studies. The Finnish Red Cross operates two biobanks, the blood service biobank and the haematological biobank. The biobanks control the research use of millions of samples primarily taken for diagnostic or research purposes, as well as associated data.[5] They also collect samples and data particularly so that the biobanks can be provided to researchers. The public hospital biobanks have large collections, collected especially from secondary and tertiary care patients, while the private hospital serves several hundred thousand occupational health clients with their particular patient profiles and obtains samples from them, among others. THL and the University of Oulu have high quality cohort collections and the Red Cross provides access to blood donor material and hosts a haematological diseases specialised sample collection together with detailed patient data.

The Biobank Act enables research use of samples and/or associated data without the need to (re)consent for each research project. The large numbers of Finnish biobank samples can be enriched with associated longitudinal patient and other data, including diagnosis, laboratory values, imaging data and medication details, for example. More and more genomic data is accumulating and can also be obtained at request from the samples.[6] The public biobank operators have established the

[3] See, for example, Southerington et al. (2019).

[4] Code 688/2012.Unofficial translation available at www.finlex.fi/fi/laki/kaannokset/2012/en20120688_20120688.pdf.

[5] The biobank register is available at www.valvira.fi/terveydenhuolto/toimintaluvat/biopankit. See also www.biopankki.fi/en/finnish-biobanks/ for information on each biobank.

[6] A large amount of genomic data from biobanks samples has accumulated, for example, in the FinnGen study (www.finngen.fi/en) and has been made available for further studies. See, for example, Palotie (2018).

Finnish Biobank Cooperative (FINBB) for national coordination and centralised access to the Finnish collections.[7]

In addition to the registered biobanks established to support research, there are numerous sample and data collections not referred to as biobanks. Also from some of them it is possible to obtain material for research under other legislation than the Biobank Act. These additional collections include, for example, health care sample archives not included within the current biobanks and collections assembled in individual research projects. With regard to data, there are several health and social care registers from which data is available for scientific research on application.

2.2 *An Overview of the Legal Framework*

The essential legislation controlling biobanks and access to samples and/or data in Finland are the GDPR, the Biobank Act, the Data Protection Act,[8] the Act on the Secondary Use of Social and Health Care Data (Secondary Use Act),[9] and the Act on the Medical Use of Human Organs, Tissues and Cells.[10] Interventional research is governed primarily by the Medical Research Act,[11] which is pending changes due to the EU Clinical Trials Regulation[12] and the EU Regulations on Medical Devices,[13] with a new Act on clinical trials in draft. Other relevant legislation includes the Act on the Status and Rights of Patients[14] and the Act on the Openness of Government Activities.[15] Table 1 sketches an overview of what the national acts govern, but it is to be noted that several of the acts can become applicable in the same study, for example, a pharmaceutical trial where potential participants are screened based on biobank samples and data.

The Finnish Medicines Agency FIMEA[16] is responsible for administering the national biobank register and for supervising and monitoring biobanks under the

[7] www.finbb.fi.

[8] Code 1050/2018. www.finlex.fi/fi/laki/alkup/2018/20181050.

[9] Code 552/2019. www.finlex.fi/fi/laki/alkup/2019/20190552.

[10] Code 191/2001. Unofficial translation available at www.finlex.fi/fi/laki/kaannokset/2001/en20010101_20130277.pdf.

[11] Code 488/1999. Unofficial translation available at www.finlex.fi/en/laki/kaannokset/1999/en19990488.pdf.

[12] Regulation 2014/536. eur-lex.europa.eu/legal-content/EN/TXT/?uri=celex%3A32014R0536.

[13] Regulations 2017/745 and 2017/746. eur-lex.europa.eu/legal-content/EN/TXT/?qid=1559211487967&uri=CELEX:32017R0745 and eur-lex.europa.eu/legal-content/EN/TXT/?qid=1559211487967&uri=CELEX:32017R0746.

[14] Code 785/1999. Unofficial translation available at www.finlex.fi/en/laki/kaannokset/1992/en19920785_20120690.pdf.

[15] Code 612/1999. Unofficial translation available at www.finlex.fi/en/laki/kaannokset/1999/en19990621.pdf.

[16] www.fimea.fi

Table 1 Overview of Finnish national legislation affecting health research

Legislative instrument	Scope with regard to research	Notes
Data Protection Act[a]	National *lex generalis* complementing the GDPR. Legal bases and derogations for scientific research.	GDPR art 6.1(e) is applicable to processing necessary for scientific research and proportionate to the public interest pursued. GDPR art 9.1 is not applicable to scientific research (based on 9.2(j)). Safeguard requirements for processing special category data. Derogations possible from GDPR articles 15, 16, 18 and 21 with specific safeguards.
Biobank Act[b]	Requirements for the registration and operations of biobanks. Access to biological samples and related data from biobanks for research for promoting health, understanding diseases and for developing health and medical care products and treatments.	New biobank act in drafting. Processing data for biobanking is expected to be clarified to be based on GDPR art 6.1(e) and 9.2(g). Biobank operations in general rely on broad consent or a notification and opt-out process stipulated in the Act enabling the transfer of older sample and data collections to the biobanks. For legal bases for processing in research, see Data Protection Act above.
Act on the Medical Use of Human Organs, Tissues and Cells[c]	Among many other purposes, governs secondary use of human tissue for research, if not available from registered biobanks.	Does not govern access to or use of data, only tissue. Several research related sections applying to different situations or material (autopsies, unused transplants, diagnostic samples).
Medical Research Act[d]	Research involving intervention in the integrity of a person, human embryo or human foetus for the purpose of increasing knowledge on health, the causes, symptoms, diagnosis, treatment and prevention of diseases or the nature of diseases in general. Establishes statutory medical research ethics committees.	Governs obtaining and using tissue for the purposes of a particular research project (interventional research). Pharmaceutical trials are to be partly taken apart from the Act to be governed by the EU Clinical Trials Regulation and a new national Clinical Trials Act.
Act on the Openness of Government Activities[e]	*Lex generalis* concerning freedom of information and bases for secrecy in the public sector. Includes rules for providing access to public records for scientific research purposes. To get access to personal data, the applicant must have a valid legal basis for processing.	The Secondary Use Act governs access to public sector records for research. Access to public records which are not covered by the Secondary Use Act is primarily decided based on this Act.

(continued)

Table 1 (continued)

Legislative instrument	Scope with regard to research	Notes
Act on the Status and Rights of Patients[f]	Among other things governs taking medical records, their confidentiality, storage times and use.	Under this Act confidential records can be shared with patient's consent.
Secondary Use Act (2019)[g]	Use of social and health care data for several secondary purposes, including also scientific research and non-scientific R&D. Establishes a new centralised permissions authority (www.findata.fi) for obtaining permission when needing data from several controllers, from controllers who have delagated their permissions authority, and from any private health or social care providers. The authority will also compile the data and make it available in a secure processing environment.	Centralised permissions and access to several health and social care registers' data. Except for aggregate statistical data, data will be available to be accessed and handled in certified secure processing environments only. Permissions authority Findata has monopoly over anonymisation and creating aggregated statistics to be provided to research or R&D. Anonymity control for research results intended to be published.

[a]Code 1050/2018. www.finlex.fi/fi/laki/alkup/2018/20181050
[b]Code 688/2012. Unofficial translation available at www.finlex.fi/fi/laki/kaannokset/2012/en20120688_20120688.pdf
[c]Code 191/2001. Unofficial translation available at www.finlex.fi/fi/laki/kaannokset/2001/en20010101_20130277.pdf
[d]Code 488/1999. Unofficial translation available at www.finlex.fi/en/laki/kaannokset/1999/en19990488.pdf
[e]Code 612/1999. Unofficial translation available at www.finlex.fi/en/laki/kaannokset/1999/en19990621.pdf
[f]Code 785/1999. Unofficial translation available at www.finlex.fi/en/laki/kaannokset/1992/en19920785_20120690.pdf
[g]Code 552/2019. www.finlex.fi/fi/laki/alkup/2019/20190552

Biobank Act. It has powers to remove biobanks from the register, which effectively means revoking their licence to operate, and to overrule individual decisions made by the biobank operators. In addition, the national data protection authority, the Office of the Data Protection Ombudsman, has the rights provided under the data protection regime in relation to personal data processing.

There are two initiatives for new legislation in preparation which could materially affect access to samples and data for research:

1. A new Biobank Act is in drafting to replace the existing one. It is expected to update the legal bases of personal data handling. Access to data may in part be moved under the Secondary Use Act.

2. A Genome Act is in drafting. The draft includes requirements for health care providers and biobanks to store genomic data in a genome centre, which will be a new expert organisation and public authority established within the THL.

2.3 Legal Foundation for Processing Personal Data in Biobanks and Biobank Research

The current Biobank Act relies on two mechanisms for bringing samples and associated data to biobanks: a broad biobank consent (Section 11) and, as an alternative for older diagnostic or research collections, a personal or public notification process with an opt-out possibility (Section 13). Data related to the collected or transferred samples can also be stored in the biobank (Section 14).[17] The Biobank Act gives biobanks the right to maintain records on the samples and related information, including personal data (Sections 20–23). Once legally obtained, the biobank operator can provide access to the collections for research projects within the scope regulated by the Biobank Act, which is research utilising the biobank samples or data for the purposes of promoting health, understanding the mechanisms of disease or developing products and treatment practices used in health and medical care. Research can be academia- or industry-driven. Scientists can obtain additional data from other registers where necessary for their scientific research project, for example, socio-economic data or reimbursement data on prescribed medicines from the Social Insurance Institution of Finland (KELA).

Access to biobank samples or data is always based on a case by case decision for each research project in accordance with Sections 26 and 27 of the Biobank Act. The research proposal must correspond to the biobank's registered research area. The proposal must also meet all legal requirements for the type of research in question and the criteria and conditions established for sample processing, some of which may also be set by the biobank. The recipient personnel must hold appropriate professional and academic qualifications for processing the samples and information, and access must be related to their occupational duties. A material transfer

[17] Based on guidance from the supervisory authority Valvira and the data protection ombudsman (available at www.valvira.fi/terveydenhuolto/toimintaluvat/biopankit), this data can include generic information on the sample donor (like identification data, dates of birth and death, cause of death), information related to the sample (like type, date stamps, diagnostic information, DNA analyses, etc.), health information closely related to the sample donor (relevant diagnoses, medication, treatments obtained etc.) and research results related to the sample (results from research to which samples were provided). Based on this, biobanks have accumulated fairly broad clinical data collections from which they can provide data with (or even without) samples for research. Based on discussions with the Ministry of Social Affairs and Health, this may change with the new biobank act. Decisions concerning the majority of the data would be taken in accordance with the Secondary Use Act instead of the Biobank Act.

agreement must be concluded between the biobank and the recipient, including also an obligation to make research results public.

To obtain access, in accordance with Section 27 the applicant must provide a research plan, an ethical evaluation and an account of the planned processing. The biobank may reject access (only) if justified based on (1) the biobank's research area and other criteria for access, (2) the need to secure intellectual property rights related to earlier research to complete ongoing research projects or to preserve the samples or collecting samples, (3) reasons pertaining to data protection, or (4) reasons pertaining to research ethics.

In the area of processing personal data for scientific research, Finnish law enables other available legal bases, not just consent, and in particular makes use of GDPR Article 6.1 subparagraph e and the Article 9.2 subparagraphs i and j. This is expected to extend to interventional studies where traditionally consent has been the legal basis for processing, together with consent for physical or psychological intervention.[18] This direction seems warranted as GDPR-governed consent increasingly seems like an unstable and in many circumstances unattainable premise for processing personal data in research, considering especially the right to withdraw at any time, which potentially greatly affects the research project and the validity of its results, and the demands for circumstances in which a valid consent can be obtained.[19]

3 Individual Rights and Safeguards Related to Data Protection

Individuals have rights and safeguards under the GDPR as well as under national law, which in part also provides limitations to the rights established in the GDPR. Scientific research has a special status in the GDPR and nationally. In Finland, biobanking itself is not considered to be within the scientific research provisions, such as those in the GDPR Article 89, but scientific research based on biobank material naturally is.

The Biobank Act Section 39 stipulates that everyone has the right to request and receive information from the biobank on:

---

[18] For appropriate legal bases in clinical trials, see the EU Commissions Question and Answers on the interplay between the Clinical Trials Regulation and the GDPR, ec.europa.eu/health/sites/health/files/files/documents/qa_clinicaltrials_gdpr_en.pdf.

[19] See Guidelines on Consent under Regulation 2016/679 (wp259rev.01), endorsed by the European Data Protection Board. Basing data processing on the law rather than consent seems unproblematic and warranted from the legal point of view, but for those emphasising data subject control or the so-called right of informational self-determination, a concept introduced by the German Bundesverfassungsgericht in 1983, the strict limitations for the possibilities to validly consent, which make it necessary to restrict, even exclude, self-determination by law to enable necessary processing, may seem less desirable. For an overview of the 1983 decision and the newly invented right, see, for example, Hornung and Schnabel (2009).

(i) whether or not samples concerning them are being stored in a biobank,
(ii) the criteria based upon which the samples are stored (meaning consent or the personal or public announcement process with an opt-out possibility),
(iii) the source of data concerning them, and
(iv) the recipients who have obtained samples taken from them and of the associated data.

In addition, Section 39 provides sample donors the right to, at their request, receive health-related information determined from their sample. When the biobank provides this information, it must also provide an opportunity to the donors to receive an account of the significance of the information. The biobank can charge an at-cost fee for providing this account.

In addition to the rights provided in the Biobank Act, the data subjects' rights under the GDPR will apply, for example, the right to obtain a copy of all of their personal data. However, the Data Protection Act Section 34 provides some exemptions to this right. This allows the data controller to withhold data, for example, if providing the data could seriously endanger the health of the data subject or his or her care or the rights of the data subject or some other party.[20]

The GDPR rights of rectification (Article 16), to data erasure (right to be forgotten, Article 17) and to restrict (Article 18) and object to processing (Article 21) will also remain more or less intact concerning processing within biobanks, but under the Data Protection Act they can be derogated from for scientific research, as will be discussed further on. The Biobank Act Section 12 states that the biobank consent can at any time be withdrawn, changed or restricted. However, data sets already formed for a particular research project and information contained within research results may continue to be used for the purposes of biobank research in accordance with the Act. In practice, any data set formed but not provided to researchers would be modified to remove data from any person withdrawing their consent. However, it may not always be possible to do the same for data sets already provided or used for research and there are legal bases for continued processing, such as scientific research in the public interest under the GDPR and the Data Protection Act.

The right to data portability (GDPR Article 20) may apply to at least some of the data stored in the biobanks, namely the data provided by the data subjects themselves under consent, if any. The extent of what should be considered data provided by the data subjects themselves is not entirely clear.[21]

With regard to decision-making concerning the data subject, including also any automated decision-making (GDPR Article 22), the Biobank Act Section 19 states that access to biobank samples or data may not be granted, and that they may not be used, for the purpose of criminal investigations or in administrative or any other decision-making concerning the sample donor. The section also specifically bans

[20] The Data Protection Act makes use of the possibility provided in the GDPR article 23 to nationally derogate from any of the GDPR articles on data subject rights.

[21] See, for example, Chassang et al. (2018).

use for the purposes of determining the person's ability to work and any decision-making of credit and insurance institutions.

As for safeguards, in accordance with the Biobank Act Section 16 the biobank samples and data must be pseudonymised by a code replacing direct identifiers, and the code key must be stored separately. There are also requirements for biobank information systems, which must be safe and enable verification of any re-identification event. When samples or data are provided to research projects, they must normally be coded again with a secondary, project specific code. The biobank may exceptionally provide identifiable material if, for example, this is necessary to link additional data from outside of the biobank to the sample donor material. In this case, the data controller who obtains the identifiable material must pseudonymise the combined material with a code provided by the biobank before providing (or using) it for the research project.

Accordingly, researchers who receive material from biobanks will in most cases not have access to any identifying information so although the data could still include personal data, the exemptions under GDPR Article 11 apply. In addition, the Finnish Data Protection Act provides for exceptions to the data subject rights in scientific research in accordance with GDPR Article 89. Under Section 31 of the Data Protection Act, GDPR Articles 15, 16, 18 and 21 can be derogated from if needed provided that 1. processing is based on an appropriate research plan, 2. a particular person or group is responsible for the research, and 3. personal data are handled and transferred only for historical or scientific research or other compatible purposes and unauthorised disclosures are prevented. If processing involves health data or other special category data or GDPR Article 10 data, then as an additional safety measure the researchers must either 1. perform a GDPR Article 35 compliant data processing impact assessment, which is then to be provided to the data protection ombudsman prior to processing, or 2. comply with GDPR Article 40 compliant code of conduct, which appropriately takes into account the derogations from data subject rights.

The new Secondary Use Act is not applied to biobank (samples or) data.[22] However, the Secondary Use Act will govern access to many types of information often combined with biobank samples and data, like additional clinical data or data on pharmaceutical prescriptions and use. When these data are required from *one* public social or health care service provider (and data controller), that service provider will decide over permissions to the data. When data are required from *more than one* public social or health care service provider, or from any private social or

[22] This is actually not evident from the Act itself but based on discussions with officials at the Ministry of Social Affairs of Health who plan to clarify this in the renewed Biobank Act being drafted. The scope of the Secondary Use Act is defined by different sections of the Secondary Use Act, in particular Section 2 'Scope' referring to Sections 1 'Objectives', 6 'Authorities and organisations responsible for services and data collection limitations' and 7 'Exceptions concerning statistics authorities'. In addition to what can be deduced from these sections, the Act governs access to private health and social care providers' personal data records for secondary purposes (see Sections 35 and 44 in particular).

health care service provider, the new public administrative authority Findata will act as a centralised permissions office for an access request.[23] Findata will also collect and combine data from the original registers and provide the combined data set to the researchers.[24] Subject to the Secondary Use Act, the data will be available for researchers only within Findata's secure processing environment, or exceptionally at Findata's permission another secure processing environment certified by an approved certification agency unless the data are aggregated statistics to ensure their anonymity—a limitation which may prove challenging in some research projects.[25] The data processing environment requirement also seems to mean that any data to be combined and analysed together with the data made available under the Secondary Use Act will need to be brought into that environment.[26] Another new requirement is that Findata will have control over the publication of results obtained based on the register data to ensure their anonymity. It can either anonymise the results itself or leave this to be done by the researchers, in which case the researchers must provide their anonymised results to the authority afterwards.[27]

---

[23] See Section 44 for division of powers.

[24] Section 5 and 14.

[25] Consider for example EU or multinational research projects which would like to control and analyse their data combined from different countries.

[26] Some requirements for the secure environments are described in sections 17–24. The Act places major expectations for the secure data environments, which will need to be able to facilitate research on any kind of data in many different formats, medical imaging formats, text, video, audio, genomic data formats, etc., combine them from various sources, include the required analytics tools and provide a user-friendly remote access interface.

[27] Section 52. Data protection and security concerns were considered so critical that the centralised permissions authority was given exclusivity over anonymisation of data. Anonymised data were considered as data with residual risk of re-identification as opposed to aggregated statistics, also exclusively produced by the permissions authority and presumed absolutely anonymous. Despite the centralised anonymisation to ensure adequate anonymity, even anonymised data obtained under this Act cannot be handled freely but only in certified secure environments and only aggregated statistics can be handled elsewhere (even though in reality also statistics can reveal information about identifiable persons when complemented with other data). The concern over publications arose fairly late in the process and the argumentation for increased control was that even when the research data are well secured, publication of the results could reveal identifiable data. This was apparently considered an unbearable risk that needed to be avoided, although there is evidence that when discussing the act in session, the parliament or at least some of the MPs did not actually realise that the restrictions to the right to publish scientific results were actually included in the final proposal they decided on—See MP Puska's statement from March 6th 2019 plenary session, www.eduskunta.fi/FI/vaski/Puheenvuoro/Sivut/PUH_171+2018+5+1+1.aspx. For the *travaux preparatoires* and expert opinions collected during the parliamentary process, see www.eduskunta.fi/FI/vaski/KasittelytiedotValtiopaivaasia/Sivut/HE_159+2017.aspx.

All in all, the parliament seems to have aimed at absolute universal anonymity, going far beyond the requirements of the GDPR for data not to be considered as personal data and discarded considerations for balance between fundamental rights. This could present a major threat to the freedom and autonomy of science and also for other justified uses of social and health care data. For example, there is probably no way of irrevocably, universally anonymising X-ray (or similar) images so that no-one, in no circumstances, could even in theory identify anyone from them. Yet sharing this kind of data is customary, necessary and presumably in most cases of little or no actual risk to anyone's rights or freedoms, or at least represents a good balance between different rights and interests.

4 Law in Context: Individual Rights and Public Interest

The Biobank Act increased the transparency of use of tissue and data for research and introduced new informational rights to sample donors.[28] The system is based on consent and an alternative opt-out mechanism with information made individually or publicly available. With the strict requirements for obtaining a valid consent, and potentially also the restrictions to how broad the consent for data processing can be, consent will become less useful as a legal basis for biobanks and research related purposes in general. This could appear to be against basic medical research ethics requirements but processing based on the law properly enacted, with transparency and real possibilities to influence, should not be ethically questionable and it does not affect the need to obtain consent for interventions. It is expected that in the new Biobank Act the legal bases for biobank activities will be processing in substantial public interest in accordance with GDPR Articles 6(1)(e) and 9(2)(g). Interventions to obtain samples would still require consent but this would not extend to data processing. This may somewhat reduce sample donor control in comparison to the current situation where processing is at least in part based on a broad biobank consent, but with the consent for interventions, safeguards and other data subject rights, the various rights and interests seem balanced.

The measures adopted in the new Secondary Use Act to protect the data extend beyond the GDPR requirements and contradict its objective to enable the free movement of data in Europe. Limitations related to the publication of results interfere with the autonomy and freedom of science protected under Section 16 of the Constitution of Finland and Article 10 of the EU Charter of Fundamental Rights and may raise concerns about appropriate reporting of scientific findings. Impacts of the Act will in practice depend largely on the resources, efficiency and mindset of the new permissions authority Findata. It is hoped major improvements will arise from the Act based on the new centralised permissions and data collection process, the new requirements for social and health care service providers to have their data available and also from new supporting services. Data from different social and health care registers were available for researchers before this Act but often access was decided by several different data controllers and their decisions on the same research proposal could vary. The application processes could also be prohibitively long and there were not always sufficient services with which to actually compile the data from the many information systems of the data controllers.

Individual rights and public interests are sometimes seen as opposites but these tensions can be exaggerated. Firstly, biobanking or research can often be both in the public and in the private interest. A biobank sample may prove valuable for a person's health care later in life or an incidental finding from research may provide important, actionable information. It could even be perceived as a patient right to be able to participate in biobanking and research. Secondly, research itself is typically not directed at individuals but at statistical, generalizable phenomena. In many

[28] See, for example, Soini (2013) and Forsberg (2013).

cases research is performed without any need, right or reasonable chance to access identifiers and without the right to use the data to affect the data subjects. Few seem to have major concerns over blood donations for health care purposes, even though it also requires precise health information on the donor, and biobanking has several parallels to it. Some of the perceived tensions could be caused by obscurity which may relate to the origin of or rationale for the right to the protection of personal data and to seeing this right as one form of property right. But data are not owned, and where there are rights then those rights may be spread between various persons and over each copy of each datum, making personal control an illusion.[29]

5 GDPR Impact and Future Possibilities for Biobanking

The GDPR seems to have brought about a move from consent as a legal basis of processing towards processing legitimised by the law as serving a public interest. This may be beneficial for research and clarify the legality of research projects. However, consent is still a possible basis for processing, and where it is used the GDPR Recital 33 recognises a 'broad consent' and this may expand current national interpretations of the borders of the consent when all information about the research is not available at the time of consenting. The GDPR Recital 159 on the other hand may expand the current national interpretation of what is considered scientific research, clearly including also technological development, and demonstration and applied research, not just academic fundamental research, for example. Consent could also be used as a form of safeguard, even if not a legal basis, though this might be confusing to the data subjects (and the controllers).

In general, the GDPR may bring better practices to data protection in research, although in health research awareness has probably been on a high level for some time because of the confidential nature of health data and the research often being pursued by health care professionals. The heightened awareness of data protection issues and uncertainty on how best to comply may have led to unnecessarily excessive measures to protect data, for example, in the case of the Secondary Use Act. The GDPR continues to recognise scientific research as a special processing purpose, even if not in itself a legal basis for research, and to further clarify what should be considered scientific. However, the GDPR fails to support the European research area by properly harmonising data protection rules. All central provisions from legal bases to data subject rights can be affected by national legislation or the lack of it, especially so in the field of scientific research, which makes cross-border collaboration challenging. The data protection regime continues to be a complex combination of EU and national rules, and understanding the rights and requirements continues to be a challenge for authorities, controllers, processors and data subjects alike.

---

[29] Expanding on these themes is beyond the scope of this book. Cf. Koops (2014) who states that the aim to give individuals control over personal data is a delusional fallacy.

6 Conclusions

Finland continues to develop its comprehensive legislatory environment for biobanks and research use of tissue and data in a complex European and international setting. It has made use of the GDPR Article 89 to enable derogation from some data subject rights for scientific research but also implemented strict safeguards extending even over non-personal data. While the aims are to enable and facilitate, new types of restrictions have also been enacted, some beyond the requirements of the GDPR and even contrary to its objective to enable the free movement of data. The eventual success and the effects of the new legislation on research and innovation as well as on the rights and freedoms of data subjects should be monitored carefully. However, with its biobanks and other research infrastructures, new legislation, new support services and continuously improving information systems, Finland is well positioned to support and deliver efficient, legal, ethical and high quality research. An area perhaps requiring more careful attention is proper international regulatory alignment.

References

Chassang G, Southerington T, Tzortzatou O, Boeckhout M, Slokenberga S (2018) Data portability in health research and biobanking: legal benchmarks for appropriate implementation. Eur Data Protect Law Rev 4(3):296–307

Forsberg J (2013) Finsk biobankslag till fördel för alla. Uppsala Universitet

Hornung G, Schnabel C (2009) Data protection in Germany I: the population census decision and the right to informational self-determination. Comput Law Secur Rev 25(1):84–88

Kääriäinen H, Muilu J, Perola M, Kristiansson K (2017) Genetics in an isolated population like Finland: a different basis for genomic medicine? J Community Genet 8(4):319–326, Published online 2017 Jul 20. https://doi.org/10.1007/s12687-017-0318-4

Koops B-J (2014) The trouble with European data protection law. Int Data Priv Law 4(4):250–261

Palotie A (2018) FinnGen-tutkimus luo perustaa genomitiedon hyödyntämiseksi terveydenhuollossa: Lähes joka kymmenes suomalainen osallistuu. Duodecim 134(16):1545–1547

Snell K, Tarkkala H (2019) Questioning the rhetoric of a 'willing population' in Finnish biobanking. Life Sci Soc Policy 15:4. https://doi.org/10.1186/s40504-019-0094-5

Soini S (2013) Finland on a road towards a modern legal biobanking infrastructure. Eur J Health Law 20(3):289–294

Southerington T, Vainio S, Pitkäranta A (2019) Biopankkilainsäädännön muuttuva kenttä: uhkat ja mahdollisuudet. Duodecim 135(10):973–974

Research Biobanking, Personal Data Protection and Implementation of the GDPR in France

Gauthier Chassang, Michael Hisbergues, and Emmanuelle Rial-Sebbag

Abstract Since 1978 and the initial French data protection law (Loi n°78-17 du 6 Janvier 1978), consecutive modifications regarding the protection of personal health data, especially in 2004, 2016 and 2018, set up a strict legal regime for processing sensitive personal data, including for research purposes. In recent years, French law has evolved proactively and in parallel with the work of the European Union (EU) on the preparation of what became the General Data Protection Regulation (GDPR), which has been in force since May 2018. This Chapter performs a state-of-art analysis (as of 1 July 2019) of the French legal framework for research biobanks and data protection rules applying to biobanking, in particular those related to data subjects' rights and Article 89 of the GDPR. Firstly, it provides updated information about the national landscape of active research biobanks in France (Sect. 1). Secondly, it explores how the French law embodies the developments brought by the GDPR and how it envisages individuals' rights in the context of research biobanking (Sects. 2 and 3). Thirdly, this Chapter analyses existing and potential national exemptions to individuals' rights, including with regard to Article 89 GDPR, and how France conceives of processing activities of 'public interest' (Sect. 4). Finally, the authors address ongoing debates around bioethics law in France and argue for the creation

G. Chassang (✉)
LEASP, Inserm, Université Paul Sabatier Toulouse 3, Toulouse, France

Infrastructure Nationale Biobanques, Institute for Public Health, Clinical Research Department, Paris, France

Plateforme "Ethique et Biosciences", Genotoul Societal, Toulouse, France

M. Hisbergues
Infrastructure Nationale Biobanques, Institute for Public Health, Clinical Research Department, Paris, France
e-mail: michael.hisbergues@inserm.fr

E. Rial-Sebbag
Infrastructure Nationale Biobanques, Institute for Public Health, Clinical Research Department, Paris, France

Plateforme "Ethique et Biosciences", Genotoul Societal, Toulouse, France
e-mail: emmanuelle.rial@univ-tlse3.fr

S. Slokenberga et al. (eds.), *GDPR and Biobanking*, Law, Governance and Technology Series 43, https://doi.org/10.1007/978-3-030-49388-2_14

of a specific Act focused on biobanking as a means of integrating, clarifying and developing not only data protection rules but also other activities related to samples, human or not, in a unique, operational and compact act (Sect. 5).

1 Introduction

France is known for having one of the stricter legal regimes worldwide regarding personal data protection. Since 1978, France has regularly updated personal data protection rules to maintain a high level of protection for individuals' rights and freedoms—something that can be considered a necessity in a democratic State.

Since 2006, this regulatory dynamism has intensified, notably in consideration of the debates which led to the European Commission proposal to adopt a European Union (EU) General Data Protection Regulation (GDPR) in 2012 and its formal adoption in 2016. Between 2016 and 2018, the French government and parliamentary bodies, in collaboration with the National Data Protection Authority (CNIL), scrutinised existing personal data protection law and adopted several acts modifying the Law on informatics and freedoms[1] (Loi Informatique et Libertés n°78-17 (LIL)), in particular regarding health data processing. These regulatory advances have inevitably impacted scientific research practices at large, including, to a certain extent, research biobanking. Indeed, biobanks which process, store and control the sharing of bioresources for research uses are stewards of the collections of human biological samples and their associated data.[2]

In this Chapter, we intend first to describe the updated regime applied to biobanking activities under French law and related procedures. Second, we concentrate on the relevant provisions of the LIL introduced in 2018, and unmodified since the last revision of 2019, that affect personal data processing for health research and cover biobanking. We consider in particular the implementation of Article 89 of the GDPR which enables national exemptions to several data subjects' rights in research contexts.

2 Biobank Infrastructure and Regulatory Environment

2.1 What Is the French Biobanks Landscape?

For 20 years, the government, through its associated ministries (research and health), supported and structured the French landscape of Biological Resource Centres (BRCs). Inserm (Institut National de la Santé et de la Recherche Médicale) played a leading role as national operator in association with various national

[1]Loi n°78-17 du 6 janvier 1978 relative à l'informatique, aux fichiers et aux libertés (LIL), 2019 version. https://www.cnil.fr/fr/loi-78-17-du-6-janvier-1978-modifiee.

[2]E.g. clinical and biological personal data qualifying the sample.

stakeholders. These actions led to the establishment of a French BRC network. This continues to be at the forefront of European countries as, since 2008, France has been the only country with a national standard for quality management in biobanking [NFS 96-900].[3] In 2011, another step was taken with the creation of a national infrastructure to support quality assurance and certification processes in biobanks, support technological innovations, provide expertise on ethical and regulatory aspects and participate in international working groups. This French BIOBANQUES Infrastructure has been decidedly oriented towards Europe with its active participation in the establishment of the European infrastructure BBMRI-ERIC.[4]

In 2001, 58 tumor biobanks attached to health care institutions were set up to improve the organisation of care and accelerate cancer research. Now, the French network of BRCs identified in health and research institutions consists of 96 biological or microbiological resource centres distributed throughout the country, which are organised into 15 thematic or regional networks. The Paris area represents a 'hot spot' of biobanks concentration (44%), which is in line with the historical distribution of large institutions and hospital groups. The remaining 56% is spread over the 13 administrative regions.[5]

The distinctiveness of the French network is that it implemented, early on, a quality management system (based on NFS 96-900) leading to the certification of almost 70% of the network (see footnote 5). The NFS defines standards for the qualification of the personal, material and dedicated biobanking processes. BIOBANQUES supports the preparation of BRCs certification process with qualified personal. The typology of the French BRC landscape varies a great deal in terms of size, expertise and therapeutic area, which gives it a richness and complexity.

A large part of BRCs in the French network is multi-thematic. The therapeutic areas of the collections and associated data housed in these structures are, by order of representativeness, according to the ICD-10 nomenclature,[6] oncology, central nervous system diseases, heart and vessel diseases, and infectious, parasitic and HIV diseases. Moreover, almost 40% are involved in the collection and preservation of biosamples and data from large national cohorts (population-based or disease-specific), the majority of which include clinical collections.

Generally, data protection law applies whatever the biobank's specificities. Challenges regarding both the sustainability of the biobanks and the clarity of the attached regulatory regime have been identified in the literature[7] and will need further political actions.

---

[3] AFNOR. NFS 96-900 for Biological Resource Centers. https://certification.afnor.org/qualite/certification-des-centres-de-ressources-biologiques-nf-s96-900.

[4] Biobank and BioMolecular Research Infrastructure - European Research Infrastructure Consortium.

[5] Hisbergues M (2019). Analysis of the French BIOBANQUES Network Characteristics. Unpublished.

[6] World Health Organisation, International Statistical Classification of Diseases and Related Health Problems, 10th Revision. https://www.who.int/classifications/icd/en/.

[7] Clément et al. (2019).

2.2 How Is Biobank Research Regulated in France?

French law does not use the term 'biobank' but refers, as a similar notion, to 'any organisms' which 'ensure the preservation and preparation for scientific purposes of tissues and cells from the human body, of organs, blood and its components and derived products' whose 'activities include the constitution and use of human biological samples collections'.[8] 'Human biological sample collection' means 'the pooling, for scientific purposes, of biological samples procured from a group of identified and selected persons according to the clinical or biological characteristics of one or several members of the group, as well as the derived products of these samples'.[9]

France has no unique, comprehensive biobank law. Successive laws, decrees and regulatory acts from government and authorities have directly or indirectly impacted research biobanking and BRCs. These have progressively constituted the current legal framework. In a nutshell, this framework is constituted by bioethics laws;[10] biomedical research laws;[11] and the data protection law that fixes data subjects' rights and special conditions for processing personal data for research purposes.[12] These major acts cross-reference themselves and interact on a number of topics. They are completed by applicable ethical, technical and scientific guidelines intended to ensure high quality and security of research.[13] This framework is mainly codified in the Public Health Code (PHC) and the Civil Code (CC), but the French biobanking legal regime remains complex and fragmented. Also, some of the provisions presented below could evolve based on ongoing debates on revising the last bioethics law.

[8] Article L.1243-3 and 4 PHC. Unofficial translation.

[9] Ibid. footnote 8.

[10] Protecting human dignity, human body integrity, non-availability, non-patrimoniality and rules regarding the procurement, collection, storage and use of human samples for research purposes. Adopted in 1994, 2004, 2011. Re-examined at the latest every 7 years after publication of the last bioethics law, presently under revision. For a summarised history of French bioethics laws, see CCNE (2018). Etats Généraux. Rapport de synthèse. Opinions du Comité Citoyen. Fig. 1.

[11] Regulating research involving human person, fixing research participants' rights, rules and procedures to set up, submit, pilot and implement interventional or non-interventional research projects since 1988. Currently: Loi n°2012-300 du 5 mars 2012, JORF 6 mars 2012.

[12] Loi n°78-17 ibid. footnote 1, as modified by Loi n°2004-801 du 6 août 2004, JORF 7 août 2004, implementing the European Data Protection Directive 95/46; Loi n°2016-41 du 26 janvier 2016 de modernisation de notre système de santé, JORF 27 janvier 2016. Loi n°2016-1321 du 7 octobre 2016 pour une République numérique, JORF 8 octobre 2016. And lastly, for implementing the GDPR, by Loi n°2018-493 du 20 juin 2018 relative à la protection des données personnelles. JORF 21 juin 2018. Décret n°2018-687 du 1er août 2018, JORF 3 août 2018, texte n°12. Ordonnance n°2018-1125 du 12 décembre 2018, JORF 13 décembre 2018, texte n°5. Décret n° 2019-536 du 29 mai 2019, JORF n°0125 du 30 mai 2019, texte n° 16.

[13] E.g. Good clinical practices in clinical trials on medicinal products for human use. Décision du 24 novembre 2006 fixant les règles de bonnes pratiques cliniques pour les recherches biomédicales portant sur des médicaments à usage humain, JORF 30 novembre 2006, texte n°64.

Biobanking for research purposes is often included within broader health research projects but can also be envisaged on its own, for example, as a parallel activity to healthcare in order to serve future undefined research. These different contexts involve different legal considerations. Today, the applicable rules for biobanking activity are identified on a case-by-case basis, depending on the nature of the activity,[14] on the purpose of the research project,[15] on the individuals concerned,[16] on the nature of the samples,[17] and on the nature of the data collected and used (personal, anonymised or anonymous data).

The legal procedures regarding personal data processing for research (ruled by LIL) and those applying to biobanking and the setting up of a biobank (ruled by the PHC, in close connection with biomedical research laws) rely on two specific frameworks. Both must ultimately be respected. Here we concentrate on the procedures for setting up a research biobank. The next section will present the procedures regarding personal data processing in research biobanking.

Two procedures exist for setting up a biobank depending on the context in which the collection of human samples is implemented and on the use envisaged for the collection, regardless of whether or not the collections are anonymised or anonymous.

- First procedure: the collection is constituted within the frame of a Research Involving Human Person (RIHP) project.

In 2016, the implementation of the Law n°2012-300[18] and its related Decree,[19] Ordinance[20] and 'Arrêtés'[21,22] on RIHP affected the rules regarding biomedical research and biobanking, essentially through new research classification and

[14] Samples procurement, non-invasive collection or reuse of existing biosamples and data.

[15] Involving human persons or not according to the French law criteria.

[16] Patients, healthy participants, minors, adults, vulnerable people and deceased persons.

[17] Organs: Articles L.1232-1 to L.1232-3, third paragraph of Article L.1235-1 and Article L.1235-2 PHC.

- Blood: Articles L.1221-4, L.1221-8-1 and second paragraph of Article L.1221-12 PHC.
- Tissues, cells, liquids and other body products such as stool: Articles L.1241-5, L.1243-3, L.1243-4, L.1245-2, L.1245-5 and L.1245-5-1 PHC.
- Embryos, fetuses and derived cells: Articles L.2151-2 and L.2151-5 to L. 2151-7 PHC.
- Micro-organisms of human origin, such as viruses, parasites: for these samples, specific biosecurity and biosafety rules could apply to their storage, handling and use, for proper protection of staff and society. See Société Française de Microbiologie (2014).

[18] Loi n°2012-300 du 5 mars 2012 relative aux recherches impliquant la personne humaine, JORF 6 mars 2012. Consolidated version.

[19] Décret n°2016-1537 du 16 novembre 2016, JORF 17 novembre 2016, texte n°27.

[20] Ordonnance n°2016-800 du 16 juin 2016, JORF 17 juin 2016, texte n°19.

[21] Arrêté du 12 avril 2018 fixant la liste des recherches mentionnées au 2° de l'article L. 1121-1 du code de la santé publique, JORF 17 avril 2018, texte n°10.

[22] Arrêté du 12 avril 2018 fixant la liste des recherches mentionnées au 3° de l'article L. 1121-1 du code de la santé publique, JORF 17 avril 2018, texte n°11.

associated procedures towards competent authorities according to the type of research and updated informed consent requirements regarding individual's participation to the research activities (consent to research participation required under PHC should not be confounded with consent as to personal data processing as referred to in the LIL).

The PHC defines a RIHP as research organised and carried out on human persons to develop biological or medical knowledge.[23] Three types of RIHP are defined according to their risks for research participants,[24] from the more risky or invasive research (RIHP1) to the less risky or less-invasive ones (RIHP3). Activities related to the procurement, collection, preservation and use of biological samples and attached data can occur in the three types if justified and detailed within the research protocol.[25]

Every RIHP project needs to be registered[26] prior to the submission to the competent authorities. Drug clinical trials covered by the EU Clinical Trial Regulation[27] will need a EudraCT number. RIHP1 ones (e.g. interventional research on medical devices) will need to obtain an ID-RCB number with registration at the National Agency for the Safety of Medicines and Health Products (ANSM). The protocol must be reviewed and approved by a competent Research Ethics Committee (Comité de Protection des Personnes—CPP). The CPP should scrutinise[28] the project in particular regarding the respect for research participants' rights, informed consent procedures, forms, the necessity and proportionality of the planned activities regarding the research purposes, including data protection measures, and in particular data minimisation. The CPP is designated randomly.[29] A CPP decision can be appealed

[23] Article L.1121-1 PHC.

[24]

- RIHP1: interventional research involving an intervention upon the person that is not justified by his or her usual care. It aims to deal with risky research such as clinical trials on experimental drugs or other health products (e.g. cell therapies' products; products in the field of human feeding).
- RIHP2: interventional research involving only minimal risks and constraints whose list is fixed by the Minister of Health, after consulting with the Director General of the National Agency for the Safety of Medicines and Health Products (ANSM). It includes research that uses health products used in their usual way and research including minimal invasive acts (blood procurement by drawing, medical imagery, etc.). See footnote 21 for a list of activities qualifying as RIHP2.
- RIHP3: non-interventional research involving no risk nor constraints and in which all acts are performed, and products are used in the usual manner. It includes for example observational research on treatment observance, on healthcare practices, the use of surveys and the collection of small quantities of supplementary samples during routine acts in healthcare or through non-invasive acts. See footnote 22 for a list of activities qualifying as RIHP3.

[25] Clear information on the nature of the interventions, attached risks, samples and data nature, sources, flows, storage and expected uses shall be, among others, presented and argued.

[26] https://ansm.sante.fr/Services/Obtenir-un-numero-d-enregistrement-pour-une-RIPH.

[27] Regulation (EU) n°536/2014 on clinical trials on medicinal products for human use, and repealing Directive 2001/20/EC. OJEU L.158/1. 27 May 2014.

[28] Article L.1123-7 PHC fixing the non-limitative list of assessment criteria used by CPP.

[29] Article L. 1123-14 PHC.

once through the same randomised process. ANSM authorisation is required only for RIHP1.[30] In RIHP2, the ANSM is only notified of the project details and CPP opinion. ANSM is not involved in RIHP3. Any substantial modifications[31] of the declared elements must be submitted to the CPP for approval and, if required, to the ANSM for authorisation.

The CPP has 45 days to approve or reject the project proposal. Silence means acceptance. Where ANSM authorisation is required, delays can vary according to the products used; if there is silence past the delay, this means refusal.

The storage of a biological collection after a project comes to an end is allowed when concerned individuals have been properly informed and are able to exercise their right to oppose. Sufficiently clear indications must have been provided about the storage duration, conditions, the scientific purposes for which samples and data will be made available and where to find further information. Only in this case do the initial ethics approval and authorisations obtained for the research project suffice to continue storage in a research biobank after a project ends. However, where individuals were not able to provide a valid informed consent for long term storage, the promoter shall consult a CPP for proper approval and follow the second procedure.

- Second procedure: the collection is not constituted within a RIHP project and/or the storage is prolonged after the end of a RIHP to cede rights on the materials for research uses, including without proper informed consent.

This procedure covers projects to create new bio-collections or biobanking sites outside any particular RIHP project (i.e. systematic collection of residual surgical samples for future research or reuse of existing samples without any additional act on human persons or a purely technological project). This procedure also concerns biobank activities where long-term storage for cession[32] to third parties is planned and, subject to a new CPP approval, where RIHP participants have not been properly informed in the initial consenting process about materials storage or cession after the project ends.

In these cases, the organism in charge of the collection is either subject to a declaration[33] to the Ministry of Research where collections will be used for their own research program needs, or to an authorisation, for those wishing to transfer

[30] Article L.1123-12 PHC fixing the non-limitative list of assessment criteria used by ANSM.

[31] As defined in Article R.1123-42 PHC. See examples in clinical trials where ANSM authorization is required: ANSM (2015). Avis aux promoteurs d'essais cliniques de médicaments - Tome 1 - Annexe 14: Exemples de modifications substantielles et non substantielles pour l'ANSM. V.01/06/2015. https://ansm.sante.fr/var/ansm_site/storage/original/application/564a06fb30def9d36ad3f0c17e3bd0b9.pdf.

[32] 'Cession' can be defined as a particular transfer of the samples including to cede rights upon the material to a third recipient, for its own uses. It shall be differentiated from collaboration with the biobank where the latter keeps custodianship and attached management rights on the material.

[33] Articles L.1243-3 and R.1243-49 to R.1243-56 PHC.

samples to third parties for research uses,[34] in application of a Decree of 2017[35] (CODECOH procedures),[36] and where individuals' information is lacking. The Ministry, and the Regional Agency of Health (ARS) where hospitals are located, have 2 months to approve a declaration, with silence meaning approval, and 3 months regarding authorisations, with silence meaning rejection. Declarations have no validity deadline. Authorisations are valid for 5 years and must be renewed after submission of an activity report.[37] Any substantial modifications to the elements[38] presented in the application dossier must be submitted to the Ministry and, where relevant, to the ARS.[39] A new CPP approval could be needed.

Whatever the procedure, biobanks wishing to export/import human biological samples[40] for research uses need specific authorisation from the Ministry of Research. The Ministry of Research will check that the principles of free donation, informed consent rules and transport standards for labelling[41] and packaging dangerous goods have been respected. This authorisation is delivered within a 3 months delay maximum.

Promoters of research using ethically sensitive biological elements, such as human embryos, gametes, or organs coming from deceased persons, need specific authorisation from the Biomedicine Agency (Agence de la Biomédecine).

Biobanks are accountable and must be able to answer to requests from competent authorities at any time, notably on the nature and characteristics of the stored samples, on the research projects using the samples, on consent or non-opposition from source individuals and on the fate of the samples. In all cases, specific rules and procedures fixed by the LIL regarding personal data collection, storage and other processing for health research purposes must be respected.

---

[34] Articles L.1243-4 and R.1243-57 to R.1243-66 PHC.

[35] Décret n°2017-1549 du 8 novembre 2017 relatif à la conservation et à la préparation à des fins scientifiques d'éléments du corps humain, JORF du 10 novembre 2017, texte n°30.

[36] Ministry Online Application: https://appliweb.dgri.education.fr/appli_web/codecoh/IdentCodec.jsp.

[37] Article R.1243-63 PHC.

[38] Articles R.1243-54 regarding declared activities and R.1263-64 PHC regarding authorised activities.

[39] Article R.1243-55 PHC.

[40] Article L.1221-12 PHC for import/export for scientific uses of blood, blood components and derived products; Article L.1235-1 for organs and Article L.1245-5 for tissues and cells.

[41] Article R.1235-3 PHC.

3 Safeguards and Individual Data Subjects' Rights in Research Biobanks

3.1 How Research Biobanks Are Integrated Within the Data Protection Framework

The LIL is not focused on biobanks, or even mentions them, but it does directly apply to them and to the various operators implied in biobanking activities that fall under the scope of the LIL Title II, Chapter III.[42]

From a data protection law perspective, those responsible for biobanks are either the data controller, join-controller, processor or third party, depending on the processing context. Indeed, biobanks essentially function as platforms for controlling access and sharing biosamples and associated personal data for external research uses, although they can also develop their proper internal research programmes. In both cases, activities performed with personal data, including pseudonymised data, are qualified as data processing that pursues one or multiple, present or future, research purposes. Like the GDPR, the research activities covered are scientific, historical research, statistics and archiving in the public interest,[43] and includes technological research (e.g. on medical devices) and innovation.

The LIL, following its amendment in 2018, did not fundamentally change the existing framework but incorporated some of the GDPR provisions, notably those updating the right to information, and provisions regarding Data Protection Officers[44] (DPO), Data Protection Impact Assessment[45] (DPIA), data transfers[46] and CNIL remits. The LIL directly refers to the GDPR in several articles. New rules were inserted into Chapter III on accessing the National Health Data System (SNDS) databases for research purposes.

Definitions of 'personal data' and 'processing'[47] are identical to the GDPR ones. Sensitive personal data[48] are a special category of personal data whose processing is forbidden in principle, with limited exemptions including processing that is necessary for scientific research.[49] Sensitive data include data concerning health, genetics or biometrics, as defined in the GDPR. The CNIL developed a flexible approach to

---

[42] Articles 57–79, Section 4 fixing specific rules for health research, study or evaluation purposes.

[43] Articles 44(3) and (6) LIL.

[44] CNIL (2018) Referentials for the certification of DPOs' skills. https://www.cnil.fr/fr/certification-des-competences-du-dpo-la-cnil-adopte-deux-referentiels.

[45] CNIL (2018) List of activities requiring DPIA: https://www.cnil.fr/sites/default/files/atoms/files/liste-traitements-avec-aipd-requise-v2.pdf; DPIA guidelines and tools: https://www.cnil.fr/fr/PIA-privacy-impact-assessment.

[46] Title III, Chapter IV LIL.

[47] Article 2 LIL.

[48] Article 6(I) LIL.

[49] Article 6(II) and (III) referring to Article 9(2) GDPR for the list of exemptions to the initial prohibition of processing.

the notion of health data which could be so qualified due to their nature, as a result of cross-processing or by destination.[50] This allows operationalisation of the qualification. The principles[51] of lawfulness, fairness and transparency, purpose limitation, data minimisation, accuracy, integrity and confidentiality, accountability and storage limitation are identical to the GDPR.

The LIL preserves important provisions for biobanking. First, regarding the purpose limitation principle, it is with the presumption of compatibility[52] for repurposing personal data processing for scientific or historical research and statistics provided that the rules and procedures[53] are satisfied. Second, the specific exception to storage limitation for personal data to be stored after the achievement of the initial processing purpose solely for archiving purposes in the public interest, scientific, historical research or statistical purposes, in accordance with Article 89(1) GDPR.[54] In both cases, data shall be at least pseudonymised and will not serve individual decision-making.

Biobanks, as samples and data repositories, have a prominent custodian role over the legal and ethical compliance monitoring in both the deposit, the management of, and the access to, the bioresources.[55,56] Confidential and secure data management is essential, notably through the definition of access rights and procedures considering the data nature or sensitivity (anonymised/anonymous data; pseudonymised data; directly identifiable data) and through efficient mechanisms to check the adequacy of the applicant's processing purposes.[57] Biobanks' duty to ensure database security applies to facilities and ICT systems used to store, process and make available the data, including measures for external data users.[58] French quality norm NFS-96-900 on BRCs and the ISO norms, in particular ISO 20387:2018 on Biotechnology and Biobanking, together with potential new labels[59] on personal data protection, allow a certain alignment of management practices. Also, biobanks can apply to the Ministerial ASIP for specific certification of health databases hosting.[60]

---

[50] CNIL. Qu'est-ce qu'une donnée de santé? See: https://www.cnil.fr/fr/quest-ce-ce-quune-donnee-de-sante.

[51] Article4 LIL.

[52] Article 4(2) LIL.

[53] Under Title I, Chapter IV, V and Title II Chapter III LIL.

[54] Article 4(5) LIL.

[55] This presupposes the existence of a right of biobanks to refuse deposit or access requests based on legal or ethical non-compliance or uncertainties and of attached responsibilities they could endorse.

[56] E.g. Borella et al. (2006).

[57] For the biobank entry/exit points.

[58] Articles 99–102, 121–122 LIL.

[59] https://www.cnil.fr/fr/les-labels-cnil. Since March 2018, personal data protection labels are no longer issued by the CNIL itself but by certified organisations.

[60] Article L.1111-8 CSP. See Agence Française de la Santé Numérique (ASIP) website: https://esante.gouv.fr/labels-certifications/hebergement-des-donnees-de-sante.

Since 2006, the CNIL has followed the GDPR approach based on operators' accountability and modified the declaration/authorisation system to create simplified procedures intended to ensure data subjects' protection while favouring research, innovation and competitiveness. The CNIL adopted referentials (Méthodologies de Référence, MR) specifying data protection rules in research contexts. Processing within a MR scope can be implemented after a commitment of compliance with the CNIL. We will concentrate on MR001,[61] MR003[62] and MR004[63] which are particularly relevant for biobanks. The use of a particular MR depends on the qualification of the research activity. In any cases, samples and data collection must be justified. The MRs articulate the LIL and the PHC. Processing falling outside the MRs' scope need CNIL authorisation.[64] Biobanks receiving samples and data will be checkpoints.

For each selected MR, Table 1 summarises the data protection rules impacting depositors to biobanks and biobanks' users.

3.2 *Overview of Data Subjects' Rights in Research Biobanking*

Generally, in France, data subjects participating in research biobanks have similar rights to participants in classical biomedical research projects. The French law functions by analogy.

The LIL approach of research is based on opt-out (non-opposition). Opt-in consent can be required under other laws (e.g. for participating in RIHP1 and 2; MR001). Consent to sensitive personal data processing with several purposes is accepted where these are clearly, intelligibly and explicitly presented to the individuals who can opt for or refuse each one.[65] Genetic data processing is only authorised for medical or scientific purposes and based on opt-in, written, free and informed consent as required by Article 75 LIL. Nevertheless, Article L.1131-1-1 PHC explicitly allows opt-out consent where the genetic analysis is based on the reuse of already collected samples. A renewal of an individual's consent will only be necessary in case of the procurement of new samples for genetic analyses. The scope of this PHC article can be questioned as it does not explicitly cover the reuse of genetic databases without attached samples. We favour a broad interpretation with the same opt-out process for the reuse of genetic data.

Table 2 provides an overview of the 3 MRs data protection principles and individual rights to be respected by depositors and access applicants to biobank

[61] Délibération n°2018-153 du 3 mai 2018, JORF 13 juillet 2018, texte n°108.

[62] Délibération n°2018-154 du 3 mai 2018, JORF 13 juillet 2018, texte n°109.

[63] Délibération n°2018-155 du 3 mai 2018, JORF 13 juillet 2018, texte n°110.

[64] Article 66(III), 76 LIL.

[65] CNIL. Conformité RGPD: comment recueillir le consentement des personnes? See: https://www.cnil.fr/fr/conformite-rgpd-comment-recueillir-le-consentement-des-personnes.

Table 1 Scope and basic rules of CNIL MR001, MR003, MR004 for personal sensitive data processing in health research

	MR001 regarding health research requiring prior informed consent	MR003 regarding health research that does not require consent	MR004 regarding research that does not involve human persons, studies and evaluations in health
Type of research potentially including biobanking or access to biobank materials	– RIHP1. – RIHP2. – Genetic research.	– Cluster clinical trials of drugs for human use. – RIHP3. – RIHP2 for which only general public information will be provided, with CPP approval. – Genetic research.	Other research and evaluation including further uses of existing samples and data from clinical or research activities, e.g. from existing databases/biobanks/National System of Health Data (SNDS).
Impact on participant's medical taking in charge	Allowed. New acts and supplementary measures with identified risks and attached response plans.	Only minimal. Can include some supplementary measures during usual taking in charge, e.g. limited additional blood procurement.	Not allowed.
Data minimisation	Strict application of the personal data processing necessity and proportionality regarding each research purposes.		
Purpose limitation	Research with a public interest purpose only.		
Research protocol	Required in respect of the disciplinary standards		
Kind of data excluded	Any unlisted data, including geocoding data, National Identification Number, religious data, data relating to infractions.		
Possible activities connected to biobanking	– Samples' procurement (invasive) or collection (non-invasive); – Setting up of a biobank; – Access and reuse of stored samples and data.	– Samples' procurement (minimally invasive) or collection (non-invasive); – Limited sample quantity; – Setting up of a biobank; – Access and reuse of stored samples and data.	– Access and reuse of stored samples and data for this research; – Samples' pooling (existing materials); – Setting up of a biobank.
Data controller (Declarant)	Research promoter		Research manager
Administrative procedures	– Prior CPP approval. – Commitment of compliance with CNIL. – Recording of processing in DPO's registry. **Research settings falling outside the MR:** CNIL authorisation.		– Commitment of compliance with CNIL. – Recording of processing in DPO's registry. – Recording of the project in a special public registry held by the INDS. **Research settings falling outside the MR:** INDS authorisation with potential CNIL advice.

Table 2 Data subjects' rights and data protection measures in the CNIL MR001, MR003, MR004 for personal sensitive data processing in health research

	MR001 regarding health research requiring prior informed consent	MR003 regarding health research that does not require consent	MR004 regarding research that do not involve human persons, studies and evaluations in health
Prior information	Yes. General information (e.g. on site) AND individual information complying with Articles 13, 14 GDPR and with the MR rules regarding minors or legally incapable participants.	Yes. General information (e.g. on site) AND individual information complying with Articles 13, 14 GDPR and with the MR rules regarding minors or legally incapable participants. Exceptionally, only general information where justified by the methodology and with competent REC approval.	Yes. General information (e.g. on site) AND individual information complying with Articles 13, 14 GDPR and with the MR rules regarding minors or legally incapable participants. For the reuse of samples, individual information is not needed when the participants already received the information about further uses for scientific research AND about a specific device available to him for acquiring knowledge of any new processing (e.g. biobank website).
Consent rules	Free, informed, explicit and written consent (Opt-in) for participation to the research or for undertaking genetic examinations for research.	Free, informed, non-opposition (Opt-out) both for participation to the research and for underlying personal data processing. Except where opt-in consent is required for primo-processing genetic data.	
Right to refuse, to withdraw or object	Yes	Yes (refusal/objection)	
Right to erasure	Yes		
Right to restrict the processing	Yes		
Right to access	Yes		
Right to portability	The MR does not address it explicitly. Conditional application according to Article 20 GDPR.		
Data recipients	Can access directly identifying data, for specific missions related to the research: – Research professionals and stakeholders in quality assurance subject to professional secrecy; Teams from the data controller's organisation and processors acting on his/her behalf; – Teams from participating research centres. A general rule excludes the same processor from processing both directly identifying data and health data of the same individual.		

(continued)

Table 2 (continued)

	MR001 regarding health research requiring prior informed consent	MR003 regarding health research that does not require consent	MR004 regarding research that do not involve human persons, studies and evaluations in health
Storage limitation	Patients' personal data: – Until the commercialisation of the product; – Until 2 years after the last publication of results; – Until the signature of the final report of the research. Professionals' personal data: until 15 years after the end of the research. Then all the data are archived according to applicable law.		
Pseudonymisation	Yes		
DPIA[a]	Yes		
Transfers	Only where necessary to the research purposes. Only with pseudonymised data (from participants or professionals). Professionals' identifying data can exceptionally be transferred if necessary for a specific mission.		
Territorial application	Applies in France and other countries where the processed data concerns persons residing in France. Controllers established outside France can engage in compliance.		

[a]The CNIL created a software, open source and free, available in English and 18 languages, to perform and manage DPIA in compliance with the GDPR: https://www.cnil.fr/en/pia-software-20-available-and-growth-pia-ecosystem

bioresources. Biobanks verify the adequacy of deposit/access requests regarding applicable ethico-legal frameworks and ensure a continuum regarding stored materials. This table reveals that the leeway provided under Article 89(1) GDPR is not used in the MRs for particularly derogating to data subjects' rights in research.

Once personal data enter a biobank, data subjects must continuously be able to exercise their rights. Privacy policies should be easily available to the public. Most of the French biobanks certified NFS-96-900 meet specific requirements that are in line with transparency such as in maintaining external communication regarding availability of the collections, terms of access and quality measures.

4 The National Exceptions to Individual Rights and the Role of Public Interest

4.1 Exceptions Regarding Data Subjects' Rights for Personal Data Processing in Research

Biobanking necessitates special measures to be able to process personal data over the long-term for future, quite broadly defined, uses. The GDPR has made available several means for Member States to derogate from individual rights for the benefit of scientific developments under certain conditions. The GDPR's flexibility is preserved in French law.

Regarding in particular the right to access, the LIL includes a special derogation 'where the personal data are stored in a form that manifestly excludes any risk as regard to privacy and data protection'. This exemption will last only for the duration necessary to reach the statistical or research processing purposes.[66] Nevertheless, it is difficult to determine which situations are being targeted. Does that open a notion of 'relative anonymity' or '*de facto* anonymity'[67] based on each processing context, purpose, and technical and organisational measures in place to protect identity and the means reasonably likely to be used for (re)identifying the data subject?

Like the GDPR, the LIL explicitly provides exceptions regarding the right to information prior to the processing when respect for this right proves impossible or involves disproportionate efforts compared to the risks of the processing. These derogations are only planned in the context of indirect data collection and in the context of further uses of already collected data, either for storage, for historical, statistical or scientific purposes, or for further processing for statistical purposes.[68] So, these exceptions could be invoked either before including the indirectly collected data in the biobank or after, at the time of accessing the bioresources, for the reuse of existing biobanks' samples or databases in research, including for genetic research. The data subject can also decide not to be informed where it would lead to reveal a diagnosis or prognosis.[69] Such exceptional circumstances necessitate justification and could trigger, for the research promoter, the CNIL authorisation procedure, the MRs requiring data subjects to be informed, and REC approval for reuses in RIPH.

Article 110 LIL allows derogations to the right to oppose to a processing where this latter answers to a legal obligation imposed to the controller or processor or where it is explicitly planned by the act authorising the processing.

Recently, lawyers criticised[70] the way the GDPR forces communication of the research promoter's DPO contact details within information notices provided to data subjects in clinical trials, claiming that DPO involvement could breach medical secret of which the sole investigator is the guarantor. Furthermore, they claim that the Clinical Trial Regulation is the special law that makes the investigator the only contact of the participants for exercising their rights. Therefore, in their opinion, DPO contact should not be provided. To date, the CNIL has not gone against GDPR.

The LIL refers to the GDPR provisions regarding the implementation of other rights, in particular regarding the right to limit processing, the right to data portability, the right to oppose and the data breach notification process.

Research exemptions to individual rights are not entirely fixed in France. Ordinance n°2018-1125 mentions the future adoption of a Decree determining the conditions and guarantees under which exemptions to data subjects' rights planned by Article 89.2 GDPR regarding its Articles 15 (access), 16 (erasure), 18

---

[66] Article 49(II) LIL.

[67] Sariyar and Schlünder (2016).

[68] Articles 116(II) and (III), 79 LIL.

[69] Article 69 LIL.

[70] Roche (2018).

(restriction) and 21 (right to object) could apply.[71] At the same time, exceptions to certain of these rights remain possible on a case-by-case basis. As the GDPR provides, such derogations could be accepted where the processing is necessary for scientific research purposes, it is lawful, where data minimisation is strictly respected, in so far as such rights are likely to render impossible or seriously impair the achievement of the specific purposes and such derogations are necessary for the fulfilment of those purposes.[72]

4.2 *The Public Interest Purpose of Processing in French Law*

Since 2016, the notion of 'public interest' has been central for processing personal data in health research. Any processing in this field must contribute to the public interest,[73] including for using simplified procedures (above-mentioned MRs). The public interest purpose is an actionable means to derogate from some general principles of personal data processing. Regarding the initial prohibition of processing sensitive data, Article 6(II) and (III) LIL allows controllers to process personal health data where the research processing pursues the public interest in respect of Title II Chapter III, including public health. The public interest purpose of the research processing also explicitly allows justified exceptions to the right to erasure[74] and base adaptations of the right to information, to oppose and to data access for minors participating in certain types of research (further detailed below, Sect. 5.1).[75] Outside archiving, the public interest purpose is not mentioned to exempt from the storage limitation principle in a research context. Data controllers involved in archiving in the public interest can derogate[76] from the rights established under Articles 15, 16 and 18 to 21 of the GDPR.

But this blurry notion is problematic, in particular where competent authorities (CNIL and INDS) can refuse data processing requests based on this criterion. In 2016, under the auspices of the INDS, a legal interpretation[77] of the notion enabled the identification of useful specifications for avoiding misunderstandings. This expertise provides that 'public interest' is a synonym of 'general interest' and 'collective benefit'. Therefore, any uses essentially motivated by private purposes or aiming at re-identifying patients, or targeting prescription behaviours of health professionals for commercial purposes (e.g. in order to promote health products) are excluded from the public interest. The notion can be further understood by considering details provided

[71] Ordonnance n°2018-1125, JORF 13 décembre 2018, Article 78.

[72] Décret n°2018-687 du 1er août 2018, op.cit. Article 23, Section 5; Article 100-1 of the consolidated version.

[73] Article 66 LIL; Article L.1460-1 PHC.

[74] Article 78 LIL ; see previous 40(II) old LIL.

[75] Article 70 LIL.

[76] Article 78 LIL.

[77] Polton and Caillé (2017). In particular pp. 48–49 list forbidden or admissible acts regarding the requirement of public interest.

within Article L.1461-1 (III) PHC dedicated to the SNDS, access to which is only granted to applicants pursuing the public interest. Without explicitly mentioning it, this Article states that SNDS makes available health data in order to contribute to the information on health and health service provision; on medico-social care and their quality; to the definition, implementation and assessment of public health and social protection policies; to the knowledge of health, social security and medico-social expenditures; to the information of professionals, structures and health or medico-social establishments on their activity; to health monitoring and safety; to research, studies, evaluation and innovation in the fields of health and medico-social taking in charge. Furthermore, Article 66(1) of the LIL explicitly identifies personal data processing implemented for ensuring a high level of quality and security of healthcare, drugs and medical devices as a public interest purpose. The CNIL can always consult the INDS to evaluate a public interest purpose.

5 GDPR Impact and Future Possibilities for Biobanking

5.1 French Specificities

French law integrates the GDPR and further develops individual rights on several points of interest for researchers.

First, the LIL states that personal data stored as research results are only accessible and modifiable by persons authorised by the data controller, in the respect of deontology. Personal data as research results must be anonymised before communication to thirds, except where the third's interest in the communication overweigh data subject's ones. In this regard the CNIL can approve anonymisation mechanisms.[78] Then, anonymised data are no longer subject to the LIL.

Second, while the GDPR excludes its application to deceased persons, the LIL ensures privacy protection after a data subject's death with a new right to write and record advanced directives on personal data management. The directives will be implemented by a trustee identified by the data subject before his death or by a person designated by law. Here, the French legislator conceives of and protects the privacy of individuals as a continuum that death does not break. It is thus possible that a data subject can ask for restricted processing or erasure or, interestingly, to donate personal data from various sources to research organisations, which includes a biobank. These instructions shall be legally valid.

Data subjects' rights adaptations have been introduced to ease the implementation of RIHP2, T3 and other studies or assessments in the field of health that pursue a public interest purpose and involve minors. By derogation, Article 59 LIL allows prior information on the processing to be provided to only one of the holders of the parental authority if it is impossible to inform the other or if he/she cannot be consulted within a timeframe compatible with the specific methodological

[78] Article 8(II)(i) LIL.

requirements of the research with regard to its purposes. This does not restrict the exercise, later on, by each holder of the parental authority, of the data subject's rights they have by law. Article 70 also enables new rights that increase the minor's autonomy in such research. The minor (aged 15 or more) may oppose the holders of parental authority receiving prior information about research participation where this leads to revealing information about an action of prevention, a screening, a diagnosis, a treatment or an intervention for which the minor expressly opposed the consultation of the holders of parental authority,[79] or when family ties are broken and the minor personally benefits from appropriate insurance. The minor may also oppose data access exercised by the holders of parental authority to personal data collected during the project. The minor exercises his/her rights alone or accompanied by a major of his/her choice.

5.2 *Perspectives Regarding Research and Biobanking*

While a decree about national derogations from certain data subjects' rights under Article 89 GDPR is expected, France launched in 2016 its national plan for genomic-medicine[80] with the aim of completing every year 200,000 human genome sequences. This will necessitate efforts in terms of samples and data storage and processing capacities but also a clear and appropriate legal and ethical framework. These new activities, plus the current revision of the bioethics law, highlight the new challenges for research biobanking.

A first set of challenges relates to the development of new techniques in genomics and the future capability to store and use bigger sets of genomic data in the form of Whole Genome/Exome sequencing. The CCNE[81] and the State Council[82] have taken a position on this matter, both favouring the practice of 'enlarged informed consent' or 'consent by delegation' based on the monitoring functions of competent and independent trusted third parties[83] for genetic research, notably for the purpose of reuse of data. Of course, both acknowledge the need to ensure respect for the fundamental rights of individuals involved in such research and that there will be some difficulty to enforce those rights during the duration of the research. As such, they proposed to rely on new mechanisms involving either research ethics

[79] In application of articles L.1111-5 and L.1111-5-1 PHC.

[80] Aviesan. Genomic Medicine France 2025. https://www.aviesan.fr/mediatheque/fichiers/version-anglaise/actualites-en/genomic-medicine-france-2025-web.

[81] CCNE, Avis 129, 2018. https://www.ccne-ethique.fr/sites/default/files/avis_129_vf.pdf. See p. 67.

[82] Conseil d'Etat (2018). Révision de la loi de bioéthique: quelles options pour demain? 28 June 2018. https://www.conseil-etat.fr/ressources/etudes-publications/rapports-etudes/etudes/revision-de-la-loi-de-bioethique-quelles-options-pour-demain. See p. 157.

[83] E.g. Research ethics committees. Biobanks' internal independent review mechanisms could qualify.

committees or an independent trusted third party in conjunction with supplying a high level of information of participants. However, the Council rejected solutions such as broad unspecified consent and dynamic consent because of their legal or technical implications (see footnote 10).

A second set of issues relates to research on human embryos, notably the creation, in research, of transgenic, chimeric embryos; the use of induced pluripotent stem cells and their ethical impact on the use of 'natural' human embryos; and the need to recognise by law the 14-day deadline limiting embryo cultures in research. A final challenge is the upcoming debate from a collective perspective of the implications of the production and use of large datasets through artificial intelligence or genetic testing/sequencing to be routinely provided in the health care system and/or commercially. This should take in their negative effects on solidarity, equality, the risk of genetic reductionism, stigmatisation and discrimination.

6 Conclusions

Currently, the French regulatory environment for research biobanking remains complex and fragmented due to the fragmented nature of the legislation to comply with. Data protection law is a common feature of any type of health research and biobank processing of personal data, whether the latter are attached to, or generated from, a biological sample, with a risk-based approach for identifying requirements to be met by researchers and biobankers. The GDPR has been fully implemented, with the potential for further developments offered by its Article 89. We acknowledge the efforts made by the CNIL to provide operators with explanatory and practical toolkits that ease both procedures and GDPR-compliance. CNIL action is pragmatic and proactive, which are good qualities that can be used by DPO networks for the purpose of boosting the understanding and adoption of a data protection culture, and will lead to innovations in data protection.

Nevertheless, we think that important deficiencies remain in biobanking regulation. The very specific role of biobanks is not fully addressed or recognised and some contexts of biobanking need further regulatory clarification. Thus, we call for the elaboration of a French Biobank Management Act to compile and develop further the rules applicable to research biobanking that would consider existing and new issues encountered by operators and the views of citizens.

References

Borella L, Dupont M, Hebert JC, Janin A, Lubin R. Pour l'INCA (2006) Charte Ethique des Tumorothèques. Ed. 2010

Clément B, Duyckaerts C, Hauw JJ, Ardaillou R (2019) Rapporteurs au nom de la Commission Biologie-génétique-technologie biomédicales. Académie Nationale de Médecine. Rapport. Sustainability of biological resource centres: a major challenge for biomedical research

Polton D, Caillé Y (2017) Cabinet Simmons & Simmons, pour l'INDS. Expertise juridique sur l'intérêt public dans le contexte des données de santé. V.2

Roche T (2018) Delsol Avocats. Article. ePub. Les coordonnées du DPO du promoteur ne doivent pas figurer sur les fiches d'information destinées aux personnes se prêtant à des recherches cliniques ! http://www.delsolavocats.fr/sdv/en/les-coordonnees-du-dpo-du-promoteur-ne-doivent-pas-figurer-sur-les-fiches-dinformation-destinees-aux-personnes-se-pretant-a-des-recherches-cliniques/

Sariyar M, Schlünder I (2016) Reconsidering anonymization-related concepts and the term "identification" against the backdrop of the European legal framework. Biopreserv Biobank 14(5):367–374

Société Française de Microbiologie (2014) Manuel de Sécurité et de Sûreté Biologiques, 1st edn. ISBN: 978-2-87805-030-1

The Regulation of Biobanking in Germany

Nils Hoppe

Abstract Biobanking in Germany is currently not subject to *sui generis* regulation. Instead, a plethora of norms from differing areas of law form the bundle of regulation that applies to biobanking. The exact shape and extent of the bundle depends on the exact configuration of the biobank. In the context of data protection, the rather fragmented nature of the regulation is to a certain extent alleviated by the direct impact of the EU General Data Protection Regulation (GDPR). In particular, the federalized system of data protection in Germany is simplified by an overarching set of norms that apply equally across the board. Whilst this is a welcome systematization of this part of the regulation of biobanking in Germany, the exact nature of the implementation of the Regulation raises novel issues in its own right. In this paper, I will outline the fragmented nature of biobank regulation in Germany, illustrate the issues on the basis of Germany's population biobank NaKo and then discuss some of the more significant issues raised by the GDPR in the context of biobanking.

1 Introduction

Despite lengthy public debate and consultation between 2010 and 2012, and a subsequent attempt to introduce biobank-specific legislation, there is still no specific statutory basis for the regulation of tissue- and biobanks in Germany.[1] Instead, there is an historically grown thicket of norms of varying pedigree and weight. In many cases, these norms come from associated areas and have simply been applied to the context of biobanking. In other cases, very abstract norms of civil liability or privacy protection are applied to biomaterials for research. In this chapter I will briefly outline the general regulatory environment, before turning my attention to Germany's large population-based biobank (*Nationale Kohorte*) as an illustration of biobank operation in the German regulatory sphere. I will then briefly address

[1] Herbst (2016), p. 371.

N. Hoppe (✉)
CELLS - Centre for Ethics and Law in the Life Sciences, University of Hannover, Hannover, Germany
e-mail: nils.hoppe@cells.uni-hannover.de

S. Slokenberga et al. (eds.), *GDPR and Biobanking*, Law, Governance and Technology Series 43, https://doi.org/10.1007/978-3-030-49388-2_15

general issues in biobanking before turning my attention exclusively on the scenario of regulating a research biobank. This is where I will discuss issues of data protection, privacy and informational self-determination, before turning to a discussion of individual rights, which are then, finally, put into the context of derogating from those rights under the provisions of Article 89 GDPR.

2 Biobanks and the Regulatory Environment

2.1 General Remarks

Based on the lack of specific legislation in relation to biobanks, commentators often turn to the definitions developed by the German Ethics Council over time in order to identify the scope of what constitutes a biobank. Given the disparate nature of regulation in this area, it makes sense to settle a definition for the purpose of this analysis. The most common and broad definition is that of a collection of human biological material, connected with corresponding personal data.[2] In the absence of specific legislation, it is this combination of tangible and intangible artefacts that provides the starting point for the identification of the current regulatory environment and further defines the legal challenges which this area poses.[3] The law has, traditionally, a strong tendency to compartmentalize the regulation of tangible and intangible assets, and therefore also the rights associated with those assets.[4] Human biomaterials represent a challenge to the clear dichotomy expected by the law and this is why biobanking represents a particularly fascinating regulatory target.

The difficulties caused by the sheer volume of the resulting regulation are further exacerbated by the fact that, if we accept this broad definition, biobanks may serve purely research purposes, or they may serve clinical and diagnostic purposes. For any of these scenarios the regulatory framework is specific and not easily transferable.[5] In the clinical context, in particular where a biobank explicitly stores biomaterials for future therapeutic use in humans, the German implementation of Directive 2004/23/EC contains provisions which incorporate the law relating to pharmaceutical products. This would increase the complexity of the discussion by an order of magnitude. For the purposes of this paper I will therefore concentrate on the regulation of research biobanks but will outline the basic regulatory requirements of other types of biobanks in Sect. 2.2 below.

[2] Ethikrat (2004).
[3] Albers (2013), p. 486.
[4] Hoppe (2009).
[5] Robienski (2010), pp. 57ff.

2.2 Germany's Population Biobank: Nationale Kohorte

Germany's large-scale population biobank *Nationale Kohorte* (NaKo) is still the most informative case study for outlining regulatory approaches to biobanking in Germany. NaKo's aim was to recruit 200,000 participants aged between 20 and 69 in 18 centres distributed across Germany, which it succeeded in doing five years ago. Biological samples were taken and subsequently stored, and participants were interviewed in relation to their lifestyle circumstances, with the second round of interviews (in order to pinpoint changes) being imminent.[6] Up to 20% of the participants provided extended health data, and around 30,000 participants underwent full-body medical imaging. NaKo is therefore a sizeable operation the scope of which gives rise to an illustrative set of regulatory issues.

NaKo's aim is to track individual participants' health over an extended period (25–30 years) and it is therefore established for the long term. The biobank is incorporated as a charitable entity (*eingetragener Verein)* led by a board of directors (similar to trustees). The charitable objective of NaKo is the support and development of epidemiological long-term research in the interests of society. The internal regulatory framework of the biobank (such as data access and use policies) are decided by the membership of the charity. Samples and data are generated, stored and processed in each of the 18 centres, though the main facility is the Helmholtz Centre in Munich. Personal data are pseudonymised, or coded, and NaKo pursues a trusted-third-party concept of code custodianship (*Treuhandstelle*) to control the keys for decoding datasets.

The incorporation of NaKo as a charity had direct impact on the scope of relevant regulation, as the controlling interest in the charity rested with public bodies, rendering NaKo a public body in its own right. In the absence of a specific statutory right to process personal data within the biobank, full informed consent is acquired.[7] The overarching duty to reduce the amount of identifiable personal data as far as technically possible[8] necessitates the custodianship coding of data for the vast majority of data points. A full anonymisation of the data would render the proposed research impracticable. German law knows additional regulatory sources for the protection of what are termed 'social data' (i.e. data processed for the purposes of providing health and social care related services). These are covered by specific statutory duties of confidentiality.[9] Any sharing of data with third parties is only permitted with the explicit consent of the individual participant[10] and in accordance with a licence granted by the appropriate authority.[11] NaKo's staff are also bound by

---

[6] https://nako.de/blog/2019/05/03/die-nako-gesundheitsstudie-geht-in-die-zweite-runde/.

[7] §4(1) BDSG (German Federal Data Protection Act).

[8] §3(a) BDSG.

[9] §35 SGB I (German Social Security Act).

[10] §67b SGB X.

[11] §75 SGB X.

a statutory duty to keep personal secrets confidential.[12] In addition, whilst individual participants sign a release waiving their treating physicians' duty to maintain confidentiality as regards NaKo, all registered medical professionals are bound by their professional duties of confidentiality (depending on which profession they belong to).

NaKo's consent is initially time limited to five years. This period is extended by a further five years respectively in perpetuity unless the participant withdraws consent in the meantime. Within each consent time span, the consent continues to have effect even if the participant loses capacity or dies. One exception to the five-year rule is the ongoing processing of health and register data which have to be regularly re-consented.

NaKo has established their consent documentation as a bundle of individual consents with differing quality and reach. Consent is sought separately to the initial interview and health data gathering, to data processing and storage of data, permission to share data with funders, procurement, storage and use of biological samples, feedback of incidental findings, further procurement of health and social data (secondary and register data), recontacting, and exclusion of commercial use.

The participants can withdraw any or all of these individual consents with the subsequent use of the data and material then depending on what is still permissible. The participant's withdrawal has to be communicated in writing, on a specific form provided by NaKo, though the process can be triggered by telephone or by e-mail. The withdrawal is then communicated to all centres as well as to the custodian of the coding keys, and recorded in NaKo's information management system. Where there is doubt in relation to the exact extent of the participant's withdrawal, NaKo interprets the withdrawal in the widest possible way. The scale of NaKo has enabled the biobank to establish some pioneering processes which are likely to serve as best practice models to other establishments that fall into the same category. It is worth briefly addressing the regulatory challenges of biobanking in general, before turning our attention to individual rights in research biobanking.

2.3 *Biobanking in General*

The general regulatory framework for histological and pathological collections is insufficient to capture the complexity of the work in research biobanks, such as the one outlined above. Indeed, this is what poses the bulk of the legal challenge in the regulation of biobanking.[13] The very broad definition of biobanking which was outlined at the outset does, however, also capture other types of biobanks[14] and it is useful to briefly outline these here.

[12] §203 StGB (German Penal Code).

[13] Albers (2013), p. 486.

[14] Robienski (2010), pp. 57ff.

The EU's Human Tissue Directive (2004/23/EC) was transposed into domestic law through a collection of amendments in the Tissue Act (*Gewebegesetz*). This path to implementation, rather than through a single, consolidated instrument, has led to scattered and unhelpfully structured regulation. Licensing for tissue establishments, for example, were incorporated into the Pharmaceutical Products Act (*Arzneimittelgesetz*). The scope of tissue establishments follows the provisions of the Directive, incorporating tissue banks, hospital departments and all other establishments within which any activities are carried out that involve the processing, preservation, storage or distribution of human tissues and cells. This also includes the procurement and testing of such materials. Following the German Ethics Council's definition of biobank, where an establishment collects tissues, bloods or organs for clinical purposes (including diagnostics), these would fall under the scope of *tissue establishment* as defined by the Directive. This difficult juxtaposition of regulatory approaches makes it necessary to clearly delineate research biobanks (following the definitions in 2013/701/EU) in order to systematize the different normative frameworks. When following this, narrower, definition of biobank (which we will do for the purposes of this paper), it becomes increasingly clear that a specific regulation for research biobanking in Germany is still a long way off.[15]

2.4 Data Protection, Privacy and Informational Self-Determination in Biobanking

Article 8 of the *European Convention for the Protection of Human Rights and Fundamental Freedoms* (ECHR) provides for protection of an individual's private and family life. This foundational principle, naturally, also applies in Germany and it is directly relevant to questions of privacy and informational self-determination in biobanking: the European Court of Human Rights has held that Article 8 rights also extend to collections of biometric data.[16] The Council of Europe does provide additional protection in Article 10 of the *Convention for the Protection of Human Rights and Dignity of the Human Being with Regard to the Application of Biology and Medicine* (the 'Oviedo Convention'). Whilst the Oviedo Convention has no immediate impact as Germany has neither signed nor ratified it, there is a compelling argument that, when applied to life sciences cases, Convention jurisprudence emanating from Strasbourg is always also likely to be imbued with Oviedo considerations, assumptions and precedent. Convention rights can only be enforced against states and not against private entities. Any privacy-related action on the basis of Convention rights cumbersome or even impossible where the biobank in question is

[15] Herbst (2016), p. 371; Schmidt am Busch et al. (2016), p. 365; Albers (2013), p. 484; Robienski (2010), p. 63.

[16] S and Marper v. The UK [2008] ECHR 1581, (2009) 48 EHRR 50, 25 BHRC 557, 48 EHRR 50, [2009] Crim LR 355.

a private or quasi-private entity (which gives additional weight to the question whether a biobank qualifies as an emanation of the state, or quasi-public body—see the NaKo discussion above).

Previously, common data protection norms were introduced through relevant OECD guidelines (1980)[17] and Conventions (1981).[18] In 1995 the EC Directive *on the Protection of Individuals with Regard to the Processing of Personal Data and on the Free Movement of Such Data* (95/46/EC) was enacted. Commentators have described it as

> [...] by far the most influential, comprehensive and complex international policy instrument, enacted to enshrine two of the oldest ambitions of the European integrations project, namely [...] an Internal Market [...] and the protection of fundamental rights and freedoms [...] [20].

As European Directives are not directly applicable in the member states but have to be implemented by way of enacting national legislation, member states were given until 24 October 1998 to make appropriate domestic provisions.

The broad cornerstones were common across the European Union: any data collected had to be accurate; the collection had to be legitimated (for example through appropriate consent, or by way of a statutory right); the data subject had to be given access to information about themselves, as well as the right to object; the data had to be secure and treated confidentially; data collection, storage and processing had to be notified to a public oversight body. Additionally, the Directive established certain categories of data which enjoyed special protection: data revealing racial or ethnic origin, political opinions, religious or philosophical beliefs, trade union membership, and health or sex life. For the purposes of Convention rights, the European Court of Human Rights has previously held that genetic information, in particular, is inherently in this category of sensitive data[19] and there is no reasonable argument that this was not also the case in relation to genetic data under Directive 95/46/EC. The widespread entry into force of the EU General Data Protection Regulation (GDPR) has not manifestly changed these fundamental considerations of approaches to data protection, but has put on a statutory footing the consensus that genetic and biometric data are special by allowing member states to create special provisions.[20]

The aim having been to create a certain degree of convergence in data protection law, a nonetheless rather eclectic mix of '[...] legal and quasi-legal instruments on

[17] OECD: Recommendation of the Council Concerning Guidelines Governing the Protection of Privacy and Transborder Flows of Personal Data of 23 September 1980, available at http://www.oecd.org/sti/ieconomy/oecdguidelinesontheprotectionofprivacyandtransborderflowsofpersonaldata.htm.

[18] Council of Europe: Convention for the Protection of Individuals with regard to Automatic Processing of Personal Data, available at http://conventions.coe.int/Treaty/en/Treaties/Html/108.htm.

[19] Marper (at no. 16 above), at para. 75.

[20] Recital 53, GDPR.

data protection [...]'[21] was the result in the Member States. The effect of the directive was therefore that there was still significant variance across member state borders on privacy protection. In addition, the German implementation of privacy is found in a combination of constitutional and data protection norms, having existed in a very similar form well before any legislative initiative at EU level. The constitutional norms, having developed over decades of finely tuned jurisprudence, do not easily yield to supranational efforts at reform. Only minimal impact of more recent legislative interventions such as the EU GDPR is therefore to be expected.

Addressing the pre-existing domestic German setting, concepts of privacy feature strongly in German constitutional law by virtue of Article 2(1) and Article 1(1) of the German constitution (*Grundgesetz*). Article 2(1) implements 'general personality rights' of individuals, and Article 1(1) establishes the inalienability of the individuals' dignity. Taken together, these two constitutional principles form the basis for an individual's right to informational self-determination, based on a 1983 decision by the Federal Constitutional Court (*Bundesverfassungsgericht*). In a landmark ruling caused by the national census,[22] the Court held that the activity of large-scale collection, storage and processing of personal data is capable of infringing an individual's fundamental right to privacy, and thereby impinge on their dignity. Each individual is entitled to decide autonomously about providing information about themselves, and how this information is subsequently used. These fundamental concepts and the doctrine of informational self-determination apply equally to data storage in the context of biobanking, and significantly limit a biobanks' ability to work without specific consent or refuse withdrawal of consent.

The combination of supranational, constitutional and ordinary domestic frameworks mean that German data protection law is fragmented across instruments and jurisdictions. The entry into force of the GDPR has to a certain extent reduced this fragmentation but by no means eliminated it. At the same time, the common, pre-existing principles as outlined already overlap with generally accepted notions of privacy protection and there is therefore no prima facie conflict between the relevant instruments: The data subject has to be informed about the extent and quality of the data processing, only as much data should be collected as absolutely necessary and any data use must be proportionate, the data may only be used for the purpose for which they were collected, the data subject has significant control over the data, there has to be a due process for disputes in relation to data, and the data must be kept secure and confidential. These fundamental requirements are mirrored across all of the instruments and jurisdictions which are in play in this context.

[21] Forgó et al. (2010), at no. 245.

[22] BVerfG, Judgment of 15.12.1983, Az. 1 BvR 209, 269, 362, 420, 440, 484/83.

2.5 Other Sources of Regulation

Despite the lack of specific regulation for biobanks, a great deal of governance can be found in various instruments which apply to this context. As briefly outlined above, international and supranational norms within geographical and political Europe provide a strong human rights-based framework for the protection of privacy, and individuals are able to take complaints in relation to a domestic failure to implement these protections to the European Court of Human Rights in Strasbourg (in the case of Convention rights) or as an infringement action to the European Commission who may subsequently take it to the European Court of Justice.[23]

The German domestic framework consists partly of norms which have been developed in parallel to international regulatory efforts, and partly the implementation of supranational legislation. It is deeply rooted in constitutional law and data protection law, both of which provide for a high level of protection of the individual's privacy. It opens up a number of possible remedies for individuals to lodge a complaint and enforce their rights through courts and regulatory bodies. The fragmented nature of data protection law in Germany has given rise to the development of a backdrop of regulatory law, steered originally by the states' individual data protection laws, together with additional secondary or canonic norms, which are regulated and enforced by data protection offices at state level. In addition, the generally applicable rules found in civil law (e.g. on property rights and liability) and criminal law (e.g. on confidentiality) imbue this framework with further rights and obligations.

3 Individual Rights

3.1 General Remarks

In common with other jurisdictions, the valid consent of individuals who provide data and material is the starting point for addressing individual rights in biobanking. In Germany, the origins of this analysis stem from Articles 2(1) and 1(1) GG, which, as we have already seen, guarantee the free expression of an individual's personality rights, and the inalienability of that individual's dignity. This also means that a patient is the final arbiter of what is to be done with or to their own body. In German civil law, this means that the patient can permit or refuse interactions based on general restitution norms.[24] This applies equally to interactions with a biobank, ranging from procurement of material and data to continuous storage and processing of material and data. Additionally, there is in many cases a private contractual duty for a physician to ensure that patients are fully informed and has adequately consented

[23] Article 258 of the Treaty on the Functioning of the European Union.

[24] §§823ff BGB (German Civil Code).

to the proposed procedure.[25] It is the full, valid consent of the individual which negates the criminality of the touching, which would otherwise amount to an assault.[26]

3.2 *Professional Regulation*

In addition, individual rights can be found in a range of professional regulations covering the exact duties of registered medical professionals to obtain and document informed consent. These types of professional norms are only binding on physicians and other regulated medical professionals, thereby leaving biomedical researchers (who are not also physicians) outside of their remit. This is particularly relevant when analysing the regulatory context of biobanking, as most staff will likely not be registered medical practitioners §8 of the Bundesärztekammer's (German General Medical Council) code of conduct for physicians[27] includes a duty to specifically inform a patient and obtain consent. The lower the clinical need for an intervention, the higher the duty to provide specific information in order to obtain an adequate consent. Where material is procured purely for research biobanking purposes, the information obligation on the physician is correspondingly high. In §15 the code of conduct incorporates the provisions of the Declaration of Helsinki, as well as a requirement to obtain advice from an appropriate ethics committee where the research concerns identifiable individuals' material and data.

3.3 *Constitutional Rights*

There is a long history of public debate on the protection of privacy in Germany. Shaped by the twentieth century experience of two oppressive regimes with utter disregard for individual liberties, there is a great deal of sensitivity around the inviolability of individuals' private spheres. In 1983, the German constitutional court had to decide how much control individuals have over personal information collected as part of a national census.[28] In this decision, the court developed the doctrine of *informational self-determination*, based on fundamental constitutional rights.

---

[25] Deutsch and Spickhoff (2014), no. 103ff.

[26] §§ 223ff StGB.

[27] BÄK (2018) (Muster-)Berufsordnung für die in Deutschland tätigen Ärztinnen und Ärzte. https://www.bundesaerztekammer.de/fileadmin/user_upload/downloads/pdf-Ordner/MBO/MBO-AE.pdfhttps://www.bundesaerztekammer.de/fileadmin/user_upload/downloads/pdf-Ordner/MBO/MBO-AE.pdf. Accessed 10 Sep 2020

[28] *Volkszählungsurteil, BVerfG,* Judgment of *15.12.1983, Az. 1 BvR 209, 269, 362, 420, 440, 484/83.*

3.4 Data Subject Rights

The recent incorporation of the EU's General Data Protection Regulation into the fragmented domestic legislative framework underpinned and explicated existing data subject rights. These include the right to access one's own health information.[29]

Where the data in question are genetic data, there may be a statutory bar to divulging this information even to the data subject, save in circumstances where a specially trained geneticist can convey and interpret the information.[30] This provision only applies to genetic information that is congenital in nature or acquired during the process of fertilisation.[31] Where the data concerns other types of stored tissue, for example in the context of a tumour biobank, these provisions do not apply. In addition, these safeguards only apply in the context of the first communication of the data to the data subject and not thereafter.[32] It is not immediately obvious whether the GenDG distinguishes clearly between raw genetic data and diagnoses or findings based on the raw data, though given that patients are able to us the raw data to pinpoint possible mutations using nothing more than a targeted internet search, it seems plausible that raw data are also captured by these restraints.[33]

Where the data in question are generated by the biobank in a research context only, there is still a prima facie right to access these data on the basis of the federal data protection legislation. Some commentators also suggest that there is a concurrent contractual obligation (based on §810 BGB) between the processor of the data and the data subject which entitles the data subject to inspect these data.[34] In the case of biobanks that are attached to a clinical setting (i.e. hospital-based biobanking), data generated through research activities (rather than diagnostic processes) may be considered part of the patient's health record,[35] which carries great significance when discussing obligations in relation to incidental findings in biobanks. There is therefore an assumption of strong data subject rights flowing from both the provisions of the GDPR, as well as from pre-existing German constitutional and civil law. The practice of requiring data subjects to contract out of these data subject rights (as is sometimes attempted through general terms and conditions, or as part of the consent documentation) is not permitted.[36] It is, however, possible to derogate from a data subject's rights on the basis that the process of providing access to data is disproportionately onerous.[37] It is these provisions that attempt to strike the difficult balance between the data subjects' rights (flowing from Article 2 (1) and 1 (1)

[29] § 630g BGB; § 16 NDSG; §§ 34, 57 BDSG; Article 15 Regulation (EU) 2016/679.

[30] §11 GenDG.

[31] Erbs (2017), GenDG (German Genetic Diagnostics Act) § 3 no. 1.

[32] Fleischer et al. (2016), pp. 481ff.

[33] Fleischer et al. (2016), p. 484.

[34] Fleischer et al. (2016), pp. 481–491.

[35] §630g BGB.

[36] §56 BDSG.

[37] §27 (2) BDSG.

GG) and the researchers' corresponding constitutional rights of academic freedom (Article 5 (3) GG, but also in Article 13 of the Charter of Fundamental Rights, and—to a certain extent—Article 179 TFEU). In both the pure research biobank setting, as well as the hospital-based biobank setting, there are strong data subject rights entitling individuals to access to their personal data, albeit on different legal bases. Additional complexity is the result where genetic diagnoses are involved. The adequate balancing of data subject rights and the biobank's socially desirable research activity is a matter for highly nuanced contractual, consent and information documentation and appropriate protocols. On the basis of these norms, it is evident that data in a biobank ought to always be re-identifiable, otherwise the targeted deletion of personal data upon request, or the granting of access to the data would be frustrated by design. The same is true for the transfer of data to third parties (i.e. it must be ensured that the data subject's rights are not frustrate through such transfers). In some cases, the individual's data has already been included in aggregated datasets for the purposes of analysis and subsequent publication. It is generally agreed that it is acceptable to define a pragmatic 'point of no return' after which the deletion of individual personal data from such datasets would be disproportionately onerous and therefore no longer necessary.

4 Article 89 and the Impact of GDPR

A number of issues arise following the entry into force of the General Data Protection Regulation. In particular, for the purposes of biobanking, some important terms remain undefined in domestic law. This concerns the term 'research'[38] which has no corresponding explication in the German federal data protection legislation, as well as the exact scope of 'personal data'[39] or 'pseudonymisation'.[40] Neither does the German implementation provide for any purpose limitation.[41] Where this is the case, the provisions of the GDPR apply directly. The rules pertaining to the consent of individual biobank participants correlate with the established informed consent and the impact of the GDPR is limited to a more express requirement to make the withdrawal of consent as easy as possible.[42] In terms of the giving of broad consent, recital 33 opens up the possibility of giving consent to certain *areas of research* and refers back to 'recognised ethical standards'. This is, in part, a departure from the paradigmatic principle of specific, informed consent that has until now been a particular challenge to data-driven biomedical research. A debate on whether biobanks fall within the scope of the term research—given that they, in most cases, are

[38] Recital 159 GDPR.

[39] Article 4 (1) GDPR.

[40] Article 4 (5) GDPR.

[41] Articles 5 (1) b. and 6 (4) GDPR.

[42] Articles 9 (1) a, 89, recital 33 GDPR; §§ 51, 27 BDSG.

repositories rather than research-active entities does not seem to be in any way meaningful. It is in my submission clear from the drafting of Art. 89 that a biobank, as a combination of archiving and scientific research-facilitation, falls squarely within the envisaged exemptions of the GDPR. Recital 158 GDPR makes it clearer what kind of archiving the European legislator had in mind, as it limits the scope to those archives that fulfil a public duty and are therefore public entities.

The derogations contained in Art. 89 of the Regulation create an important window of opportunity for research-related processing of personal data. At the same time, there is an almost inevitable collision between the right of informational self-determination (as outlined above) and the right to academic freedom. Most importantly, the research-focused derogations from the stringent provisions of the GDPR, such as those provided for in Articles 5 (1) e. and 89 GDPR can be found in the German federal legislation.[43]

The German implementation immediately derogates from Article 9(1) of the Regulation, making it lawful to process personal data for scientific and historical research purposes in the teeth of an individual's dissent, as long as it is proportionate to do so under the circumstances, and as long as there are technical measures in place to protect the data subjects' rights.[44] Interestingly, the German data protection law provides the possibility of derogation only for the rights established in Articles 15 ('Data Access'), 16 ('Rectification'), 18 ('Restriction on Processing') and 21 ('Objection'). As far as the Article 15 is concerned, there is a further express limitation which removes the obligation to provide information about an individual's data in cases where it is scientifically necessary to hold the data and it would be too onerous to provide the information.[45] Data that are used for scientific research should be anonymized, where this does not go against the grain of proposed research or against specific individual data subjects' rights.[46] The latter is, for example, the case where data might yield information which must be communicated back to the data subject (such as serious, clinically relevant incidental findings). In other cases, the datasets ought to be pseudonymized effectively, unless the purpose of the research would be impossible to be achieved in such a case.

The 'right to be forgotten' as well as the 'right to data portability' are not captured by the derogations, which has implications for biobanking. Exactly how German biobanks are supposed to provide for data portability, in particular in the context of the unique combination of material and data, remains open.

[43] § 27 BDSG.

[44] § 27 (1) BDSG.

[45] § 27 (2) BDSG.

[46] § 27 (3) BDSG.

5 Conclusions

Biobanking is an activity that is clearly societally desirable, and is key to answering some of the most vexing health issues that society faces. At the same time, the activities of (especially large-scale) biobanks touch upon some fundamental individual rights. The density of the data held by these establishments can represent a significant risk to the informational self-determination, and therewith to the well-being, of data subjects and their family members. It is therefore somewhat unusual that the area of biobanking has not attracted clear and systematic *sui generis* legislation. Whilst the strong top-down governance of the General Data Protection Regulation assists to some extent in clearing the thicket of regulation in this area, there is still significant fragmentation and a sustained lack of legal certainty. In particular, the challenge of finding a combined legal approach to a repository of tangible and intangible material remains unaddressed and is one of the remaining grey areas of unclear regulation. Large-scale population-based biobanks, such as NaKo, are in the privileged position of establishing governance mechanisms that can fill these blank spaces with approaches which, by virtue of being novel and singular, have the potential to become best-practice models. At the same time, even an establishment like NaKo is only one variety of biobank in a complex ecosystem of diagnostic, archival, therapeutic and research data and material repositories, each of which configuration attracts its own regulatory mixture. The concurrent development of international and supranational norms, as well as domestic constitutional norms in Germany have meant that there is to this day no absolute clarity on the extent to which norms are applicable in which scenario. If there was hope that the Regulation will bring answers to domestic legal questions, the implementation of Art. 89 shows that whilst some answers are provided, new questions arise, such as why some biobanks will have to make provisions for giving effect to research participants' data portability rights. It is clear that this will remain an area where debate and explication of the law continue to be necessary; the law's principal duty to create certainty has still not fully been met.

References

Albers M (2013) Rechtsrahmen und Rechtsprobleme bei Biobanken. Medizinrecht 31:483–491

Deutsch E, Spickhoff A (2014) Medizinrecht, 7th edn. Springer, Heidelberg

Erbs G, Kohlhaas M, Häberle P (2017) Strafrechtliche Nebengesetze 224. EL (March 2019)

Fleischer H, Schickhardt C, Taupitz J (2016) Das Recht von Patienten und Probanden auf Herausgabe ihrer genetischen Rohdaten. Eine rechtliche und ethische Analyse samt einer Empfehlung für die Praxis. Medizinrecht 34:481–491

Forgó et al (2010) Ethical and legal requirements for transnational genetic research. CH Beck, Munich, No. 245

Herbst T (2016) Rechtliche und ethische Probleme des Umgangs mit Proben und Daten bei großen Biobanken. Datenschutz und Datensicherheit 6:371–375

Hoppe N (2009) Bioequity – property and the human body. Ashgate Publishing, Farnham

Nationale Kohorte. Die NAKO-Gesundheitsstudie geht in die zweite Runde
Nationaler Ethikrat (2004) Biobanken für die Forschung
OECD. OECD Guidelines on the Protection of Privacy and Transborder Flows of Personal Data. http://www.oecd.org/sti/ieconomy/oecdguidelinesontheprotectionofprivacyandtransborderflowsofpersonaldata.htm. Accessed 14 April 2019
Robienski J (2010) Die Auswirkungen von Gewebegesetz und Gendiagnostikgesetz auf die biomedizinische Forschung. Verlag Dr. Kovac, Hamburg
Schmidt am Busch B, Gassner UM, Wollschläger F (2016) Der Augsburg-Münchner-Entwurf eines Biobankgesetzes. Datenschutz und Datensicherheit 6:365–370

Mapping the Biobank Landscape in Greece

Olga Tzortzatou and Anastasia Siapka

Abstract The biobank landscape in Greece is mainly defined by tissue and data collections created in the course of clinical practice whose samples are subsequently repurposed for research. Given that there is no specific Greek biobank law, these collections have been so far governed through provisions drawn from the domestic civil and constitutional legal armamentarium concerning (biomedical) research as well as soft and hard EU and international laws. This chapter provides an empirical overview of the biobank landscape in Greece, describing existing biobanks and tissue collections potentially used for research in a non-exhaustive manner. Next, it explores how the Greek Law on the Protection of Personal Data envisages individuals' rights in the context of biobanking research and how these rights are weighted against the public interest. Finally, it evaluates the potential impact of the GDPR on biobanking in Greece.

1 Introduction

The biobank landscape in Greece mainly consists of tissue and data collections created in the course of clinical practice whose samples are subsequently repurposed for research. Given that there is no specific Greek biobank law, these collections have been so far governed through provisions drawn from the domestic civil and constitutional legal armamentarium concerning (biomedical) research as well as soft and hard EU and international laws. These provisions combined aim at

Dr. Tzortzatou would like to acknowledge the contribution of George Malamis, Human genetics—History of life sciences, University of National and Kapodistrian University of Athens, for his valuable input in chapter 2.i, in describing the current biobanking landscape in Greece.

O. Tzortzatou (✉)
Biomedical Research Foundation of the Academy of Athens, Athens, Greece
e-mail: otzortzatou@bioacademy.gr

A. Siapka
Centre for IT & IP Law, Faculty of Law, KU Leuven, Leuven, Belgium

S. Slokenberga et al. (eds.), *GDPR and Biobanking*, Law, Governance and Technology Series 43, https://doi.org/10.1007/978-3-030-49388-2_16

safeguarding research participants' rights, primarily their privacy and autonomy, and the public interest. Whilst preserving such protective measures, the Greek law transposing GDPR into national legislation alongside the expected creation of a national population biobank have the potential to facilitate biobank research in Greece.

2 Biobank Infrastructure and Regulatory Environment

2.1 *Biobank Infrastructure: The Greek Reality*

In the Greek legislative corpus, there is neither a definition nor any reference to the term *biobank*. According to the definition offered by the Organization for Economic Co-operation and Development (OECD), biobanks are 'structured resources that can be used for the purpose of genetic research and which include: (i) human biological materials and/or information generated from the analysis of the same; and (ii) extensive associated information'.[1] In the same vein, it has been argued that the definition of a biobank should clearly state its research purpose,[2] whereas matters such as the size of sample collections or the richness of data should be of secondary importance.[3] The hereinafter analysis takes into consideration these definitional requirements by the OECD and Shaw et al. Hence, collections of samples and, more broadly, data which have been created in the course of clinical routine (clinical biobanks), without a specific research purpose or with the objective of applying these tissue samples on humans, will fall outside its material scope.

Issues regarding retrospective research arise commonly in Greece when human samples originating from clinical biobanks are reused for research activities without the patients having been informed at the time of their tissue collection about the possibility of their samples being used for future research. So far, retrospective research was lawfully conducted even without patients' informed consent as long as three authorising decisions were in place: one from the competent Research Ethics Committee (REC) examining ethical and deontological concerns arising from the study and two from the Hellenic Data Protection Authority (hereafter HDPA or DPA) addressed to both the data controller/legal entity and the researcher acting as data controller.[4] Upon the GDPR coming into effect and the subsequent absence of DPA authorisations, the role of RECs in securing lawful retrospective research is enhanced.

---

[1] Tzortzatou (2015).

[2] Hallinan (2018).

[3] Shaw et al. (2014).

[4] On the DPA's double authorization see Decisions ΑΠΔΠΧ 31/2013, 46/2004, 47/2004. However, the law did not apply for retrospective research on data from deceased.

Overall, biobank researchers in Greece encounter practical difficulties, which prevent them from establishing and administering biobanks. Firstly, to obtain the patient's informed consent, a researcher needs to collaborate both with the clinician, which is hindered by the lack of preoperative reflexes in clinical practice, and the patient, which occurs rarely given the lack of awareness about biobanking research among the general public in Greece. Secondly, all peripheral laboratories need to be informed of the required processing, which is in practice difficult, because all laboratories would need to apply a single processing protocol. Thirdly, record-keeping is not sufficiently thorough in hospitals, resulting in incomplete historical data of patients' clinical course, including long-term monitoring.

The latter is further thwarted by the fact that patients often change their preferred doctors and/or medical practices, while at the same time there is no central record-keeping or guidance by the National Health System. Lastly, pseudonymisation and tissue registration presuppose bioinformatics support by qualified staff. The unavailability of research funding renders this requirement one of the main hindrances to biomedical research in general and consequently complicates biobanking (inter) operability and sustainability. In this regard, initiatives such as the Greek Infrastructure for Personalised Medicine enhance collaboration among researchers, the interoperability of future biobanking activities, and the lawful conduct of retrospective research in Greece.

A considerable, yet not officially registered in its entirety, number of research biobanks is found in hospitals, medical universities and research institutions across Greece.[5] Specifically, outside Athens and Thessaloniki, the two major Greek cities, these are developed and maintained exclusively at University Medical Schools. Most research biobanks in Greece comprise biological material which is or could be used in the analysis (e.g. cardiovascular, many types of cancer, metabolic, respiratory, hereditary, neurodegenerative, infectious). They are originally developed during clinical practice as clinical biobanks, storing heterogeneous biological samples. At the time of collection, these samples are destined for clinical/diagnostic activities, but they are afterwards repurposed usually through the route of a broad consent to any research purpose granted by the patient. In some cases, research biobanks include samples from groups of the general population, meaning healthy individuals whose data serve as control samples. Existing tissue collections, research biobanks amongst them, fall under the supervision of the Ministry of Health, the Ministry of Education, Research and Religious Affairs and, specifically, its General Secretariat for Research and Technology.[6]

[5] Due to the lack of any official documentation, Dr. Tzortzatou acknowledges the existence of more biobanks in Greece but has chosen to include only those for which confirmed data was received. This study does not include the charting of biobanks from the private sector which are mainly paraffin-tissue blocks in private pathology clinics, in large centers of analysis (BIOMATRIKI, EUROMEDICA etc) and in private hospitals with a Pathological Laboratory (Health Medicine Metropolitan, Medical ThessalonikiMedicine, Euromedica General Clinic of Thessaloniki.

[6] See also http://biobank.bioacademy.gr/.

The largest tissue collection whose samples are mainly intended for diagnostic services but might be used for research purposes is the First Department of Pathology which belongs to the Medical School of the National and Kapodistrian University of Athens established in 1850. It is the oldest laboratory of pathological anatomy in Greece, serving also research and educational needs. The total number of examinations conducted by the laboratory amounts to 30,000 cases per year, the majority of which involves patients with malignant diseases. The samples are stored in the laboratory's premises in paraffin blocks with corresponding documented diagnoses from the 'Laiko' Hospital as well as from thirty other hospitals across Greece.[7] The patients' consent to the use of their tissues for research is given at the time of the tissue collection and is then archived. During the last decade, the department has been actively involved in a European brain tissue bank network BrainNet Europe II (Network of European Brain and Tissue Banks for Clinical and Basic Neuroscience) project funded by the European Commission's 6th Framework Program for Research.

The Laboratory of Medical Genetics of the University of Athens (Horemeio), also providing diagnostic services mainly, is based at the Children's Hospital 'Agia Sofia'. Due to its long experience, it is a reference centre for issues related to the diagnosis, treatment and prevention of genetic diseases across Greece. It holds an important tissue collection on genetic diseases, storing DNA samples for research purposes with an informed consent procedure since 2010. Similarly to the Laboratory of Medical Genetics, the Report Centre for Thalassemia offers diagnostic examinations for thalassemia and, at the time of collection, it obtains individuals' consent to the use of their tissue for research, provided that their data are anonymised.

Furthermore, the Hellenic Cooperative Oncology Group (HeCOG) runs from 1990 its own tissue collection, with 14,000 formalin-fixed paraffin-embedded blocks, all fully annotated with clinical data from patients treated in network centers, accompanied with consent forms for research purposes. There is a HeCOG molecular oncology laboratory in Thessaloniki, with a second smaller laboratory in Athens.[8] The National Retrovirus Reference Centre (NRRC) based in the Athens University Medical School (Athens) has an active biobank of 370,000 saved samples (plasma, serum, biopsies, DNA, dry specimens), including samples preserved in liquid nitrogen, from 1991. The NRRC specializes in virology research on human pathogenic micro-organisms (AIDS, Hepatitis B and C, other viral infections) as well as cancers of viral origin.[9]

A research biobank outside clinical practice, set up through the European Prospective Investigation into Cancer (EPIC) study in 1994 and currently held in the premises of the Hellenic Health Foundation (Athens), contains samples from 28,572

[7] See also https://www.laiko.gr/index.php?option=com_content&view=article&id=74&Itemid=113.

[8] See also https://www.hecog.gr/el/.

[9] See also http://www.mednet.gr/archives/2018-3/pdf/358.pdf.

adults from all over Greece, representing a broad range of sociodemographic traits.[10] Data collection for this biobank was accomplished with participants' informed consent by means of two questionnaires during a baseline examination in which the following information was recorded: medical and reproductive history, sociodemographic and lifestyle factors, and habitual diet. Anthropometric data and blood pressure were measured, while blood samples were also collected.[11]

From 1998, the National Centre for Scientific Research 'Demokritos' operates the Molecular Diagnostics Biobank on inherited types of cancer with approximately 15,000 germline DNA samples accompanied with pedigrees describing the family history of the disease (e.g. genes BRCA1, BRCA2, TP53, PALB2).[12] As from 2009, the Laboratory of Molecular Oncology in collaboration with HeCOG, the Hellenic Collaborative Oncology Group and Aristotle University of Thessaloniki operates a biobank, which includes biological material from more than 15,000 patients who participated in clinical trials and have provided their informed consent to the use of the biological material for research purposes.[13]

Since 2007, the University of Ioannina hosts the Cancer Biobank, with samples from 600 patients with hematologic neoplasia and an unregistered number of patients with solid organ neoplasia.[14] Research participants have signed an informed consent form, which, thanks to the creation of a GDPR compliance office on site, is being reviewed to become more nuanced, tiered and fully compliant with the requirements of the GDPR. Data collection was specific to each research project but generally focused on the disease, its status, and DNA and RNA extraction data. Another important biobank is that of Idiopathic Intermediate Pulmonary Diseases (IOP) and for Idiopathic Pulmonary Fibrosis. This biobank collects clinical and epidemiological data and biological material (blood, plasma, biopsy etc.).[15]

---

[10] See also http://epic.iarc.fr/centers/greece.php.

[11] The first phase of the study consists information provided upon filling of specific questionnaires. In the lifestyle questionnaire there are included socio-demographic characteristics and sensitive information related to them such as the medical, family as well general information such as the professional history, the level of physical activity and how the volunteer lives. Reported diagnoses of interest are further ascertained through consultation of medical files in hospitals and clinics all over Greece or, in case of death, through the collection of death certificates from the regional death registries. The dietary questionnaire describes the dietary habits of the volunteer e.g. the frequency and quantity of consumption of alcoholic and non-alcoholic beverages and intake nutritional supplements. The second phase involves the somatometric examination of the volunteer and the third and final phase of the baseline examination includes blood sampling. The collected fractions of blood samples (serum, plasma, leucocytes, erythrocytes) are kept at −2000C on a specially formulated biological basis.

[12] http://www.iprctca.dcmokritos.gr/indcx.php?option=com_content&task−view&id−23&Itemid=40.

[13] See also https://www.eliek.gr.

[14] See also http://old.uoi.gr/services/lab-net/net-web/Cancer_Biobank_gr.pdf.

[15] See also http://www.pneumon.org/assets/files/789/file578_166.pdf and http://ipf.fleming.gr/ipf_biobank/.

The Biomedical Research Foundation of the Academy of Athens (BRFAA) is the Central Node of the BBMRI-GR network from 2008, which is officially a member of the Pan-European Biomedical Infrastructure Consortium (BBMRI-ERIC).[16] Within BRFAA operates the Hellenic Biobank for Parkinson's Disease on patients with Parkison's Disease (PD).[17] It contains 708 samples of PD patients and 351 of control samples, which are all numbered and allocated pseudonomysided codes corresponding to clinical information such as demographics, history of exposure to environmental influences, clinical history, and relevant clinical scales. All information, including informed consent forms, is both stored in hard copy and uploaded to the database of the biobank. BRFAA also has also a normal population samples biobank (placental connective tissue) collected for research purposes. The Hellenic Cord Blood Bank operates within the Center of Clinical, Experimental Surgery & Translational Research in BRFAA and also obtains informed consent from the parents for further research use of their children's stored biospecimens. BRFAA, along with the Fleming Institution, is also part of the Greek Research Infrastructure for Precision Medicine (pMedGR). This infrastrusture is coordinated by the University of Athens and 'aims to bring together intersectoral partners', such as Biotechnology SMEs, diagnostics developers, biomedical and clinical researchers and policy makers, in order to advance precision medicine in Greece. It could prove to be of obvious support to biobanking activities in Greece, as it has stated that it 'will determine strategies and implement best practices for collecting, cataloguing, and storing samples and specimens (fresh, frozen or FFPE samples)'.[18]

Since 2013, samples (including serum, plasma and DNA) are obtained from patients attending the 'Out-Patient Clinic for the Prevention and Treatment of Overweight and Obesity in Childhood and Adolescence', in the 'Aghia Sophia' Children's Hospital (Athens). This research biobank functions within the 'National Program for the Prevention and Treatment of Overweight and Obesity in Childhood and Adolescence', and approximately 3000 children and adolescents have been followed-up at the Out-Patient Clinic. All data and samples are being provided with the participants' explicit and written informed consent and the approval of the local REC. Another biobank is that of the Institute of Applied Biosciences (INAB) of the Centre for Research and Technology Hellas (CERTH), which is affiliated with the Hematology Department and the HCT Unit of the 'G. Papanicolaou' Hospital in Thessaloniki. It has a collection of 60,000 samples coming from different types of biospecimens on 24 hematologic malignancies.[19]

Finally, a national BBMRI.GR network of existing tissue collections among different institutions, which shall be based in the Biomedical Research Foundation of the Academy of Athens (BRFAA), has been established. Once set in operation, this

[16] See also https://www.tovima.gr/2008/11/25/science/epiteloys-biotrapeza/.

[17] See also http://www.bioacademy.gr/lab/stefanis/H8yK/research?lang=en.

[18] See also https://www.precisionmedicine.gr/units.

[19] See also https://directory.bbmri-eric.eu/menu/main/app-molgenis-app-biobank-explorer/biobankexplorer?country=GR.

biobank will comply with the quality standards of the EU infrastructure BBMRI-ERIC. This nationwide endeavour will initiate a new era of biomedical research in Greece, during which large-scale and high-quality biological samples of patients and healthy individuals will be gathered for analysis employing not only latest technologies, such as Next Generation Sequencing (NGS), but also suitable for integrated analyses that will include the full range of omics technologies, which is necessary to make new treatments possible in the context of Precision medicine.[20] Furthermore, the country's contribution to the BBMRI-ERIC infrastructure and its concomitant compliance with the BBMRI ERIC Code of conduct aim to create a network of Greek biobanks and connect them with the infrastructure in order to expedite Greece's integration into the European Research Area (ERA) regulations.[21]

2.2 *Regulatory Framework*

Within the Greek legal context, general rules on (biomedical) research are applicable to biobank research as a more specific type thereof. Provisions governing research participants' personal data and autonomy derive from the following soft and hard legal instruments:

i. Convention for the Protection of Individuals with regard to Automatic Processing of Personal Data (Convention 108) of the Council of Europe;
ii. Convention for the Protection of Human Rights and Dignity of the Human Being with regard to the Application of Biology and Medicine: Convention on Human Rights and Biomedicine of the Council of Europe (Oviedo Convention);
iii. Law 2619/1998 ratifying the Oviedo Convention;
iv. Law 3418/2005 (Code of Medical Ethics/Deontology) and specifically Article 24 (2) d, requiring that the research project is approved by the competent administrative authority, following a consenting opinion of the competent Scientific Council of the hospital and/or the Ethics Committee;[22]
v. Regulation EU No 536/2014 on clinical trials of medicinal products for human use;
vi. Ministerial Decision DYG 3/89292/2003 implementing Directive 2001/20/EC on the approximation of the laws, regulations and administrative provisions of the Member States relating to the implementation of good clinical practice in the conduct of clinical trials on medicinal products for human use;
vii. Law 4386/2016 on Regulations for Research and other provisions, regulating administrative aspects of research.

[20] See also https://www.precisionmedicine.gr/.

[21] More information about this initiate can be found at http://code-of-conduct-for-health-research.eu/.

[22] Research on human is specifically regulated in Article 21-27, Law 3418/2005.

viii. Law 4624/2019, Personal Data Protection Authority, implementing measures for Regulation (EU) 2016/679 of the European Parliament and of the Council of 27 April 2016 on the protection of individuals with regard to the processing of personal data and their integration into national law legislation of Directive (EU) 2016/680 of the European Parliament and of the Council of 27 April 2016 and other provisions.
ix. Additional regulations including sample quality, standard operational procedures, ISO certifications such as ISO/IEC 17025 and Good Laboratory Practice Regulations.[23]

The only relevant piece of law wherein collections of tissues are referred to in a systematic way, in terms of structure and operability, is the Presidential Decree 26/2008, which implements the Directive 2004/23/EC of the European Parliament and of the Council in the Greek legislation. This Decree sets quality and safety standards for the donation, procurement, testing, processing, preservation, storage, disposal of dangerous substances, and distribution of human tissues and cells. In general, this Decree does not apply to research biobanks, since it refers exclusively to the application of tissues and cells on humans.[24] However, it applies to both public and private biobanks which store stem cells for transplantation, in which case the Hellenic Transplant Organization (HTO/EOM) as well as sperm and IVF biobanks are responsible for authorization.

Researchers acting within a biobank are, furthermore, subject to obligations of professional secrecy,[25] securing in this way participants' privacy. When collected

[23] The following framework applies:

i. PD. 273/2000/2000 (Government Gazette 1370/B'/9.11.2000) Implementation of Good Laboratory Practice Principles (GLP), GLP Compliance Monitoring in Controlled Data Studies and Inspection and Accreditation System for GLP Testing Units and Testing Sites.
ii. Ministerial Decision 452/1997/1998 (Government Gazette 294/B'/26.3.1998) Implementation of Good Laboratory Practice (GLP) principles, GLP testing in the Chemicals—Chemicals Studies and Inspection and Accreditation System of Experimental Of GLP Units
iii. Ministerial Decision 22/94/1994 (Government Gazette 706/B'/20.9.1994) Accreditation and control system for laboratories of good laboratory practice
iv. Ministerial Decision 1282/91/1992 (Government Gazette 669/B'/13.11.1992) Amending and supplementing the 1285/89 CFD Decision in compliance with Directive 90/18/EEC on the inspection and verification of good laboratory practice (republication of Government Gazette 80/B/92
v. Decision 1285/1989 Harmonization of Directive 88/320/EEC on the inspection and verification of good laboratory practice (GLP)
vi. Decision 1146/88/1988 (Official Gazette 669/B'/12.9.1988) Approval of the application of the principles of good laboratory practice and control of their application during tests of chemical substances—chemical products.

[24] It should however be noted that in several cases the collections described in the law may proceed to research activities on the donated tissues, provided that specific informed consent has been provided. Of paramount importance is the example of the Hellenic Cord Blood Biobank (HCBB) http://hcbb.bioacademy.gr/, where specific informed consent is required for parents who donate blood at the Unrelated Cord Blood Bank, in order for the latest to be used for research purposes.

[25] Article 13 (1) Law 3418/2005.

within the practice of medical care/services, personal information concerning health is subject to medical confidentiality. This confidentiality can be lifted with the subject's consent. In addition, medical confidentiality along with sanctions for its violation are enshrined in the Greek Penal Code (Article 371). In practice, researchers who do not abide by obligations of medical confidentiality are still subject to confidentiality by a bilateral legal act with the controller, such as a Non-Disclosure or Confidential Disclosure Agreement (NDA/CDA).[26]

On the research participants' side, their privacy is further safeguarded by the application of relevant GDPR provisions related to the protection of genetic and health data. Already before the GDPR, health-related data used in biomedical research and formed as part of a file were protected as sensitive data under Law 2472/1992 (Act on the Protection of Individuals with regard to the Processing of Personal Data), which had implemented the Directive 95/46/EC (Data Protection Directive) in Greece. This law (Article 7 (1)) prohibited the processing of sensitive data, health and genetic ones among them, and allowed it only under specific exceptions (Article 7 (2)), with consent being one of the legal bases for lawful processing.

3 Individual Rights and Safeguards

Biobank participants have access to multi-level protection of their rights in Greece. First of all, in the realm of private law, the Greek Civil Code establishes the right to personality (Article 57), a more specific aspect of which is–according to the dominant scholarly view–the subjects' right to monitor and allow the use of their health data (informational self-determination). Concurrently, a web of constitutional provisions directly applicable to biobank research guarantees individuals' privacy and autonomy at a higher level.[27]

Additionally, the autonomy of biobanks' participants is protected by Law 4521/2018, which in Chapter 5 establishes Research Ethics and Deontology Committees (REDCs) in all universities and research institutions. Funded research projects involving studies on humans or on samples deriving from humans, such as genetic material, cells, tissues and personal data, need prior authorisation from the institution's REDC before launching. REDCs examine whether research projects respect humans' inherent value as well as participants' autonomy, private life and personal data. Regarding the latter, though, it remains unclear how data protection issues could be reviewed by REDCs, given that, on the one hand, their boards often

[26] Such agreements contain provisions regarding the duration of the confidentiality agreement, the liability of the researcher, the scope of the research, the description of the exact confidentiality duties etc.

[27] Greek Constitution Article 9A on the right to data protection; Article 2 (1) on the protection of human dignity; Article 9 on the right to private life; and Article 5 (1) on the free development of personality. The Article 5 (5) on the right to the protection of one's health and genetic identity could also be interpreted as protective of the aforementioned informational self-determination.

do not include a data protection expert and that, on the other, their pre-GDPR responsibility was to verify whether controllers had obtained the required authorisation from the Hellenic Data Protection Authority. In any case, this provision should not be interpreted as indicative of a legislative will to have the duties of DPAs replaced by REDCs in research, as the former remain solely responsible for assessing data protection violations.[28]

More recently, GDPR and the Law 4624/2019 or 'Law on the Protection of Personal Data', hereinafter the 'Greek law', containing a total of 42 Articles which transpose derogations and points left to the national legislator's discretion into Greek legislation, apply directly as foreseen to the protection of participants' privacy. One of the most significant changes brought about by them is the abrogation of the HDPA authorisation. Specifically, before GDPR came into force in Greece, the HDPA provided a 'double authorisation' for the collection and processing of personal data: one to the controller who owned the data and one to the researchers who requested those data for the purpose of scientific research in case the data where not in their ownership, rendering therefore the latter controllers of the data.[29]

GDPR and the provisions included in Article 30 of the Greek law apply to the processing of personal data for scientific or historical research purposes or for the collection and maintenance of statistical data. Research is not further defined in the Greek law, but following GDPR it is mentioned in its scientific and historical type. The objective of a European Research Area is not mentioned or implied either, as cross-border processing is examined only with regards to crime-related data. Furthermore, pursuant to Article 9(4) GDPR, a further limitation on the processing of genetic data is identified under Article 23 of the Greek law, strictly prohibiting the processing of genetic data for health and life insurance purposes. It is however worth noting that the national legislator chose not to prohibit the processing of genetic data which have been generated in the course of predictive genetic tests.

Of extreme importance to participants' right to privacy in biobanking is the above mentioned breakthrough provision which refers to the data controller's 'interest' that must be carefully examined on a case-by-case basis when it comes to data processing for research purposes.[30] More specifically, the Greek law specifies that '... processing of specific categories of personal data ... is permitted without the consent of the data subject, when the processing is necessary for the purposes of scientific or historical research or for the collection and maintenance of statistics, and the interest of the data controller is superior to the data subject's interest not process its personal data. The controller shall be required to take appropriate and

[28] The role of REDCs in ensuring participants' autonomy is further established in Code of Medical Ethics/Deontology Article 24(2)(d).

[29] Particularly, as far as the extraction of health data from hospitals for the purpose of carrying out scientific research is concerned, the concurring opinion of the scientific council of the hospitals and Committees of Deontology of the institutions who will carry the research, is additionally required.

[30] Greek law Article 30.

specific measures to protect the data subject's legitimate interests. These may include in particular: (a) restrictions on data access by data controllers and processors; (b) pseudonymization of personal data; (c) encryption of personal data (d) appointments of a DPO.' Through this provision, for the first time the Greek legislator allows researchers to process the personal information of research participants, without the latter's consent or the HDPA's authorisation. This is definetely a positive step for biobanking research, where until now the model of informed written consent was rigorously followed and was thereby impeding research activities.[31]

However, the above provision should be interpreted as the 'exception' from seeking the participant's informed consent for research purposes and not the rule which should remain the controller's obligation to seek the subject's informed consent to the processing of their data, especially in the cases of prospective research studies. Otherwise, this provision risks to be wrongfully used as a 'carte blanche' enabling researchers to override individuals' autonomy by using their data without a priori informing them for the intended data processing. Therefore, examining on a case-by-case basis if the researcher's interest is in fact harmed or not is crucial to the right interpretation of this provision. Furthermore, the researcher's obligation to seek the research participant's informed consent to data processing should not be conflated with the obligation to request the participant's consent to take part in the research study per se. Consequently, the researcher's responsibility to guarantee that all information relevant to the research study, including information about personal data processing, has been provided to the participant remains part of the established obligation provide study participants with all the necessary information about each research protocol.[32]

The Greek law postulates[33] that processing of special categories of data is permitted, among other reasons, for the purpose of 'preventive medicine'. Assuming that the technological progress taking place in biobanking research will be soon conducive to direct health benefits for the general population and given the fact that biobanks are already described as 'the driving force of technological development and preventive medicine',[34] it is not excluded that the aforementioned provision may in the near future be directly applicable to biobanks. This would mean that biobanks would have become an indispensable part of the healthcare system, serving also the purposes of preventive medicine.[35]

---

[31] Tzortzatou (2015).

[32] Relevant provisions in Greek legislation for research involving humans in research apply such as the Chapter IIa.5 and IVa.16 of the Law 2619/1998 transposing the Oviedo Convention into Greek legislation where it is specifically stated that research with human participants can only take place after the person concerned gives his/her specific consent, upon prior informed notice and that the consent can be freely withdrawn at any time.

[33] Greek law Article 22.

[34] Dabrock (2012).

[35] Notably, Article 22(1)(b) and (3) imposing additional safeguards in comparison to Article 30, is the appropriate legal basis for Biobanking research as biobanks have a higher risk for the individ-

Therefore, personal data processing in the case of biobanking research would be lawful, without the data subject's informed consent, under the condition that additional (compared to the provision for research process) specific measures and safeguards are in place, including mainly the following: 'a) technical and organizational measures to ensure that the treatment is in conformity with GDPR; (b) measures to ensure that ex-post verification can be carried out and the determination of whether and by whom personal data has been entered, modified or removed; (c) measures to increase awareness of the staff involved in the personal data processing; (d) restrictions on access by data controllers and processors; (e) the pseudonymization of personal data; (f) encryption of personal data; (g) measures to ensure the capacity, confidentiality, integrity, availability and durability of processing systems and services related to the processing of personal data, including the ability to quickly restore availability and access in the event of a physical or technical incident; (h) procedures for regularly testing, evaluating and evaluating the effectiveness of technical and organizational measures to ensure the safety of processing; (i) specific rules to ensure compliance with this Act and the ISG in the event of transmission or processing for other purposes; (j) DPO appointment'. It is, therefore, clear that the above two provisions (Article 30 and Article 22 respectively) contravene the Greek legal tradition in processing health and genetic data, which relied upon the informed written consent, and foster a new model for conducting research without the individual's consent, as long as the data controller's interest supersedes that of the subject.[36] In support of biobanking research is also the fact that the Greek law postulates no further specification or addition regarding storage limitation; therefore, in the case of research, only the relevant provisions of Article 5(1)(e) GDPR apply.

As seen above, pursuant to Article 89(1) GDPR, the Article 30 of the Greek law enumerates several safeguards, which data controllers are required to enact for the data processing to be in accordance with individuals' rights and freedoms. Contrary to the previous data protection regime, and following the GDPR, the current law introduces into Greek legislation the concept of pseudonymisation. More

---

ual's privacy from data processing in such settings where data are stored for indefinite periods and unknown at the time of collection purposes.

[36] Something, which also the former draft of the Greek law recognized as a necessary precondition when it came for processing specific categories of personal data for research purposes. Specifically, draft of the Greek law Article. 19(1) posited: 'Personal data processing for scientific or historical research is allowed provided that: a) data subjects have granted their consent; b) the data controller already possesses the relevant data from respective previous researches and data subjects have consented to further use or use for related purposes.[…]'. Similarly, draft Article 19(2) posited: 'Processing personal data that are included in the special categories of Article 9 GDPR or concern criminal proceedings, security measures or convictions for scientific or historical research purposes or for statistical purposes is allowed in the following cases: a) data subjects have granted their explicit consent. Provided that participation in scientific research activities in the context of clinical trials is concerned, provisions of Articles 28 to 34 of the Regulation EU No 536/2014 of the European Parliament and of the Council on clinical trials on medicinal products for human use, and repealing Directive 2001/20/EC shall apply.; b) the data controller already has access to the relevant data from related previous scientific or statistical researches and data subjects had consented to further use or use for related purposes.'

specifically, further introduces the concept of data encryption as a technical means strengthening data protection, without however defining the term. Although anonymisation is not defined in the law, it is mentioned in Article 30(3), where it is stated that the data controller must anonymise the data as soon as the scientific or statistical purposes permit so, unless this is contrary to the data subject's legitimate interest. In addition, the Greek legislator provides that, until anonymisation takes place, features that can be used to correlate details of personal or actual situations of an identified or identifiable individual must be stored separately. Furthermore, these features can be combined with individual details only if required by the research or statistical purpose, adding in this way further safeguards for the data subject's protection.[37]

When it comes to publishing the results of scientific research, the Greek law requires compiance with specific conditions for the publication or disclosure of personal data. In particular, personal data processed in the context of research can be published by the data controller, provided that either the concerned data subjects have given their relevant explicit and written consent or the publication is absolutely necessary to present the results of historical research; in this later case, all personal data are pseudonymised.[38]

Furthermore, the Greek law allows for overriding, inter alia, the data subject's right to access, rectify, restrict and object to the processing (Article 15, 16, 18 and 21 GDPR). More specifically, it grants such an exception in so far as, on the one hand, exercising these rights may render impossible or seriously impair the purposes of scientific or historical research and, on the other hand, restricting these rights is necessary to achieve the aforementioned purposes. For the same reason, the right of access (Article 15 GDPR) does not apply where personal data are necessary for scientific purposes and providing information to the data subject requires disproportionate effort. The right to data portability (Article 20 GDPR) may apply to at least some of the data stored in the biobanks, namely the data provided by the data subjects themselves under consent, if any. What should be considered as such data, though, is not entirely clear.[39] Lastly, there is no specification or addition in the Greek law providing particular research exemptions to the right to erasure ('right to be forgotten'); therefore, the GDPR provision applies as it stands.

---

[37] However, it is worth noticing that the concept of anonymization is not new in relation to data protection of research participants in the Greek legislation. In fact, it is a provision consistent with the former Data Protection Law 2472/1997 where anonymization of data was a prerequisite for research.

[38] Greek law Article 30(4).

[39] Chassang et al. (2018).

4 Law in Context: Individual Rights and Public Interest

The ultimate objective of a biobank is to serve the public interest by improving public health. Yet, this objective might be in contrast to the need to guarantee individual rights such as the ones examined in the previous part. Traces of this tension between individual rights and public interest in the domain of research are found in the Greek Constitution and particularly in its Article 16, which establishes the right to research and endows it with both a status negativus, in the sense of a state obligation not to interfere with research, and a status positivus, in the sense of a state obligation to assist researchers in their work.

In addressing conflicts between this constitutional right to research/science and the likewise constitutionally protected individual rights examined above, the principle of proportionality becomes key. A more straightforward scenario is when the scientific research contravenes the public interest or fundamental rights of third parties. In such cases, according to the principle of lawfulness, which was already in force through the former data protection law, processing personal data is forbidden.

There are no specifications regarding the private or public character of research in the Greek law. However, the law allows access to special categories of personal data that are held for archiving purposes in the public 'interest under the condition that relevant safeguards for the protection of data subjects are in place. However, the fact that the mere appeal to public interest is deemed sufficient to grant access to health and genetic data, e.g. within the context of registries, significantly weakens individuals' position and might prove to be problematic.'

Finally, since the authorisation procedure by the Hellenic Data Protection Authority is abrogated, possible risks to public interest should be taken into consideration by the controller within the framework of a Data Protection Impact Assessment (DPIA). This is why, especially in the context of biobanking, DPIAs should be seen as a dynamic process that needs to be constantly updated based on relevant technical developments. Of great importance is the role of the biobank's Data Protection Officer (DPO), who is by law responsible for informing and advising the controller (biobank as a legal entity) and the employees (researchers) on their obligations pursuant to GDPR; monitoring their compliance with the Regulation; advising on the development of the DPIA and monitoring its performance; cooperating with the DPA and acting as the contact point for issues related to processing, including the prior consultation of Article 36 GDPR.

All in all, the regulatory as well as empirical research landscape in Greece is for the first time slightly distancing itself from the model of informed consent, under the condition that specific technical means and safeguards are in place. We are still however far from witnessing a 'communitarian turn' from models of informed consent to consent based on the values of trust, solidarity, reciprocity, citizenry, or even moral obligation towards fellow human beings and the greater social benefit.[40]

[40] Kongsholm and Kappel (2017) and Knoppers and Chadwick (2005).

Moreover, it is remarkable that neither the Greek constitution nor the Greek law or the GDPR are preoccupied with group-level threats to privacy and autonomy. Adopting a strictly individualistic lens in data protection implies that entire social groups might be stigmatised and disadvantaged because of their genetic dispositions or that the particularities of vulnerable social groups such as minors or incompetent persons might be disregarded.

Such concerns become even more imperative in the context of biobank research, whose process and outcomes are primarily group- and population-based. Contrariwise, these are issues which could be addressed through targeted legal instruments, as is indicatively the case with the Estonian Human Genes Research Act, which includes provisions on genetic discrimination, or the Swedish Biobanks in Medical Care Act, which contains specific rules on samples from newborns.[41] What is more, a suggested collective consideration of data protection is not necessarily at odds with greater individual autonomy. Instead, by indicatively adopting a Kantian perception of autonomy, the welfare of others could serve as a guiding principle in reaching personal autonomy.[42]

Hence, it remains to be seen in practice how the national DPA will respond to such societal and ideological specificities and strike a balance between individual and group/public interests. Alternatively, the absence of legal provisions related to crucial biobank-related issues, including discrimination based on health and genetic data processing, the treatment of specific social groups, data ownership, benefit sharing and consent withdrawal, risks deriving from the commercialization of biobanks and/or their findings, incidental findings and disclosure of research results, could set forth the case for a tailored, unified biobank law in Greece.

5 GDPR Impact and Future Possibilities for Biobanking

GDPR brought significant changes to the data protection framework in Greece, and its overall impact can be deemed as further enabling biobanking activities. By implicitly establishing research as the legal basis for data processing, it addresses one of the main impediments of retrospective research and satisfies one of the most enduring demands of the Greek scientific community. Similarly, by eliminating the need for prior authorisation from the HDPA, it simplifies the research process. Before the GDPR, the double HDPA authorisation was required for all kinds of data processing, even data transfer, which means that now researchers have been relieved from a substantial bureaucratic burden. Yet, this does not come at the expense of individuals' protection, as they are equipped with measures and safeguards such as encryption, pseudonymisation of their data and the DPO appointment, which come as a guarantee of their rights.

[41] Swedish Act can be accessed at http://biobanksverige.se/wp-content/uploads/Biobanks-in-medical-care-act-2002-297.pdf.

[42] Wood (2009).

Moreover, the fact that all Member States must comply with the same minimum level of protective safeguards demanded by the GDPR, notwithstanding any national deviations, will make it easier for Greece to participate in cross-border consortia and biobank research projects. Last but not least, the GDPR has brought some necessary terminological clarity by introducing the newly brought in data protection legislation term of 'pseudonymisation' as oposed to anonymisation. Also, by promoting the former in lieu of the—widely rejected among Greek researchers–anonymisation it allows for information-heavy and thereby safer scientific outcomes, thus rendering biobank research more effective. Hopefully, the advent of the GDPR in tandem with the expected national population biobank will gear the public opinion towards a positive reception of biobank research.

6 Conclusions

The brief overview provided in this chapter is by no means intended to be exhaustive; rather, it aspires to have provided a first documentation of the empirical and regulatory landscape of biobanks in Greece. Absent an ad hoc law, biobanks in Greece have been so far governed through an assemblage of laws regulating biomedical research and data protection, which includes constitutional and civil law provisions protecting, on the one hand, the freedom of research and, on the other, individuals' privacy. When it comes to participants' data protection rights, the Greek Law makes use of Article 89 GDPR, as derogations for specific subject rights for scientific research have been proposed and it allows the processing of personal data without the subject's prior consent, when specific safeguards are implemented. However, as analysed above, numerous existing practical difficulties have prevented researchers from establishing biobanks. It is, therefore, anticipated by the research community that the national population biobank network, once established, will bring to the forefront discussions for the articulation of a specific legal framework for biobanking. By supplementing or specifying the current data protection regime in Greece, such framework would significantly contribute to legal certainty in the realm of biobanking research. As a result, it could enable the processing of an extensive amount of samples and data stored in biobanks for research purposes, ultimately benefiting the Greek society as a whole.

References

Chassang G, Southerington T, Tzortzatou O, Boeckhout M, Slokenberga S (2018) Data portability in health research and biobanking: legal benchmarks for appropriate implementation. Eur Data Prot Law Rev 4(3):296–307

Dabrock P, Taupitz J, Ried J (2012) Trust in biobanking: dealing with ethical, legal and social issues in an emerging field of biotechnology. Springer Editions

Hallinan D (2018) Feeding Biobanks with Genetic Data: What role can the General Data Protection Regulation play in the protection of genetic privacy in research biobanking in the European Union? Dissertation thesis at Vrije Universiteit Brussel
Knoppers BM, Chadwick R (2005) Human genetic research: emerging trends in ethics. Nat Rev Genet 6(1):75–79
Kongsholm NCH, Kappel K (2017) Is Consent Based on Trust Morally Inferior to Consent Based on Information? https://www.ncbi.nlm.nih.gov/pubmed/28240791
Regulation (EU) 2016/679 of the European Parliament and of the Council of 27 April 2016 on the protection of natural persons with regard to the processing of personal data and on the free movement of such data, and repealing Directive 95/46/EC (General Data Protection Regulation)
Regulation (EU) No 536/2014 of the European Parliament and of the Council of 16 April 2014 on clinical trials on medicinal products for human use
Shaw D, Bernice E, Colledge F (2014) Clinical genetics. https://pdfs.semanticscholar.org/6214/09329391228dbfdc8937a5a75e3fe09350ad.pdf
Tzortzatou O (2015) The protection of sensitive data in the field of biomedical research. Sakkoulas Editions, Athens
Wood A (2009) Duties to oneself, duties of respect to others. Wiley-Blackwell

The Italian Way for Research Biobanks After GDPR: Hybrid Normative Solutions to Balance the Protection of Individuals and Freedom of Research

Simone Penasa and Marta Tomasi

Abstract The Italian context of biobanking is made up of a vast number of collections, in some cases well-organised and connected in virtuous networks and in others not identifiable as structured biobanks. From a comparative perspective, Italy can be regarded as a hybrid model, positioned between countries with full and detailed legislation concerning biobanks and those that rely only on guidelines published by national ethics committees or professional societies that have no binding legal value. In countries like Italy where the need for specific regulation is more urgent, the entry into force of the GDPR could have offered a chance to fill the gap in the legislation with regard to biobanking for medical scientific research purposes. This overview highlights the improvements made and the obstacles that persist.

1 Introduction

The Italian context of biobanking is made up of a vast number of collections, in some cases well-organised and connected in virtuous networks and in others not identifiable as structured biobanks. Italy lacks ad hoc regulation for biobank research activities. Thus, the protection of participants and donors' rights must be derived from different legal sources, and these concern, in particular, personal data protection. Among these, a key role is played by non-legislative regulations adopted by administrative authorities upon delegation by the legislator. This approach has

Although the work is the result of a joint reflection of the two authors, paragraphs 2 and 5 can be attributed to Marta Tomasi and paragraphs 3 and 4 to Simone Penasa. Paragraphs 1 and 6 were elaborated by both authors. In writing the chapter the authors also took advantage of their previous publications, in particular, of Macilotti M, Penasa S, Tomasi M (2015) Consent, Privacy and Property in the Italian Biobanks Regulation: A Hybrid Model within EU?. In: Mascalzoni D (ed) Ethics, Law and Governance of Biobanking. Springer, Dordrecht, pp 53–77.

S. Penasa (✉) · M. Tomasi
University of Trento, Trento, Italy
e-mail: simone.penasa@unitn.it; marta.tomasi@unitn.it

S. Slokenberga et al. (eds.), *GDPR and Biobanking*, Law, Governance and Technology Series 43, https://doi.org/10.1007/978-3-030-49388-2_17

created a hybrid model of protection that positions Italy comparatively between countries with full and detailed legislation concerning biobanks and countries which only rely on guidelines published by national ethics committees or professional societies that have no binding legal value. The main reference points in Italy are the general Authorisations issued by the Italian Data Protection Authority (DPA): Authorisation no. 8/2016 on the processing of genetic data, and Authorisation no. 9/2016 on the processing of personal data for scientific research purposes.

The GDPR offered Italian legislators the opportunity to reconsider the whole system and to design a more comprehensive framework of protection. The Italian legislature decided to take advantage of the possibility given by the GDPR to Member States to introduce further limitations with regard to the processing of some kinds of data[1] and to instruct the DPA to identify the special conditions for the processing of health and genetic data.[2] To update the general Authorisations adopted in the past, the DPA opened up a public consultation which it was hoped would prove an effective instrument for different stakeholders involved in biobanking activities to highlight the deficiencies of the existing regulatory framework and to suggest structural improvements.

2 Biobank Infrastructure and Regulatory Environment

2.1 The Italian Biobank Landscape

The Italian biobank landscape is composed of a vast number of collections of samples and data, not always identifiable and organized as structured biobanks. The main categories of biobanks are clinical and research biobanks. *Clinical* biobanks are deposits of human tissue samples stored in a clinical context and obtained from patients who have been tested and received treatment in healthcare services. *Research* biobanks are ones established with a research aim and with samples obtained from research participants or from other (clinical) biobanks.

The only official collection at the national level is the Italian DNA database, the establishment of which was provided for by Law no. 85/2009 titled 'Adhesion of the Italian Republic to the Prüm Treaty. Establishment of national DNA database (NDNADB) and the central laboratory for the NDNADB', with the aim to facilitate

[1] See Article 9.4 of the GDPR which allows Member States to maintain or introduce further conditions, including limitations, with regard to the processing of genetic data, biometric data or data concerning health.

[2] See Penasa et al. (2018), pp. 1–15.

the identification of those who might have committed crimes.[3] With regard to clinical and research biobanks, there is no central register. Consequently, the exact number of biobanks and stored biological samples is unknown.

To improve and strengthen the Italian infrastructure for biobank research and to provide an overview and easier access to samples for both Italian and international researchers, the Italian node of BBMRI was established through a joint effort by the Ministry of Health and the Ministry of University & Research. This brings together the National Institute of Health (Istituto Superiore di Sanità), the National Center for Research (Consiglio Nazionale delle Ricerche), 18 universities, 22 institutes for care and research (IRCCS), institutions for hospitalisation and care closely linked to translational research, and patient associations. BBMRI-IT has two main goals: to provide new common services for the community of the Italian biobanks, and to contribute to pan-European research infrastructure BBMRI-ERIC.[4]

According to their website, a survey has been designed to assess and select well-established Italian biobanks in terms of quality and richness of samples and data and to identify biobanks available to provide services to the BBMRI network. Indeed, according to their website, 'the Italian node has specific scientific skills that it can share with the other national nodes about informatics, molecular analysis in archive tissues and ELSI'.[5] BBMRI-IT includes 90 biobanks/biological resource centres/collections, mainly disease-oriented (oncological, genetic, multi-specialist), and organised into thematic and regional networks.

With regard to participation in activities organised as partnerships which give birth to national and international networks focused on specific objectives, a relevant example is the *Telethon Network of Genetic Biobanks*. It was founded in 2007 and is a research project financially supported by Fondazione Telethon. It is presently composed of 11 biobanks and stores about 100,000 biological samples, representing approximately 950 distinct rare genetic diseases.[6]

The Italian biobank landscape is completed by networking initiatives carried out at the regional level: Italian Regions, in fact, are in some cases involved in a series of initiatives to organise activities connected with biobanking and are in charge of the recognition of regional accredited biobanks.[7]

Population biobanks are also an important reality, given the existence in Italy of populations that can be considered genetic isolates. A recent example that was widely reported concerns the events that affected a collection of biological samples and data in the region of Sardinia.[8] The collection belonged to Shardna, a company

[3] Act no. 85/2009, 14 July 2009, published on the Official Journal (G.U.) no.160 Supp.Ord. no.108/L G.U. General series.

[4] More information at https://www.bbmri.it.

[5] http://www.bbmri-eric.eu/national-nodes/italy/.

[6] More information at http://biobanknetwork.telethon.it/.

[7] More information at https://www.bbmri.it/regioni.

[8] See Piciocchi et al. (2017), pp. 1–14.

created in 2000 through a public-private partnership as the first of its kind in Italy in the field of genomics research. Shardna's research focused on identifying genetic and environmental factors that carry a predisposition to common multifactorial diseases through the study of a genetically homogeneous population from the isolated communities in the Ogliastra region in Sardinia. The biobank included 230,000 biological samples from the almost 13,000 fully genealogically-linked residents of that region. Nearly 10 years after its creation a controversial bankruptcy case engulfed the company, which sparked concern among the participants. The case led to a couple of decisions by the national DPA and one by the Tribunal of Cagliari which represent a fascinating point of reference to investigate how the interests of participants and freedom of research can be assessed in the Italian regulatory framework.[9]

2.2 Regulation of Biobank Research and Collection of Samples

In contrast to many countries, there is no special biobank legislation in Italy. The regulation of biobank research can be framed under the general data protection legislation and also in terms of the processing of biological samples.

More precisely, Italy can be regarded as a 'hybrid model',[10] as mentioned earlier. The hybrid nature of the Italian model is mainly due to the role played by the national DPA, an independent administrative authority which is also established as the supervisory authority responsible for monitoring application of the GDPR. In the broader framework of the Italian legislation primarily related to the protection of personal data, it is the DPA which implements the GDPR and is in charge of identifying the conditions under which some personal data processes can occur. In particular, the DPA issued a general Authorisation concerning the processing of genetic data, considered as a category deserving special conditions of protection (general Authorisation no. 8/2016) and a general Authorisation for the processing of personal data for scientific research purposes (general Authorisation no. 9/2016). The conditions set out by the DPA mainly give regard to the purposes of use, the requirements for collection and storage, and communication and information duties. However, as will be explained below, the contents of both Authorisations are being reconsidered in the light of the new framework created by the entry into force of the GDPR.

In general terms, in Italy samples can be collected for clinical purposes or for research purposes. The patient/participant's informed consent is normally required

[9] See Italian Data Protection Authority, decision no. 389, 6 October 2016; Tribunal of Cagliari, Sez. I, decision no. 1569, 18 May 2017; Italian Data Protection Authority, decision no. 561, 21 December 2017.

[10] Macilotti et al. (2015), pp. 53–77.

as procedures involve intrusion into the body. Beyond international and European provisions (such as Article 5 of the Oviedo Convention[11] and Article 3 of the Charter of Fundamental Rights of the European Union[12]) the principle of consent is enshrined in Article 32.2 of the Italian Constitution and it has recently been reinforced in ordinary legislation.[13]

After having served their clinical purpose, some tissue samples can be stored in a biobank and may subsequently be used for research or other purposes. In this case, unless anonymisation occurs, the rules relating to the processing of personal data apply. Biological samples, which are considered as mere 'supports', basically follow the rules relating to the processing of personal data.

Before the entry into force of the GDPR, the Code of Privacy[14] provided that data disclosing health and sex life should be kept separate from any other personal data and that they might not be disseminated[15] without the written consent of the data subject.[16] The Code strictly specified the cases in which the processing of health data could be allowed—under the prior DPA's authorisation and when the purposes concerned either a third party or the community—even without the data subject's consent in the cases expressly provided for by the legislation.[17] With regard to genetic data, the Code of Privacy provided that their processing was legitimate only under the conditions set by the Authorisation released by the DPA. Legislative decree no. 101/2018, which was adopted to implement the provisions of the GDPR, introduced art. 2-septies to the Italian Code of Privacy that provides for special guarantees for the processing of genetic, biometric and health-related data, and modified Article 110 of the Code of Privacy. The normative changes introduced by this reform uphold the mechanism of general Authorisations to be issued by the DPA, but their contents are undergoing a process of revision and reconsideration, also through a public consultation.[18]

The general Authorisation for the processing of personal data for scientific research (no. 9/2016) allows the processing of data suitable for disclosing health, even without the data subjects' consent, for scientific research purposes in the

---

[11] Convention for the Protection of Human Rights and Dignity of the Human Being with regard to the Application of Biology and Medicine: Convention on Human Rights and Biomedicine, Oviedo, 4 April 1997, Article 5—General rule: 'An intervention in the health field may only be carried out after the person concerned has given free and informed consent to it.'

[12] Charter of Fundamental Rights of the European Union, article 5: '1. Everyone has the right to respect for his or her physical and mental integrity. 2. In the fields of medicine and biology, the following must be respected in particular: the free and informed consent of the person concerned, according to the procedures laid down by law.'

[13] Law no. 219/2017 on informed consent and advanced directives.

[14] Legislative decree no. 196 of 30 June 2003.

[15] Legislative decree no. 196 of 30 June 2003, Article 22.

[16] Legislative decree no. 196 of 30 June 2003, Article 76.

[17] Legislative decree no. 196 of 30 June 2003, Article 110.

[18] The process was concluded, after this Chapter was submitted for publication, with the approval by the DPA of Document no. 146/2019, which confirms most of the contents of the previous Authorisations.

medical, biomedical or epidemiological sectors, subject to compliance with the limitations and conditions laid down by the same Authorisation and exclusively if the data are indispensable to achieve the purposes of the research. The Authorisation, in particular, sets out four requirements: (i) the processing must be necessary to conduct studies; (ii) the research project should not have any significant, personal impact on the data subjects themselves; (iii) the research project should rely on data or samples collected beforehand for healthcare purposes or should implement prior research projects; in addition (iv) the project must obtain a reasoned and favourable opinion from the competent ethics committee.[19]

In the case of genetic data, Authorisation no. 8/2016 requires the written informed consent of the 'person concerned', who can freely, and at any time, withdraw consent. With specific regard to the processing for scientific and statistical purposes, the Authorisation requires the data subject to be informed about whether the data and/or biological samples are to be retained and used for other scientific and statistical research purposes, which shall also be specified appropriately. Where it is impossible to inform the data subjects, and all reasonable efforts have been made to contact them, further retention and use of the data or samples is allowed for research projects other than the initial one. However, this is only when: (i) research for similar purposes cannot be performed by processing data relating to individuals who can, or have been able to, provide their informed consent; (ii) the processing does not allow the identification of the data subjects; (iii) there is no proof that the data subjects have objected; and (iv) an ad hoc authorisation by the national DPA is released after obtaining a reasoned and favourable opinion from the competent ethical committee.

It is clear that neither of the two Authorisations contains provisions directly addressing biobanks. Their regulation should therefore be based on general provisions concerning storage of samples and data and the possibilities of secondary uses for research purposes.

3 Individual Rights and Safeguards

3.1 General Remarks

The way in which the balance between the interests of the participants and the interests of the research is configured can be deduced from the joint reading of some legislative provisions that have been introduced following changes brought by the GDPR and of some provisions adopted by the national DPA.

[19] Section 2.1 of Authorization no. 9/2016.

3.2 'Further Conditions' and the Role of the National DPA

Legislative decree no. 101/2018 introduced Article 2-septies in the Italian Code of Privacy that provides for special guarantees for the treatment of genetic, biometric and health-related data. It specifically implements the clause provided by Article 9, paragraph 4 of the GDPR (processing of special categories of personal data), according to which 'Member States may maintain or introduce further conditions, including limitations, with regard to the processing of genetic data'. Further conditions, in particular, have to be found in Authorisations issued by the national DPA.

At the legislative level, Article 110 of the Code of Privacy, which has been amended by the Legislative decree no. 101/2018 in order to adapt it to the GDPR, states that consent of the data subject for the processing of health data, for the purpose of scientific research in the medical, biomedical or epidemiological fields, is not necessary when the research is conducted on the basis of laws or EU law, in accordance with Article 9, paragraph 2, point j) of the GDPR.[20] According to the same provision, consent is also not necessary when, due to particular reasons, informing the interested parties is impossible or implies a disproportionate effort, or risks seriously damaging or making the achievement of the aims of the research impossible. The Legislative decree does not clarify the exact scope of the concept of 'particular reasons' which makes it impossible to contact the interested person, thus leaving quite a broad margin of appreciation.

At the same time, in order to balance the lack of consent with other conditions, Article 110 provides that in such cases:

(a) the data controller adopts appropriate measures to protect the rights, freedoms and legitimate interests of the data subject;
(b) the research programme is the object of a motivated favourable opinion by the competent ethical committee at the territorial level; and
(c) the research must be submitted to prior consultation of the guarantor pursuant to Article 36 of the Regulation.[21]

[20] According to art. 9, para. 2, letter j), 'processing is necessary for archiving purposes in the public interest, scientific or historical research purposes or statistical purposes in accordance with Article 89(1) based on Union or Member State law which shall be proportionate to the aim pursued, respect the essence of the right to data protection and provide for suitable and specific measures to safeguard the fundamental rights and the interests of the data subject'.

[21] 'Article 36 (Prior consultation): 1. The controller shall consult the supervisory authority prior to processing where a data protection impact assessment under Article 35 indicates that the processing would result in a high risk in the absence of measures taken by the controller to mitigate the risk. 2. Where the supervisory authority is of the opinion that the intended processing referred to in paragraph 1 would infringe this Regulation, in particular where the controller has insufficiently identified or mitigated the risk, the supervisory authority shall, within period of up to 8 weeks of receipt of the request for consultation, provide written advice to the controller and, where applicable to the processor, and may use any of its powers referred to in Article 58. That period may be extended by 6 weeks, taking into account the complexity of the intended processing. The supervisory authority shall inform the controller and, where applicable, the processor, of any such extension within 1 month of receipt of the request for consultation together with the reasons for the delay. Those periods may be suspended until the supervisory authority has obtained information it has requested for the purposes of the consultation.'

3.3 Balance Between the Lack of Consent and Further 'Appropriate Measures' of Protection: Secondary Use of Data and Samples

The possibility to bypass the need to receive the written consent of the data subject is counterbalanced by the establishment of a set of requirements that are both substantive and procedural. These should be 'appropriate measures'[22] to protect rights and freedoms, and involve an ethical committee (favourable opinion) at the local level and the authority at the national level (consultation).

This regulatory framework is further developed by the national DPA Authorisation no. 9/2016. When it is not possible to acquire the consent of the data subjects, the data controller must document in the research project the existence of the reasons, considered entirely special or exceptional, why informing the interested parties is impossible or entails a disproportionate effort, or seriously prejudices or makes impossible the achievement of the aims of the research. This occurs, in particular, in three cases.

The first is when ethical reasons arise related to the circumstance that the data subject ignores his/her condition. This category includes research for which the information on the processing of data to be made to the interested parties would involve the disclosure of information concerning the conduct of the study whose knowledge could cause material or psychological harm to the data subjects themselves (for example, epidemiological studies on the distribution of a factor that predicts or can predict the development of a morbid state for which there is no treatment).

The second is when it is not possible to acquire consent due to organisational impossibility attributable to the fact that the failure to take into account the data referred to the estimated number of data subjects that cannot be contacted to inform them, with respect to the total number of subjects involved in the research, would have significant consequences for the study in terms of alteration of the relative results; this related in particular to the inclusion criteria included in the study, the recruitment modalities, the statistical number of the chosen sample, as well as the period of time elapsed since the data referring to the interested parties were originally collected (for example, in cases where the study concerns subjects with diseases with a high incidence of mortality, in the terminal phase of a disease, or in old age and with serious health conditions).

The third is when health reasons exist which are attributable to the severity of the clinical status of the person in question because of which he/she is unable to understand the indications given in the information and to give valid consent. In such cases, the study must be aimed at improving the clinical status of the person concerned. Furthermore, it is necessary to prove that the purposes of the study cannot be achieved through the treatment of data referring to persons able to understand the

[22] This expression seems to recall those 'appropriate safeguards' to which Article 89.1 GDPR refers.

indications given in the information and to provide valid consent or other research methodologies. This should have regard, in particular, to the inclusion criteria foreseen by the study, to the enrolment modalities, to the statistical number of the chosen sample, as well as to the reliability of the results achievable in relation to the specific aims of the study. When the genetic data treatment is due to health reasons, the consent of persons with an incapacity or inability to act must be acquired as soon as health conditions allow it.

The deontological rules for treatments for statistical or scientific research purposes apply to all treatments carried out for statistical and scientific purposes.[23] These should be in accordance with the methodological standards of the relevant disciplinary sector which are held by universities, research institutes and scientific societies, as well as researchers operating within them. In expressing his/her consent to a medical or epidemiological investigation, the interested party is required to declare whether he or she wants to know about any unexpected discoveries that emerge about him/her during the research. If the party declares such an interest, the personal data that can reveal the state of health can be disclosed to him/her or, in the case of physical incapacity or inability to understand, to those who legally exercise representation, to a near relative, a family member or a trustee (Article 8).

3.4 Pseudonymisation, Minimisation and the Storage of Data and Samples

In the light of Article 89 GDPR, general Authorisation no. 9/2016 concerning the processing of personal data for scientific research purposes provides that encryption or pseudonymisation techniques or other solutions are to be adopted where the research cannot achieve its goals without the identification, even temporary, of the interested parties. These techniques, considering the volume of the data processed, the nature, the object, the context and the purposes of the processing, make data not directly traceable to the interested parties, allowing them to be identified only when necessary. In these cases, in general, codes cannot be deduced from the personal identification data of the data subjects. This rule can be overturned upon written justification in the research project if the particular characteristics of the treatment require so and if it implies a manifestly disproportionate use of resources. The link between the research material and the data identifying the interested party, which is temporary and essential for the result of the research, is also justified in writing. In application of the principle of minimisation, the processing of personal data for scientific research purposes in the medical, biomedical or epidemiological fields may concern data able to reveal the health status of the data subjects, their sex life or their racial and ethnic origin, only if they are indispensable for the achievement of the research objectives (Article 5, paragraph 1, letter c) GDPR).

---

[23] National DPA, January 2019.

According to Article 99 of the Code (as modified by Legislative decree no. 101/2018), the processing of personal data for archiving purposes in the public interest, for scientific or historical research or for statistical purposes may be carried out even after the period of time necessary to achieve the different purposes for which the data were previously collected or processed. For the purposes of archiving in the public interest, for scientific or historical research or for statistical purposes, the personal data of which, for any reason, the processing of which has ceased, may be stored or transferred to another data controller in compliance with the provisions of Article 89, paragraph 1 of the GDPR. According to Article 106 of the Code, the Guarantoris allowed to establish ethical rules suitable to integrate the rules of the legislative decree, also with reference to the length of data conservation.

Authorisation no. 9/2016 provides that data and biological samples must be maintained only for a period of time not exceeding that necessary for the purposes for which they were collected or subsequently processed. A research project must declare a conservation period for the retention period, following the conclusion of the study, at the end of which the aforementioned data and samples should be anonymised.

According to Article 110-bis, the national DPA may authorise the further processing of personal data, including the special categories referred to in paragraph 9 of the GDPR (genetic data, biometric data or data concerning health) for the purposes of scientific research or for statistical purposes by third parties who mainly carry out such activities. This requirement is needed when, due to particular reasons, informing data subjects is either impossible, involves a disproportionate effort, or risks seriously prejudicing or making the achievement of the aims of the research impossible. In any case, appropriate measures to protect the rights, freedoms and legitimate interests of the interested party must be adopted in accordance with Article 89 of the GDPR, including preventive forms of data minimisation and anonymisation. Genetic data are subject to more restrictive rules.

3.5 *Special Rules for Genetic Data*

With specific regard to genetic data processing, Legislative decree no. 101/2018 introduced art. 2-septies of the Code of Privacy, which provides specific guarantees for the processing of genetic data, biometric data and data related to health conditions. It implements Article 9, paragraph 4 of the GDPR by confirming that these data can be processed when one of the conditions provided by paragraph 2 of Article 9 GDPR are fulfilled and measures introduced by the national DPA are satisfied. The latter measures shall introduce specific safeguards related also to the way of communicating to the interested person of diagnosis and health-related data. Guarantee measures shall identify security measures, including those techniques of encryption and pseudonomisation, minimisation measures, specifications modality for the selective access to the data and to communicate the information to interested parties, as well as any other measures necessary to guarantee the rights of the data subjects.

In the context of genetic data treatment, guarantee measures can identify, in the event of a particular and high level of risk, consent as a further measure to protect the rights of the data subject, pursuant to Article 9, paragraph 4 of the GDPR, or other specific precautions. In any case, genetic and health-related data cannot be diffused.

In the context of information and consent to genetic data processing, Authorisation no. 8/2016 (processing of genetic data), as amended in accordance with the GDPR on 13 December 2018), provides that information given to interested persons must particularly highlight:

(a) results achievable, related also to unexpected information which can be derived from data processing; and
(b) the right to limit the scope of communication of genetic data and transfer of biological samples, and the possible use for of the latter further purposes.

The same Authorisation also set out the cases in which consent for genetic data processing is mandatory, among which the processing for research purposes not provided for by the law is listed. Accordingly, genetic data and biological samples processing is allowed only when aimed at the protection of interested individuals, third parties or public health in medical, biomedical and epidemiological fields. Also, clinic experimentation or scientific research aiming at developing genetic analysis techniques is allowed. Specific requirements for individuals who are not able to give their consent are provided by the Authorisation (§ 4.11.2).

The research project must clarify adopted measures for guaranteeing that the conferring of biological samples is voluntary. Special attention must be given to the communication of measures adopted to allow for the identification of interested persons only for the time necessary for collecting and processing of data/samples (in accordance with Article 25 GDPR); and the procedures through which interested persons, upon request, can access the information contained in the research project.

In the event that the data subject withdraws his/her consent to the processing of data for research purposes, the biological sample is destroyed provided it has been taken for such purposes, when the sample cannot longer be referred to an identified or identifiable person.

The biological samples taken and the genetic data collected for health protection purposes can be stored and used for purposes of scientific or statistical research, without prejudice to the need to acquire the informed consent of the persons concerned, except in cases of statistical surveys or scientific research required by law or limited to the pursuit of scientific and statistical purposes directly connected with those for which the informed consent of the interested parties was originally acquired. This is set out in Authorisation no. 8/2016, § 4.11.3.

When, due to particular reasons, it is not possible to inform the interested parties in spite of having made every reasonable effort to do so, the conservation and further use of biological samples and genetic data collected for the realisation of research projects, other than the original ones, are allowed if similar research cannot be carried out by processing data that refers to persons from whom informed consent may or has been acquired and:

(a) when the research programme involves the use of biological samples and genetic data that originally did not allow identification of the interested parties, or that, following treatment, did not allow identification of the same interested parties and it does not appear that the latter have previously provided contrary indications;
(b) or when the research programme that was the object of a justified and favourable opinion of the competent ethical committee at a territorial level is subject to prior consultation with the national DPA pursuant to Article 36 of the GDPR.

4 Law in Context: Individual Rights and Public Interest

The above discussion indicates that the Italian legislature has opted for an integrated system of substantial and procedural guarantees. On the one hand, it recalls the conditions set forth by Article 9, paragraph 2 of the GDPR while, on the other, it delegates to the national DPA the establishment of further conditions and guarantee measures in an ad hoc authorisation. Furthermore, the Authorisations issued by the DPA have a general value and they have to be integrated by ethics committees' evaluations and approvals of single research projects. By doing so, the Italian legislature, coherently with the approach implemented at the EU level, strengthens the standards provided at the statutory law level by introducing ad hoc provisions for genetic data treatment. At the same time, it reaffirms the hybrid approach of the Italian legal system to biobanks and specifically genetic data and biological samples treatment because it expressly delegates to the competent administrative authority the function of further developing the regulatory framework.

Especially when compared with other relevant national legal systems (such as those of the UK and Spain), the lack of an ad hoc legislative Act on biobanking for research is stark and inevitably provokes a certain level of uncertainty in all involved subjects (researchers, participants and data subjects).

In the light of the central role played by the national DPA in setting the regulatory framework in this context, it is worth referring to its 2017 Annual Report[24] in order to understand possible areas of special relevance in the interplay between scientific research needs and the rights protection of individuals. In 2017, the DPA authorised, in the context of an international multi-centre research project requiring the treatment of data relating to the health of patients suffering from acute respiratory distress, the processing of data in the absence of prior information and consent of the patients when they were temporarily unable to provide it and this capacity was not expected to be reacquired before the end of the follow-up period. The authorisation was limited to the data and operations strictly necessary and relevant for the conduct

[24] 2017 Annual Report, 69 ff.

of the study. In particular, taking into account the state of unconsciousness, the DPA considered that the aims pursued could not be achieved through the processing of personal data on health, referring only to persons able to understand the indications given in the information sheet and to validly consent.[25] This further clarifies that if the health conditions of the interested party will improve during the survey and the interested party is able to understand the content of the information and to give valid consent to the processing of the data, the consent of the latter will be collected after the beginning of the survey, subject to appropriate information.

5 GDPR Impact and Future Possibilities for Biobanking

In countries like Italy where the need for specific regulation is more urgent, the entry into force of the GDPR might contribute to filling the gap in the legislation with regard to biobanking for medical scientific research purposes. The GDPR, in fact, beyond producing direct binding effects, requires the Italian legislature to intervene in order to provide a comprehensive and general legal framework concerning research biobanking. So far, the main impact of the GDPR on the Italian legal regulation of research biobank has been in the aforementioned amendment of the Data Protection Code of 2003. As already said, Italy decided to take advantage of the clause provided by Article 9, paragraph 4 of the GDPR, according to which 'Member States may maintain or introduce further conditions, including limitations, with regard to the processing of genetic data'. Beyond the substantial modifications and the limitations introduced, as described in the previous paragraph, what is worth mentioning is the procedure followed to build the whole framework of regulation. The legislator confirmed the old mechanism of delegating to the national DPA the duty to identify the conditions under which the treatment of specific kinds of data can be considered legitimate. In the past years, the DPA accomplished its task by means of adopting general authorisations for different kinds of processing. Taking advantage of its previous activity, in order to implement the GDPR the DPA selected the provisions contained in the old general authorisations which can be considered to be compatible with the GDPR and opened a public consultation to acquire observations and proposals around them. It should be stressed that public consultations are an instrument to which the Italian law is quite unfamiliar. It might be the case that the importance given by the GDPR to decentralisation strategies and institutionalised ethics (such as standards, codes of conduct and ethical thresholds) and the suggested risk-based approach, motivated the DPA to at least consider the voices of relevant stakeholders (e.g. associations or representatives from the field of scientific research). The public consultation offered the biobanking community the chance to present its viewpoints on the practical implications and problems with the asystematic, existing regulatory framework. How many of these observations will be considered is yet to be seen.

[25] Authorisation no. 6503911, 11 May 2017.

6 Conclusion

The Italian regulatory framework for biobank research is composite, complex and strongly focused on the protection of individual rights, in some cases creating obstacles to the development of research. The main feature of this regulatory model is its hybrid nature, where standards set forth by the DPA play an essential role in defining the concrete balance between the protection of participants' fundamental rights and freedom of research. The Italian legislature took advantage of the 'incomplete harmonisation' offered by the GDPR (see in particular Article 9, paragraph 4) and entrusted the DPA with the task of identifying the conditions for processing genetic and health data, in the hope of setting higher standards of protection. A key issue, which is common to other national systems, is the special regimen dedicated to genetic data. In this case the requirement of informed consent—characterised in terms of specificity—is still deemed fundamental. Where, exceptionally, informed consent for scientific research is not specifically required (see Part II), the protection of individual rights is rebalanced by requiring specific measures of protection, such as pseudonymisation and—in case of further use of samples and data – an ad hoc authorisation by the competent authority and a favourable opinion by the competent ethical committee.

References

Macilotti M, Penasa S, Tomasi M (2015) Consent, privacy and property in the Italian biobanks regulation: a hybrid model within EU? In: Mascalzoni D (ed) Ethics, law and governance of biobanking. Springer, Dordrecht, pp 53–77

Penasa S, de Miguel Beriain I, Barbosa C, Białek A, Chortara T, Dias Pereira A, Nicolas Jimenez P, Sroka T, Tomasi M (2018) The EU general data protection regulation: how will it impact the regulation of research biobanks? Setting the legal frame in the Mediterranean and Eastern European area. Med Law Int XX(X):1–15

Piciocchi C, Ducato R, Martinelli L, Perra S, Tomasi M, Zuddas C, Mascalzoni D (2017) Legal issues in governing genetic biobanks: the Italian framework as a case study for the implications for citizen's health through public-private initiatives. J Community Genet 9(2):1–14

Norwegian Biobanks: Increased Complexity with GDPR and National Law

Anne Kjersti Befring

Abstract Norway is generally regarded as having good opportunities for biobank research because of Biobank Norway—its national infrastructure of biobanks—which represents one of the world's largest existing resources within biobanking. It covers both consented population-based and disease-specific clinical biobanks. However, the regulatory framework in Norway for biobanking is fragmented, which makes navigating the legal landscape challenging.

The Personal Data Act (PDA) implements the General Data Protection Regulation (GDPR), and a few adjustments were made in the national health legislation in order to bring it into line with the GDPR. The Health Research Act (HRA) enables the use of biobanking and personal data in research with and without the consent of individuals. There are some disagreements about the changes brought about by the GDPR when it comes to research on biological material that includes personal data. When implementing GDPR Article 89, it was emphasised that the Data Protection Officer (DPO) has an important role even though the research ethics committee has allowed the use of data (the regional committee for medical and health research ethics (REC)). This has created conflicts. This article highlights key issues and ambiguities related to the GDPR and national legislation, and the relationship between the two.

1 Introduction

Norway is not a member of the European Union (EU) but it is part of the European Economic Area (EEA). EU legal acts must be incorporated into the EEA Agreement before they can be implemented into national law in Norway. The PDA—including the GDPR in Norwegian translation—entered into force in Norway on July 20th 2018 by reference to the incorporation of the GDPR into the EEA Agreement through a Joint Committee Decision on July 6th 2018.

The GDPR has not revolutionised the approach to privacy and data protection but it has increased the sector's awareness of the need to use health data and the need to

A. K. Befring (✉)
Law Faculty, University of Oslo, Oslo, Norway
e-mail: a.k.befring@jus.uio.no

S. Slokenberga et al. (eds.), *GDPR and Biobanking*, Law, Governance and Technology Series 43, https://doi.org/10.1007/978-3-030-49388-2_18

protect such information through the duty of confidentiality and created uncertainty about who should make decisions about sharing data in health and research organizations the potential to ensure more awareness of research participants' rights versus the societal and scientific interest in research.

All research and medical treatment includes processing of personal data, and the relationship between GDPR and national law provides the basis for several issues. This article raises issues related to how GDPR has been implemented, interpreted and what effects it has had, in fact and in law when it comes to biobanking and research. The GDPR provides for a two-level framework to enable derogations from these rights when scientific research is concerned, first, by directly invoking in provisions of the GDPR on a condition that safeguards that must include 'technical and organisational measures' are in place and second, through the Member State law.[1] These derogations can be challenging in light of the legal and ethical standards in biobanking that have been set forth in international treaties, national legislation, and how GDPR has been implemented through changes in the health legislation, and other legal instruments, as soft law.

There is also an ongoing discussion about the various roles and decision-making authority with regard to data sharing, and the division of responsibilities between the Data Inspectorate, regional ethical committees (RECs), Directorate for Health and E-Health, and the Norwegian Board of Health Supervision. An important change was that the health laws made reference to the legal definitions in the GDPR and that national regulations on the access to use personal data processing basis under the GDPR. Several examples show that there are different perceptions of the application of the GDPR in research on biological material. Some argue that the GDPR has made significant changes to the terms of research that include biological material and personal data, while others believe that it has not led to such changes with reference to the exemptions for research. Some claim that consent has become more important for the regulation of research and the publication of research results, while others claim that this is not the case.

The GDPR provides the possibility for implementation of national, sector-specific regulations as long as these regulations are not in conflict with the GDPR. In preparation for the implementation of the GDPR in Norway, the Norwegian Ministry of Health and Care Services (HOD)[2] made some amendments to ensure compatibility with it (Prop. 56 LS (2017–2018)).

[1] Staunton et al. (2019).

[2] HOD is responsible for providing good and equal health and care services to the population of Norway.

2 Biobanks Infrastructure and Regulatory Framework

2.1 Biobanks in Norway

Norway is working on establishing a health analysis platform and a note on legislative amendments has been sent from the Ministry at a hearing which took place during the last half of 2019. The health analysis platform will gather the many health registers for research and innovation purposes. Norway has a long history of establishing and maintaining health registers used to track specific societal or health-related aspects. Norway has established 70 health registries and 20 are central health registries that are mandatory and nationwide. There are currently more than 50 national disease and medical quality registries.[3] They may contain health data and personal identification information. Some registers contain human biological material in biobanks that are associated with the quality registers. More detailed information on the different health registries and how to access them is available online.[4]

Biobank Norway is a national infrastructure of biobanks and represents one of the world's largest existing resources within biobanking. It covers both consented population-based and disease-specific clinical biobanks.[5] Biobanks in Norway also have access to unparalleled longitudinal health data in health registers. Hence, it is a unique asset for global research and innovation projects within life sciences, disease prevention and treatment. Below are some examples of Norwegian biobanks.

The Norwegian Mother and Child Cohort Study is a birth cohort and biobank that collected samples from 95,000 pregnant women, 114,000 children and 70,000 fathers, from 1998 to 2008. The Janus Serum Bank is a unique cancer specific cohort with blood samples from 318,628 Norwegians collected from 1974 to 2004. The biobank is reserved for cancer research and is globally unique in terms of size and number of cancer cases.[6] The Tromsø Study was initiated in 1974 in an attempt to help combat the high mortality in Norway due to cardiovascular diseases. Over the years the cohort has been expanded and now includes samples from over 40,000 people and holds unique phenotypic data. The NoPSC Biobank for primary sclerosing cholangitis (PSC) is one of the largest PSC biobanks in the world. It collects a range of different matrices and high-quality phenotypic data.

The Nord-Trøndelag Health Study (HUNT) is one of the largest health studies ever performed, comprising samples from 140,000 people collected in four rounds since the mid-1980s. It is a unique database of genetics, questionnaires, clinical

[3] Norwegian Institute of Public Health (2019). From 2007 to 2016, the number of quality registers with national status increased from 13 to 54. The definition of a medical quality register is a health register where results for a limited patient group are continuously documented.

[4] Norwegian Institute of Public Health: https://www.fhi.no/en/shortcuts/about-the-health-registries/. Norwegian Directorate of eHealth: www.helsedata.no, and https://www.kvalitetsregistre.no/.

[5] BBMRI.NO (2019).

[6] Langseth et al. (2017).

measurements and biobanked samples. HUNT Biobank is a national biobank for Cohort of Norway (CONOR) with 250,000 DNA samples from all the large Norwegian Health Surveys gathered in one place. HUNT Databank contains information on the health of and samples from participants in the HUNT study conducted in three waves of data gathering.[7] The data collection was carried out with questionnaires, interviews, clinical studies and analyses of blood and urine samples. In addition, the HUNT Databank contains blood and urine samples stored in the HUNT Biobank which can be requested and defrosted for genetic analyses and other biological markers.[8]

2.2 *Norwegian Regulations*

When the GDPR was implemented, it was pointed out by the Norwegian authorities that health services are subject to extensive regulations in Norwegian law. As the confidentiality protection applies within the health service and research, there was no need for any limited additional regulations. The Ministry has not uncovered a need to design new supplementary legal bases, for the processing of personal data within the scope of health legislation, nor has the Ministry identified the need for new national provisions that make exceptions to the prohibition on processing specific categories of personal data, which also include health information.[9] The health legislation with regulations provides a number of such guarantees, with the duty of confidentiality a particularly significant guarantee in this context. Another measure is, for example, the requirement for encryption in section 21 of the Health Register Act (HREG) or a decision on the disclosure of information.[10]

There are minimal changes in the health laws, possibly because the regulation does not define how clear and specific the national regulations must be with regard to providing legal grounds for the processing of data. However, some changes are of great importance because they change the procedures of processing personal data and decision-making systems. The GDPR regulates questions that the national health legislation does not regulate specifically. References from the GDPR to national laws include the basis for processing data and exceptions from the prohibition against processing particularly sensitive data.[11]

The exceptions in the GDPR Article 89 for rights in scientific research etc. are incorporated into the national laws through referrals but there are ambiguities about how they should be interpreted. Several derogations have been made in national

[7]The HUNT1 Survey (1984–1986), the HUNT2 Survey (1995–1997) and the HUNT3 Survey (2006–2008) In addition to data from the main studies, the HUNT databank also contains data from a number of additional studies.

[8]hunt-db.medisin.ntnu.no/hunt-db/#/, 2019.

[9]GDPR Art. 6 (1) (c) and (e) and (3), and 9.

[10]Prop. 56 LS (2016-2017) pp. 183-184. This legal provision refers to GDPR art. 32.

[11]GDPR Art. 6.1, 9.2 and 89.

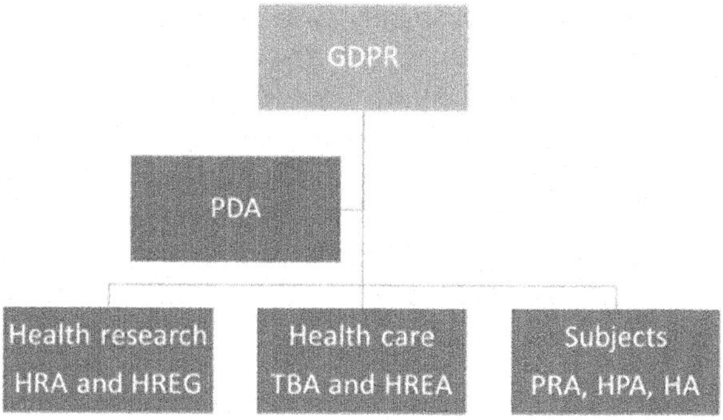

Fig. 1 Relationship between GDPR and central national laws regulating biobanking. Human rights underpin both GDPR and national laws

legislation, and these are discussed below.[12] According to Norwegian law, biobanks and personal data are regulated in different laws. The PDA refers to the laws that regulate biological material and the processing of personal data.[13] Several laws regulate the storage of biological material and data in research and in connection with healthcare. These play an important role in the implementation of the GDPR (see Fig. 1).

Public and private biobanks are divided into three main groups: diagnostic biobanks, treatment biobanks and research biobanks. The first two, both of which store material gathered during the course of treatment, are regulated by the Treatment Biobank Act (TBA), and the latter by the Health Research Act (HRA).[14] Before the TBA was adopted in 2003, there was no separate law governing the large collections of biological material that had been systematically obtained and stored over several generations from the 1930s.[15]

Since 2008 the HRA[16] has regulated research involving people, biological material and data, and describes medical and health research as use of 'scientific methodology to provide new knowledge about health and disease.'[17] This definition is relatively broad and includes all interventions on humans, living and dead, on human biological material and on health information, as well as regulation of pilot studies, testing and performance of experimental studies.[18] The HRA regulates the establishment of *research biobanks*.[19]

---

[12] With reference to the GDPR Article 89.

[13] PDA section 2.

[14] TBA: 2003-02-21. no. 12. HRA: Act 2008-06-20 no. 44. There are also biobanks regulated by the Penal Code and the Criminal Procedure Act.

[15] Halvorsen (2006).

[16] HRA: Act 2008-06-20 no. 44.

[17] HRA section 4 a.

[18] HRA section 2. See Ot.prp. nr. 74 2006–2007. Clinical testing of medicinal products on humans follows from the Medicines Act section 3, cf. § 2 (3). Clinical testing of medical equipment is regulated by the Medical Devices Act. The HRA complements in both cases as far as it suits.

[19] Biobanks used in medical treatment are regulated by TRA.

There may be uncertainty about what research is and what is the development of method and quality assurance. The term 'scientific methodology' refers both to general principles of scientific theory of reasoning and to the more specific techniques developed within various scientific disciplines to produce 'valid knowledge'.[20] This excludes quality assurance.[21] Research on human beings requires prior approval from a research committee. With the implementation of GDPR, the Norwegian authorities have assumed that a pre-approval from the ethics committee is not sufficient to process personal data. The requirements for 'state of art' in healthcare will be indicative of when diagnostics and healthcare should be organised as research.[22]

The TBA regulates biobanks, which are defined as 'a collection of human biological material delivered for medical examination, diagnosis and treatment.'[23] These tissue samples have been collected from all organs of the body, from all age groups, that have been taken for medical tests, diagnostics and treatment as part of healthcare for more than 100 years. In recent years, it has included samples from all newborns. The purpose of the TBA is to secure storage of material and data in healthcare and to ensure that the collection, storage, processing and destruction is carried out in an ethically responsible and legal manner for the good of the individual and society. The storage of biological material and data for use in healthcare is aimed at achieving continuity and reliability of treatment.

Registers used for health research are regulated by the HREG.[24] This includes data transferred from patient records. Duties and rights also follow from the laws mentioned above. The HREG aims to facilitate the collection and processing of health information, to provide better health and care services through increased knowledge.

Health registers based on personal data derived from biological material in hospitals and health care providers, should mainly be processed in accordance with the Health Records Act (HREA).[25] This means that a distinction is made between the law that regulates registers in the health service and registers based on data from the health service for the purpose of health research. When giving medical treatment, healthcare professionals are required to store relevant and necessary information in the health record.[26] This means, among other things, that data must be stored when the health care is given without consent, for example because the patient is unable to consent or when using force. Data and biological material obtained in the health

[20] See Ot. prp. nr. 74 (2006–2007) pp. 11–13.

[21] The scope of the Act can come across as limited because of its requirement for scientific methodology and the purpose limitation that includes knowledge about health and illness.

[22] It can also be an argument in favour of a more lenient interpretation of scientific methodology.

[23] TBA section 2.

[24] HREG: Act 2014-06-20 no. 43.

[25] HREA: Act 2014-06-20 no. 44. See also TBA section 5 number 7, which refers to this law that regulates patient data stored with biological material.

[26] Also called Patient records and medical records. HPA sections 39 and 40, and HREA section 8. HPA: 1999-07-02 no. 64.

service can be used for research through transfer to health registers or by pre-approval from ethical research committee and data controller.

The legislation clearly distinguishes between activities that are justified on the grounds of healthcare and research and other activities, as well as between storing and processing of data and biological material for purposes of health research and for purposes of healthcare (Simonsen and Nylenna (2005), Simonsen 2014). The medical development has blurred the lines between medical treatment and health research, and this raises new issues about how to apply the law. One example is that genetic mapping as part of personalised medicine means that biological material is the starting point for knowledge about the genetics and diagnostics of patients, and for clinical testing (Befring 2019).[27] When healthcare and research are needed to safeguard and protect the vital interests of individuals, it can include using material and data according to the exceptions in HRA, HREG and GDPR.[28] Another issue that can be raised but will not be dealt with here is the question of ownership of the biobank and the material it contains, and about intangible assets that can be acquired on the basis of biobanks.

The prohibition against commercial exploitation of research participants, human biological material and health information should be assessed on the basis of the need for development of methods and if there is a trade relationship between the public health service and private actors. A central question for states is who should own and dispose of biological material obtained over several generations. Biobanks built up in public health services could be perceived as common property that should be used for the common good to develop new knowledge and new methods. Ownership and intellectual property may be a more important starting point for discussions on intellectual property rights when algorithms and costly treatment methods are developed based on biological material.

Subjects for regulation in the relevant laws are research participants and patients, researchers, health personnel and healthcare companies. The Patients' and User Rights Act (PRA)[29] regulates them as rights subjects, and the HPA and the Hospital Act (HA)[30] regulate them as duty subjects.

The HRA requires a designated person to be in charge of the research, who must ensure that competent personnel and satisfactory equipment is available and that the research is carried out under safe conditions.[31] The person shall also ensure that the applicable regulations are followed and that the research process is cancelled immediately if the interests of the research participant so indicates. The Act also requires an ethics committee to pre-evaluate research projects and ensure compliance with the regulations for research and privacy, as well as the international obligations regarding the position of subjects. The committee's view on whether the research project is ethically acceptable or not must be substantiated.

[27] Chapters 7 and 8.

[28] HRA section 28 and 35. GDPR art. 6 (1)(d), 9(2) (j) and (h). and 89.

[29] PRA: 1999-07-02 no. 63.

[30] HA: 1997-07-02 no. 61.

[31] HRA section 5.

3 Individual Rights and Safeguards

3.1 Article 89 and the Right to Information

The legislation shall be carried out in accordance with fundamental privacy considerations that include the basic principles of respect for human dignity and for human autonomy and equality norms. The health legislation is based on three key principles for health research and storage of biological material and data in healthcare: principles of justification, of confidentiality and of autonomy. The confidentiality principle applies also after the death of persons. Research on biological material taken from a deceased person is correspondingly subject to the provisions in the Transplantation Act (TA) and Autopsy Act (AA), relating to transplantation, hospital autopsies and the donation of bodies etc. and regulations issued pursuant to this Act.[32]

The ban on processing sensitive personal information, is not applicable when processing is necessary for archiving purposes in the public interest, scientific or historical research purposes or statistical purposes in accordance with Article 89 (1), based on Union or Member State law.[33] Such a law must be proportionate to the aim pursued, respect the essence of the right to data protection and provide for suitable and specific measures to safeguard the fundamental rights and interests of the data subject.[34]

The Norwegian legislation—in accordance with GDPR Article 89 (2)—explicitly derogates from the rights of the data subjects laid down in GDPR Articles 15, 16, 18 and 21. These exemptions are considered by the authorities to be in accordance with the regulation. It is specified in the narrative, including Recital 65, that further retention of the personal data 'should be lawful where it is necessary' for the performance of a task carried out in the public interest, on the grounds of public interest in the area of public health, for archiving 'scientific or historical research purposes'.

In the national consultation round, research environments emphasised the need for several exceptions. Where the aforementioned provisions of Article 9 (2) require a 'basis' for the processing or that the processing is 'permitted', they may, in their wording, hardly be expected to make an unconditional claim that there must always be a completely explicit and specific legal basis. In connection with the implementation of the GDPR, it was stated that it does not provide a clear answer to the clear or specific national provisions that allow the processing of particular categories of personal data.[35]

In connection with the implementation of GDPR, disagreement on art 89 was uncovered. The Norwegian Center for Research Data stated that an exception from

---

[32] HRA section 21. TA: 2017-05-07 no. 25. AA: 2017-05-07 no. 26. Act of 9 February 1973 no. 6.

[33] GDPR Article 9 (1). HRA section 28 and 35.

[34] GDPR Article 9 (2) (j).

[35] Prop. 56 LS (2016–2017) pp. 40–41.

the right to data portability is also necessary when processing for statistical purposes.[36] They also stated that exemptions from the duty to notify pursuant to Article 19 of the Regulation should be made for processing for research and statistics purposes. GDPR Article 21, which entitles the data subject to protest against the processing of personal data when processing is based on Article 6 (1) (e) or (f), may be relevant when processing personal data for scientific or historical research purposes, unless the processing is necessary to perform a task in the public interest. This right has not been included in the Norwegian legislation and will probably be covered by the trade-offs that are made of interests that can offset consent.

HOD points out that Article 89 allows for exemptions from the right to protest under Article 21 for research purposes.[37] A separate provision in national legislation was therefore not proposed or adopted. On the other hand, exceptions to the right of access were adopted for research purposes on the basis of Article 23 (1) (e) and Article 89 (2) and (3) of the Regulation, and these are crucial for the data subject. If research participants should be able to claim their personal information, this will be at the expense of legitimacy and ethics in research. It is important to ensure that research data through the registrant's right to data portability is not subject to merchandise and commercial activities.[38] Exemptions from the right of access can therefore be made pursuant to Article 15 in the PDA.[39] The right of access under GDPR Article 15 does not apply to the processing of personal data for archival purposes in the public interest, purposes related to scientific or historical research or statistical purposes in accordance with GDPR Article 89 (1) as far as: (a) it will require disproportionate efforts to provide access or (b) access rights are likely to make it impossible or severely prevent the achievement of the objectives of the treatment. The third paragraph is further formulated as an exception instead of a condition, but this is not intended to have any significance to the scope of the article.

The HREG gave the data subject the right to require the erasure of 'bothersome information', as a result of interest shown in it.[40] The HREG gives the data subject a right to delete or block health information that has already been processed if processing of the information 'feels strongly distressing for the data subject' and there are no 'strong general considerations' that indicate that the information is being processed.[41] This form of balancing of interests exists in several laws and is also reflected in the GDPR and in human rights conventions.[42] The general provision on limitations with regard to rectification and deletion in the PDA will also apply to health information in research.[43]

---

[36] Prop. 56 LS (2016–2017) chapter 11.

[37] Together with the exemption in Article 21 (6).

[38] Prop. 56 LS (2016–2017) pp. 83–84.

[39] Section 17 (1, a cf) makes exceptions from the right to access to information.

[40] HREG section 25.

[41] HREG sections 8 to 11.

[42] HPA section 43. See also HRA section 36. PDA section 11.

[43] PDA section 17 second and third paragraphs.

Pursuant to the HPA and the PRA, there are limitations on access to data that have been stored in connection with healthcare. This narrow access must be seen both in the light of the fact that data storage is based on a statutory requirement and because that information may be excluded from the person's entitled to access or information insight.[44] The local health authority (Fylkesmannen) decides on the question of erasure.

3.2 Consent

Consent is not required for the use of anonymised human biological material and anonymous data. Anonymous data is nevertheless covered by the standard of care in research and medical care. In Norwegian legislation there are different forms of consent when researching personal data and biological material: expressed consent, broad consent in HRA sections 13 and 14, explicit and silent consent. The consent scheme has many limitations in Norwegian health legislation—these are discussed in more detail in my doctoral thesis.[45]

In Norway, biological material from large parts of the population is stored without consent and it varies widely how much the emitter knows about the purpose of storing and processing the material. Storage of biological material in treatment biobanks is not based on independent and explicit consent.[46] Most of the population has biological material stored in treatment biobanks without having explicitly consented to storage. There is no general right to information, but if the material is going to be used in a different manner than originally planned then informed consent must be obtained.

All newborns are screened for different genetic diseases and the material is stored in a separate biobank.[47] Parents can refuse screening, but few do so. This material can be used for 'method development' without consent. The scope of this activity is not further defined. This can open up the potential for the wide use of the material. With the new newborn database in the health service, biological material from all inhabitants of the country will be stored. However, with regard to the further use of tissue samples stored in clinical biobanks for research purposes, patients' right to self-determination may be better protected. In comparison, patients are not entitled to receive individual information about storage and further use of tissue samples. Each individual research participant must be able to give his or her consent to participate in research and has the right to receive the necessary information. An important exception to this requirement is access to research on biological material

[44] PRA sections 5-1 and 3-2.

[45] Befring (2019), and specifically chapters 5 and 10.

[46] TBA section 11.

[47] Oslo University hospital.

and health data without consent.[48] The HREG allows use of data obtained in the health service without the consent of the patient.[49]

The main rule in HRA section 13, is that research on people must be based on a voluntary, informed and specified consent. The information must be sufficient for the person to understand the consequences of receiving healthcare or to participate in research.[50] It is possible to conduct research on material saved in treatment biobanks or personal data if the REC approves it.[51]

The HRA section 14 allows 'broad-based consent' on certain conditions for research on human biological material and personal health data but not on research involving humans. The broad consent must define the research purposes for use of biological material and personal health data and a REC may specify conditions for use of broad consent and may order the project manager to obtain new consent if the committee deems it necessary.[52] A REC may approve new or changed use of previously collected human biological material or personal health data without new consent being obtained if it is difficult to obtain new consent and the research in question is of significant interest to society.[53] This may only be approved if the participants' welfare and integrity are ensured. Participants who have given broad consent are entitled to receive information about the project at regular intervals.

Consent to take part in a research project may be withdrawn at any time with some exceptions.[54] The ability to withdraw consent does not apply to the researcher's necessary requirement of fulfill his obligations, for example, to publish research results.[55] It is an obligation to have openness in research and to publish research results. Participants must receive information about this as the basis for consent. At the same time, the identity of participants must be adequately protected. A person who has withdrawn their consent may demand the destruction of their biological material and the erasure of the personal health data within 30 days.[56] The right to demand destruction, erasure or surrender of biological material or health data pursuant to the second paragraph does not apply if the material or data have been anonymised, or if the material has been processed and is now part of another biological product, or if the data have already been included in completed analyses. RECs may allow continued research on the material and defer destruction and erasure until the

---

[48] HRA section 28 and 35.

[49] Registers with person-identifiable data can be created without the consent of regulations, see sections 8 and 11 of the Health Register Act.

[50] The right to information in HRA section 13 and PRA section 3-2.

[51] RECs shall consider and give prior approval to health research that includes people, biological material and health data, se HRA sections 9 and 10. Exceptions have been made for health registers, cf. HREG.

[52] In the event of substantial changes to the research project that are deemed to have consequences for the participant's consent, new consent must be obtained in accordance with HRA section 13.

[53] HRA section 15.

[54] HRA section 16.

[55] Befring (2019) chapters 10.

[56] Upon withdrawal, research on the material or information must cease.

research project has been completed when particularly strong social or research considerations so warrant.

The law stipulates that the biological material must be stored in some situations, e.g. when the information is anonymised, when the material or processing is part of another biological product, and when the material is already included in a scientific work.[57] The right to destruction can be limited due to the same reasons. This means that there are several exceptions to the main rule of consent when researching biological material and health data provided they are proportionate.[58] This may only be applied if the research in question is of significant interest to society and the participants' welfare and integrity is ensured. The prior approval from REC may replace individual consent after a specific consideration and REC may specify conditions for use. The patient must have been informed in advance that human biological material may be used for research and must have been given the opportunity to refuse to be involved in research on human biological material. In my doctoral thesis I assess whether biological material can be used for genome sequencing under this provision.[59] Extensive mapping of the human genome is understood as analyses that provide detailed information on large portions of the human genome of individuals whereby large volumes of information are typically generated. In the mentioned mother-child survey, the genetics of a large number of children, mothers and fathers were mapped without the affected persons being made aware of the mapping and without explicit consent. I argue that the Norwegian law was interpreted incorrectly in this case. It is assumed that the requirement for consent for invasive research in the UN Convention on Civil and Political Rights Article 7 represents a legal barrier to mapping the genetics. Public interest cannot justify interventions such as genetic mapping in normal circumstances. It can also be considered disproportionate when the patient does not benefit from the procedure or consent. At the same time, there is an argument that the law should be reassessed based on the possibilities that may arise from new technology and the GDPR.

The PDA has several general exceptions to the requirement for information and allows processing of personal data and health data for research without consent.[60] The GDPR art. 89 has an exemption for the rights of registered persons, including medical research, if it is 'in the public interest' (Recital 51) when the processing is proportionate.

These provisions refer to the purposes set out in GDPR Article 89 and require that it is for the benefit of society and that it is necessary for archiving which is in the public interest for scientific or historical research purposes or statistical purposes. Article 89 can be perceived as a proportionality provision that balances interests through formulations that reasonably relate to the objective sought, are consistent with the fundamental content of the right to the protection of personal

[57] HRA section 15.

[58] HRA sections 14, 15, 28 and 35.

[59] Befring (2019) chapter 10.

[60] PDA section 8 and 9.

data and take appropriate and specific action to safeguard the data subject's interests. This includes assessments of what is 'necessary', 'proportionate' and what constitutes 'due care' when using biological material and personal data. However, the further retention of the personal data should be considered lawful when it is necessary on the grounds of public interest in the area of public health, for archiving purposes in the public interest, or for scientific or historical research purposes.

A specific question is whether the research subjects that have consented to participating in research can refuse the publishing of research results from research that is based on the interests of society. In the preparatory work for the PDA, there is disagreement on what is sufficient security in accordance with art. 89 when there are strong public interests. A central question is whether there is sufficient pseudonymization when there is public interest. Emphasis shall be placed on whether access will 'make it impossible or substantially impede its own safeguarding of statutory duties' regarding the storing and handling of the material.[61]

The primary purpose of the measures or guarantees is to ensure that the treatment is in line with the basic principles of the processing of personal data, taking into account the sensitivity of the information, the purpose of the treatment, the risk of the treatment, etc. Hence the guarantees or measures may vary considerably.

3.3 Confidentiality Protection

Confidentiality protection is governed by several laws and includes persons in healthcare facilities who process personal data as well as health researchers.[62] Irrespective of consent and confidentiality, personal data stored in the health service can be shared for research, health analyses, quality assurance, administration, planning or management of the healthcare service.[63] However, this is limited in scope. The definition of 'health information' in GDPR Article 4 (15) has been incorporated into the health laws and is no longer linked to the scope of confidentiality as in previous legislation. One consequence of this change is that biological material and raw data may be covered by the duty of confidentiality but not by the definition of health information.[64] In the preparations for the incorporation of the GDPR, it is pointed out that statutory exemptions from the duty of confidentiality imposed on researchers and health personnel will be a legal basis for processing personal data. This also includes exceptions to the duty of confidentiality and has an impact on who can make decisions about sharing data.

[61] Compared to the requirements for a supplementary legal basis pursuant to GDPR art,. 6 (1) (f), and (3), there is an assessment of what is sufficient based on the purpose and risk.

[62] E.g. HPA section 21, HRA section 7 and Patient Journal Act section 15.

[63] HPA section 29 a-c.

[64] Befring (2019) chapter 12.

The Norwegian confidentiality protection can constitute a source protection that includes biological material.[65] It covers both personal data and the use of biological material as the source of information, and can include protection of deceased persons who cannot consent. As the GDPR refers to the European Convention on Human Rights, it can be argued that the GDPR also entails a confidentiality protection of biological material.[66]

The degree of personal identification for health information should not be greater than is necessary to achieve the objectives. Pseudonymisation is a valuable tool to reduce the risk of computing. Names, personal identification numbers and other identifiers are obscured by replacing them with a particular key, such as a number code, which is kept separately from the information. This will reduce the risk of re-identification and may give greater freedom in the use of the information. This method is not as useful for data that can be identifiable in itself, such a genetic data.

3.4 Purpose Limitation

The right to correction and the limitation of processing in GDPR Articles 16 and 18 do not apply to the same purposes under GDPR 89 (1) as far as the rights are likely to make it impossible or severely prevent the achievement of the objectives of the treatment. However, these exceptions do not apply if the processing has legal effects or direct actual effects on the data subject. PDA section 17(2) makes exceptions in the right to rectification (GDPR Article 16) and the right to restriction of processing (GDPR Article 18).

The legislator argues that there is no need for further exceptions at this stage. According to HRA section 36, the data subject may require rectification and erasure according to GDPR Articles 16 and 17, unless this exception is applicable.[67] If the necessary data are already available (i.e. have been obtained from individuals), they can be used for further research purposes regardless of what purposes they were initially obtained for. Even where data are initially obtained based on informed consent for specific purposes, they can be used for (different) research later on, irrespective of the storage and purpose limitations (Articles 5 (1) (b) and (e)).

In 2006, the Norwegian Supreme Court decided on the disclosure of material to identify a possible deceased participant in connection with a serious robbery where

[65] HPA section 21 and HRA section 7.

[66] Recital 1. The protection of natural persons in relation to the processing of personal data is a fundamental right. Article 8(1) of the Charter of Fundamental Rights of the European Union (the 'Charter') and Article 16(1) of the Treaty on the Functioning of the European Union (TFEU) provide that everyone has the right to the protection of personal data concerning him or her.

[67] In HRA it is shown that the exceptions in the Personal Data Act sections 16 and 17, from the right to information and access and from the duty to notify of breaches of personal data security apply correspondingly to access pursuant to HRA section 42, and sections 40 and 41.

a police officer was killed.[68] The conclusion was that the police could not receive the biological material from the hospital as there was neither consent nor weighty interests present. In a case from 2014, the Supreme Court granted permission for the use of biological material to determine paternity.[69] The right to know one's father was crucial in this judgment.[70] There is no deadline for a child to raise a case as it the case for parents. The information is not in itself sufficient to change paternity, but can be a basis for the child to require the question of paternity settled by the courts. DNA information is crucial for determining paternity.

However, in another case the court reached the opposite conclusion. Biological traces on a bag of drugs found on a patient could not be delivered from the hospital to the police as this would constitute a breach of the duty of confidentiality.[71] We find a similar approach in a judgment of the European Court of Human Rights. In the Great Chamber case *S and Marper v. UK*, Article 8 was argued to include protection of cell samples (sections 68 to 72). The ECHR concluded that biological materials were stored in an inappropriate way. The Court pointed to some of the fundamental challenges that arise when storing genetic information, amongst them that storing of data must safeguard the protection of privacy: 'The mere storing of data relating to the private life of an individual amounts to an interference within the meaning of Article 8' (section 67). Each case must also be considered with regard to its specific context. The Court also emphasised that the emergence of new technology makes storing of genetic data more risky that what we can foresee at this point in time (section 71).

Biobanks and the comprehensive national registers with personally identifiable information are used for very different purposes. Questions can be raised as to whether national registers are contrary to purpose limitations. In Norway, emphasis has been placed on establishing 'platforms' for compiling biobanks and health registers, and for broad access to health research. Patients are often not aware that their data is being transferred from hospitals to the national registers. Even though new medical knowledge may be of public interest, the use of information must satisfy the balance between individual and public interest, as expressed in the HREG ('pressing social need' (section 8)). It might exclude commercial research that has no evidence of benefit sharing or address issues of public importance.

A REC must approve the establishment of research biobanks. A biobank can be established without being connected to a specific research project, and material collected for specific research may be transferred to a biobank after the project is carried out.[72] The sharing of biological material from a research biobank with other

[68] See Rt. 2006 p. 90 (Nokas Decission).

[69] See Rt. 2014 p. 585.

[70] See the discussion of paternity examinations and rights in NOU 2009: 5 (*Paternity and other motherhood*).

[71] See Rt. 2013 p. 1442.

[72] HRA section 25. Article 27 defines the rules for processing and storing of biological material.

countries requires consent and prior approval from the REC.[73] The HRA stipulates that human biological material from research biobanks may not be released for insurance-related purposes to an employer, a prosecuting authority or a court. This applies even if the person from whom the material stems gives consent to its release. The intention is to prevent persons in vulnerable positions from feeling pressured into disclosing sensitive information about their own health.

Transmission of data from the medical records to national health registers can take place without consent when it is stipulated in HREG section 8 and 11.[74] The provision applies only to the disclosure of information from statutory registers pursuant to the HREG section 11. It is uncertain whether this automated transfer of patient data to health registers is consistent with the GDPR's purpose limits.[75] In the HRA there are limitations in section 38 which prohibits the storage of data beyond the time necessary for carrying out the research project. There is no corresponding restriction on storage time when it comes to biological material but it is required that material be stored and handled properly with respect for the donor of the material.[76] Health information in the health service must be relevant and necessary to maintain storage.[77]

4 Law in Context: Individual Rights and Public Interest

After the implementation of the GDPR, processing of health personal data for research purposes should be limited to the legal grounds therein. Public interest require biological material and health data to be shared without consent and that the research is transparent and verifiable.[78] With regard to research on biological material, the considerations of self-determination and integrity apply in a somewhat different manner, most particularly in the form of a need for protection and right of control of sensitive information, i.e. privacy. In Norway, there are currently discussions on how data protection is weighed against the opportunities for research and medical treatment. Sharing of biological material and health data may increase patient safety, for example, through increased knowledge of medical methods. The proportionality assessment implies that this value must be weighed against risk of data processing, such as sharing data through systems that are not sufficiently secure.[79] For several of the areas of application, it is required that the information is of significant interest to the society and that the patient's integrity and welfare is

[73] Furthermore, the requirements for processing of data must be fulfilled, cf. Section 29 of the HRA.

[74] HREG section 20.

[75] GDPR art. 5.

[76] HRA section 27.

[77] HPA section 39 and 40.

[78] This is achieved through publication, cf. Article 9 (2), (i) and (j), and Recitals 156 and 157.

[79] Befring (2019), chapter 1, 7 and 14.

sufficiently safeguarded, i.e. by ensuring that the degree of personal identification is not greater than is necessary for the purpose in question. This proportionality assessment requires routine checks to assess whether it is necessary to use personal data. The GDPR's principles are applicable and will be important in the trade-offs that need to be made.

Approval from the REC was previously considered a necessary and adequate legal ground for processing of health personal data for research purposes. With the implementation of the GDPR, the Norwegian ministry of Health have assumed that the pre-approval from the REC is no longer sufficient when processing data in research.[80] The research activity that has previously based the processing of data on a concession must self-assess whether there is an adequate treatment basis. This has created uncertainty about who will make final decisions about research that includes data.

The HRA reflects the need for more nuanced requirements for consent depending on whether the research concerns individuals, human biological material or personal data derived from such material. In Norway the focus on what can be perceived as a legal and correct balance between requirements for safety when biological material and personal data are used, and who will make decisions about data sharing, which is about both statutory authority, competence and legal responsibility.

Firstly, little emphasis is placed on the need for confidentiality protection to vary—even within the categories in GDPR art. 9. Genetic data can range from being insensitive to being very sensitive and meaningful to more people than the one who has given consent.

Secondly, a great deal of emphasis has been placed on consent, which may have an impact on the opportunities for implementing research results that have been initiated and in connection with the obligation to publish research results, including with a view to verification.

Thirdly, questions have arisen as to who should take data processing decisions. The disagreement concerns who should take decisions, and the relationship between the data controller, the research manager, the privacy officer and the supervision of health research and the processing of personal data. The research manager according to the law (HRA) is an institution or a legal or natural person who has the overall responsibility for the research project and who has the necessary prerequisites to fulfil the research manager's duties under the HRA section 4 e.

It may be the same legal entity as the data controller but not necessarily. Health personnel have legal responsibility for medical treatment and research, for example, due diligence, documentation and verifiability. When conducting research on health services, the hospital's management is responsible both for ensuring that the research is sound and that the healthcare provided is up to certain standards. Through these regulations, correlations are created between the health service's duties, the healthcare personnel's duties and the rights of the patient, the subject and the data

[80] Prop. 56 LS (2016–2017) pp. 184–185, chapter. 32.3 refers to the relationship between the GDPR and the HRA.

subject.[81] Finally, a controversial issue in Norway is what role the DPO has in relation to decisions made by health personnel and hospital management.

When implementing GDPR Article 89, it was emphasised that the DPO should assess whether data can be processed in research. In health and research organizations the management has delegated decision-making authority to DPOs, despite the fact that they have no legal responsibility, and that many decisions about sharing personal data require medical assessments. At Oslo University Hospital, the largest hospital in Norway (and across all Nordic countries), 32 researchers have spoken out against how the DPO acts in assessments of research projects.[82] In this context, it was pinpointed that research projects of great value to the population have been halted by the DPO, who has been given wide authority from the data controller. This petition was formulated as a warning and was sent to the Board of Health. Previously, examples were given that the DPO had also stopped data sharing in connection with medical treatment, beyond their advisory role and their competence to advise.[83] This has created conflicts and public debate.[84] Discussions in the media may indicate that this has led to variations in practice, some of which are far stricter than before the implementation of the GDPR. The question is, which qualifications are required to make the necessary balances. Insight into different aspects of data processing may be necessary to prevent any consideration from being over-emphasised at the expense of other considerations, e.g. that the data processing is being too restrictive at the expense of opportunities for safeguarding patient safety and proper research. In order to achieve the balance between considerations discussed in the GDPR, it is assumed in many questions that competence is to be considered for research and academic issues.

One conclusion will be that the adoption of the GDPR has led to various interpretations of national law and how to implement it, and informal effects, that is, effects beyond what can be justified by law. This means that the actual effects of the GDPR have been greater than the legal ones.

A fundamental interest may be the opportunities for providing effective healthcare based on medical knowledge gained through the sharing of biobank material when data are the key ingredients of new medical knowledge. The ability to share data is a competitive parameter whose relevance will continue to increase with

---

[81] The institutions have a responsibility to ensure that the health personnel will be able to comply with their statutory duties and fulfil their obligations, see HPA section 16.

[82] More information is available in Aftenposten 6. januar 2019. https://www.aftenposten.no/meninger/debatt/i/VRnber/Nar-personvern-truer-folkehelsen%2D%2D32-forskere-ved-Oslo-universitetssykehus 16. februar 2019. https://www.aftenposten.no/norge/i/OnxKmV/Stor-varslersak-om-personvern-ved-Oslo-universitetssykehus.

[83] More information is available in Aftenposten 18. desember 2018 'Dødelig personvern'. https://www.aftenposten.no/meninger/debatt/i/VR7jEW/Dodelig-personvern%2D%2DTorkel-Steen.

[84] For examples of contributions to the debate, see https://www.aftenposten.no/meninger/debatt/i/VRnb1W/Helseministeren-bor-lytte-mindre-til-byrakratene-og-mer-til-de-som-faktisk-leverer-helsetjenestene%2D%2DTorkel-Steen. And https://www.aftenposten.no/meninger/debatt/i/VRnPJ6/Beskyttelse-av-pasientsikkerhet-er-overordnet-andre-hensyn%2D%2DAnne-Kjersti-Befring.

machine learning and artificial intelligence. It is challenging to develop legislation that allows use of materials and sufficient protection in all different types of research as they entail different issues. Where it is not possible to provide detailed rules on such conditions, for example, because the rules cover many different categories of treatment, it becomes necessary to establish more general rules. If the purpose of application is wide, it will be difficult to establish guarantees. An alternative is to determine mechanisms or procedures that the treatment manager should follow. Pre-approval by the supervisory authority is an example of such a mechanism.

5 Conclusions

Different interpretations of GDPR Article 89 has led to uncertainty about the legal basis for research and datasharing. A biobank contains both biological material and data, and questions arise as to whether the regulation should be the same. One argument for similar national legislation is that biological material represent a higher risk of violations due to new technology. The evolution of technology has made it possible for hospitals, companies and research institutions to collect, store and use biological material and large amounts of data from biological material. With the aid of technological methods, it can be difficult to distinguish between the protection of human biological material and data because biological material can be traced back to individuals and provide a lot of information about those individuals. This makes it even more necessary to develop new rules and arrangements for consent.[85] The indirect consent form (see Sect. 3.2) for storing biological material in the health service may be too weak to meet the requirements of the GDPR. Indirect consent means that there is no explicit consent related to the actual storage of biological material, and that the general consent to health care is used as a legal basis.

The storage of biological material should therefore rest on an independent legal basis. At the same time, the emphasis on consent regarding the preparation and publication of research could weaken the opportunities for sharing medical knowledge. As mentioned above, this is discussed in Norway on the basis of GDPR Article 89.

There are also discussions on when the individual protection of biological material occurs and whether this protection can be an obstacle to developing new medical knowledge. This applies in particular to research on human genetics and genetic variants. It may be crucial to use data and biological materials in order to achieve an appropriate management of biobanks and personal data that can be derived from such banks. This can be justified by the fact that medical assessments, research ethical assessments and legal assessments are required. The Norwegian Board of Health Supervision supervises the research to ensure that it is in accordance with legal requirements and this includes biological material.

[85] Befring (2019), Chapter 13.

Cooperation between the Norwegian Data Protection Authority, ethical committees (REC) and health authorities, may be essential in order to provide guidance and to make decisions regarding supervision and pre-approval (REC), when the question assumes considerations of interest under the GDPR and the legislation.

The Ministry of Health and Care Services (HOD) has prepared a circular that addresses some of the challenges with GDPR and Norwegian legislation, and points out how standards for research can be developed with reference to GDPR.[86] Furthermore, it recommended that a Code of Conduct for Health Research should be developed for biobank research. In this guide, it was recommended that the health authorities should be involved in issues concerning the processing of personal data in research. Apart from this, no new regulations have been proposed.

In any case, a code of conduct must be based on an understanding of what are duties and rights in GDPR and the national law. This is hardly sufficient given that the law does not provide a sufficient basis for processing data. Norway should instead adopt new legislation that can complement the GDPR to create greater clarity when it comes to processing biobank material/data for research purposes.

New technology provides new opportunities to build up medical knowledge but also comes with new challenges, including privacy breach risks. The freedom of both the people and the country depends to a large extent on how the comprehensive data is processed. On the one hand, to achieve the necessary security and to maintain democracy and openness about what influences governance. On the other hand in order to utilize knowledge. New questions arise about public organizations and commercial use of data.

References

Befring AK (2019) Persontilpasset medisin. Rettslige perspektiver. Gyldendal, Oslo

Halvorsen M (2006) Norsk biobankrett. Fagbokforlaget, Bergen

Langseth H, Gislefoss RE et al (2017) Cohort profile: the Janus Serum Bank Cohort in Norway. Int J Epidemiol 46(2):403–404g. https://doi.org/10.1093/ije/dyw027

Simonsen S (2014) Kommentarer til behandlingsbiobankloven. In: Tjomsland S, Simonsen S (eds) Helseforskningsloven. Kommentarutgave. Oslo, Gyldendal juridisk

Simonsen S, Nylenna M (2005) Helseforskningsrett. Den rettslige regulering av medisinsk og helsefaglig forskning. Gyldendal Akademiske, Oslo

Staunton C, Slokenberga S, Mascalzoni D (2019) The GDPR and the research exemption: considerations on the necessary safeguards for research biobanks. Eur J Hum Genet 27:1159–1167. https://doi.org/10.1038/s41431-019-0386-5

[86] Helse- og omsorgsdepartementet: Rundskriv 12. April 2019. https://www.regjeringen.no/no/dokument/dep/hod/rundskriv/2019/rundskriv-i-32019-om-informasjonshandtering-i-spesialisthelsetjenesten/id2642049/.

Norwegian Legislation

Personopplysningsloven: 2018- 06- 15 no. 38 (Personal Data Act: PDA)
Behandlingsbiobanken: 2003-02-21. no. 12 (Treatment Biobank Act: TBA)
Helseforskningsloven: 2008-06-20 no. 44 (Health Research Act: HRA)
Helseregisterloven: 2014-06-20 no. 43 (Health Register Act: HREG)
Pasientjournalloven: 2014-06-20 no 44 (Health Record Act: HERA)
Helsepersonelloven: 1999-07-02 no. 64 (Health Personell Act: HPA)
Pasient – og brukerrettighetsloven: 1999-07-02 no. 63 (Patient and user right Act. PRA)
Spesialisthelsetjenesteloven: 1999-07-02 no. 61 (Hospital Act: HA)
Transplantasjonslova: 2017 – 05- 07 no. 25
Obduksjonslova: 2017-05-07 no 26

Public Documents

NOU 1993: 22 Pseudonyme helseregistre
NOU 2009: 1 Individ og integritet — Personvern i det digitale samfunnet
NOU 2009: 5 Paternity and other motherhood
Prop.56 LS (2017–2018) Lov om behandling av personopplysninger (personopplysningsloven) og samtykke til deltakelse i en beslutning i EØS-komiteen om innlemmelse av forordning (EU) nr. 2016/679 (generell personvernforordning) i EØS-avtalen
Ot. prp. nr. 74 (2006-2007) Om lov om medisinsk og helsefaglig forskning (helseforskningsloven)
The Norwegian Institute of public health: Gode helseregistre – bedre helse. Strategi for modernisering og samordning av sentrale helseregistre og medisinske kvalitetsregistre 2010–2020

The Supreme Court of Norway

Rt. 2006 p. 90 (Nokas)
Rt. 2013 p. 1442 (narkotikapose)
Rt. 2014 p. 585

The European Court of Human Rights

S. og Marper v. United Kingdom. Application no. 30562/04 og 30566/04

Media

Aftenposten (2018) Dødelig personvern. https://www.aftenposten.no/meninger/debatt/i/VR7jEW/Dodelig-personvern%2D%2DTorkel-Steen. Accessed June 2019
Aftenposten (2019a) Når personvern truer folkehelsen. https://www.aftenposten.no/meninger/debatt/i/VRnber/Nar-personvern-truer-folkehelsen%2D%2D32-forskere-ved-Oslo-universitetssykehus. Accessed June 2019
Aftenposten (2019b) Stor varslersak om personvern ved Oslo Universitetssykehus. https://www.aftenposten.no/norge/i/OnxKmV/Stor-varslersak-om-personvern-ved-Oslo-universitetssykehus. Accessed June 2019

Aftenposten (2019c) Beskyttelse av pasientsikkerhet er overordnet andre hensyn! https://www.aftenposten.no/meninger/debatt/i/VRnPJ6/Beskyttelse-av-pasientsikkerhet-er-overordnet-andre-hensyn%2D%2DAnne-Kjersti-Befring. Accessed June 2019

Aftenposten (2019d) Helseministeren bør lytte mindre til byråkratene og mer til de som faktisk leverer helsetjenestene. https://www.aftenposten.no/meninger/debatt/i/VRnb1W/Helseministeren-bor-lytte-mindre-til-byrakratene-og-mer-til-de-som-faktisk-leverer-helsetjenestene%2D%2DTorkel-Steen. Accessed June 2019

Norwegian Institute of Public Health (2019). https://www.fhi.no/en/shortcuts/about-the-health-registries/. Accessed June 2019

Norwegian Directorate of eHealth (2019) Helsedata. www.helsedata.no. Accessed June 2019

Nasjonalt servicemiljø for medisinske kvalitetsregistre (2019). https://www.kvalitetsregistre.no/. Accessed June 2019

Biobanks and GDPR: A Look at the Portuguese Panorama

Carla Barbosa and Andreia da Costa Andrade

Abstract The need for the existence of biobanks for health research purposes is something of which government authorities have been aware for several years. One year after the full entry into force of the GDPR, the Portuguese legislature has finally passed the law that ensures the full implementation of the data protection regime's points left open by the European legislature. However, Portugal has also in place a range of legislation regulating the establishment and functioning of biobanks. The regulation of biobanks for research purposes imposes special protection duties on scientific research activity in which biological samples and associated data are used in order to guarantee protection of privacy and confidentiality.

1 Introduction

Medical research is recognized vital in enabling general improvement of citizens' health through progress achieved by medicine. Nonetheless, the benefits are not immune to the risks inherent in the indispensable intervention of human beings, either by the provision of biological samples or by the mere sharing of personal data. Prevention of risk and possible damage entails compliance not only with the principles and rules elaborated by the scientific community, but also with technical and clinical rules, and respect for the dignity of the human person (as the overriding principle of the international legal order) and its various dimensions.

The guiding and conforming principles for the treatment of biological samples and the personal data of participants in scientific research studies are derived from the conjunction of the provisions set out in the Convention 108 of the Council of Europe, of January 28, 1981; in the UE Regulation 2016/679 of the European Parliament and the European Council, of April 26, 2016, on the protection of natural persons with regard to the processing of personal data and on the free movement of such data, and repealing Directive 95/46/EC (General Data Protection Regulation;

C. Barbosa (✉) A. da Costa Andrade
Biomedical Law Institute, Law Faculty, University of Coimbra, Coimbra, Portugal
e-mail: cbarbosa@fd.uc.pt

S. Slokenberga et al. (eds.), *GDPR and Biobanking*, Law, Governance and Technology Series 43, https://doi.org/10.1007/978-3-030-49388-2_19

hereafter GDPR); but also in national law as article 26°/1, article 35° and article 73°/4 of the Constitution of the Portuguese Republic (hereafter CPR); Law n° 21/2014, of April 16, and repealing Law n° 73/2015, of 27 July, Law on Medical Research (hereafter LMR); and the Law n° 12/2005, of 26 January, on personal genetic data and health data, as well as the regulation thereof made by Decree-Law n° 131/2014, of August 29.

Given the aforementioned legal framework, and the guiding principles, one year after the full entry into force of the General Data Protection Regulation (GDPR), the Portuguese legislature has finally passed the law that ensures the full implementation of the data protection regime's points left open by the European legislature. Law n. 58/2019, from August 8th, that ensures the implementation, in the national legal order, of Regulation (EU) 2016/679 of the Parliament and of the Council of 27 April 2016 on the protection of individuals with regard to the processing of personal and free data circulation of this data.[1] The long period without national laws adopted to adapt personal data protection norms to the Portuguese reality largely affected the development of scientific research, in that on the one hand most projects entail analysis of data and biological samples, in the absence of a safe, conclusive regulatory framework, and on the other hand they rely on EU funding which required the resolve and the guarantee of compliance with national and EU norms on data protection, thereby putting Portuguese researchers at a disadvantage vis-à-vis their counterparts. There is still ongoing discussion about the national law adopted.

Meanwhile, precisely in light of the untouchable value of the dignity of the human person, the Portuguese legislature considered it lawful to impose special protection duties on scientific research activity in which biological samples and associated data are used. The purpose of regulation is to ensure that scientific research into human health is conducted in a transparent way and in accordance with ethical standards, promoting its excellence and credibility as well as the protection of society and the individual. Draft Law n° 142/XIII,[2] which aims at approving the legal framework for the harvesting, processing, analysis, provision and destruction of human cells (stem cells included) and tissues for scientific purposes, although it has expired it should be discussed again.

---

[1] Available for consultation at https://dre.pt/web/guest/pesquisa/-/search/123815982/details/maximized.

[2] Available for consultation at https://www.parlamento.pt/ActividadeParlamentar/Paginas/DetalheIniciativa.aspx?BID=42877.

2 Biobank Infrastructure and Regulatory Environment

2.1 General Remarks

Portugal has in place a range of legislation regulating the establishment and functioning of biobanks. There is legislation in force to regulate stem cells biobanks,[3] biobanks for criminal and civil purposes,[4] and biobanks (so called bio data banks) for health care provision, including disease diagnosis and prevention, and basic or health research.

2.2 Legal Framework

To biobanks for research purposes we are applying Law n° 12/2005, of January 26 (hereafter Law 12/2005) repealed by Law n° 26/2016, of August 22, and regulated by Decree-Law n° 131/2014, of August 29. Article 19/1 of Law 12/2005 defines biobanks as 'any repository of biological samples or their derivatives, with or without limited storage life, whether using prospective harvesting or previously harvested material, or being obtained as part of routine health care, whether in screening programmes, or for research purposes, which must include personally identified, identifiable, anonymized or anonymous samples'.

For a biobank to be created, prior authorization is needed from an entity duly accredited by the department in charge of the protection of health (Law 12/2005). Until the application of General (EU) Data Protection Regulation,[5] in May 25, 2018,

[3]With regard to the use of stem cells, we should first consider Law n.° 12/2009, of March 26 (amended by Law n.° 1/2015, of January 8, and Law n.° 99/2017, of August 25), which establishes the legal regime governing quality and safety relating to the donation, collection, analysis, processing, preservation, storage, distribution and application of human tissues and cells, transposing into the domestic legal order Directive 2004/23/EC of the European Parliament and of the Council of March 31, 2006/17/EC of the Commission, of February 8, and 2006/86/EC of the European Parliament. However, it is the legal provision itself that removes its application with regard to stem cell research. Thus, in all matters relating to stem cell research, we must resort to the general laws regulating clinical research in Portugal, namely Law N.° 21/2014, of April 16. The law regulates clinical research, defined as 'any systematic study to discover or verify the distribution or effect of health factors, states or outcomes, processes or disease, performance, or safety of interventions or provision of health care, thus transposing into Portuguese law two European directives (Directive 2001/20/EC, of the European Parliament and of the Council, of April 4, on the approximation of Member States' laws, regulations and administrative provisions relating to the application of good clinical practice into the conduct of clinical trials on medicinal products for human use and the partial transposition of Directive 2007/47/EC of the European Parliament and of the Council, of September 5)'.

[4]Law n° 5/2008, of February 12, Database of DNA profiles—for purposes of civil and criminal identification, amended by Laws n° 40/2013, of June 25, and Law n° 90/2017, of August 22.

[5]Regulation (EU) 2016/679 of the European Parliament and of the Council, of April 27, 2016, on the protection of natural persons with regard to the processing of personal data and on the free movement of such data and repealing Directive 95/46/EC (General Regulation on Data Protection).

prior authorization of the National Data Protection Commission was required too, to the extent that personal data were involved. Currently, therefore, these entities (i.e. the biobanks) are mostly under the regulatory authority of the Health Authority and the National Data Protection Commission. However, full compliance with the legal requirements also entails a favorable opinion from the Ethics Commission.

2.3 *Collection of Samples*

Once biobanks are lawfully established, their functioning is subject to tight rules, especially with regard to consent. Collection of biological products and the taking of DNA samples for genetic testing must be the subject of separate informed consent for the purpose of medical tests and for research purposes stating the purpose of the collection and the shelf life of samples and products derived from them.[6] In other words, purpose determines the use of the sample obtained and included in the biobank.

A sample obtained and incorporated into a biobank for medical purposes cannot be used for research purposes, save in cases where retrospective use is possible, as we will see below.

Informed consent shall be in writing, and it is required to get and use the material in a bank of biological products; in the written consent form, the purpose of the biobank, the person responsible, the types of research to be undertaken, potential risks and benefits, conditions and duration of storage, measures taken to ensure privacy and confidentiality of the persons involved and the provision as to the possibility of communicating or not the results obtained with this material, must be stated (article 19°, n° 5 of Law 12/2005). Hence, it is necessary to obtain two consents: a first consent to obtain the biological sample, and a second one to inclusion of that sample in the biobank.

The law that ensures the implementation, in the internal legal order, of GDPR, provides in article 31°/4 that the general rules on consent provided for in the GDPR shall apply, in that such consent may cover several areas of research, and the ethical standards recognized by the scientific community must be respected. This is an opening vis-à-vis the specificity previously required, and one that will have a huge impact on the development of scientific research in the field of health.

Consent to inclusion in the biobank may be revoked at any time. Consent may be withdrawn at any time by the person to whom the biological material belongs or, after his/her death or disability, by his/her family members, in which case the biological samples and stored derivatives must be destroyed for good (article 18°/3 of Law 12/2005). At stake here is the application of the fundamental medical principle—the patient's self-determination—to the holders of the samples incorporated

[6] Article 18°/1 of Law 12/2005.

into a given biobank. It is always (or almost always) the subject of that sample who agrees to withdraw the sample, or include the sample in the biobank, or revoke consent to include that sample in the biobank.

In exceptional cases, consent may be waived. This occurs in those situations—which we have already mentioned—where retrospective use of samples is made, or in special situations where the consent of the persons concerned cannot be obtained due to the amount of data or individuals, their age or other comparable reason; the material and the data can be processed, but only for scientific research purposes or the collection of epidemiological or statistical data (article 19°/6 of Law 12/2005). The fact that this situation is provided for in the legislation is of paramount importance for health research using biological samples, especially in research cases with secondary use of samples, that is, samples collected for use in a given research, a use that proves relevant to further research not covered by the original consent.

The fact that someone agrees that their biological sample is incorporated into a biobank does not mean that s/he loses the possibility of exercising any rights over that sample. In fact, the law establishes that stored biological material is considered property of the person from whom it was obtained or—after his/her death or disability—of their relatives, and should be stored as long as it is of proven use for current and future family members (article 19°/13). In other words, despite being delivered to a biobank, the sample still never ceases to be the property of the person who has delivered it. This raises another issue directly related to it. In the case of information relevant to the health of the individual who yielded the sample (for research purposes) being discovered during the research process, should this information be communicated to him/her? It is our contention that this should always be taken into account when consent is sought, and the person who provides the sample and gives consent should inform the researchers whether or not s/he would like to be contacted, in the case of information that is relevant to his/her health is discovered—incidental findings. The law pointed in this direction by providing that, if the bank has personally identified, or identifiable samples, and if the possibility of reporting results of the studies carried out is provided, a medical expert in genetics must be involved in this process (article 19°/12).

2.4 *Regulation of Biobank Research*

Another aspect of great importance in the regulation of biobanks for research purposes in Portugal is the protection of privacy and confidentiality. The storage of personally identified material should be avoided by controlling access to collections of biological material, by limiting the number of authorized personnel to do so, and by ensuring its safety with respect to loss, alteration or destruction. In this regard, and similarly to what happens with respect to the current legislation on protection of personal data, the use of anonymized biological samples is required. Article 19° states in this regard, that only anonymous or irreversibly anonymized samples may be used, and the personally identified or identifiable samples should be limited to studies that cannot be done otherwise (n° 9). It also stresses that if there is an absolute need to use personally identified or identifiable samples, they should be coded, with the codes being stored separately, but always in public institutions (n° 11). In this connection, it is very interesting that article 19°/10 here provides for the impossibility of storage of non-anonymized (identify or identifiable) human biological material by commercial entities. It is also interesting to note that for several years, until the entry into force of Law n° 12/2009, of March 26, there was in Portugal a ban on stem cell biobanks which had a double mission—health care and research—and entirely owned by private entities; precisely because of this legal provision, these for-profit, private entities used do store personally identified biological samples. This situation ceased to exist with the entry into force of the aforementioned legislation in 2009, as stocks of stem cell biobanks owned by for-profit, private entities became permitted.

Although at no point does it refer to the legislation in force on the subject, the draft law on the legal framework for the harvesting, processing, analysis, provision and use, storage and destruction of human cells and tissues for scientific purposes, including stem cells, that was under discussion at the Assembly of the Republic, maintains the general principles, while introducing some innovation in relation to the requirements of the establishment of the biobank, in particular as regards its sustainability. In fact, article 18° of the draft law lists a dense set of requirements for the establishment of a biobank for scientific research purposes, which if it is approved in its current version (there is an expectation to be presented again in this version), will determine the elaboration and submission to the (still to be created) Committee for the Coordination of Research in Human Cells and Tissues, of a strategic plan of operation and medium term financial viability.

And this, of course, in addition to the descriptive document of the purposes of the bank, the characteristics of the collections and inclusion criteria of the samples, as well as the organic and operating regulation of the bank, and the strategic plan of operation and medium term financial viability, and the terms of consent and information to the donors.

2.5 The Portuguese Biobank Landscape

Over the last decade, we have witnessed a proliferation of these infrastructures in Portugal, with numerous biobanks dedicated to research. We find very different examples: some biobanks are larger and some of a smaller size, some dedicated to a specific pathology and some to several. Given their relevance we will give here four examples: two national biobanks (of particular note, due to their size in a country like Portugal), a network of tumor banks and a consortium of biobanks.

The biobank of the Oporto University Institute for Public Health (Instituto de Saúde Pública da Universidade do Porto—ISPUP) is in place for almost two decades. With over 200,000 samples, this is a pioneer structure in Portugal, the biobank was created to be useful for research in the area of determinants of human health, and focus on relatively frequent conditions in the general population, such as diabetes, cardiovascular disease, rheumatic diseases and cancer or obesity, and behavioral disorders. The biobank of ISPUP has an immense amount of data from the participants of four Portuguese population *cohorts* (longitudinal studies that assess the evolution of population health over time), spanning different generations: EPIPorto (Oporto's adult population), EPITeen (Oporto's young adults) Generation XXI (Oporto's children) and Bitwin (twins), and also cross-cutting samples representative of the Portuguese continental population. These samples preserved in the biobank are linked to data on an immense diversity of variables such as socioeconomic class, housing, food, cognition, among others.

The biobank of IMM, a structure created by the Institute of Molecular Medicine (IMM) within the Lisbon Academic Center of Medicine (CAML), about 6 years ago, which hosts and stores a collection of biological samples, voluntarily donated, with the aim of boosting biomedical research. Currently with thousands of samples (200,000, approximately) and their clinical data, the IMM-Biobank is a unique platform of technical support for research into the origin of diseases with a major impact on public health, such as cancer or osteoporosis. The IMM-Biobank collects samples in several ways. Through people who spontaneously donate their samples, or, for example, in the case of patients, samples are collected mainly in hospitals, at the proposal of a doctor, which is then examined by an ethics committee.

Subsequently, collections of biological material are coded with a separate number to safeguard the identity of their donor. The biobank of IMM CAML currently comprises 14 collections in areas as diverse as Neurology, Rheumatology, Orthopedics, Oncology, Cardiology, Endocrinology, among others. The IMM CAML Biobank creates conditions for the study of the pathogenesis of several diseases with a huge impact on human health, making it possible to identify new diagnostic and prognostic tests, as well as new therapeutic targets. It should be noted that the IMM-Biobank is part of the BBMRI—European Network of Biobanks.

Another very interesting example is the National Network of Tumor Banks (RNBT). 'A Tumor Bank (TB) is a particular type of biobank consisting of the organized collection of tumor samples (neoplasias), which may comprise non-neoplastic tissue. The purpose of a TB is to record this type of material and the associated data (epidemiological, clinical, anatomic-pathological and molecular), under ideal conditions for biomedical research. The availability of this type of material, when collected under optimum conditions, allows the development of translational research and the application of basic biomedical research knowledge to clinical problems'.[7]

Finally, we should also mention the existence in Portugal of a consortium of biobanks: Biobanco.pt. It is a biomedical research infrastructure that aims to

[7] Health Authority, available at www.dgs.pt. In Portugal there are several individual initiatives of TBs, some of which meet the requirements of the current Portuguese legislation, while others correspond to organized collections of samples. 9 Tumor Banks—Hospital São João; IPATIMUP; IPO—Porto; Centro Hospitalar e Universitário de Coimbra; ACIMAGO, centro Hospitalar Lisboa Norte; IPO Lisboa; IMM; Hospital Garcia da Orta—are part of the Portuguese RNBT.

maximize national and international scientific collaboration based on the use of human biological samples and their clinical data.[8] It presents as its commitments the following: *(i)* facilitate access to high quality biological samples and related clinical data; *(ii)* standardize the infrastructures, and the procedures of existing biobanks such as the processing and storage of the samples, to ensure quality; *(iii)* share resources and services so as to promote a global characterization of the sample as well as knowledge exchange; and *(iv)* assist the development of the BBMRI platform, fostering Portuguese participation in the infrastructure (BBMRI-ERIC.pt).

3 Individual Rights and Safeguards

In the national legislative framework set out above, a definition of scientific research that meets the demand in Recital 159 of the GDPR, is not offered in clear and distinct terms. Although a definition of scientific research that spells out the scope of the concept is not advanced, the legislator uses the concept in the normative stipulations pertaining to the theme, as in the case of Article 19°/3 of Law n° 12/2005, which limits the establishment of biobanks (or to use the legal expression: biological product banks) to the purpose of health care provision, and basic or applied health research.

Recital 159 of the GDPR sets out in general terms the characteristics of data processing for scientific research purposes, including technological development and demonstration, the fundamental and applied research as well as privately funded research. The national legislature has acknowledged that the GDPR leaves open the possibility for each Member State to establish weighting standards where data processing for scientific research purposes is concerned, and the legislature considered it appropriate to enshrine specific standards in this area. Article 31° of the law that ensures implementation of the GDPR in the national legal order, while not exclusively focused on the subject of the protection of personal data in the context of scientific research using biological samples, here discussed, refers it without providing a definition, nor detailing what should be considered scientific research; still, it goes on recognizing that 'treatment for scientific research purposes shall respect the principle of data minimization and include the anonymization or pseudonymization of the data, provided that the objectives can be achieved by one of these means'.

[8]This national scientific infrastructure will facilitate the integration of national researchers into international consortia, involving academic centers and the pharmaceutical industry, and fostering the development of science and economics. This consortium is composed of the most representative biobanks for research purposes in the country: IMM-biobank (Lisbon Academic Center of Medicine); CEDOC—NOVA Biobank; ICG Biobank (Calouste Gulbenkian Foundation); Champalimaud Biobank (Champalimaud Foundation); ISPUP Biobank (Oporto University); INSA Biobank (Ricardo Jorge National Public Health Institute); Coimbra Biobank (University of Coimbra); Azorbio Biobank (Terceira Island Santo Espírito Hospital, EPE); National Network of Tumor Banks.

Within the framework of the GDPR, the national law also states that in these cases, 'rights of access, rectification, limitation of treatment and opposition provided for in articles 15°, 16°, 18° and 21° are inhibited, where the exercise of those rights has become impossible, in particular in the event of anonymization of the data collected', or is likely to seriously jeopardize to achieve the purposes underlying the processing of the data. The national law further states that 'the general rules on consent, as provided for in the GDPR, apply [to data processing for scientific research], considering that it may cover several research areas, and the ethical standards recognized by the scientific community must be complied with'. In this context, it should also be noted that the national legislature has made no distinction between public sector—or private sector-funded data processing for scientific research purposes, thereby demonstrating the unwillingness to develop the crux of the matter, to wit: public interest linked to scientific research.

In the national law, the national legislature does not develop in sufficient detail the concepts of personal data or pseudoanonymization, in that they are referred as set out in Article 4 of the GDPR. While it is true that the previous legislation, now repealed, defined in the exact terms of the directive that transposed the concept of personal data, the new proposal does not deal with this particular aspect, limiting itself to stating that 'treatment for scientific research purposes should comply with the principle of data minimization'—without expanding further on the concept—and to 'include their anonymization or pseudonymization where the aimed ends can be reached by one of these ways', in Article 31° thereof, included in a chapter that seeks to summarize all specific situations of processing of personal data. It is true that the scientific community and researchers from the various centers and areas of biomedical research have long resorted to the coding technique as a safe and efficient means to protect participants' privacy while still promoting satisfactory results in the studies developed on the basis of samples and data collected and processed.

The clause in Article 5(b) of the GDPR is critically important in particular in the health care research sector, as it admits that further processing for record purposes in the public interest, or for scientific, historical research or statistical purposes, is not considered to be incompatible with the initial purposes, in accordance with Article 89(1).

Article 5(1)(e) of GDPR states that personal data must not be kept in a form which permits the identification of subjects for no longer than is necessary for processing purposes. However, an exceptional clause has been added concerning data processing for scientific research purposes, which allows personal data to be kept for longer periods, in accordance with Article 89(1), although they are subject to the application of appropriate technical and organizational measures to safeguard the rights and freedoms of the data subject.

While debatable whether this is a real exception or an additional constraint regime, the Portuguese legislature has only put forward a general proposal as to the data retention period. In Article 21° of the law on adaptation to the GPDR, the legislature makes the period of retention of personal data dependent on a legal stipulation or imposition or, in cases where by the nature and purpose of the treatment, it is not possible to determine in advance the time when it is no longer necessary, the preservation of personal data for an unlimited period is lawful. This might clearly be the case with medical scientific research.

GDPR Articles 4(1), 11 and 7, articulate a concept of informed consent that is based on a free, specific, informed and explicit manifestation of will, through which the data subject accepts, by means of a declaration or unequivocal positive act. However, Recital 33 admits that it is often not possible to fully identify the purpose of personal data processing for scientific research purposes at the time of data collection. Therefore, data subjects should be allowed to give their consent to certain areas of scientific research when in keeping with recognized ethical standards for scientific research. Data subjects should have the opportunity to give their consent only to certain areas of research or parts of research projects to the extent allowed by the intended purpose. We have already referred the primary character of Informed Consent in the development of scientific research based on the processing of personal data, health data, and especially genetic data and biological samples. Hence, it will suffice here to highlight the requirement made by the Portuguese legislature in the draft law on the regulation of biobanks for scientific research purposes.

In accordance with Article 5° of that proposal, donors should be informed in advance, in a manner suitable to their level of literacy, in writing, of the objectives of the collection, the research to be carried out, the known benefits and risks inherent in the procurement of cells and tissues of human origin for the purposes of scientific research, as well as their ethical, social and legal implications, storage conditions, confidentiality and access, as well as the conditions for alteration or destruction of samples. Therefore, the validity of informed consent has not been restricted to a defined area or study, as provided for in the legislation still in force.

Prohibition in principle of the processing of sensitive personal data such as health data, genetic data and biometric data, is subject to the exceptions in article 9 (2), with special focus on the provisions in paragraph i), according to which the processing of the aforementioned data is permitted if the processing is necessary on public interest grounds in the field of public health. In this respect, legal, European or national provisions ensuring appropriate and specific measures to safeguard the rights and freedoms of the data subject, in particular professional secrecy, are required, as already mentioned in Recital 156.

In this particular point, Law of Public Health Surveillance System, governs in Portugal. It establishes a public health surveillance system that identifies risk situations, collects, updates, analyzes and disseminates data on transmissible diseases and other public health risks, as well as prepares contingency plans in the event of emergency situations, or as serious as those of public disaster.[9] This system

[9] Law 81/2009, of August 21 establishes SINAVE, a public health surveillance system, through the organization of a set of entities from the public, private and social sectors, carrying out public health activities, according to their respective organic laws and statutory assignments, enforcing measures of prevention, alert, control and response, regarding communicable diseases, in particular the infectious ones, and other public health risks, with a view to ensuring citizens' right to health protection. Further Information at: https://dre.pt/pesquisa/-/search/488301/details/maximized.

replicates the guidelines of the World Health Organization (WHO) in the control of compulsory notifiable diseases by collecting data to fulfill the obligations falling within the scope of the national and international epidemiological surveillance competences.

Also with regard to the treatment of sensitive data, such as genetic and biometric health data, the GDPR allows Member States to determine new conditions or limitations. In the bill that was under discussion, the Portuguese legislature merely cited the principle set out in the regulation, without further ado on this.

Normally, data processed for scientific research purposes are not collected by researchers, but rather communicated by an entity (health care provider or other) who reports them without any identification, as this is not relevant to the success of the study. In compliance with the principle of minimization, Article 11 of GDPR allows the maintenance of such treatments without connection with the identification of the data subject. In the same vein, the national law on the implementation of the GDPR in Portugal provides in article 31° of the discussed draft, that treatment for record purposes in the public interest, and for scientific research purposes, should comply with the principle of data minimization, limiting itself to the data essential for the success of the study, and include anonymization or pseudonymization of the data, where the objectives can be achieved by one of these ways. This is certainly the best privacy by concept strategy.

In cases where the personal data were not collected by the person in charge of processing them—i.e. the researcher, for the matter at stake here—and where it is possible to identify the subjects, the reporting obligations set out in Article 14 of the GDPR will not apply, as this would constitute a disproportionate effort for researchers. However, protective measures will have to be taken, and measures that in some way materialize the transparency advocated in the legal statement, such as the publication of the study.

It is also important to highlight the provisions of Article 31°/ 2 of the law that adapt the GDPR norms, according to which 'where personal data are processed for purposes of record in the public interest, scientific or historical research or official statistical purposes, the rights of access, rectification, limitation of the processing and opposition provided for in GDPR articles 15, 16, 18 and 21 of the are undermined where the exercise of those rights has become impossible, namely where the data collected are anonymized, or liable to seriously undermine the attainment of those objectives'.

In with the possibilities for exceptions in GDPR, the Portuguese legislature did not recognize data subjects within the scope of scientific research purposes as being entitled with the right to be forgotten, Article 17 GDPR.

4 Law in Context: Individual Rights and Public Interest

At the moment of the establishment of a biobank and during the management performance process, in the overwhelming majority of cases the public interest and markedly individual values and interests are pitted against each other, as if they were antagonistic realities. Still, it is possible to strike a balance between science development and individual rights by means of a legal regime that, fully compliant with the primacy of the dignity of the human person, provides the scientific community with the right conditions for the development of scientific research activity, thus opening the way to generate new knowledge in the health area that will ultimately benefit individuals in the civil community.

With the new draft law on the establishment of biobanks for scientific research purposes, the Portuguese legislature sought a balance solution between the injunction to strengthen research institutions and scientific output, as well as boost innovation and the development of new products and processes by the institutions that in Portugal are dedicated to scientific research and technological development in those areas. And the requirements that scientific research in human health be carried out in a transparent manner, in accordance with ethical principles, which promotes its excellence and credibility as well as the protection of society and the individual.

To this end, it sought to establish the legal framework for the collection, processing, analysis, distribution and use, storage and destruction of cells and tissues of human origin for scientific research purposes, including stem cells, based on the principles of Autonomy, Vulnerability, Scientific Integrity, Confidentiality, Gratuitous donation of samples of human origin, Non-discrimination and Non-stigmatization, which together conform and apply the principle of the dignity of the human person (Article 3° of the bill).

The bill sets out that in practice the establishment and management of the biobank to be created under the terms of the draft law under consideration will be previously controlled by the National Data Protection Commission (CNPD), and also by the Commission for Coordination of Research in Human Cells and Tissues, still to be created.[10] In addition to technical requirements regarding infrastructure conditions and storage of samples and associated data, these entities will assess the other requirements directly associated with the rights of subjects of samples and data kept in the biobank. For this, ethical and legal standards will be mobilized, namely those in the GDPR as well as in the Law of Personal Genetic Information and Health Information, approved by Law n° 12/2005, of January 26, regulated by Decree-Law n° 131/2014, of August 29, with a special focus on the rules of conformation of

[10]This Commission will be composed of six members from the Ethics Committee for Clinical Research, the National Council for Medically Assisted Procreation, the National Ethics Council for the Life Sciences, the Portuguese Society of Stem Cells and Cell Therapy, the Foundation for Science and Technology, IP, INSA, IP, and INFARMED—National Authority for Medication and Health Products, IP.

Informed Consent, and regarding measures for the protection and organization of the data.

Concerning this point, the legislature can only determine how the various laws dealing with the collection and preservation of samples and personal (health and genetic) data will be combined, especially in conflicting norms. For example: Law 12/2005 lays down in Article 19°/10 the ban on storage of non-anonymized material by for-profit private entities, even if the samples are intended for scientific research. However, the draft law that was under discussion is mute on this point, always referring to entities and public or private repositories.

Still in the framework of the protection of individual rights, the Portuguese legislature innovated vis-à-vis the previous legislation in that it lays down a set of guarantees, with emphasis on the requirement to present a strategic plan of financial viability in the medium term (Article 18°/4 c) of the draft law), and also periodical control (Article 20°) and rules for the extinction of the biobank (Article 19°/2).

5 GDPR Impact and Future Possibilities for Biobanking

Most biobanks have a personal database aggregated to the biological samples repository. These infrastructures are therefore subject to rules not only on biobanks legislation but also on the protection of personal data. This was the case before the application of the GDPR started; however, it is now clearer, in the sense that the Regulation explicitly refers biobanks. In terms of national law, the law that will operationalize the application of various aspects related to the GDPR makes no reference to biobanks. Moreover, the bill is also very parsimonious with regard to the provisions concerning research using personal data, almost doing a transposition of what is laid down in the Regulation.

The only distinguishing aspect that the Portuguese case may bring is that it provides for a *vacatio legis* of three years for public institutions. That is, for the latter the application of the rules of the GDPR will not begin on May 25, 2018, having instead an additional three year period to adapt, after the entry into force of the Portuguese law. Considering that most (or at least the largest) biobanks for research purposes in Portugal are dependent on public institutions, this would mean that the GDPR rules do not apply to them. This, in our view, does not favor these infrastructures, considering that the GDPR is clearer and facilitates research using personal data.

Thus, apart from this aspect—the creation of a double scheme for the private sector and the public sector—the application of the GDPR in Portugal will not bring major differences regarding research using biobanks with personal data.

We believe that research will be easier, but this will be the result of greater permissiveness in research—a result stemming from the Regulation itself, and is not tied to Portugal alone.

The new regulation seems to have adopted principles which, at first sight, facilitate the pursuit of scientific research using personal data. Personal data for research purposes may be defined as '*the generation of knowledge about human populations through scientific and/or statistical methods, which does not need to contribute to the common interest, through the determination of new insights in a particular field of research*'.[11]

From a practical point of view, the Regulation continues to establish a clear preference for conducting scientific research using anonymous data to establish that, if the purpose of the research can be achieved through this type of data; in such case this 'can be fulfilled by further processing which does not permit or no longer permits the identification of data subjects (paragraph 1)'. However, where this is not possible, the pursuit of scientific research is possible with the use of personal data, provided that adequate safeguards are adopted in accordance with the Regulation itself. Those safeguards include technical and organizational measures to ensure respect for the principle of data minimization (i.e., appropriate processing which is relevant and limited to what is needed for research purposes) which includes the pseudonymization explicitly mentioned in GDPR Article 89 (1) that we will analyze below.

A comparison with the 1995 Directive shows a number of differences worth being reported. While the Directive adopted a more conservative stance by establishing the general principle of prohibiting personal data processing for scientific research purposes and only allowing it to be carried out through case analysis and the corresponding authorization from the regulatory authorities of each Member State,[12] the new regulation allows such research to be carried out. It does demand the adoption of such appropriate safeguards. In this regard, one difference between the two texts that we should point out is that the Regulation expressly refers pseudonymization as an appropriate measure, whereas the Directive never mentions this process.

Nevertheless, we think that the new Regulation establishes a general principle, in theory more favorable to research. However, there are points that only practice shall clarify the way Member States will be applying it. Therefore, the derogation of the rights of access, rectification, opposition and limitation on processing is unclear and has not been implemented. It can also be left to each Member State's discretion. The expression used is 'Union or Member State law may provide for derogations'. The question that remains unclear is: 'In what form? And what about consent? Is it possible to talk about broad consent?

[11] Ploem (2004).

[12] Recital 34 of the Directive states that Member States were authorized, where reasons of public interest so justify, 'to derogate from the prohibition on processing sensitive categories of data where important reasons of public interest so justify in areas such as public health and social protection - especially in order to ensure the quality and cost-effectiveness of the procedures used for settling claims for benefits and services in the health insurance system - scientific research and government statistics; whereas it is incumbent on them, however, to provide specific and suitable safeguards so as to protect the fundamental rights and the privacy of individuals'. Rules can also be found in Articles 11 and 13 of the Directive for the exceptions and situations where data have not been obtained from the owner.

The recital 33 of the Regulation does meet researchers' actual needs. Personal data are often collected for health research purposes, but the specific area of research is not actually identified, because at the time of collection that area is still unknown. However, how can this recital be harmonized with the requirement set forward in the wording of Article 9 of the Regulation? This rule establishes a prohibition on the processing of special categories of personal data. This limitation shall not apply if the data subject has given explicit consent to the processing of those personal data for one or more specified purposes, except where Union or Member State law provide that the prohibition referred to in paragraph 1 may not be lifted by the data subject (Article 9(2)(a)).

Research carried out in the health sector has kept the issue of consent and its various forms very much alive in Portugal. Research using health data, where the model used for consent is provided by the subjects of this data, is no exception to this rule. On the one hand, this is a traditional model of informed consent (the one set forward in the wording provided in the legal section of the Regulation) in which required informed consent—which is free and explicit—from the data subject makes it difficult to advance scientific research. On the other hand, new currents are emerging with alternative models such as broad consent (the one that appears to be mentioned in recital 33), which we can define as those situations where the donor consents to his/her sample(s) being used once at the beginning of the research experiment. If additional analyses need to be performed or new experiments are designed, the donor is not contacted again, provided the new research is not a significant deviation from what was agreed to initially.[13] Apologists for the traditional model argue that such broad consent is not true consent, as it cannot be taken into account. However, we agree with David Townend, who argues that *the difficulty behind this problematic debate is that informed consent and broad consent are presented as opposites of each other. However, informed consent and broad consent are not polar opposites, neither are they points on a continuum or spectrum. They refer to different issues within consent. Informed consent concerns the quality of the consent, whereas broad consent concerns the subject matter of the consent.*[14]

The future and the practical application of the Regulation will tell what will be the option of the member states regarding consent models. However, in the best interest of research, we hope that flexibility will begin to be implemented in the area of consent requirements, provided protective measures appropriate to the rights of personal health data subjects are duly safeguarded.

Another aspect not covered by the regulation is the secondary use of personal information for research purposes—secondary use refers to the use of data originally collected for a purpose other than the current one. This is a point on which the Regulation is mute. Hopefully, it will not prevent this secondary use, which, though essential for research using personal health data, is impossible to anticipate. Very often, a new purpose is only known after the processing of personal health data has begun, and the reality is that 'all data derived from genome-wide associated studies

[13] Steinsbekk et al. (2013).

[14] Townend (2012)

and large-scale population studies which increasingly use electronic health records (EHRs) and/or electronic medical records will fall under this legislation.[15] There is also no doubt that data sharing and provision of secondary data access can have a profoundly beneficial impact on progress in biomedicine and the health sciences'.[16]

Finally, the Regulation does not specifically address the processing of personal data for research developed with the use of biological samples. However, the Regulation will necessarily apply to research, developed using samples stored in biobanks, where it is possible for researchers to relate these biological samples to personal data (the Regulation explicitly defines personal health data as information obtained from the analysis or examination of a body part or bodily substance, including genetic data and biological samples).[17] With regard to research biobanking, the approval of the Regulation could hamper or halt various medical research procedures, including retrospective as well as prospective research.

It is indisputable that biobanks are essential tools for the development of research. Still, these infrastructures face various challenges: whether at the level of governance or economic sustainability. The truth is that biobanks create bio-value, which is defined by Catherine Waldby as 'the surplus of in vitro vitality produced by the biotechnical reformulation of living processes'.[18] Portugal is a small country, and for this reason one of the main problems that often arises, and one that frequently comes up whenever biobanking-related issues are discussed, is the economic sustainability of biobanks. Now, sustainability is a critical element in the development of these infrastructures.

Biobanks maintenance and their economic sustainability might rely for the most part of it on their being integrated into public institutions with public funding (considering that these biobanks do not have nationwide scope, and to that extent they may not have problems similar to those of biobanks such as in the case of Iceland). Hence the need national biobanks have felt to be increasingly integrated into European or international biobank networks.

In this respect, the fact that Europe has a common legislation—the *GDPR*—might facilitate as far as personal data processing is concerned. However, this can only be said from an abstract point of view. In practice, though, what I think will happen is that very different national laws will lead to different legal systems with regard to the use of biobanks.

The other problem directly related to sustainability is, as we have said, governance. In Portugal we have biobanks for research purposes in private and public institutions; in the case of private institutions, with the limitation we have seen above: the legislation prohibits private for-profit institutions from having identified samples. For the most part, however, the financing and governance system stems from a public model. It has been the government, either through its direct

[15] Salvaterra (2015).

[16] Burton et al. (2017).

[17] This did not happen with the Directive.

[18] Waldby (2012).

administration or through decentralized institutes (such as universities or hospitals), that has borne the costs of these infrastructures. In fact, few private institutions have biobanks for research purposes or biobanks that have been created in accordance with existing regulations. For example, of the consortium existing in Portugal which we have mentioned above, only two of the infrastructures are located in private institutions: the Biobank of the Calouste Gulbenkian Foundation, and the Biobank of the Champalimaud Foundation. It is interesting that the institutional nature of the two of them is the same: a Foundation.

We believe that Portugal will continue above all, to be committed to support public biobanks. Not so much the establishment of more biobanks, but rather the expansion of the existing ones, and also their inclusion into international networks of biobanks. The need for the existence of biobanks for health research purposes is something of which government authorities have been aware for several years. The allocation of public funds and the financing of some reputable private entities will therefore allow the growth of these infrastructures in terms of size in Portugal. This is actually what we have been witnessing: the increase in the number of samples in existing biobanks; integration into networks; creation of biobanks consortia. As for the GDPR, we think it will facilitate the research developed in Portuguese biobanks. However, only future practice and the National Data Protection Commission's own stance in this regard will confirm this perception.

6 Conclusion

Portugal has various laws regulating the establishment and functioning of biobanks. The legislation in force includes the law regulating stem cell biobanks, biobanks for civil and criminal purposes, and biobanks (or biological product banks, as the Portuguese law prefers to label them) for health care purposes (including diagnosis and disease prevention), or basic research and applied medical research.

One year after the full validity of the GDPR the country, Portugal finally has a law to adapt European standards to the national predicament. The approved law is unsatisfactory and merely repeats what was already established in the European law, since the legislator has so far not exploited the room left open by the GDPR for each Member State's arrangements, which limits all sectors of activity, but in particular the scientific research carried out by the national research centers which, due to this gap, are in unequal circumstances vis-à-vis their peers.

Once the process of discussion and approval of the bill on the establishment and management of biobanks for scientific research purposes is complete (that we don't know when it ends as the process has to be restarted), it is likely that Portugal will continue to focus on the expansion of existing structured biobanks, and also on their inclusion in international biobanks networks. The existing structures will have to adapt themselves to new legal requirements and seek to comply with national and international legal requirements that seek a balance between the development of scientific research and the protection of the rights of individuals.

References

Burton PR, Banner N, Elliot MJ, Banks J, Knoppers BM (2017) Policies and strategies to facilitate secondary use of research data in the health sciences. Int J Epidemiol 46(6):1729–1733

Ploem CM (2004) Tussen privacy en wetenschapsvrijheid. Regulering van gegevensverwerking voor medisch-wetenschappelijk onderzoek, (diss. Amsterdam UvA). Sdu, Den Haag

Salvaterra E (2015) Philosophy of Science, Philosophy of Mind, University eCampus, Novedtrate, Italy. http://www.biostorage.com/blog-posts/2015-eu-data-protection-regulation/

Steinsbekk KS, Myskja BK, Solberg B (2013) Broad consent versus dynamic consent: pros and cons for biobankers to consider. Eur J Hum Genet 21:897–902

Townend DMR (2012) The politeness of data protection exploring a legal instrument to regulate medical research using genetic information and biobanking. PHD thesis, author's version

Waldby C (2012) Biomedicine, tissue transfer and intercorporeality. Fem Theory 3(3):239–254. https://doi.org/10.1177/146470002762491980

The New European Legal Framework on Personal Data Protection and the Legal Status of Biological Samples and Biobanks for Biomedical Research Purposes in Spanish Law

Carlos M. Romeo-Casabona

Abstract Biomedical research has increasingly resorted to biological material, particularly in view of the enormous potential for the future of a better knowledge of the DNA of all living beings and even the possibility of modifying it by means of various techniques, including gene editing. For Precision Personalised Medicine the support of biobanks is also a very important tool.

In relation to the protection of personal data, Spain has quickly implemented and adapted its internal laws to the GDPR through its new Organic Act 3/2018 of 5 of December on Protection of Personal Data and guarantee of digital rights. The new Act implements and completes some features of the GDPR, including those related to the provisions of Articles 9 and 89, in particular health related data and big data. In this way and by means of this 'bridge' Act, an attempt has also been made to guarantee the harmony between the GDPR and the pre-existing legislation, trying to ensure at the same time in effectiveness in promoting scientific research and in respecting for the rights of samples' donors.

1 Introduction

For several decades now, biomedical research has increasingly resorted to biological material, particularly in view of the enormous potential for the future of a better knowledge of the DNA of all living beings and even the possibility of modifying it by means of various techniques, including gene editing. Precision Personalised Medicine (PPM) is based on adapting the treatment to the individual genetic characteristics of each patient.[1] For PPM the support of biobanks is also a very important tool.

---

[1] See further Romeo Casabona et al. (2018), p. 29.

C. M. Romeo-Casabona (✉)
University of the Basque Country, Faculty of Law, Bilbao, Spain

S. Slokenberga et al. (eds.), *GDPR and Biobanking*, Law, Governance and Technology Series 43, https://doi.org/10.1007/978-3-030-49388-2_20

Spain has been a pioneer in the creation of systematic collections of human biological samples and, subsequently, of biobanks for different purposes.[2] Policy-makers and legislators have been particularly concerned about the use of human samples for biomedical research and biobanks as a very useful tool for this purpose. Maintaining a balance between scientific needs and progress, on the one hand, and an environment very respectful of the fundamental rights of those affected (i.e., the so-called 'source subject' of the samples), on the other, has been a constant concern for the Spanish authorities involved.

Spain has also been a relevant reference (i.e., some European countries and Latin America) to achieve a regulatory environment on these issues and for the collection and use of human biological samples for various scientific purposes.[3]

In relation to the protection of personal data, some European countries have quickly implemented and adapted their internal laws to the GDPR. This is the case of Spain, which its new Organic Act 3/2018 of 5 of December on Protection of Personal Data and guarantee of digital rights is generally applicable. The new Act implements and completes some features of the GDPR, including those related to the provisions of Articles 9 and 89, in particular health related data and big data. In this way and by means of this 'bridge' Act, an attempt has also been made to guarantee the harmony between the GDPR and the pre-existing legislation, trying to ensure at the same time in effectiveness in promoting scientific research and in respecting for the rights of samples' donors.

2 Biobank Infrastructure and Regulatory Environment

2.1 Biobank Infrastructure

2.1.1 General Remarks

The legal regime of each type of biobank is different according to its specific purpose, although there are some common points. In order to situate ourselves better in the Spanish regulatory context, I will now mention only the different banks of human material and/or the data extracted from these materials, which are managed in the biobanks.

[2] Orfao de Matos (2011), p. 89.

[3] Romeo Casabona and Simon (2013), p. 7.

2.1.2 Banks for Diagnostic and Biomedical Research Purposes

First of all, we can mention biobanks for diagnostic and biomedical research purposes. In Spain, some of these biobanks specialise in human samples of diverse nature: cells, tissues, tumours, DNA, fluids, etc. The study of these banks and their impact on the regulatory framework established by the GDPR, especially Article 89, will be the main focus of this study.

We will advance at this point only that Spanish regulations legally define what is to be understood by a 'biobank': a public or private, non-profit establishment that houses a collection of biological samples conceived for diagnostic or biomedical research purposes and organised as a technical unit with criteria of quality, order and destination (Act on Biomedical Research—Ley de Investigación Biomédica, LIB-, Article 3 (d)).

2.1.3 Banks for Therapeutic Purposes (Transplantation of Cells, Tissues and Organs)

The coordination of the procurement of human organs and tissues for transplant purposes, and more recently of cells of the same origin, has been a priority for Spanish health authorities. The National Transplant Organisation has led this national coordination activity worldwide in order to identify potential live and deceased donors and more suitable recipient patients, according to the established protocols. Thanks also to an adequate legal framework, which has persisted unaltered over time,[4] Spain is the country that leads, in relative terms and for many years, the number of donors and transplants performed.[5] For this reason, the concept of bank in the strict sense, that is, as a deposit of organs or tissues for transplantation, is relative in this sector, disregarding the fact that it can occur with some cells and tissues (e.g. bone marrow and other bone and cartilage elements).

2.1.4 Banks for Reproductive Purposes (Gametes and Embryos)

Specific legislation on assisted human reproduction techniques provides for the preservation of cryopreserved in vitro embryos as well as gametes for reproductive purposes and for scientific research relating to human reproduction.[6] If another

---

[4] Act 30/1979, of 27 October, on Organ Extraction and Transplantation. Royal Decree-Law 9/2014, of 4 July, establishing quality and safety standards for the donation, procurement, evaluation, processing, preservation, storage and distribution of human cells and tissues and approving coordination and operating standards for their use in humans.

[5] During 2017, 2183 effective organ donors were registered in Spain, bringing the rate per million population to 46.9.

[6] Act 14/2006, of 26 May, on Techniques of Assisted Human Reproduction (LAHRT), Articles 16 et seq.

scientific purpose is pursued, it will be governed by the law that regulates biomedical research.[7] The centres that apply these techniques are considered exclusive banks of these materials and embryos in vitro, but require prior authorisation, which means that it is the centres that select their reproductive use according to the criteria established by law. Consequently, gametes donors do not have any power to decide on the reproductive destination of the donated material, nor recipient women.

There is a duty of confidentiality in the access and use of donors' personal data, and the protection of donors' identity is guaranteed by law. Gametes and embryo banks are legally considered as health centres and services. There is an obligation to register the embryos deposited in a specific register. Embryos will be deposited for a limited time. The National Commission for Assisted Human Reproduction is legally entrusted with various functions that may include the use of embryos and gametes intended for reproduction or for scientific research purposes related to human reproduction.[8]

2.1.5 Population Studies Banks

Spain has not created a national database nor has it collected massive biological samples from citizens for purposes of population studies, mainly referring to the health of citizens; there are some local banks for purposes of epidemiological studies or studies of the prevalence of certain diseases in certain territories or in certain sectors of the population (genetic screening), which in any case will require the consent of the interested parties (LIB Article 54 (5).[9] The competent authorities and various social sectors consider that in the interest of observing the principle of proportionality, this practice could significantly affect certain fundamental rights of citizens.

2.1.6 Forensic Investigation Database (DNA Profiles)

As in many other countries, in Spain there is a national police database of identifiers obtained from the analysis of non-coding DNA profiles. It is in charge of the Ministry of the Interior and pursues two main purposes: criminal investigation and identification of cadaveric remains and investigation of missing persons.[10] That means that the use of these biological materials for biomedical research is not allowed, nor scientific research biobanks samples for criminal investigation purposes.

---

[7] Act 14/2007, of 3 July, on Biomedical Research (LIB), Articles 34 et seq.

[8] LTRHA, Article 20.

[9] Spain, through the National DNA Bank and the Genotyping Centre, participates in the international programme 1000 genomes.

[10] Organic Act 10/2007, of 8 October, which regulates the police database of identifiers obtained from DNA.

Obviously, although people may voluntarily offer to have some biological material extracted for any of these purposes, DNA profiles may be included in the database without the consent of the subject under investigation.[11] Only identifiers obtained from DNA, in the framework of a criminal investigation, which exclusively provide genetic information revealing the identity of the person and his or her sex and ethnic group may be registered in this police database.[12]

2.2 *Biobanks for Biomedical Research Purposes: Their Implementation in Spain*

2.2.1 General Remarks

There are a high number of biobanks for biomedical research purposes in Spain. Several of them got the rank of national that, according to the law, cover the needs of samples whose availability is not assured by the territorial banks or that due to the importance of certain biological materials are intended to ensure coverage throughout the Spanish territory. The Carlos III Health Institute (Instituto de Salud Carlos III), an autonomous body that belongs to the Ministry of Health, coordinates in some way the different existing biobanks, notwithstanding the autonomy enjoyed by the biobanks dependent on the Autonomous Communities (autonomous and local biobanks). National banks depend directly on this Institute.

2.2.2 The National Banks Are as Follows

(i) *The National Bank on Cell Lines* (Banco Nacional de Líneas Celulares) is structured in the form of a network (with nodes in Granada (central node), Barcelona and Valencia) and covers the entire national territory. It has a specific regulation,[13] according to which other biobanks for biomedical research purposes are obliged to make available to the National Bank a certain number of free samples, which the National Biobank also distributes free of charge among Spanish researchers, once they have justified the need for the samples requested and the research objectives pursued. In reality, the structure of the National Bank is not based on the deposit, treatment, storage, conservation and distribution of biological material, but on the registration of the existing samples in each biobank associated to the National Bank and on a part of them the latter directly takes the assignment decisions.

[11] Article 3(1) Org. Act 10/2007.

[12] Article 4 Organic Act 10/2007.

[13] Act 3/2007 and Order SCO/393/2006.

(ii) *The National DNA Bank* (Banco Nacional de ADN) is based at the University of Salamanca and has been linked for some years to the Carlos III Health Institute, on which the biobank is organically dependent.[14]

2.2.3 The So-Called Autonomous Communities Banks

They have been created in some Autonomous Communities (institutional territorial units in which the whole country is organised) in order to supply the needs for biological samples of researchers from the respective Autonomous Community, although they also attend to requests that may be made by researchers from other Spanish territories (e.g. BIOEF, in the Autonomous Community of the Basque Country).

2.2.4 Health Centre Banks (Hospitals)

They are located in large hospitals throughout Spain, mainly to meet the needs of researchers linked to each hospital (e.g. university hospitals).

2.2.5 Banks Specialised in Specific Biological Samples

Since most of the local and some autonomous banks do not have the capacity and infrastructure to have all kinds of samples that researchers may need, some biobanks have been created that specialize in collecting and treating some biological materials necessary for certain lines of research, and in fact cover the entire national territory. The most important that exist in Spain are the *Neurological Research Centre Foundation* (Centro de Investigaciones Neurológicas, CIEN) and *The Cancer Tumor Bank* (Banco de Tumores Oncológicos).

Neurological Research Centre Foundation biobank is dedicated to having biological samples of the central nervous system (mainly brain tissue, muscle and nerve, cerebrospinal fluid, blood and derivatives, and DNA). While the donation of brain tissue is carried out logically *post mortem* ('brain bank'), the other samples can be obtained in life from the donor or source subject.

The Cancer Tumor Bank specializes in the collection of tissue and cancer cells, usually extracted in the course of surgery. It is a precious biological material in order to carry out studies on the various types of cancer that exist. The Bank of the Centro Nacional de Investigaciones Oncológicas (CNIO) maintains samples of this nature but also others of interest for research other than cancer.

---

[14] In 2018 has a collection of biological samples from approximately 39,000 donors (healthy and sick) and more than 120,000 aliquots (units) have been distributed to 270 research projects.

Finally, some of these banks (firstly local biobanks) can meet the custody and maintenance needs of certain samples that are linked to a given private research project, without actually being incorporated into the overall structure of the biobank in which they are deposited and therefore cannot be transferred to third parties and the agreement is established in a remunerated basis.

Different are the *collections* called by the Law, whose existence is exceptionally permitted insofar as biological samples have been obtained to carry out one or more specific research projects on similar matters from the remaining samples or for diagnostic purposes for the treatment of the source subject (Articles 60 (2) and 67 LIB). Once the research project or projects similar to the project for which the remaining biological samples were initially consented are concluded, they must be destroyed or transferred to a biobank, depending on the terms of the consent given by the source subject (Article 61 LIB). This regulation means that so-called blank consent has been excluded.

2.3 The National Network of Biobanks (Red Nacional de Biobancos)

Spain has a stable network of biobanks to promote scientific cooperation in the field of biomedical research. With the National Network having a fundamentally hospital base, its creation seeks to ensure that the existing multiplicity of biobanks is not uncoordinated or chaotic, while ensuring rapid access to the set of existing biobanks by researchers in the biomedical sector. Its network configuration allows to know in greater detail the type of samples existing in each biobank, their characteristics and their availability, so that by being united in a network the scientific community can obtain the maximum performance from all the biobanks existing in the country.[15] The main objective of the National Network of Biobanks is to provide a public service to biomedical researchers throughout the country, assuming in any case the relevant ethical principles and strict compliance with current legislation. The National Network has been promoted and is funded by the Carlos III Health Institute.

The National Network of Biobanks is made up of 63 institutions distributed in 15 Autonomous Communities. Of these institutions, 52 correspond to hospital biobanks of the National Health System and the other 11 are associated centres and are distributed among private hospitals, networks of territorial biobanks, national banks and other institutions with biobank activity, such as some universities. The samples that make up the National Network of Biobanks are very varied and their characteristics are easily identifiable as the different biobanks that guard them are part of the Network: oncological samples (tumor bank), nervous system samples (brain banks),

[15] Spanish biobanks are not yet a part of the BBMRI-ERIC Network. A main challenge for the future is to analyse the possible fit of Spanish biobanks in this structure through the National Network of Biobanks.

samples that collect nucleic acid derivatives, solid samples of various pathologies, serotheques and plasmotheques and diagnostic collections.

2.4 Applicable Regulatory Framework

The regulatory framework that can most directly affect the creation, structure, organization and operation of biobanks is found in the first place in the Act on Biomedical Research,[16] whose Title V (Chapter IV Articles 63 to 71) is devoted to biobanks, as well as to genetic tests and biological samples (Chapters II and III). Probably this Act was innovative at the time of its approval (i.e., giving the option for a flexible or 'open' consent for further use of samples for related biomedical researches and promoting anonymisation of personal data that are collected in biobanks) and remains still with respect to the conception and purposes of biobanks, having managed to make compatible and facilitate access by scientists to well-ordered biological samples of human origin identified in aspects of interest for research with respect for the rights of the people from whom these samples come, such as their autonomy and privacy.[17]

The implementation of this Act regarding biobanks and human biological samples has been achieved by a Royal Decree of 2011, which regulates biobanks for biomedical research purposes, the treatment of biological samples and the National Registry of Biobanks.[18]

In relation to the protection of personal data, Organic Act 3/2018 is generally applicable,[19] which succeeds the previous Organic Act on the Protection of Personal Data of 1999 and is adapted to the GDPR, as well as GDPR itself. The new Act 3/2018 implements and completes some features of the GDPR (in no case modifies or replaces it), including those related to the provisions of Article 89, in particular data related to health, that have been established in great detail. In this way and by means of this 'bridge' Act, an attempt has been made to guarantee, and it can be stated that quite correctly, the harmony between the regulations of the GDPR and the pre-existing legislation, adding details that in many cases try to ensure that the normative framework is at the same time effective in promoting scientific research and respect for the rights of donors of biological samples.

---

[16] Act 14/2007, of 3 July.

[17] Seoane and Casado da Rocha (2008), p. 131.

[18] Royal Decree (RD) 1716/2011, of 18 November, establishing the basic requirements for the authorization and operation of biobanks for biomedical research purposes and for the treatment of biological samples of human origin, and regulating the operation and organization of the National Registry of Biobanks for biomedical research.

[19] Organic Act 3/2018, of 5 December, on Protection of Personal Data and guarantee of digital rights.

3 Guarantees for the Rights and Interests of Source Subjects

3.1 Legal Requirements

The provisions of Chapter III of Title V of Act 14/2007 (Articles 58 to 62, LIB) regarding obtaining, prior information, consent, confidentiality, transfer, conservation of data and samples, access to data and the right not to be informed, as well as the provisions of RD 1716/2011 and the concordant regulations mentioned above, shall apply to biological samples deposited in biobanks. The biological samples incorporated into biobanks may be used for any biomedical research, under the terms prescribed by this Act, provided that the source subject or, as the case may be, its legal representatives have given their consent under the terms and conditions provided by law.

It is possible to highlight some demands that reinforce the safeguard of the rights of the people involved, or that suppose a certain non-essential weakening of the same justified, as established in the new Organic Act 3/2018. In any case, it must be borne in mind that this Act does not deal directly with human biological samples for research and biobanks, but only with data relating to health. Therefore, the application to biological samples of the provisions relating to health data will be acceptable to the extent that the samples have given rise to some personal data, but not the sample itself, if no information has yet been obtained from it. In conclusion, Organic Act 3/2018 does not provide for an automatic equation between data and samples.[20] It will be necessary to combine this latter with specific provisions in LIB and RD 1716/2011.

3.2 The Collection of Samples

The collection of samples will be carried out in accordance with the provisions for direct biomedical research with biological samples (research projects). The following requirements must be met: justify the purpose for which the samples are to be used and describe the lines that will make up the collection; indicate the identity of the person responsible for the biobank; these will be specific transfers for specific purposes; description of the characteristics of the biobank. The source subject shall also be informed that the sample is to be transferred for biomedical research and of the availability of information. The possibility of the donor establishing some restriction for its use has been discussed.

[20] Sobre esto último véase, p. ej., Add. Prov. 17.2, e) Act 3/2018.

3.3 *The Informed Consent of the Involved Person*

3.3.1 General Rule

The consent of the person concerned shall always be required.[21]

3.3.2 Reuse of Personal Data

However, the reuse of personal data for health and biomedical research purposes shall be considered lawful and compatible when, having obtained consent for a specific purpose, the data are used for purposes or research areas related to the area in which the initial study was scientifically integrated.[22]

3.3.3 Public Health Research

For public health reasons, scientific studies may be carried out without the consent of those concerned in situations of exceptional relevance and seriousness to public health.[23]

3.3.4 Pseudonymisation of Data

In cases of transfer of samples, the principle of transfer of pseudonymised data/samples is enshrined, which currently no longer requires additional consent when the researcher makes a transfer to third parties (e.g. to other researchers working on the same project).

The new regime established in 2018 for the use of data for biomedical research purposes is as follows:

The use of pseudonymised personal data for health research purposes, and in particular biomedical research, is considered lawful and will be required:

1. a technical and functional separation between the research team and those who carry out pseudonymisation and conserve the information that makes re-identification possible;
2. that pseudonymised data are only accessible to the research team when:

   (i) there is an express commitment to confidentiality and not to carry out any re-identification activity;

[21] Add. Prov. 17 (2) (a) Org. Act 3/2018.

[22] Add. Prov. 17 (2) (b) Org. Act 3/2018 and Article 13 GDPR.

[23] Add. Prov. 17 (2) (b) Org. Act 3/2018.

(ii) specific security measures are adopted to prevent re-identification and access by unauthorised third parties. Data may be re-identified at source when an investigation using pseudonymised data reveals a real and specific risk to the safety or health of an individual or group of individuals, or a serious threat to their rights, or is necessary to ensure adequate health care.[24]

As a general rule, the biobank will deliver samples in a anonymised or pseudonymised basis according to the case. When the characteristics of the research require the identification of the samples, this should be evaluated previously by the Biobank Ethics Committee (see below, Sect. 5.1, b: External Committees).

3.4 *Free Nature of Assignments*

The biobanks will operate on a non-profit basis for research projects that have been scientifically approved, without prejudice to charging for the costs of obtaining, purifying and preserving and managing the application for biological samples, including their transport,[25] which will have to be paid by the applicant researcher.[26]

This requirement implies that biobanks must in fact act for non-commercial purposes, whether they belong to public or private institutions (e.g. private foundations promoted by patient associations).[27]

3.5 *Incorporation Into the (Clinical) Research Ethics Committees of the Data Protection Officer*

It is a standard that all clinical trials and other research projects involving an intervention in human beings, access to their personal data or their biological material be subject to prior evaluation by an independent clinical research ethics committee, whose opinion must be favourable in order to carry out the research (in addition to any other necessary authorisations).[28] The new Organic Act (3/2018) establishes the

[24] Add. Prov. 17 (2) (d) Org. Act 3/2018.

[25] See Art 30 Royal Decree 1716/2011.

[26] See, e.g. the National DNA Bank's price list: http://www.bancoadn.org/docs/tarifas-banco-adn-2018.pdf.

[27] The ruling of the Supreme Court of 24.02.2010 declared null and void the Decree 10.11.2006 of the Autonomous Community of Madrid, which approved the establishment of private umbilical cord blood banks for profit, basing its annulment on the fact that the exclusive use of biological material for a person or his/her family cannot be reserved in a biobank, whether public or private, without making it available to the list of potential registered patients. This issue is currently regulated by the State Government, Royal Decree-Law 9/2014 of 4 July, cited above.

[28] See Article 12 LIB and RD 1090/2015, which regulates clinical trials with medicines, Research Ethics Committees with medicines and the Spanish Registry of Clinical Research.

incorporation of a Data Protection Officer to all Ethics (Clinical) Research Committees with Medicines or, failing this, an expert with sufficient knowledge of Regulation (EU) 2016/679 when dealing with research activities involving the processing of personal data or pseudonymised or anonymised data.[29]

3.6 *Situations of Special Risk*

Those responsible for or in charge of the files must assess the risks and, where appropriate, adopt the opportune measures when, among other cases:

- The processing of data of affected groups in a situation of special vulnerability and, in particular, of minors and persons with disabilities is carried out.
- There is a massive processing that involves a large number of affected or entails the collection of a large amount of personal data.
- The personal data are routinely transferred to third States or international organisations for which an adequate level of protection has not been declared.[30]

3.7 *The Transfer of Samples*

All researchers in Spain may apply for getting human biological samples to the competent biobank. The application shall contain information about the project to be developed and the explicit commitment of the applicant centre and/or of the researchers participating in the project not to use the material requested for any use other than that indicated therein. The transfer of samples may be accompanied by the associated clinical information, which entails the use of procedures that guarantee the protection of personal data, unless they have been previously anonymised or pseudonymised. The refusal to transfer the samples requested will be motivated by the responsible person, who will have at sight the respective previous reports of the scientific director and both of the biobank scientific and ethical committees (see below, Sect. 5.1, b).

4 Law in Context: Individual Rights and Public Interest

The Act on Biomedical Research explicitly includes a principle that comes from the 1997 Council of Europe Convention on Human Rights and Biomedicine (Oviedo Convention, Article 2), which forms part of the Spanish internal legal system: the

[29] Add. Prov. 17 (2) (h) Org. Act 3/2018.

[30] See Article 28 (2) (e) (f) and (g), Org Act 3/2018.

health, interest and well-being of the human being who participates in biomedical research will prevail over the interest of society or science (Article 2(2)(b) LIB), adding that research from human biological samples will be carried out within the framework of respect for fundamental rights and freedoms, with guarantees of confidentiality in the treatment of personal data and biological samples, especially in the performance of genetic analysis (Article (2)(c) LIB). The applicable regulations are consistent with these general principles of this Act and are reflected in numerous provisions of the same that guarantee information, consent (notwithstanding this in a more open way than the GDPR), confidentiality and other rights of affected persons.[31]

On the other hand, it is also established that freedom of research and scientific production in the biomedical sciences will be guaranteed (Article (2)(d) LIB), which could not be otherwise, since it is a fundamental public freedom proclaimed by the Spanish Constitution. In this way Spanish legislation maintains a balance between the priority interest of individuals, but at the same time promotes biomedical research, in this case facilitating access to human biological material. However, it should be remembered that the new Organic Act 3/2018, introduces some exceptions to the interest of parties, specifically on a more extended consent approach than the GDPR to the detriment of the widespread accessibility of data (and samples) by researchers,[32] although it can be considered that they are still in agreement with the framework of the latter.

5 GDPR Impact and Future Possibilities for Biobanking

5.1 Biobanking and Samples Research Governance

Spanish previous legislation (LIB and RD 1716/2011) has paid special attention to issues directly or indirectly related to the governance of biobanks and biological samples. In this place we will only mention which are the aspects most linked to governance that have been regulated:[33]

(a) Requirements for the Creation of a Biobank
Authorisation is required (Article 64 LIB); the scientific interest of the biobank must be justified (Article 63 LIB); non-commercial purpose must be guaranteed, as the profit motive is excluded; a distinction is made between holders, managers and director of the biobank.

---

[31] Vivas Tesón (2012), p. 1.

[32] As explained above (Sects. 3 and 3.1), according to Organic Act 3/2018 a starting consent is necessary prior to the use of personal data for biomedical research purposes, but this is not more necessary or only in a very limited way for posterior use thereof.

[33] See Articles 4–19, Royal Decree 1716/2011.

(b) External Committees to Biobanks

Two independent committees are established within the biobank and between themselves: the scientific committee and the ethics committee.[34] Its main functions are:

(i) *Ethics Committee*: the ethical evaluation of applications (binding nature of the report if negative), advice on quality procedures and on the ethical aspects of the good practice document, responding to consultations presented by the director of the biobank and deciding cases of individualised sending of information.[35] It is therefore a different committee from the Research Ethics Committee, as that one has specific functions exclusively related to the transfer of samples by biobanks.

(ii) *Scientific Committee*: the scientific evaluation of applications (binding nature of the report if negative), advice on quality procedures and on scientific aspects of the good practice document, responding to queries from the director.

5.2 National Register of Biobanks

Registration is mandatory for all biobanks that provide for primary or secondary research purposes.[36] The Register depends on the Instituto de Salud Carlos III, but it is also necessary to register the biobank, like any other file, in the Register of the Spanish Data Protection Agency (Agencia Española de Protección de Datos, AEPD).

5.3 The Future of Biobanking and of the Related Norms

We can state that with the current European regulatory framework, and the Spanish regulation itself, obstacles have been eliminated and procedures have been facilitated to be able to research with human biological samples, without posing serious risks to individual's fundamental rights.

The availability of big data is a new and very important legal challenge that is not yet certain that the GDPR has effectively addressed. For its part, the Spanish Data Protection Organic Act 2018 deals with an issue arising from the use of big data: the risk of re-identification. It is a matter that requires a great deal of attention, especially in sectors that are more vulnerable to it, such as health data and genetic data. The foreseeable appearance of illegal re-identification cases will test the effectiveness of the legal provisions in this respect, which at the moment seems doubtful.

There are several ways in which it will be necessary to go further in the future to ensure effective protection of the subjects who are the source of biological samples:

---

[34] See Article 15 Royal Decree 1716/2011.

[35] Tatay Pérez (2015), p. 185.

[36] See Article 67 LIB.

extend and reinforce the duties of confidentiality of any person who, for any circumstance or legal provision, has access to the data of third parties, including those known unexpectedly; extend the anonymisation practices of personal data before handing over data or biological samples to third parties; this category should include, as the current regulations already do, pseudonymised data whose identification codes are under the exclusive control of responsible persons and are not transferred to third parties when they receive the data and/or biological samples. Practices (e.g. unjustified addition of mass data, mass analysis of data of one or more persons) which, intentionally or accidentally, allow the re-identification of the persons from whom the data originate will be discouraged, the personal data protection regulations will then be fully re-applied and immediate anonymisation of these data will be obligatory. The principles of data quality must also be reinforced, in the sense that data that have been processed are only used for the declared purpose for which they were collected and are not passed on to third parties, save for very strictly established exceptions.

6 Conclusion

The GDPR represents a major challenge for the authorities of the EU MS, in particular for their lawmakers. The Spanish legislator, by means of Organic Law 3/2018, has made a great effort to implement the GDPR and to harmonise it with pre-existing domestic law, particularly in relation to personal data in the field of biomedical research. It is certain that the new internal legal regime, with the support of the GDPR, will decisively facilitate biomedical research which requires the processing of personal data and human biological samples.

However, it is also probable that this Act has not been sufficiently clear in relation to some key issues, since in addition to going beyond the GDPR in such decisive matters as the consent of the interested party, it presents relevant interpretative doubts in other matters, possibly due to ambiguous wording, such as, for example, the process of pseudonymisation (not the use of data that are already pseudonymised), that is, whether or not it also requires the prior consent of the interested party.

References

Orfao de Matos A (2011) Biobancos (Técnico). In: Romeo Casabona CM (ed) Enciclopedia de Bioderecho y Bioética, Cátedra Interuniversitaria de Derecho y Genoma Humano - Ed. Comares, Granada, pp 89–97

Romeo Casabona CM, Simon WJ (eds) (2013) LatinBanks. Study on the legal and social implications of creating banks of biological material for biomedical research. Comares, Granada

Romeo Casabona CM Nicolás Jiménez P, De Miguel Beriain I (eds) (2018) Retos éticos y necesidades normativas en la actividad asistencial en Medicina Personalizada de Precisión. Fundación Instituto Roche, Madrid
Seoane JA, Casado da Rocha A (2008) Consentimiento, biobancos y ley de investigación biomédica. Rev Der Gen H / H Gen Law R 29:131–150
Tatay Pérez DG (2015) Los Comités de Etica externos del Biobanco: distinción de figuras afines y ordenación en una legislación dispersa. Rev Der Gen H / H Gen Law R 42:185–204
Vivas Tesón I (2012) Bioinvestigación, biobancos y consentimiento informado del sujeto vulnerable. LL 7911:1–5

Swedish Law on Personal Data in Biobank Research: Permissible But Complex

Magnus Stenbeck, Sonja Eaker Fält, and Jane Reichel

Abstract This chapter describes the regulatory and organisational infrastructure of biobank research in Sweden, and how the introduction of the GDPR affects the possibilities to use biobank material in future research. The Swedish legislator has chosen a rather minimalistic approach in relation to the research exception in Article 89 GDPR and has only enacted limited general exceptions to the data protection rules. This may be partly explained by the comprehensive right to public access to official documents which gives researchers vast access to information held in registries, albeit conditioned on abiding by secrecy and confidentiality rules. The Swedish legislation implementing the GDPR includes a general exception from the data protection rules in relation to the right to access to official documents, which researchers also benefit from. However, confidentiality rules for different categories of information differ between sectors, which hinders an effective use of the registries in research. The regulatory regime for using biobank and registry data in Sweden thus involves both data protection and secrecy rules, which makes the legal landscape permissible but complex. The operationalisation of the research exception in Article 89 GDPR is analysed against this background. Special attention is given to the possibility to link personal information derived from biobanks with personal information from other data sources, including large national population based statistical registries as well as information from national clinical registers.

M. Stenbeck (✉)
Karolinska Institute, Department of Clinical Neuroscience, Division of Insurance Medicine, Stockholm, Sweden
e-mail: magnus.stenbeck@ki.se

S. E. Fält
Regional Biobank Centre in Uppsala Örebro healthcare region, Uppsala, Sweden
e-mail: sonja.eaker.falt@rbcuppsalaorebro.se

J. Reichel
Stockholm University, Faculty of Law, Stockholm, Sweden
e-mail: Jane.Reichel@juridicum.su.se

S. Slokenberga et al. (eds.), *GDPR and Biobanking*, Law, Governance and Technology Series 43, https://doi.org/10.1007/978-3-030-49388-2_21

1 Introduction

The history of collecting human biological samples in pathology clinics of Swedish hospitals goes far back, and there are today examples of tissue samples in paraffin blocks dating back to the end of the 1800s. However, the large collections at the university hospitals consist mainly of samples dating from the 1940s onwards. Biobanks in Sweden are under the supervision of the Health and Social Care Inspectorate (IVO), which holds an official register of the biobanks.[1]

The biobanks provide an invaluable asset for medical research and are also extensively used for that purpose, albeit hitherto not to their full potential. This is partly due to the lack of a national biobank information system through which information about stored samples can be retrieved for research purposes. This chapter describes the proposed development of such a system. It also covers the general regulatory framework of biobanking, the regulation of personal data in research, and the impact that the General Data Protection Regulation (GDPR) may have on biobank research.

2 Biobank Infrastructure and Regulatory Environment

2.1 *Biobanks in Sweden*

In 2018, there were around 450 biobanks registered in the official registry for biobanks that held samples taken in a health care setting. In the 250 biobanks kept by the 21 county councils/regions which are responsible for healthcare and the 7 universities with medical faculties, there are over 150 million samples stored and 3 to 4 million samples are added annually. The largest biobanks are located in the county councils/regions, where an estimated 90% of all biobank samples in Sweden are stored. There are also biobanks at private companies such as pharmaceutical companies, private hospitals and caregivers, and at some public authorities, for example, the Public Health Agency and the National Food Agency.[2] The largest biobanks within healthcare are in the areas of pathology and cytology, carrying around 90% of samples, followed by microbiology, the PKU-biobank and biobanks generated in research, altogether around 7%. The PKU-biobank holds samples collected from the screening of all newborn babies in Sweden since 1975 (the screening started in 1965). The biobank is named after the first disease that was screened for. Today, 25 rare diseases are screened for,[3] and inclusion of a further disease is under way.

---

[1] Governmental Inquiry (SOU) 2018:4, Future Biobanks [Framtidens biobanker], p. 87.

[2] www.biobanksverige.se.

[3] Governmental Inquiry (SOU) 2018:4, Future Biobanks [Framtidens biobanker], p. 383 and https://www.socialstyrelsen.se/stod-i-arbetet/sallsynta-halsotillstand/nyfoddhetsscreening/.

Information about patients and their samples is maintained in the county council/region laboratory information systems (LIS). There are several such systems in different fields of medicine and run by various software providers. The LIS information is part of a patient's medical record. Some information from LIS is transferred to the Swedish Biobank Register (SBR), which aids in the tracking of patient samples across county councils/regions. The SBR is currently under construction.[4] Information on collections of samples mainly collected for research is handled in the parallel laboratory information management system (LIMS).[5] Besides SBR, a nationwide search register to aid researchers to find biobank samples and data is being proposed, as described in the following sections. Such a system would make it possible for authorities holding the register to find samples and link the information to other patient health data using the national personal identification number (PIN) at the request of researchers. Thereafter, an application to the biobanks for access to the samples of interest could be made.

A PIN is provided to each resident of Sweden by the Tax Authority[6] at birth or at a later point after immigration and is used to identify individuals in all sectors of society. National registers and databases using the PIN include not only medical records, statistical health data and vital statistics over long time periods but also demographic and socioeconomic data.

2.2 *Regulatory Framework*

This section describes the regulatory framework that exists for biobanking in general. Regulation of the use of biobanks in research is covered in subsequent sections.

The Swedish Biobank Act was enacted in 2002.[7] The Act covers tissue samples collected in healthcare and kept in Swedish biobanks, except samples that are not preserved for an extended time period.[8] The initiative to regulate biobanks came after a debate on the HUGO-project, which was an international project that conducted human genome organization to map the human genome.[9]

In the Biobank Act, consent based on sufficient information is of central importance for sample processing. Samples may only be collected and stored in a biobank after the sample provider or, if the donor is a minor, his or her custodian, has been informed about that intention and the purposes for which the biobank may be

---

[4] Governmental Inquiry (SOU) 2018:4, Future Biobanks [Framtidens biobanker], p. 88.

[5] Cramer (2016).

[6] 18 § Census Act [Folkbokföringslag (1991:481)].

[7] Act on Biobanks in Medical Care (Lag (2002:297) om biobanker i hälso- och sjukvården m.m.).

[8] 3§ Act on Biobanks in Medical Care.

[9] Governmental Bill [prop.] 2001/02: 44 Biobanks in Medical Care [Biobanker inom hälso- och sjukvården].

used. Only after this can his or her consent be obtained.[10] The Biobank Act requires that this is recorded in the sample provider's medical records.[11] Specific rules are in place for collecting and storing samples from embryos, foetuses and deceased persons.[12]

The narrow scope of the Biobank Act has been seen as a problem, specifically because biobanks created outside healthcare are not covered. Further, the Act sets out rather complex consent rules, which are discussed further in Sect. 3.2. In addition, the provisions on the release of tissue samples and the transfer of biobanks have led to administrative burdens for the biobank organizations, which in turn led the government in 2008 to commission a committee to draft a new Act. The report was presented in 2010 but no legislation was enacted based on it.[13] Another committee, commissioned in 2016, presented its report in 2018.[14] As of Summer 2020, no legislation has been proposed, but it can be assumed that the government will do this in the near future. Meanwhile, the 2002 Act has been updated to be in conformity with the GDPR and the EU Clinical Trials Regulation.[15]

With respect to the handling of information derived from the biobanks, there have been two issues to deal with: firstly, the possibility to search for and find samples of a certain type or pertaining to an identified person, and secondly, the handling of test results based on the samples. Proposals to handle these issues by creating a national register were put forward by a government inquiry in 2014,[16] in which a national register with information on sample characteristics as well as test results was suggested, and then another inquiry in 2018,[17] in which a national register was suggested, this time with information on sample characteristics such as PIN, type of sample, the time of sampling and contact information. All this information would be passed on to the responsible biobank, although test results on individual persons would be left out. Government action on these proposals is also expected in the near future.

[10] Chapter 3, Section 1 and 2 Biobank Act.

[11] Chap. 3, 7 § Biobank Act.

[12] Chap. 3, 3-4 §§ Biobank Act.

[13] Governmental Inquiry (SOU) 2010:81 A New Biobank Act [En ny biobankslag].

[14] Governmental Inquiry (SOU) 2018:4, Future Biobanks [Framtidens biobanker].

[15] Regulation (EU) No 536/2014 of the European Parliament and of the Council of 16 April 2014 on clinical trials on medicinal products for human use.

[16] Governmental Inquiry (SOU) 2014:45, Unique Knowledge through Register Based Research [Unik kunskap genom registerforskning].

[17] Governmental Inquiries (SOU) 2018:4, Future Biobanks [Framtidens biobanker] and (SOU) 2018:36 Right to research [Rätt att forska].

3 Personal Data and Research

3.1 Implementing GDPR in Swedish Law: Introductory Remarks

Directly or indirectly identifiable samples and data must be handled in accordance with the rules pertaining to personal data in the GDPR and other international and national legislation. Sweden has enacted a Data Protection Act which lays down general, complementary rules to the GDPR. Both pieces of legislation are relevant for handling personal data deriving from biological samples as well as any other type of personal data.[18] In addition, there are special rules in the Biobank Act on how samples from a biobank may be accessed for research purposes.[19] In the handling of biobank samples for research purposes, the legislations concerning the processing of biological samples and the processing of personal data must both be taken into account.

Before going into these issues, the Swedish tradition of transparency and the principle of public access to official documents will be introduced briefly. This principle plays an important role in research by providing broad access to publicly-held health data, such as the many registries on health and living conditions held by Swedish authorities.[20] Openness and transparency have been part of the national constitutional identity of Sweden for centuries; the first Freedom of the Press Act that contained this principle was enacted in 1766.[21] According to the current Freedom of the Press Act, 'everyone shall be entitled to have free access to official documents'; this is a right that can only be restricted on certain legal grounds and under a specific Act—the Public Access to Information and Secrecy Act.[22] All types of document are covered under this right to access, including electronic ones.

Article 86 GDPR allows Member States some regulatory space to ensure that personal data in official documents is disclosed in accordance with Member State law, in order to 'reconcile public access to official documents with the right to the protection of personal data'.[23] Sweden has included such provisions in the Data Protection Act, stating that the GDPR and the Swedish Data Protection Act is not to be applied to the extent that it would be contrary to the Freedom of the Press Act or

---

[18] Data Protection Act [Lag (2018:218) med kompletterande bestämmelser till EU:s dataskyddsförordning].

[19] Chap. 4 Biobank Act.

[20] See further Sect. 4.1.

[21] His Majesty's Gracious Ordinance Regarding the Freedom of Writing and of the Press, 1766 and Hirschfeldt (2017), p. 22.

[22] Chapter 2, 1–2 §§ Freedom of the Press Act (1949:105) [Tryckfrihetsförordning] and The Public Access to Information and Secrecy Act (2009:400) [Offentlighets- och sekretesslag.

[23] See also Recital 154.

the Freedom of Expression Act.[24] Due to the strict regulatory regime set out in the Freedom of the Press Act, the right to access to documents can only be restricted by the Public Access to Information and Secrecy Act. Otherwise the document is public. This Act includes a legal basis for keeping personal data secret on condition that there is a risk that the data, after the document has been released, will be processed in conflict with the GDPR, the Data Protection Act or the Ethical Review Act.[25] Further, documents including information on health, sexual issues, etc., or statistical information, are covered by secrecy, based on different conditions for each category of information.[26] Researchers may be granted access also to confidential information subject to appropriate conditions, for example, that the information remains confidential and that all documents are returned or destroyed after the research project is finalized.[27]

The Freedom of the Press Act also excludes the possibility to claim some other rights of the individual included in the GDPR. For example, an official document can only be culled in certain specific conditions, notwithstanding the rights to rectification or to be forgotten in regards to personal data recorded in an official document.[28] Further, the Freedom of the Press Act only recognises a right to appeal the denial of access to an official document.[29] A data subject cannot appeal the denial of the right of rectification in such a document or appeal the release of personal data from an official document based on the Freedom of the Press Act.

3.2 *Consent and Processing of Samples from Biobanks*

As described in Sect. 2.2, consent is of central importance for processing of biobank samples when the sample is included in a biobank as well as for the further use of the sample. How the information is to be provided, however, is not regulated in Swedish law, and the preparatory works state that this may vary depending on the purpose.[30] In Article 4(11) the GDPR has included a clear definition of consent for the purpose of personal data processing. In addition, the GDPR provides guidance

[24] Chapter 1, 7 § Data Protection Act. The previous Personal Data Act, 1998, had an equivalent wording in 7–8 §§. However, according to Chap. 1, 13 § the Freedom of the Press Act, the processing of sensitive personal data within the sphere of application of the Act may be regulated by ordinary law. As of summer 2019, no such legislation has been enacted.

[25] Chap. 21, 7 § Public Access to Information and Secrecy Act.

[26] For example, Chap. 21, 24 and 25 Public Access to Information and Secrecy Act.

[27] Chap. 10, 14 § Public Access to Information and Secrecy Act.

[28] 4 Chap., 4 § Public Access to Information and Secrecy Act and 10–17 §§ Archives Act (1990:752) [arkivlag]. See further the Swedish Administrative Court verdict in HFD 2015 ref. 71 and Reichel (2018), p. 298.

[29] 2 Chap, 19 § Freedom of the Press Act.

[30] Governmental Bill (prop.) 2001/02: 44 Biobanks in Medical Care [Biobanker inom hälso- och sjukvården], p. 38.

on which information should be provided where personal data are collected directly from the data subject at the time of data collection or from another source at a later point in time.[31] These rules apply to any data derived from biological samples.

Research on human biological samples taken from a living person, and which may be linked to that person, must obtain ethical approval before it can be conducted.[32] Such a review is conducted by the Swedish Ethical Review Authority. The requirement also applies to research conducted on samples that are collected outside healthcare, and thus outside the scope of application of the Biobank Act. For samples taken within healthcare, rules on consent are made complicated by multiple consent rules since the collection and storage of samples for treatment and other medical purposes are also regulated in the Patient Act.[33]

Further, according to the Biobank Act, samples may not be used for purposes other than those covered by prior information and consent without the donor being informed and consenting to the new purpose, unless permission has been granted by the Swedish Ethical Review Authority.[34]

3.3 Consent and Processing of Personal Data in Research

As seen above, consent is of primary importance in the Biobank Act. Somewhat in contrast to the heavy reliance on consent in that Act, according to the GDPR consent is only one of several available legal grounds for processing personal data in research.[35] The Swedish legislator has not enacted a general rule regulating research in the context of the GDPR, but the issue was discussed in the preparatory works (an important source of law in the Swedish legal tradition) to the Data Protection Act. The government has stressed that the legal basis for processing personal data in a public context is normally public interest under Article 6(1)(e).[36] The public interest is spelled out in legal documents governing public authorities and other organizations, as required in GDPR Article 6(2). In general, this requirement is recognized as the principle of legality whereby governments must operate. If processing of personal data is necessary to fulfil the general commission or a specific task of the government organization, then public interest becomes the relevant legal basis for the processing. Legal documents may include laws, ordinances, government

[31] Articles 13 and 14 GDPR.

[32] 4 § p. 3 and 6 § Ethical Review Act (2003: 460 [Lag (2003:460) om etikprövning av. forskning som avser människor Act].

[33] Chap. 4 Patient Act (2014:821) [Patientlag].

[34] Chapter 3, Section 5 Biobank Act.

[35] a. 6.1a of the General Data Protection Regulation (EU) 2016/679 (GDPR).

[36] Government Bill 2017/18:105 New Data Protection Law [Ny dataskyddslag], p. 49.

decisions and instructions to public agencies as well as some decisions made by public agencies, such as permissions granted by the Swedish Ethical Review Authority.[37]

A general commission to perform academic research was established in the Higher Education Act.[38] The ordinance applies to higher education institutions for which the Government is the accountable authority, which includes the majority of Swedish research universities. This means that the legal ground for research under this Act is public interest and not consent. In many cases also research conducted by private entities qualifies if the research is regulated by any of the legal documents types listed above or based on a government or government agency decision. In some cases private entities conduct research that does not fall under the Act, for example, some of the research by pharmaceutical companies. When that occurs, the processing of personal data may be allowed by consent or under Article 6(1)(f), i.e. legitimate interest, which entails a case-by-case weighing between the controller's legitimate interest of processing and the registered subject's right to privacy protection. In general, the Swedish interpretation of the GDPR puts a strong emphasis on public interest as the default legal ground for processing personal data in research and other publicly-motivated activities.

This also applies to the processing of special categories of personal data (sensitive personal data) as regulated in Article 9.(2)(g). The Ethical Review Act requires that research in Sweden on categories of personal data listed in Article 9.1 GDPR as well as criminal convictions and offenses must be approved by the Swedish Ethical Review Authority.[39] Accordingly, the Act provides the legally based safeguard required for research performed in Sweden.[40] The ethical approval of a research project sometimes requires consent as a safeguard, but the legal basis of processing is normally public interest, as discussed above. The traditional requirement for consent in the area of medical studies may therefore be waived under special circumstances, including practical considerations when processing historical data collected across long time periods or very large volumes of data from national registries.

The collection and preservation of samples in biobanks, as well as their general availability for medical treatment and research purposes, is based on mandatory consent according to the Biobank Act as described above. In line with this, for research on biological material from a living person, the Ethical Review Act also prescribes mandatory consent.[41]

As mentioned above, the GDPR offers a definition of consent in Article 4(11), which is further elaborated in Recital 42. When consent is used, that definition should be followed. It is almost identical to earlier definitions based on the Swedish

[37] Ibid., pp. 56–59.

[38] 2 § Higher Education Act (1992:1434) [Högskolelag].

[39] 3 and 6 §§ Ethical Review Act.

[40] Note that ethical permits cannot be received, and hence not used as safeguards, for research conducted outside of Sweden. In that case, some other safeguard must be in place.

[41] 17 § Ethical Review Act.

Personal Data Act which implements the EU Data Protection Directive.[42] But processing of genetic data has now been added to what is considered to be special categories of data (Article 9(1) GDPR, in Sweden referred to as 'sensitive personal data'[43]). Hence, consent must be freely given, specific, informed, unambiguous and, in the case of sensitive personal data, explicit. It should be based on a statement or a clear affirmative action. The person providing consent must be given sufficient information before making the decision.

The possible scope of consent given for research has been widely discussed.[44] Article 4(11) GDPR states that consent must be specific and explicit. Swedish medical and social research is frequently based on large data collections preserved over long time periods. Modern epidemiological theories highlight the necessity of very long follow-up periods to investigate the effects of sometimes inherited individual properties and long term exposures to risks starting far back in time. This is relevant, not least for medical research using biological samples. The need to be more open to a broad description of the final purpose of the research is acknowledged in Recital 33 of the GDPR. At the current point in time, the practical importance of Recital 33 for how consent can be obtained for research has not been definitively resolved in Swedish law.

A couple of additional remarks regarding the requirement of explicit consent for sensitive data are needed. According to the current Swedish interpretation, this additional requirement does not exclude consent given orally or by a clear affirmative action, such as knowingly participating in a clinical study.[45]

Further elaboration is needed with respect to the possibility to collect samples and derive data from them for widely defined research purposes. An exception to the rules in Article 5.1(b) GDPR on specific purposes is found in the Biobank Law, which allows for the long-term preservation of biobank samples in repositories together with data on the sample providers. The samples and data may only be used for the purposes for which they have been collected and received consent, unless it is for a research purpose which has been approved by the Swedish Ethical Review Authority or is located within an approved clinical trial.[46]

[42] Personal Data Act (1998:204 [Personuppgiftslag)].

[43] Government Bill 2017/18:105 New Data Protection Law [Ny dataskyddslag], p. 75.

[44] A summary of the national discussion can be found in the Governmental Inquiry (SOU) 2017:50 Processing of Personal Data for Research Purposes [Personuppgiftsbehandling för forskningsändamål], pp. 168–171.

[45] Governmental Inquiry (SOU) 2017:50 Processing of Personal Data for Research Purposes [Personuppgiftsbehandling för forskningsändamål], pp. 175–176.

[46] Chap. 3, 5 § Biobank Act.

4 Individual Rights and Safeguards

4.1 General Legislation on Derogations from GDPR Rights in Swedish Law

As mentioned above, in addition to the rights described in Chapter 3 of the GDPR, individuals are protected by the Public Access to Information and Secrecy Act[47] for any information held by a public authority. This law is based on the constitutional Freedom of Press Act[48] and provides strong protection against unwarranted disclosure of personal information from official records.

In addition, Sweden has enacted a Data Protection Act which lays down general complementary rules to the GDPR. Initially, a specific Act for research data was planned[49] but in a rather late stage of the legislative process rules concerning processing personal data for research were included in the Data Protection Act instead. With this approach, the possibility to make research exemptions and derogations has been implemented in a minimalistic manner, relying on the rules in the GDPR to be applied directly or with already-existing Swedish rules that correspond to the allowable derogations. The government has been delegated the power to enact further regulations to implement exemptions under Article 89.2 GDPR, though no such rules have been enacted as of Summer 2020. The view taken has been that existing national legislation sufficient covers the needs, while being in accordance with the GDPR. Some small and predominantly formal changes have been made in a number of laws and ordinances pertaining to specific registries in the social and medical sector which are frequently used by researchers. As an example, the existing national legislation provides a possibility for a donor to withdraw consent for use of the sample at any time. If the withdrawal applies to all types of use, the sample must be destroyed or anonymized immediately.[50]

4.2 Technical and Organizational Safeguards

According to Article 89.1 GDPR, safeguards must be included to protect personal data in research. In the case of sensitive personal data, such safeguards have to be based on legislation. Procedures for informed consent in biobanking and in research, and requirements for ethical approval, were discussed above (Sects. 3.2–3.3). In the proposed law on processing personal data in research it was initially planned to explicitly state that the existing procedure for ethical review was a legal requirement

[47] The Public Access to Information and Secrecy Act (2009:400)] [Offentlighets- och sekretesslag].

[48] Freedom of the Press Act (1949:105) [Tryckfrihetsförordning].

[49] Governmental Inquiry (SOU) 2017:50 Processing personal data for research purposes [Personuppgiftsbehandling för forskningsändamål].

[50] Chapter 3, 6 § Biobank Act.

for sensitive data in order to strengthen pseudonymization as a preferred safeguard and to make the possibility to opt out from a research project a non-disputable right. In the end, however, the corresponding rules in the GDPR were seen as providing sufficient levels of protection with respect to the right to object to processing and the option to use pseudonymization as a safeguard. In addition, the Swedish Ethical Review Act was considered to already meet the requirement of being a legally grounded safeguard for sensitive personal data. The Swedish Data Protection Act includes a general safeguard rule for purpose limitations in research according to which researchers may only use personal data collected for research purposes to take action vis-a-vis the data subject, if there are particular reasons for the vital interests of the data subject.[51] Further, the so-called 'Life Gene Act', enacted as a response to regulatory difficulties to collect information for a major long term research infrastructure project named Life Gene, states that a data controller must limit the electronic access to personal data to what each person needs to be able to fulfil his or her work tasks in relation to the register.[52] Direct access to personal data in the register is forbidden.[53]

4.3 *Further Adaptions on Rules for Informed Consent in Biobank Research*

As mentioned above, all research on human biological samples, sensitive personal data and personal data on criminal offenses must obtain ethical approval before being conducted.[54] Further, the Biobank Act requires specifically informed consent for collecting and storing samples.[55] With the proposed Biobank Act, it is suggested that the rules for information, consent and withdrawal in healthcare and research should be applied to biobanks. Accordingly, the Data Protection Act, the Patient Data Act [56] and the Ethical Review Act for research on identifiable biological samples should be applicable also for samples stored in biobanks.[57] No rules for consent were therefore proposed to be included in the new Biobank Act. According to the proposal, the Patient Act would give the patient a right to be informed and a right to either withdraw the sample or limit the allowable use of the sample.[58]

---

[51] Chap. 4, 1 § Data Protection Act.

[52] 10 § Act on Certain Registries for Research on what Inheritance and the Environment Mean for Human Health [Lag (2013:794) om vissa register för forskning om vad arv och miljö betyder för människors hälsa ('Life Gene Act')].

[53] 11 § 'Life Gene Act'.

[54] 6 § Ethical Review Act.

[55] 3 Chap. 1 § Biobank Act.

[56] Patient Data Act (2008:355). [Patientdatalag].

[57] Governmental Inquiry (SOU) 2018:4 Biobanks of the Future [Framtidens biobanker], p. 274.

[58] Ibid., p 284 and Patient Act (2014:821) [Patientlag].

The obligation to inform and the right to object to processing in the Patient Data Act does not meet the general GDPR requirement of valid consent. It is not based on a statement or a clear affirmative action but instead requires action by the data subject if he or she wishes to be excluded. But the rule does correspond to the right to object to or restrict processing stated in Articles 18 and 21 GDPR. The Patient Data Act strengthens this right by removing the limitation of the right to object included in Article 21(6) GDPR so that it applies to all patient data, except to those that fall under the communicable diseases legislation on public health hazards.[59]

4.4 Proposals for Further Legislation

Two further legislative Acts have been proposed but not yet enacted, namely, as mentioned above, a new Biobank Act,[60] and further, an Act that provides long-term regulation of research databases.[61] Both would be important for regulating the processing of personal data for healthcare and other population-based registries in research, as well as for the creation of a national biobank register where samples can be traced for utilization in research and combined with other clinical data.

5 Law in Context: Individual Rights and Public Interest

5.1 Minimalistic Regulatory Approach, But Hardly a Restrictive View on Research

As seen above, the Swedish legislator has taken a minimalistic approach when it comes to implementing exemptions for handling personal data for research purposes. No general exemptions have been introduced. Instead, the Swedish legislator has chosen to rely on the GDPR directly and on general Swedish law already in place. This could be interpreted as an indication that Swedish law is restrictive in relation to the use of personal data in research, but this is not a correct conclusion.

First, the preparatory works for implementing rules on processing of research data clearly state that the exemptions in the GDPR are to be applied in Sweden.[62] As described above, according to the government much of the previously-existing Swedish legislation provides such exemptions. The motive for not including any further exemptions is thus that they are already in place and are GDPR-compatible.

[59] Chap. 2 and 3, Communicable Diseases Act [Smittskyddslag (2014:168)].

[60] Governmental Inquiry (SOU) 2018:4 Biobanks of the Future [Framtidens biobanker].

[61] Governmental inquiry (SOU) 2018:50 Right to Research [Rätt att forska].

[62] Governmental Bill (prop.) 2017/18:298 Processing personal data for research purposes [Behandling av. personuppgifter för forskningsändamål], pp. 116, 120, 124 and 128.

Further, it may be argued that the wide access to personal data via Swedish public registries in itself calls for a high level of protection for the data subjects concerned.

Second, as mentioned above, academic research is widely seen as a public interest laid down in the law,[63] which makes it the basic legal ground for research that uses personal data in the field of public health as well as in other areas. This extends to much research carried out also by private research entities[64] which otherwise would have to rely on consent or legitimate interest.[65] Hence, public interest opens up the possibility to use large databases with personal data collected over long time periods in health-related research.

Third, Sweden has a long tradition of keeping registries with information on identified persons and deceased individuals for the entire or large parts of the population. Statistics Sweden, a government agency producing official statistics, keeps at least 40 registers that are interesting for research. The National Board of Health and Welfare keeps some 15 registers on health, healthcare and social services, such as the national cancer register, the national patient register, the causes of death register, etc. The county councils collaborate around a system of clinical care registers (so-called healthcare quality registers). Currently, there are over 100 clinical registers in different fields that have attained certification as national registers and are partly intended for research use. All of these resources can be used together with biobank data in research.[66]

As mentioned above, since 1947 all Swedish residents have been assigned a PIN, a personal identification number, that applies to all sectors of society and is used by private as well as government organizations as a common mean of identification. The PIN consists of a date of birth and an additional four digits. This provides a fertile ground for register-based research, which can include personal data from biobanks if there is a system whereby biobank data can be found and combined with other register-based data. This would make it possible to combine data from all the registers on the individual level and make retrospective cohort studies of a number of important health problems. Such a searchable national register of biobanks holdings is being proposed as part of the new biobank legislation but has not yet been implemented.

5.2 *Further Legislative Reform: Research Databases*

There are currently three legislative Acts in force providing possibilities for researchers to build research databases based on personal data from public registries for research purposes which can be used for several purposes within a broadly

[63] Governmental Bill (prop.) 2017/18:298 Processing personal data for research purposes [Behandling av. personuppgifter för forskningsändamål], p. 34. In the case of research the appropriate regulation is found in 2§ Higher Education Act (1992.1434).

[64] Governmental Bill (prop.) 2017/18:298 Processing personal data for research purposes [Behandling av. personuppgifter för forskningsändamål], pp. 35–36.

[65] Article 6(1)(f) GDPR.

[66] https://www.registerforskning.se/en/.

specified field of research.[67] A recent governmental inquiry proposed a new Act on research databases which may replace these Acts. The inquiry pointed out that Sweden has a world-leading position in terms of statistics about living conditions and health, and that the proposed Act could provide a stronger regulatory framework to promote an effective use of existing registers and databases in research adapted to modern database and data protection technology. This would make it possible to build new infrastructure for research within broadly defined subject matter areas consisting of both new data and data collected from the public registers. It is proposed that the instrument of ethical review be expanded so that universities can be granted permissions to build national research databases which are accessible exclusively for research and not available for other purposes. The inquiry recommends as an additional safeguard to use remote access to such national research databases when possible instead of distributing a great number of copies of personal data files across the research community. Similar proposals have been discussed in neighbouring countries but have not, to the knowledge of the authors, been proposed as legislation.

As mentioned above, a national biobank register intended for tracing samples collected in Swedish biobanks is also being proposed, which would be accessible for researchers.[68] Efforts have been made to develop comprehensive patient-oriented medical records which would also be accessible for researchers.[69]

6 Future Possibilities for Biobanks in Research

6.1 Consent and Public Interest

The future role of consent is a matter of uncertainty in the context of biobank research where the handling of samples legally based on consent has to go hand in hand with the processing of personal data in research based on public interest. A similar problem exists in how the pharmaceutical and medical technical industry can obtain permission to collect and keep data for partly proprietary research purposes, given that the basis for processing and preserving data in this area is also based on consent at the time of data collection. The consent given in both these contexts is a general purpose consent, which is at odds with the GDPR principles. The interpretation of Recital 133 on the scope of consent for research processing

67 Act on Certain Registers for Research on what Inheritance and the Environment Mean for Human Health [Lag (2013:794) om vissa register för forskning om vad arv och miljö betyder för människors hälsa], Act on Forensic Psychiatry Research Register [Lag (1999:353) om rättspsykiatriskt forskningsregister], and Act on Processing of Personal Data at the Institute for Evaluation of Labour Market and Education Policy [Lag (2012:741) om behandling av. personuppgifter vid Institutet för arbetsmarknads- och utbildningspolitisk utvärdering].

68 Governmental Inquiry (SOU) 2018:4, Future Biobanks [Framtidens biobanker], p. 229.

69 Governmental Inquiry (SOU) 2018:4, Future Biobanks [Framtidens biobanker], p. 307.

will be of importance here, as well as the reliance on public interest as the basis for the processing of large data holdings preserved over long time periods where renewed consent becomes impossible in practice.

6.2 *Public Disclosure, Secrecy and International Collaboration*

Beyond the GDPR and the proposed national laws on biobanks and research databases, the Freedom of the Press Act and the Public Access and Secrecy Act establish important rules governing the access to official documents, including personal data held by the authorities. The secrecy rules of statistical authorities and healthcare providers differ. This has created legal obstacles for the possibility to use a national biobank register to search for samples and combine them with clinical information from healthcare or clinical registers, which has not yet been resolved. The Public Access and Secrecy Act seems to limit the possibility to make the wide searches in population registries that are necessary to find matching cases in morbidity/mortality registries and biobanks in order to build relevant research databases for cohort studies of the biological and social determinants of health.

In addition, the Public Access and Secrecy Act may make it more difficult to achieve the cross-country free flow and exchange of data within the EU that is a goal of the GDPR.[70] The exchange of personal data for research purposes with third countries is still curtailed by this Act as well, since it requires a guarantee that Swedish law on freedom of information and secrecy will be upheld in the country receiving the personal data. The enactment of the GDPR did not change this fact as it respects existing national legislation in this area.[71]

The matter is further complicated by the difficulty to create international agreements that will extend GDPR data protection rules to territories outside the EU. For instance, this applies to research collaboration with the USA. It has not been granted an 'adequacy decision' demonstrating that appropriate data protections are in place, which would enable transfers to proceed without additional justification or safeguards.[72] The US-EU Privacy Shield does not serve that purpose for public agencies since it is focused on commercial transfer.[73] US authorities are not able to agree to all of the contractual provisions set forth by European counterparts due to statutory conflicts with US legislation.[74] Whether the derogations listed for important reasons of public interest in 49(1)(d) GDPR would apply to some specific transfers of research data without the receiving country's adherence to the GDPR has not yet been sufficiently explored.

[70] Recital 5 and Article 1(3) GDPR.

[71] Recital 154 and Article 86 GDPR.

[72] Article 45 GDPR.

[73] EU-US Privacy Shield Framework Principles issued by the U.S. Dept of Commerce and approved by the EU Commission on February 2, 2016.

[74] Personal communication with Robert Eiss, legal expert National Institutes of Health (NIH), USA.

7 Concluding Remarks

In conclusion, the Swedish regulatory framework for allowing the use of health data for research is, on the one hand, rather permissive, giving researchers wide access to registries, but, on the other hand, a bit ambiguous. No specific legal basis for processing personal data in research has been introduced in law, but the government has indicated that this is not needed given the legal context that already exists in which public interest is the default.

In general, the research exemptions in the GDPR have not been implemented in a clear and unequivocal manner in Swedish law, thus leaving researchers with an imprecise and ambiguous framework. Lastly, several governmental inquiries have been undertaken over the years, and these have made proposals for clearer and, to some extent, less burdensome regulations for biobanking and register-based research. As of Summer 2020, these have not been enacted. To what extent the GDPR has affected the policy choices of the Swedish legislator is therefore uncertain.

References

Cramer K (2016) What is a LIMS?. sapiosciences.com

Hirschfeldt J (2017) Free access to public documents – a heritage from 1766. In: Lind A-S, Reichel J, Österdahl I (eds) Transparency in the future – Swedish openness 250 years. Ragulka, Visby

Reichel J (2018) Public access or data protection as a guiding principle in the EU's composite administration? An analysis of the ReNEUAL model code in the light of Swedish and European case law. In: Wahlgren P (ed) 50 years of law and IT, Scandinavian studies in law. Jure, Stockholm

Part IV
Fragmentation and Ways Forward

Biobanking Across Europe Post-GDPR: A Deliberately Fragmented Landscape

Olga Tzortzatou, Santa Slokenberga, Jane Reichel, Andreia da Costa Andrade, Carla Barbosa, Sofie Bekaert, Evert-Ben van Veen, Carlos M. Romeo-Casabona, Katharina Ó. Cathaoir, Gauthier Chassang, Annelies Debucquoy, Jean-Jacques Derèze, Laurent Dollé, Sonja Eaker Fält, Radek Halouzka, Mette Hartlev, Michael Hisbergues, Nils Hoppe, Isabelle Huys, Els Kindt, Anne Kjersti Befring, Lukasz Kozera, Dorota Krekora-Zajac, Teodora Lalova, Michaela Mayrhofer, Anastassia Negrouk, Jakub Pawlikowski, Simone Penasa, Kärt Pormeister, Emmanuelle Rial-Sebbag, Anastasia Siapka, Tom Southerington, Magnus Stenbeck, Maja Šutalo, Marta Tomasi, Peggy Valcke, and Ruth Vella Falzon

O. Tzortzatou (✉)
Biomedical Research Foundation of the Academy of Athens, Athens, Greece
e-mail: otzortzatou@bioacademy.gr

S. Slokenberga
Faculty of Law, Uppsala University, Uppsala, Sweden
e-mail: santa.slokenberga@jur.uu.se

J. Reichel
Stockholm University, Faculty of Law, Stockholm, Sweden
e-mail: Jane.Reichel@juridicum.su.se

A. da Costa Andrade · C. Barbosa
University of Coimbra, Law Faculty, Biomedical Law Institute, Coimbra Area, Portugal
e-mail: cbarbosa@fd.uc.pt

S. Bekaert
Department of Public Health and Primary Health Care, Faculty of Medicine and Health Sciences, Ghent University, Ghent, Belgium
e-mail: sofie.bekaert@ugent.be

E.-B. van Veen
MLC Foundation, Hague, Netherlands
e-mail: eb.vanveen@medlaw.nl

C. M. Romeo-Casabona
University of the Basque Country Faculty of Law, R.G. Chair in Law and the Human Genome, Bilbao, Spain

S. Slokenberga et al. (eds.), *GDPR and Biobanking*, Law, Governance and Technology Series 43, https://doi.org/10.1007/978-3-030-49388-2_22

K. Ó. Cathaoir · M. Hartlev
University of Copenhagen, Faculty of Law, Copenhagen, Denmark
e-mail: katharina.o.cathaoir@jur.ku.dk; mette.hartlev@jur.ku.dk

G. Chassang
Université Paul Sabatier Toulouse 3, Toulouse, France

Infrastructure Nationale Biobanques, Institute for Public Health, Clinical Research Department, Paris, France

Plateforme "Ethique et Biosciences", Genotoul Societal, Toulouse, France
e-mail: gauthier.chassang@inserm.eu

A. Debucquoy
BBMRI.be, Belgian Cancer Registry, Brussels, Belgium
e-mail: annelies.debucquoy@kankerregister.org

J.-J. Derèze
UZ Leuven, Leuven, Belgium
e-mail: jean-jacques.dereze@uzleuven.be

L. Dollé
Université Libre de Bruxelles, Department of Pathology, Brussels, Belgium
e-mail: laurent.dolle@erasme.ulb.ac.be

S. E. Fält
Regional Biobank Centre in Uppsala Örebro healthcare region, Uppsala, Sweden
e-mail: sonja.eaker.falt@rbcuppsalaorebro.se

R. Halouzka
Masaryk Memorial Cancer Institute, Brno, Czech Republic
e-mail: halouzka@mou.cz

M. Hisbergues
Infrastructure Nationale Biobanques, Institute for Public Health, Clinical Research Department, Paris, France
e-mail: michael.hisbergues@inserm.fr

N. Hoppe
CELLS - Centre for Ethics and Law in the Life Sciences, University of Hannover, Hannover, Germany
e-mail: nils.hoppe@cells.uni-hannover.de

I. Huys
Clinical Pharmacology and Pharmacotherapy, Department of Pharmaceutical and Pharmacological Sciences, KU Leuven, Leuven, Belgium
e-mail: isabelle.huys@kuleuven.be

E. Kindt · P. Valcke
Centre for IT and IP Law (CiTiP), KU Leuven, Leuven, Belgium
e-mail: els.kindt@kuleuven.be; peggy.valcke@kuleuven.be

A. K. Befring
Law Faculty, University of Oslo, Oslo, Norway
e-mail: a.k.befring@jus.uio.no

L. Kozera
BBMRI-ERIC, Graz, Austria
e-mail: lukasz.kozera@bbmri-eric.eu

D. Krekora-Zajac
Univeristy of Warsaw, Institute of Civil Law, Warsaw, Poland
e-mail: d.krekora@wpia.uw.edu.pl

T. Lalova
Department of Pharmaceutical and Pharmacological Sciences, KU Leuven, Leuven, Belgium

Centre for IT and IP Law (CiTiP), KU Leuven, Leuven, Belgium
e-mail: teodora.lalova@kuleuven.be

M. Mayrhofer
BBMRI-ERIC, Graz, Austria
e-mail: michaela.th.mayrhofer@bbmri-eric.eu

A. Negrouk
International Policy Office, European Organisation for Research and Treatment of Cancer, Brussels, Belgium
e-mail: anastassia.negrouk@eortc.org

J. Pawlikowski
Department of Ethics and Medical Law, Chair of Social Medicine, Lublin, Poland
e-mail: j.pawlikowski@uksw.edu.pl

S. Penasa · M. Tomasi
University of Trento, Trento, Italy
e-mail: simone.penasa@unitn.it; marta.tomasi@unitn.it

K. Pormeister
University of Tartu, Law Faculty, Tartu, Estonia

E. Rial-Sebbag
Infrastructure Nationale Biobanques, Institute for Public Health, Clinical Research Department, Paris, France

Plateforme "Ethique et Biosciences", Toulouse, France
e-mail: emmanuelle.rial@univ-tlse3.fr

A. Siapka
Centre for IT & IP Law, Faculty of Law, KU Leuven, Leuven, Belgium
e-mail: anastasia.siapka@kuleuven.be

T. Southerington
University of Turku, Hospital District of Southwest Finland, Finnish Biobank Cooperative – FINBB, Turku, Finland
e-mail: tomsou@utu.fi

M. Stenbeck
Karolinska Institutet, Department of Clinical Neuroscience, Division of Insurance Medicine, Stockholm, Sweden
e-mail: magnus.stenbeck@ki.se

M. Šutalo
Law Office Maja Šutalo, Zagreb, Republic of Croatia
e-mail: maja@sutalo.hr

R. Vella Falzon
University of Malta, Valetta, Malta
e-mail: ruth.vella-falzon@um.edu.mt

Abstract This chapter seeks to provide insight into the ways in which Member States leveraged the regulatory discretion afforded to them by the GDPR. Specifically, it reviews the biobank regulatory environment; whether and how derogations under Article 89(2) GDPR are enabled; the legal basis for scientific research and the role of consent in biobanking post-GDPR; the balance between individual rights and public interest in national law; and finally, the GDPR's impact and future possibilities for biobanking. In exercising self-determination, Member States can, to a certain extent, align data protection requirements with their values and aspirations. Such alignment, though, could jeopardize collaborative research. In light of the need to bridge divergent legal and ethical requirements at a national and supranational level, the role of Research Ethics Committees (RECs) might prove to be essential.

1 Introduction

1.1 Background

The GDPR has had considerable impact on biobanking. Despite foreseeing rather stringent measures to ensure that personal data are adequately protected and placing strict obligations on controllers, the GDPR has relaxed the regulation of research in two important ways. First, through lawfulness requirements for data processing, including the conditions set forth in Article 9(2) GDPR for lifting the prohibition of health and genetic data processing. Second, through derogations from certain individual rights under Article 89 GDPR. These requirements, possibilities and further regulatory opportunities offered by the GDPR co-exist with and relate to national regulatory frameworks on biobanking.

Even though the GDPR is a regulation and, therefore, establishes a uniform framework across national legal orders, Member States' ability to maintain existing or even introduce new national exceptions allows the preservation of the fragmented landscape of biobanking law in Europe. The GDPR offers several lawfulness avenues in the form of legal grounds for data processing that lift the general prohibition of genetic and health data processing. Particularly important among these are broad consent - a possibility offered by Article 6(1)(a) in conjunction with Articles 9(2)(a) and 7 and as guided by Recital 33. The application of these provisions does not, in principle, require further implementing measures by the Member States. Furthermore, Article 9(2)(j) GDPR grants the possibility to adopt either national law or EU law that permits processing of health and genetic data for research purposes without the data subject's consent, provided that such processing is proportional to the aim pursued, respects the essence of the right to data protection and is accompanied by suitable and specific measures to safeguard the data subject's fundamental rights and interests.[1] Therefore, should there be a law in place providing

[1] Article 9(2)(j) GDPR.

these guarantees, even broad consent to the processing of health and genetic data for research purposes might not be necessary.

The derogations from individual rights under the research regime set forth in the GDPR have two limbs: one that relies on the direct applicability of GDPR and does not require further implementation measures, but requires compliance with Article 89(1) GDPR; and another that provides EU/EEA Member States with the possibility to derogate from four rights foreseen in the GDPR on the condition that a national law is in place and that the requirements of Article 89(1) GDPR are met (notably, adequate safeguards are in place) and in so far as such rights are likely to render impossible or seriously impair the achievement of the specific purposes, and such derogations are necessary for the fulfilment of those purposes. These rights are enshrined in Articles 15, 16, 18 and 21 GDPR. Additionally, the GDPR enables further regulatory opportunities for research falling within the domain of public interest.

The opportunities that the GDPR has created for research raise questions on whether they have been operationalized nationally and what implications they create for collaborative research between EU/EEA Member States. This chapter seeks to provide insight into the fragmented landscape and the research-related implications of GDPR implementation across Member States. It is not an exhaustive comparison of GDPR implementation across these countries. Rather, it reviews the legal basis for data processing, with a particular emphasis on consent, and examines the national application of Article 89(2) GDPR, specifically, whether derogations from Articles 15, 16, 18 and 21 GDPR are enabled and what safeguards are in place. Additionally, it considers what, if any, consideration for balancing individual rights and public interest has been advanced nationally. Thereafter, it considers implications for scientific research in the area of biobanking.

1.2 Method and Limitations

To provide a pan-European overview of the GDPR's impact on the biobanking regulatory framework, experts in health law and/or data protection law, commonly with experience in the area of genetic and genomic research and biobanking, were invited to contribute their insights with respect to the following issues:

(1) biobank infrastructure and regulatory environment;
(2) the questions of legal basis and consent in biobanking;
(3) individual rights and derogations under Article 89(2) GDPR, including adequate safeguards;
(4) the balance between individual rights and public interest in national law; and
(5) GDPR impact and future possibilities for biobanking.

Additionally, BBMRI-ERIC[2] prepared and circulated a research-facilitator tool in the form of a screening table, based on which national laws were screened for

[2] More information on BBMRI-ERIC infrastructure can be found at http://www.bbmri-eric.eu/.

further details related to the operationalization of the GDPR in the national context. The experts who participated in the study represented nineteen EU/EEA countries: Belgium, Croatia, Czech Republic, Denmark, Estonia, Finland, France, Germany, Greece, Ireland, Italy, Latvia, Liechtenstein, Malta, the Netherlands, Norway, Poland, Portugal and Spain. Each collaborator's answers along with the BBMRI-ERIC hosted table constituted a national report, and all data were analyzed, summarized and grouped into categories based on similarities or significant differences. The authors of these national studies have subsequently verified the accuracy of this work. All collaborators are co-authors of this study.

2 Biobank Regulatory Environment Across Europe

In the absence of a supranational actor with competence and authority to regulate biobanking and set uniform, comprehensive and binding requirements within and across borders, it falls on the national legal orders to regulate biobanking with due regard to their external commitments.[3] To identify the approach that national legal orders have taken with respect to regulating biobanks, the hereinafter analysis reviews national regulatory frameworks and governance approaches.

There are countries that have opted for a sector-specific legislation for biobanking research. Among these are Spain, where the Act on Biomedical Research[4] has devoted specific chapters to biobanks; Portugal, where the Biobank Act for Research Purposes has been in place since 2005;[5] and Latvia, where the Human Genome Research Law was adopted in 2002 and came into effect in 2004. Parallel to biobanking regulations, in all countries participating in the present study, national and European laws on privacy and personal data protection, namely Convention 108 and the GDPR, apply collectively. This is certainly the case for Belgium. With a network of biobanks that are linked to public institutions such as hospitals, universities and research centers, it has a number of European and Belgian provisions which regulate biobanking activities. Most notably, there is the Belgian Act on the Procurement and Use of Human Body Material (Act on HBM)[6] and the Royal Decree of 2018,[7]

---

[3] Slokenberga et al. (2017).

[4] Ley de Investigación Biomédica, LIB, 14/2007, de 3 de julio 2007.

[5] Article 19/1 of Law 12/2005 defines biobanks as 'any repository of biological samples or their derivatives, with or without limited storage life, whether using prospective harvesting or previously harvested material, or being obtained as part of routine health care, whether in screening programs, or for research purposes, which must include personally identified, identifiable, anonymized or anonymous samples'.

[6] Act of 19 December 2008 regarding the procurement and use of human bodily material destined for human medical applications or for scientific research applies.

[7] Royal Decree of 9 January 2018 on biobanks, in implementation of Article 22 of the Act of December 2008.

which provides the legal basis for the entry into force of the provisions on biobanks contained in the Act on HBM and further specifies their application.

However, even where a biobank Act is in place, other laws apply concurrently. For example, Finland's regulatory framework for obtaining and using tissue and data from biobanks and other such repositories for research comprises mainly the Biobank Act, the Data Protection Act,[8] the Act on the Secondary Use of Social and Health Care Data,[9] and the Act on the Medical Use of Human Organs, Tissues and Cells[10]. Of particular interest is Estonia, where the national Biobank EBB[11] is regulated by a sector-specific Act, as opposed to other tissue collections and biobanks in the country which are regulated by a combination of provisions on biomedical research.[12] Sweden has two specific Acts on research databases, the Act on Certain Registers for Research on what Inheritance and the Environment Mean for Human Health and the Act on Forensic Psychiatry Research Register, which both apply to biobanks.

Other countries, such as France, Germany, Denmark, Greece,[13] Croatia,[14] Czech Republic, Ireland,[15] Liechtenstein, the Netherlands and Poland,[16] regulate biobanks through a combination of national provisions on biomedical research and data protection, without a lex specialis on biobanks. In the absence of a specific biobank Act, ethical, technical and scientific guidelines supplement the regulation of biobanks.[17]

Italy's approach could be characterized as an 'hybrid model', since the national Data Protection Authority (DPA) issued in 2016 two specific Authorizations concerning the processing of genetic data and the processing of personal data for

[8] Code 1050/2018. www.finlex.fi/fi/laki/alkup/2018/20181050.

[9] Code 552/2019. www.finlex.fi/fi/laki/alkup/2019/20190552.

[10] Code 191/2001 www.finlex.fi/fi/laki/kaannokset/2001/en20010101_20130277.pdf.

[11] Order no 177 of the Government of the Republic of Estonia, Sihtasutuse Eesti Geenivaramu Asutamine, adopted 13 March 2001.—RTL 2001, 37, 512.

[12] Human Genes Research Act (HGRA), RT I 2000, 104, 685. Official English translation. https://www.riigiteataja.ee/en/eli/518062014005/consolide.

[13] Tzortzatou (2015).

[14] See the Law on Protection of Patients' Rights (official gazette 169/04, 37/08), Law on Implementation of General Regulation on Data Protection (official gazette 42/18), Ethical Codex of the Institute for Medical Research and Occupational Health.

[15] See the Section 5(1), Data Protection Act 2018 (Section 36(2)) and Health Research Regulations 2018 (S.I. No. 314 of 2018).

[16] E.g. in the case of Poland, the Polish biobanks guidelines of good practices or standards of conduct are based on international, European and other regulations and recommendations created by international organizations (such as BBMRI-ERIC and ISBER). For more information on Biobanking in Poland, see also, Witoń et al. (2017).

[17] See for example in the case of France the Good clinical practices in clinical trials on medicinal products for human use Décision du 24 novembre 2006 fixant les règles de bonnes pratiques cliniques pour les recherches biomédicales portant sur des médicaments à usage humain, JORF 30 novembre 2006, texte n°64.

scientific research, which include specific provisions for biobanking research.[18] The Malta BioBank has two main arms, the Clinical Bank and the Population Bank.[19] Apart from the GDPR, which has been transposed into Maltese law by means of the Data Protection Act, no specific law regulates research, except for the Clinical Trial Regulation and laws regulating higher education and health. The biobank's governance is regulated by the Statute for the Centre for Molecular Medicine and Biobanking.

Finally, Biobank Norway is a national infrastructure of biobanks which includes consented population-based and disease-specific clinical biobanks, and offers access to unparalleled longitudinal health data in health registers.[20] Biobanks and personal data are regulated in different laws. The Personal Data Act regulates the processing of personal data when these relate to specific biological material, while public biobanks are regulated by the Treatment Biobank Act and the Health Research Act.

As seen above, the approaches taken to biobanking regulation vary across Europe, with most countries choosing not to introduce a sector-specific piece of law into their domestic legal order. However, where countries have opted for such specific instruments, these do not sufficiently address all the issues arising from biobanking research, especially those related to the processing of participants' personal data. Hence, national law still needs to be applied in conjunction with the GDPR and other sources of European/international law.

3 Legal Basis for Biobanking. The Place and Role of Consent as One of the Legal Bases for Data Processing in Biobanking: Informed, Broad or None?

Participants' written and informed consent has undeniably been the most common legal basis upon which the processing of health and genetic data for biomedical research on humans has been legally justified. However, the scope of consent differs substantially across the countries included in the current study, which obstructs the transfer of data across borders within the framework of collaborative projects. The informed consent procedure has been heavily criticized as the route least likely to enhance research participants' autonomy in biobanking, given the large amount of samples and data that need to be stored and processed for long periods of time and, most importantly, for research purposes unknown at the time of their collection. In contrast to the informed consent model, which originates in clinical practice and has a longstanding tradition in the field of medical law that aims to protect

[18] The contents of the two Authorisations that were deemed compatible with the GDPR were, more recently, collected in Document No 146 of 2019, concerning the processing of special categories of data.

[19] More information can be found at the Biobank's website https://www.um.edu.mt/biobank.

[20] See more information can be found at the Biobank's website at https://www.ntnu.edu/biobanknorway.

individuals from research interventions, the broad consent model is arguably best suited to biobanking research.[21]

The critical question regarding consent is how countries chose to delineate its scope. Recital 33 is the only place in the GDPR where broad consent is implied, stating that 'data subjects should be allowed to give their consent to certain areas of research'.[22] Still, nowhere in the regulation is broad consent explicitly established. It is, therefore, of particular comparative interest how Member States used their granted discretion to introduce further conditions for health and genetic data processing (Article 9(4) GDPR), and, more specifically, what approach they adopted in regards to the scope of consent. Nonetheless, as noted in the introduction of this chapter, it is not precluded that broad consent could be directly applied by invoking the provisions of the national law, unless a Member State, following the discretion left under Article 9(2)(a) or 9(4) GDPR, precludes the use of consent as a means to lift the prohibition of health and genetic data processing.

Belgium established the controller's obligation to inform data subjects about the anonymization of their personal information and the reasons for which the exercise of their rights would render the achievement of the objectives impossible or seriously impede them from the time of the data collection. Prior to the data collection, according to the Belgian Privacy Act and without prejudice to the GDPR provisions on the controller's responsibilities, including those on record keeping, the controller shall add specific elements to the registration of processing activities for purposes of scientific research. As stated in the law, these requirements consist in the justification of the use of the data, which may or may not be pseudonymized; the reasons why the exercise of the data subject's rights threatens to render the achievement of the objectives impossible or seriously impedes them; and, if applicable, the data protection impact assessment, when the data controller processes special categories of data for the purposes of scientific or historical research or statistical purposes.

The Irish legislation normally requires data subjects' explicit consent to the processing of special categories of data for research. The Health Research Regulations (2018) define consent broadly as for the purpose of specified health research, either in relation to a particular area or more generally in that area or a related area of health research, or part thereof. Specific measures must be taken to safeguard personal data, including: limitations on access; strict time limits for the erasure of personal data and mechanisms to ensure this; targeted training; logging mechanisms; designation of a data protection officer (where not mandatory) and, where processing health-related data, a requirement that the processing is undertaken by a health practitioner or a person bound by an equivalent duty of confidentiality; pseudonymization and encryption. The Health Research Regulations list further measures, such as appropriate governance structures. Researchers can apply for an exemption

[21] Dynamic consent, have also been proposed as the suitable way for individuals to consent to their data process, when it comes to biobanking research activities, see also Steinsbekk et al. (2013).

[22] More information on broad consent can be found at: https://www.nature.com/articles/ejhg2012282, https://journals.plos.org/plosmedicine/article?id=10.1371/journal.pmed.0050192, https://www.sciencedirect.com/science/article/pii/S1470204506706180, https://www.nature.com/articles/ejhg2012282, https://journals.sagepub.com/doi/pdf/10.1177/096853320901000201.

when they are 'of the view that the public interest in carrying out the research significantly outweighs the public interest in requiring the explicit consent'.

Croatia leaves no room for broad consent to medical research. The Croatian Law on Patients Protection states that consent to medical research has to contain detailed explanations of involved procedures and risks.[23] In the Czech Republic, the legislator laid down no further specific conditions for consent to medical research, adopting the informed consent approach elaborated in the GDPR. In the case of Latvia, the Human Genome Research Law requires specific consent.[24] Furthermore, this consent shall be documented on a form approved by the Cabinet.[25] These rules have not been amended since the GDPR entered into force. Nonetheless, work on a new law regulating biobank research has commenced and could lead to a different approach to consent. In Spain, the data subject's consent is required. However, the reuse of personal data for health and biomedical research shall be considered lawful if consent was obtained for the first use. Furthermore, scientific studies may be carried out without the consent of those concerned for public health reasons and in situations of exceptional relevance and seriousness to public health. Interestingly, in France, the law functions on the basis of opt-out consent (non-opposition), although opt-in consent can be required under special laws. Consent to several purposes is accepted, where these are clearly, intelligibly and explicitly presented to the individuals, who can opt for or refuse each one.[26]

In Portugal, consent may cover several areas of research. This is an improvement compared to the specific consent previously required. However, consent can only be waived in exceptional cases, where samples are used retrospectively, or when the consent of the persons concerned cannot be obtained due to the number of data or individuals, their age or other comparable reasons. In these cases, data and biospecimens can only be processed for scientific research purposes or for the collection of epidemiological or statistical data.

Along the same lines, but with an even broader scope, the Finnish Biobank Act allows research participants to give their informed consent to the storage and use of samples (to be) taken from them, to the purpose of biobank research, to the transfer of their personal information (to researchers) and to linking personal data from

---

[23] Law on Protection of Patients' Rights (official gazette 169/04, 37/08)—Article 19.

[24] Section 10(1) states 'Before a person participates in the genetic research, a doctor shall issue to the person written information regarding: 1) the purpose, content and duration of the genome research project; 2) potential risks; 3) the right to freely express his or her consent and to revoke it at any time; and 4) a possibility to perform genetic research outside of Latvia'. Human Genome Research Law, Latvijas Vēstnesis, 99 (2674), 03.07.2002.

[25] Cabinet (of Ministers) holds the executive power. Provisions on the specimen of the gene donor consent form and the procedure for its completion and storage Provisions on the specimen of the gene donor consent form and the procedure for its completion and storage. Latvijas Vēstnesis, 128 (3076), 13.08.2004.

[26] See also the referentials adopted by the CNIL (Méthodologies de Référence, MR) specifying data protection rules in research contexts and specifically MR001 (regarding health research requiring prior informed consent), MR003 (regarding health research that does not require consent) and MR004 (regarding research that do not involve human persons, studies and evaluations in health).

other sources and other processing of samples and information obtained with the samples to the extent required by biobank research. Furthermore, the Biobank Act does not require a new consent to the use of biospecimens and associated data by each research project. The Biobank Act is being reviewed, however, and it is expected that the legal bases for processing by the biobank will be Articles 6(1)(e) and 9(2)(g) instead of consent (draft government bill for a new Biobank Act, May 2018), while the Data Protection Act already provides that, under certain conditions, processing personal data for scientific research is lawful based on 6(1)(e) and that the restrictions of Article 9(1) will not apply.

In Italy, data subjects' consent to the processing of health data for scientific research is not necessary when the research is carried out on the basis of (national or EU) law, in line with Article 9(2)(j) GDPR, including when the research is part of a biomedical or health research program, provided that an impact assessment pursuant to Articles 35-36 GDPR is conducted and published. Furthermore, consent is not necessary when, due to specific reasons, informing the interested parties is impossible or involves disproportionate effort, or risks making it impossible or seriously impairing the achievement of the aims of the research. In such cases, the data controller shall take appropriate measures to protect the rights, freedoms and legitimate interests of the interested party, and the research program should receive the favorable opinion of the competent Research Ethics Committee (REC) at a territorial level which must be submitted for preventive consultation to the Garante.

In a similar vein, Germany allows biomedical research to be conducted after data subject's informed consent, which is freely given and easily withdrawn, has been provided. However, public interest, instead of consent, may be used as the legal basis for processing special categories of personal data in the context of scientific research, if appropriate safeguards for the legally protected interests of data subjects are implemented. Such safeguards may consist of anonymizing personal data as quickly as possible, taking measures to prevent unauthorized disclosure to third parties, or processing them in an organizationally and spatially separate manner from other tasks.

In implementing GDPR, Sweden has not introduced any specific rule providing a legal basis for processing personal data in research. Existing rules on research conducted by public and private entities have been deemed sufficient. In particular, Sweden has two specific Acts on research databases providing the legal basis for researchers to access data without further consent, under certain conditions and after ethical approval, namely the Act on Certain Registers for Research on what Inheritance and the Environment Mean for Human Health and the Act on Forensic Psychiatry Research Register. Both have been adapted to the GDPR requirements. When processing is not based on informed consent, there will be a different legal basis for research conducted by public research entities (public interest as legal basis) and private ones (commonly, legitimate interest as legal basis). The Netherlands has taken further steps by adopting an opt-out approach when the personal data come from a health care provider, as the patient should not have objected to such use for research. When seeking consent is impossible and the research serves a public interest which cannot be fulfilled without these data, then research is permitted as long as appropriate guarantees are in place. Concerning Denmark's

Data Protection Act,[27] it includes a provision on the processing of personal data for scientific and statistical purposes without the data subject's consent. Consequently, the Act makes use of the options provided by Article 9(2)(j) and Article 89 GDPR. It is a precondition that the research project is of significant societal interest, and safeguards are outlined in the Act.

Similarly, Norway's Personal Data Act dictates that special categories of personal data can be processed without data subject's consent if it is necessary for archiving purposes in the public interest, scientific or historical research purposes or statistical purposes.[28] This requires that the benefit to society as a whole clearly exceeds the disadvantages experienced by the subject whose personal data is processed without consent. Furthermore, processing must be subject to appropriate safeguards in accordance with Article 89(1) GDPR. It is required that the controller confers with the data protection officer to make sure that such safeguards are in place. Norway also predicts that in the future, and under certain conditions, broad-based consent will be adopted for research on human biological material and personal health data.[29] When using biological material and health-related personal data, the broad consent must define the research purposes, and new consent may in specific cases be requested by the competent REC if the conditions for use of broad consent need to be specified.

The Estonian Data Protection Act takes quite a liberal approach to the research use of personal data beyond informed consent. Processing personal data in research without consent is permissible in line with GDPR requirements as long as the data are pseudonymized or any other equally effective method is followed, but (upon certain conditions) also when the data enables identification of the individual.[30] Likewise, Liechtenstein and Greece allow the processing of special categories of data for the abovementioned purposes without consent if such processing is necessary for those purposes and the processor's interests outweigh those of the person concerned, given that specific measures are in place. Greek law, specifically refers to data pseudonymisation and encryption, DPO designation and data access restriction on behalf of the data processor and/or controller, as such measures.

Similarly, the Maltese Data Protection Act implementing the GDPR provides a derogation for scientific or historical research purposes provided that adherence to the GDPR provisions would be likely to render impossible or seriously impair the achievement of those purposes and the data controller reasonably believes that such derogations are necessary for the fulfillment of those purposes. In these cases,

[27] Act no. 502 of 23 May 2018 on supplementary provisions to the regulation on the protection of natural persons with regard to the processing of personal data and on the free movement of such data.

[28] See PDA sections 8 and 9.

[29] See the chapter of Norway.

[30] However, it is worth noting that in the case of the Estonian Biobank (EBB), exceptionally broad consent remains as it was prior to the GDPR the legal basis for the use of data for research, something that can be regarded as an exercise of the discretion referred to in Recital 33 GDPR. See further Kärt Pormeister (2018).

processing for scientific or historical research shall be subject to appropriate safeguards for the data subject's rights and freedoms, including pseudonymization and other technical and organizational measures in order to ensure respect for the principle of data minimization. The conditions imposed for processing in the field of public health have been made applicable to processing genetic data and biometric data. Hence, the controller must consult with and obtain prior authorization from the Commissioner. The Commissioner in turn must consult with a REC.

As a review of the national approaches demonstrates, different possibilities for lifting the prohibition of Article 9 GDPR to process health and genetic data have been operationalized in the national legal orders. Often, several possibilities co-exist, in particular, a consent-based approach with a public interest-based approach or similarly regulated approach, following which the consent requirement may be misapplied or derogated from. When these derogations apply, in some countries a legal requirement to consult RECs emerges.

4 Derogations from Individual Rights Under Article 89(2) Subject to Article 89(1)

4.1 Enabling Derogations

Article 89(2) GDPR enables Member States to lay down derogations from data subjects' rights to access, rectification, restriction of processing and objection when personal data are processed for scientific purposes. Such discretion is subject to safeguards as set out in Article 89(1), but its boundaries are not clearly defined by the Regulation. At the same time, the non-binding Recital 156 highlights that Member States also retain the ability to provide specifications and derogations from the rights to erasure and data portability. Moreover, Recital 41 indicates that 'where this Regulation refers to a legal basis or a legislative measure, this does not necessarily require a legislative act adopted by a parliament, without prejudice to requirements pursuant to the constitutional order of the Member State concerned' provided it is clear, precise and foreseeable. Hence, what follows examines whether and how Member States did actually make use of this margin of maneuver and establish specific exceptions to the rights found in Articles 15, 16, 18 and 21 GDPR.

To begin with, it can be noted that seven of the countries participating in the study, specifically, Croatia, Germany, Greece, Malta, the Netherlands, Portugal and Sweden refrained from prescribing further derogations in their GDPR adapting legislation. The Dutch implementing Act did not embed the right to object (Article 21 GDPR) as a research exemption. According to the same Act, research institutions acting as data controllers are allowed not to give effect to Articles 15 (access), 16 (rectification) and 17 (erasure) GDPR.[31] Germany and Greece are slightly more

[31] See article 44 of the Dutch implementing Act.

specific when it comes to overriding the right to access for research purposes by adding that in such cases the provision of information should involve disproportionate effort. Finland lists specific safeguards that are required for the derogations to apply (appropriate research plan, designated responsibilities, confidentiality[32]), including additional safeguards in case of special category personal data (DPIA provided to national supervisory authorities or compliance with an appropriate and approved code of conduct). It also enacted derogations from the controller's obligations to provide information to the data subject under Article 13 and Article 14.

The Italian Legislative Decree 101/2018 mentions, in particular, derogations from the right to rectification, noting that in exercising data subjects' rights pursuant to Article 16 GDPR the rectification and integration of data are noted without modifying the latter when the result of these operations does not produce significant effects on the result of the research. In Liechtenstein, under certain conditions, limitations are also possible with regard to the right to data portability of Article 20 GDPR.

Latvia adopted the Personal Data Processing Law that enables a general derogation when research is carried out in the public interest. It states that 'if data are processed for scientific or historical research purposes in the public interest, the rights of a data subject specified in Articles 15, 16, 18, and 21 of the Data Regulation shall not be applied, insofar as they may render impossible or seriously impair achievement of the specific purposes, and derogations are necessary for the achievement of such purposes'.[33] This derogation is not aligned with the key law regulating human genome research, and consequently, until a new Act is adopted and the current one repealed, or until the current law is amended, these derogations might have limited effect. A similar approach was adopted by Denmark. The Danish Data Protection Act specifically states that Articles 15, 16, 18 and 21 GDPR do not apply to data processed for scientific or statistical purposes.

In the Czech Republic, the Act on Personal Data Processing allows for derogations from data subject rights when personal data are being processed for scientific research pursuant to Article 89(2) GDPR. Specifically, it states that the data subject's rights to access, rectification, restriction of processing and objection to processing apply adequately or can even be postponed if this is necessary and proportional to the fulfillment of the purpose of processing. It also states that the right to access shall not apply if processing is necessary for scientific research and the provision of such information would involve disproportionate effort. However, several national legislators merged derogations from data subjects' rights for research purposes with those for reasons of public interest, or focused only on the latter. Portugal posits the anonymization of data as an additional condition under which derogations for the sake of public interest or research purposes are allowed. The legislation to be proposed in Portugal states that in processing data for purposes

[32] Biobank Act Section 16 specifically requires that the biobank samples and data must be pseudonymised by a code replacing direct identifiers, and the code key must be stored separately.

[33] Personal Data Processing Law, Latvijas Vēstnesis, 132 (6218), 04.07.2018.

of archiving in the public interest, scientific or historical research or official statistical purposes, the rights of access, rectification, restriction of processing and opposition are superseded when their exercise is impossible, namely when the data collected are anonymized, or liable to seriously hinder the attainment of the aforementioned objectives.[34]

In addition to acknowledging the possibility of derogations for research purposes, Italy and Malta regulate further obligations of data controllers and rights of data subjects when such derogations occur.

More specifically, Italy provides that ethical rules, to be approved by the Italian Personal Data Protection Authority, may indicate the cases in which the rights listed in Articles 15, 16, 18 and 21 of the GDPR can be limited, pursuant to Article 89(2) of the same Regulation. The Maltese Data Protection Act provides that processing for scientific or historical research purposes, shall be subject to appropriate safeguards for data subjects' rights and freedoms, including pseudonymization and other technical and organizational measures, to ensure respect for the principle of data minimization. When such purposes can be fulfilled by processing, which does not permit, or no longer permits, the identification of data subjects, those purposes shall be fulfilled in that manner. Furthermore, controllers must consult with and obtain prior authorization from the Commissioner when they intend to process genetic data, biometric data or data concerning health for statistical or research purposes in the public interest. The Commissioner must, in turn, consult with a REC.

Of comparative interest is also the way in which national laws treat derogations from the right to object. Norway dictates exceptions from the right to access to information, the right to rectification and the right to restriction of processing, but the national legislator argues that there is no need for further exceptions. As a result, there is no exception or extension of the scope of derogations with regard to the right to object. Equally, the Dutch GDPR Implementation Act did not embed the right to object as a research exemption, although research institutions are allowed not to give effect to Articles 15, 16 and 17 GDPR.

In Italy, derogations from the right to object are permitted when processing is necessary in the public interest. Contrary to the countries examined above, this is the only right for which research and public interest merge in the Italian law. Malta takes a different approach regarding the right to object, which may be overridden when personal data are processed for purposes of academic expression. However, neither the Maltese Data Protection Act[35] nor the GDPR offer any guidance on what is considered 'academic expression', making it unclear whether scientific and health research would fall under this provision. In the UK, where controllers reasonably require further information and have informed the data subject of that requirement, they are not obliged to comply with the data subject's notice not to process their data unless this further information has been provided. Finally, both in Ireland and Greece when processing data for scientific research purposes, the rights

[34] Legislation to be proposed.

[35] Chapter 586 of the Laws of Malta.

of the data subject under Articles 15, 16, 18 and 21 GDPR are restricted to the extent that is necessary and the exercise of the rights would be likely to render impossible, or seriously impair, the achievement of the research.

Overall, the Member States are split between enabling and not enabling derogations from individual rights under Article 89(2) GDPR and the extent to which these derogations are enabled. The fragmentation of the regulatory landscape might have further implications for collaboration, and could open up the possibility of forum shopping. How Member States address this issue will be reviewed in the concluding analysis of this chapter.

4.2 *Insights in Appropriate Safeguards*

Derogations from the rights indicated in Article 89(2) GDPR, namely Articles 15, 16, 18 and 21 GDPR, not only require the existence of a national law, but are also subject to the conditions and safeguards referred to in paragraph 1 of this Article in so far as such rights are likely to render impossible or seriously impair the achievement of the specific purposes, and such derogations are necessary for the fulfilment of those purposes. Therefore, it is clear that derogations are possible. What is less clear is whether the relevance of appropriate safeguards and case-by-case assessment likewise needs to be established by law, or whether direct applicability and effect of the GDPR provisions will suffice. The formulation of the provision in Article 89(2) GDPR is rather ambiguous, but could be argued to be related to national law. Therefore, this section reviews how the requirement for safeguards is approached nationally.

Article 89(1) GDPR generally refers to 'safeguards and technical measures' that need to be in place to assure lawful processing of the special categories of personal data, and indicates that '[t]hose measures may include pseudonymization (...)'. Pseudonymization in Article 4(5) GDPR is defined as the 'processing of personal data in such a manner that the personal data can no longer be attributed to a specific data subject without the use of additional information'. Such additional information should be kept separately and be subject to technical and organizational measures so that the personal data can not be attributed to an identified or identifiable natural person. This explicit introduction of pseudonymization aims at minimizing risks against data subjects and is especially considered an appropriate safeguard when processing is conducted for research purposes based on Article 89(1) GDPR. Yet, according to Recital 28 GDPR, data controllers are not prevented from applying other technical measures in order to comply with their data protection obligations. In fact, this requirement is rather to be approached as an obligation, given that data controllers are bound by the duty to ensure that subjects' personal data are adequately safeguarded, and this duty applies regardless of whether a Member State has regulated safeguards in any further way.

This study has showed the national legislators' preference for pseudonymization when it comes to choosing among other measures for enhancing privacy. It is worth mentioning that, until the GDPR entered into force, other terms were also used in practice across Europe, such as 'anonymized data', 'coded data', 'codified data', 'linked data', 're-identifiable data', 'masked data', 'de-identifiable data', in order to describe what now falls under the general term 'pseudonymized data'. Consequently, the latter are for the first time in a data ptotection piece of legislation distinguished from the 'anonymous data', meaning those unable to identify the subject.[36]

In terms of what constitutes pseudonymization, the majority of countries included in this study do not provide further definitions of the term, which means that Article 4(5) GDPR applies as it stands. In particular, Croatia, Czech Republic, Finland, France, Greece, Norway, Portugal, Sweden, Latvia and Liechtenstein refrain from further specifying pseudonymization, whereas Germany, Ireland and Malta repeat the definition offered by the GDPR. Interestingly, before the advent of the Regulation, Norway used to define pseudonymous data as indirectly identifiable ones, while now pseudonymization is considered to encompass all means of de-identification. In Finland, the Data Protection Ombudsman is unequivocal in classifying pseudonymized data as personal data universally. Concerning the French legislation, the implementation of pseudonymization is presumed in order to preserve confidentiality, although previous iterations of the law referred to it as coding. In Spain, both definitions of data coded and of biological sample coded are provided by the Spanish Biomedical Research Law.[37]

Where most national laws present slight differentiations is the distinction between anonymization and pseudonymization as well as the relation between the two. Specifically, the Belgian legislator grants priority to the use of anonymous data. Only if controllers cannot achieve their research purposes should they turn to pseudonymous data. If the research objective remains unattainable even with the usage of pseudonymized data, then data controllers are allowed to process non-pseudonymized ones. In choosing among different methods of pseudonymization and anonymization, data controllers benefit from the guidance of a data protection officer, when such person has been designated, who advises with regard to the suitability of these methods for data protection.

In Portugal, no priority is attributed to either anonymization or pseudonymization. More specifically, 'anonymization or pseudonymization' is selected when the target goals can be reached through either of these. This corresponds with the Portuguese empirical reality, given that, in practice, biomedical researchers and

---

[36] Nevertheless, the longstanding use of above terms such as 'anonymized data', has led to confusion many researchers who are now progressively starting to familiarize themselves with the 'pseudonymous' as opposed to 'anonymous' data. This can be clearly reflected in the study protocols were most often researchers refer to 'anonymized codified data' instead of the right term which is 'pseudonymized data'.

[37] The Spanish Biomedical Research Law of 2007 provided following terms: 'Data coded or reversibly dissociated: data not associated with an identified or identifiable person because the information has been replaced or unlinked identifies that person by using a code that allows for the inverse operation' (Article 3 (k)).

'Biological sample encoded or reversibly dissociated means a sample not associated with an identified or identifiable person as a result of the replacement or disassociation of that person information that identifies that person by using a code that allows reverse operation' (Article 3(r)).

scientists have been implementing coding techniques as a way to reconcile the protection of data subjects' privacy with the deduction of satisfactory research outputs. Interestingly, in regards to anonymization, the Greek law further states that the data controller must anonymize the data as soon as the scientific purposes permit so, unless this is contrary to the legitimate interest of the data subject. In addition, it predicts that until anonymization takes place the features that can be used to correlate details of personal or actual situations of an identified or identifiable individual, must be stored separately. These features can be combined with individual details only if it is required by the research or statistical purposes. Furthermore, the Greek law also indicatively refers to the data controller's and/or data processor's data access restriction, the data encryption and the DPO designation, as additional safeguards when it comes to the processing of specific categories of data for scientific purposes. In regards to scientific publications containing personal data, these can take place either after the data controller obtains the explicit written informed consent of the data subject or after the controller pseudonymizes the data, in case no consent is obtained, however, the publication is necessary for the presentation of the scientific research results.

Italy demands that the Italian DPA provides for further conditions under which genetic, biometric and health-related data can be processed, namely encryption and pseudonymization techniques, minimization measures, specific methods for selective access and any other measure necessary to safeguard the rights of those concerned.[38] In all these cases, the Italian regulations interpret these terms based on the volume of data processed, the nature, object, context and purposes of the processing, and denote methods of rendering data not directly traceable to the concerned parties but identifiable only when necessary.

In the Czech Republic, pursuant to the Act on Personal Data Processing, if it is consistent with the purpose of personal data processing (scientific research), the personal data referred to in Article 9(1) GDPR should be processed in a form which does not allow the identification of the data subject. This does not apply when legitimate interests of data subjects prevent this.

In contrast, Norway clearly advances pseudonymization over anonymization. Norway used to define pseudonymous data as 'indirectly identifiable' ones, while now pseudonymization is considered to encompass all means of de-identification that meet certain requirements for whomever has access to the key. Provided that data subjects' identity is sufficiently protected or pseudonyms are being applied, data controllers can proceed with processing data for health research. Requiring that all data used in research be anonymous is deemed unrealistic, as it would impede controlling and verifying research outcomes. Moving on to the Netherlands, it is still unclear how pseudonymization is perceived. Before the GDPR, the DPA issued

[38] The same formulation, i.e. encryption or pseudonymization techniques, was also adopted in the General Authorisation 9/2016 concerning the processing of personal data for scientific research purposes and in the General Authorisation 8/2016 concerning genetic data treatment, and can now be found in the Document No. 146 of 2019, concerning the processing of special categories of data.

a decision mentioning that pseudonymization does not per se lead to anonymization, which has regrettably opened up space for diverse, inconclusive interpretations regarding the connection between pseudonymous and anonymous data.

The NHS Health Research Authority in the UK clarified that personal data, which have been pseudonymized (e.g. key-coded), fall under the remit of the GDPR depending on how difficult it is to attribute the pseudonym to a particular individual. This echoes the provisions of Recital 26 GDPR which posits that if pseudonymized data could be attributed to a natural person by the use of additional information, then they should be considered to be information on an identifiable natural person. Furthermore, data that have been anonymized are excluded from the scope of GDPR, with the act of anonymization being viewed as data processing.

Finally, a few Member States examined pseudonymization in relation to third-party transfers. In Denmark, the Data Protection Authority is authorised to issue general rules on the transfer of data processed for research purposes to third parties, with pseudonymization being among the possible requirements in the preparatory works. At the same time, in France, pseudonymization is indicated as obligatory before transferring data to non-EU countries.[39]

Overall, even though Member States conformed in their incorporation of pseudonymization, this newly-suggested measure is still ambiguously phrased and examined in relation to other alternative technical measures, which raises questions about its sufficiency in eliminating risks to data subjects' rights. Given that whether a set of data is considered anonymized or pseudonymized will determine the applicability of the GDPR provisions at each instance, it is vital that the definitions, characteristics and legal status of these techniques are further illuminated. Regarding the states that have opted for enabling the derogations but have not further specified them in their data protection legal frameworks, it is too early to conclude that these safeguards do not exist. They could be included in research-specific regulations adopted at a later stage or interpreted in light of the pre-GDPR research regulations, for example, as rules on coding and decoding of the samples under the Human Genome Research Law in Latvia. Moreover, even if the national law does not refer to or specify applications of safeguards in any way, controllers are not released from their obligation to ensure compliance with the GDPR.

5 Public Interest

Benefit sharing from research, return of the results, incidental findings and intellectual property policies are means to ensure a balance between the protection of participants' interests, on the one hand, and the promotion of the public interest, on the other. Specifically, when it comes to biobanking, public interest has long been debated as one of the suitable legal bases for processing special categories of

[39] See reference 11, and specifically the CNIL Reference methodologies MR001 and MR003.

personal data as per Article 9(2)(j) GDPR and in opposition to consent.[40] Furthermore, as elaborated by Slokenberga in the introductory chapter, classifying biobanking as public research enables further derogations from individual rights.[41] It is crucial to see how national legislators chose to handle the abovementioned provision, which stands in close relation to Article 89(1) GDPR on technical and organizational measures and safeguards requirements.

Belgium, chose to impose two further obligations on the data controller when it comes to archiving personal data for scientific research in order to ensure public interest, namely the justification of the public interest, of the stored archives and the reasons according to which the exercise of the rights of the person concerned threatens to render the achievement of the objectives impossible or seriously impedes them. In contrast, Italy avoided imposing further obligations on the controller. Instead, it enhanced the role of the DPA in setting the regulatory framework, as reflected in the Annual Report of the DPA, where the interplay between scientific research needs and individuals' rights protection is prominent. Similarly to Italy, Portugal's legislation to be proposed on the establishment of biobanks for scientific research purposes sets specific requirements for transparency in scientific, health-related research. Public interest is safeguarded through the control of biobanks by the National Data Protection Commission and the Commission for Coordination of Research in Human Cells and Tissues, which will be created.

Finland's, new Biobank Act is expected to adopt substantial public interest as a legal basis for biobanking activities. Concerns have also been raised regarding the new Act on the Secondary Use of Social and Health Care Data when it comes to the public interest, and specifically, the dissemination of research results. In particular, this Act introduces limitations to the publication of results, which interferes with the autonomy and freedom of science. In the case of Malta, society's participation in biobanking is paramount, as reflected by the steps taken towards the creation of a portal that would allow participants to grant their digital consent. In this way, participants could track the use of their samples and associated data as well as access information and updates about the research projects in which their samples are involved. Research results would also be made available on the portal, thus turning research participants into research partners.

Since 2016, in France, 'public interest' has been seen as a synonym for 'general interest' and 'collective benefit', and has become important to the processing of personal data in health research. Data controllers claiming public interest research purposes should be able to justify this assertion. They can, then, process data through a simplified route. However, public interest is only mentioned as an exception to the principle of storage limitation in research when it comes to archiving reasons. Furthermore, data controllers who are involved in archiving in the public

[40] See paragraph 3 'Consent as one of the legal basis for data processing in biobanking across EU Member States: informed, broad or none?'

[41] See Articles 18(2), 20(3) and 21(6) GDPR. See further Santa Slokenberga, Setting the foundations: Individual rights, public interest, scientific research and biobanking.

interest can derogate from the rights of access, rectification, restriction of processing and to object.

Germany and Greece, following the letter of the GDPR, provided specific rules, such as limitations on data subjects' rights or technical measures that safeguard special categories of personal data. The Danish Data Protection Act does not include a provision specifically referring to public interest, but provides for processing of personal data for the purposes listed in Article 9(2)(h) and (g) GDPR, which seems to cover purposes outlined in GDPR Article 9(2)(i). Similarly, the Netherlands, which has many quality registries and a comprehensive cancer registry, has not implemented Article 9(2)(i) for biobanking purposes. Such registries, which are usually not based on informed consent, find a 'workaround', e.g. using a common data processor and/or relying on the implementation of Article 9(2)(j). The Estonian approach seems to be shifting the balance between individual rights and public interest strongly towards public interest since research is seen as a task carried out in the public interest.

Ireland allows processing special categories of data in the public interest to protect against serious cross-border threats, ensure high standards of quality and safety of health care and for archiving purposes. The obligations of controllers and rights of data subjects are restricted to the extent necessary and proportional to, inter alia, national security and enforcement of civil law claims. The relevant minister has the power to issue regulations further restricting data subjects' rights in the public interest. Spain introduced exceptions to the interest of parties, specifically in a more extended consent approach than the GDPR, to the detriment of the widespread accessibility of data (and samples) by researchers, although it can be considered that they are still in agreement with the framework of the latter with the new Privacy Act.[42] In Latvia, even though it is not defined what research falls in the area of public interest, when it does so, derogations from Articles 15, 16, 18, and 21 GDPR are possible.[43]

Finally, Croatia has no explicit definition of medical scientific research, and this has been one of the causes of discussion of the balance between the individuals' right and public interests.[44] Specifically, where the scientific and experimental zone ends, the public interest begins where there is no such broad rights for the individuals. Such blurred boundaries might, in practice, cause challenges due to different interpretations of scientific research and experimental medicine in the country.

The analysis above illustrates that the countries implemented Article 9(2)(j) GDPR in their legislations vis-a-vis their longstanding research tradition. In those

[42] Organic Act 3/2018 of 5 of December on Protection of Personal Data and guarantee of digital rights.

[43] Personal Data Processing Law, Latvijas Vēstnesis, 132 (6218), 04.07.2018, Section 31.

[44] The Ethical Codex of the Institute for Medical Research and Occupational Health (https://www.imi.hr/en/) explicitly states that the wellbeing of the examinees should prevail over the interests of science and society. Therefore, within the research studies conducted by the Institute, there is obvious misbalance between the individual rights and public interest for the benefit of the individual rights. There are also numerous public discussions and cases pending in front of the Court with respect to question whether the vaccination is related to the individual freedom or should be seen as an obligatory action in favor of the public interest.

countries where the public interest had already been synonymous to general interest and a solidarity-based approach to research was already cultivated, the relevant provision was adopted as a means to further promote the balance between the public interest and individuals' rights. However, even in cases where certain societies were already familiar with biobanking research, the national legislator did not further specify the requirements of Article 89(1), and instead chose to stick to the letter of GDPR.

6 Conclusion

As the chapter shows, the approach to regulating biobanks differs significantly across EU and EEA Member States. Differences have emerged not only on whether and to what extent biobanking is regulated, but also on the requirements set forth by laws. These differences apply to key elements such as lawfulness requirements, in particular, the appropriate legal basis for biobanking as well as the legal basis for lifting the prohibition of health and genetic data processing. Through the approach that GDPR has taken, it has opened up room for the Member States to move away from the long-established model of informed consent in biobanking, at least regarding personal data processing. Whether this room will be widely used or if Member States will stick to the generic consent requirements under the GDPR remains to be seen. Similarly, it will be interesting to examine how this will be received by RECs. Additionally, the protection of data subjects' rights, and approaches for alternative measures to ensure high level of data protection when derogations are enabled. Finally, differences emerge in how Member States approach public interest and whether biobanking is subsumed into it. While it is often argued that biobanking research is in the public interest, not all Member States have explicitly or legally acknowledged this. Such research may benefit from the generally generous data protection regime enacted with the GDPR, but may not benefit from the additional measures concerning 'public interest' under the GDPR. Even though in principle these variations should not affect the free movement of personal data under the GDPR, in so far as RECs have the discretion to declare research as non-compliant with ethical principles and regulations, fragmentation will remain a challenge facing researchers in collaborative projects. This conclusion suggests the need for further research on the interaction of law and ethics nationally as well as under the GDPR. It also indicates the necessity for pan-European, sector-specific, Codes of Conduct, as encouraged by GDPR. Towards this direction, relevant initiatives have been launched with the aim of enhancing data flows across EU/EEA countries for research purposes.[45] Such initiatives, though, should be developed in coalition with

[45] See also the European Data Protection Supervisor, A Preliminary on data protection and scientific research, 6 January 2020. The preliminary opinion, refers to two current initiatives. First, sector-specific a Code of Conduct for Health Research is currently underway from BBMRI-ERIC. Second, a Code of Conduct from GEANT, the pan-European data network for the research and education community

comparable ones originating in the healthcare sector. Especially in the field of biomedical research, where present and foreseeable technological progress enables extraction of valuable information from existing healthcare datasets, research and healthcare reveal themselves as the two sides of the same coin. Therefore, drafting sector-specific Codes of Conduct, which will call attention to this interaction and will incorporate non-conflicting data protection provisions, particularly in relation to data flows or exchanges, should be a priority for all multi-sector actors involved in the aforementioned initiatives.

Acknowledgements The author wishes to thank Anastasia Siapka for her support during all the stages of this Chapter.

References

Council of Europe, Convention 108 for the Protection of Individuals with regard to Automatic Processing of Personal Data

Pormeister K (2018) Genetic research and applicable law: the intra-EU conflict of laws as a regulatory challenge to cross-border genetic research. J Law Biosci:706–723

Regulation (EU) 2016/679 of the European Parliament and of the Council of 27 April 2016 on the protection of natural persons with regard to the processing of personal data and on the free movement of such data, and repealing Directive 95/46/RC (General Data Protection Regulation)

Slokenberga S, Martinez RM, Reichel J (2017) Legal and ethical governance of intercontinental biobanking – some experiences from a H2020-project. Förvaltningsrättslig tidskrift

Steinsbekk KS, Myskja BK, Solberg B (2013) Broad consent versus dynamic consent in biobank research: is passive participation an ethical problem? Eur J Hum Genet 21(9)

Tzortzatou O (2015) The protection of sensitive data in the field of biomedical research. Sakkoulas Editions, Athens

Witoń M, Stapagiel D, Gleńska-Olender J, Chrościcka A, Ferdyn K, Skokowski J, Kalinowski L, Pawlikowski J, Marciniak B, Pasterk M, Matera-Witkiewicz A, Kozera Ł (2017) Organization of BBMRI.pl: The Polish Biobank Network, Biopreservation and Biobanking

Allocation of Regulatory Responsibilities: Who Will Balance Individual Rights, the Public Interest and Biobank Research Under the GDPR?

Jane Reichel

Abstract In this chapter, an analysis is undertaken of the division of legislative power in the space created by the GDPR, regarding the balancing of individual rights, the public interest and biobank research. The legislative competences of the EU, international obligations within bioethics, and the regulatory space left for Member States are all examined. The conclusion of the chapter is that in spite of the aim of the GDPR to further legal harmonisation, it is more likely that unity will be brought about through administrative cooperation and soft law tools.

1 Introduction: Balancing Individual Rights and Public Interest in Biobank Research Post-GDPR

Balancing the individual right to data protection and the public interest in biobank research involves a number of constitutional and statutory rules within the EU. The individual right to data protection enjoys a strong constitutional protection within the EU legal order, being included both in Article 8 of the EU Charter of Fundamental Rights (Charter) and Article 16 of the Treaty of the Functioning of the European Union (TFEU). The General Data Protection Regulation (GDPR) further provides a comprehensive set of legislation on how the right is to be upheld in practice, according to what the EU refers to as 'a gold standard'.[1] Research also benefits from some protection since freedom of science is protected in several international treaties. The 1948 Universal Declaration on Human Rights includes a right to share in scientific advancements and benefits, although this is not exactly directed at research itself. The International Covenant on Economic, Social and Cultural Rights contains an

[1] Regulation (EU) 2016/679 of the European Parliament and of the Council of 27 April 2016 on the protection of natural persons with regard to the processing of personal data and on the free movement of such data, and repealing Directive 95/46/EC (GDPR) and Slokenberga et al. (2019), p. 32.

J. Reichel (✉)
Stockholm University, Faculty of Law, Stockholm, Sweden
e-mail: Jane.Reichel@juridicum.su.se

S. Slokenberga et al. (eds.), *GDPR and Biobanking*, Law, Governance and Technology Series 43, https://doi.org/10.1007/978-3-030-49388-2_23

obligation on the Member States to 'respect the freedom indispensable for scientific research and creative activity'. The EU Charter declares in Article 13 that arts and scientific research shall be free of constraint. Framed like this, freedom of science can hardly be said to be an individual right that researchers can rely on, but nevertheless it does represent recognition of the importance and value of science.[2]

The protection of individual rights is, however, not the only objective of the GDPR. According to Article 1, the GDPR has as its dual aim to protect natural persons with regard to the processing of personal data and provide rules relating to the free movement of personal data.[3] Within the understanding of free movement of personal data also lies the possibility to use the data for different aims, such as research. The tension between these aims and objectives has been analysed throughout this book.

One of the more salient aims of the EU's data protection law reform which led to the enactment of the GDPR was to diminish the discrepancies between national laws implementing the EU Data Protection Directive.[4] For the biobank community, this step was more than welcome. The fragmentation of European biobanking law has been identified as a major hurdle to prosperous biobank research.[5] In a report on the subject commissioned by the EU Commission in 2012, the first recommendation out of nine was the following:[6]

> Member states and European institutions should develop a consistent and coherent legal framework for biobanking that should protect participants' fundamental rights, in particular in the areas of privacy, data protection and the use of human tissue in research.

The legislative form of the GDPR, a regulation instead of a directive, was chosen in order to ensure that the same law would be applicable throughout the EU. In Recital 10 of the GDPR it is stated that '(c)onsistent and homogenous application of the rules for the protection of the fundamental rights and freedoms of natural persons with regard to the processing of personal data should be ensured throughout the Union'. As has been widely discussed, and is also apparent from the contributions in this book, in the area of scientific research, this objective has only been partially achieved. In the same recital it is also stated that '(t)his Regulation also provides a margin of manoeuvre for Member States to specify its rules, including for the processing of special categories of personal data ("sensitive data")'. In this

[2] Ruffert and Steinecke (2011), p. 30.

[3] See Article 1 GDPR which defines the dual objective of the regulation as protection of natural persons with regard to the processing of personal data and rules relating to the free movement of personal data. It may further be reiterated that the Directive 95/46/EC of the European Parliament and of the Council of 24 October 1995 on the protection of individuals with regard to the processing of personal data and on the free movement of such data, the Data Protection Directive, was enacted as an internal market instrument, under Article 100a Treaty establishing the European Community (today Article 114 TFEU).

[4] Recital 9 and 13 GDPR.

[5] Gottweis et al. (2012), p. 8. See, for a global perspective, Dove (2015), p. 681.

[6] Gottweis et al. (2012), p. 6.

way, the GDPR offers considerable room for inconsistencies at the individual project and Member State levels.

The core data protection principles are laid down in the GDPR, but the detail, the prerequisite for performing the balancing test between individual right and public interest in biobank research, is defined in the laws of the Member States. What does this mean for biobankers in the EU, and for biobank networks, such as the BBMRI-ERIC? A central question is thus the relationship between the core principles and the details in the derogations. How far does the regulatory space of the Member States reach when implementing the research exceptions? In the *Schrems* case the Court of Justice of the European Union (CJEU) held there limits to how far restrictions on the individual right to privacy, in this case based on Article 7 of the Charter, could go; restrictions may not compromise 'the essence of the fundamental right to respect for private life'.[7] These boundaries are to be upheld also by the Member States.[8] The question, thus, is how a legitimate and foreseeable regulatory regime for processing of health data in biobanking is to be achieved. Does the GDPR contain mechanisms that provide a level playing field for biobanks within the EU today?

The analysis in this chapter draws on the conclusion presented in this book, in an effort to answer these questions. In Sect. 2, the background to the diversity in the regulatory landscape was analysed from the perspective of legislative competence of the EU. In Sect. 3, the outcome of the implementation of the GDPR in the Member States was discussed. In Sect. 4, the potential consequences of the differences in regulatory regimes were addressed in relation to forum shopping, and Sect. 5 did the same in relation to administrative cooperation and soft law tools for harmonisation. In the final Sect. 6, the question of how a level playing field for biobanks can be achieved is discussed.

2 Diversity in Regulatory Responses to the GDPR in the Member States

2.1 Components for Regulating the Processing of Personal Data in Biobank Research

There are two core principles in the law and ethics of biomedical research that can be considered to be universally accepted: in all bio-scientific research activity the principle of informed consent of the individual involved must be respected, and all bio-medical research should be reviewed by research ethics committees before

[7] Case C-362/14 Schrems v Data Protection Commissioner, EU:C:2015:650, p. 94.

[8] See Joined Cases C-203/15 and C-698/15 Tele2 Sverige AB v Post- och telestyrelsen and Secretary of State for the Home Department v Tom Watson, Peter Brice, Geoffrey Lewis, EU:C:2016:970, p. 129.

being conducted.[9] These principles have also gained an increasing acceptance in connection to processing of personal data in research.[10] However, at the global level, there is still no legally binding document regulating these issues.

As has been discussed throughout this book, and in line with the GDPR, processing of personal data can be lawfully conducted based on either informed consent or public interest, legitimate interest, contract, etc.[11] If the personal data belong to a special category, for example, health data or genetic data, further requirements set forth in Article 9 apply. According to Article 9(2)(j) and Article 89, this type of data may be processed in research under the condition that there are appropriate safeguards available, normally via ethical approval from research ethics committees.[12] The value of research will thus be balanced against the risk of harm from privacy intrusion experienced by data subjects.[13] Regulating the processing of personal data in biobank research therefore involves at least three separate regulatory areas: data protection, research and bioethics.

2.2 *EU Regulatory Competences in Data Protection, Research and Bioethics*

As discussed previously in this book,[14] the regulatory competence of the EU is central to the understanding of the regulatory regime for the processing of personal data in research. In contrast to national states, the EU does not have a general legislative competence but may only enact binding law in areas where the Member States have conferred powers to legislate.[15] This notion is generally referred to as the principle of conferral and is codified in Article 5(2) of the Treaty of the European Union.

In regards to data protection, the question is unproblematic. With the Lisbon Treaty the EU was conferred a specific competence in the area of data protection in Article 16(2) TFEU. According to the Article, the EU may enact 'rules relating to the protection of individuals with regard to the processing of personal data' and 'rules relating to the free movement of such data'.[16] The EU also has some competence in the area of research, but it is limited in several ways. The EU may, for example, carry out activities to define and implement programmes and set up joint

[9] Ruffert and Steinecke (2011), pp. 94–96.

[10] Slokenberga et al. (2019), p. 32.

[11] Article 6(1) GDPR.

[12] Article 9(2)(J) and Article 89(1) GDPR and the contributions to this book.

[13] See the chapter by M.G. Hansson in this book, and Whitley (2016) p. 39.

[14] See the chapter by S. Slokenberga in this book.

[15] See further Reichel (2016), p. 174.

[16] The previous Data Protection Directive was enacted as an internal market act, under Article 100 a Treaty establishing the European Community (EC) at the time of the enactment of the Directive, today Article 114 TFEU.

undertakings or any other structure necessary for the efficient execution of Union research, technological development and demonstration.[17] One example of the latter is the regulation introducing a procedure for Member States to establish a European Research Infrastructure Consortium (ERIC), under which the BBMRI-ERIC was established.[18] However, when it comes to ethical issues, the EU does not have any competence to enact legislative acts.[19]

Even though the lack of sufficient legislative competence to fully regulate the processing of health or genetic data in biobank research arguably could have been overcome through an extensive interpretation of the competence to regulate data protection issues, as has been done in the area of administrative cooperation, which is another area where the EU has only limited competence to regulate,[20] the strong connection between governance of research and bioethics and national legal culture may have made it politically impossible. Moreover, even though the underlying values and ideas of the bioethical aspects of law can to a large extent be described as universal, there are still national and regional differences, not least when it comes to health and genetics.[21] The differences in the regulatory responses of the Member States, discussed throughout this book, seem to confirm this.

2.3 Aligning the GDPR with Other International Obligations of the Member States

One central regulatory aspect of biobank research is the definition of informed consent. The GDPR permits using what is known in research circles as 'broad' consent. However, as noted several times throughout this book, consent in itself is not a

---

[17] Article 179 and 187 TFEU.

[18] Council regulation (EC) No 723/2009 of 25 June 2009 on the Community legal framework for a European Research Infrastructure Consortium (ERIC).

[19] See, for example, the Amended Proposal for a Directive of the European Parliament and of the Council on Setting Standards of Quality and Safety for the Donation, Procurement, Testing, Processing, Storage, and Distribution of Human Tissues and Cells, COM (2003) 340 final, p. 4, where the Commission rejected certain proposals from the European Parliament on ethical issues on the grounds that Article 168 TFEU, which at the time was Article 152 EC, does not give the EU competence in that field. See further Busby et al. (2008).

[20] The GDPR contains elaborated rules on administrative governance and cooperation, which will be discussed briefly in Sect. 3. Further, in regards to clinical trials, the EU has adopted certain rules on administrative cooperation in bioethical matters, Regulation (EU) No 536/2014 of the European Parliament and of the Council of 16 April 2014 on clinical trials on medicinal products for human use and the European Data Protection Board issued Opinion No 3/2019 which concerns the interplay between the EU Clinical Trials Regulation (CTR) and the GDPR.

[21] For example, Article 23.1 World Medical Association, Declaration of Helsinki—Ethical Principles for Medical Research Involving Human Subjects holds that the law of the land is to be applied, together with relevant international norms and standards as long as these do not undermine the Helsinki Declaration itself.

necessity for personal data to be lawfully processed. In that way, the GDPR paves a rather smooth path for research on residual samples and data. In itself, this approach is not novel. It has previously existed in different national legal orders, as well as internationally. For example, when referring to the collection of human specimens, Article 22 of the Biomedicine Convention states:

> When in the course of an intervention any part of a human body is removed, it may be stored and used for a purpose other than that for which it was removed, only if this is done in conformity with appropriate information and consent procedures.

In the explanatory report to the convention it is noted that an appropriate information and consent procedure does not necessarily mean that the patient or his or her representative must give a formal informed consent. It indicates that '[i]n some cases, it will be sufficient for a patient or his or her representative, who have been duly informed (for instance, by means of leaflets handed to the persons concerned at the hospital), not to express their opposition'.[22] The GDPR addresses the information requirement in this regard under Article 14, allowing exceptions if 'the provision of such information proves impossible or would involve a disproportionate effort'.[23]

From this, the question emerges whether the EU has attempted to re-define the minimum level of protection for individuals when research concerns their residual biological material. If so, this creates a conflict of laws between the Council of Europe and the EU legal orders, and it is questionable whether those Member States of the EU that have ratified the Biomedicine Convention will be able to take full advantage of what the GDPR offers. Additional questions can be raised regarding those states that have signed the convention only, and are thus obliged not to defeat the object and purpose of the treaty. A solution here could be found in Article 26 of the Biomedicine Convention which does not place Article 22 in the cluster of core values of the convention, and thus permits the state parties to restrict these rights in some situations.

However, from an ethical standpoint and at least on the surface, this can be seen as rather problematic. The control expressed by the research participant/datasubject through the possibility to decide on whether or not to participate in a particular study may not necessarily relate to the desire to control personal data. As noted by Staunton et al., it may well be attributed to the aim of the particular study and an unwillingness of the research participant/data subject to have their data used in studies that do not conform to their ethical beliefs.[24] Has the GDPR therefore stripped the data subjects of their ability to control the use of their data in research? In our view, as *expressis verbis* stated in Article 9(2)(j), it is in the hands of the Member States and the EU. The ability to avoid consent-based research has been subordinated to the EU competence

[22] Explanatory Report—ETS 164—Human Rights and Biomedicine (Convention), https://rm.coe.int/16800ccde5, para 137.

[23] Art 14(5)(b) GDPR.

[24] Staunton et al. (2019), p. 2.

limitations and prevailing values in a particular national legal order. It may well be the case that a particular Member State will choose not to operationalise Article 9(2)(j) GDPR, but up until now, at least according to the country laws that have been reviewed in this book, this approach has not been taken.

3 Regulating Safeguards at the National Level: Heterogeneity Remains

Article 89(1) and (2) divides the responsibility for ensuring that appropriate conditions and safeguards are in place for the lawful processing of personal data in research between the EU and the Member States. The first paragraph, Article 89(1), does not clearly point out who is responsible for ensuring safeguards but merely holds that 'processing for (...) scientific or historical research purposes (...), shall be subject to appropriate safeguards, in accordance with this Regulation, for the rights and freedoms of the data subject'. Safeguards may be provided via national law, but it is required that they are regulated 'in accordance this Regulation', the GDPR. Article 89(2), on the other hand, refers to either Union law or national law to allow derogations from Articles 15, 16, 18 or 21, subject to appropriate conditions and safeguards.[25] Accordingly, the conditions and safeguards for processing personal data in biobank research are regulated in a decentralised manner. Also, Article 9(4) GDPR contributes to the decentralisation by allowing Member States to maintain or introduce further conditions, including limitations for the processing of genetic data, biometric data or data concerning health. In addition, Article 23 GDPR allows for further general derogations in the public interest, for example, for public health.[26]

As the pan-European survey by Tzortztou et al. in chapter 'Biobanking Across Europe Post-GDPR: A Deliberately Created Fragmented Landscape' in this book illustrates, the Member States have taken different approaches in implementing these conditions and safeguards in regard to both the form and content. Whilst Sweden has taken a minimalistic approach and has only made use of the possibility in Article 89(2) GDPR to adopt general derogations in a limited manner, the regulatory framework for allowing researchers to access and process data held in public population-based health registries remains wide.[27] In Italy, the entry into force of the GDPR has, on the other hand, had the function of filling the gap in the legislation with regard to biobanking for medical scientific research purposes.[28] In France and in Finland, the

[25] See the chapter by A.G. Duguet and J. Herveg in this book for further details.

[26] The concept of public interest in the GDPR is analysed by S. Slokenberga, see the chapter by S. Slokenberga in section 4.3.4 in this book.

[27] See the chapter by M. Stenbeck, S. Eaker Fält and J. Reichel in this book.

[28] See the chapter by S. Penasa and M. Tomasi in this book, section IV.

national regulatory approach seems to a certain extent to uphold a stricter standard than required by the GDPR, whereas in Estonia, the legislator has chosen a more lenient approach.[29] The national regulatory responses thus remain heterogeneous.

4 Addressing Regulatory Differences Via Forum Shopping?

A relevant question to pose is whether this heterogenous regulatory landscape may lead to forum shopping, in the sense that research proposals are allocated to Member States with the most beneficial regulatory regimes. The question of forum shopping, or in other words, regulatory competition, is far from unknown in the EU Internal Market and not always seen as problematic in itself. Within the Internal Market, Member States should allow a free flow of goods, services, labour and capital, unless there is a legitimate reason to hinder it.[30] It is for the economic actors in the Internal Market to allocate their business to the forums that offer the most advantageous conditions. In the *Centros* case, the CJEU held that it was contrary to the rules of the Internal Market for a Member State to refuse to register a 'letterbox-company' merely on the basis that the company wanted to allocate its business in a less restrictive regulatory environment. Only on suspicion of fraud would it be legitimate for the Member State to take action.[31] The practice is also well known in labour law where employers might want to place their headquarters in a state with a more lenient labour law regime. Even if this is often criticised, it has proven difficult to combat the practice without distorting the Internal Market.[32] As mentioned in the introduction, the GDPR has as its objective to promote free movement of personal data. In global medical research, the concepts of 'ethics dumping', the practice of exporting unethical research practices to lower-income settings, has been recognised as an ethical problem.[33] The differences between Member States of the EU should not be exaggerated, but at the same time researchers allocating research proposals to certain states in order to circumvent ethical regulation can be seen as problematic and will in the long run undermine social trust in biobanking. The next issue to consider is therefore whether the GDPR contains any mechanisms that may bridge the regulatory differences.

---

[29] See the chapter by G. Chassang et al., section 5.1; Chapter by T. Southerington, section III and chapter by K. Pormeister, section 4.

[30] Article 26 TFEU.

[31] Case C-212/97 Centros Ltd v Erhervs- og Selskabsstyrelsen EU:C:1999:126, p. 39.

[32] Houwerzijl (2014), p. 98.

[33] See, for example, The Global Code of Conduct for Research in Resource-Poor Settings, in particular Article 14. The code was developed within the TRUST, Equitable research party projects, see further www.globalcodeofconduct.org/.

5 Addressing Regulatory Differences Via Administrative Cooperation and Soft Law Tools

As mentioned briefly above and as also discussed by Dara Hallinan in chapter 'Biobank Oversight and Sanctions Under the General Data Protection Regulation' of this book, the GDPR contains an elaborated governance structure for both European and national administration within the data protection area. Here, focus is laid on the potential of this structured cooperation of authorities to overcome differences in interpretations of data protection rules and concepts. It is in this context of interest to note that the administrative structure is partially regulated also in EU primary law. Both Article 8 of the Charter and Article 16 TFEU state that compliance with data protection rules shall be subject to control by an independent authority. This independency is regulated in Chapters VI and VII of the GDPR, together with the competence, tasks and powers of the national data protection authorities (DPAs) and the newly established European Data Protection Board (EDPB), which has taken over after the previous Article 29 Working Party Group.

One of the tasks of the EDPB is to issue guidelines, recommendations, best practices and opinions on a wide range of subjects.[34] Even if the GDPR does not regulate biobanking directly, these documents will often be relevant both in regards to defining core principles of data protection, such as informed consent, and in relation to processing personal data across sectors, such as clinical trials.[35] The GDPR also introduced several new tools with which DPAs can cooperate; two of these will be discussed here. These are a one-stop-shop mechanism for appointing a lead authority in cases involving monitoring of cross-border processing and a procedure for composite decision-making, labelled a consistency mechanism.[36]

The first mechanism was established to offer a smooth and foreseeable means of supervision since it identifies one single DPA to act as a one-stop-shop for controllers and processors active in more than one Member State, thus giving the lead DPA a role as coordinator of the supervision of all the processing activities of that business throughout the EU in collaboration with other 'concerned' DPAs.[37]

The second, the consistency mechanism, provides a procedure for fulfilling the role of a dispute resolution mechanism in which the EDPB functions as a dispute resolution body.[38] According to this procedure, a DPA can refer a draft decision to

---

[34] Article 70(1) GDPR.

[35] See European Data Protection Board, Guidelines on Consent under Regulation 2016/679 (wp259rev.01) and European Data Protection Board, Opinion No 3/2019 which concerns the interplay between the EU Clinical Trials Regulation (CTR) and the GDPR. Further, the European Data Protection Supervisor (EDPS), tasked with monitoring data protection within the EU institutions and bodies under Regulation 2018/1725, has issued a Preliminary opinion on data protection and scientific research, 6 January 2020.

[36] Article 56 and 63–66 GDPR, respectively. See further Hijmans (2016), p. 369.

[37] Article 60 GDPR and Giurgiu and Larsen (2016), p. 349.

[38] Ibid, p. 350.

the EDPB before enacting a decision in different categories of situations. In the first category, consisting of six identified cases, referral is compulsory.[39] In the second category, concerning 'any matter of general application or producing effects in more than one Member State', referral is optional.[40] However, the procedure in the second paragraph can be initiated by any DPA, not merely the lead authority, the chair of the EDPB and the Commission. If the DPAs cannot agree, any one of them may trigger the consistency mechanism, thus inviting the EDPB to take a leading role. In both categories, the EDPB issues an opinion which all DPAs and the Commission may comment on.[41] The lead authority must 'take utmost account of the opinion of the Board' and communicate to the Chair of the Board whether it will maintain or amend its draft decision.[42] If the lead authority does not abide by the opinion, the EDPB may proceed with a dispute resolution. This effectively entails a decision adopted for the individual case which the DPA must implement by giving a final decision according to the requirements of the relevant national law, referring to the decision enacted by the EDPB.[43] If and to what extent this mechanism is to be used within the area of research in general or biobank research in particular remains to be seen. Within the areas where the GDPR acknowledges the regulatory competence of the Member States, such as due to the research exceptions, it is hardly conceivable that the consistency mechanism can reconcile the various approaches and traditions of the Member States, at least not in a comprehensive manner.

A more customised tool for defining the proper balance between individual right and public interest in biobank research is the code of conduct.[44] A code of conduct can be drafted by private companies and organisations for the processing of personal data by certain categories of controllers or processors.[45] The procedure for adopting a code of conduct involves both a DPA, the EDPB and the Commission, and results in a binding document specifying the proper application of the GDPR for processing within the Union and as a basis for transfer outside.[46] In June 2019,

---

[39] According to Article 64(1) GDPR, the competent supervisory authority shall communicate the draft decision to the Board when it: (a) aims to adopt a list of the processing operations subject to the requirement for a data protection impact assessment pursuant to Article 35(4); (b) concerns a matter pursuant to Article 40(7) whether a draft code of conduct or an amendment or extension to a code of conduct complies with this Regulation; (c) aims to approve the requirements for accreditation of a body pursuant to Article 41(3,) of a certification body pursuant to Article 43(3) or the criteria for certification referred to in Article 42(5); (d) aims to determine standard data protection clauses referred to in point (d) of Article 46(2) and in Article 28(8); (e) aims to authorise contractual clauses referred to in point (a) of Article 46(3); or (f) aims to approve binding corporate rules within the meaning of Article 47.

[40] Article 64(2) GDPR.

[41] Article 64(4) GDPR.

[42] Article 64(7) GDPR. See further Recital 136 GDPR.

[43] Article 65 GDPR.

[44] Also, the Data Protection Directive recognised code of conducts, Article 27.

[45] Article 40 GDPR.

[46] Article 40(2) and 46(2) (e) GDPR.

the EDPB issued guidelines on the subject.[47] These describe the codes as being able to 'help to bridge the harmonisation gaps that may exist between Member States in their application of data protection law', and to 'provide an opportunity for specific sectors to reflect upon common data processing activities and to agree to bespoke and practical data protection rules, which will meet the needs of the sector as well as the requirements of the GDPR'.[48]

The BBMRI-ERIC is currently drafting a Code of Conduct for Health Research which, according to its webpage, may 'guide researchers and administrative staff, reduce unnecessary fear relating to compliance and enhance data sharing for the purpose of stimulating progress in research'.[49] Arguably, this has the potential to define and operationalise the regulatory space provided by Art 9(2)(j), and create a balanced and proportionate approach for the purpose of achieving the public interest in research while respecting the essence of the right to data protection and upholding suitable and specific measures to safeguard this fundamental right. As argued in this book, the careful calibrating requested in this operation is a difficult yet essential factor for biobanking. If unity in central areas is reached, a code of conduct for biobanking could prove a most valuable tool in the present fragmented legal landscape. However, striving for unity must be weighed against the benefit of allowing Member States some leeway to uphold national or regional traditions. The final assessment of ethical and legal viability of the individual research project in the future will also be conducted by research ethic committees (RECs) in the Member States. In order to gain general acceptance, the code of conduct must meet the ethical standards applied by these boards, taking into account the ambiguity resulting from Article 9(4) and Article 23 GDPR. Further, the international obligations discussed above (Sect. 2.3) must also be met. In order to achieve this, the stakeholders of the code of conduct must resolve the issues that the EU legislator was unable to overcome in the legislative process. A bottom-up approach may prove more successful.

6 Concluding Remarks: Can a Level Playing Field for Biobanks Develop?

One of the more salient objectives of the EU data protection reform leading to the enactment of the GDPR was to further align national laws on data protection. Nevertheless, as the GDPR allows for derogations via Member States law to such a high degree, it could be argued that it is a regulation in name only and that its form

[47] The European Data Protection Board Guidelines 1/2019 on Codes of Conduct and Monitoring Bodies under Regulation 2016/679.

[48] Ibid, p. 4.

[49] http://code-of-conduct-for-health-research.eu. see also chapter by Lalova et al., in this book, Section 4.2.

in reality is more a directive. The regulatory regime for processing personal data in biobank research thus remains a mixed responsibility for the EU and its Member States.

The question of the relationship between the core data protection principles of the GDPR and national law that provides derogations has been analysed throughout this book. As has been seen, the regulatory differences in the Member States remain. However, the GDPR also introduces governance structures for administrative cooperation and the production of soft law documents to provide guidance for the interpretations of the GDPR and its core principles. Further, with the introduction of a new legal tool, the code of conduct, private entities and collaborative networks have also been invited to take part in the regulatory work. Thus, it may be argued that the harmonising factors in the area of research will be found in the area of soft law and governance tools rather than in the area of EU and Member State legislation.

This finding can be seen as contrary to one of the general features of fundamental rights law that derogations from a right should be set out in transparent and unequivocal rules enacted in a democratically legitimate manner.[50] This notion is also recognised in the preamble of the GDPR:[51]

> Where this Regulation refers to a legal basis or a legislative measure, this does not necessarily require a legislative act adopted by a parliament, without prejudice to requirements pursuant to the constitutional order of the Member State concerned. However, such a legal basis or legislative measure should be clear and precise and its application should be foreseeable to persons subject to it, in accordance with the case-law of the Court of Justice of the European Union (the 'Court of Justice') and the European Court of Human Rights.

Further, as discussed above, the CJEU held in the *Schrems* case that there are limits to how far the right to data protection can be restricted via legally binding acts.[52]

Soft law documents and private-public governance tools can generally be said to lack the qualities of democratic legitimacy and transparency in comparison to legislative acts enacted by a parliament.[53] However, the combination of practical need and lack of political will and/or legislative competence within the EU seems to have paved the way for these types of non-law solutions. One of the benefits of this softer form of developing a common understanding of law is that it does not call into question the formal transfer of powers from the national level to the supranational level, and therefore entails less of a commitment for the involved states.[54] Moreover, as held by Mayrhofer and Prainsack, this is a common way of regulating international biobanking as non-legally binding agreements and soft law regularly emerge in the absence of a central regulator.[55] Following the conclusions in the pan-European

[50] Compare Article 52 of the Charter and Article 8.2 of the European Convention of Human Rights.

[51] Recital 41 GDPR.

[52] Case C-362/14 Schrems v Data Protection Commissioner, EU:C:2015:650, p. 94.

[53] Reichel (2016), p. 186.

[54] Spina (2011), pp. 249, 261.

[55] Mayrhofer and Prainsack (2012), pp. 64, 70.

survey, chapter 'Biobanking Across Europe Post-GDPR: A Deliberately Created Fragmented Landscape' in this book, the assessment of the legal and ethical requirements will in the end be a question for RECs to resolve within their adjudication. The transparency and legal certainty of this adjudication would have benefitted from a fulfilment of the recommendation put forward in the 2012 Commission report, that the EU and its Member States ought to develop a consistent and coherent legal framework for biobanking that should protect participants' fundamental rights, in particular in the areas of privacy, data protection and the use of human tissue in research.[56]

References

Busby H, Hervey T, Mohr A (2008) Ethical EU law? The influence of the European group on ethics in science and new technologies. Eur Law Rev 33:803–842

Dove ES (2015) Biobanks, data sharing, and the drive for a global privacy governance framework. J Law Med Eth 43(4):675–689

Giurgiu A, Larsen TA (2016) Roles and powers of national data protection authorities. Eur Data Prot Law Rev 2:342–352

Gottweis H et al (2012) Biobanks for Europe. A Challenge for Governance, Report of the Expert Group with Ethical and Regulatory Challenges of International Biobank Research. Directorate-General for Research and Innovation, European Commission, Brussels

Hijmans H (2016) The DPAs and their cooperation: how far are we in making enforcement of data protection law more European. Eur Data Prot Law Rev 2:362–372

Houwerzijl M (2014) 'Regime shopping' across (blurring) bundaries, regulating transnational labour in Europe: the quandires of multilevel governance. Department of Private Law, Oslo University, Skriftserie 196, Oslo

Mayrhofer M, Prainsack B (2012) Being a member of the club: the transnational (self-) governance of networks of biobanks. Int J Risk Assess Manage 12:64–79

Reichel J (2016) Alternative rule-making within European bioethics – necessary and therefore legitimate? Tilburg Law Rev 21:169–192

Ruffert M, Steinecke S (2011) The global administrative law of science. Springer, Berlin

Slokenberga S, Reichel J, Niringiye R, Croxton T, Swanepoel C, Okal J (2019) EU data transfer rules and African legal realities: is data exchange for biobank research realistic? Int Data Priv Law 9(1):30–48

Spina A (2011) The regulation of pharmaceuticals beyond the state. In: Chiti E, Mattarella BG (eds) Global administrative law and EU administrative law. Springer, Berlin

Staunton C, Slokenberga S, Mascalzoni D (2019) The GDPR and the research exemption: considerations on the necessary safeguards for research biobanks. Eur J Hum Genet 1

Whitley SN (2016) Balanced ethics review. A guide for institutional review board members. Springer

[56] Gottweis (2012), p. 6.